C000053452

STREET ATLAS

Worcestershire

First published in 2003 by

Philip's, a division of
Octopus Publishing Group Ltd
2–4 Heron Quays, London E14 4JP

First edition 2003
Second impression 2004

ISBN 0-540-08336-4 (spiral)

© Philip's 2003

OS Ordnance Survey®

This product includes mapping data licensed
from Ordnance Survey® with the permission of
the Controller of Her Majesty's Stationery Office.
© Crown copyright 2003. All rights reserved.
Licence number 100011710.

Printed and bound in Spain
by Cayfosa-Quebecor

Contents

III	**Key to map symbols**
IV	**Key to map pages**
VI	**Route planning**
VIII	**Administrative and Postcode boundaries**
1	**Street maps** at 3½ inches to 1 mile
198	**Town maps** of Ludlow and Stratford-upon-Avon
199	**Index** of towns and villages
202	**Index** of streets, hospitals, industrial estates, railway stations, schools, shopping centres, universities and places of interest

Digital Data

The exceptionally high-quality mapping found in this atlas is available as digital data in TIFF format, which is easily convertible to other bitmapped (raster) image formats.

The index is also available in digital form as a standard database table. It contains all the details found in the printed index together with the National Grid reference for the map square in which each entry is named.

For further information and to discuss your requirements, please contact Philip's on 020 7644 6932 or james.mann@philips-maps.co.uk

Key to map symbols

III

22a	**Motorway** with junction number
	Primary route – dual/single carriageway
	A road – dual/single carriageway
	B road – dual/single carriageway
	Minor road – dual/single carriageway
	Other minor road – dual/single carriageway
	Road under construction
	Tunnel, covered road
	Rural track, private road or narrow road in urban area
	Gate or obstruction to traffic (restrictions may not apply at all times or to all vehicles)
	Path, bridleway, byway open to all traffic, road used as a public path
	Pedestrianised area
DY7	**Postcode boundaries**
	County and unitary authority boundaries
	Railway, tunnel, railway under construction
	Tramway, tramway under construction
	Miniature railway
Walsall	**Railway station**
South Shields	**Private railway station**
	Metro station
	Tram stop, tram stop under construction
	Bus, coach station

◆	**Ambulance station**
◆	**Coastguard station**
◆	**Fire station**
◆	**Police station**
✚	**Accident and Emergency entrance to hospital**
H	**Hospital**
✛	**Place of worship**
i	**Information Centre** (open all year)
P	**Parking**
P&R	**Park and Ride**
PO	**Post Office**
⋏	**Camping site**
	Caravan site
▶	**Golf course**
⊠	**Picnic site**
Prim Sch	**Important buildings, schools, colleges, universities and hospitals**
River Ouse	**Tidal water, water name**
	Non-tidal water – lake, river, canal or stream
	Lock, weir, tunnel
	Woods
	Built up area
Church	**Non-Roman antiquity**
ROMAN FORT	**Roman antiquity**
87 / 58	**Adjoining page indicators**

Acad	**Academy**	Inst	**Institute**	Recn Gd	**Recreation**
Allot Gdns	**Allotments**	Ct	**Law Court**		**Ground**
Cemy	**Cemetery**	L Ctr	**Leisure Centre**	Resr	**Reservoir**
C Ctr	**Civic Centre**	LC	**Level Crossing**	Ret Pk	**Retail Park**
CH	**Club House**	Liby	**Library**	Sch	**School**
Coll	**College**	Mkt	**Market**	Sh Ctr	**Shopping Centre**
Crem	**Crematorium**	Meml	**Memorial**	TH	**Town Hall/House**
Ent	**Enterprise**	Mon	**Monument**	Trad Est	**Trading Estate**
Ex H	**Exhibition Hall**	Mus	**Museum**	Univ	**University**
Ind Est	**Industrial Estate**	Obsy	**Observatory**	Wks	**Works**
IRB Sta	**Inshore Rescue Boat Station**	Pal	**Royal Palace**	YH	**Youth Hostel**
		PH	**Public House**		

■ The small numbers around the edges of the maps identify the 1 kilometre National Grid lines ■ The dark grey border on the inside edge of some pages indicates that the mapping does not continue onto the adjacent page

The scale of the maps on the pages numbered in blue is 5.52 cm to 1 km • 3½ inches to 1 mile • 1: 18103

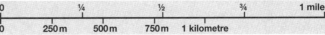

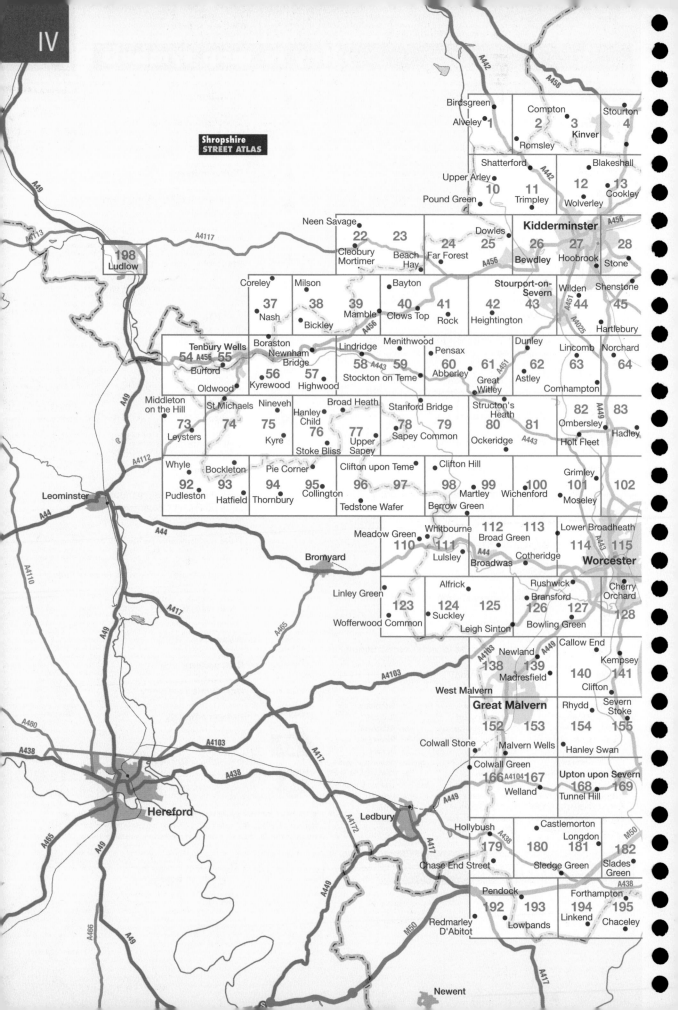

Shropshire STREET ATLAS

Birdsgreen / Alveley **1**	Compton **2**	Stourton **3** Kinver	Stourton **4**
Shatterford / Upper Arley / Pound Green **10**	Trimpley **11**	Blakeshall **12**	Cookley **13** Wolverley
Neen Savage **22** Cleobury Mortimer	Beach Hay **23**	Far Forest **24** Dowles **25**	**Kidderminster** **26** Bewdley	Hoobrook **27** Stone **28**
Coreley **37** Nash	Milson **38** Bickley	Mamble **39**	Bayton **40** Clows Top	Rock **41**	Heightington **42**	Stourport-on-Severn **43**	Wilden **44**	Shenstone **45** Hartlebury
Tenbury Wells **54** **55** Burford Oldwood	Boraston / Newnham Bridge **56** Kyrewood	Highwood **57**	Lindridge **58** Stockton on Teme	Menithwood **59**	Pensax **60** Abberley	Great Witley **61**	Dunley **62** Astley Comhampton	Lincomb **63**	Norchard **64**
Middleton on the Hill **73** Leysters	St Michaels **74**	Nineveh **75** Kyre	Hanley Child **76** Stoke Bliss	Broad Heath **77** Upper Sapey	Stanford Bridge **78** Sapey Common	**79**	Structon's Heath **80** Ockeridge	**81**	**82** Ombersley Holt Fleet	**83** Hadley
Whyle **92** Pudleston	Bockleton **93** Hatfield	Pie Corner **94** Thornbury	Collington **95**	Clifton upon Teme **96** Tedstone Wafer	**97**	Clifton Hill **98** Berrow Green	Martley **99**	Wichenford **100**	Grimley **101** Moseley	**102**
Meadow Green **110**	Whitbourne **111** Lulsley	**112** Broad Green	**113**	Lower Broadheath	**114**	**Worcester** **115**
Linley Green **123** Wofferwood Common	Alfrick **124** Suckley	**125** Leigh Sinton	Rushwick **126** Bransford	Bowling Green **127**	Cherry Orchard **128**
Newland **138**	**139** Madresfield	Callow End **140** Clifton	Kempsey **141**
West Malvern **Great Malvern** **152**	**153**	Rhydd **154**	Severn Stoke **155**
Colwall Stone	Malvern Wells	Hanley Swan	
Colwall Green **166**	**167** Welland	**Upton upon Severn** **168** Tunnel Hill	**169**
Hollybush **179** Chase End Street	**180**	Castlemorton **181** Longdon Sledge Green	**182** Slades Green
Pendock **192** Redmarley D'Abitot	**193** Lowbands	Forthampton **194** Linkend	**195** Chaceley

198 Ludlow

Leominster

Bromyard

Hereford

Ledbury

Newent

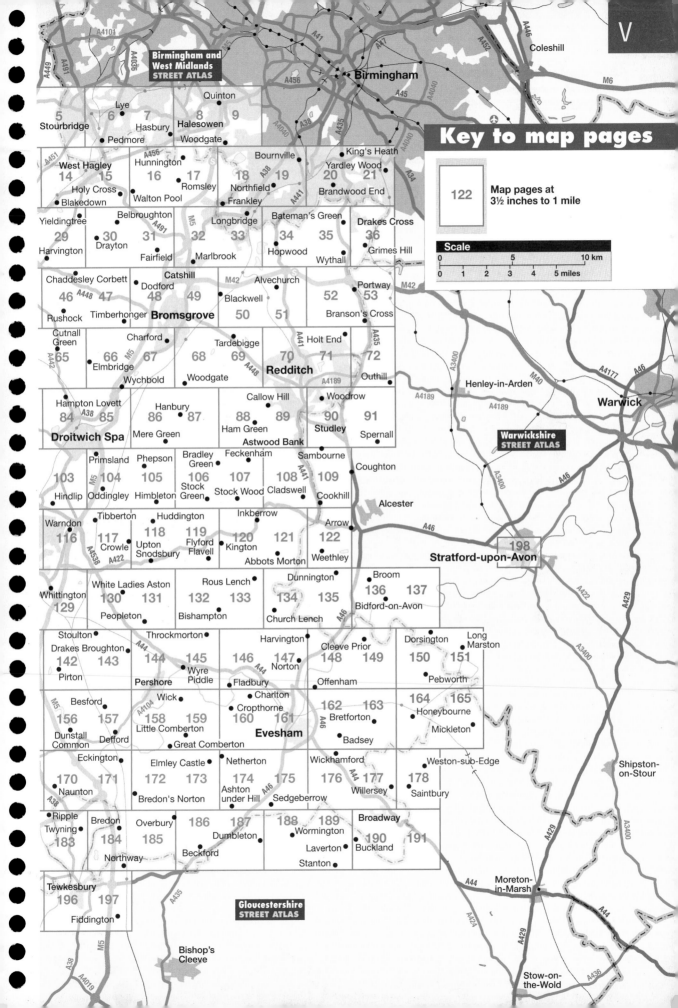

Scale

0   5   10 km
0 1 2 3 4 5 miles

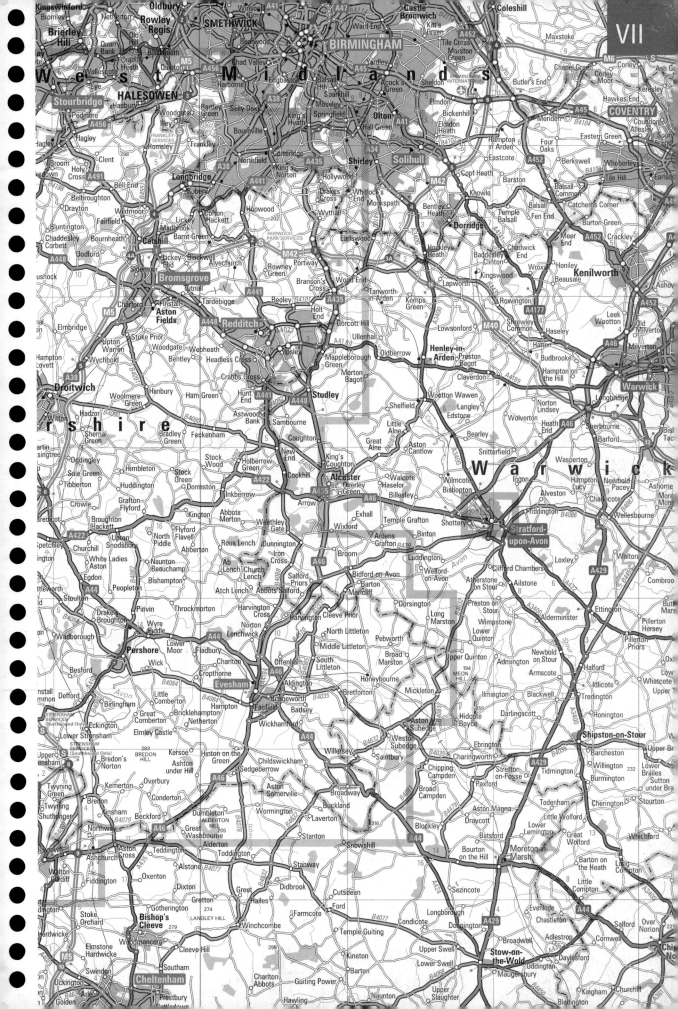

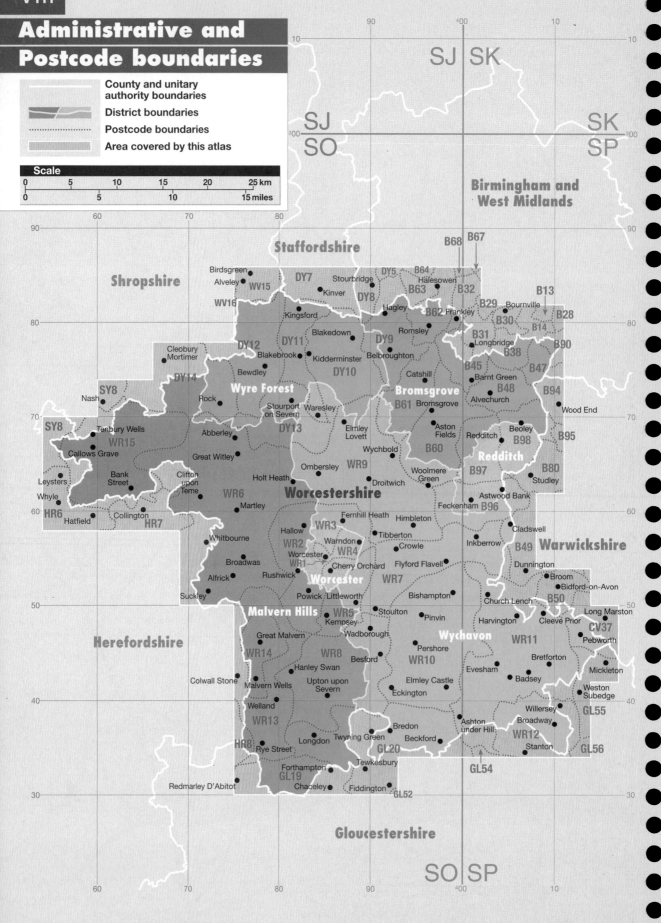

Administrative and Postcode boundaries

	County and unitary authority boundaries
	District boundaries
	Postcode boundaries
	Area covered by this atlas

Scale

| 0 | 5 | 10 | 15 | 20 | 25 km |
| 0 | | 5 | | 10 | 15 miles |

SJ SK

SJ
SO

SK
SP

Birmingham and West Midlands

Staffordshire

Shropshire

B68 B67

Birdsgreen
Alveley
WV15
DY7
Stourbridge
DY5
B64
Halesowen
B63
B32
WV16
Kinver
DY8
Hagley
B62 Frankley
B29
Bournville
B13
B30
B14
B28
Kingsford
Blakedown
DY9
Romsley
B31
Longbridge
B90
DY12
DY11
B38
B47
Cleobury
Mortimer
DY10
Belbroughton
B45
Barnt Green
B94
DY14
Blakebrook
Kidderminster
B48
Alvechurch
Wood End
Bewdley
Catshill
SY8
Wyre Forest
Rock
Bromsgrove
B61
Bromsgrove
B98
B95
Nash
Aston
Fields
Redditch
Beoley
SY8
Tenbury Wells
Stourport
on Severn
Waresley
Elmley
Lovett
B60
WR15
Abberley
DY13
Wychbold
Redditch
Callows Grave
HR6
Great Witley
Ombersley
WR9
Woolmere
Green
B97
B80
Studley
Leysters
Bank
Street
Clifton
upon
Teme
Holt Heath
Droitwich
Astwood Bank
Feckenham
B96
Whyle
HR6
Collington
WR6
Martley
Himbleton
Cladswell
Hatfield
HR7
Whitbourne
Fernhill Heath
WR3
Tibberton
Inkberrow
B49
Warwickshire
Broadwas
WR2
Warndon
Crowle
Dunnington
Broom
Alfrick
Worcester
WR4
Flyford Flavell
Bidford-on-Avon
Rushwick
WR1
Cherry Orchard
Church Lench
B50
Suckley
Worcester
WR7
Bishampton
Long Marston
Powick Littleworth
Harvington
Cleeve Prior
CV37
Malvern Hills
WR5
Stoulton
Pinvin
Pebworth
Kempsey
Wadborough
Wychavon
WR11
Great Malvern
Pershore
Bretforton
Colwall Stone
WR14
WR8
Besford
Evesham
Badsey
Mickleton
Hanley Swan
Elmley Castle
Weston
Subedge
Malvern Wells
Upton upon
Severn
Eckington
Welland
Willersey
Broadway
GL55
WR13
Bredon
Ashton
under Hill
WR12
Stanton
GL56
HR8
Longdon
Twyning Green
Beckford
Rye Street
GL20
GL54
Forthampton
Tewkesbury
GL19
Chaceley
Fiddington
Redmarley D'Abitot
GL52

Herefordshire

Worcestershire

Gloucestershire

SO SP

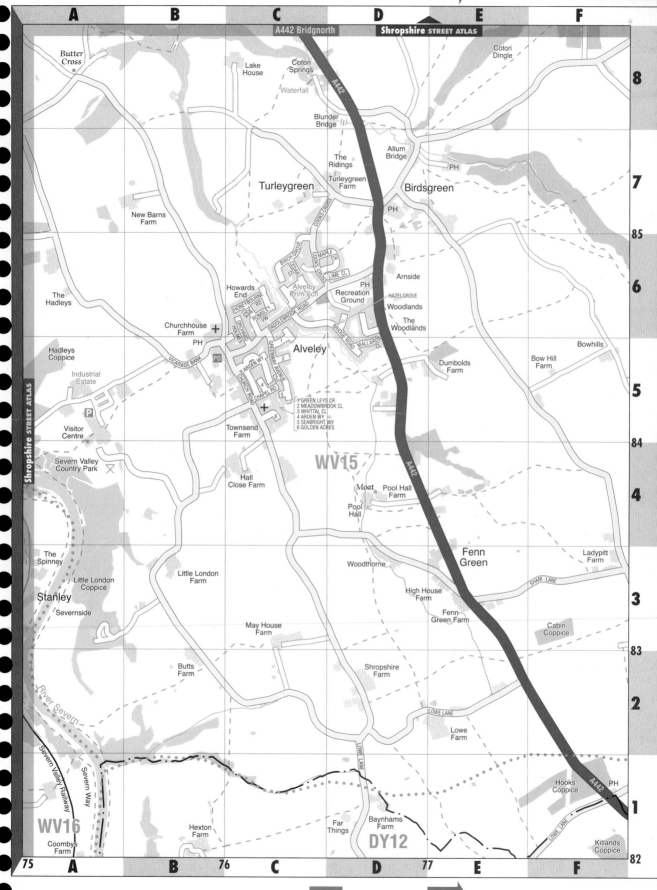

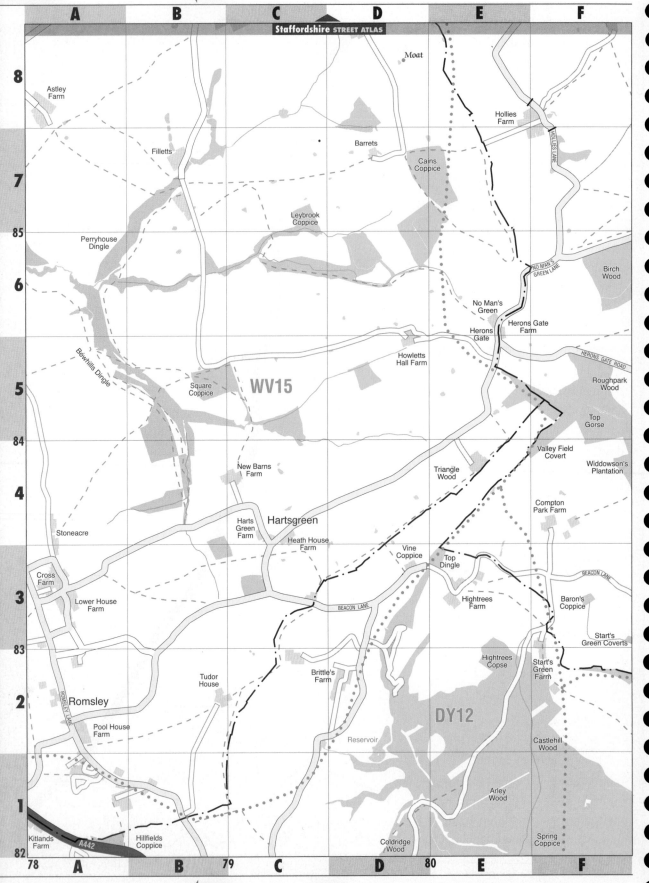

Staffordshire **STREET ATLAS**

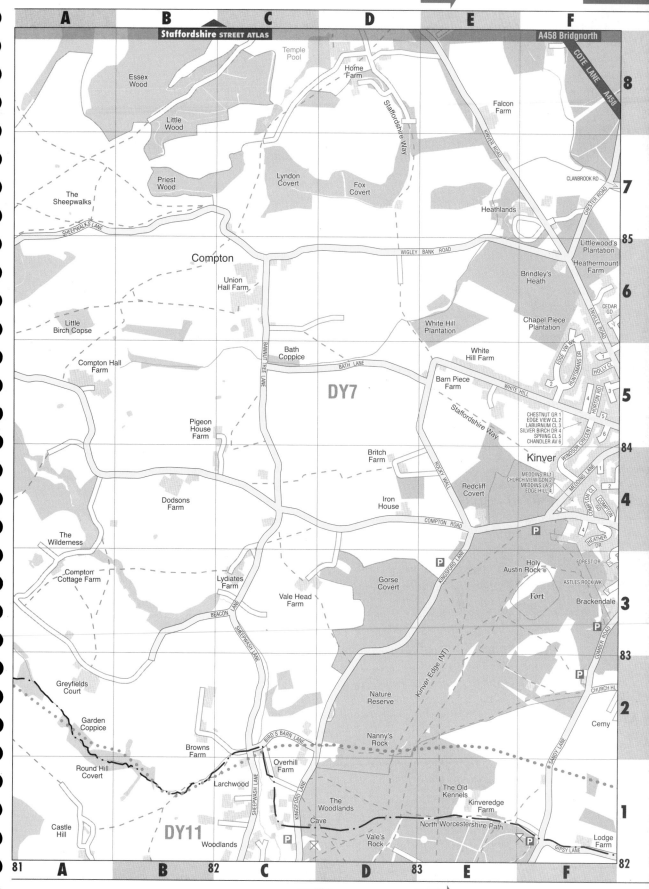

Staffordshire STREET ATLAS

A458 Bridgnorth

COTE LANE
A458

A **B** **C** **D** **E** **F**

Temple Pool

Essex Wood

Home Farm

Falcon Farm

Little Wood

CLANBROOK RD

8

Priest Wood

The Sheepwalks

Lyndon Covert

Fox Covert

Heathlands

CHESTER ROAD

7

SHEEPWALKS LANE

WIGLEY BANK ROAD

Littlewood's Plantation

85

Compton

Union Hall Farm

Brindley's Heath

Heathermount Farm

ENVILLE ROAD

6

Little Birch Copse

Bath Coppice

White Hill Plantation

Chapel Piece Plantation

CEDAR GD

BANNUT TREE LANE

BATH LANE

EDGE VW WK

HURSTMANS DR

HOLLY CL

Compton Hall Farm

White Hill Farm

WHITE HILL

HORTON RD

5

Pigeon House Farm

Barn Piece Farm

Staffordshire Way

CHESTNUT GR 1
EDGE VIEW CL 2
LABURNUM CL 3
SILVER BIRCH DR 4
SPRING CL 5
CHANDLER AV 6

84

Britch Farm

Redcliff Covert

Kinver

WINDSOR CRESCENT

DY7

ROCKY WALL

MEDDINS RI 1
CHURCH VIEW GDN 2
MEDDINS LA 3
EDGE HILL 4

MEDDINS LANE

COMPTON CL

4

Dodsons Farm

Iron House

COMPTON ROAD

COMPTON CU CL

HEATHER DR

The Wilderness

P

Holy Austin Rock

FOREST DR

ASTLES ROCK WK

Compton Cottage Farm

Lydiates Farm

Vale Head Farm

Gorse Covert

KINGSFORD LANE

Fort

Brackendale

3

BEACON LANE

SHEEPWASH LANE

P

P

CLIMBER ROAD

Kinver Edge (NT)

83

CHURCH HL

Greyfields Court

Nature Reserve

P

2

Garden Coppice

Nanny's Rock

Cemy

BIRD'S BARN LANE

Browns Farm

Overhill Farm

SANDY LANE

Round Hill Covert

Larchwood

The Old Kennels

Kinveredge Farm

The Woodlands

KINGSFORD LANE

SHEEPWASH LANE

Cave

North Worcestershire Path

1

Castle Hill

DY11

Woodlands

P

Vale's Rock

P

Lodge Farm

GIPSY LANE

81

A **B** 82 **C** **D** 83 **E** **F** 82

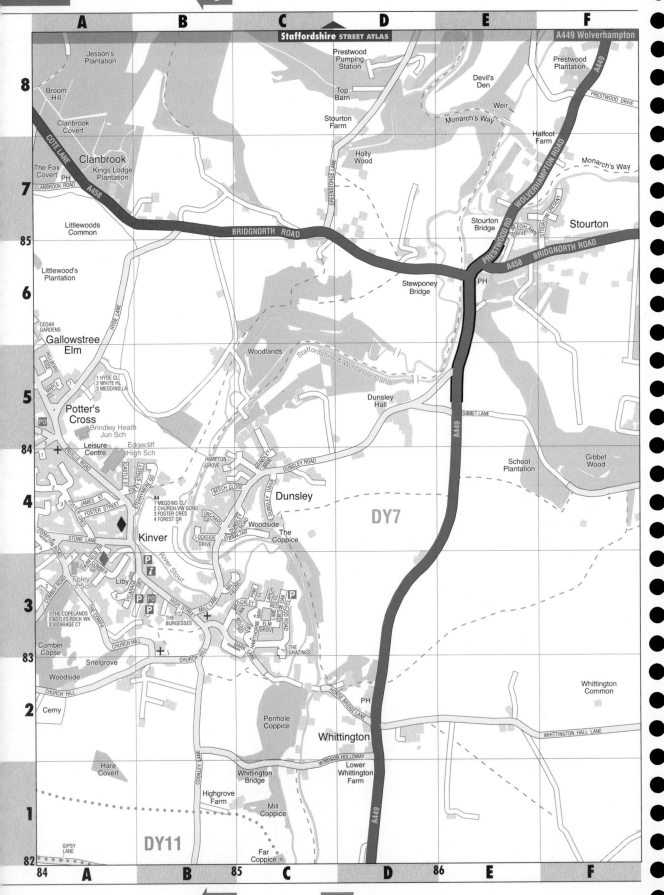

3

Staffordshire STREET ATLAS

A449 Wolverhampton

A   B   C   D   E   F

8

Jesson's Plantation

Prestwood Pumping Station

Prestwood Plantation

PRESTWOOD DRIVE

Devil's Den

Broom Hill

Clanbrook Covert

Top Barn

Weir

Monarch's Way

Halfcot Farm

Monarch's Way

7

The Fox Covert

Clanbrook

Kings Lodge Plantation

PH

CLANBROOK ROAD

A458

COTE LANE

Stourton Farm

Holly Wood

GREENSFORGE LANE

Stourton Bridge

Stourton

PRESTWOOD RD

WOLVERHAMPTON ROAD

BEECHLAWN DRIVE

STOURTON CRESENT

85

Littlewoods Common

BRIDGNORTH   ROAD

A458   BRIDGNORTH ROAD

6

Littlewood's Plantation

Stewponey Bridge

PH

CEDAR GARDENS

Gallowstree Elm

HYDE LANE

HILL ROAD RISE

Woodlands

Staffordshire & Worcester Canal

5

MAPLE CL

1 HYDE CL
2 WHITE HL
3 MEDDINS LA

Potter's Cross

Brindley Heath Jun Sch

Dunsley Hall

GIBBET LANE

A449

School Plantation

Gibbet Wood

PO

ENVILLE ROAD

84

Leisure Centre

Edgecliff High Sch

HAMPTON GROVE

BRINDLEY BRAE

DUNSLEY ROAD

4

A4
1 MEDDINS CL
2 CHURCH VW GDNS
3 FOSTER CRES
4 FOREST DR

CASTLE ST

FOX'S STREET

STERNMERE RD

JAMES ST

FOSTER STREET

FOSTER CRES

BEECH CLOSE

Dunsley

DUNSLEY DRIVE

DUNSLEY LANE

DY7

Kinver

STONE LANE

COMPTON ROAD

ORCHARD GR

GIBRALTAR

Woodside

The Coppice

LOCKSIDE DRIVE

River Stour

3

COMBER ROAD

FAIRFIELD DR

COMBER GR

Liby

VICARAGE DR

PO

P
i

P

Roley Inf Sch

THE COMPA

THE BURGESSES

HIGH STREET

MILL LANE

MILL FIELDS

BROCKLEY'S

PINE CL

LARCH

HAWTHORNE WAY

REDWD

LIME GR

ELM GROVE

OLD ROAD

P

1 THE COPELANDS
2 ASTLES ROCK WK
3 VICARAGE CT

WILLOW RD

DARK LANE

THE GRAZINGS

83

Comber Copse

Snelgrove

CHURCH HILL

CHURCH HILL

Woodside

2

CHURCH HILL

Penhole Coppice

HORSE BRIDGE LANE

PH

Whittington

Whittington Common

WHITTINGTON HALL LANE

Cemy

Hare Covert

COOKLEY LANE

Highgrove Farm

Whittington Bridge

Mill Coppice

WINDSOR HOLLOWAY

Lower Whittington Farm

A449

1

DY11

GIPSY LANE

Far Coppice

82

84   A   B   85   C   D   86   E   F

6 → E8 3 LONGBOAT LA
F8 8 CORBETT HO

Staffordshire STREET ATLAS

Bellsmill

A491 Wolverhampton (A449)   A461 Brierley Hill

Smallshire Way

River Stour

Stourbridge Canal

River Stour

8

7

85

6

5

84

4

83

2

1

82

Monarch's Way

Newtown Bridge

Stapenhill Farm

New Wood

St James CE Prim Sch

New Wood Cl

Friars Gorse

Hyperion Rd

Chantry Rd

Twickenham

Essex Gdns

Gilbanks Rd

Rugby Rd

Somerset Dr

Kent Rd

B4537

The Hawthorns

A458

Prestwood Dr

Wollaston Rd

Vicarage Rd

Meadowpark Rd

Kingsway

Rutland Pl

Cheshire Cl

Cornwall Rd

Norfolk Rd

Dorset Rd

Durham Rd

Devon Rd

Wentworth Rd

Gerald Rd

Laburnum Rd

Richmond Way

Firmstone St

Harrop Rd

Apley Rd

High St

Wollaston Rd

Brugnorth Rd

B4537

Barratt's Coppice Farm

Football Club

High Park Farm

Wollaston Way

Ridgecroft

Falcon Cres

Ridings

Meriden Ave

Blue Cedars

Larch Cl

Wildacres

Fairfield Rise

Meriden Ave

Bridle Rd

Gladstone Dr

Whitney Ave

Hamilton Ave

Vestry Ct

B4186

Liddiard Ct

Foster Pl

High St

Wollaston

Meriden

Barratt's Coppice

Sewage Works

DY7

Gibbet La

Bott's Farm

Round Hill

Roundhill Farm

Whittington Hall La

Whittington Farm

Iverley Heath

High Lodge

High Lodge Farm

Bunker's Hill Wood

Bunker's Hill

Tennis & Squash Club

Iverley Park Farm

A451

Sugar Loaf La

Roman Rd (Sandy La)

Shenstone Ave

High Park Ave

The Ridge Prim Sch

Park Rd West

Gregory Rd

Harmon Rd

Whitmore Rd

Leonard Rd

Francis Rd

Dunsley Rd

Finchfield

Heronvale Cl

Larkhill

Swallowfield

Drakes Hill Cl

Kingfisher Dr

Little Iverley Covert

Westwood Ave

Lavender Rd

Chestnut Rd

Sycamore Rd

St George's Rd

Princes Rd

Romsley Way

Hazel Gr

Elderberry La

Cedar Gr

Crematorium Cemy

Marston

STOURBRIDGE

Caslon Cres

Shenstone Ave

Rosemary

Mandal La

Maynard Ave

The Broadway

Norton

The Broadway

Windsor Rd

Greyhound La

Sandy Rd

Ridgewood High Sch

Lady Grey's Owlk

Studley Gate

Lyttelton Rd

Palfrey Rd

Park Rd

Bowling Green Rd

Dellway Ct

Tudor Gdns

Fox Covert

Acacia

Kings Ct

Kingswinford

Beechwoods Ct

Cathcart Rd

Brook St

Boro Cross

Enville St

Charles Rd

Lawn Ave

Lawn St

South Rd

B4186

Gigmill Way

Cherry St

Glebe St

Morning Pines

Poole St

Fredericks Cl

Colshaw Rd

Gig Mill Prim Sch

Kempton Way

Poplar Rd

Belbroughton Rd

Arley Dr

Harvire

Witton St

Winwood

Heath La

B4186

Worcester St

Mary Stevens Park

Grassmere Dr

Stanley Rd

Gainsborough Hill

Temple Rd

Severn Rd

Avon Rd

Beech Rd

Lea Vale Rd

Dale Rd

Lea Vale

Norton Rd

Osmaston Rd

Runcorn Cl

Eveson Rd

Harrington Dr

Rungeford Rd

Coverdale

Racecourse La

Racecourse Farm

Pedmore Common

Birkdale Cl

Sunningdale Cl

St Andrews Cl

Ainsdale Cl

Lytham

Bramber Way

Albemarle Rd

Stratton Grange

DY8

Stourbridge Coll

Enville Pl 1
Baylie Ct 2
Kennedy Ct 3

Greenfield Ave

Bath Prim Sch

Beale St

Cleveland St

Western Rd

Heathfield Gdns

Bernwall Cl

Pargeter St

Baylie St

Heath St

Oxford St

Amblecote

The Holloway

Westland Gdns

Old Wharf Rd

Canal St

Linkwood Ind Est

Bradley Rd

Foster Pl

A458

Wollaston Rd

Bath Rd

A461

Glassworks

Works

Richmond Gdns 1
Harlestones Ho 2

Corbett

Liby Sch

High St

A4102

A491

Stourbridge Canal

Monarch's Way

River Stour

Brettell La

Audnam

Park La

Collis St

School Rd

Westland Gdns

H

Norton Covert

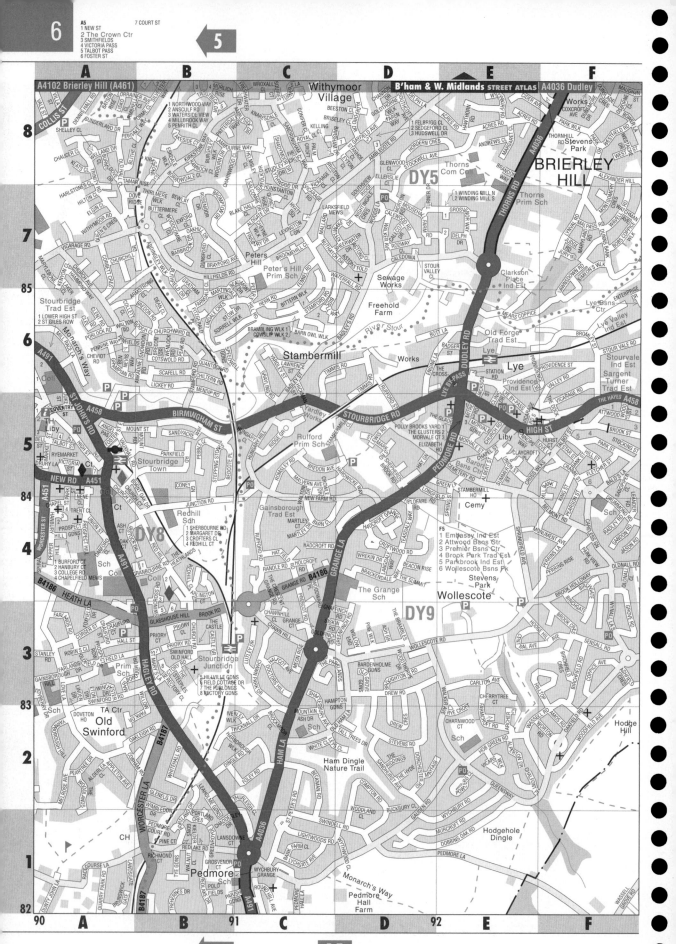

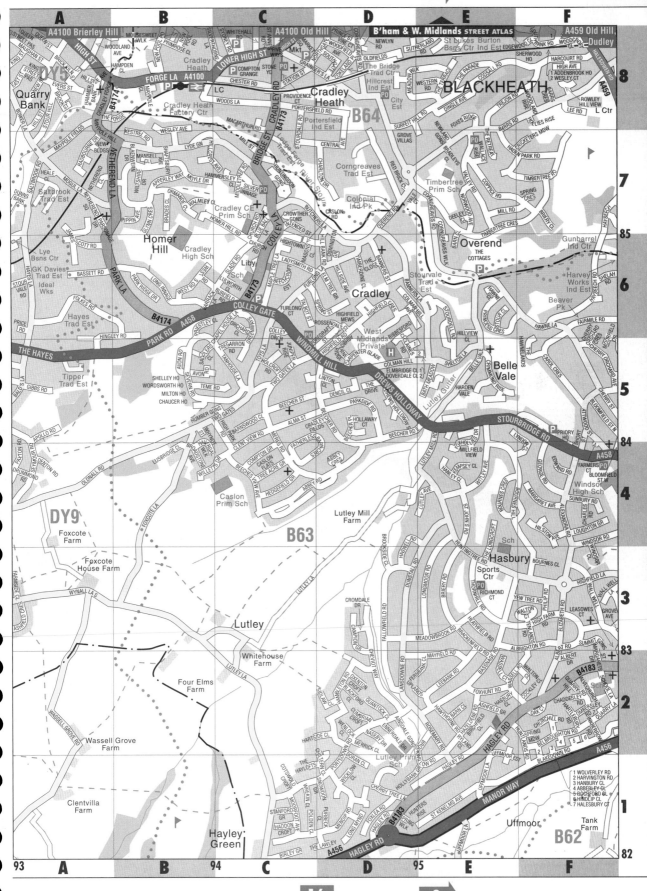

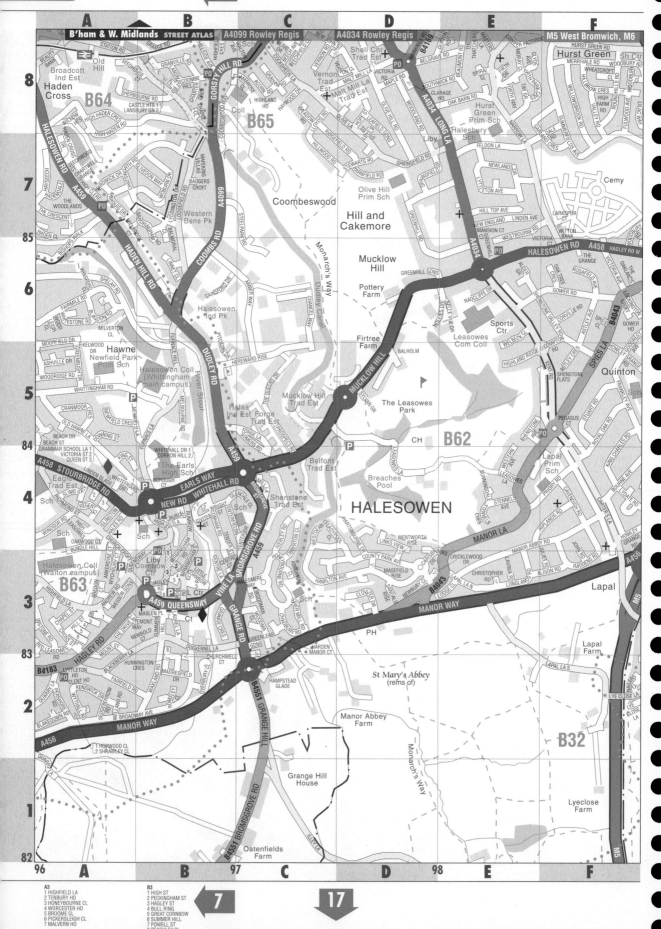

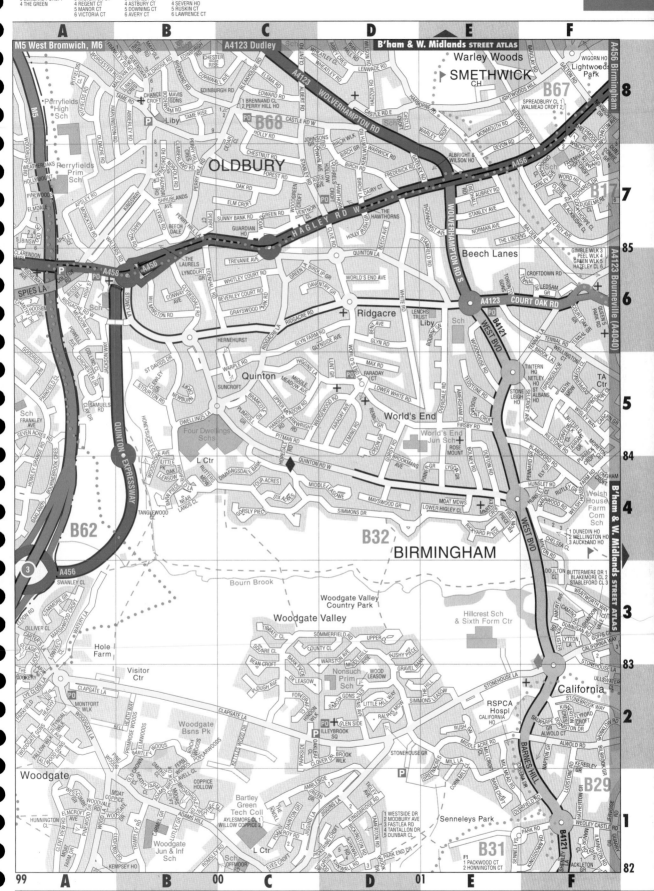

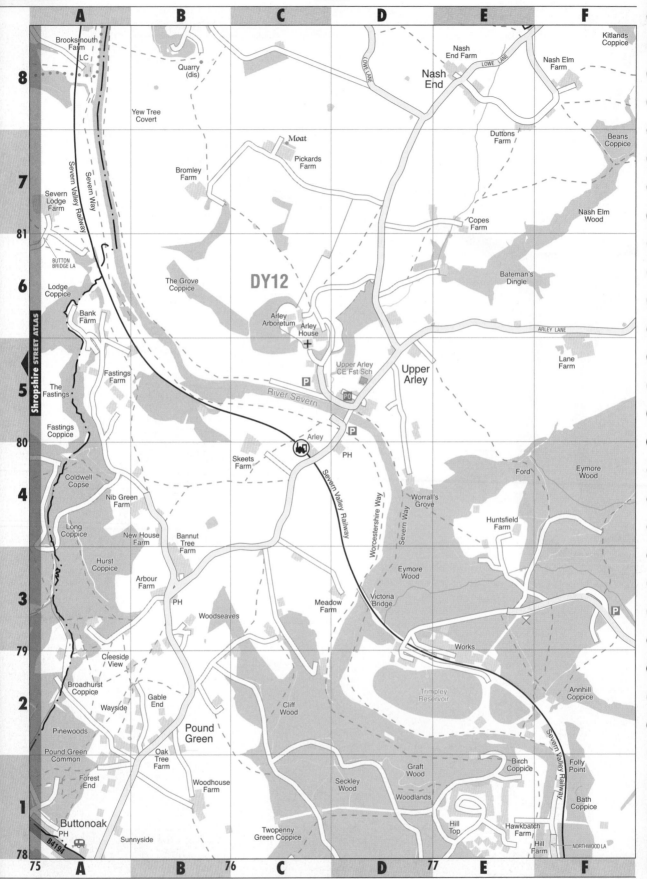

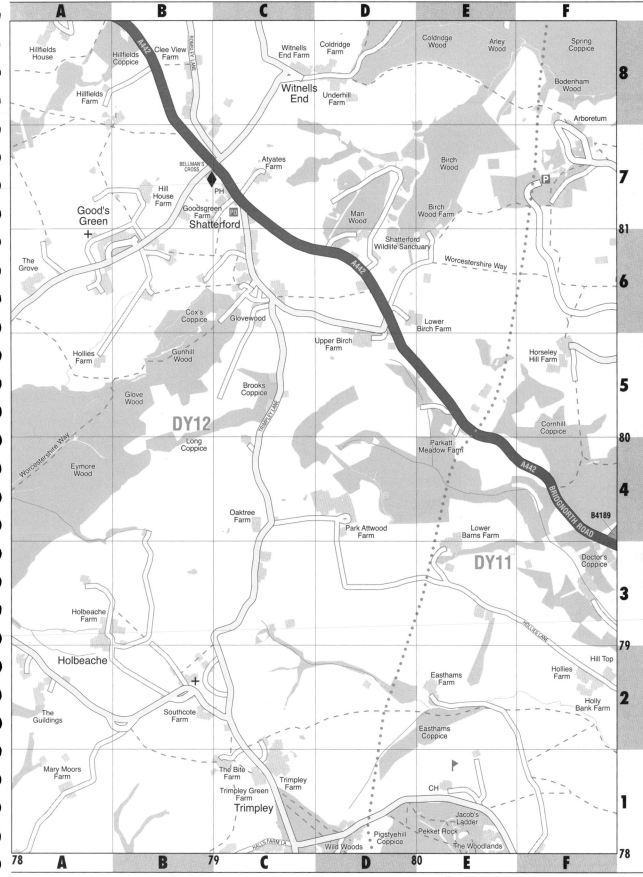

A **B** **C** **D** **E** **F**

Hillfields House

Hillfields Coppice

Hillfields Farm

Clee View Farm

ROMSLEY LANE

A442

Witnells End Farm

Coldridge Farm

Coldridge Wood

Arley Wood

Spring Coppice

8

Witnells End

Underhill Farm

Bodenham Wood

Arboretum

Atyates Farm

Birch Wood

7

BELLMAN'S CROSS

PH

Hill House Farm

Man Wood

Birch Wood Farm

P

Good's Green

Goodsgreen Farm

PO

Shatterford

Shatterford Wildlife Sanctuary

81

The Grove

Worcestershire Way

6

Cox's Coppice

Glovewood

Upper Birch Farm

Lower Birch Farm

Horseley Hill Farm

5

Hollies Farm

Gunhill Wood

Brooks Coppice

TRIMPLEY LANE

Glove Wood

DY12

Cornhill Coppice

80

Long Coppice

Parkatt Meadow Farm

A442

Worcestershire Way

Eymore Wood

BRIDGNORTH ROAD

4

Oaktree Farm

Park Attwood Farm

Lower Barns Farm

DY11

B4189

Doctor's Coppice

Holbeache Farm

3

HOLLIES LANE

Holbeache

Hill Top

79

Easthams Farm

Hollies Farm

The Guildings

Southcote Farm

Holly Bank Farm

2

Easthams Coppice

Mary Moors Farm

The Bite Farm

Trimpley Farm

CH

Trimpley Green Farm

Jacob's Ladder

1

Trimpley

Pigstyehill Coppice

Pekket Rock

HALLS FARM LA.

Wild Woods

The Woodlands

78

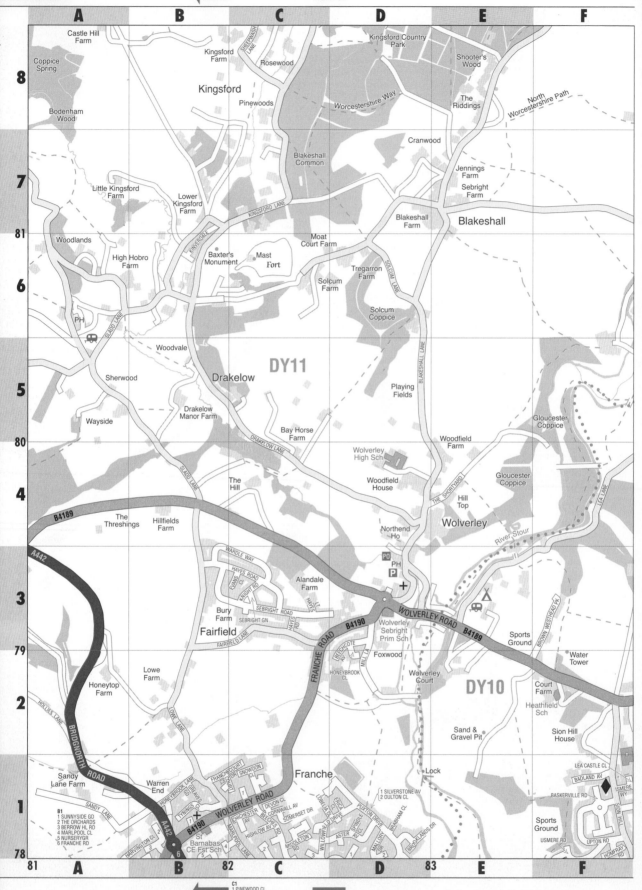

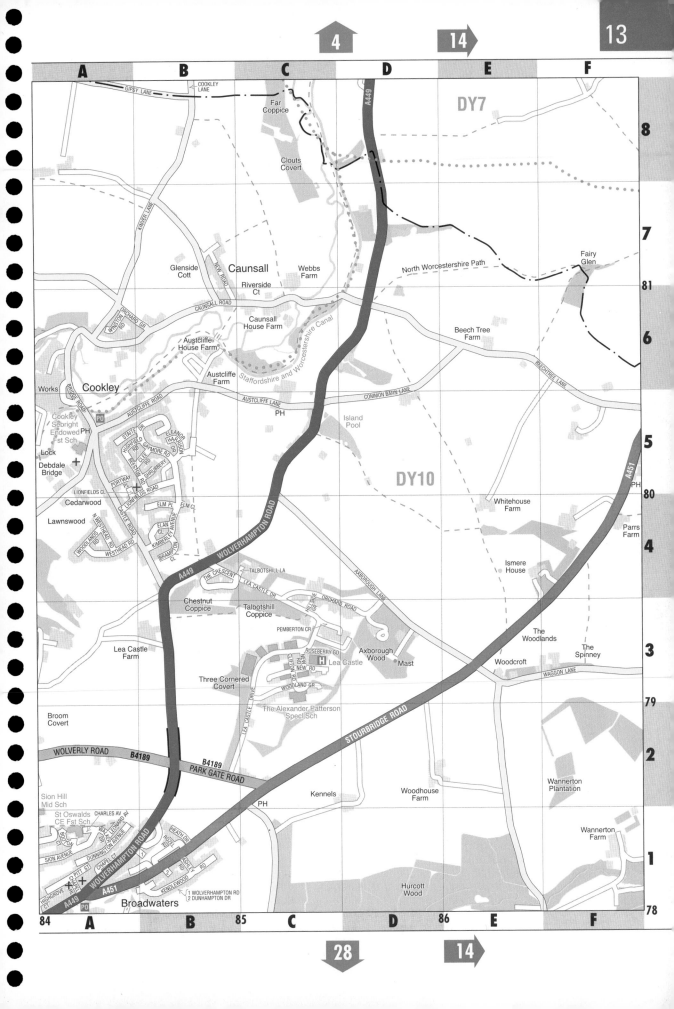

DY7

Sugarloaf Farm

OUNTY JOHN LA
Burys Hill

Mast

Crown Inn (PH)

Iverley

KIDDERMINSTER RD

Iverley House Farm

SUGAR LOAF LA

Iverley Hay Farm

The Birches

81

Highdown Cottages

North Worcs Path

Upper Brake Farm

Haybridge High Sch

DY8

BRAKE LA

STOURBRIDGE RD

CROWN LA

Common Farm

DY8

Hagley RC High Sch

THE BRAKE

Palmer's Hill

WOODLAND AVE

THE COPPICE

HOARSTONE

SWEETPOOL LA

HAYBRIDGE AVE

SUMMERVALE RD

A451

FIVE WAYS

IVERLEY LA

Brakemill Plantation

THE CRESCENT

WILLON CL

THE GREENWAY

5

Pumping Station

80

Brakemill Farm

Sewage Works

CAVENDISH DR

THE SYCAMORES 1
THE HAZELS 2
THE SPRUCES 3
THE HAWTHORNS 4
THE BRIARS 5
THE GREEN 6
LONG CL 7
SPRING CL 8

MILESTONE DR

4

Stakenbridge Farm

BEECHES MEWS 9
PINEWOODS CT 10

PINEWOODS AVE

MEADOW CROFT

A456

PINEWOODS CL

STAKENBRIDGE LA

DY10

Stakenbridge

KIDDERMINSTER RD S

THICKNALL LA

WAGGON LA

CHURCHILL LA

CHURCH FARM BARN & COTTS

Churchill

Bridge Farm

Harborough Farm

Falconry Ctr

WORCESTER RD

A450

DY9

3

Churchill Farm

Harborough Hill

Nursery

STONEY LA

79

SCULTHORPE RD

THE CROFT

WHEATMILL CL

BIRMINGHAM RD

Harborough Hall

Broome Mill

Windmill Pool

BROOME LA

2

CH

Blakedown

LC

MILL LA

MILL CL

Monarch's Way

STOURBRIDGE RD

BROOKSIDE WAY

ELM DR

LYNWOOD DR

THE AVENUE

ROXALL CL

STATION DR

Blakedown

Blakedown CE Prim Sch

Broome Lodge Farm

BROOME LA

Wannerton House

Downs Plantation

SWAN CL

FORGE LA

PO

B4188

Knoll Hill House

Hackman's Gate

Hundred Acre Farm

1

Sewage Works

Swan Pool

HALESHIRE LA

Forge Pool

New House Farm

BELBROUGHTON RD

B4188

A450

78

A456

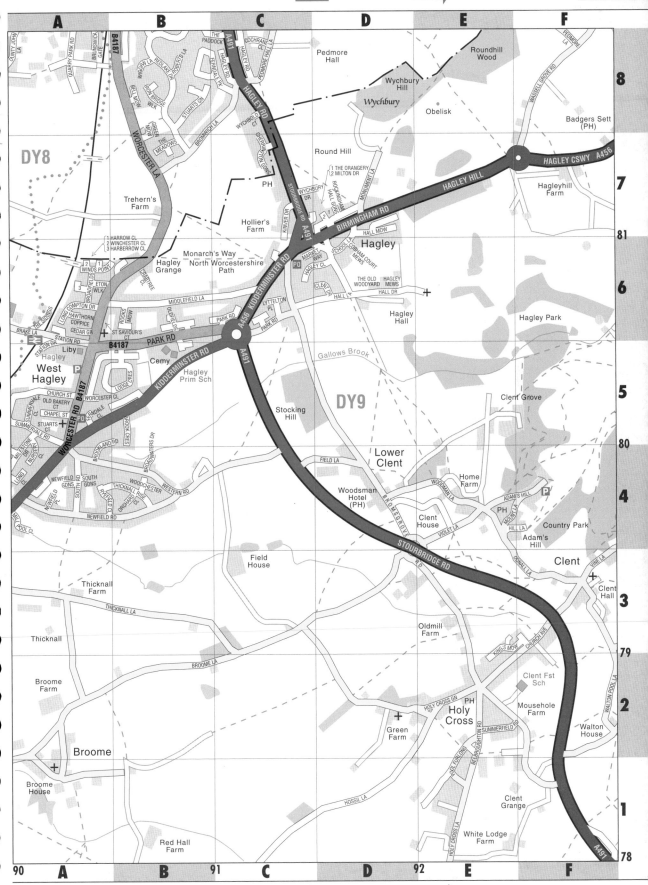

A   B   C   D   E   F

8
7
81
6
5
80
4
3
79
2
1
78

CH

HAGLEY RD   A456
LUTLEY LA
HAYLEY PARK RD
HODGETTS DR
WAUGHT DR
ABBOT RD
KEMELSTOWE CRES
CAUSEY FARM RD

B63

Uffmoor Farm

HAGLEY CSWY
A456

Hagley Wood

Bogs Wood

UFFMOOR LA

HAGLEY WOOD LA

Spring Farm

P

Uffmoor Wood

Nimmings Plantation
Nimmings Visitor Ctr

Short Wood

Penorchard Farm

CHAPEL LA
Chapel Farm

North Worcestershire Path

St Kenelm's Farm

Clent Hills

P
High Harcourt Farm

The Four Stones

P

Fox Farm

Four Oaks House

ST KENELM'S RD

B62

IVY

THE ALDERS
THE HEDGEROWS
DARK LA
WAVERLEY CRES

Monarch's Way

Clent Hills Country Park

Deep Wood

Dark Pool

HOLT LA

Holt Farm

PH
VINE LA
CLATTERBACH LA

Walton Hill

SPRING LA

Oatlands

FIELDHOUSE LA

Fieldhouse Farm

Whitehall Farm

Nag Hill

DY9

WALTON RISE

Walton Hill Farm

RUMBOW LA

HIGHFIELD LA

Rumbow Cottages

Walton Pool

Walton Farm

Calcot Hill

SHUT MILL LA

Daleswood Farm

Dales Wood

Squats Wood

MOOR HALL
Moor Hall

Calcothill Farm

WINWOOD HEATH RD
North Worcestershire Path

Great Farley Wood

FARLEY LA

ROMSLEY HILL GRANGE

Farley Farm

93   A   B   94   C   D   95   E   F

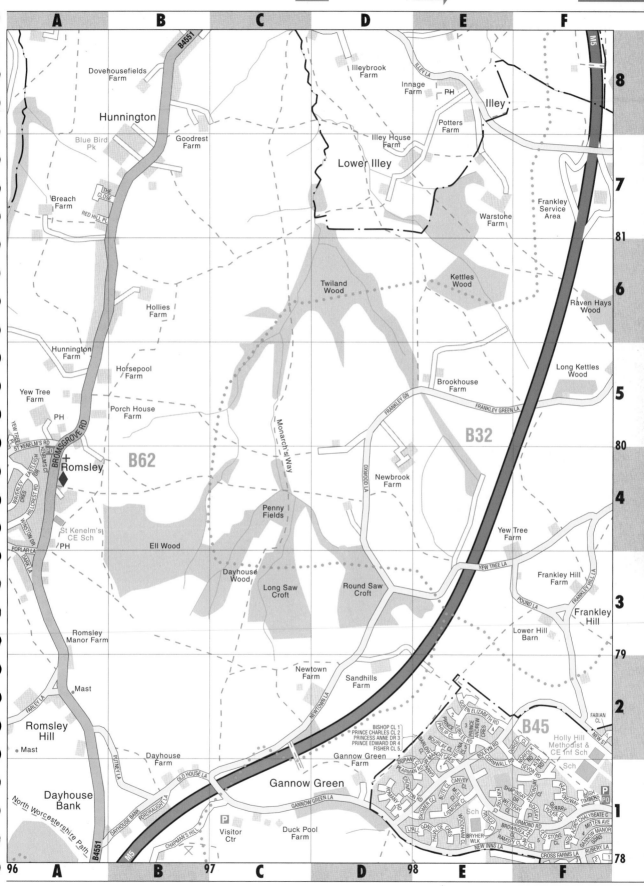

A B C D E F

8
7
81
6
5
80
4
3
79
2
1

B4551

Dovehousefields
Farm

Illeybrook
Farm

Innage
Farm

PH

Illey

Hunnington

Blue Bird
Pk

Goodrest
Farm

Potters
Farm

Illey House
Farm

Lower Illey

Breach
Farm

THE
CLOSE

RED HILL PL

Warstone
Farm

Frankley
Service
Area

Kettles
Wood

Twiland
Wood

Raven Hays
Wood

Hollies
Farm

Hunnington
Farm

Horsepool
Farm

Porch House
Farm

Brookhouse
Farm

Long Kettles
Wood

Yew Tree
Farm

PH

FRANKLEY GN

FRANKLEY GREEN LA

B32

Monarch's Way

ST KENELM'S RD
KENELM CT
EASTLEIGH
DR

BROMSGROVE RD

WAVERLEY
CRES

HILLCREST RD

YEW TREE

B62

+ Romsley

OXWOOD LA

Newbrook
Farm

80

St Kenelm's
CE Sch

WINSTON DR

POPLAR LA
DARK LA

PH

Ell Wood

Penny
Fields

Yew Tree
Farm

YEW TREE LA

Frankley Hill
Farm

FRANKLEY HILL LA

POUND LA

Frankley
Hill

Dayhouse
Wood

Long Saw
Croft

Round Saw
Croft

Lower Hill
Barn

Romsley
Manor Farm

Newtown
Farm

Sandhills
Farm

FARLEY LA

Mast

Romsley
Hill

Mast

Dayhouse
Farm

PUTNEY LA

DAYHOUSE BANK

OLD HOUSE LA

FORDRAUGHT LA

NEWTOWN LA

Gannow Green
Farm

BISHOP CL 1
PRINCE CHARLES CL 2
PRINCESS ANNE DR 3
PRINCE EDWARD DR 4
FISHER CL 5

QUEEN ELIZABETH RD

PRINCE
ANDREW
CRES

JUBILEE RD

BOLEYN RD

CORNWALL CL

FABIAN
CL

B45

NEW ST

Holly Hill
Methodist &
CE Inf Sch

Sch

Dayhouse
Bank

North Worcestershire Path

B4551

M5

CHAPMAN'S HILL

Visitor
Ctr

Gannow Green

GANNOW GREEN LA

Duck Pool
Farm

P

DURANT
CL

PEARMAN RD

RANYAL
RD

SKOMER CL

LYALL
GDNS

THURLOE
CRES

BOURLAY CL

PHILIP CL

MANOR CL

BUTE CL

CANVEY
CL

MILL
CL

WOODHAM
CL

BRYHER
WLK

NEW INNS LA

LISMORE CL

ARKSEY
CL

SHARINSAY
DR

KINTYRE CL

RAMSAY
CL

BROWNSEA
CL

ORMOND RD

RASO CL

STONE

CROSS FARMS LA

PI

DORSEY
CL

NORFOLK
CL

DEVON RD

KENT
CL

WESTRAY
DR

HIGH
TIMBERS

WIDE ACRES
CHALYBEATE C

RAILWAY
WLK

QUARRY
CL

GANNOW MANOR
GDNS

RUBERY LA

P
PO

MITTEN AVE

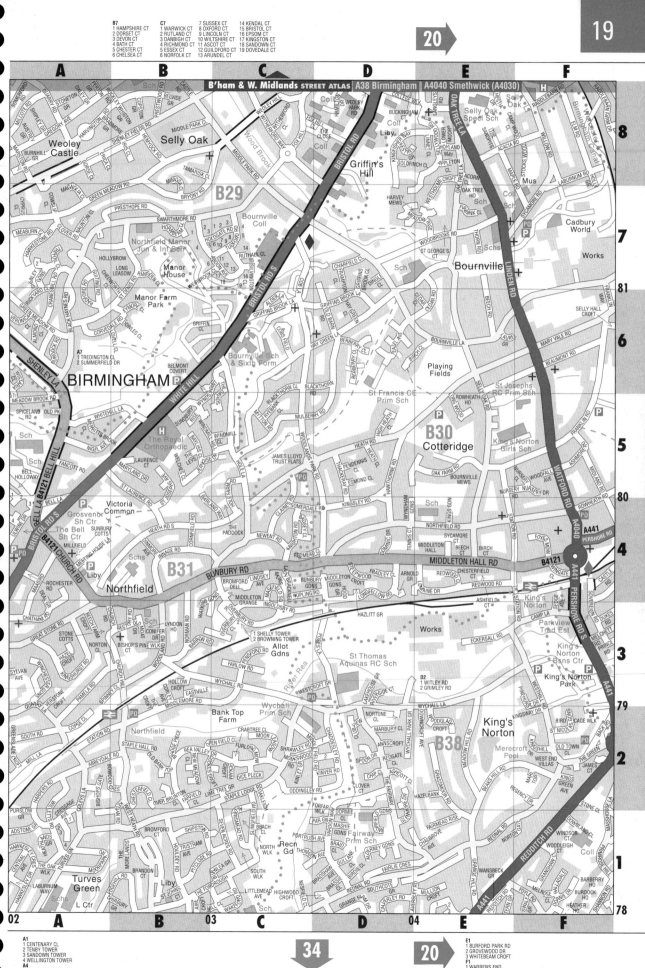

B7
1 HAMPSHIRE CT
2 DORSET CT
3 DEVON CT
4 BATH CT
5 CHESTER CT
6 CHELSEA CT

C7
1 WARWICK CT
2 RUTLAND CT
3 DANBIGH CT
4 RICHMOND CT
5 ESSEX CT
6 NORFOLK CT

7 SUSSEX CT
8 OXFORD CT
9 LINCOLN CT
10 WILTSHIRE CT
11 ASCOT CT
12 GUILDFORD CT
13 ARUNDEL CT

14 KENDAL CT
15 BRISTOL CT
16 EPSOM CT
17 KINGSTON CT
18 SANDOWN CT
19 DOVEDALE CT

B'ham & W. Midlands STREET ATLAS A38 Birmingham | A4040 Smethwick (A4030)

A1
1 CENTENARY CL
2 TENBY TOWER
3 SANDOWN TOWER
4 WELLINGTON TOWER
A4
1 CUTLERS ROUGH CL
2 SAXON WOOD CL
3 BELL HILL
4 VINEYARD RD

E1
1 BURFORD PARK RD
2 GROVEWOOD DR
3 WHITEBEAM CROFT
F1
1 WARRENS END

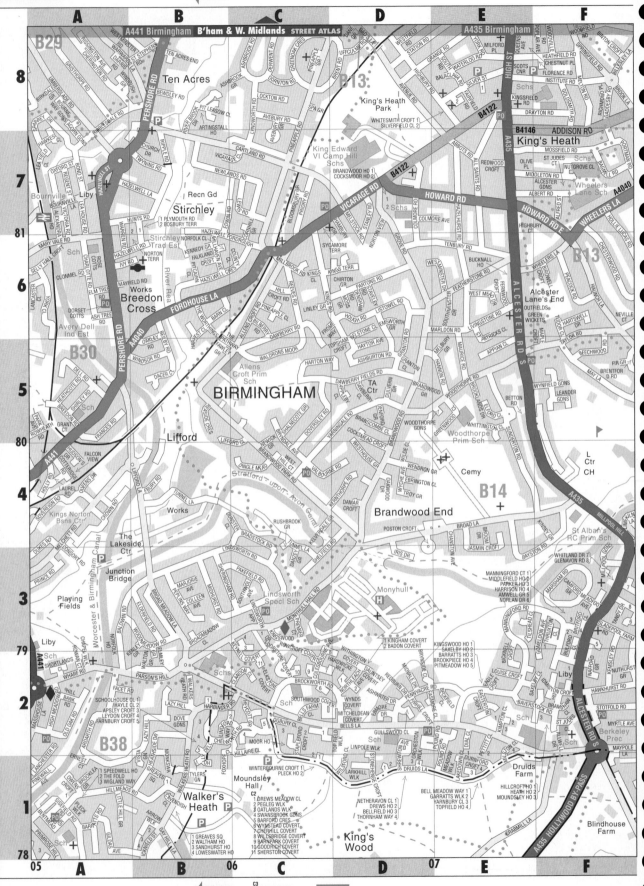

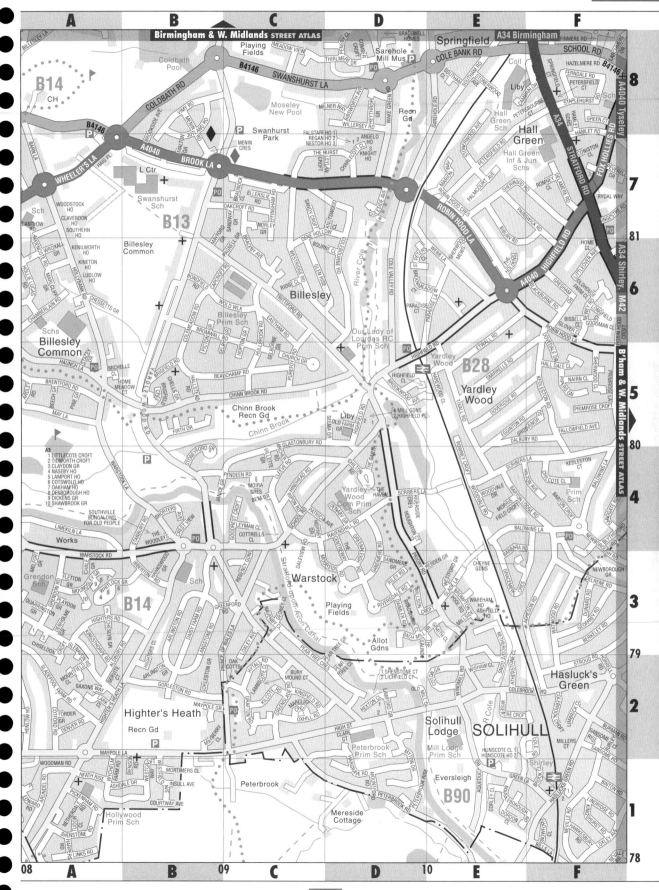

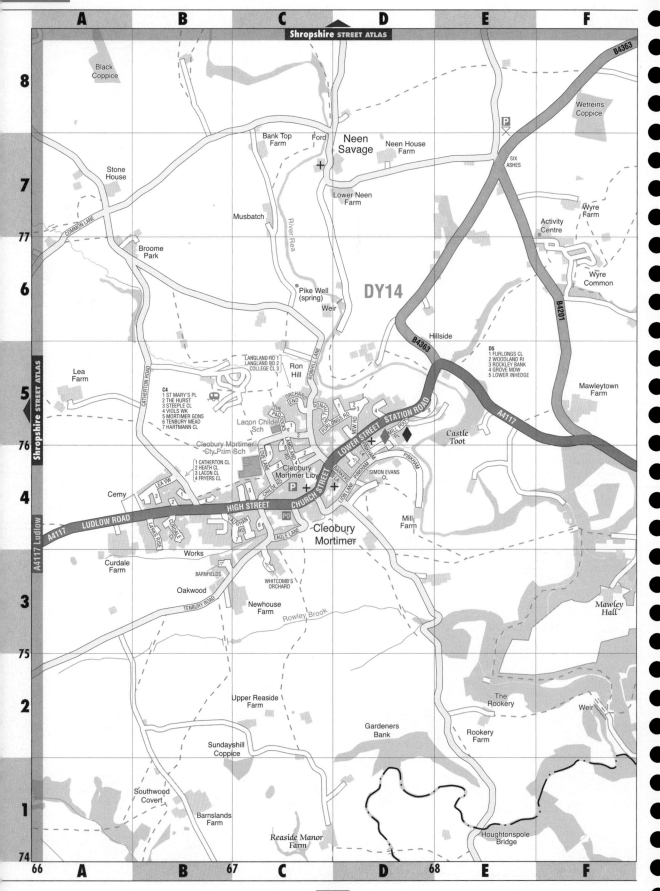

DY14

Neen Savage

Black Coppice

Stone House

Lea Farm

Broome Park

Musbatch

Bank Top Farm

Ford

Neen House Farm

Lower Neen Farm

Pike Well (spring)

Weir

Ron Hill

Wetreins Coppice

Wyre Farm

Activity Centre

Wyre Common

SIX ASHES

Hillside

Mawleytown Farm

LANGLAND RD 1
LANGLAND RD 2
COLLEGE CL 3

C4
1 ST MARY'S PL
2 THE HURST
3 STEEPLE CL
4 VIOLS WK
5 MORTIMER GDNS
6 TENBURY MEAD
7 HARTMANN CL

D5
1 FURLONGS CL
2 WOODLAND RI
3 ROCKLEY BANK
4 GROVE MDW
5 LOWER INHEDGE

Lacon Childe Sch

Cleobury Mortimer Cty Prim Sch

1 CATHERTON CL
2 HEATH CL
3 LACON CL
4 FRYERS CL

Cleobury Mortimer Lib

Castle Toot

STATION ROAD

A4117

MILL POOL

Simon Evans CL

Cemy

LEA VW

HIGH STREET

LUDLOW ROAD

A4117 Ludlow

CHURCH STREET

LOWER STREET

Cleobury Mortimer

Mill Farm

Curdale Farm

Oakwood

Works

BARNFIELDS

WHITCOMB'S ORCHARD

Newhouse Farm

TENBURY ROAD

Rowley Brook

Mawley Hall

Upper Reaside Farm

Gardeners Bank

The Rookery

Rookery Farm

Weir

Sundayshill Coppice

Southwood Covert

Barnslands Farm

Reaside Manor Farm

Houghtonspole Bridge

River Rea

Common Lane

Catherton Road

B4363

B4201

B4363

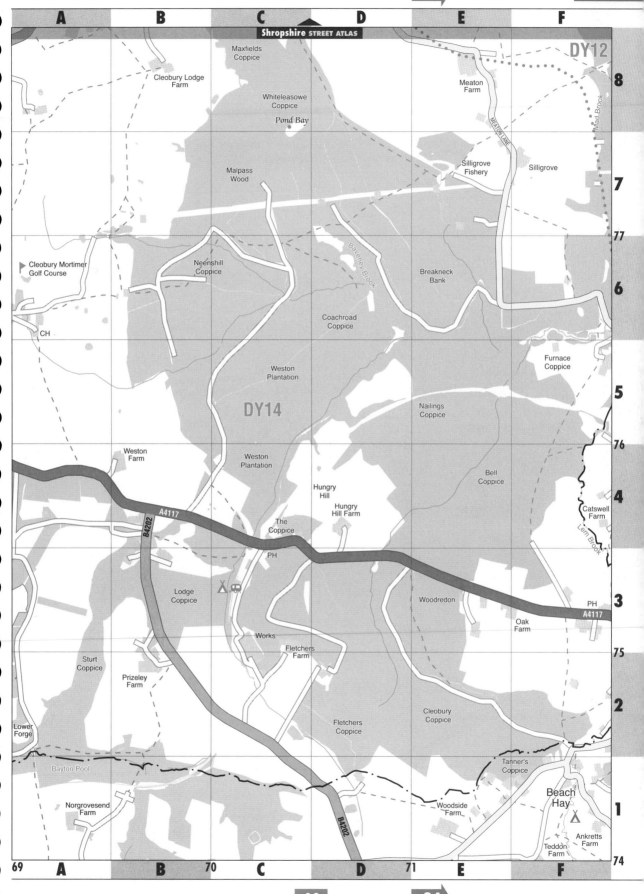

Shropshire STREET ATLAS

DY12

Maxfields
Coppice

Meaton
Farm

Whiteleasowe
Coppice

Pond Bay

Silligrove
Fishery

Silligrove

Malpass
Wood

MEATON LANE

Mad Brook

8

7

77

▶ Cleobury Mortimer
Golf Course

Neenshill
Coppice

Breakneck
Bank

Baveney Brook

6

CH

Coachroad
Coppice

Furnace
Coppice

Weston
Plantation

DY14

Nailings
Coppice

5

76

Weston
Farm

Weston
Plantation

Bell
Coppice

Catswell
Farm

Lern Brook

4

A4117

B4202

Hungry
Hill

Hungry
Hill Farm

The
Coppice

PH

Woodredon

Oak
Farm

PH
A4117

3

Lodge
Coppice

Works

Fletchers
Farm

75

Sturt
Coppice

Prizeley
Farm

Fletchers
Coppice

Cleobury
Coppice

2

Lower
Forge

Bayton Pool

Tanner's
Coppice

Beach
Hay

Norgrovesend
Farm

Woodside
Farm

Ankretts
Farm

Teddon
Farm

B4202

1

74

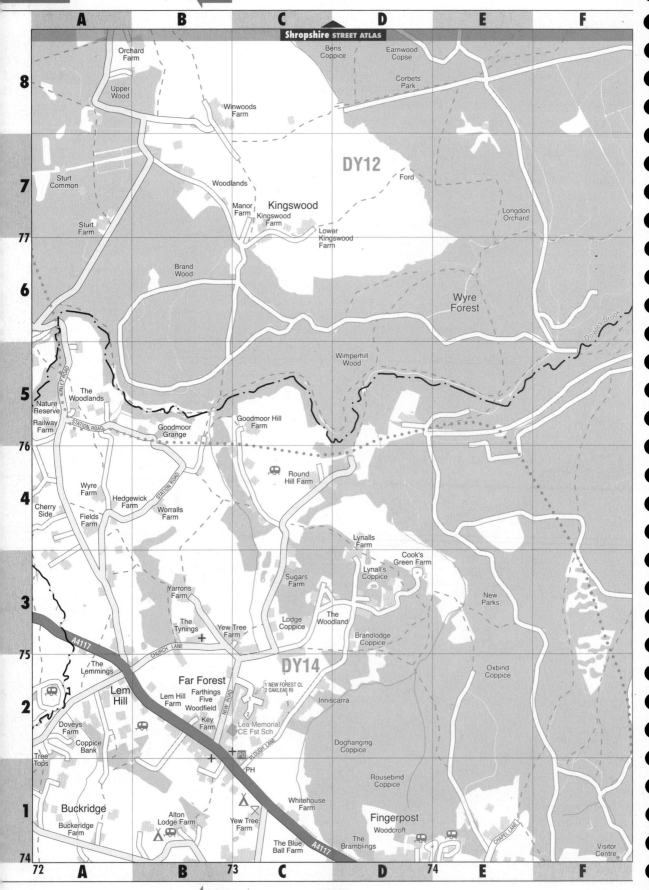

Shropshire STREET ATLAS

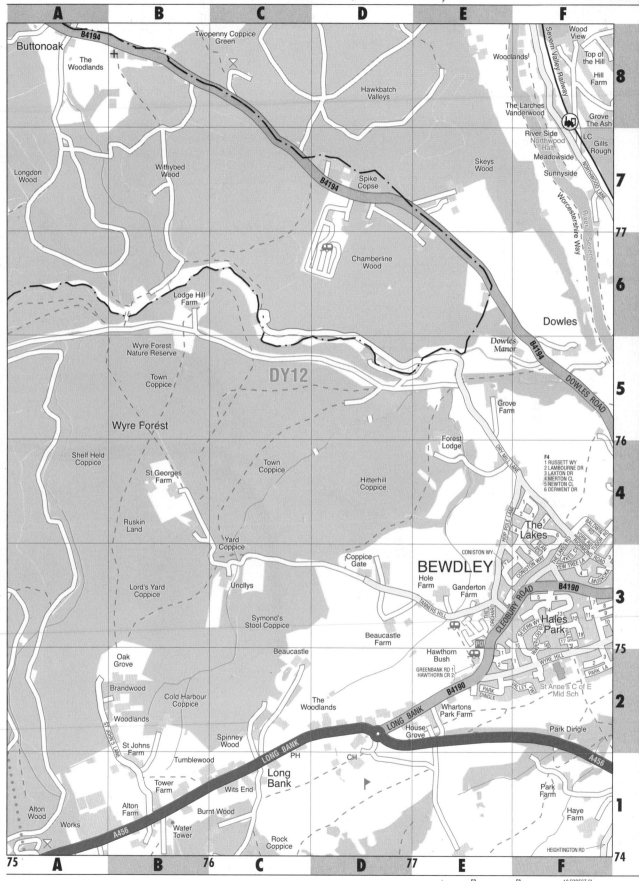

A B C D E F

8

7

77

6

Buttonoak

B4194

The Woodlands

Twopenny Coppice Green

Hawkbatch Valleys

Woodlands

Wood View

Top of the Hill

Hill Farm

The Larches
Vanderwood

Grove
The Ash

River Side
Northwood Hall
Meadowside

LC
Gills Rough

Sunnyside

Longdon Wood

Withybed Wood

Spike Copse

B4194

Skeys Wood

Severn Valley Railway

NORTHWOOD LANE

Worcestershire Way

River Severn

Chamberline Wood

Dowles

Lodge Hill Farm

Wyre Forest Nature Reserve

Town Coppice

DY12

Dowles Manor

B4194

DOWLES ROAD

5

76

Wyre Forest

Town Coppice

Grove Farm

Shelf Held Coppice

St Georges Farm

Town Coppice

Hitterhill Coppice

Forest Lodge

F4
1 RUSSETT WY
2 LAMBOURNE DR
3 LAXTON DR
4 MERTON CL
5 NEWTON CL
6 DERWENT DR

4

Ruskin Land

Yard Coppice

The Lakes

DRY MILL LANE

HOP POLE LANE

CONISTON WY

BEWDLEY

Hole Farm

Ganderton Farm

CLEOBURY ROAD

B4190

HALES
Hales Park

3

75

Lord's Yard Coppice

Uncllys

Coppice Gate

Symond's Stool Coppice

Beaucastle Farm

TANNERS HILL

Oak Grove

Beaucastle

Hawthorn Bush

GREENBANK RD 1
HAWTHORN CR 2

B4190

PO

St Anne's C of E Mid Sch

2

Brandwood

Cold Harbour Coppice

Woodlands

St Johns Farm

Spinney Wood

The Woodlands

LONG BANK

House Grove

Whartons Park Farm

PARK DINGLE

VALLEY

Park Dingle

ST JOHN'S LANE

Tumblewood

PH

CH

Long Bank

Alton Wood

Works

Alton Farm

Burnt Wood

Wits End

Water Tower

Rock Coppice

A456

Park Farm

Haye Farm

HEIGHTINGTON RD

1

74

75 A B 76 C D 77 E F 74

F2
1 PINETREE RD
2 BRANCHES CL
3 BIRCH TREE RD

F3
1 BRAMLEY WY
2 ELLESMERE DR
3 LANCASTER RD
4 YEW TREE CL
5 EARLY RIVER PL
6 ELTON RD
7 MERRICKS LA
8 FORT-MAHON PL
9 OAKWOOD RD

10 FOREST CL
11 MERRICKS CL
12 GROSVENOR WOOD
13 MORELLA CL
14 HALES PARK
15 HORNBEAM CL
16 CHERRY CL
17 IRONSIDE CL
18 WHITE HEART CL

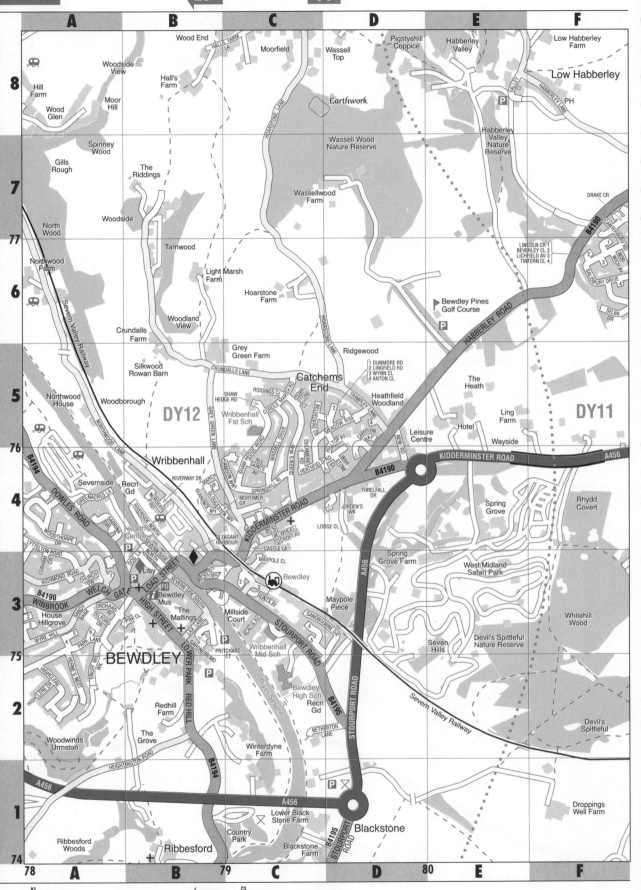

A3
1 VENUS BANK
2 OAKWOOD RD
3 FOREST CL
4 BARRATTS STILE LA
5 BARRATTS CL
6 ROSENHURST DR

C3
1 WESTBOURNE ST
2 STEPHENSON PL
3 STATION ROAD
4 BROOK VALE
5 SANDSTONE RD

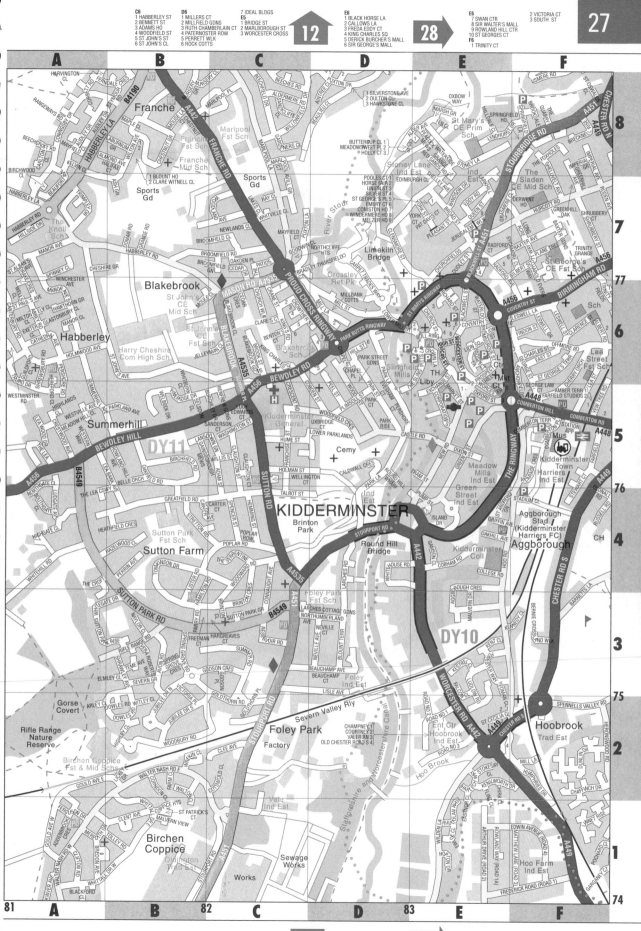

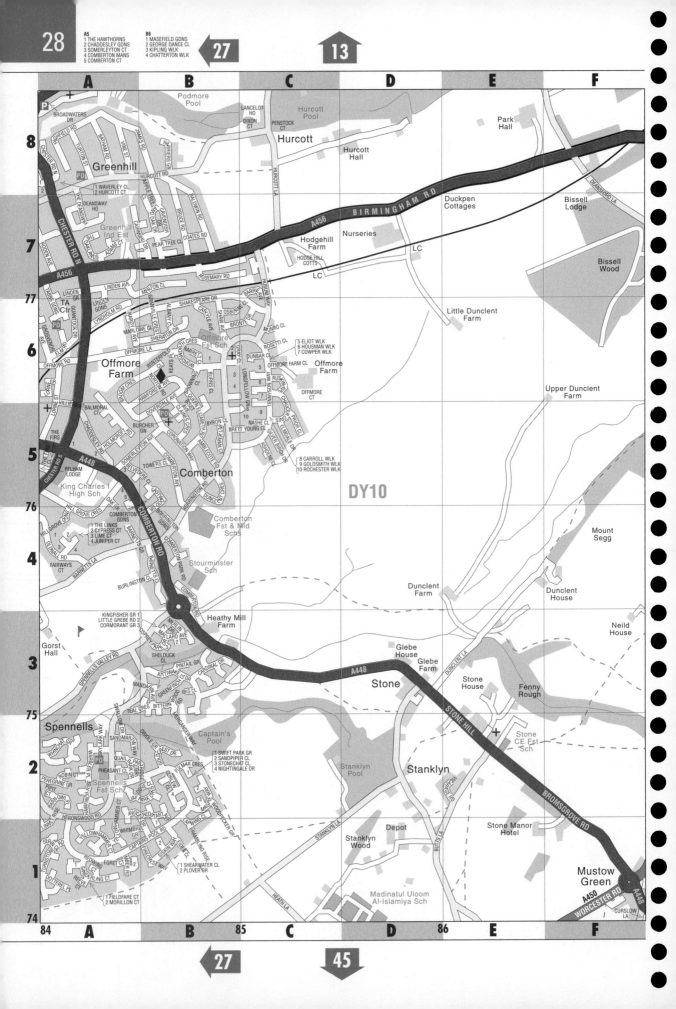

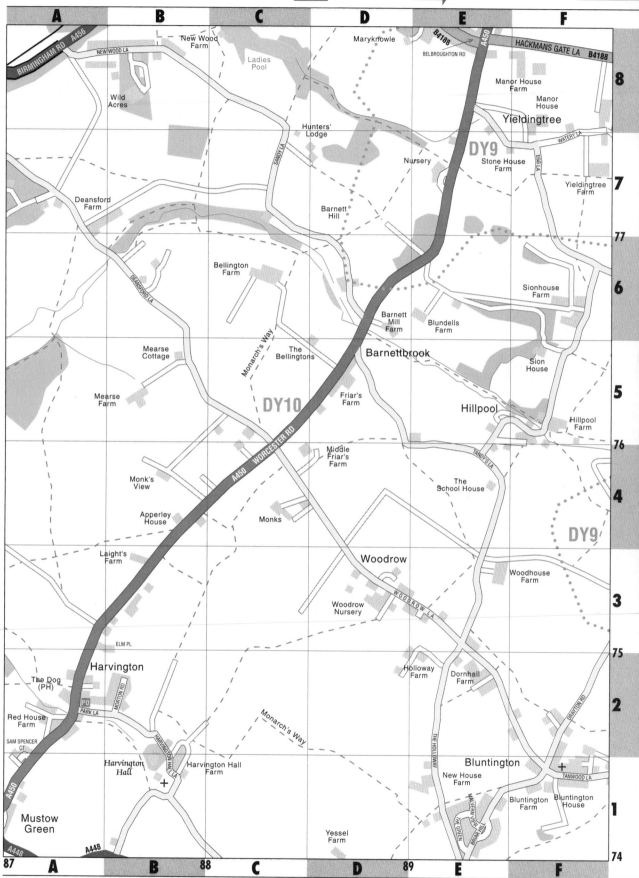

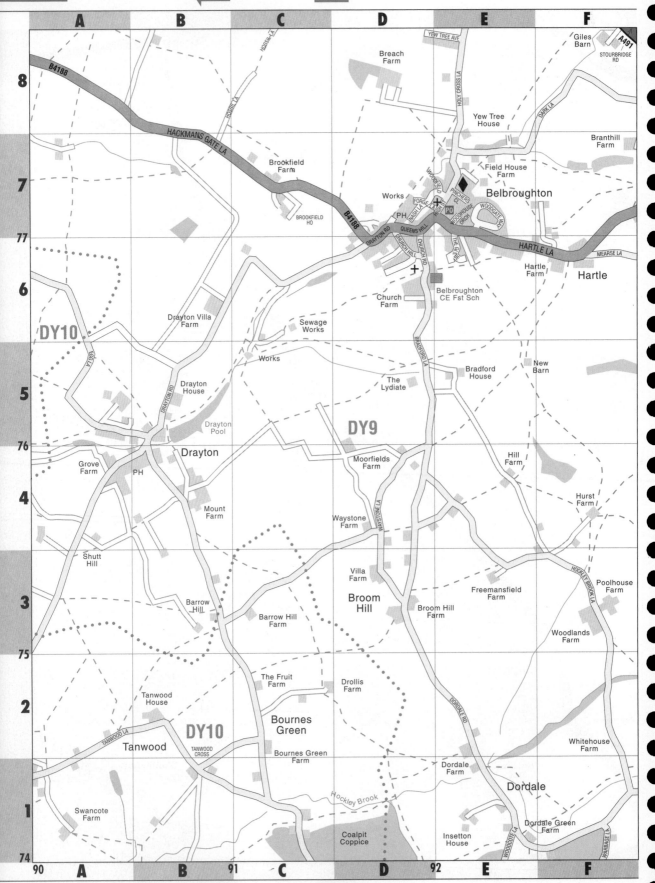

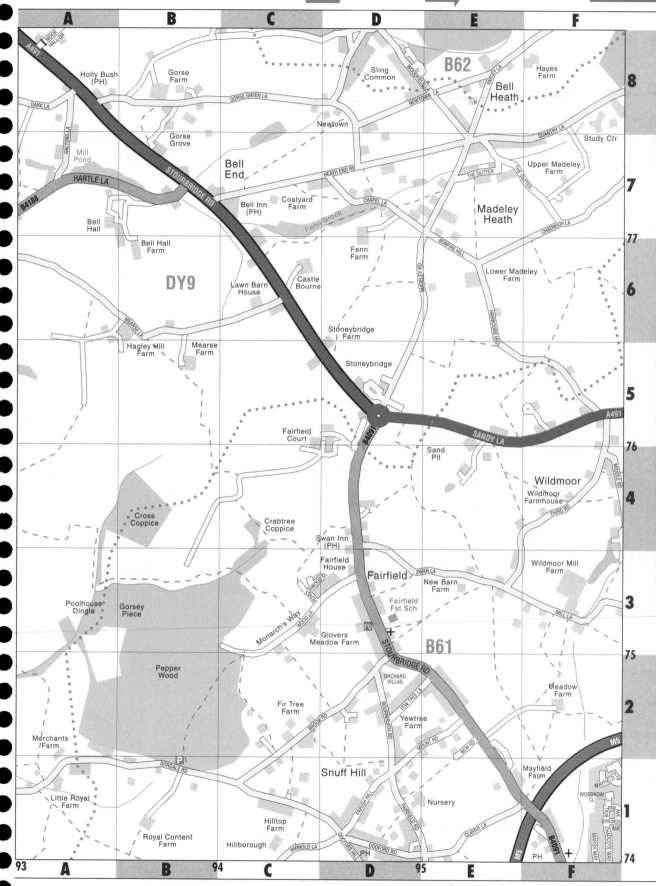

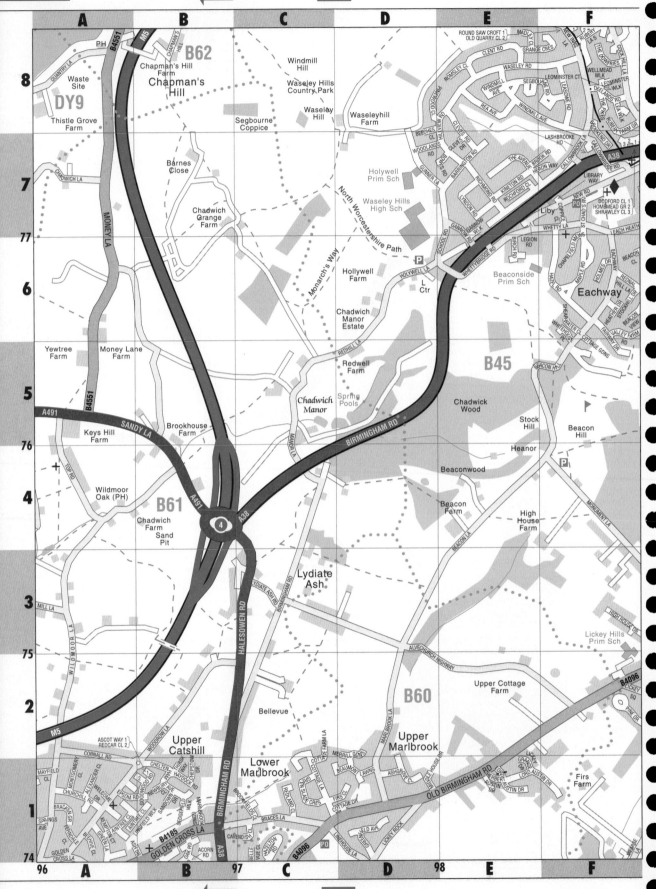

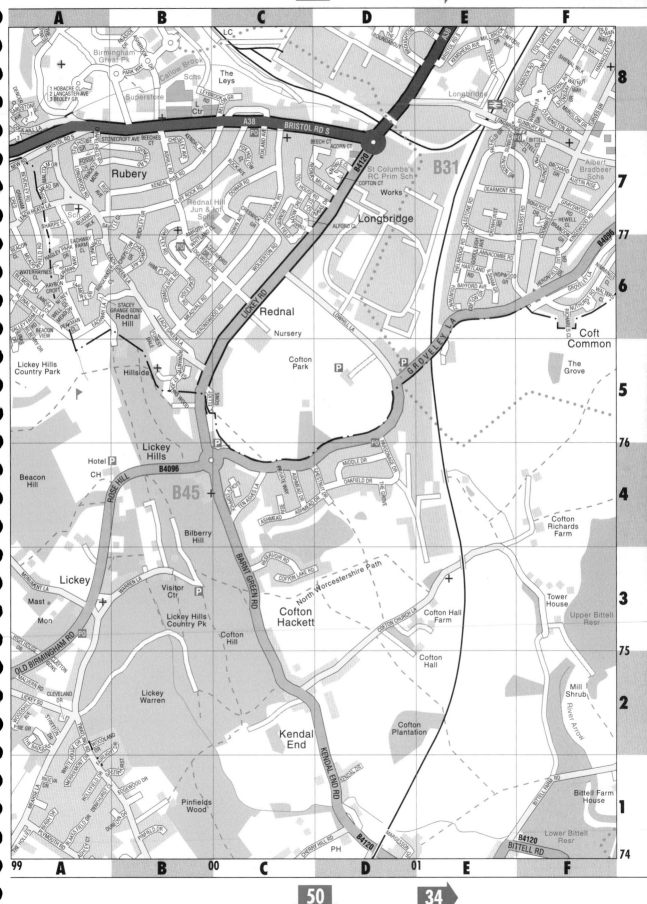

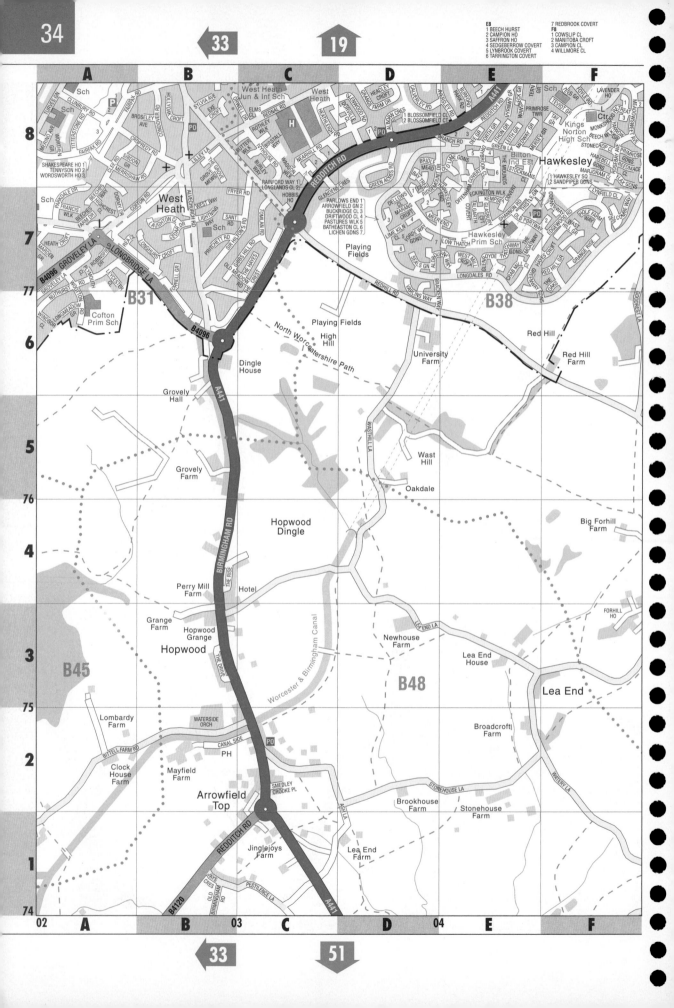

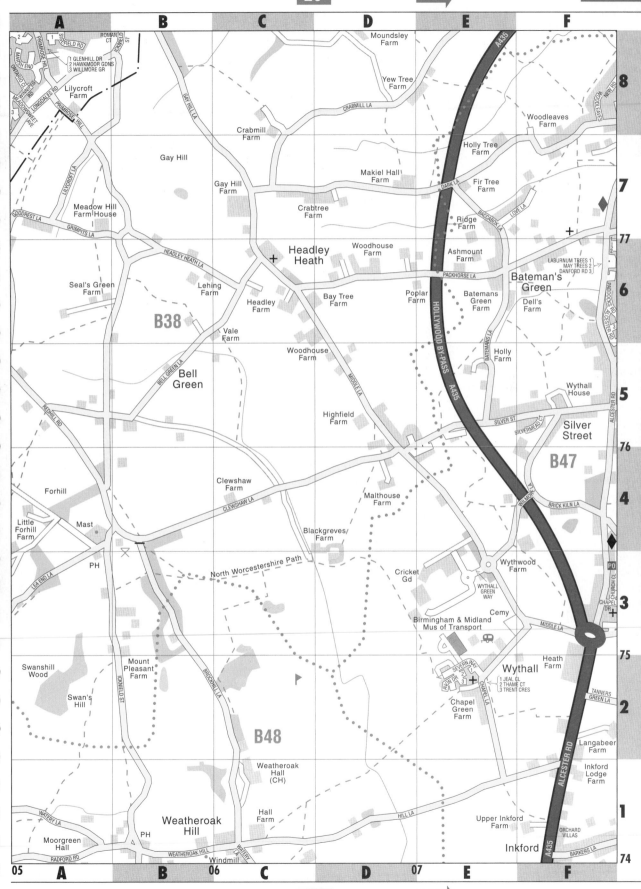

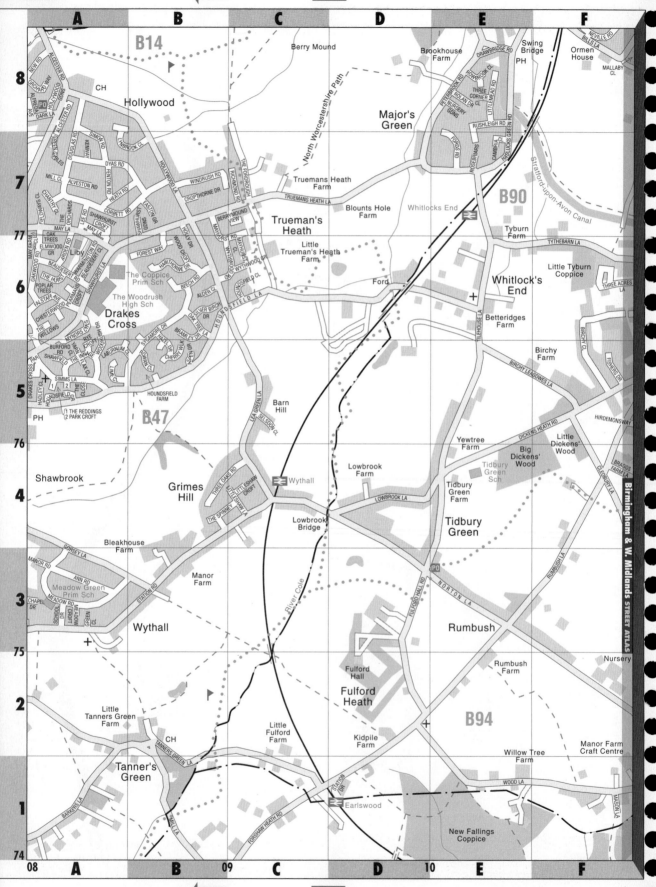

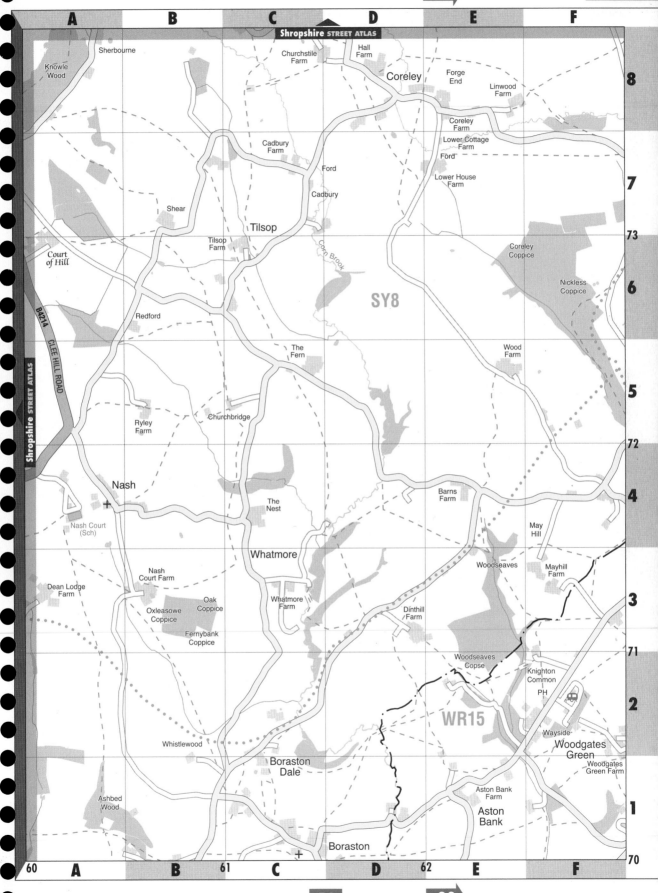

Knowle Wood

Sherbourne

Churchstile Farm

Hall Farm

Coreley

Forge End

Linwood Farm

Coreley Farm

Lower Cottage Farm

Cadbury Farm

Ford

Ford

Lower House Farm

Shear

Cadbury

Coreley Coppice

Tilsop

Tilsop Farm

Corn Brook

SY8

Nickless Coppice

Court of Hill

Redford

The Fern

Wood Farm

B4214

CLEE HILL ROAD

Ryley Farm

Churchbridge

Shropshire STREET ATLAS

Nash

The Nest

Barns Farm

May Hill

Nash Court (Sch)

Whatmore

Woodseaves

Mayhill Farm

Dean Lodge Farm

Nash Court Farm

Oak Coppice

Whatmore Farm

Dinthill Farm

Oxleasowe Coppice

Fernybank Coppice

Woodseaves Copse

Knighton Common

PH

Whistlewood

WR15

Wayside

Woodgates Green

Boraston Dale

Woodgates Green Farm

Ashbed Wood

Aston Bank Farm

Aston Bank

Boraston

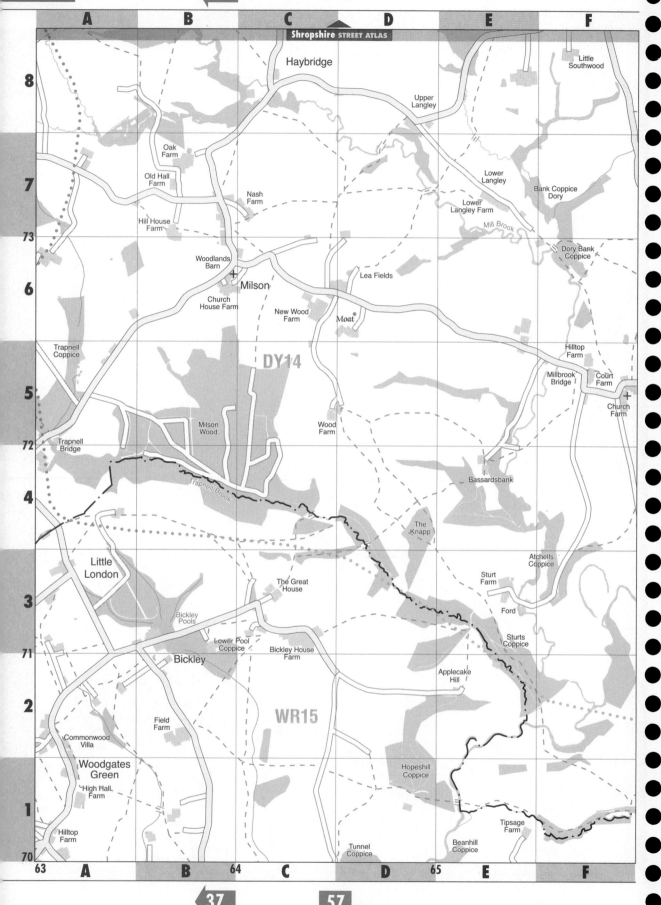

Shropshire STREET ATLAS

Haybridge

Little
Southwood

Upper
Langley

Oak
Farm

Old Hall
Farm

Lower
Langley

Bank Coppice
Dory

Nash
Farm

Lower
Langley Farm

Mill Brook

Hill House
Farm

Dory Bank
Coppice

Woodlands
Barn

Milson

Lea Fields

Church
House Farm

New Wood
Farm

Moat

Hilltop
Farm

Trapnell
Coppice

DY14

Millbrook
Bridge

Court
Farm

Church
Farm

Milson
Wood

Wood
Farm

Trapnell
Bridge

Trapnell Brook

Bassardsbank

The
Knapp

Atchells
Coppice

Little
London

The Great
House

Sturt
Farm

Bickley
Pools

Ford

Lower Pool
Coppice

Bickley House
Farm

Sturts
Coppice

Bickley

Applecake
Hill

Field
Farm

WR15

Commonwood
Villa

Hopeshill
Coppice

Woodgates
Green

High Hall
Farm

Tipsage
Farm

Hilltop
Farm

Tunnel
Coppice

Beanhill
Coppice

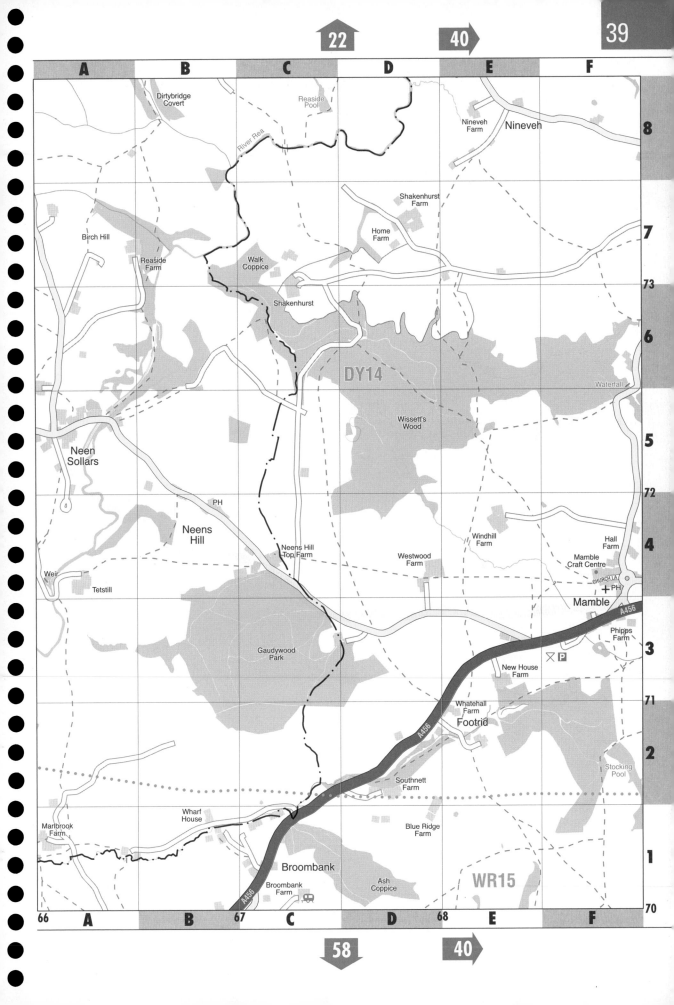

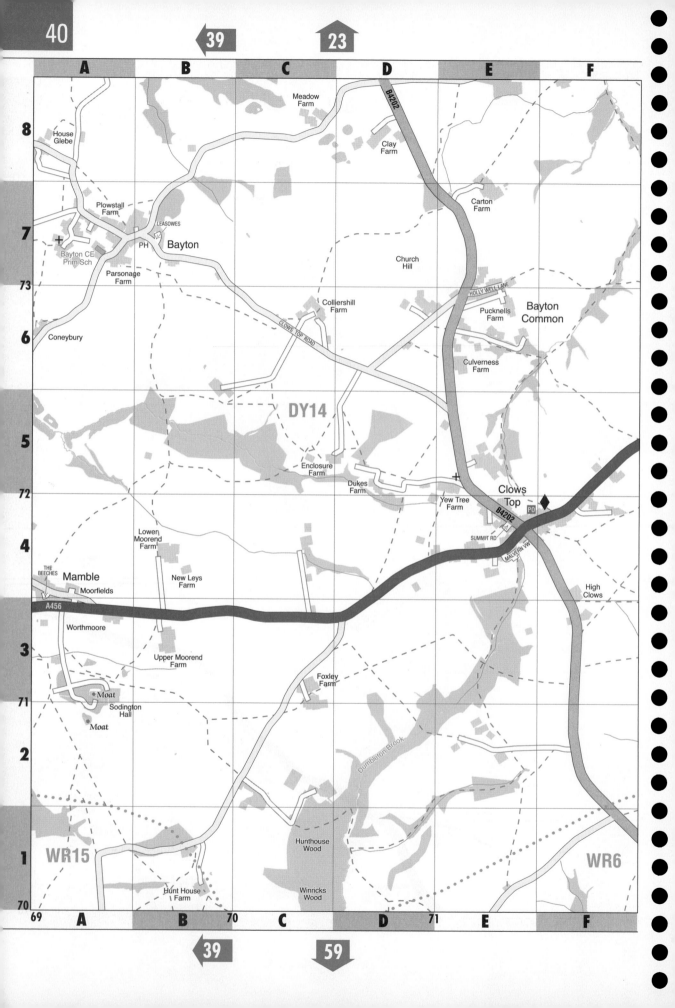

A   B   C   D   E   F

8
House
Glebe

7
Plowstall
Farm
LEASOWES
Bayton
PH
Bayton CE
Prim Sch
Parsonage
Farm

73

6
Coneybury
CLOWS TOP ROAD
Colliershill
Farm

Meadow
Farm

B4202
Clay
Farm

Carton
Farm

Church
Hill

HOLLY WELL LANE
Pucknells
Farm
Bayton
Common

Culverness
Farm

DY14

5
Enclosure
Farm
Dukes
Farm

Yew Tree
Farm

Clows
Top
B4202
PO

72

4
Lower
Moorend
Farm
SUMMIT RD
MALVERN VW

THE
BEECHES
Mamble
Moorfields
New Leys
Farm

High
Clows

A456

Worthmoore

3
Upper Moorend
Farm
Foxley
Farm

71
Moat
Sodington
Hall
Moat

2
Dumbleton Brook

1
WR15
Hunthouse
Wood
WR6

70
Hunt House
Farm
Winricks
Wood

69   A   B   70   C   D   71   E   F

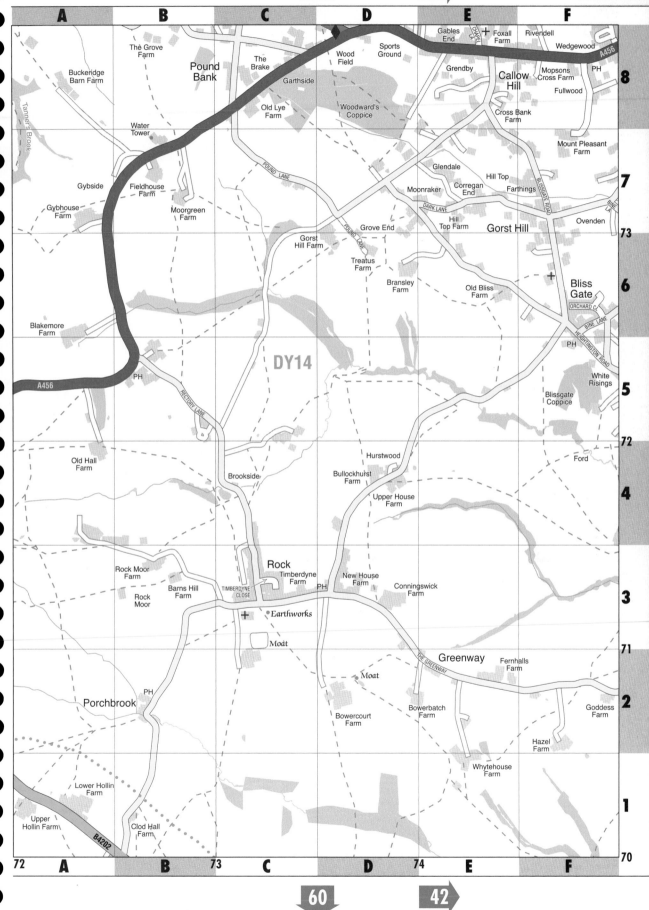

A　B　C　D　E　F

8

A456

Keens Farm

Stone House Farm

Bannut Tree Farm

Lye Head Farm

The Bramblings

Woodside

Rock Coppice

Park End Farm

Horsehill Farm

Cross Bank

Coppice Gate Farm

End Park

Park End

7

Abberley View Farm

Lye Head

Burnt Wood

Worcestershire Way

Horsehill House

Grove The

73

Ford

Little Lakes

Ford

CH

6

BINE LANE

Shades Farm

Gladder Brook

HEIGHTINGTON ROAD

Bines Farm

Lane End Coppice

5

Oak Tree Farm

Lane End Farm

Deasland Farm

Liveridge Farm

Brookside Farm

DY12

72

Latchetts Farm

4

Piggotts Farm

HEIGHTINGTON ROAD

Elm Bank Farm

Gladderbrook Farm

Hill Farm

Farman's Court

Hay Oak Farm

High Oak Farm

Organs Hill Farm

Elfords Farm

Heightington

3

Riddings Farm

Moorfield Barn Farm

Chapel Farm

DY14

The Peats Farm

Leystill Farm

The Wylde Farm

HEIGHTINGTON ROAD

71

THE GREENWAY

2

Castle Farm

Palmers Farm

Oldhouse Farm

Falklands Farm

DUNLEY ROAD

Waterfall

Worcestershire Way

Joan's Hole

1

DY13

Oakwood Barn

Hurtlehill Farm

70

75　A　B　76　C　D　77　E　F

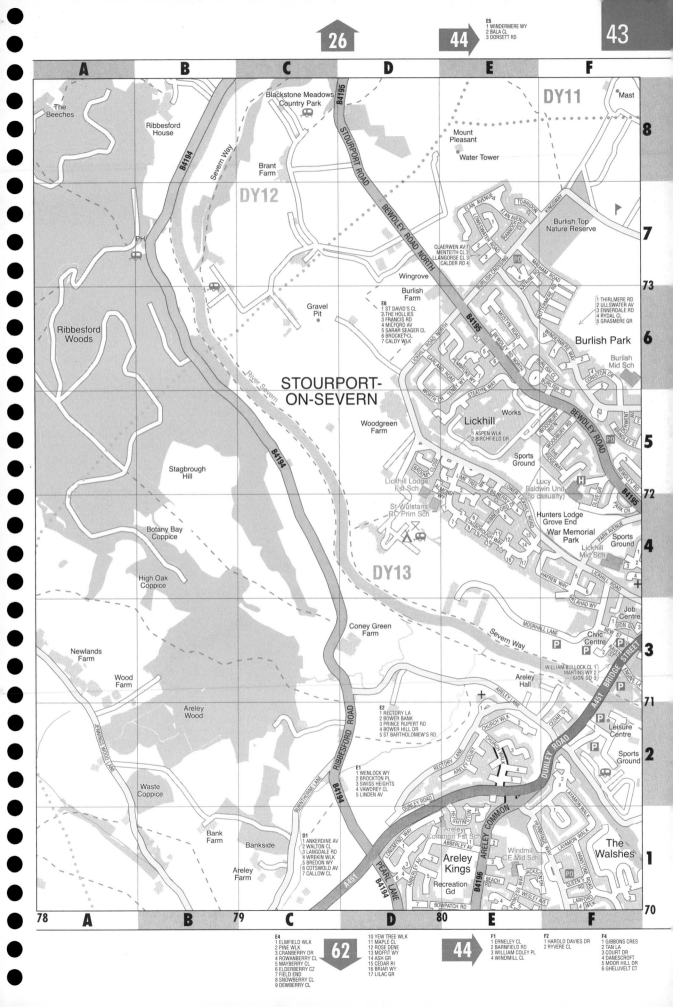

STOURPORT-ON-SEVERN

DY13

DY11

Wilden

Leapgate

Charlton

Hartlebury Common

A3
1 SION GDN
2 PARKES PAS
3 PARKES QUAY
4 STOUR LA
5 LODGE RD
6 BELL ROW
7 ENGINE LA

A4
1 BEWDLEY RD
2 BULLUS RD
3 PULLMAN CL
4 MINSTER RD
5 ST MICHAEL'S CL
6 GIBBONS CR
7 FOUNDRY ST
8 CHURCH DR
9 WORCESTER ST

B1
1 BRITANNIA GDN
2 WARD RD

B4
1 SAXILBY PL
2 SUMMERFIELD RD
3 ORCHARD CL
4 MILL CL

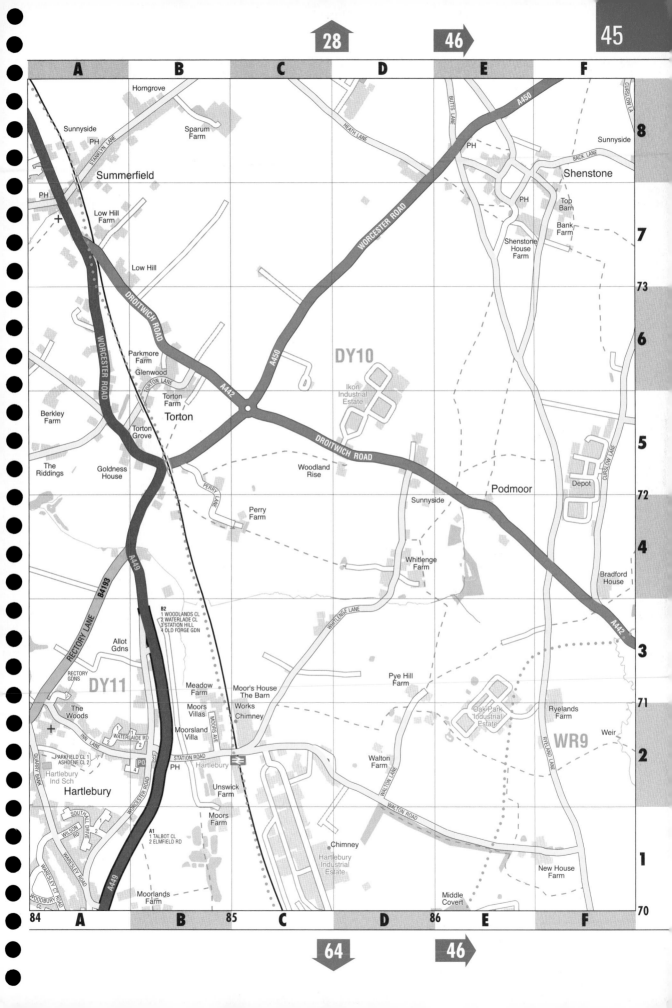

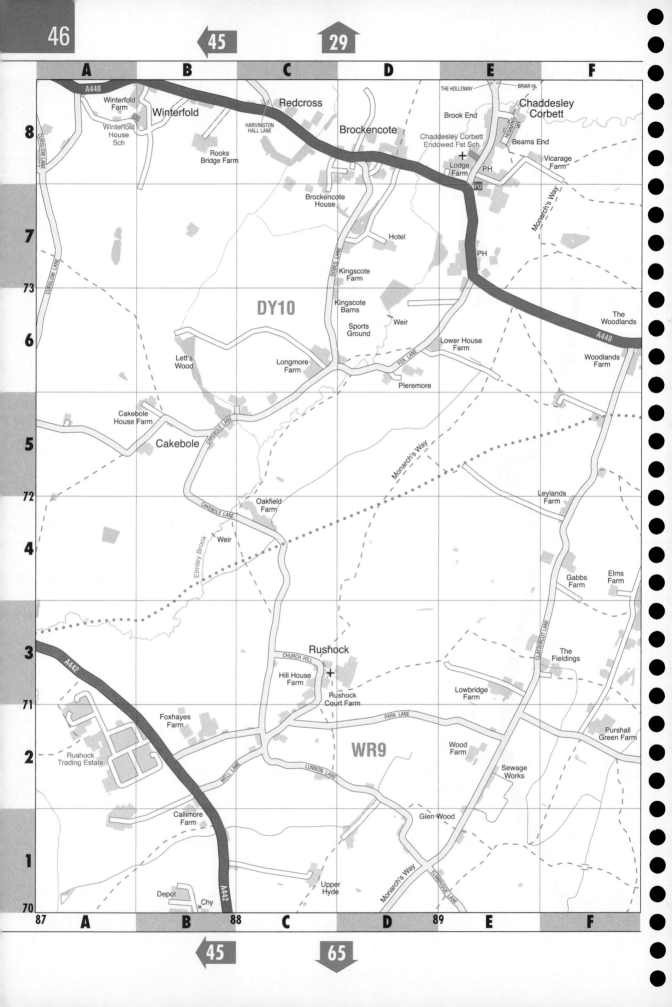

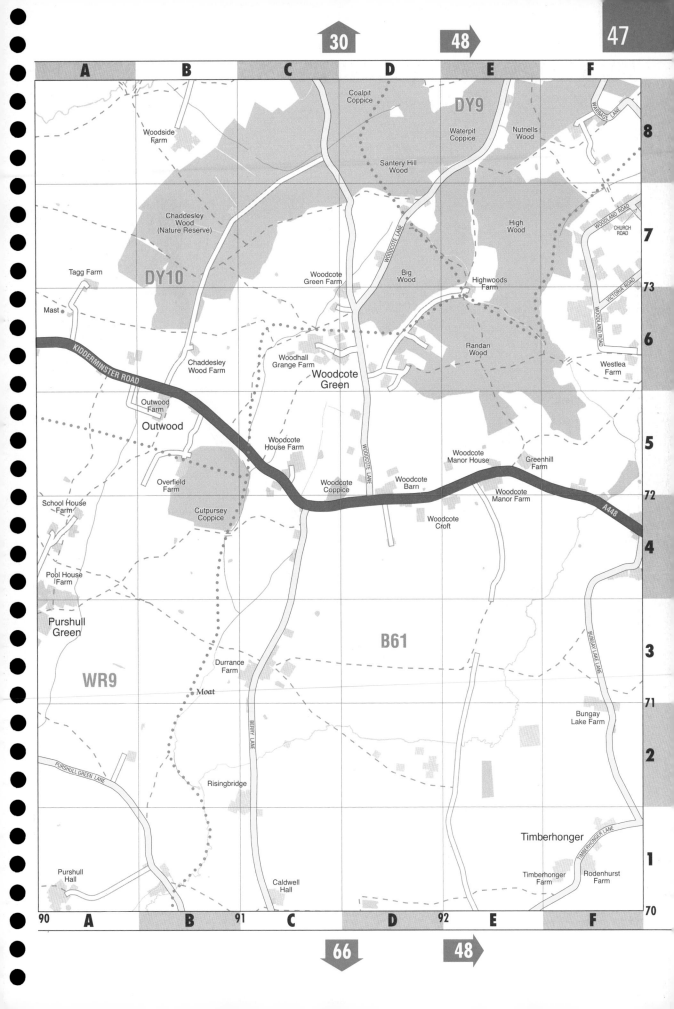

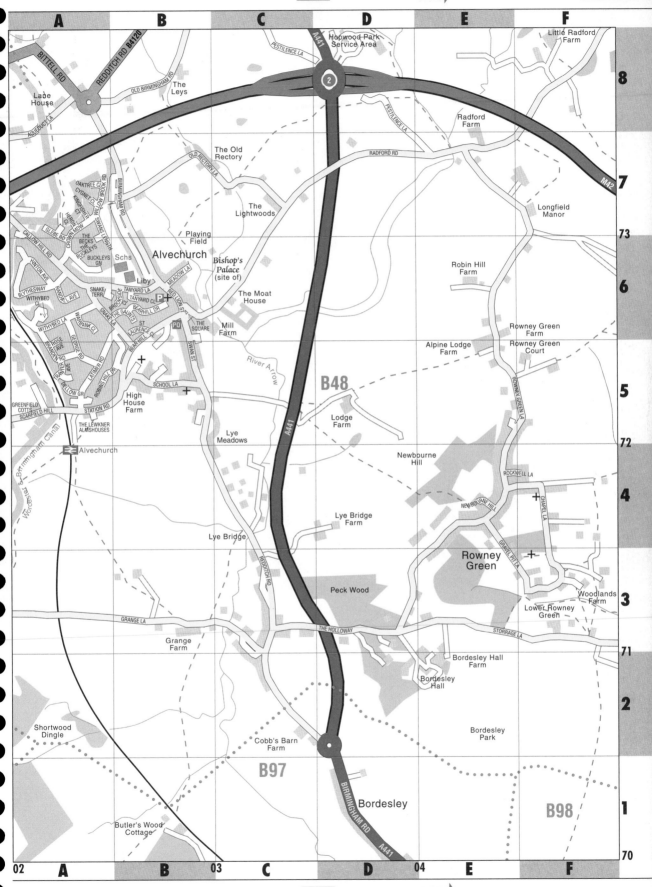

A B C D E F

8

Newhouse Farm

Lanehouse Farm

Lower Inkford Farm

Brook Priory Farm

PH

B47

7

Alcott Farm

M42

Birch Acre

Birch Acre Farm

Blackoak Wood

73

HILLCREST PK

DUMBLE PIT LA

ALCESTER RD

A435

M42

3

A435

6

Seechem Lodge

Seechem Farm

ICKNIELD ST

Brookside

Moorfield Farm

BILLESLEY LA

Billesley Farm

PH

Moorfield Coppice

Moorfield Coppice

WATERY LA

5

Old House Farm

LILLEY GREEN RD

Hob Hill Farm

Hob Hill

Newlands

HOLLY LA

Lilley Green Hall Farm

B48

Woodlands Farm

Rose Cottage Farm

SEAFIELD LA

WHITEPITS LA

72

Hill Farm

Brockhill Farm

4

Storrage Wood

Barton Farm

OLD LA

Old Farm

Chapel Farm

Heath Green Poultry Farm

3

Storrage House

STORRAGE LA

Dump House Farm

DUMPHOUSE LA

Heath Green

Heath Green Farm

71

Lower Park Farm

BROCKHILL LA

2

ICKNIELD ST

B98

Carpenters Hill Wood

Poplars Farm

Carpenters Hill Farm

Newlands Rough

1

Hall Farm

Brook Farm

Beoley Hall

Carpenter's Hill

70

05 A B 06 C D 07 E F

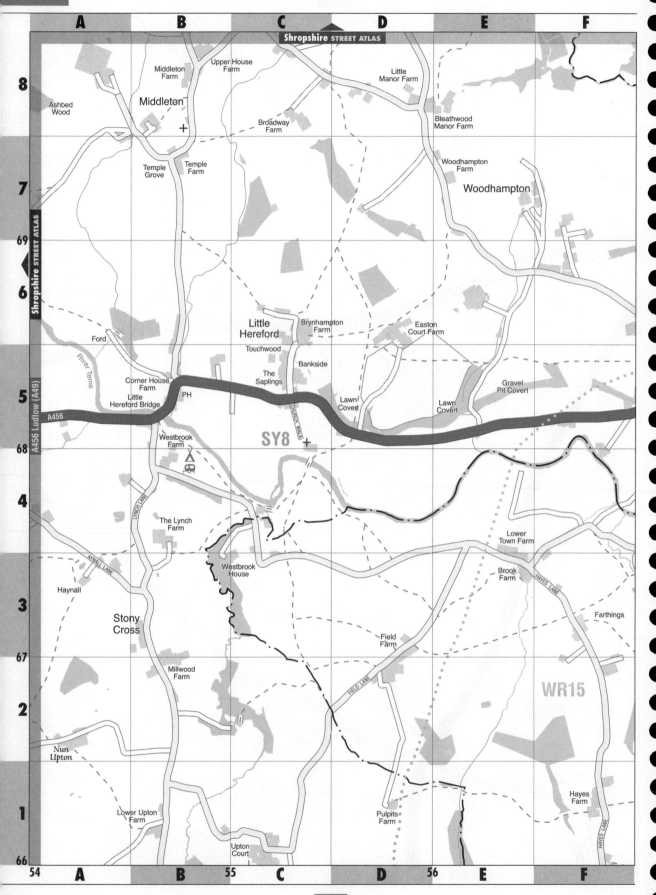

A   B   C   D   E   F

8

7

69

6

Ashbed
Wood

Middleton
Farm

Middleton

Upper House
Farm

Little
Manor Farm

Broadway
Farm

Bleathwood
Manor Farm

Temple
Grove

Temple
Farm

Woodhampton
Farm

Woodhampton

Shropshire STREET ATLAS

Ford

Little
Hereford

Brynhampton
Farm

Easton
Court Farm

Touchwood

River Teme

Corner House
Farm

The
Saplings

Bankside

Gravel
Pit Covert

A456 Ludlow (A49)

5

68

4

Little
Hereford Bridge

PH

SY8

Lawn
Covert

Lawn
Covert

A456

Westbrook
Farm

CHURCH WALK

Lynch Lane

The Lynch
Farm

Lower
Town Farm

Aynall Lane

Westbrook
House

Brook
Farm

Hayes Lane

3

67

2

Haynall

Stony
Cross

Field
Farm

Farthings

WR15

Millwood
Farm

Field Lane

1

66

Nun
Upton

Lower Upton
Farm

Upton
Court

Pulpits
Farm

Hayes
Farm

Hayes Lane

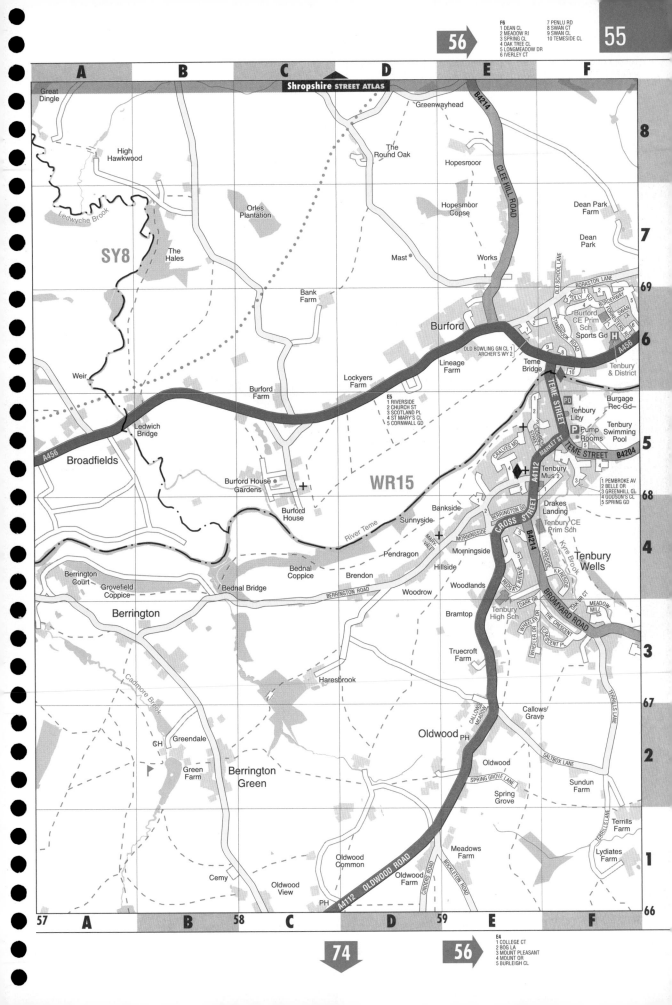

F6
1 DEAN CL
2 MEADOW RI
3 SPRING CL
4 OAK TREE CL
5 LONGMEADOW DR
6 IVERLEY CT
7 PENLU RD
8 SWAN CT
9 SWAN CL
10 TEMESIDE CL

A B C D E F

Shropshire STREET ATLAS

Great Dingle

Greenwayhead

B4214

8

The Round Oak

Hopesmoor

High Hawkwood

Ledwyche Brook

Orles Plantation

Hopesmoor Copse

Dean Park Farm

7

CLEE HILL ROAD

SY8

The Hales

Bank Farm

Mast

Works

Dean Park

OLD SCHOOL LANE

BORASTON LANE

69

HOLLY RD

BORDERWAY

Burford CE Prim Sch

SWAN LA

Weir

Burford

FORRESTERS

STANBROOK ROAD

Sports Gd

A456

6

Tenbury & District

Lineage Farm

OLD BOWLING GN CL 1

ARCHER'S WY 2

Teme Bridge

Burford Farm

Lockyers Farm

TEME STREET

Burgage Rec Gd

Tenbury Liby

PO

Ledwich Bridge

E5
1 RIVERSIDE
2 CHURCH ST
3 SCOTLAND PL
4 ST MARY'S CL
5 CORNWALL GD

Tenbury Rooms

Pump Rooms

P

Tenbury Swimming Pool

A456

Broadfields

CHURCH STREET

MARKET ST

TEME STREET

B4204

5

GRAVLES MD

Tenbury Mus 2

A4112

WR15

Burford House Gardens

Burford House

River Terne

Bankside

Sunnyside

1 PEMBROKE AV
2 BELLE OR
3 GREENHILL CL
4 GODSON'S CL
5 SPRING GD

Drakes Landing

Tenbury CE Prim Sch

68

BERRINGTON GD

CROSS STREET

Pendragon

Morningside

B4214

Tenbury Wells

4

Bednal Coppice

Brendon

Hillside

MARY VALE

MORNINGSIDE

KYRESIDE

Kyre Brook

Berrington Court

Grovefield Coppice

Bednal Bridge

BERRINGTON ROAD

Woodrow

Woodlands

BROMYARD ROAD

MEADOW MILL

Berrington

Bramtop

Tenbury High Sch

REDGATE AVENUE

THE CRESCENT

OAK DR CT

3

Truecroft Farm

WHEELER DR

CRESCENT PL

TERRILLS LANE

Haresbrook

67

Cadmore Brook

Callows Grave

2

CH

Greendale

Oldwood PH

SALTBOX LANE

Green Farm

Berrington Green

Oldwood

CALLOWS MEADOW

SPRING GROVE LANE

Sundun Farm

Spring Grove

Terrills Farm

1

Cemy

Oldwood View

PH

Oldwood Common

OLDWOOD ROAD

Oldwood Farm

CINDERS ROAD

BOCKLETON ROAD

Meadows Farm

Lydiates Farm

A4112

66

55
37

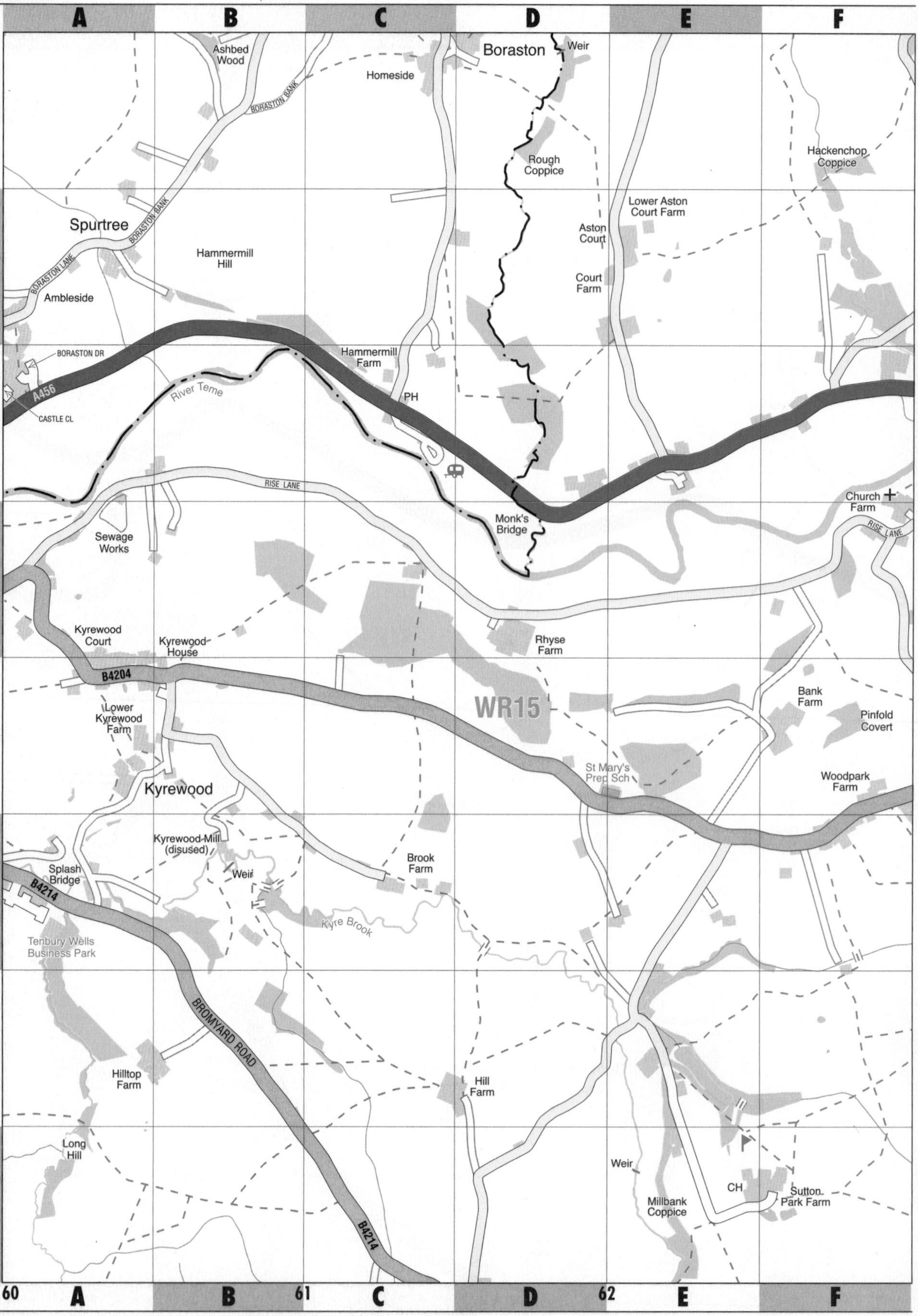

| | A | B | C | D | E | F |

Boraston
Weir
Ashbed Wood
Homeside
BORASTON BANK

8

Rough Coppice
Hackenchop Coppice

Lower Aston Court Farm

Spurtree

7
Hammermill Hill
Aston Court
Court Farm

BORASTON BANK

Ambleside

69
BORASTON DR
Hammermill Farm

6
A456
River Teme
PH
CASTLE CL

RISE LANE

Monk's Bridge
Church Farm
RISE LANE

Sewage Works

5
Kyrewood Court
Kyrewood House
Rhyse Farm
Bank Farm
Pinfold Covert

68
B4204

Lower Kyrewood Farm

WR15

4
St Mary's Prep Sch
Woodpark Farm

Kyrewood

Kyrewood Mill (disused)
Weir
Brook Farm

3
Splash Bridge
B4214
Kyre Brook

Tenbury Wells Business Park

67
BROMYARD ROAD

2
Hilltop Farm
Hill Farm

Long Hill

1
Weir
CH
Sutton Park Farm
Millbank Coppice

B4214

66

| | A | B | C | D | E | F |
| 60 | | | 61 | | 62 | |

55
75

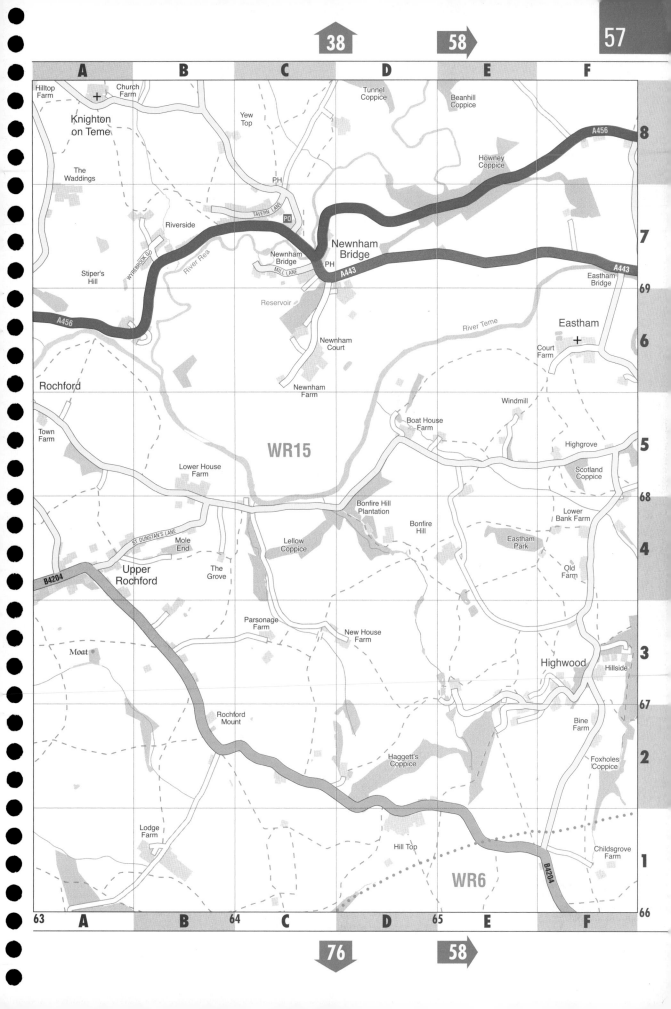

57
39

A B C D E F

8

Doddenhill Farms
A456
Archfield Farm
Upper Woodston
Middle Woodston
Woodston Byre
Woodston Manor
Oldfields Farm

7

Woodston Farm
Vicarage Wood
Lindridge
Lambswick Farms
A443
The Farm

69

Crundall Coppice
Lindridge CE Prim Sch
PH
Linkhill Wood

6

A443

5

Pipersbrook Farm
WR15
River Teme

68

ASTLEY ORCHARD
Astley Farm
Eastha Grange
Lowerhouse Farm
Puddleford Farm
ORLETON LANE

4

Holtsbank Coppice
Coldenhale Farm

Bine Coppice
Wall Hills Wood
Wall Hill Farm

3

Foxholes Coppice
NEW ROAD
Mill Coppice
Quarry Hill

67

Hillwood Farm

2

New House Farm

WR6

1

Hanley Court
Wall Hills Wood
Waterfall
Collier's Pool
NEW ROAD

66

66 A B 67 C D 68 E F

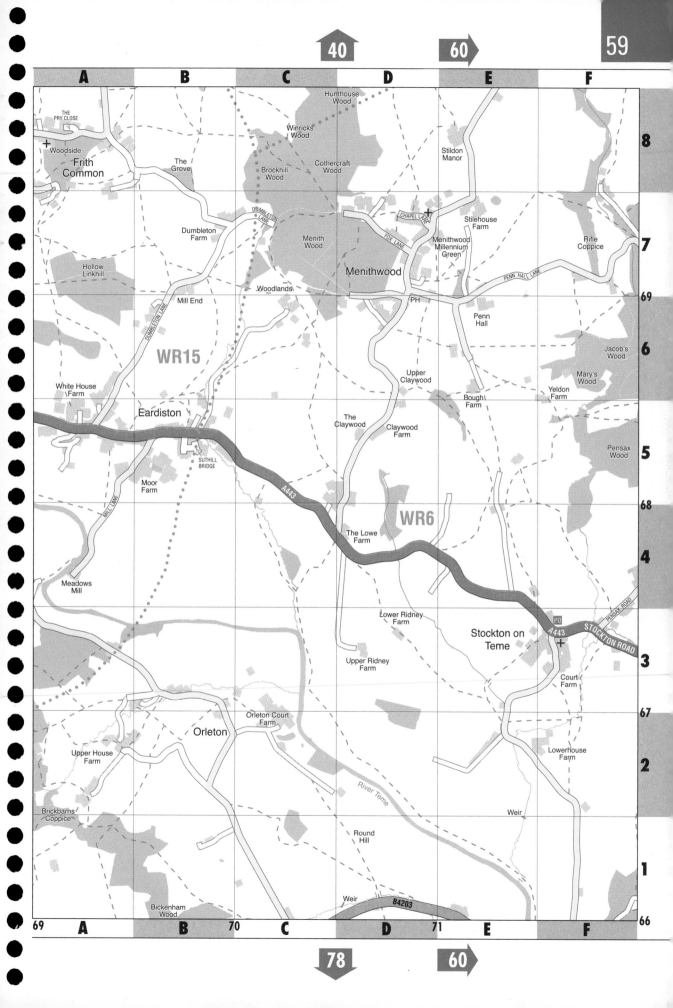

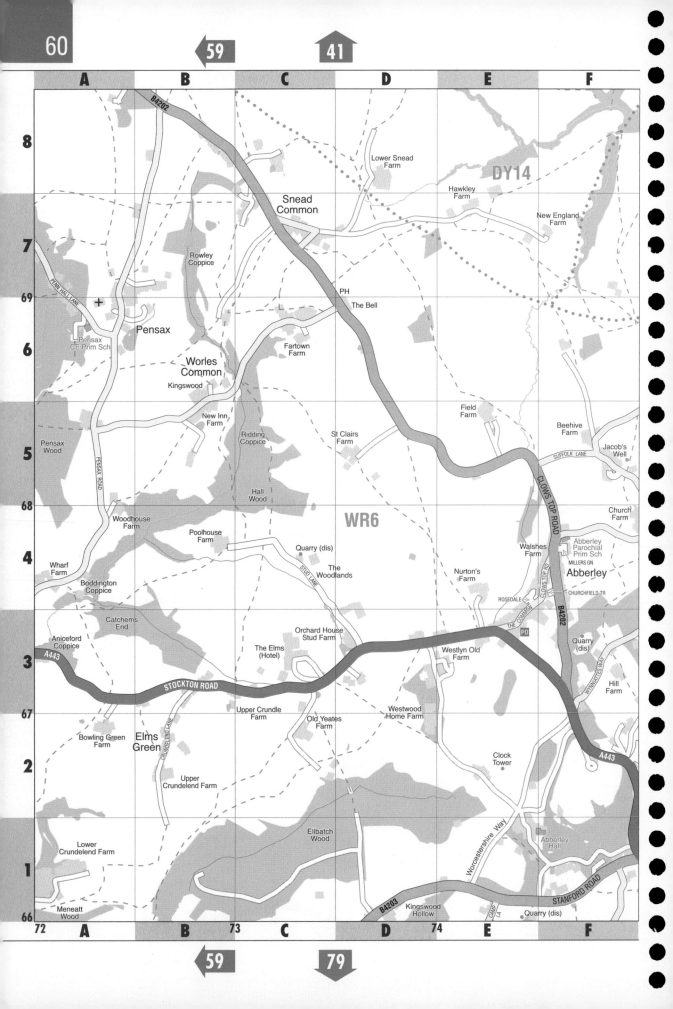

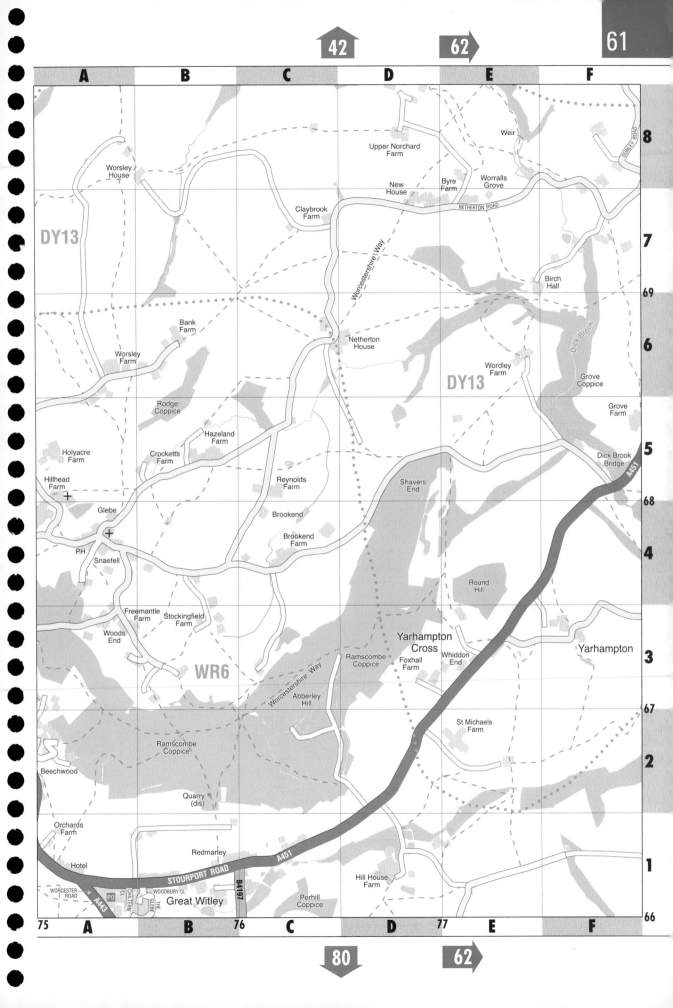

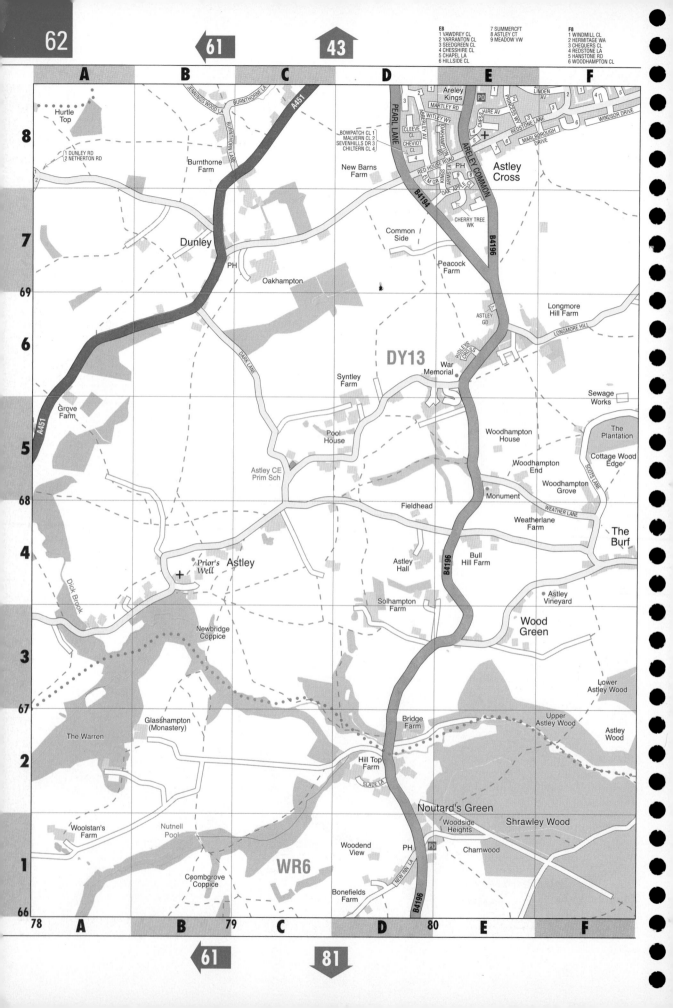

61 43

E8
1 VAWDREY CL
2 YARRANTON CL
3 SEEDGREEN CL
4 CHESSHIRE CL
5 CHAPEL LA
6 HILLSIDE CL

7 SUMMERCFT
8 ASTLEY CT
9 MEADOW VW

F8
1 WINDMILL CL
2 HERMITAGE WA
3 CHEQUERS CL
4 REDSTONE LA
5 HANSTONE RD
6 WOODHAMPTON CL

A   B   C   D   E   F

8

Hurtle Top

1 DUNLEY RD
2 NETHERTON RD

Burnthorne Farm
Burnthorne Lane

A451

JENNINGS WOOD LA

BURNTHORNE LANE

New Barns Farm

BOWPATCH CL 1
MALVERN CL 2
SEVENHILLS DR 3
CHILTERN CL 4

Areley Kings
MARTLEY RD
WITLEY WY
CLEEVE CL
CHEVIOT CL
RED HOUSE ROAD
ABBERLEY AV
OAKHAMPTON RD
ELM GR
OAK ARMS CL
OAK APPLE CL
PEARL LANE

LINDEN AV
PO
CHESHIRE AV
PRINCESS WY
REDSTONE LANE
MARLBOROUGH DRIVE
WINDSOR DRIVE

Astley Cross

7

Dunley
PH
Oakhampton

Common Side

Peacock Farm

B4194

ARELEY COMMON

CHERRY TREE WK

B4196

Longmore Hill Farm

69

6

DARK LANE

Syntley Farm

DY13

ASTLEY GD

War Memorial

RIDLEYS CROSS

Longmore Hill

Sewage Works

A451

Grove Farm

Pool House

Woodhampton House

The Plantation

5

Astley CE Prim Sch

Woodhampton End

Cottage Wood Edge

SCOTS LANE

68

Fieldhead

Monument

Woodhampton Grove

WEATHER LANE

Weatherlane Farm

The Burf

4

Dick Brook

Prior's Well   Astley

Astley Hall

B4196

Bull Hill Farm

Astley Vineyard

3

Newbridge Coppice

Solhampton Farm

Wood Green

Lower Astley Wood

67

2

The Warren

Glasshampton (Monastery)

Bridge Farm

Hill Top Farm

SLADE LA

Upper Astley Wood

Astley Wood

Woolstan's Farm

Nutnell Pool

Noutard's Green

Woodside Heights
PO

Shrawley Wood

1

Woodend View
PH

Charnwood

Coombgrove Coppice

WR6

NEW INN LA

Bonefields Farm

B4196

66

78   A   B   79   C   D   80   E   F

61 81

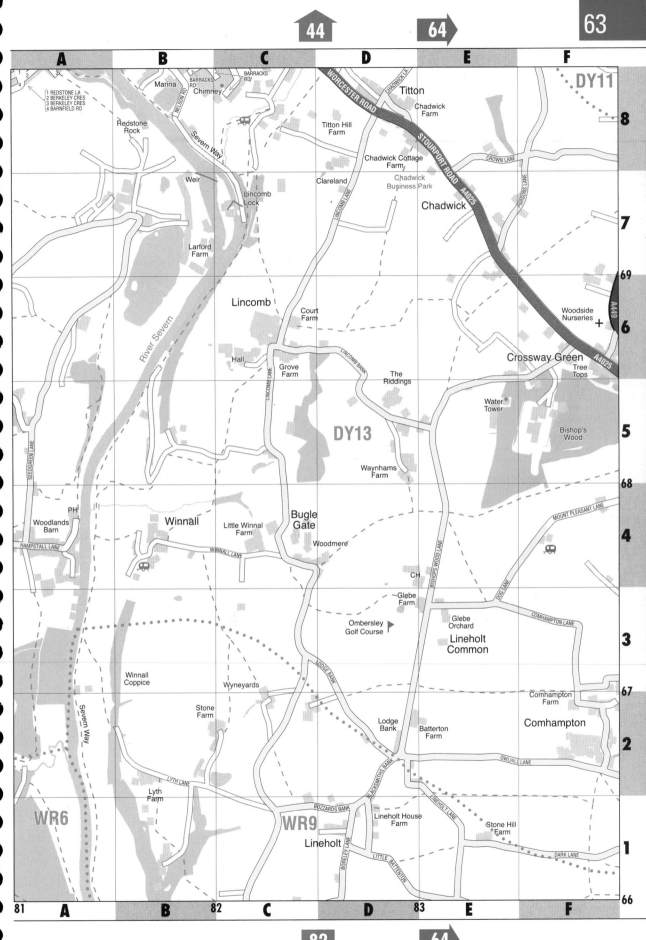

63　45

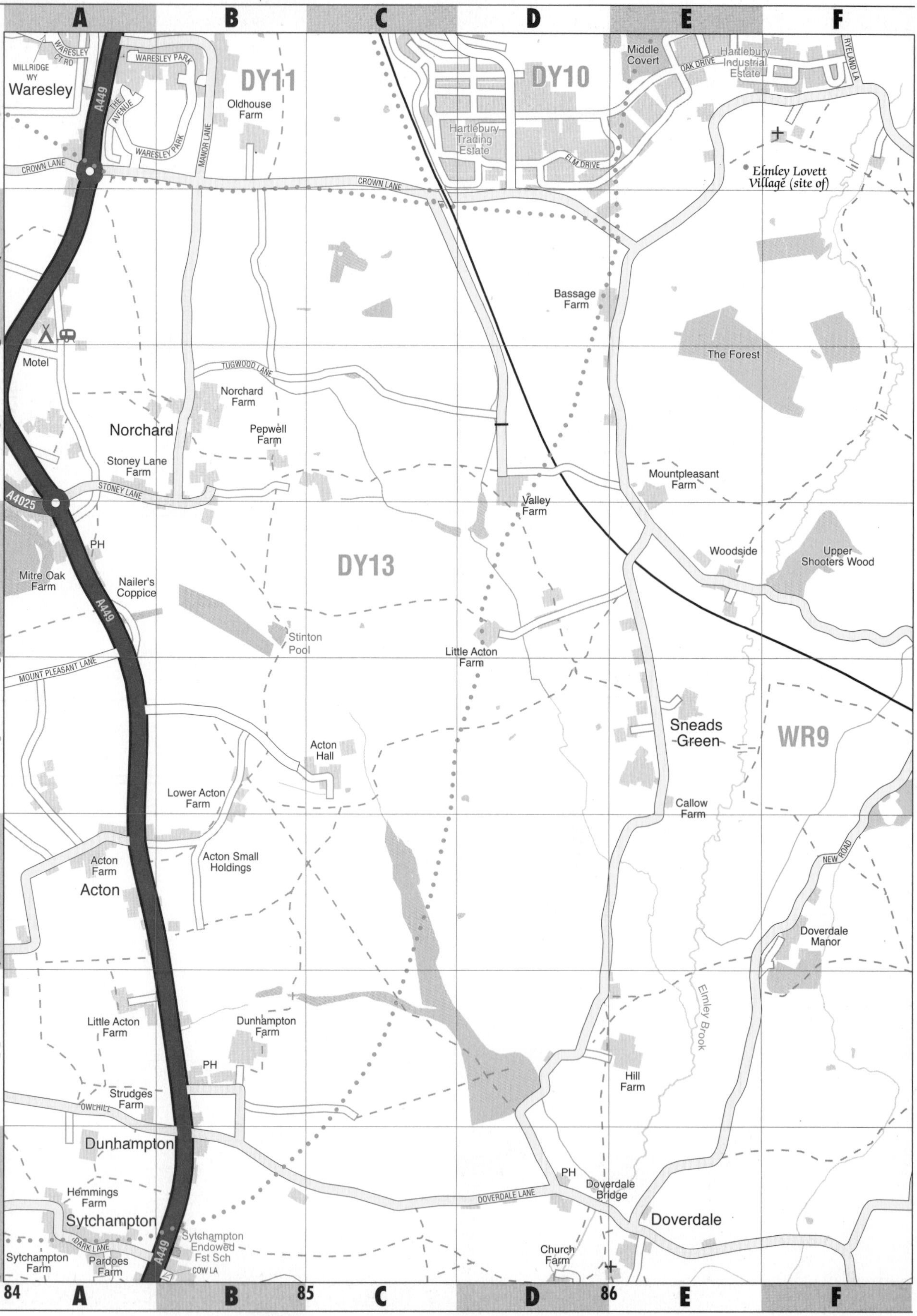

A　B　C　D　E　F

MILLRIDGE WY
Waresley
WARESLEY CT RD
WARESLEY PARK
THE AVENUE
A449
MANOR LANE
DY11
Oldhouse Farm

Middle Covert
OAK DRIVE
Hartlebury Industrial Estate
RYELAND LA
DY10
Hartlebury Trading Estate
ELM DRIVE

CROWN LANE
CROWN LANE

8

Elmley Lovett Village (site of)

7

Bassage Farm

69
Motel
The Forest

TUGWOOD LANE
Norchard Farm
Pepwell Farm

6
Norchard
Stoney Lane Farm
STONEY LANE
A4025

Mountpleasant Farm

Valley Farm

Woodside
Upper Shooters Wood

PH
Mitre Oak Farm
Nailer's Coppice
A449
DY13

5

Stinton Pool
Little Acton Farm

68
MOUNT PLEASANT LANE

Sneads Green
WR9

Acton Hall

4

Lower Acton Farm

Callow Farm

Acton Small Holdings

Acton Farm
Acton

3

Doverdale Manor
NEW ROAD

67

Elmley Brook

Little Acton Farm
Dunhampton Farm
PH

2

Hill Farm

Strudges Farm
OWEHILL
Dunhampton

Doverdale Lane
PH
Doverdale Bridge

1
Hemmings Farm
Sytchampton
Sytchampton Endowed Fst Sch
DOVERDALE LANE
Doverdale
DARK LANE
A449
COW LA
Church Farm

66
Sytchampton Farm
Pardoes Farm

84　A　B　85　C　D　86　E　F

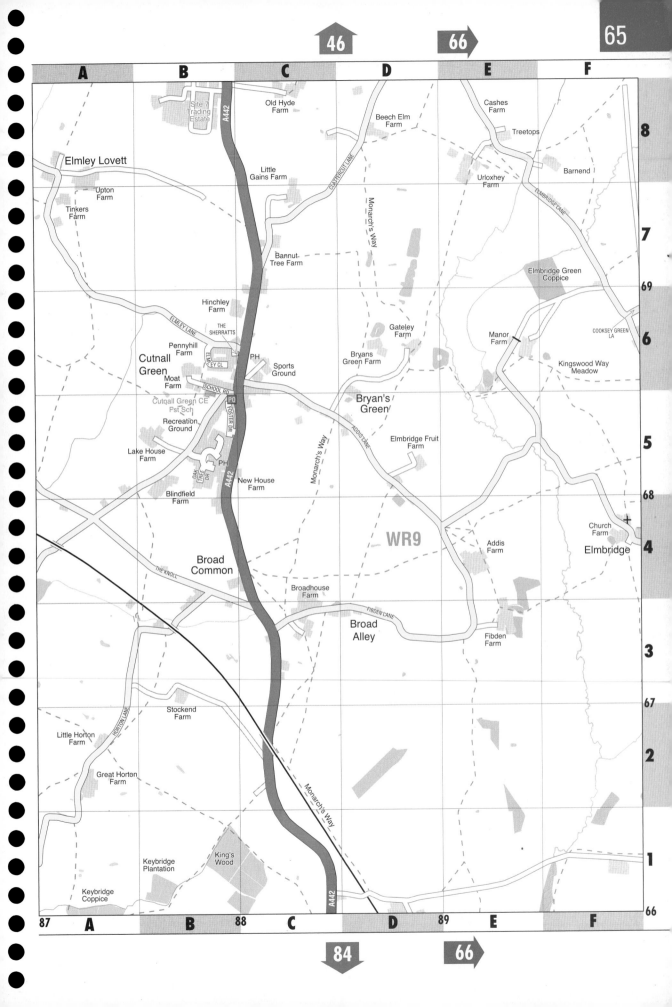

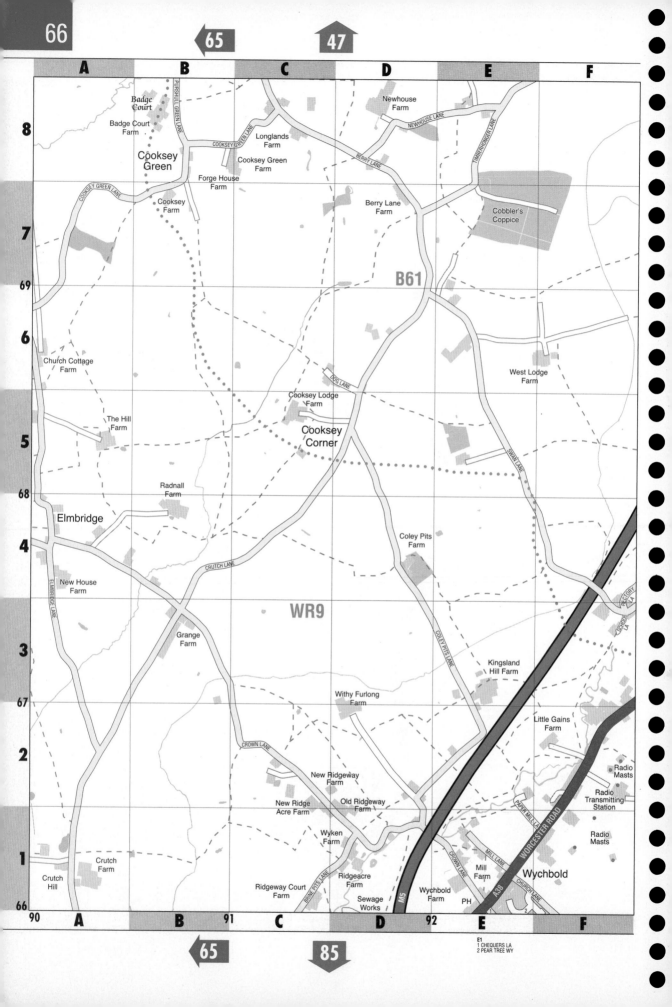

F6
1 SUGARBROOK CT
2 Aston Fields Trad Est
3 Silver Birches Bsns Pk

A B C D E F

8

South Bromsgrove
Com High Sch
(Tech Coll)

Foxhollow
Sch
REGENT
HIGHFIELD RD
B4091
Spadesbourne Brook
Breakback
Hill
Mast
Monarch's Way

ALDERLEY RD 1
WHITFORD CL 2

ROCK HILL

BROMSGROVE

Charford

Charford
Fst Sch

7

B61

Foxwalks
Farm

Grafton Manor
House
Fish Pond
GRAFTON LA

69

STOKE RD A38

Bowling Green
Farm

WORCESTER RD

B4091 HANBURY RD

6

Superstore

B4094

AVONCROFT RD

REDDITCH RD

Stoke
Heath

West Ct

Sugar Brook

A38

Avoncroft Mus
of Historic
Buildings

Tanhouse
Farm

5

Warren
House

Ottilie
Hild Sch

Windmill

Avoncroft Cattle
Breeding Ctr

E6
1 WAGGONERS CL
2 COUNTINGHOUSE WAY
3 KERRY HILL
4 MARTINGALE CL

Sunningdale

Ewe and
Lamb
(PH)

68

Rectory
Farm

THE
BEECHES

WORCESTER RD

Fieldview
House

BRICKHOUSE LA

Fish House La

4

Little Brick
House Farm

Stoke Pound
Farm

Brickhouse
Farm

Stoke Prior
Bridge

HANBURY RD

STOKE POUND LA

FARFIELD

WHITFORD BRIDGE RD

Little Intall
Farm

PH

SWAN LA

Stoke
Prior

River Salwarpe

Foley
Gardens

Upton
Warren

Nature Reserve

Moors
Farm

A38

Sailing
Lake

Upton Warren
Bridge

Hobden Hall
Farm

SHAW LA

ORCHARD
CRES

Stoke Prior
Fst Sch
PO
RYEFIELDS
CLOVERDALE

PRIOR CL
WALL'S RD

Ryefields
Farm

B60

Navigation Inn
(PH)

3

Stoke
Wharf

67

Hen Brook

Works

Shaw Lane
Ind Est

GREENSIDE

WHYNOT CL

Waste
Pit

Worcester and Birmingham Canal

THE COURTYARD

Harris
Ind Pk

Saxon
Bsns Pk

ALFRED
CT

Sports Gd

Works

FOLEY GDNS

CARTWRIGHT RD

2

WR9

Sagebury
Farm

ROSEMARY DR
CORIANDER
BASIL
WITCHE COTTS
JUBILEE TERR
VERBENA CL
SAGEBURY DR

Stoke
Works

WESTONHALL RD

Weston Hall
Farm

B4091

MOORGATE RD

Poolhouse
Farm

Harbours Hill
Farm

Little
Harbours
Farm

1

66

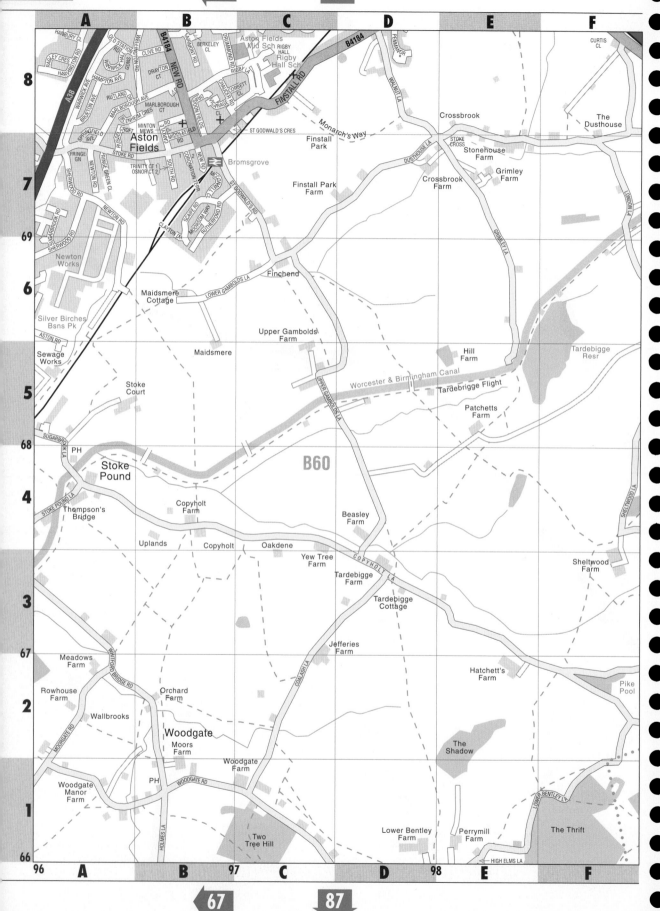

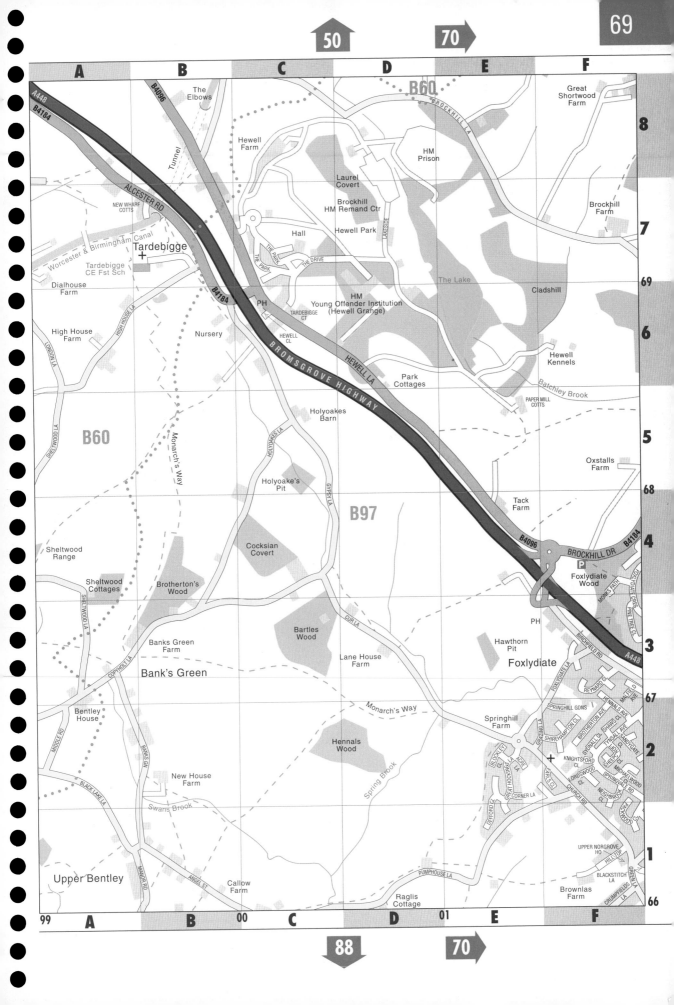

69 51

	A	B	C	D	E	F

8

Butler's Hill Wood

Bordesley

Bordesley Park Farm

A441

7

Butler's Hill

WEIGHTS FARM

WEIGHTS LA

B4101 DAGNELL END RD

Butler's Hill Farm

BIRMINGHAM RD

Bordesley Bridge

River Arrow

WITHER GREEN LA

B98

Abbey Stad

69

BROCKHILL LA

Greensleeves

Sports & L Ctr

Cemy

Crem

6

B5
1 BLACKWELL LA
2 KERSWELL CL
3 DEVONPORT CL
4 ALDBOROUGH LA
5 GISBURN CL
6 ELLENBROOK CL
7 CORNHAMPTON CL
8 AMBERGATE CL
9 DRAYCOTT CL
10 BIRCHENSALE FARM

Brockhill Wood

Lowan's Hill Farm

BORDESLEY LA

Bordesley Abbey (rems of)

Visitor Ctr

NEEDLE MILL LA

Riverside

Mus

5

LILY GREEN LA

BROCKHILL DR

APPLETREE LA

EDENFIELD

GOSCOTE

DARBY LA

PENNYFOLD

CARTHORSE LA

Mast

Red Ditch

WINDSOR RD B4184

Works

MIDDLEHOUSE LA

Enfield

Enfield Ind Est

Superstore

ALVECHURCH HIGHWAY

FORGE MILL RD

St Stephen's CE Fst Sch

HEWELL RD

Abbey Trad Intl Area

CLIVE HO

FISHING LINE RD

MEADOWHILL CRES

MEADOWHILL RD

ALBERT ST

B4160

Abbeydale

68

B4184

SHIRA LA

GREEN LA

TICKNALL CL

COOTON CL

TURNPIKE LA

ROSEDALE CL

Birchensale

BEECH TREE

OAK TREE AVE

LIME TREE

BATCHLEY RD

BRIDLEY MOOR RD

BOWOOD CL

CEDAR VIEW

CEDAR RD

ELM RD

MILL ST

ABBEY RD

St Stephen's Ho

PROSPECT

GROSVENOR

St George's

Trinity High Sch

4

FOXLYDIATE CRES

ROWAN CRES

YEW TREE CL

QUEEN'S COTTS

ST DAVIDS

CHERRY TREE WLK

PO

Pitcheroak Specl Sch

Birchensale Mid Sch

B97

Holyoakes Field Fst Sch

IZOD ST
KINGFISHER WLK

Valley Stad (Redditch FC)

Redditch

ADELAIDE ST

BATES HILL

EDWARD ST

BRITTEN ST

CHURCH RD

WILLIAM ST

PEAKMAN ST

MARKET PL

VINE ST

RED LION ST

ALCESTER ST

Coll

Coll

CHURCH RD

Liby SILVER

TH

The Trafford Pk Tudor Bsns Ctr

A4023 COVENTRY HIGHWAY

B4160

A441

ST GEORGE'S RD

PHILLIPS

TEMPLE

3

PINE TREE

Pitcheroak Cotts

Foxlydiate Wood

Batchley Fst Sch

Batchley

1 KEMERTON HO
2 WILMCOTE HO
3 HANBURY HO
4 WOODGATE HO
5 LEDBURY HO

WIDNEY HO

WOODLAND RD

BROMSGROVE RD

ALLWOOD HO

VICARAGE CRES

VICARAGE VIEW

HOLMWOOD CL

HOLMWOOD HO

PURSHULL CL

Cemy

STATION WAY

RINGWAY

IPSLEY ST

BEAUFORT ST

LUDLOW RD

ORCHARD ST

SMALLWOOD ST

SUMMER ST

MOUNT PLEASANT

HONEYBOURNE CL

CHURCH RD

SOUTHMEAD CRES

A448

STEVENSON AVE

HOLLOWAY LA

ENDICOTT RD

Sch

67

A448

FITZGUY

BOXNITT CL

1 WOODSIDE AVE
2 NOONAN CL
3 MUSKETTS CT
4 BIRCHFIELD CT

PITCHER OAK WOOD

CH

REDDITCH

PARTRIDGE HO 1
HAYNES HO 2
ROXBORO HO 3

SALOP RD

HARESFIELD RD

PARSONS RD

SMALLWOOD ALMSHOUSES

DINGLESIDE

TUNNEL DR

NAILSWORTH RD

B98

ALVECHURCH HIGHWAY

SOUTHCREST RD

BARTLEET RD

HILL

SOUTHCREST RD

2

Webheath

DOWNSELL HO

LYNDEN

Webheath Fst Sch

SHELTWOOD CL

SPRINGVALE RD

HEATHFIELD RD

MAPLE HO WESTBURY

MINWORTH CL

WOODEND CL

LOWER COMMON

BROMSGROVE HIGHWAY

BIRCHFIELD RD

B4504

Smallwood

NEWALL HO

SOUDAN

IVOR RD

MOUNT PLEASANT

MYRTLE AVE

LILAC CL

GREENFIELDS

POOL BANK

BYFORD CL

LABURNUM RD

WELLINGTON ST

Southcrest

DULAIS

COMPTON

THE MAYFIELDS

CRABTREE CL

BARLICH WAY

Lodge Pool

Lodge Park

TWINERS RD

LODGE POOL DR

1

BLACKDITCH RD

REDDITCH RD

WEATHEROAK CL

PALMWOOD

HEATHFIELD RD

PO

COLEFORD CL

DUNSTALL CL

MIDDLE PIECE DR

BASCOTE

FENWICK CL

ALTON

CARLTON CL

DORRIDGE CL

MARLPIT LA

WINDMILL DR

GOLDTHORNE CL

MALVERN HO

ASHTON CL

FECKENHAM RD

1 SPINNEY MEWS
2 SPINNEY WLK

CHARLES ST

ARCHER TERR

STONEHOUSE RD

CHAPEL CL

WOOD CT

PLYMOUTH CT

PLYMOUTH RD

EADIE MEWS

RECTORY RD

RECTORY CT

ROOKERY LA

St Luke's Cotts

St Luke's CE Fst Sch

Southcrest Wood

ASPPERTON CL

GILBERTSTONE

EASTNOR CL

CREDITCH CL

COLEFORD DR

GREENLANDS DR

BELMOORTON RD

ADDLINGTON RD

DORNASTON DR

PLENHAM CL

WIREHILL DR

HIMBLETON CL

RYDAL CL

SKILTS AVE

LODGE POOL DR

PINELOW DR

GRIMLEY CL

66

PEXDON CL

Marlpit Farm

BELMONT CL

B4504

CRAIGHAM

SHELLEY CL

THE MEADWAY

HEADLESS CROSS DR

HALLOWFIELDS CL

A441

02	A	B	03	C	D	04	E	F

69 89

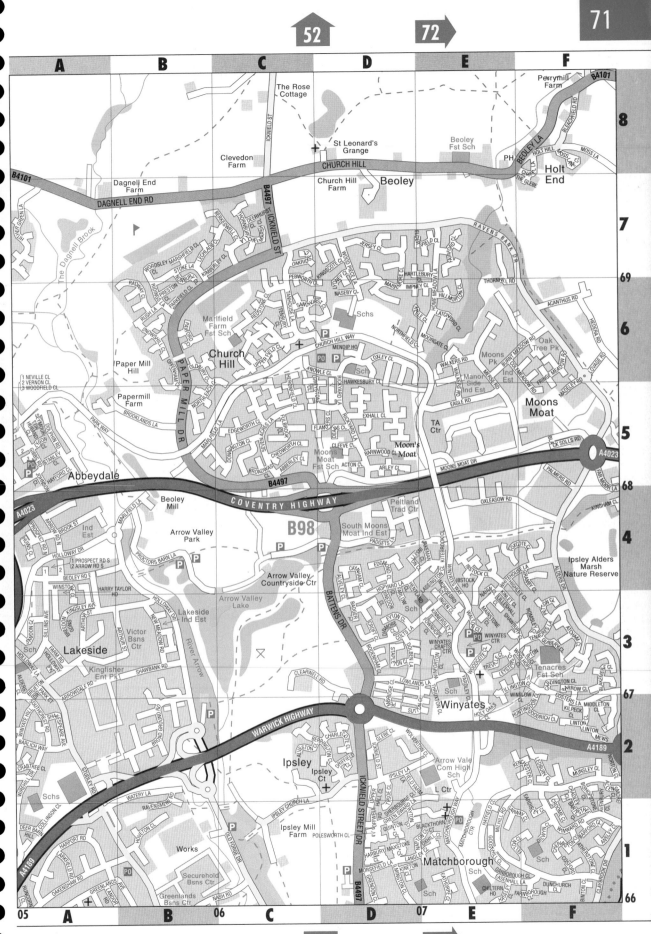

71
53

A   B   C   D   E   F

8

BEOLEY LA
B4101

FORDE HALL LA

Pink
Green

ALDERHANGER LA

Trap's
Green

PINK GREEN LA

ALDERHANGER LA

B94

7

MOSS LA

Green Hills
Farm

TANWORTH LA

A435

69

WAPPING LA

6

HEDERA RD

B98

ULLENHALL LA

GORCOTT HILL

Gorcott
Hill

Gorcott
Hall

PH

REDDITCH
Mast

Oldberrow Hil
Farm

5

A4023

COVENTRY HIGHWAY

A435

68

B95

4

KINGHAM CL
ILLSHAW CL
HOLLYBERRY CL
FURZE LA

Skilts Sch

LONGHOPE CL
FLAXLEY CL
KENDAL
BAR MOOR CL

GATELEY CL
MEPHEN
PRESTBURY CL
HINDLIP CL
DURSLEY LA
KELDAL
NEWENT
LINDRIDGE CL
OTTER CL
CHESWICK CL

+

BIRMINGHAM RD

3

ABBOTS WOOD CL
ARDENS CL
BEAULEY CL
ALDERS DR

COMMON LA

Lower
Skilts
Farm

67

CLAYBROOK DR

B80

2

A4189

WARWICK HIGHWAY

Mappleborough
Green
CE Prim Sch

Cracknut
Hill

A4189

PH

Mappleborough
Green

Outhill

1

HAYE LA

Gattax
Farm

A435

66

71
91

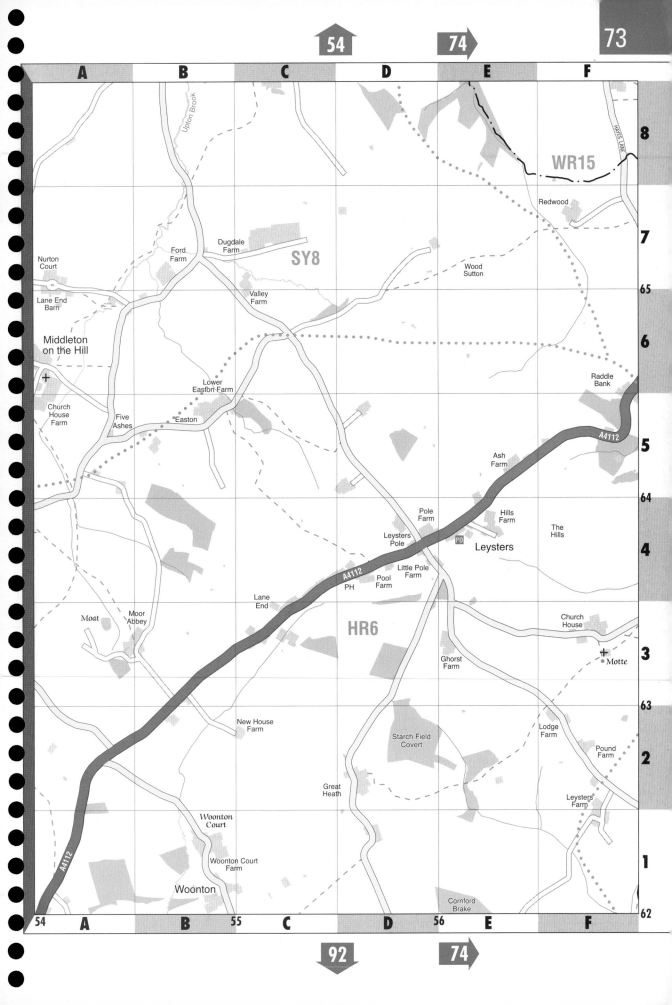

73 55

A	B	C	D	E	F

A4112

St Michaels

Oldwood Common

Currall Hall

8

New House Farm

Cadmore Brook

St Michaels Farm

College Walk

St Michael's Coll

Cinders Road

Bockleton Road

Pool House Farm

Little Redwood

Oldwood Road

Cadmore Bridge

Frith Farm

7

Cinders Wood

65

Gorsty Farm

Cinders Lane

6

A4112

Cinders

Birchley Farm

Lower Miles Hope Farm

Miles Hope

WR15

5

Wilden

64

Sunny Bank Dingle

4

Hanging Grove

Bockleton Road

Old Manor Farm

3

Hill Farm

Weston Farm

Prince's Grove

63

Ford

2

Newton Farm

Romers Common

Romers Farm

1

Cockspur Hall

Bockleton Country Study Centre

Middle Common

Home Farm

62

Cockspur Coppice

57	A	B	58	C	D	59	E	F

73 93

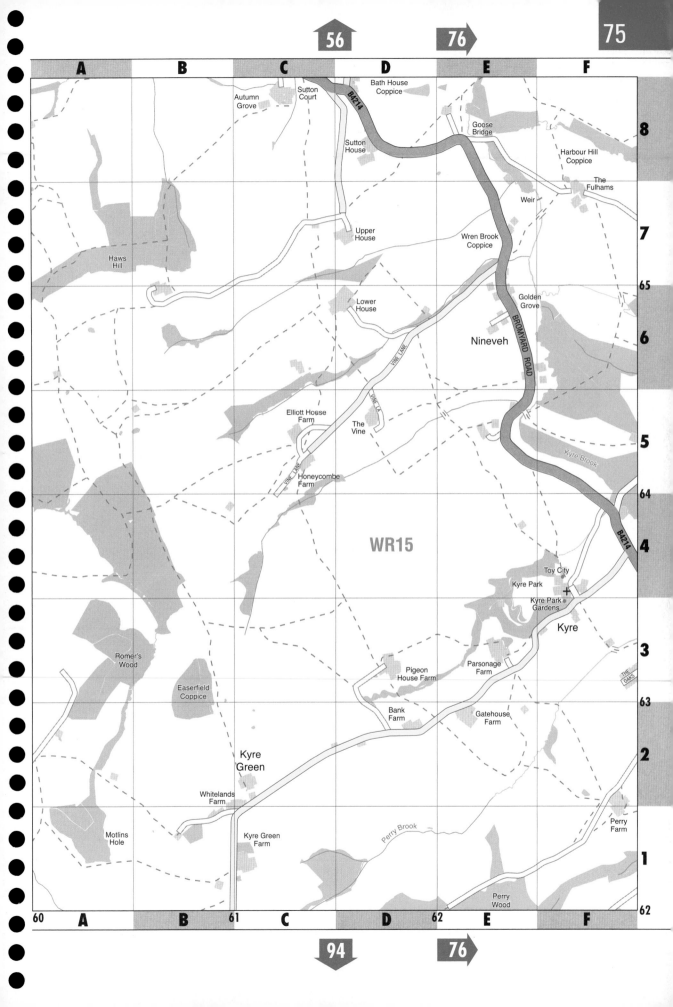

A B C D E F

Autumn Grove
Sutton Court
Bath House Coppice
B4214
Sutton House
Goose Bridge
Harbour Hill Coppice
Weir
The Fulhams
Upper House
Wren Brook Coppice
Haws Hill
Lower House
Golden Grove
VINE LANE
BROMYARD ROAD
Nineveh
Elliott House Farm
The Vine
VINE LANE
VINE LANE
Honeycombe Farm
Kyre Brook
WR15
B4214
Toy City
Kyre Park
Kyre Park Gardens
Kyre
Romer's Wood
Pigeon House Farm
Parsonage Farm
THE OAKS
Easerfield Coppice
Bank Farm
Gatehouse Farm
Kyre Green
Whitelands Farm
Perry Brook
Perry Farm
Motlins Hole
Kyre Green Farm
Perry Wood

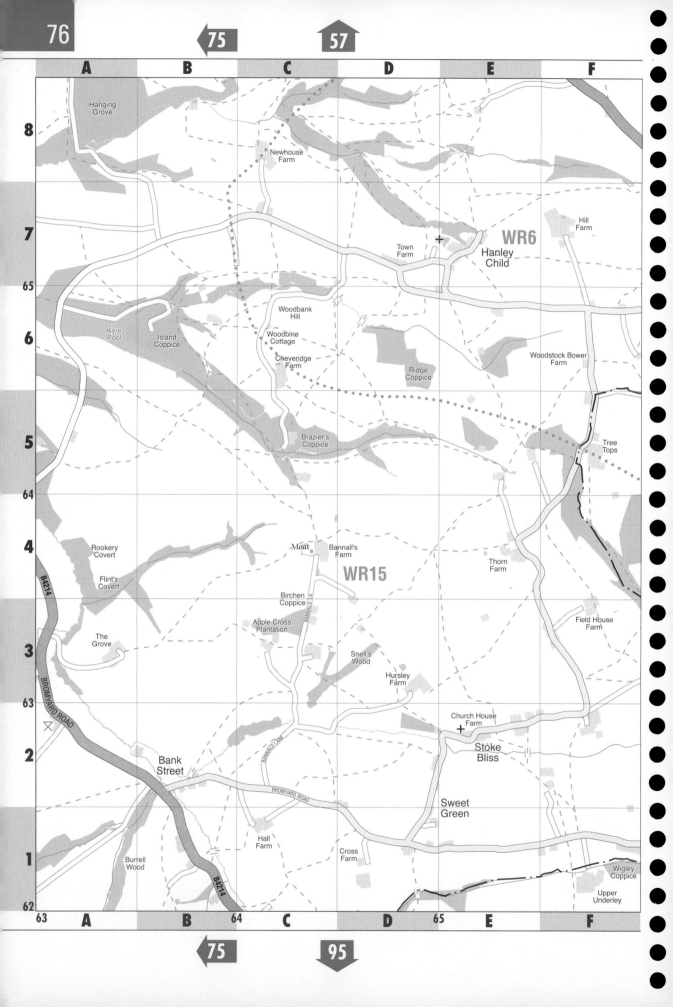

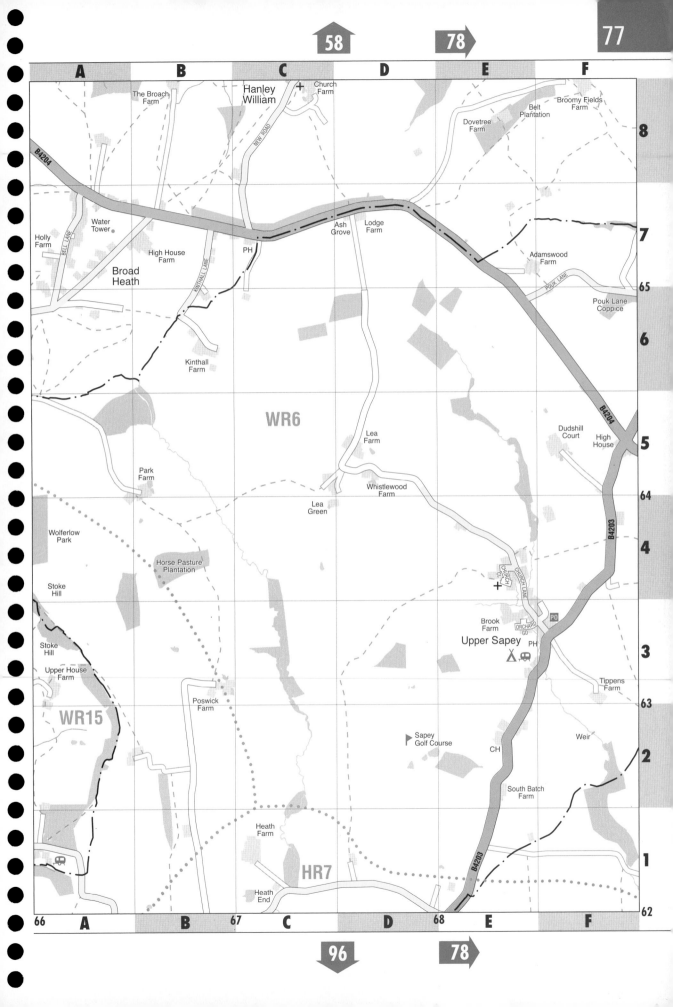

77
59

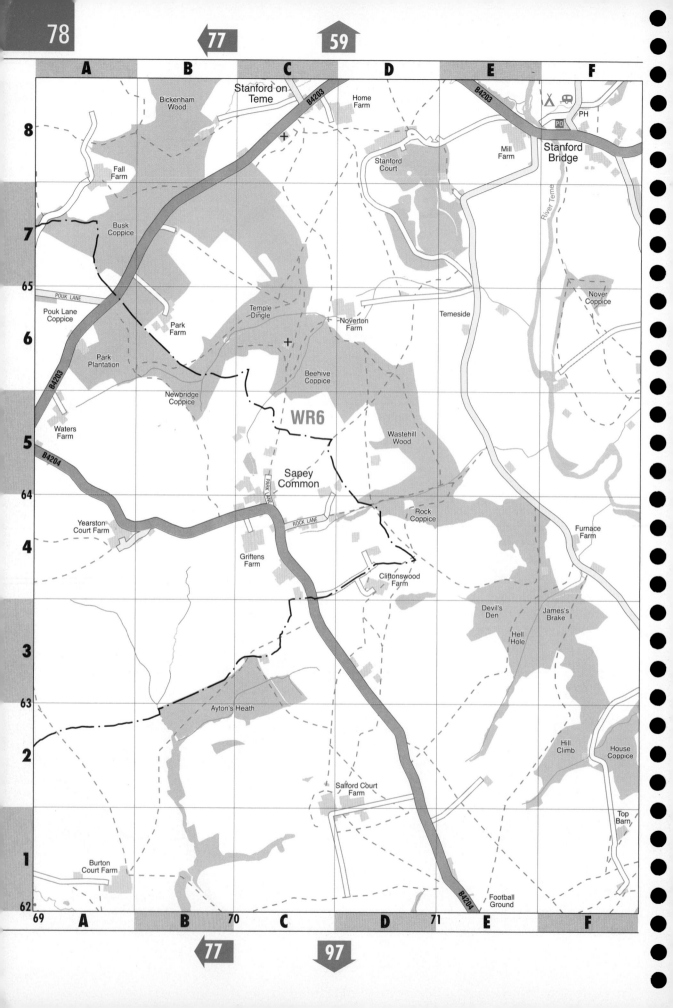

77
97

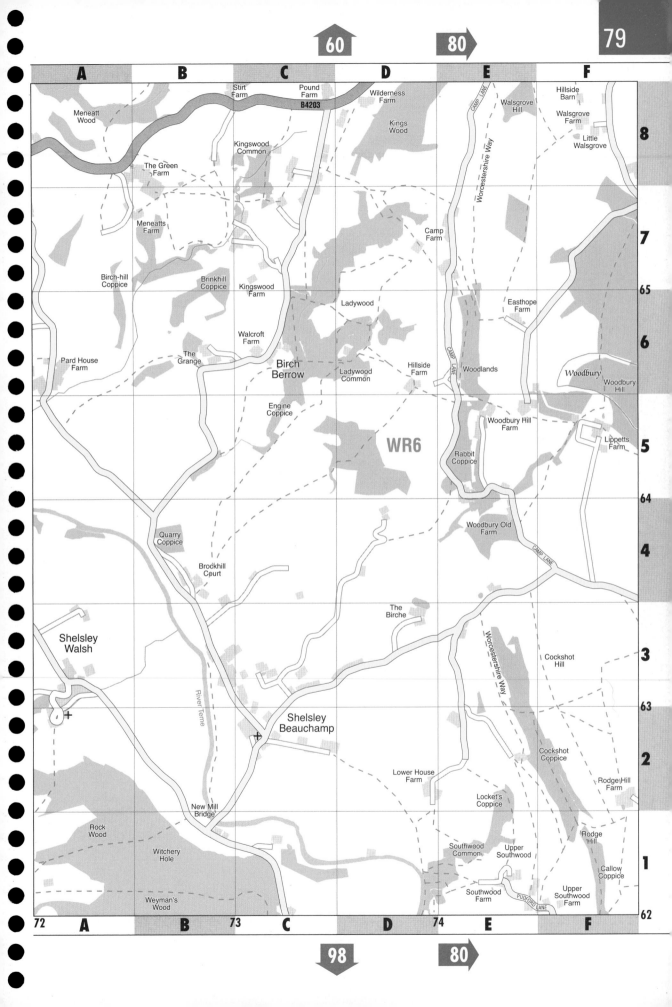

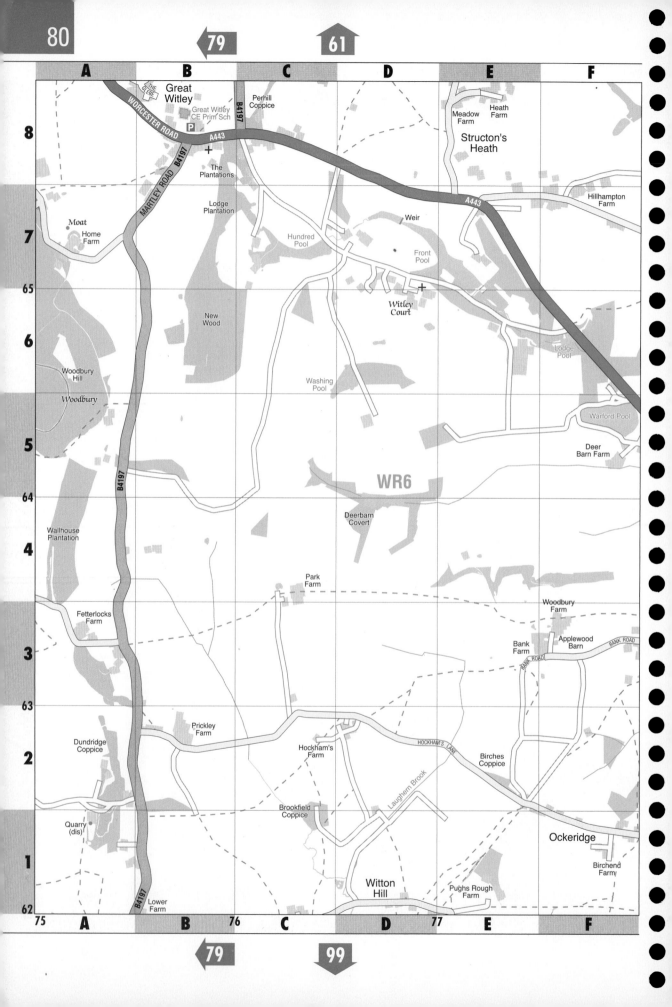

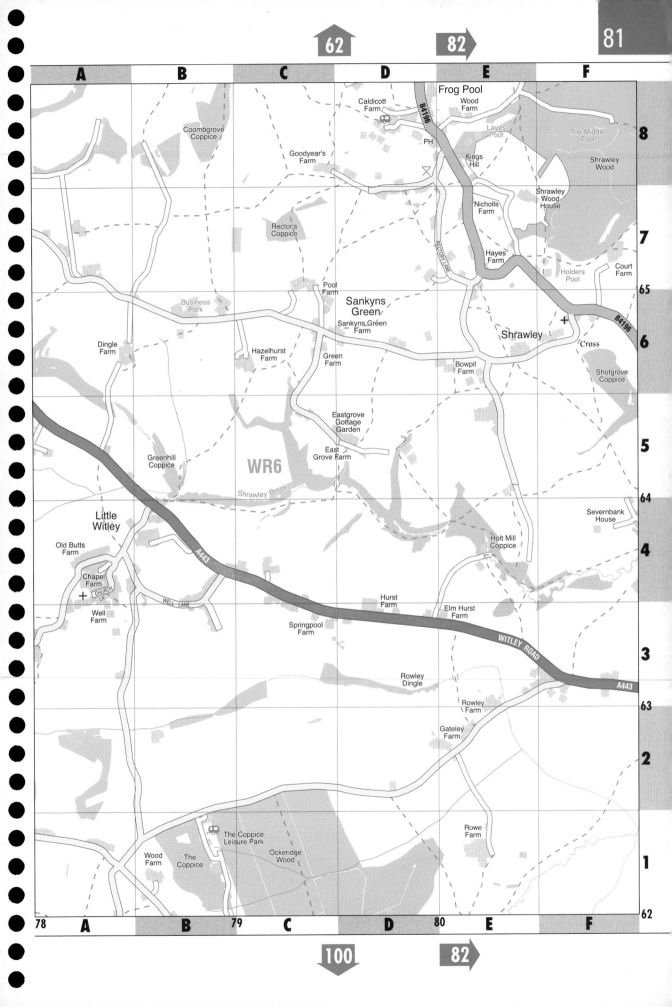

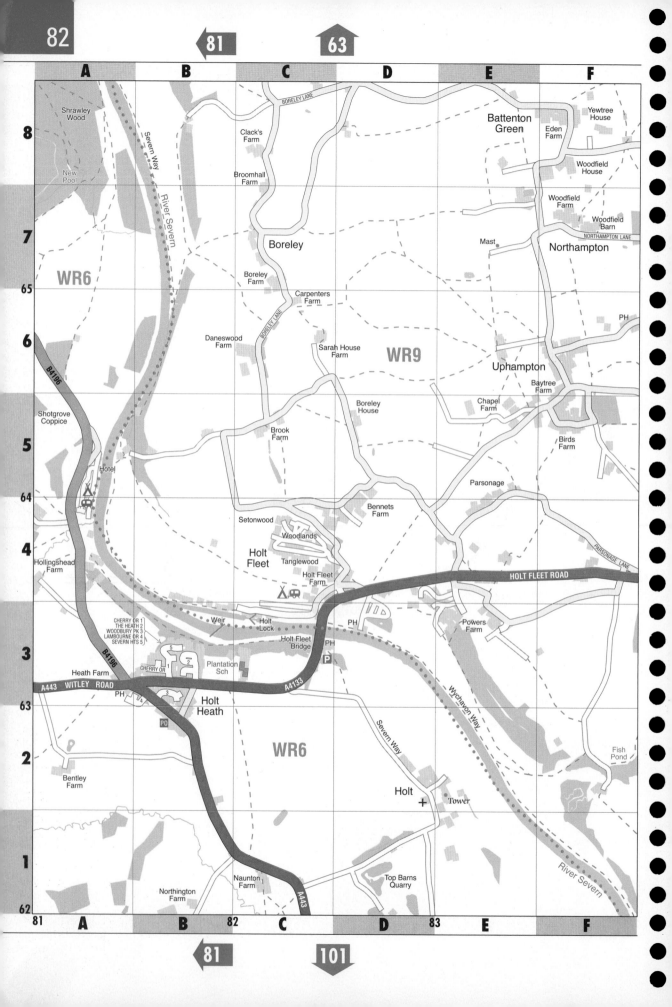

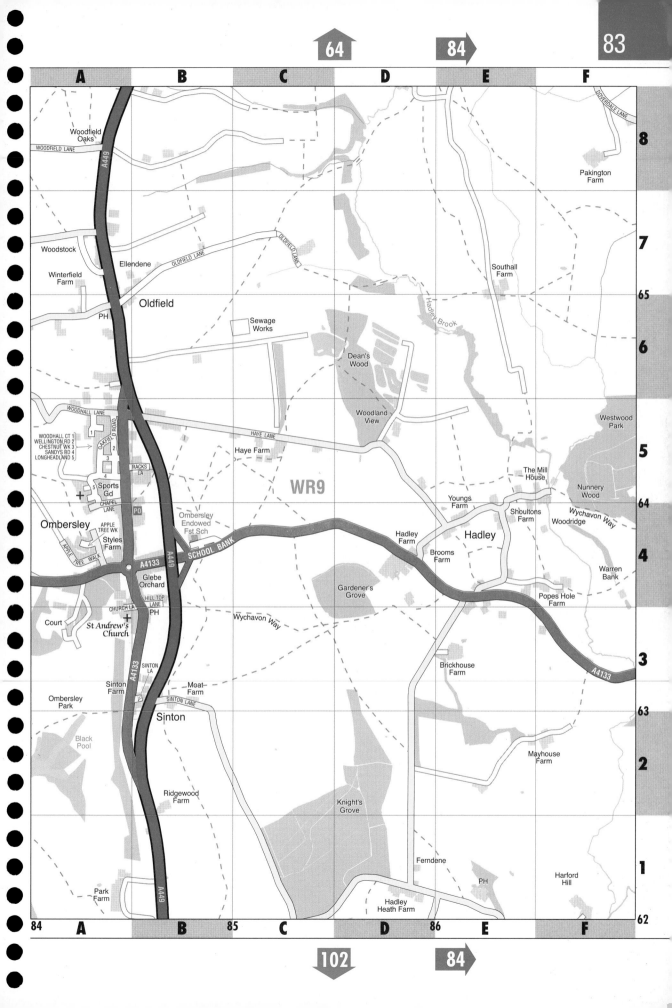

83
65

D5
1 PLOUGHMANS WY
2 DROVERS WY
3 DROVERS PL
4 SHEPHERDS HL
5 SHEPHERDS CT
6 FARMERS CT

A B C D E F

8

7

65

6

WR9

5

64

4

3

63

2

1

62

Keybridge Farm
Keybridge Coppice
Upper Hall Farm
Hampton Farm
Elmbridge Brook
Wychavon Way

Doverdale Lane
Farmbank Plantation
THE FOREST
Doverdale La
Hampton Lovett
Plantation Millgrove
Park Farm

Farm Bank Road
Kingswood Rd
Wassage Way N
Wassage Wy
Mobile Home Park
Highstank Pool

Hampton Lovett Industrial Estate
Wassage Wy S
De Salis
Lovett Rd
Forest End
Allots

Wassage Coppice
Stonebridge Cross Business Park
Pointon Way
Stoney Bridge
Crofters End
Industrial Estate

Monarch's Way
Jakeman's Hill Farm
Crofters Way
Kidderminster Road
Berry Hill
Roman Way Business Park

Nunnery Wood
Wychavon Way
Boycott Wood
Paddock Way
Archers Wy
Westwood Road
Westlands
Shepherds Wy
A442

Fish Pond
Nunnery Farm
Charland Coppice
Westlands Fst Sch
Coppice Wy
Farmers Wy
PO
Meadow Wy
Meadow Road
George Baylis Rd
Roman Way

Westwood House
Bowling Green Plantation
Woodmans Place
Woodmans Wy
Kidderminster Road
Works

DROITWICH SPA
SALINAE
Farriers Wy
South Park Dr
A38
Arrow Cft
Vines La

Westwood Park
Boycott Wood
Hunters Wy
East Park Cr
Stouton Cft
Vines Lane
Hampton Rd

Monarch's Way
Westwood Road
Park Wy
Newtown
Leigh Gr
Salwarpe Road
Union Lane

Westwood Farm
Great Pool
Roman Way
Westacre
Ledwych Cl
Droitwich Spa
Friar St
Priory Lane

Ward's Bridge
A4133
Nuffield Drive
Inett Wy
Shirley Jones Cl
Droitwich Sports & Leisure Centre
Briarmill Bridge
Westacre Mid Sch
Ombersley Way
North St
Saltway
P
P

Broadfield Plantation
Westwood Way
Droitwich High Sch
West St
Saltway
TA Ctr
BMI Droitwich Spa
Highfield Cl

Home Farm
Westwood Close
Briars Hollow
St Joseph's RC Prim Sch
Siding Lane Bridge
Recn Gd
Packington Rd
Manning Rd
Wedgber Row Cl
Droitwich Spa Brine Baths

High Park
Briar Hill Coppice
Lyttle Hill
St Joseph's Cl
Home Mdw Wy Cl
Nunnery Avenue
Blackfriars Ave
Corbett St

Oakham Dr
Galvestune Way
Bower Hl
Chawson Rd
Wych Cl
Old Coach Road
Ripple Rd
Witton Mid Sch

Chawson
New Chawson Lane
Oakham Pl
Witton Avenue
Chawson Fst Sch
College Gn
Westwood Av

Monarch's Way
River Salwarpe
Ombersley Way
Blake Ave
Long Sling
Evertons Cl
Victoria Ave
Recn Gd

Salwarpe Court
Coputt Lane
Chawson Lane
Mast
ROMAN WAY A38
Thames Dr
Witton Avenue
B4090
The Oaklands
The Parklands

83
103

C1
1 ALDERBROOK RD
2 OAKLEIGH RD
3 COLFORD CL
4 OLD CHAWSON LA
5 BRECON CL
6 BARNS CFT WY
7 WHARFEDALE CR
8 DERWENT GR

D1
1 PADGEWELL HL
2 WENSLEYDALE
3 GLENDALE
4 TEESDALE CL
5 WAVENEY RD
6 AVONDALE
7 TEME CR
8 CALDER CL

E3
1 LEDWYCH RD
2 DOWLES CFT
3 ACRE LA
4 STATION ST
5 WESTCROFT ST
6 HARRIS CL
7 ALBERT ST
8 ARCHERS GD
9 ST RICHARD'S GD

F3
1 PRIORY GD
2 CHORLEY RD
3 COVERCROFT
4 OMBERSLEY ST E
5 VICTORIA SQ
6 BOURNE CL
7 HERITAGE WY
8 ST ANDREW'S CL
9 ST ANDREWS RD

10 SEVERN CT
11 COBHAM CT
12 RICKETT'S LA

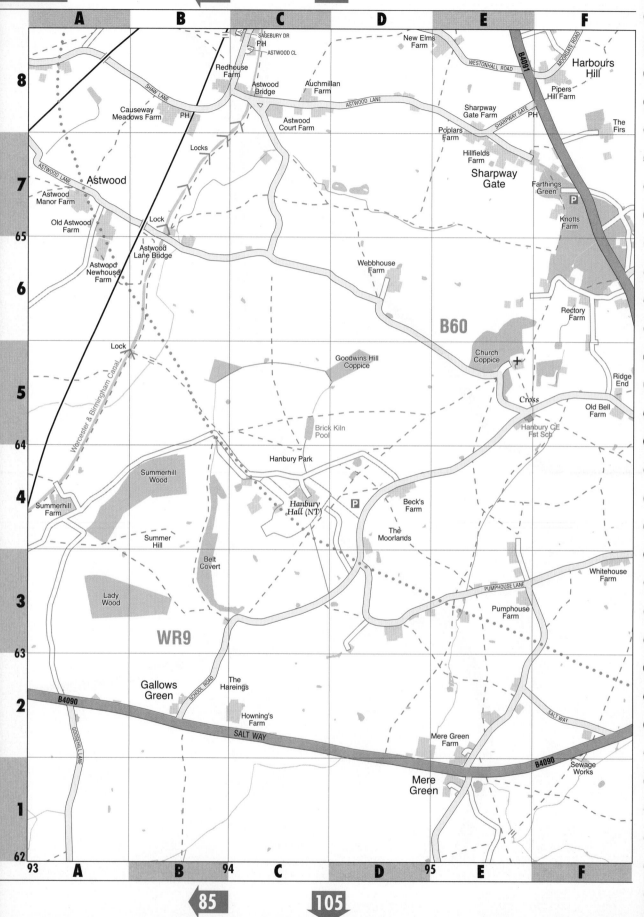

A   B   C   D   E   F

SAGEBURY DR
PH
ASTWOOD CL
New Elms Farm
WESTONHALL ROAD
B4091
MOORGATE ROAD
Harbours Hill

Redhouse Farm
Astwood Bridge
Auchmillan Farm
ASTWOOD LANE
Sharpway Gate Farm
SHARPWAY GATE
PH
Pipers Hill Farm
The Firs

8

SHAW LANE
Causeway Meadows Farm
PH
Astwood Court Farm
Poplars Farm
Hillfields Farm
Sharpway Gate
Farthings Green

P

Locks
Knotts Farm

ASTWOOD LANE
Astwood

7

Astwood Manor Farm
Lock
Webbhouse Farm
B60
Rectory Farm

Old Astwood Farm
65

Astwood Lane Bridge

Astwood Newhouse Farm
6
Church Coppice
Cross
Ridge End

Lock
Worcester & Birmingham Canal
Goodwins Hill Coppice
Old Bell Farm

5
Cross
Hanbury CE Fst Sch

64
Brick Kiln Pool

Summerhill Wood
Hanbury Park
Beck's Farm
Whitehouse Farm

4
Hanbury Hall (NT)
P
The Moorlands

Summerhill Farm
Summer Hill
Belt Covert
PUMPHOUSE LANE
Pumphouse Farm

3
Lady Wood
WR9
63

SCHOOL ROAD
The Hareings
Gallows Green

2
B4090
Howning's Farm
SALT WAY
Mere Green Farm
SALT WAY
B4090
Sewage Works

GOOSEHILL LANE
Mere Green

1

62

93   A   B 94 C   D 95 E   F

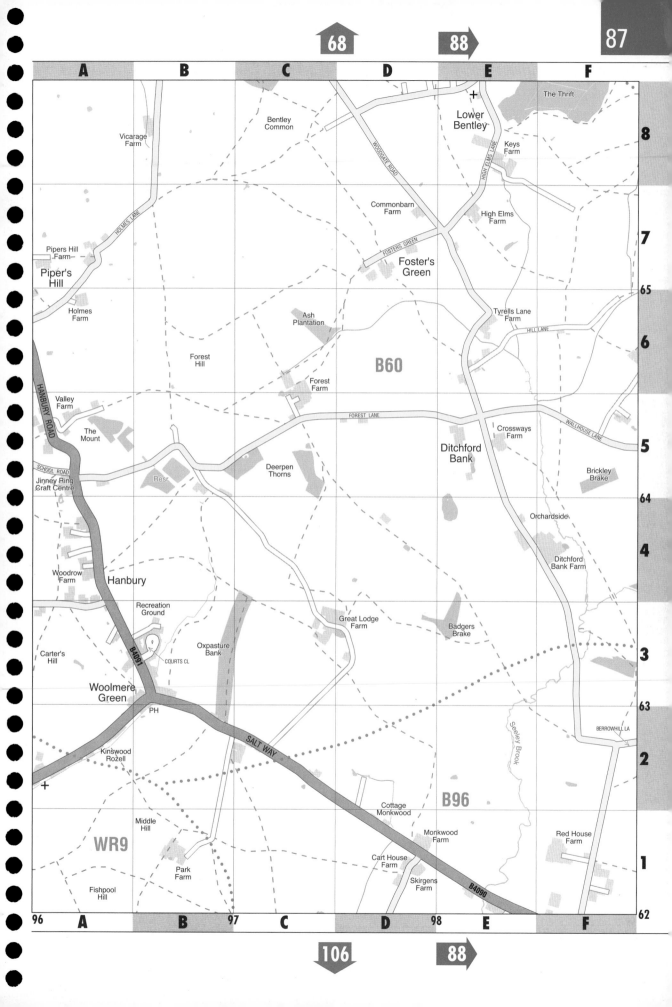

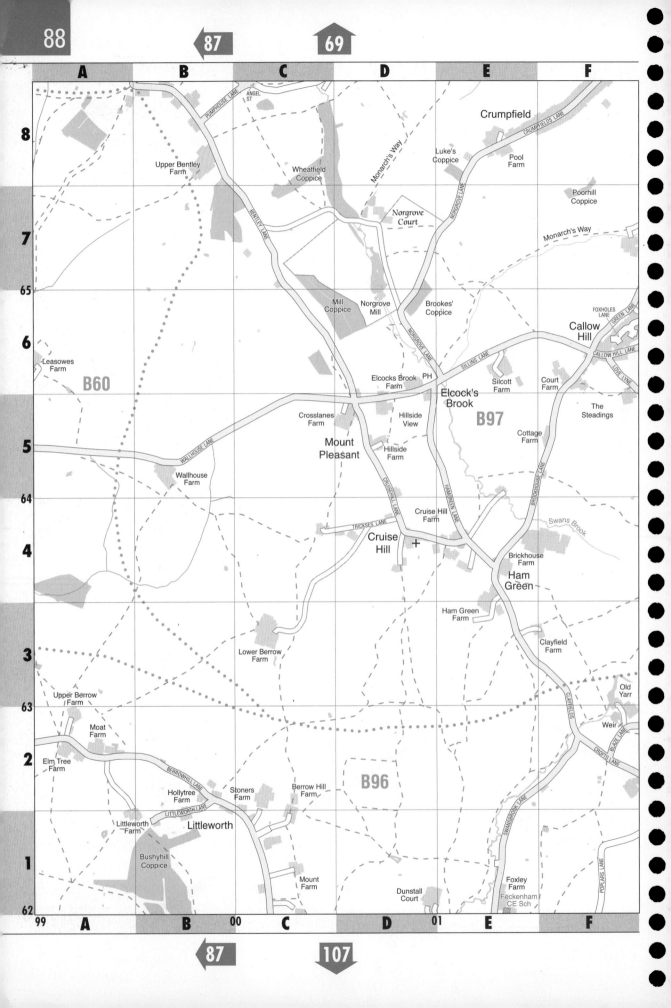

Crumpfield

CRUMPFIELDS LANE

Upper Bentley Farm

Wheatfield Coppice

ANGEL ST

PUMPHOUSE LANE

BENTLEY LANE

Monarch's Way

NORGROVE LANE

Luke's Coppice

Pool Farm

Poorhill Coppice

Norgrove Court

Monarch's Way

Mill Coppice

Norgrove Mill

NORGROVE LANE

Brookes' Coppice

FOXHOLES LANE

GREEN LANE

Callow Hill

Leasowes Farm

B60

Elcocks Brook Farm

PH

SILLINS LANE

Silcott Farm

CALLOW HILL LANE

Court Farm

LOVE LYNE

The Steadings

Elcock's Brook

B97

Crosslanes Farm

Hillside View

Cottage Farm

WALLHOUSE LANE

Mount Pleasant

Wallhouse Farm

Hillside Farm

CRUISEHILL LANE

HAMGREEN LANE

BROOKHOUSE LANE

Swans Brook

TRICKSES LANE

Cruise Hill Farm

Cruise Hill

+

Brickhouse Farm

Ham Green

Ham Green Farm

Clayfield Farm

Old Yarr

Lower Berrow Farm

Upper Berrow Farm

CLAYFIELDS

Weir

Moat Farm

BLAZE LANE

CROFTS LANE

Elm Tree Farm

BERROWHILL LANE

Stoners Farm

Berrow Hill Farm

B96

SWANSBROOK LANE

Hollytree Farm

LITTLEWORTH LANE

Littleworth Farm

Littleworth

POPLARS LANE

Bushyhill Coppice

Mount Farm

Dunstall Court

Foxley Farm

Feckenham CE Sch

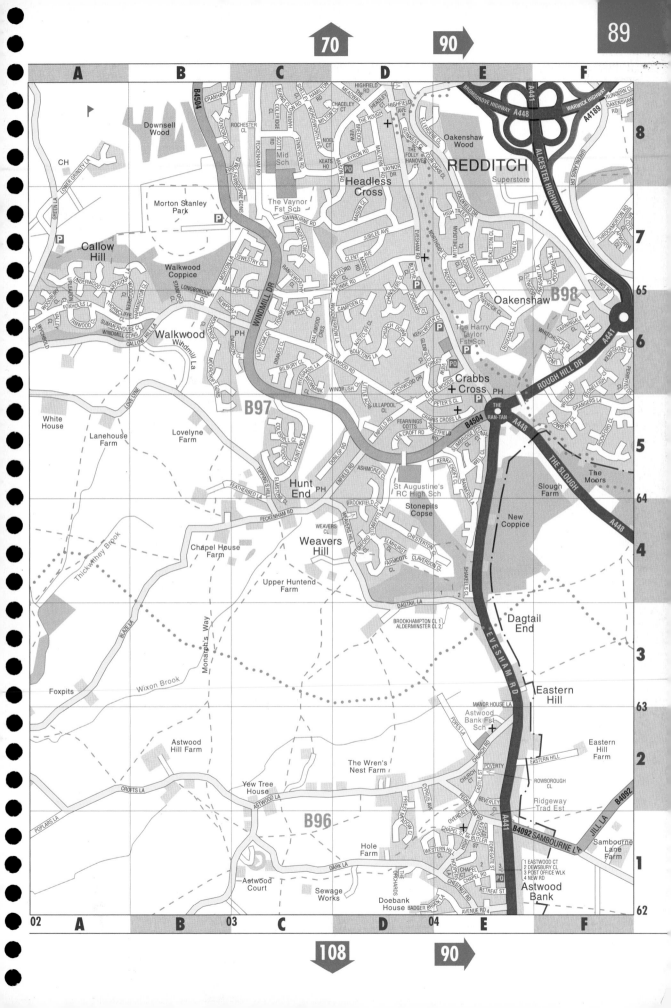

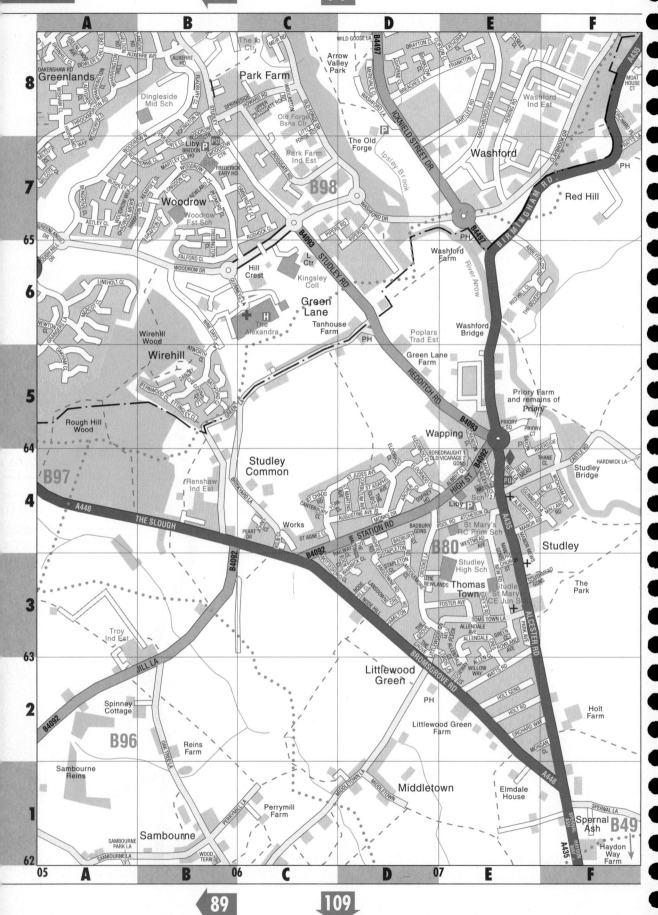

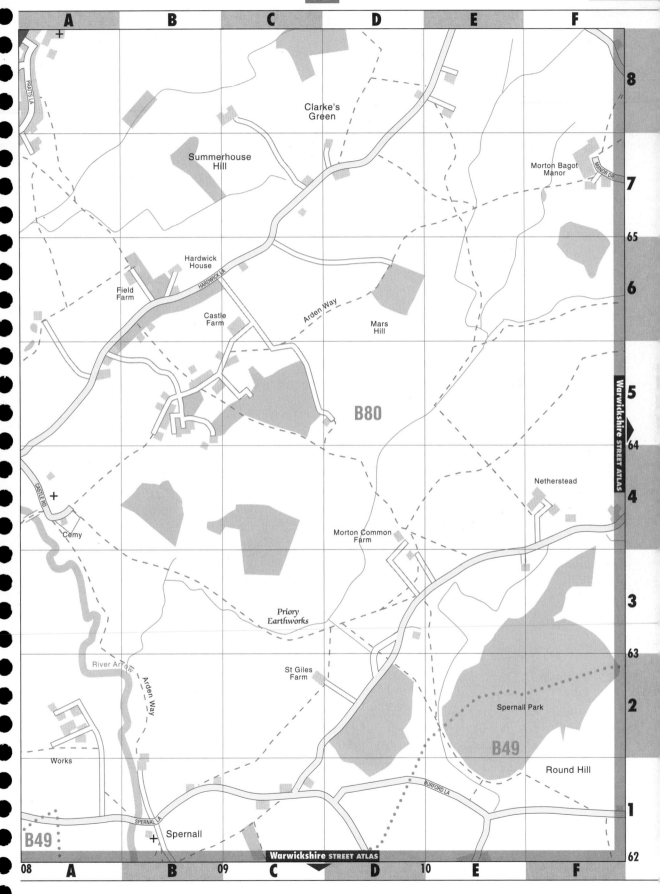

A B C D E F

8

Clarke's
Green

Summerhouse
Hill

Morton Bagot
Manor

MANOR DR

7

65

Hardwick
House

HARDWICK LA

Field
Farm

Castle
Farm

Arden Way

Mars
Hill

6

B80

5

64

Netherstead

4

CASTLE RD

Cemy

Morton Common
Farm

Priory
Earthworks

River Arrow

Arden Way

St Giles
Farm

Spernall Park

B49

Round Hill

3

63

2

Works

BURFORD LA

SPERNAL LA

B49

Spernall

1

62

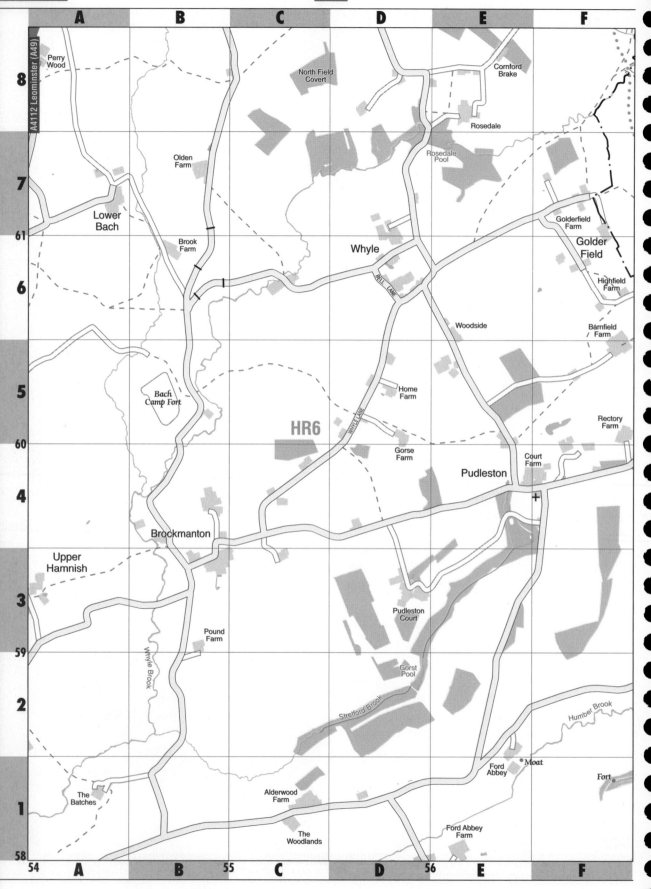

A   B   C   D   E   F

A4112 Leominster (A49)

Perry Wood

North Field Covert

Cornford Brake

Rosedale

Rosedale Pool

Olden Farm

Lower Bach

Golderfield Farm

Golder Field

Brook Farm

Whyle

BELL LANE

Highfield Farm

Woodside

Barnfield Farm

Bach Camp Fort

Home Farm

WHYLE LANE

HR6

Rectory Farm

Gorse Farm

Court Farm

Pudleston

Brockmanton

Upper Hamnish

Pudleston Court

Pound Farm

Whyle Brook

Gorst Pool

Stretford Brook

Humber Brook

Ford Abbey

Moat

Fort

The Batches

Alderwood Farm

The Woodlands

Ford Abbey Farm

54   A   B   55   C   D   56   E   F

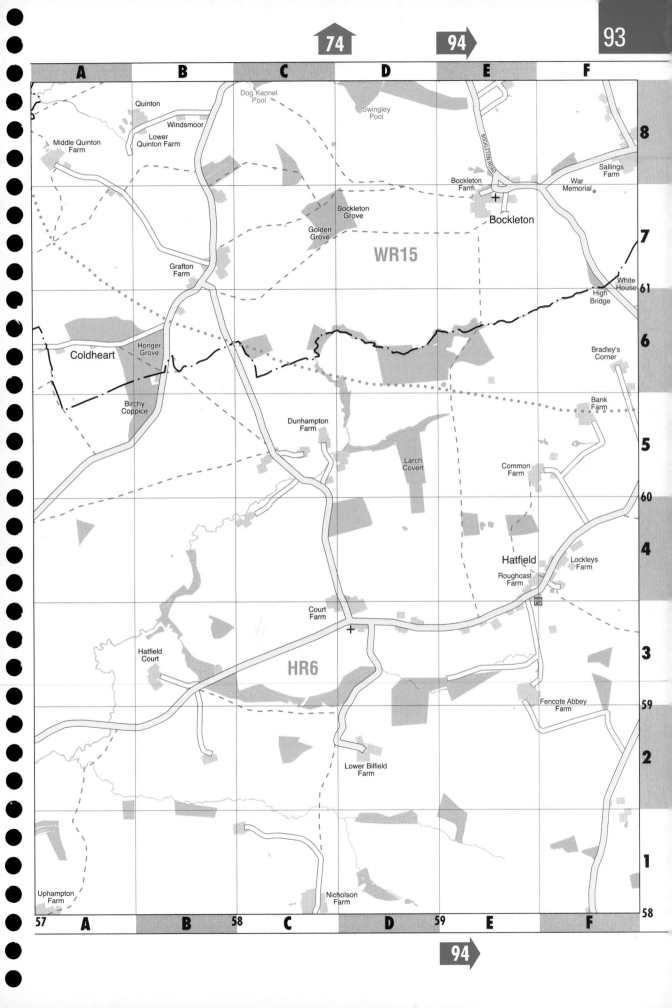

A B C D E F

8
7
61
6
5
60
4
59
3
2
1
58

Quinton
Windsmoor
Lower Quinton Farm
Middle Quinton Farm
Dog Kennel Pool
Swingley Pool
BOCKLETON ROAD
Bockleton Farm
Sallings Farm
War Memorial
Bockleton
Bockleton Grove
Golden Grove
Grafton Farm
WR15
White House
High Bridge
Coldheart
Honger Grove
Bradley's Corner
Birchy Coppice
Bank Farm
Dunhampton Farm
Larch Covert
Common Farm
Hatfield
Lockleys Farm
Roughcast Farm
Court Farm
HR6
Hatfield Court
Fencote Abbey Farm
Lower Bilfield Farm
Nicholson Farm
Uphampton Farm

A B C D E F

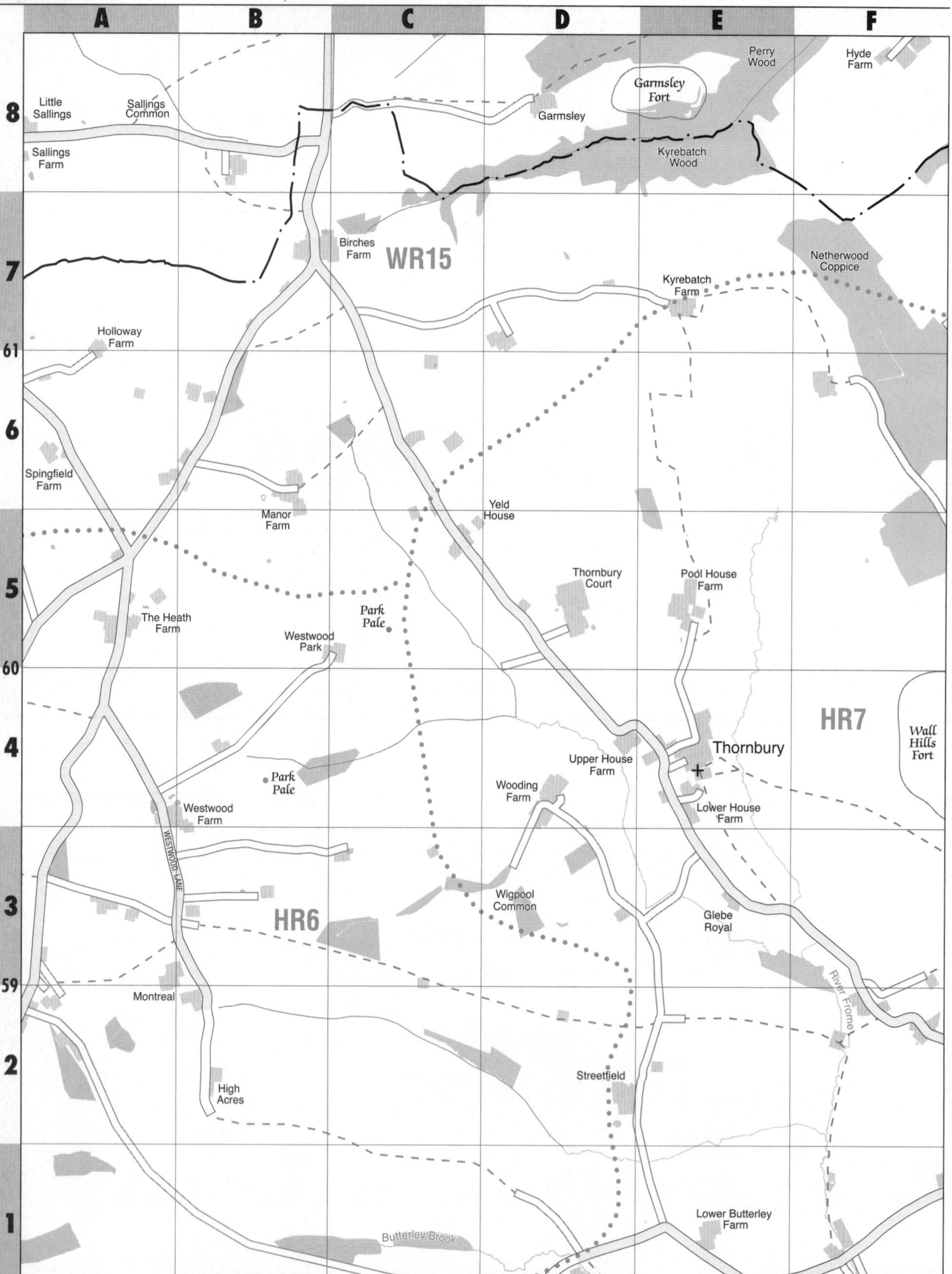

8 Little Sallings
Sallings Common
Garmsley
Garmsley Fort
Perry Wood
Hyde Farm
Sallings Farm
Kyrebatch Wood

Birches Farm
WR15
Kyrebatch Farm
Netherwood Coppice

7

61 Holloway Farm

6 Spingfield Farm
Manor Farm
Yeld House

Thornbury Court
Pool House Farm

5 The Heath Farm
Park Pale
Westwood Park

60

HR7
Wall Hills Fort

4 Upper House Farm
Thornbury
Wooding Farm
Lower House Farm

Park Pale
Westwood Farm

WESTWOOD LANE

3 HR6
Wigpool Common
Glebe Royal

59 Montreal
River Fromet

2 High Acres
Streetfield

1 Lower Butterley Farm
Butterley Brook

58

60 A B 61 C D 62 E F

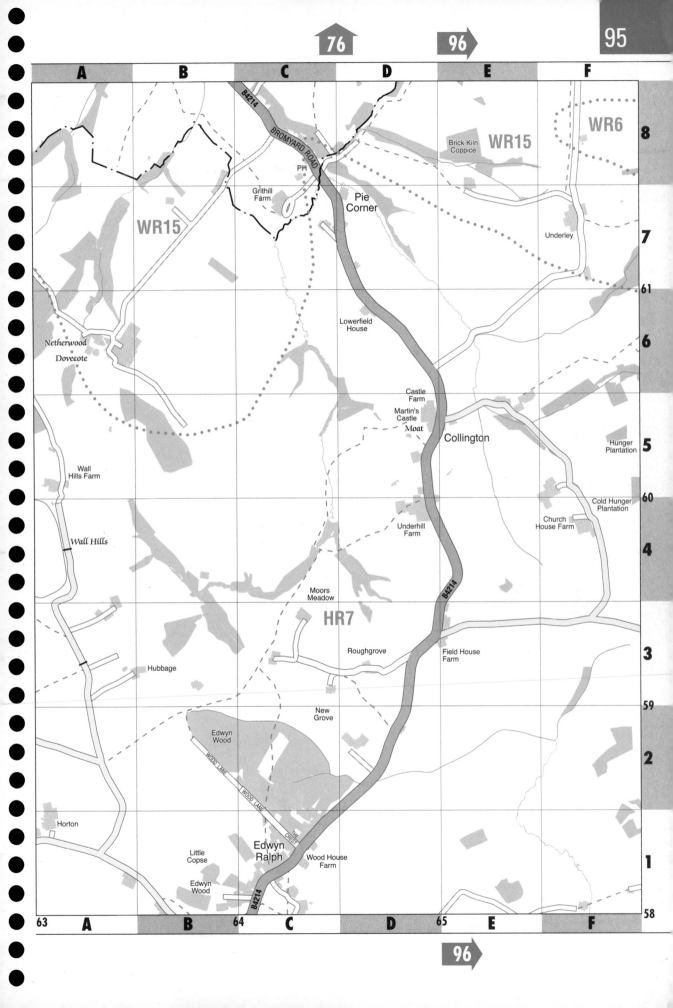

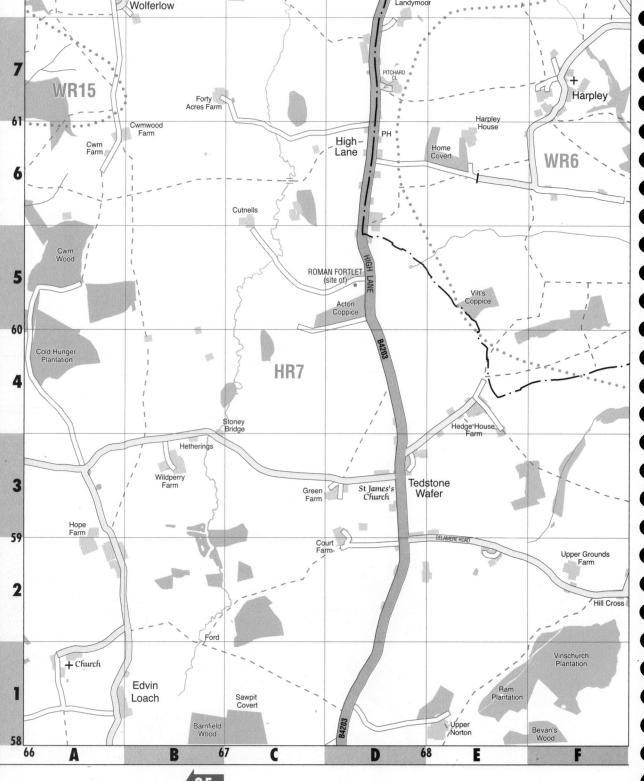

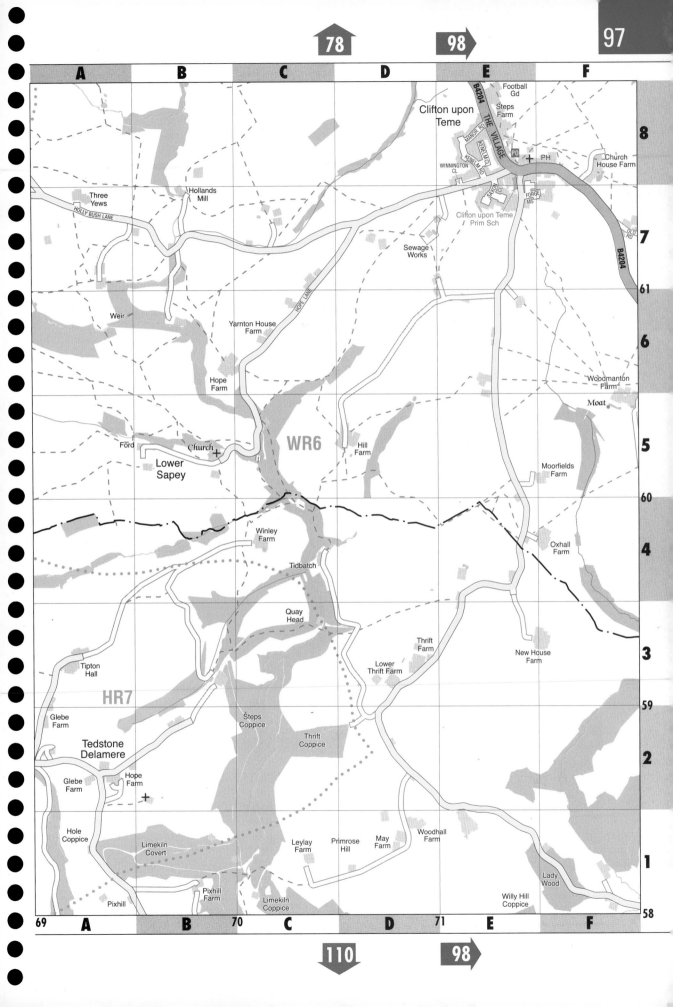

A   B   C   D   E   F

8

Clifton upon Teme

Football Gd

Steps Farm

THE VILLAGE

B4204

MANOR RD

KENELM RD

Church House Farm

WINNINGTON CL

PO

PH

SAXON CL

FORGE MS

Clifton upon Teme Prim Sch

7

OLD RD

B4204

Three Yews

HOLLY BUSH LANE

Hollands Mill

Sewage Works

61

Weir

Yarnton House Farm

HOPE LANE

6

Woodmanton Farm

Hope Farm

Moat

Ford

Church

Hill Farm

WR6

5

Moorfields Farm

Lower Sapey

60

Winley Farm

Oxhall Farm

4

Tidbatch

Quay Head

Thrift Farm

New House Farm

3

Tipton Hall

Lower Thrift Farm

HR7

59

Glebe Farm

Steps Coppice

Thrift Coppice

Tedstone Delamere

2

Glebe Farm

Hope Farm

Hole Coppice

Limekiln Covert

Leylay Farm

Primrose Hill

May Farm

Woodhall Farm

1

Lady Wood

Pixhill Farm

Willy Hill Coppice

Pixhill

Limekiln Coppice

58

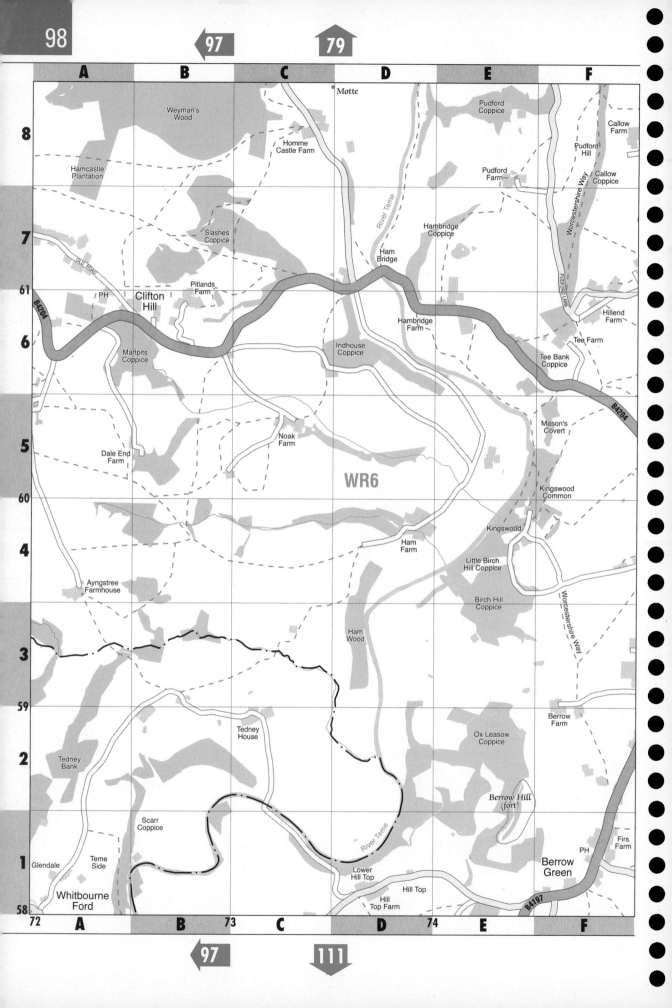

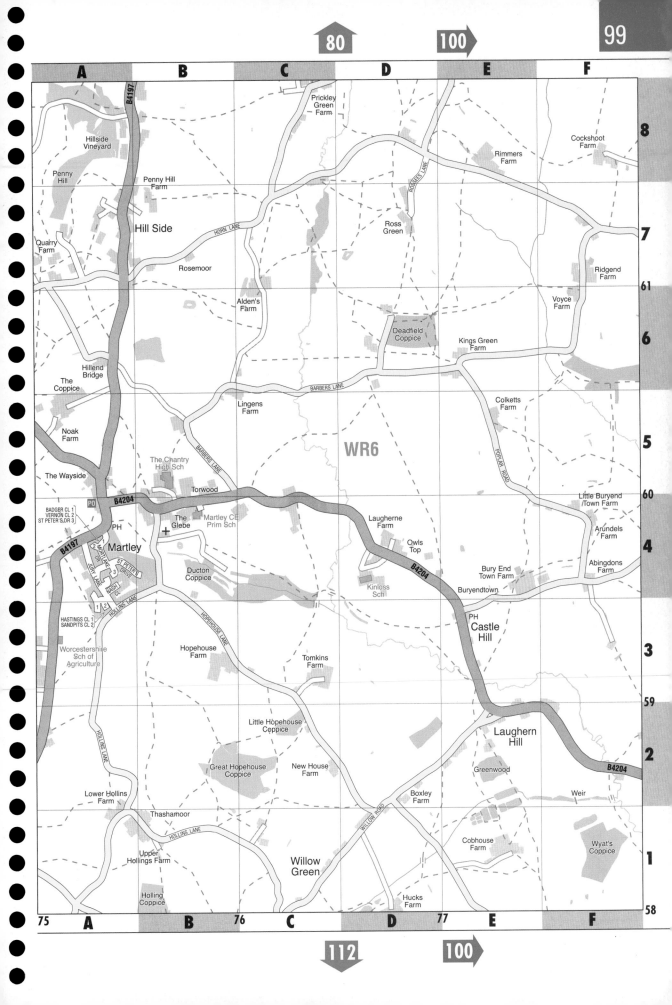

99
81

| A | B | C | D | E | F |

8

Corbett
Coppice

Ockeridge
Wood

7

Woodhouse
Farm

Monk
Wood

61

6

Ridgend
Coppice

QUEENSWAY

Bush
Farm

Monkwood
Nature
Reserve

Wichenford

WR6

Whitehouse
Farm

Green
Farm

Wichenford
Coppice

The
Woodlands

Monkwood
Green

5

Woodcote

PH

60

Moorland

Goodwins
Farm

Wichenford
Dovecote (NT)

Moat

Wichenford
Court

4

Hill
Farm

3

Greenstreet
Farm

WR2

Kedges
Wood

59

Kedges
Farm

Fitcher Brook

2

B4204

Laughern Brook

1

Moat

Kenswick
Manor

B4204

Woodhall
Farm

58

| 78 | A | B | 79 | C | D | 80 | E | F |

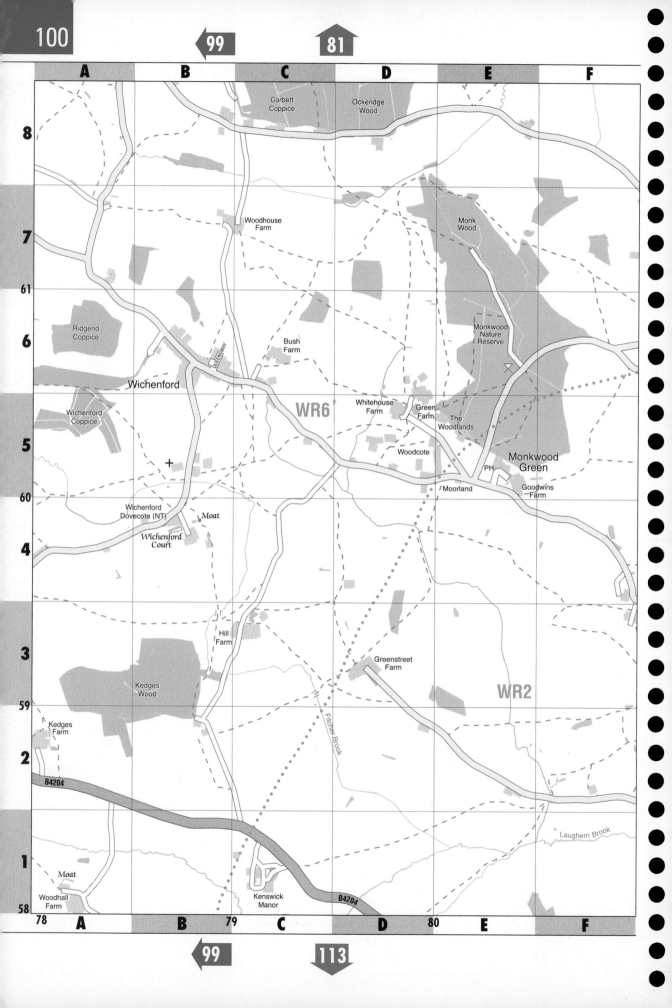

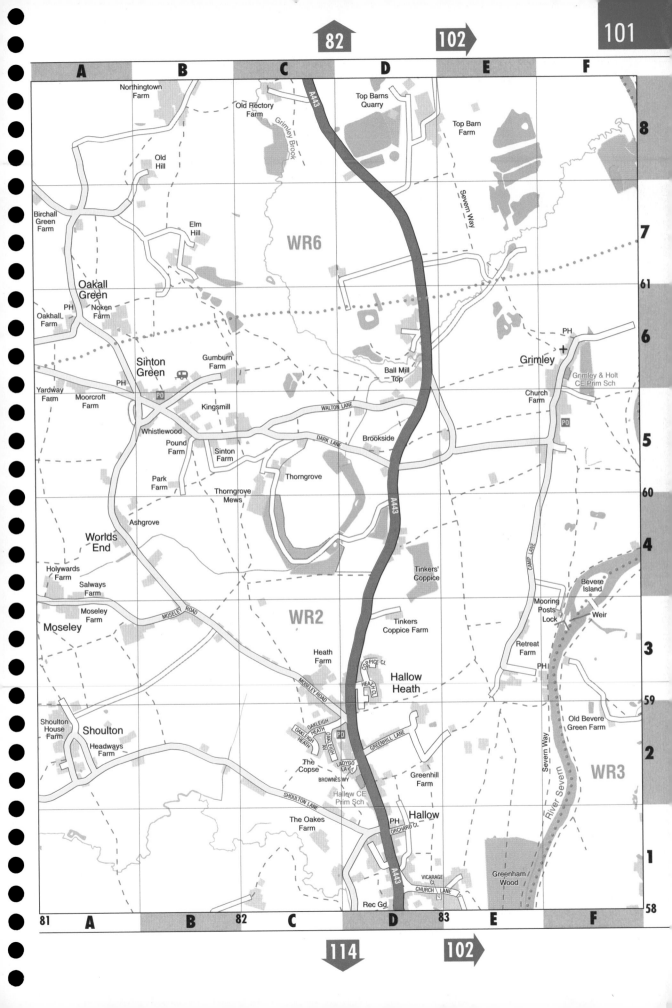

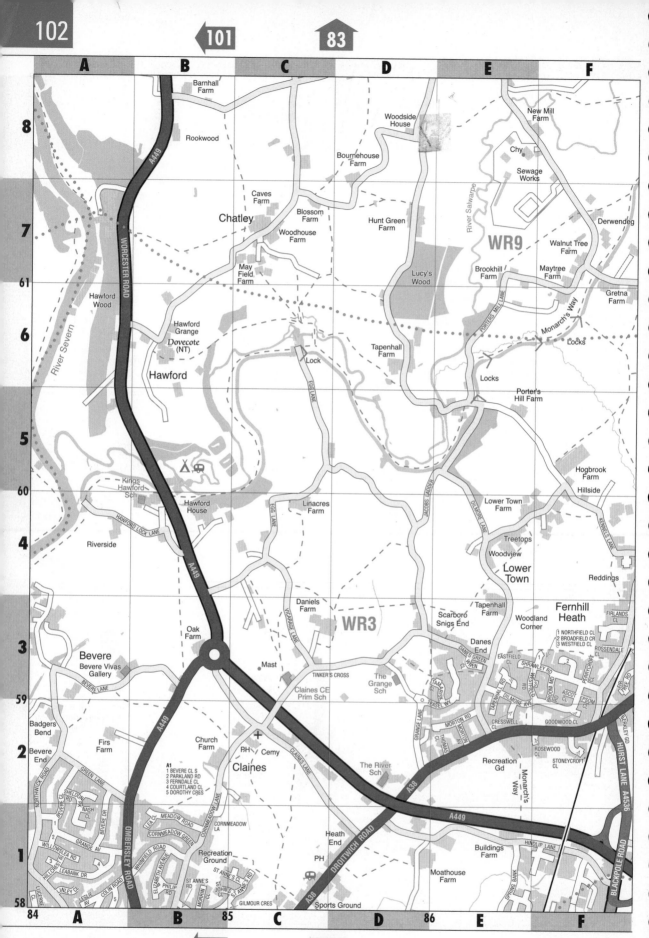

101
83

A   B   C   D   E   F

8

7

61

6

5

60

4

3

59

2

1

58

84   A   B   85   C   D   86   E   F

101
115

Barnhall Farm

Rookwood

Woodside House

New Mill Farm

Chy

Sewage Works

Bournehouse Farm

Caves Farm

Chatley

Blossom Farm

Hunt Green Farm

Derwendeg

WR9

Woodhouse Farm

Walnut Tree Farm

May Field Farm

Lucy's Wood

Brookhill Farm

Maytree Farm

Gretna Farm

Hawford Wood

Hawford Grange

Dovecote (NT)

Hawford

Lock

Tapenhall Farm

Locks

Monarch's Way

Locks

Porter's Hill Farm

River Severn

EGG LANE

WORCESTER ROAD

A449

Kings Hawford Sch

HAWFORD LOCK LANE

Hawford House

Linacres Farm

EGG LANE

JACOBS LADDER

DILMORE LANE

Lower Town Farm

Hogbrook Farm

Hillside

KENNELS LANE

Riverside

Treetops

Woodview

Lower Town

Reddings

Daniels Farm

VICARAGE LANE

WR3

Scarboro Snigs End

Tapenhall Farm

Woodland Corner

Fernhill Heath

FIRLANDS CL

Oak Farm

Mast

Bevere

Bevere Vivas Gallery

BEVERE LANE

TINKER'S CROSS

The Grange Sch

Danes End

DANES GREEN

TAM CL

GRANGE LANE

EASTFIELD CL

SHRAWLEY RD

WESTFIELD

BROOM MD

ROSSENDALE CL

PERRYCROFT

ASCOT CL

EPSOM CL

1 NORTHFIELD CL
2 BROADFIELD CR
3 WESTFIELD CL

Claines CE Prim Sch

Badgers Bend

Bevere End

Firs Farm

Church Farm

PH Cemy

CLAINES LANE

MORTON RD

MORTON AV

CRESSWELL

GOODWOOD CL

TREE RD

BERKLEY RD

HURST LANE A4536

NORTHWICK ROAD

GREEN LANE

SHELDON RD

NASH CL

BEVERE CL

BEVERE DR

Claines

A1
1 BEVERE CL S
2 PARKLAND RD
3 FERNDALE CL
4 COURTLAND CL
5 DOROTHY CRES

The River Sch

ROSEWOOD CL

STONEYCROFT CL

Recreation Gd

Monarch's Way

Heath End

PH

DROITWICH ROAD

Buildings Farm

HINDLIP LANE

BLACKPOLE ROAD

WILLOWSLEA RD

HILLCREST RD

LEABANK DR

GRANGE AV

WINFIELD ROAD

PHILIP RD

ELIZABETH AVENUE

TEA CL

MEADOW ROAD

CORNMEADOW GREEN

CORNMEADOW LANE

CORNMEADOW LA

Recreation Ground

ST ANNE'S RD

ST ANNE'S CL

ST JOHN'S CL

ST ANNE'S RD

MORRIN CL

Moathouse Farm

SPRING BANK

LUCERNE CL

INLEY CL

LESLIE AV

COLIN CL

GILMOUR CRES

A38

Sports Ground

A449

A38

OMBERSLEY ROAD

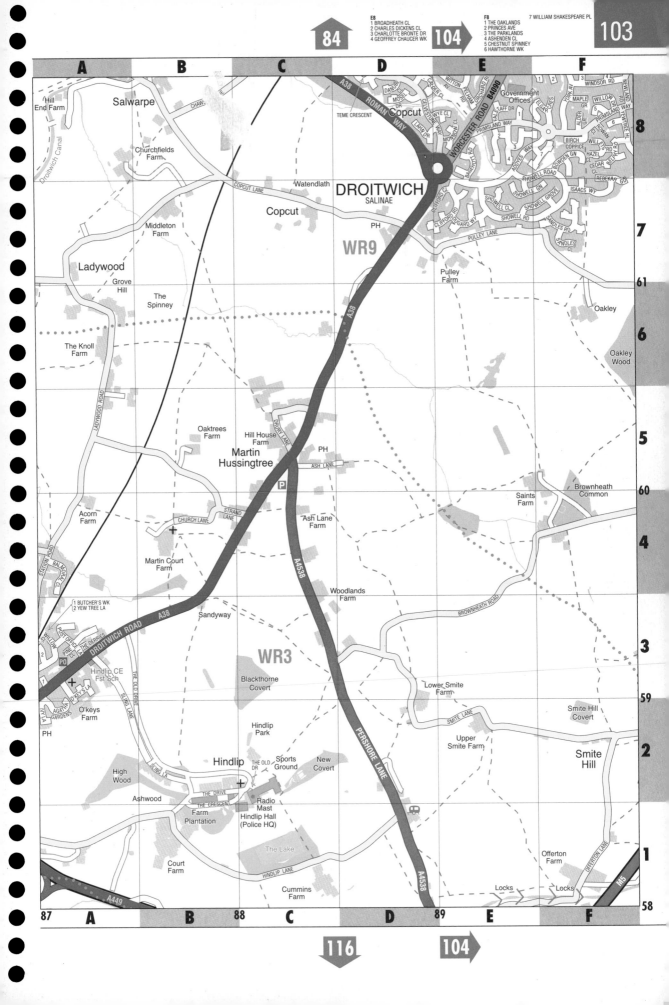

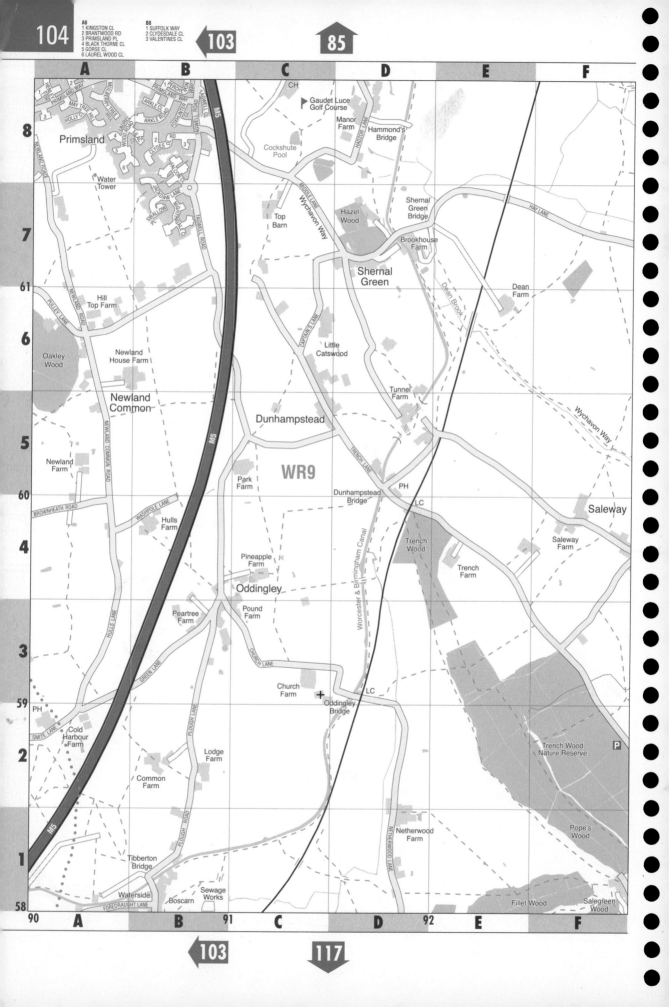

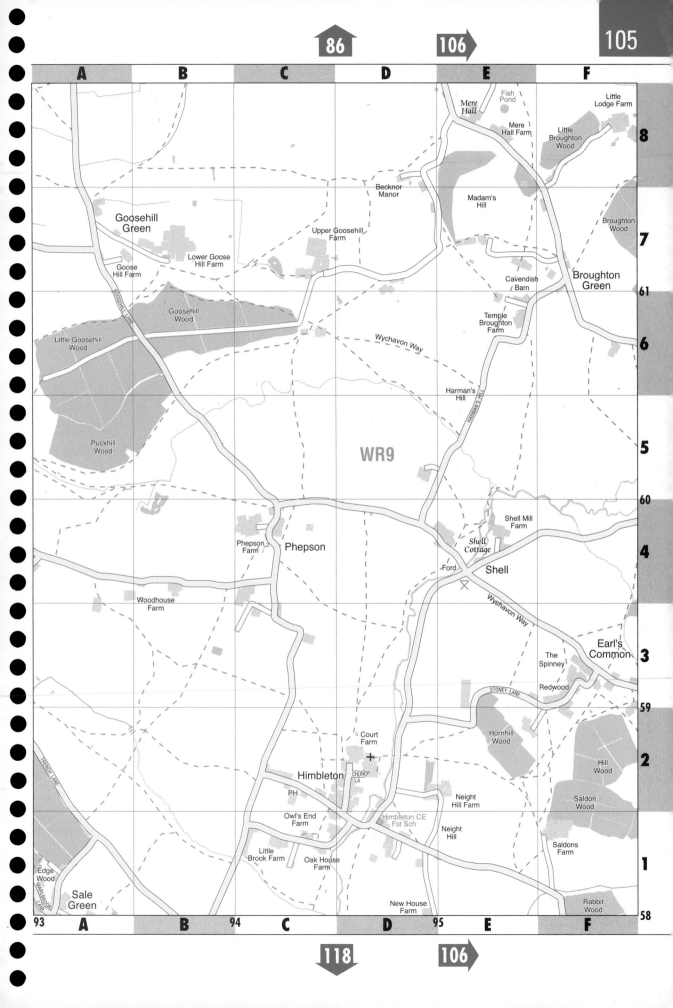

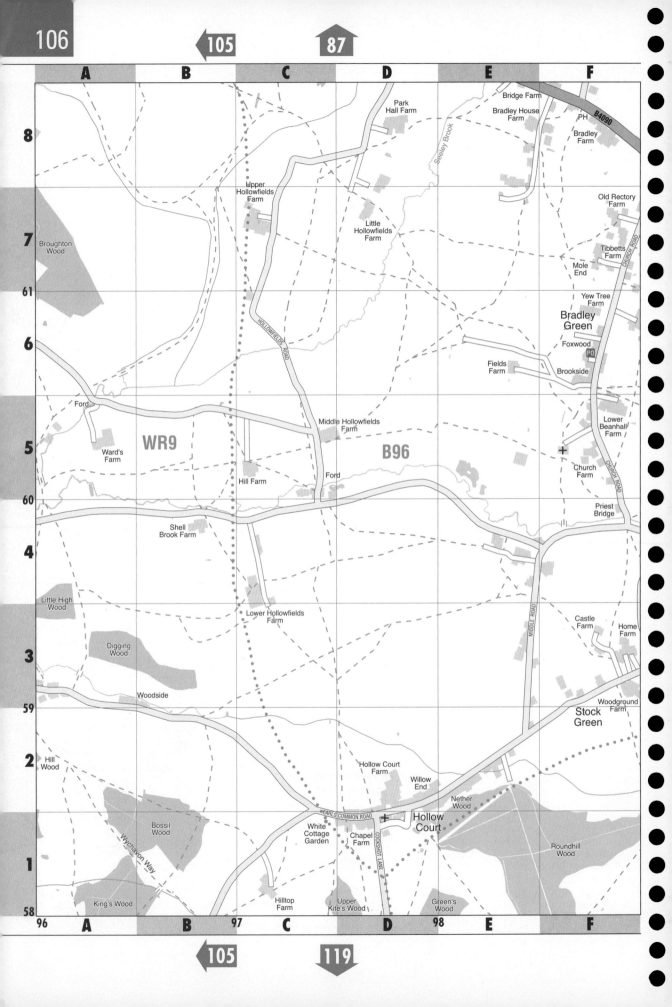

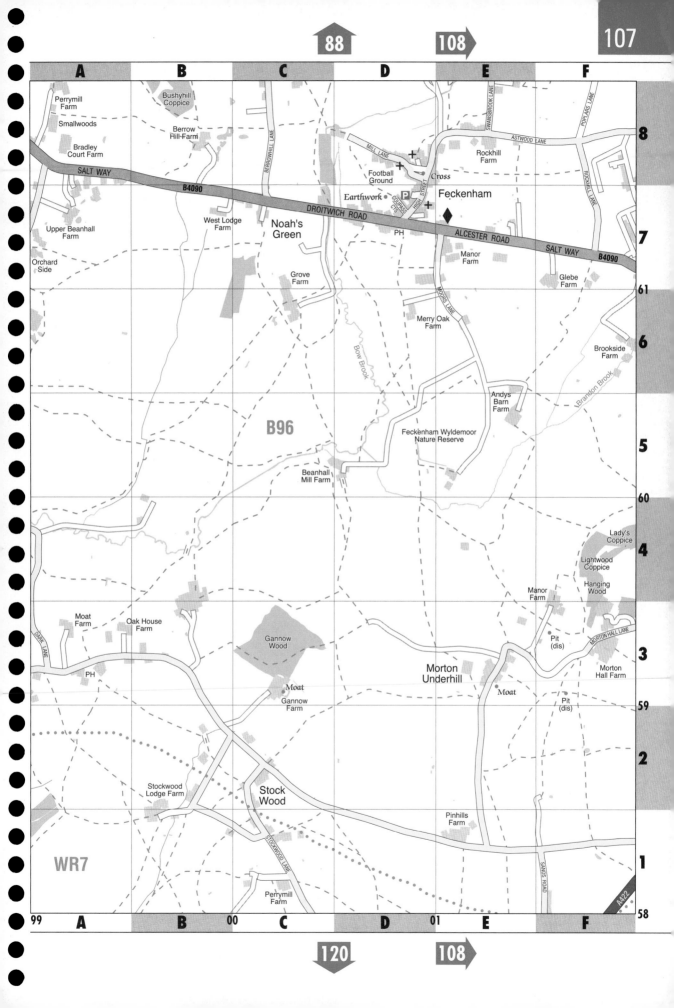

A   B   C   D   E   F

8

Perrymill Farm
Smallwoods
Bushyhill Coppice
Berrow Hill-Farm
Swansbrook Lane
Astwood Lane
Poplars Lane
Rockhill Farm
Bradley Court Farm
Mill Lane
Cross
Rockhill Lane

SALT WAY
B4090
DROITWICH ROAD
Football Ground
Earthwork
P
COMPASS CFS
HIGH STREET
Feckenham

7

Upper Beanhall Farm
West Lodge Farm
Noah's Green
PH
ALCESTER ROAD
SALT WAY   B4090
Manor Farm

Orchard Side
Grove Farm
Merry Oak Farm
Glebe Farm

61

6

Bow Brook
Brandon Brook
Brookside Farm

B96
Feckenham Wyldemoor Nature Reserve
Andys Barn Farm

5

Beanhall Mill Farm

60

Lady's Coppice

4

Lightwood Coppice
Hanging Wood

Moat Farm
Oak House Farm
Manor Farm
Pit (dis)
Morton Hall Lane

3

DARK LANE
PH
Gannow Wood
Morton Underhill
Moat
Morton Hall Farm

Moat
Gannow Farm
Pit (dis)

59

2

Stockwood Lodge Farm
Stock Wood
STOCKWOOD LANE
Pinhills Farm

1

WR7
Perrymill Farm
SANDS ROAD
A422

58

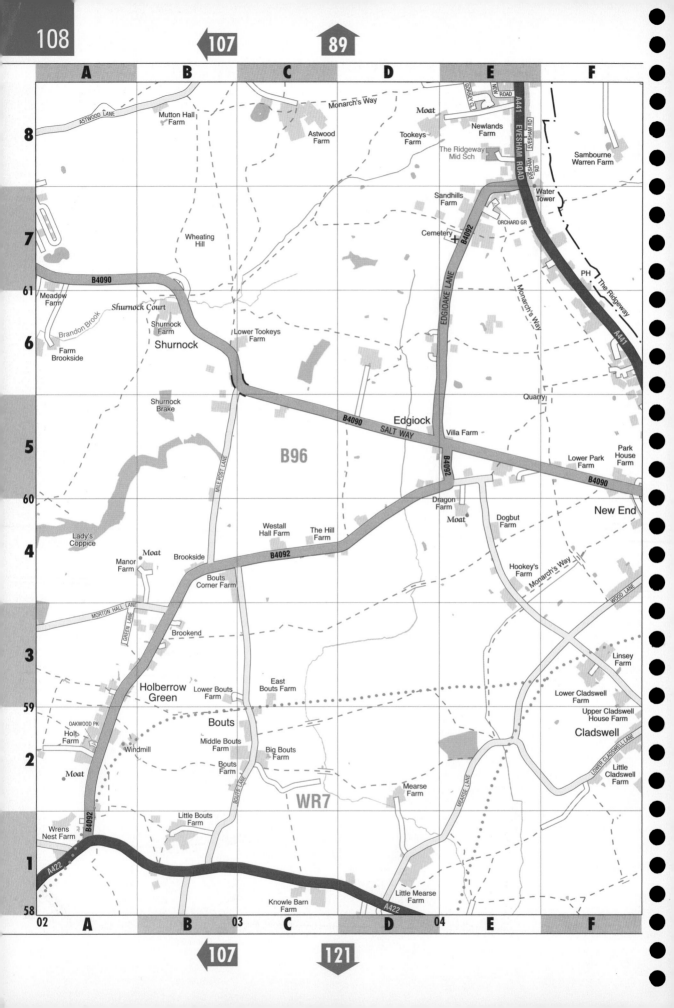

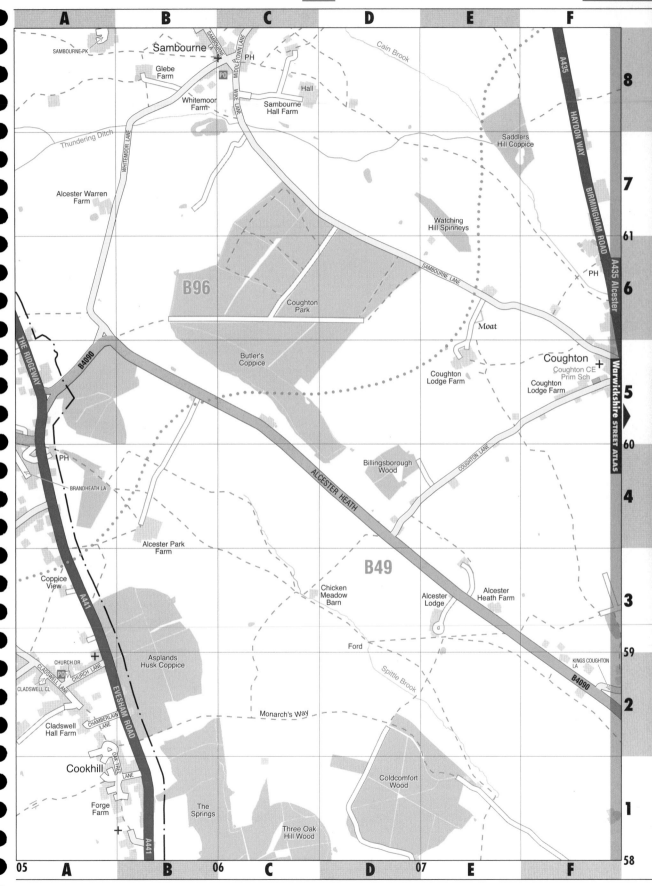

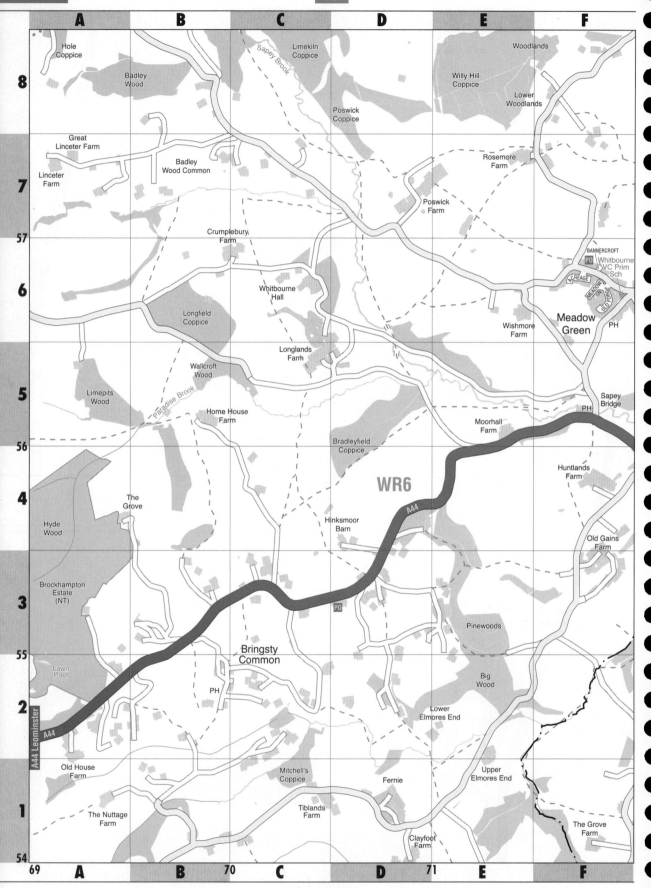

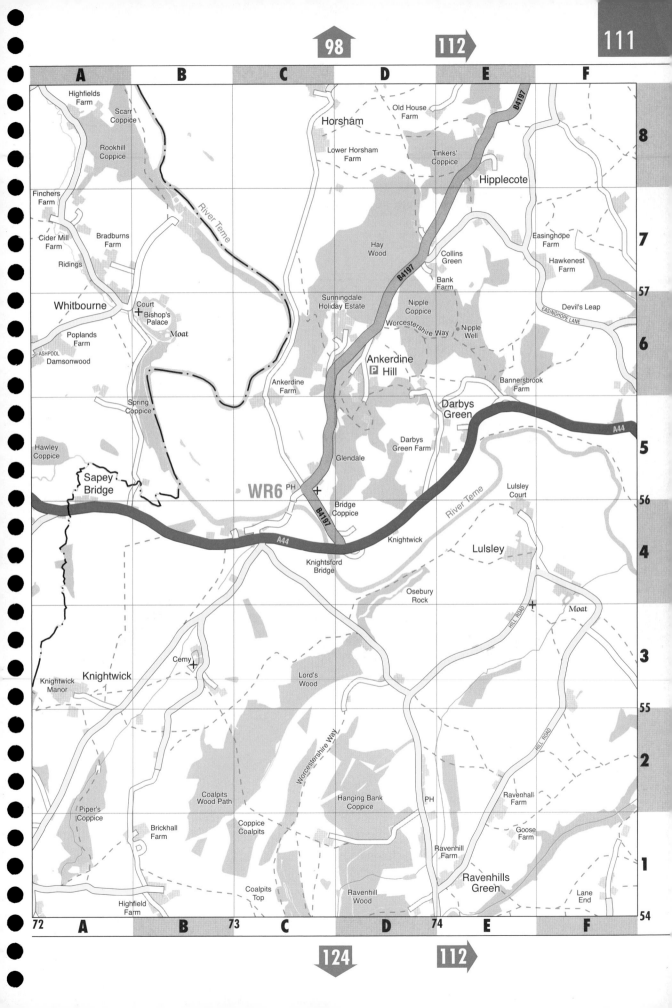

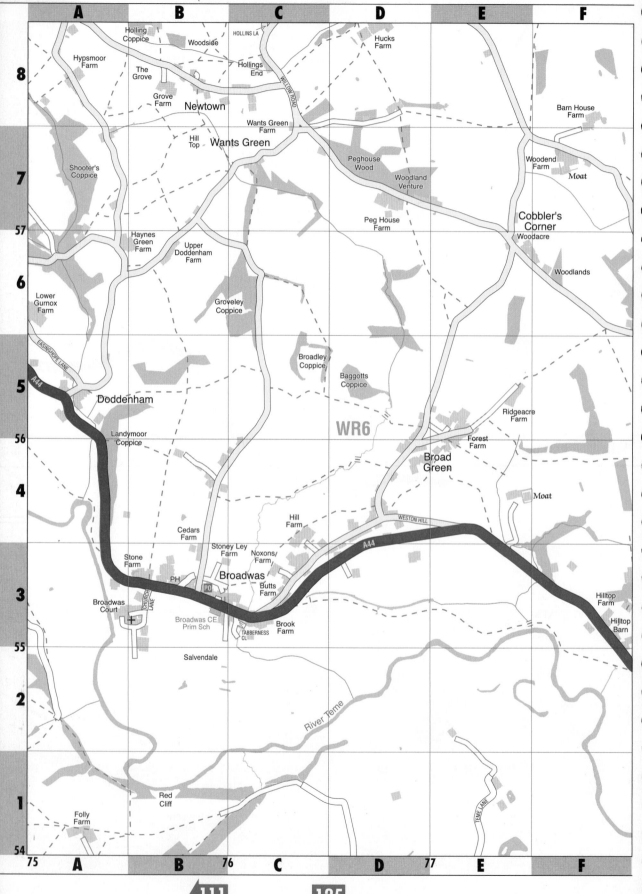

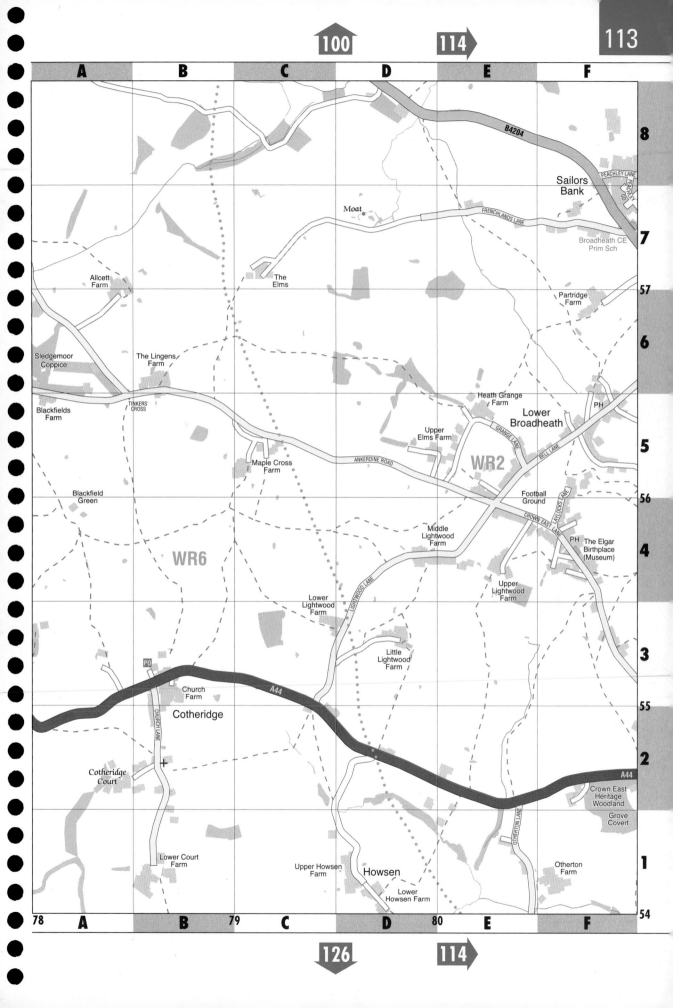

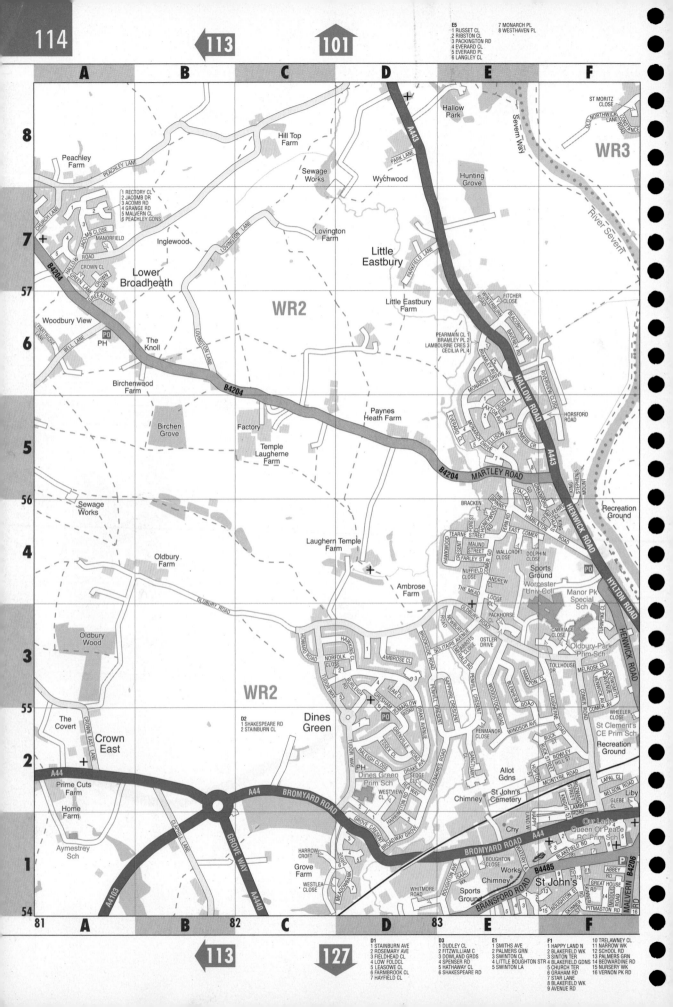

E5
1 RUSSET CL
2 RIBSTON CL
3 PACKINGTON RD
4 EVERARD CL
5 EVERARD PL
6 LANGLEY CL
7 MONARCH PL
8 WESTHAVEN PL

WR3

8

Hallow Park

St MORITZ CLOSE

OLD NORTHWICK LANE

CONSTANCE

Peachley Farm

PEACHLEY LANE

Hill Top Farm

Sewage Works

Wychwood

Hunting Grove

River Severn

Severn Way

7

1 RECTORY CL
2 JACOMB DR
3 ACOMB RD
4 GRANGE RD
5 MALVERN CL
6 PEACHLEY GDNS

Inglewood

LOVINGTON LANE

Lovington Farm

Little Eastbury

PARKFIELD LANE

MANORFIELD

57

Lower Broadheath

WR2

Little Eastbury Farm

FITCHER CLOSE

WINTERBURN RD

BEACONHILL DR

BATLEY RD

B4204

CHURCH LANE

HALLOW ROAD

GREEN LANE

CROWN CL

6

Woodbury View

The Knoll

LOVINGTON LANE

PEARMAIN CL 1
BRAMLEY PL 2
LAMBOURNE CRES 3
CECILIA PL 4

RIVERVIEW CLOSE

HALLOW ROAD

PORTHOUSE LANE

BELL LANE

Birchenwood Farm

B4204

MONARCH DRIVE

BRAMLEY RD

LAXTON AV

CECILIA

LECHMERE CR

HORSFORD ROAD

5

Birchen Grove

Factory

Paynes Heath Farm

Temple Laugherne Farm

EVERARD CL

MONTROSE

ALLISON AV

ANDREW DRIVE

KING STEPHENS MOUNT

A443

B4204   MARTLEY ROAD

56

Sewage Works

Laughern Temple Farm

BRACKEN

THE SPINNEY

STALFORD RD

GREENDOL

KING

MELROSE AV

Recreation Ground

HENWICK ROAD

4

Oldbury Farm

OLDBURY ROAD

Ambrose Farm

HAWKWOOD

TEARNE STREET

FOREST WOOD

FERN RD

EAST COMER

COMER RD

HIMBLETON RD

FARLEY ST

MAUND STREET

WALLCROFT CLOSE

DOLPHIN CLOSE

Sports Ground

Worcester Univ Coll

Manor Pk Special Sch

PO

HYLTON ROAD

NUFFIELD CLOSE

COMER RD

ANDREW CL

THE MEAD

LODGE

PACKHORSE

CARRIAGE CLOSE

TURNPIKE CL

Oldbury Park Prim Sch

HENWICK ROAD

3

Oldbury Wood

OLDBURY ROAD

HOWARD ROAD

NORFOLK CLOSE

HANTING CL

AMBROSE CL

NEWBURY RD

BROOKSIDE ROAD

SOLITAIRE AVENUE

ABBOTS CL

MEAD RD

SAPPHIRE CRESCENT

PENHILL CRESCENT

OSTLER DRIVE

WOODSTOCK ROAD

BLENHEIM ROAD

LAUGHERNE ROAD

TOLLHOUSE DR

MELROSE CL

ACKSMITH AVENUE

HENWICK AV

COMER RD

WHEELER CLOSE

55

WR2

D2
1 SHAKESPEARE RD
2 STAINBURN CL

Dines Green

TUDOR WAY

BIRLEIGH

GRESHAM RD

BARLOW

DRAKE AVENUE

GRENVILLE CL

PENHILL CRESCENT

ANDREW RD

PENMANOR CLOSE

WINDSOR AVE

BUCK

St Clement's CE Prim Sch

Recreation Ground

The Covert

CROWN EAST LANE

2

Crown East

A44

Prime Cuts Farm

OLDPHIL LANE

RALEIGH CLOSE

ESSEX CL

SEDGE

PH

Dines Green Prim Sch

GREENACRES ROAD

DRAKE AVE

SANCTUARY

Allot Gdns

St John's Cemetery

McINTYRE RD

BUCK STREET

ROWLEY

HILL ST

HOPTON

KNIGHT

LAMBER

LAPAL CL

NELSON ROAD

GLEBE

Liby

A4103

GROVE WAY

A44   BROMYARD ROAD

WESTVIEW CL

RACE WAY

HARBISTON RD

Chimney

St John's

Chy

LAND W

HAPPY

Our Lady Queen Of Peace RC Prim Sch

A44

P

MALVERN RD

B4206

1

Home Farm

Aymestrey Sch

A4103

A440

Grove Farm

HARROW CROFT

WESTLEA CLOSE

MEADOWBANK DRIVE

BROADWAY GROVE

WHITMORE ROAD

A44   BROMYARD ROAD

BRANSFORD ROAD

Sports Ground

BOUGHTON AVE

ISAAC

Chimney

Works

BLAKEFIELD RD

St John's

B4485

CHURCH TER

GREAT HOUSE RD

ABBEY RD

PITMASTON RD

SKINNER

VERNON PK RD

54

81   82   83

A   B   C   D   E   F

D1
1 STAINBURN AVE
2 ROSEMARY AVE
3 FIELDHEAD CL
4 LOW FOLDCL
5 LEASOWE CL
6 FARMBROOK CL
7 HAYFIELD CL

D3
1 DUDLEY CL
2 FITZWILLIAM C
3 DOWLAND GRDS
4 SPENSER RD
5 HATHAWAY CL
6 SHAKESPEARE RD

E1
1 SMITHS AVE
2 PALMERS GRN
3 SWINTON CL
4 LITTLE BOUGHTON STR
5 SWINTON LA

F1
1 HAPPY LAND N
2 BLAKEFIELD WK
3 SINTON TER
4 BLAKEFIELD GDNS
5 CHURCH TER
6 GRAHAM RD
7 STAR LANE
8 BLAKEFIELD WK
9 AVENUE RD
10 TRELAWNEY CL
11 NARROW WK
12 SCHOOL RD
13 PALMERS GRN
14 BEDWARDINE RD
15 NURSERY WK
16 VERNON PK RD

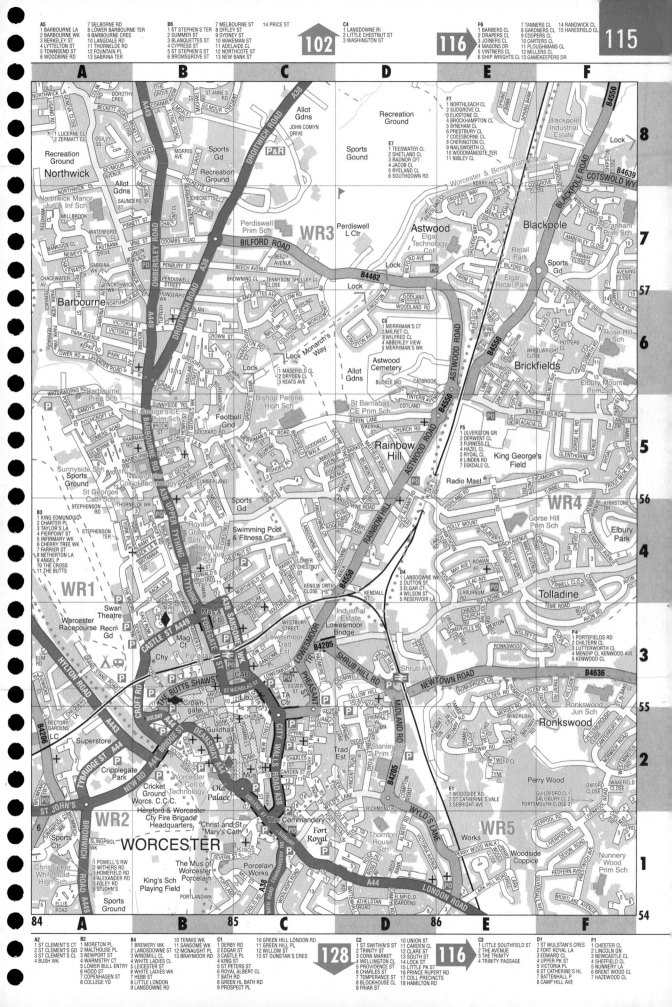

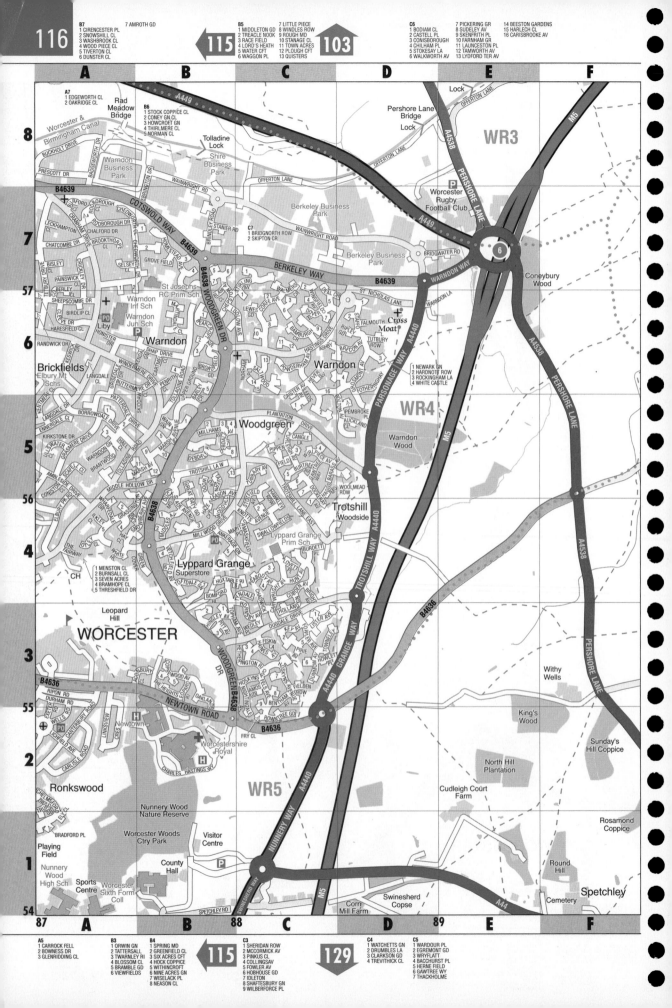

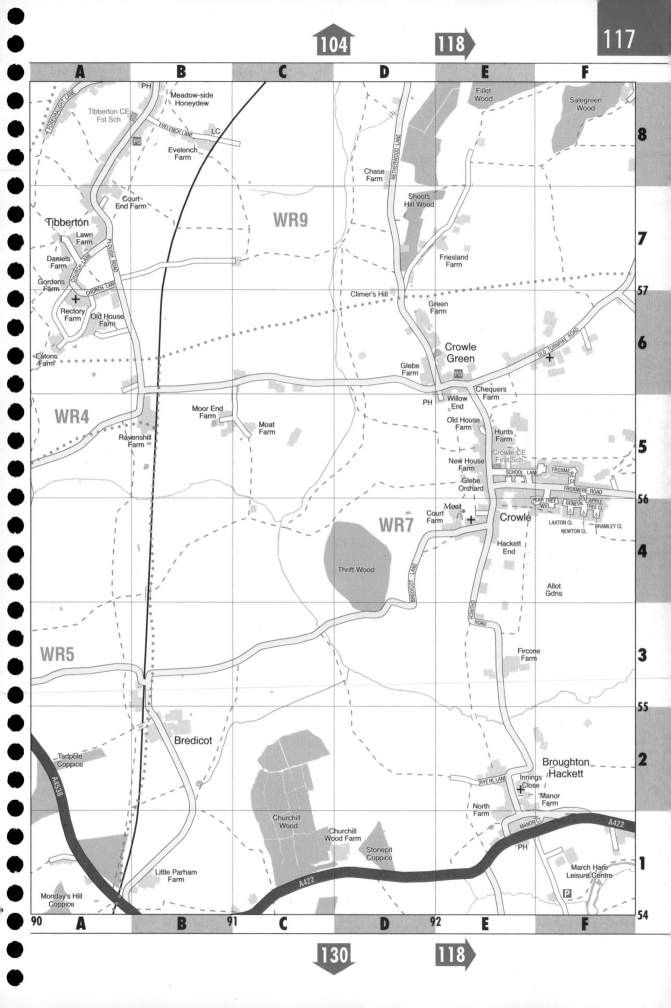

A   B   C   D   E   F

90   A   B   91   C   D   92   E   F   54

8
7
57
6
5
56
4
3
55
2
1

FOREDRAUGHT LANE

PH
Meadow-side
Honeydew
Tibberton CE
Fst Sch
EVELENCH LANE
LC
PO
Evelench
Farm

Court
End Farm

Tibberton

Lawn
Farm

Daniels
Farm

PLOUGH ROAD

CHURCH LANE

Gordons
Farm

CHURCH LANE

Rectory
Farm

Old House
Farm

Eatons
Farm

WR9

Chase
Farm

NETHERWOOD LANE

Fillet
Wood

Salegreen
Wood

Shoots
Hill Wood

Friesland
Farm

Climer's Hill

Green
Farm

Crowle
Green

OLD TURNPIKE ROAD

Glebe
Farm

PO

PH

Willow
End

Chequers
Farm

WR4

Moor End
Farm

Moat
Farm

Ravenshill
Farm

Old House
Farm

Hunts
Close

New House
Farm

Crowle CE
First Sch

SCHOOL LANE

FROXME

FROXMERE ROAD

Glebe
Orchard

PEAR TREE
WY

GENEV

APPLE
TREE CL

56

LAXTON CL

NEWTON CL

BRAMLEY CL

Moat

Court
Farm

Crowle

WR7

Hackett
End

Thrift Wood

BREDICOT LANE

Allot
Gdns

CHURCH ROAD

Fircone
Farm

WR5

55

Bredicot

Broughton
Hackett

Tadpole
Coppice

A4538

RYE HL LANE

Innings
Close

Manor
Farm

North
Farm

MANOR CT

A422

Churchill
Wood

Churchill
Wood Farm

Stonepit
Coppice

PH

March Hare
Leisure Centre

P

Little Parham
Farm

A422

Monday's Hill
Coppice

117 105

A B C D E F

8

Sale Green
Sale Green Farm
SHAFTLAND CROSS
TRENCH LANE

Rabbit Wood

Diamond Hall Farm

Hall Farm

Huddington **WR9**

7

Huddington Court

Mill Farm

Hill Court

57

Bow Brook

6

Huddington Hill Farm

Commandry Farm

5

56

FROXMERE ROAD

Froxmere Court

4

Sewage Works

Bow Wood

WR7

3

Libbery

Yew Tree Farm

55

Little Hall Farm

Elms Farm

Libbery Farm

Humblebee Hall

Bow Brook

2

A422

Court Farm

PH

PH

Moorend Barn

A422

Upton Snodsbury

CROFT RD

PO

B4082

HILLSIDE CL

FLAX PIECE

1

Upton Snodsbury CE Fst Sch

CHURCH LA

SCHOOL LA

COLLEGE RD

PERSHORE ROAD

Holyoak Farm

CHAPEL LA

PERSHORE RD

CUTTS POOL

54

93 A B 94 C D 95 E F

117 131

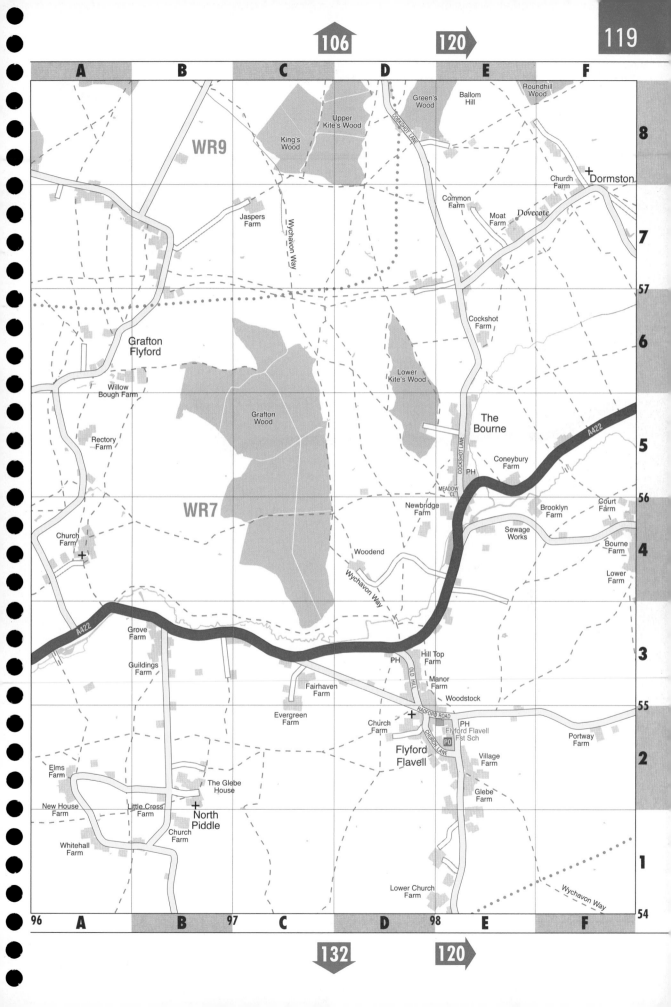

A B C D E F

8
7
57
6
5
56
4
3
55
2
1
54

96 A B 97 C D 98 E F

WR9

Upper Kite's Wood

King's Wood

Green's Wood

Ballom Hill

Roundhill Wood

COCKSHOT LANE

Church Farm

+ Dormston

Common Farm

Moat Farm

Dovecote

Jaspers Farm

Wychavon Way

Grafton Flyford

Willow Bough Farm

Cockshot Farm

Lower Kite's Wood

The Bourne

A422

Grafton Wood

Rectory Farm

Coneybury Farm

Cockshot Lane

PH

WR7

MEADOW CL

Newbridge Farm

Brooklyn Farm

Court Farm

Church Farm +

Woodend

Sewage Works

Bourne Farm

Lower Farm

Wychavon Way

A422

Grove Farm

Guildings Farm

Fairhaven Farm

PH

Hill Top Farm

OLD HILL

Manor Farm

Woodstock

Evergreen Farm

RADFORD ROAD

Church Farm +

PH

Portway Farm

Flyford Flavell Fst Sch

PO

CHURCH LANE

Flyford Flavell

Village Farm

Elms Farm

The Glebe House

New House Farm

Little Cross Farm

Church Farm

+ North Piddle

Glebe Farm

Whitehall Farm

Lower Church Farm

Wychavon Way

119
107

A B C D E F

8

Little Inkberrow

Manor Farm

Pit (dis)
Stonehouse Farm

Recreation Gd

STOCKWOOD LANE

A422

SANDS RD

Berrowsfield Farm

All Saints Farm

Stonehouse Farm

STOCKWOOD LANE

Allendale

Wood Croft

Bredon Cl

Inkberrow Fst Sch

HIGH STREET

WINDMILL LANE

THE PLECK

CHURCHWAY

7

Dormston Manor

Broadclose Farm

Tree Tops

MALTHOUSE CR

HIGH HO DR

TUER WAY RD

ORCHARD RD

Inkberrow

Moat

Pit (dis)

Stonepits

BROADCLOSE LANE

BROADCLOSE LANE

Hillside

STONEPIT LANE

CAT WY

MD

PH

CHURCH

Perryfields Farm

57

Newhouse Farm

Lower Farm

Quarry (dis)

Hill Farm

Littleworth Farm

PEPPER ST

RAMBLE CL

DEVON CL

BRECON CL

CHESTNUT LA

CHRISTOW

PO

6

Hill Farm

Cottage Farm

Brooklyn Ct

MUMMER MD

PEPPER ST

ROCK HL

NODBURY HL

POPLAR PIECE

DINGLE END

WR7

Springfield Farm

Sewage Works

5

A422

Quarrypit Farm

Quarry (dis)

Quarry (dis)

56

Earthworks

Thorn Dene

4

Piddle Brook

Moat

Kington

Thorn Farm

Little Ashdene Farm

Pit (dis)

Tip (dis)

3

Red House Farm

Grove Farm

MILL LANE

Radford

55

Ridge Farm

PH

2

Radford Fruit Farm

WR10

RADFORD ROAD

Westol Hall Farm

WR11

1

54

99 A B 00 C D 01 E F

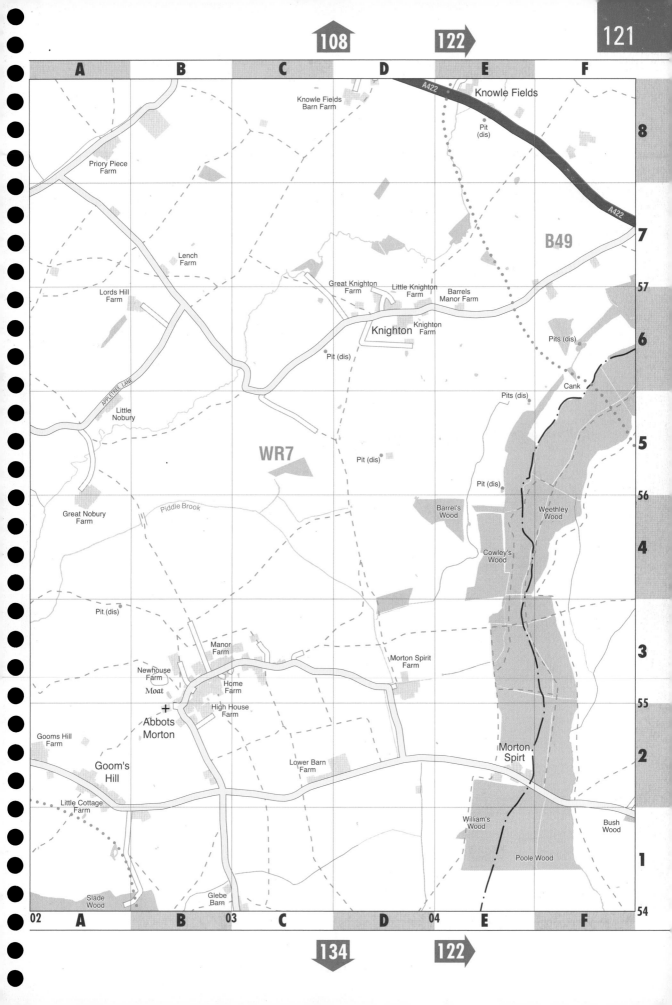

A   B   C   D   E   F

8

Three Oak Hill Wood

The Old House

Coldcomfort Farm

COLD COMFORT LA

Priory Farm

Mill Mound

Old Park Wood

A441

EVESHAM ROAD

A422

7

Priory (site of)

57

The Woodlands

Newman's Plantation

Nunnery Wood

B4088

Thornhill Farm

A422

6

Arrow Lane Plantation

A422

A422

Arrow

A422 Alcester

PARK VW

Thornhill Wood

Warwickshire STREET ATLAS

5

B49

56

Ridgeway Farm

Weethley Farm

EVESHAM ROAD

Deerings Hill

Ragley Park

4

Icehouse Grove

Ragley Hall

Dumfries Grove

Weethley

3

WR7

Pearson's Wood

B4088

55

Big Grove

Little Grove

2

Weethley Bank

Ladies Wood

Bush Wood

Cockerham's Wood

Evesham Lodge

Ennister Wood

1

Weethley Gate

Berry Coppice

Holly Bush Farm

54

Wood Bevington Farm

B4088

Dunnington Heath Farm

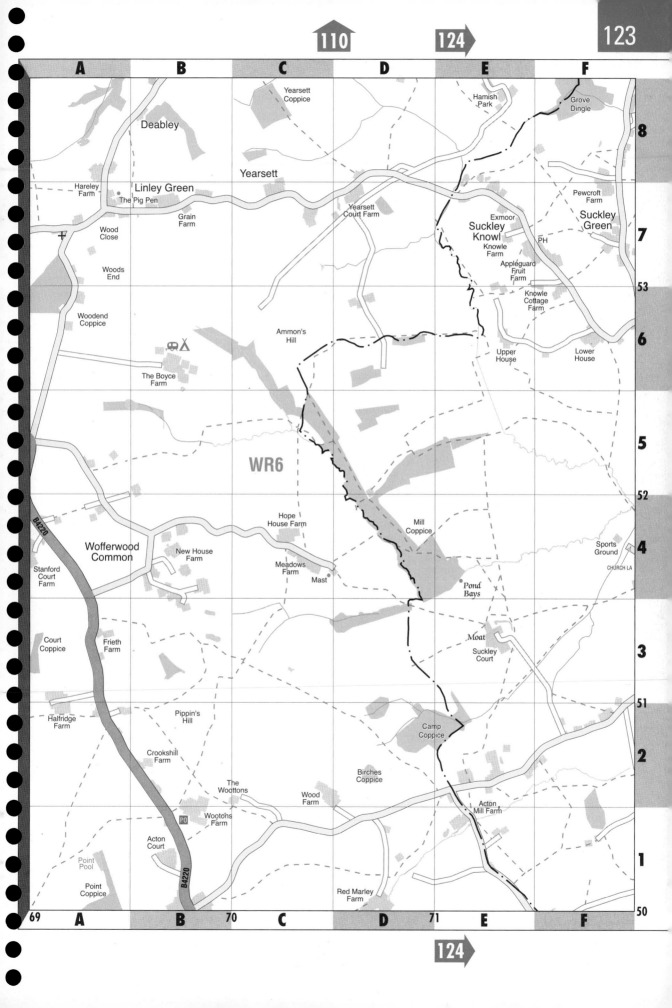

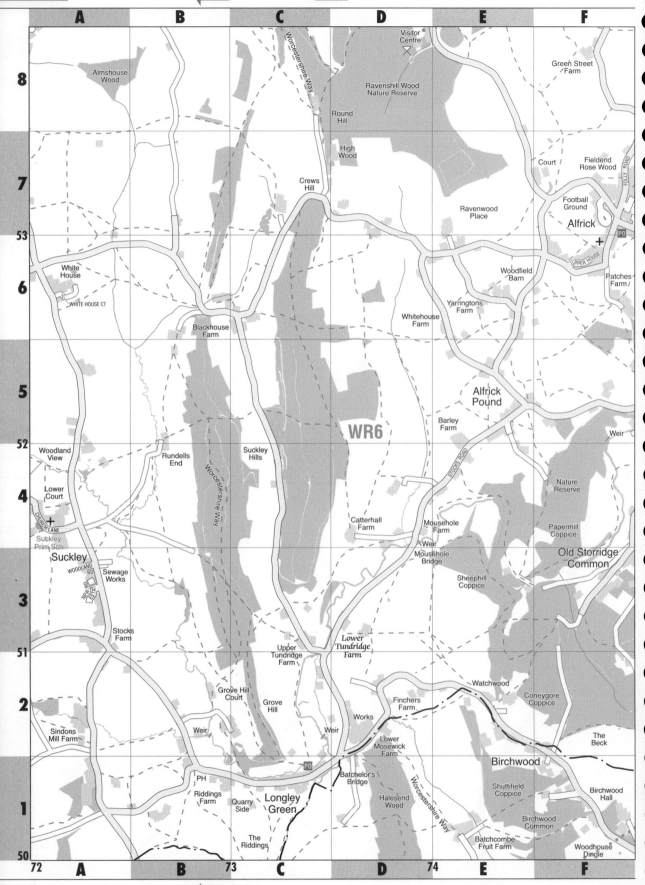

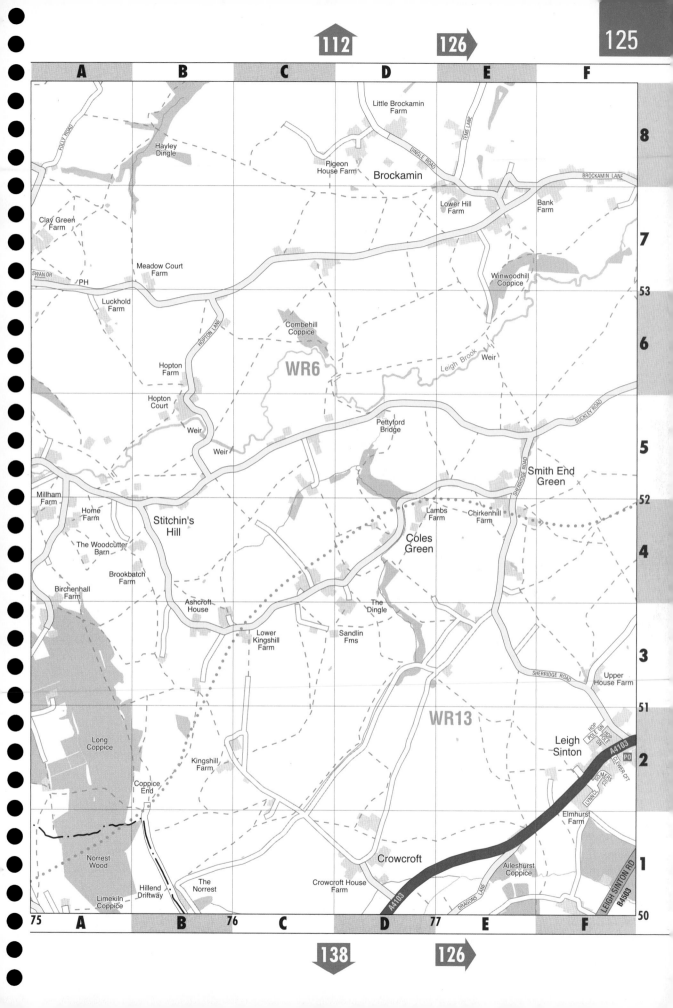

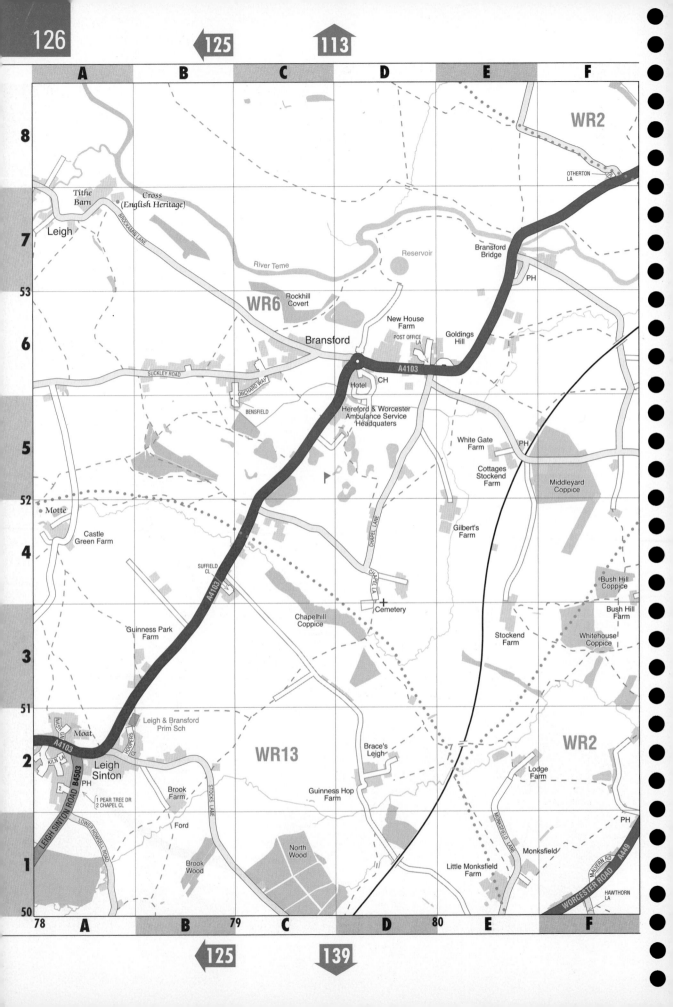

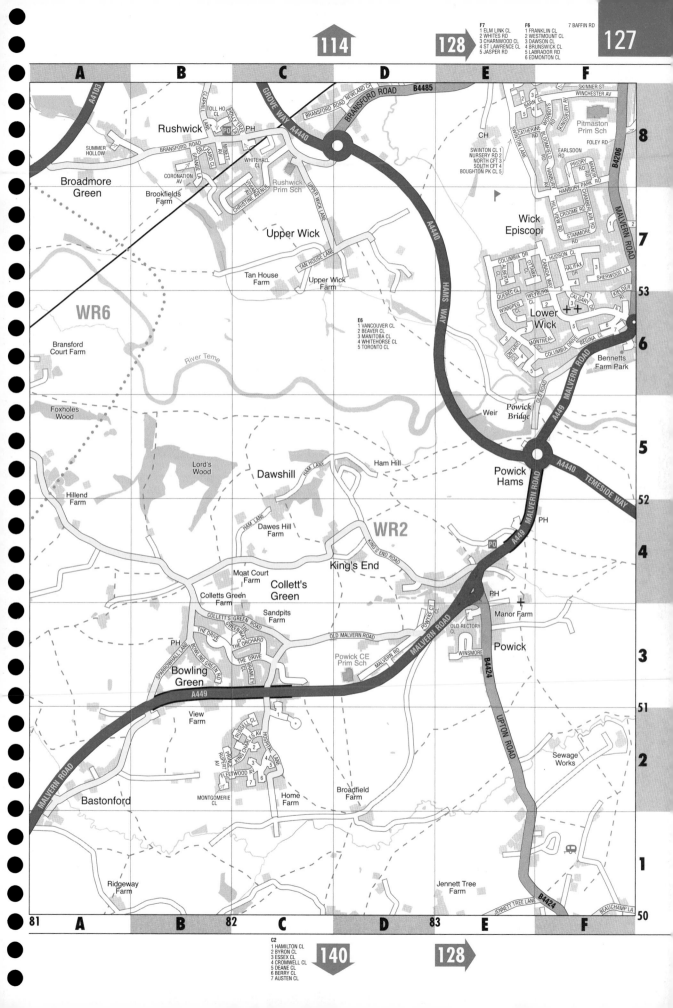

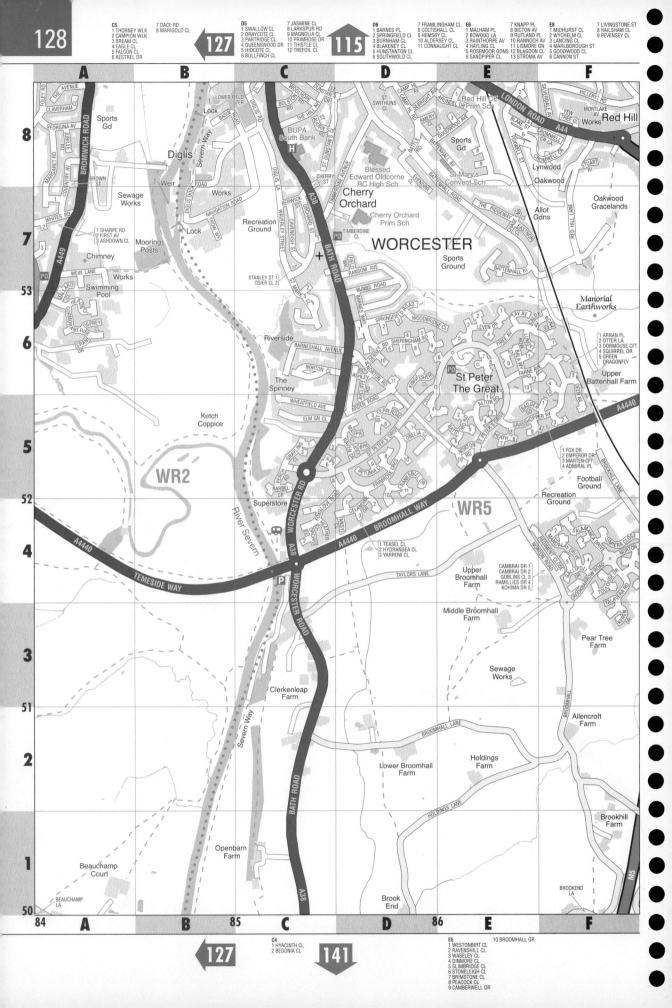

WR2

WORCESTER

WR5

129
117

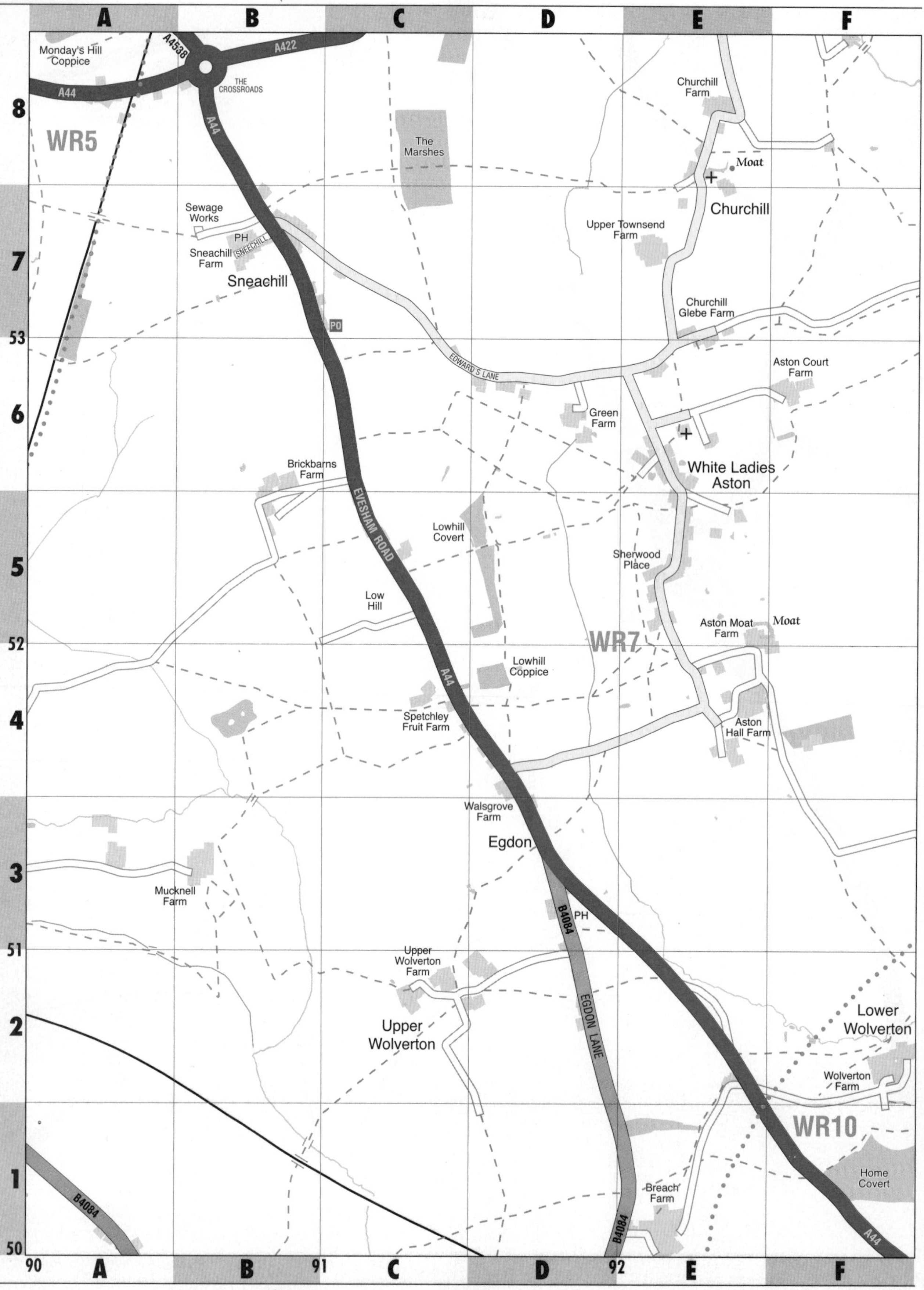

A B C D E F

8

Monday's Hill Coppice

A4538 A422 THE CROSSROADS

A44

WR5

The Marshes

Churchill Farm

Moat

Churchill

Sewage Works

PH
Sneachill Farm
SNEACHILL

7

Sneachill

Upper Townsend Farm

53

Churchill Glebe Farm

EDWARD'S LANE

Aston Court Farm

6

Green Farm

White Ladies Aston

Brickbarns Farm

EVESHAM ROAD

Lowhill Covert

Sherwood Place

5

Low Hill

Aston Moat Farm   Moat

52

A44

WR7

Lowhill Coppice

4

Spetchley Fruit Farm

Aston Hall Farm

Walsgrove Farm

3

Egdon

Mucknell Farm

B4084   PH

51

Upper Wolverton Farm

EGDON LANE

Lower Wolverton

2

Upper Wolverton

Wolverton Farm

WR10

1

B4084

Breach Farm

A44

Home Covert

50

90 A B 91 C D 92 E F

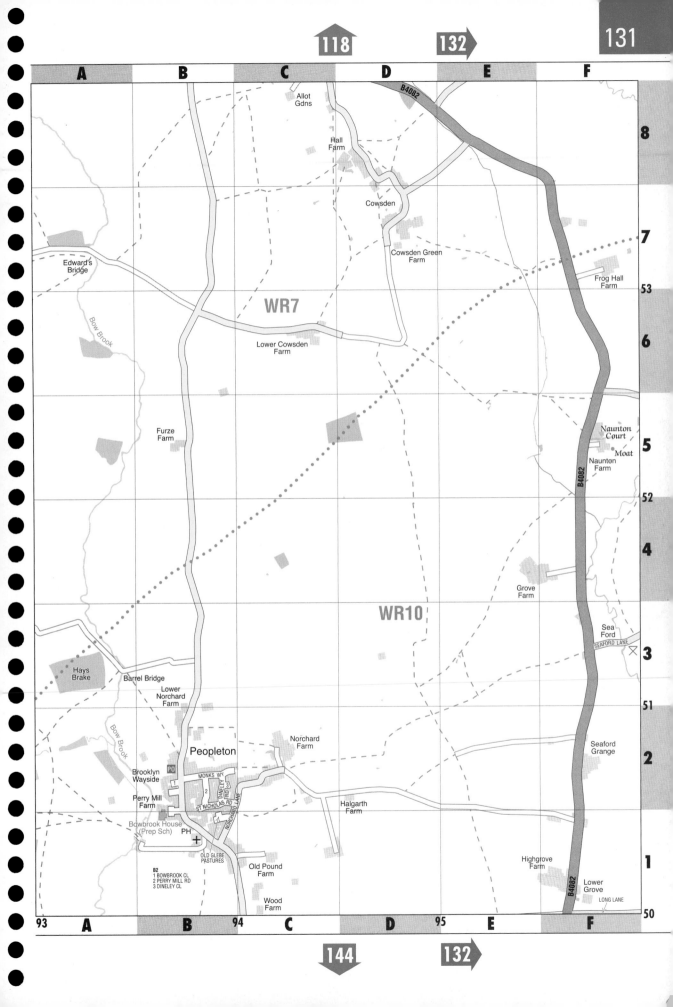

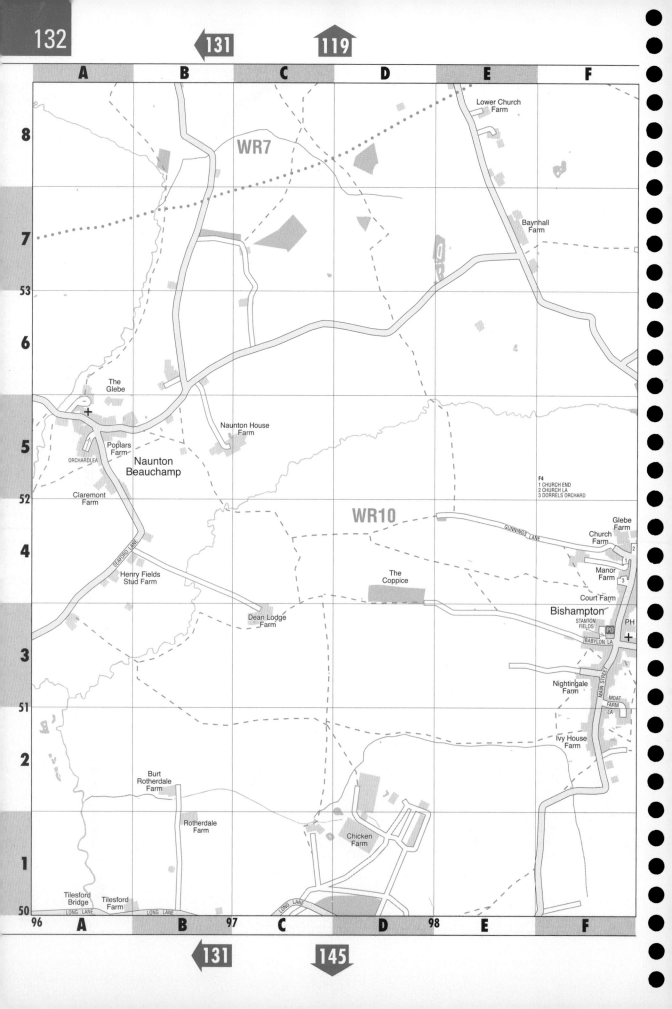

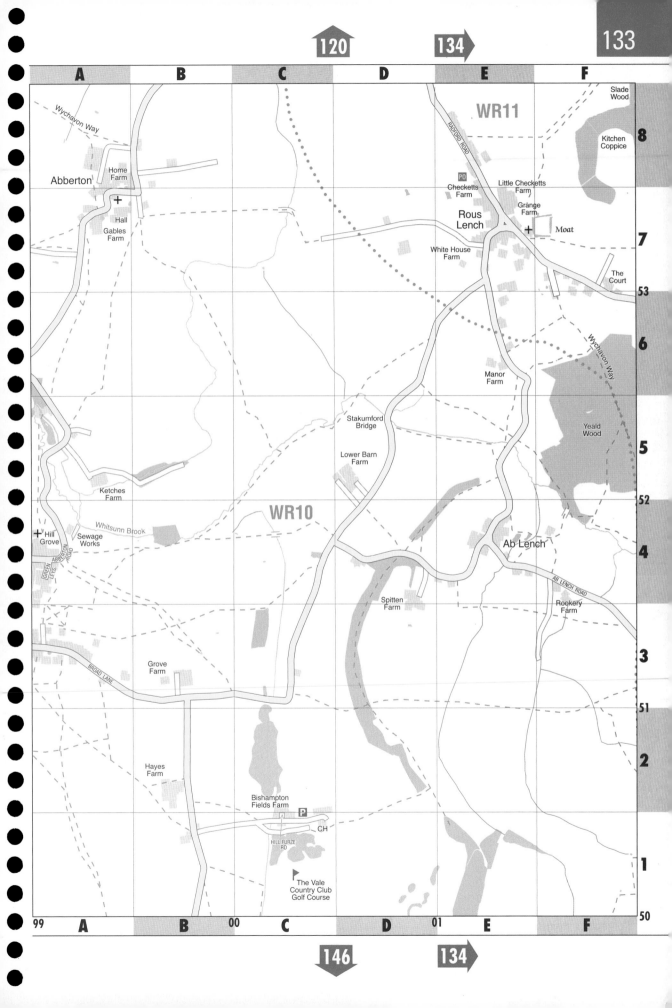

133
121

A B C D E F

8

Slade
Wood

Morton Low
Wood

Morton
Wood Farm

Bevington Waste

WR7

7

53

Commissioners
Wood

Long
Wood

6

Hill
View Farm

Rough
Hill

FRANKLIN'S LANE

Yeald
Wood

King Edward's
Plantation

5

Old Yew
Hill Wood

52

Atchlench
Wood

Wychavon Way

White Rails
Farm

North
Farm

4

The Low

LOW ROAD

Woodend
Farm

WR11

Salford
Coppice

Church
Farm

AB LENCH ROAD

MAIN STREET

THE CROFT

MALT HO LA

PO
THE TURN

ATCH LENCH ROAD

3

Church Lench
CE Prim Sch

Church
Lench

Spring
Hill Farm

Salford Lodge
Farm

51

Atch
Lench

EVESHAM ROAD

2

Manor
Farm

1

LEYS ROAD

50

02 A B 03 C D 04 E F

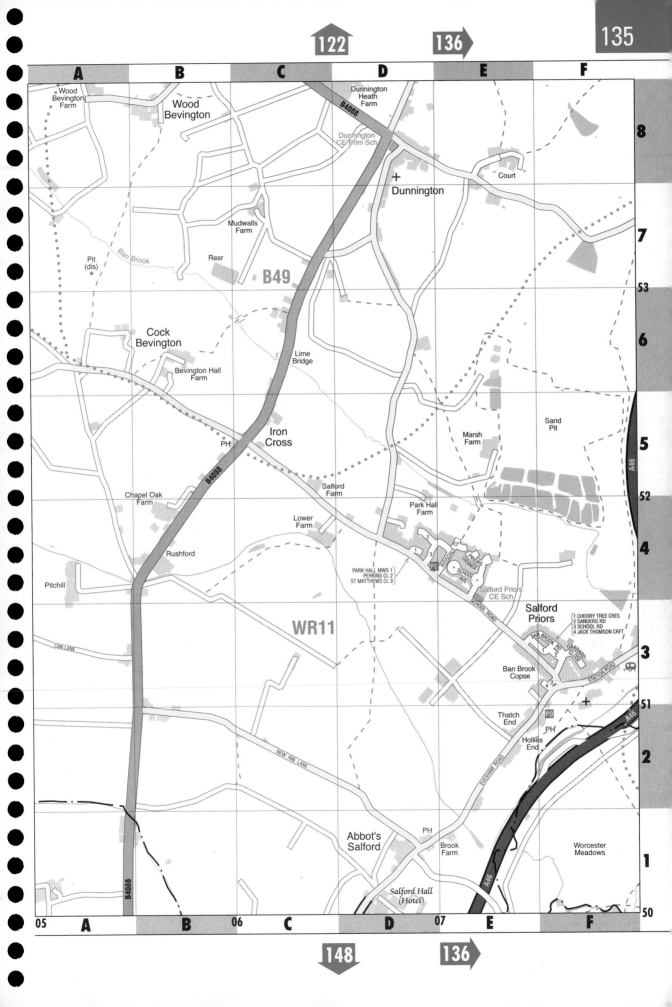

A   B   C   D   E   F

8

7

53

6

5

52

4

3

51

2

1

50

Wood Bevington Farm

Wood Bevington

Dunnington Heath Farm

B4088

Dunnington CE Prim Sch

Dunnington

Court

Mudwalls Farm

Ban Brook

Pit (dis)

Resr

B49

Cock Bevington

Lime Bridge

Bevington Hall Farm

Sand Pit

A46

Marsh Farm

Iron Cross

PH

B4088

Salford Farm

Park Hall Farm

Chapel Oak Farm

Lower Farm

PARK HALL MWS 1
PERKINS CL 2
ST MATTHEWS CL 3

Salford Priors CE Sch

Salford Priors

1 CHERRY TREE CRES
2 SANDERS RD
3 SCHOOL RD
4 JACK THOMSON CRFT

Rushford

Pitchill

WR11

CAN LANE

SCHOOL ROAD

BAN BROOK RD

GARRARD CLOSE

STATION ROAD

Ban Brook Copse

Thatch End

PO

PH

Hollies End

A46

NEW INN LANE

EVESHAM ROAD

Abbot's Salford

PH

Brook Farm

Worcester Meadows

A46

Salford Hall (Hotel)

05   A   B   06   C   D   07   E   F

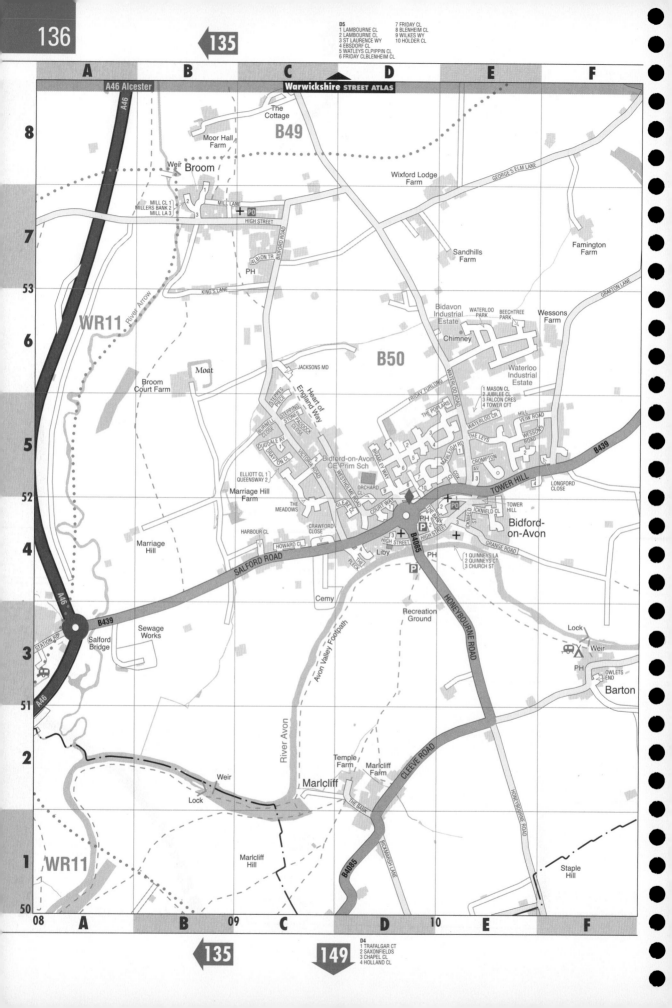

D5
1 LAMBOURNE CL
2 LAMBOURNE CL
3 ST LAURENCE WY
4 EBSDORF CL
5 WATLEYS CLPIPPIN CL
6 FRIDAY CLBLENHEIM CL
7 FRIDAY CL
8 BLENHEIM CL
9 WILKES WY
10 HOLDER CL

Warwickshire STREET ATLAS

A46 Alcester

The Cottage

B49

Moor Hall Farm

Wixford Lodge Farm

GEORGE'S ELM LANE

Weir Broom

MILL CL 1
MILLERS BANK 2
MILL LA 3

MILL LANE

PO
HIGH STREET

Sandhills Farm

Famington Farm

ALBION TR

PH

BIDFORD ROAD

KING'S LANE

WR11

River Arrow

GRAFTON LANE

Bidavon Industrial Estate

WATERLOO PARK

BEECHTREE PARK

Wessons Farm

Chimney

B50

Moat

Jacksons MD

Waterloo Industrial Estate

Broom Court Farm

1 MASON CL
2 JUBILEE CL
3 FALCON CRES
4 TOWER CFT

HILL VIEW ROAD

STEPPES PIECE

Heart of England Way

FRIDAY FURLONG

THE POPLARS

WATERLOO ROAD

WESSONS ROAD

STEPPING STONES

BURNELL CLOSE

PADDOCK CLOSE

WATERLOO CR

WATERLOO CR

THE LEYS

B439

DUGDALE AV

DRAYTON CL

VICTORIA ROAD

Bidford-on-Avon CE Prim Sch

BRANLEY WAY

MARLEIGH RD

COX

CROMPTON AV

TOWER HILL

LONGFORD CLOSE

ELLIOTT CL 1
QUEENSWAY 2

WESTHOLME ROAD

ORCHARD CL

Longford Close

TOWER HILL

Bidford-on-Avon

Marriage Hill Farm

THE MEADOWS

GLEBE CL

COURT WY

PO

ICKNIELD CL

ICKNIELD ST

PH

HARBOUR CL

CRAWFORD CLOSE

THE BANK

HIGH STREET

HIGH STREET

Marriage Hill

HOWARD CL

PLECK

Liby

PH

1 QUINNEYS LA
2 QUINNEYS CT
3 CHURCH ST

GRANGE ROAD

SALFORD ROAD

B4085

P

Cemy

Recreation Ground

Lock

Weir

B439

A46

STATION RD

Salford Bridge

Sewage Works

Avon Valley Footpath

HONEYBOURNE ROAD

PH

OWLETS END

Barton

A46

River Avon

Weir

Lock

Temple Farm

Marlcliff Farm

CLEEVE ROAD

Marlcliff

THE BANK

HONEYBOURNE ROAD

WR11

Marlcliff Hill

B4085

BICKMARSH LANE

Staple Hill

D4
1 TRAFALGAR CT
2 SAXONFIELDS
3 CHAPEL CL
4 HOLLAND CL

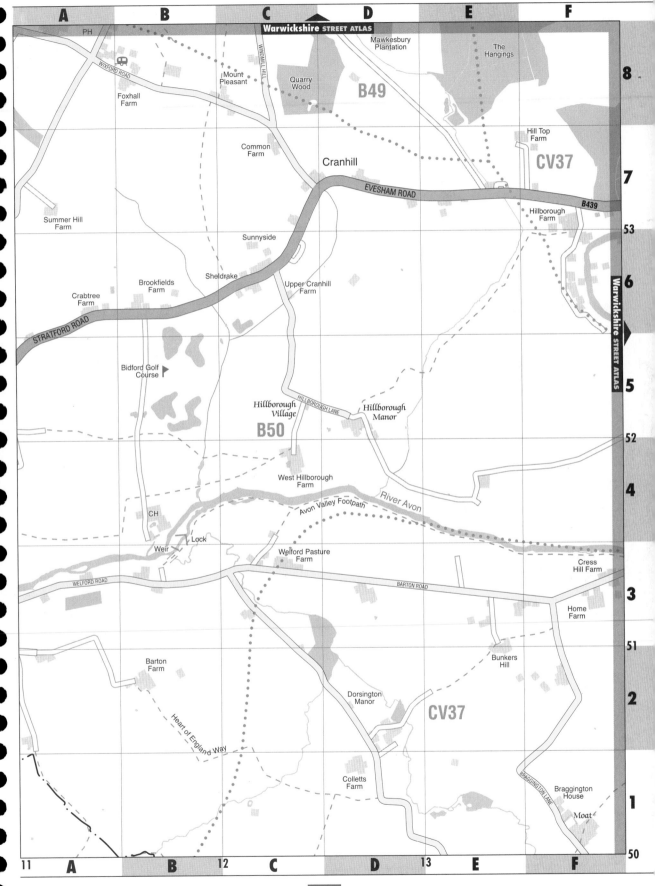

Warwickshire **STREET ATLAS**

A   B   C   D   E   F

PH

WIXFORD ROAD

WINDMILL HILL

Mount Pleasant

Mawkesbury Plantation

The Hangings

Quarry Wood

B49

Hill Top Farm

CV37

Foxhall Farm

Common Farm

Cranhill

EVESHAM ROAD

B439

Hillborough Farm

Summer Hill Farm

Sunnyside

Sheldrake

Brookfields Farm

Upper Cranhill Farm

Crabtree Farm

STRATFORD ROAD

Bidford Golf Course

HILLBOROUGH LANE

Hillborough Village

Hillborough Manor

B50

West Hillborough Farm

River Avon

Avon Valley Footpath

CH

Cress Hill Farm

Weir

Lock

Welford Pasture Farm

BARTON ROAD

WELFORD ROAD

Home Farm

Barton Farm

Bunkers Hill

Heart of England Way

Dorsington Manor

CV37

BRAGGINGTON LANE

Braggington House

Colletts Farm

Moat

8

7

53

6

5

52

4

51

3

2

1

50

11   A   B   12   C   D   13   E   F

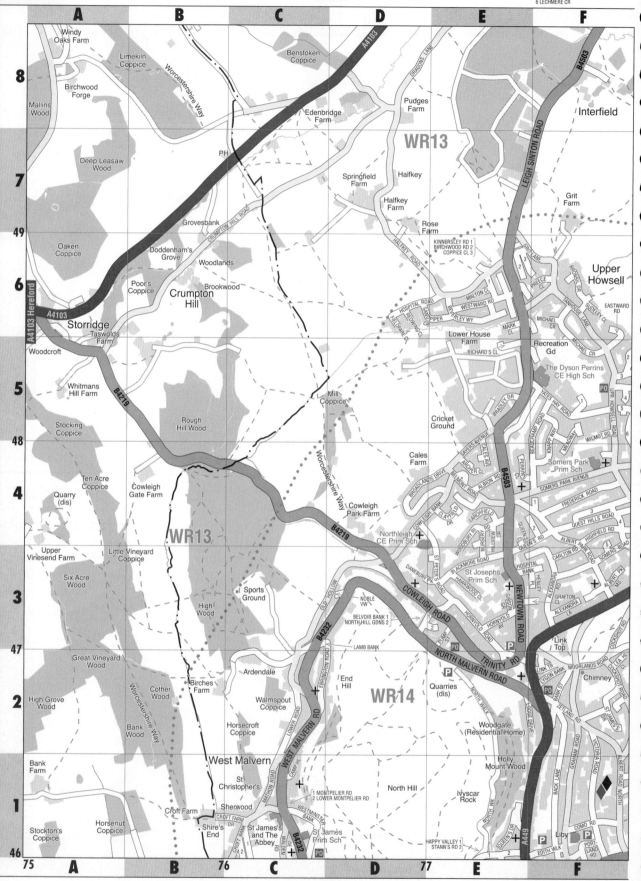

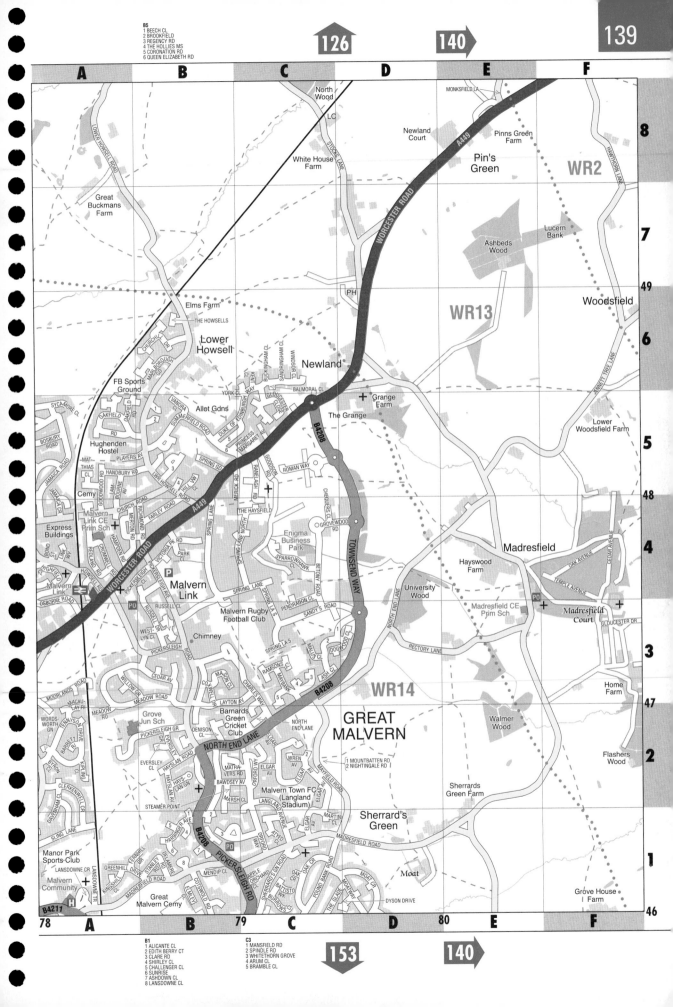

A B C D E F

8

7

49

6

WR2

WR13

Woodsfield

North Wood
LC

White House Farm

MONKSFIELD LA

Newland Court

Pinns Green Farm

A449

Pin's Green

WORCESTER ROAD

Lucern Bank

Ashbeds Wood

HAWTHORN LANE

KENNET TREE LANE

Great Buckmans Farm

LOWER HOWSELL ROAD

Elms Farm

THE HOWSELLS

Lower Howsell

PH

Newland

Grange Farm

Lower Woodsfield Farm

5

The Grange

FB Sports Ground

Allot Gdns

B4208

CHURCH DR

MARLBOROUGH GD

SUMMERFIELD ROAD

BUCKINGHAM CL

SANDRINGHAM CL

WINDSOR

YORK CL

KENT CL

DUKE OF EDINBURGH WAY

BALMORAL CL

GLOUCESTER CL

Roman Way

48

Hughenden Hostel

PLAYERS AV

VANDRA

OAKFIELD RD

OAKFIELD RD

HANDBURY RD

SPRING GD

PRINCESS MARGARET AV

MERRICK RD

RANELAGH RD

GOODSON

THE HAYSFIELD

CHEQUERS CL

GROVEWOOD RD

Madresfield

SYCAMORE CL

BOSBURY ROAD

JAMAICA ROAD

JAMAICA CR

MATTHIAS CL

MAT

DODGWOOD RD

BOURNE

CHURCH ROAD

FARLEY ROAD

LWR HOWSELL ROAD

HILL VW

SPRING LANE

SPRING LANE NORTH

SPRING LA S

Enigma Business Park

SPARROWHAWK

BETONY ROAD

University Wood

Hayswood Farm

OAK AVENUE

CEDAR AVENUE

TEMPLE AVENUE

4

Express Buildings

Cemy

Malvern Link CE Prim Sch

RICHMOND RD

MERTON RD

HAMPTON RD

REDLAND RD

CROMWELL

VICTORIA PK RD

PARK RD

Malvern Rugby Football Club

PENDRAGON CL

SANDY'S ROAD

NORTH END LANE

Madresfield CE Prim Sch

PO

Madresfield Court

GLOUCESTER DR

HIGHFIELD RD

BOND ST

LINK RD

HOWSELL RD

Malvern Link

WORCESTER ROAD

A449

PICKERSLEIGH CL

PO

RUSSELL RD

Chimney

RUSSELL CL

PICKERSLEIGH ROAD

WEST-LYN CL

CEDAR AV

MACAULEY

COLWELL RD

LAYTON AV

Spring LA S

MALLS CL

DOGW RD

ASH CL

RAMSONS CL

MAYBANK

RECTORY LANE

Home Farm

47

OSBORNE ROAD

B4211

Manor Park Sports Club

Malvern Community

WORDSWORTH GN

MOORLANDS ROAD

MEADOW RD

MACAULAY RD

Grove Jun Sch

WILLOW GR

MEADOW ROAD

PICKERSLEIGH GR

DENISON CL

Barnards Green Cricket Club

B4208

NORTH END LANE

GREAT MALVERN

WR14

Walmer Wood

Sherrards Green Farm

Flashers Wood

2

LANSDOWNE CR

LANSDOWNE TR

CLERKENWELL CR

DALEHAM CL

BYRON RD

TENNYSON DRIVE

BARRETT RD

KIPLING RD

Eversley CL

HAYSLAN RD

HAYSLAN AV

PICKERSLEIGH RD

EVERSLEY RD

MATRAVERS RD

HAYS GN

BAWDSEY AV

MARSH CL

ORFORD RD

Malvern Town FC (Langland Stadium)

LANGLAND AVENUE

WREN AV

ELGAR AV

ELGAR AV

MAYFIELD RD

1 MOUNTBATTEN RD
2 NIGHTINGALE RD

MARTIN CL

Sherrard's Green

MADRESFIELD ROAD

1

SLING LANE

H

Malvern Community

LANSDOWNE CR

KINGSHILL CL

GREENHILL DRIVE

FERNHILL CL

STANLEY RD

MADRESFIELD ROAD

DELAMERE RD

MENDIP CL

COTSWOLD RD

ELM EY

Great Malvern Cemy

PICKERSLEIGH RD

B4208

PO

HARBINGER AVE

Apple Orchard

SHERRARD GN ROAD

BATTISTO WK

OAK CR

OAK CR

MOAT CR

ROUND BANK ROAD

THE GLADE

BURROWS

ALYED WAY

ELGAR AV

Moat

DYSON DRIVE

Grove House Farm

46

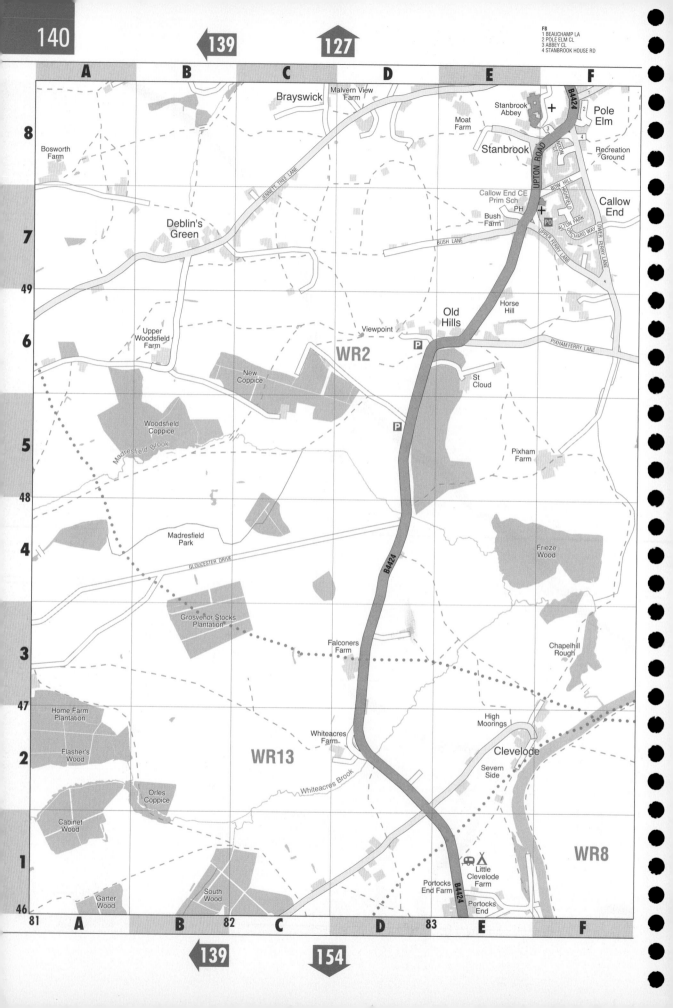

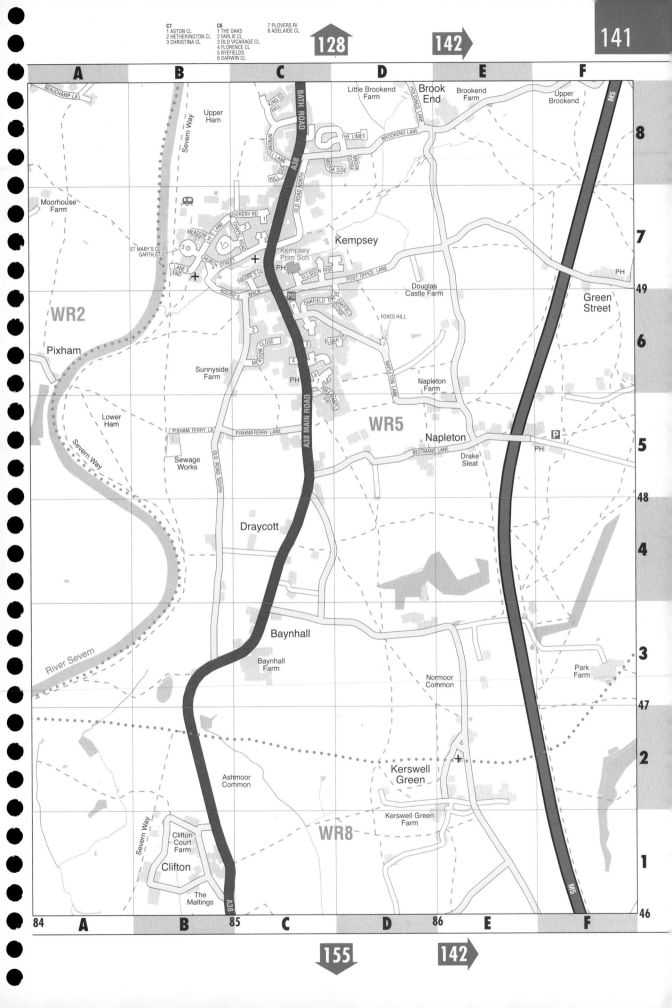

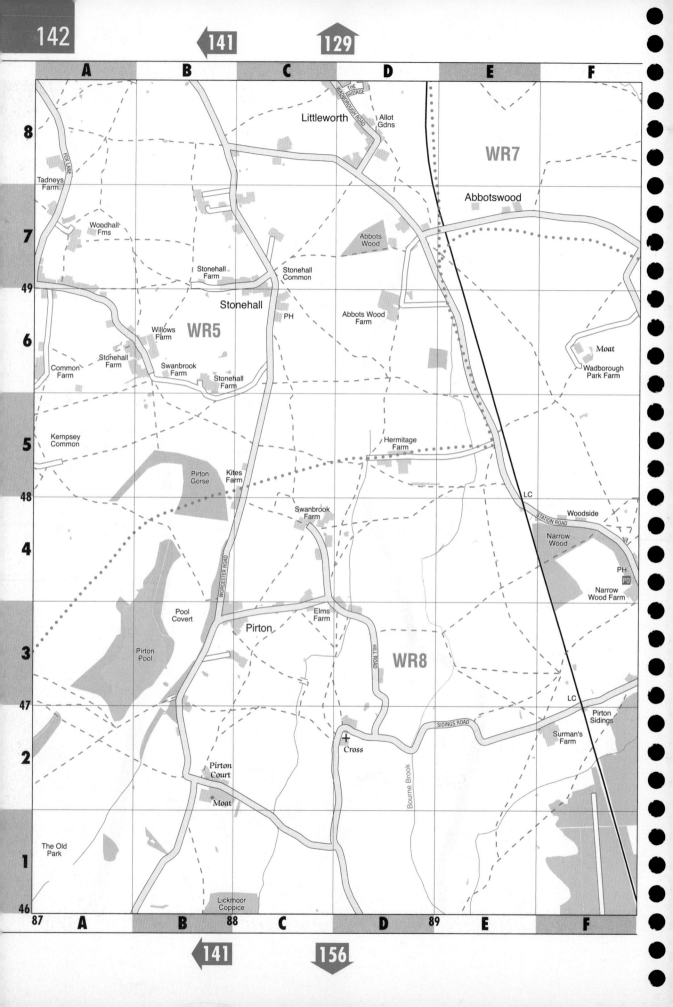

141
129

A   B   C   D   E   F

8

Littleworth

Allot
Gdns

WR7

Tadneys
Farm

Abbotswood

7

Woodhall
Fms

Abbots
Wood

Stonehall
Farm

Stonehall
Common

49

Abbots Wood
Farm

Stonehall

PH

WR5

Willows
Farm

6

Moat

Stonehall
Farm

Common
Farm

Swanbrook
Farm

Stonehall
Farm

Wadborough
Park Farm

Kempsey
Common

Hermitage
Farm

5

Pirton
Gorse

Kites
Farm

LC

48

Woodside

Swanbrook
Farm

STATION ROAD

Narrow
Wood

4

WORCESTER ROAD

PH
PO

Narrow
Wood Farm

Pool
Covert

Elms
Farm

Pirton

3

WR8

Pirton
Pool

HILL ROAD

LC

47

Pirton
Sidings

SIDINGS ROAD

Surman's
Farm

2

Cross

Pirton
Court

Bourne Brook

Moat

1

The Old
Park

46

Lickmoor
Coppice

87   A   B   88   C   D   89   E   F

141
156

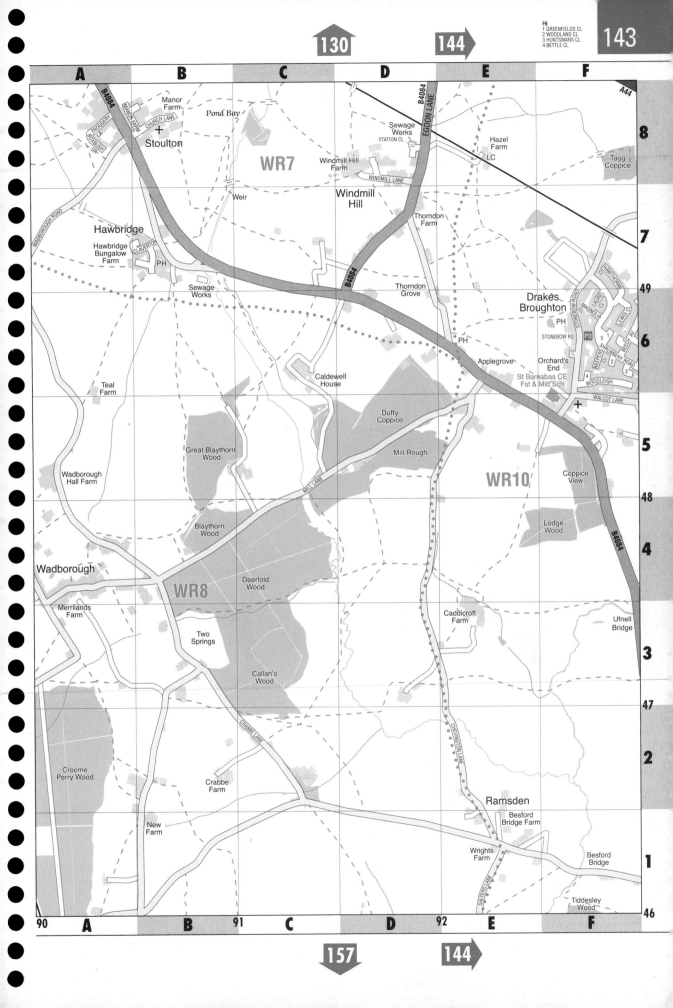

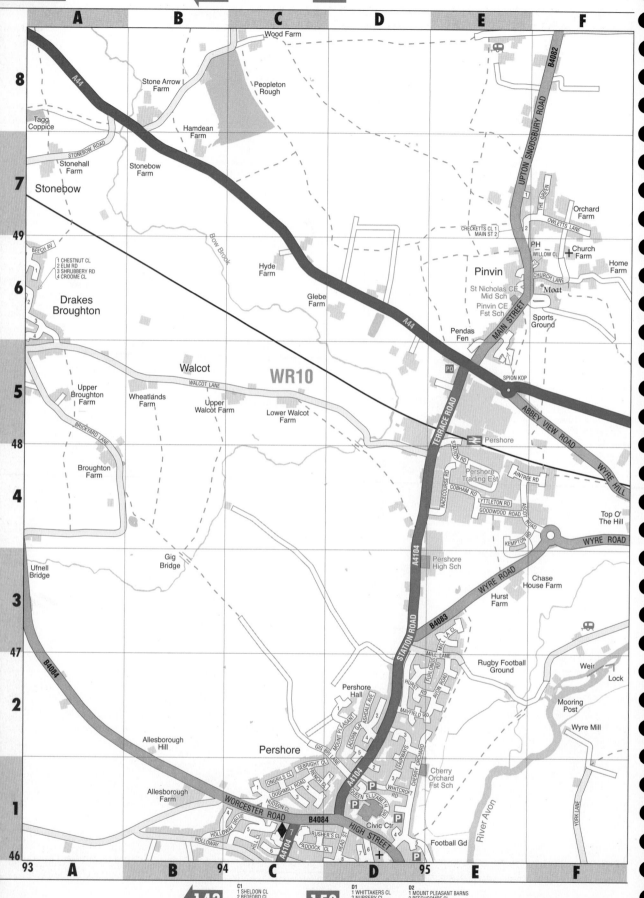

C1
1 SHELDON CL
2 BEDFORD CL
3 SCOBELL CL
4 WILLOW CL
5 ALLESBOROUGH DR
6 RAIL GROUND
7 THREE SPRINGS RD

D1
1 WHITTAKERS CL
2 NURSERY CL
3 FAIRWAYS WLK
4 REDLANDS
5 KING GEORGE'S WY
6 PRIEST LA
7 ST AGATHA'S CL
8 ST AGATHAS RD

D2
1 MOUNT PLEASANT BARNS
2 BEECHCOMBE CL
3 APPLE TREE RD
4 BIRCHTREE GR
5 MAPLE AV

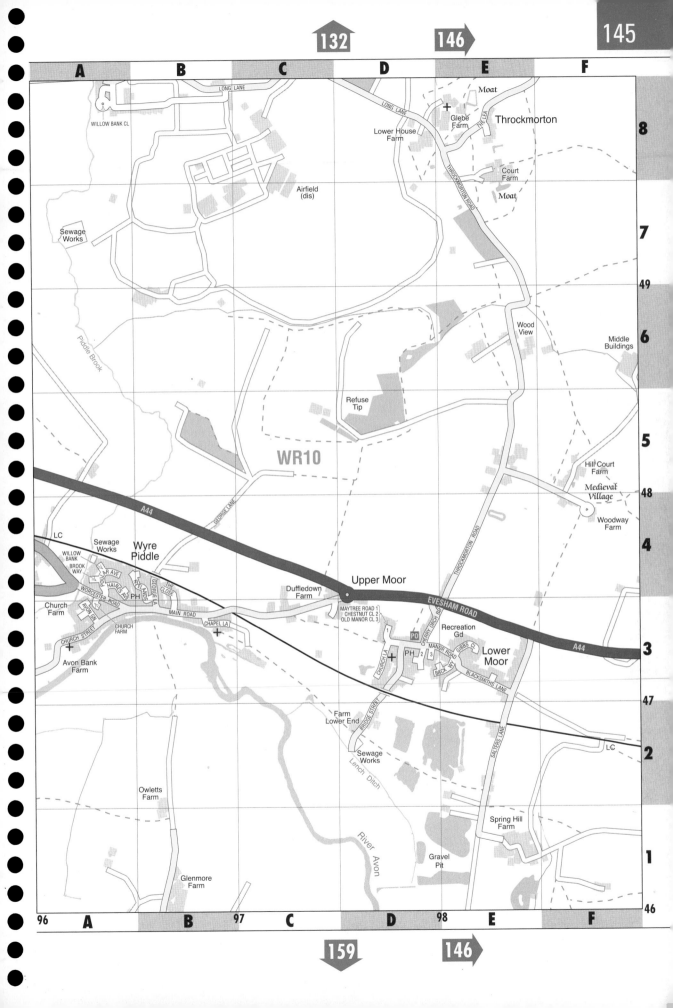

145
133

A B C D E F

8

7

49

WR10

6

Sheriff's
Lench

Bishampton Bank

The Larches
Farm

Badger's
Hill

Five
Oaks Farm

Protheroughs
Farm

Badgers Hill
Farm

Hill
Furze

WR11

Underwood
Farm

5

Whitsun Brook
Farm

48

Hillside

Hillside Machine
Farm

Craycombe
Hill

Slade
Wood

Bittern Bank
Machine Farm

Machine
Farm

Craycombe
Coppice

Blue Bank
Coppice

4

Wychavon Way

Cold
Knap Wood

Glebe
Farm

Tunnel
Hill Wood

A44

The
Scar

Mast

Woodnorton
Farm

Little
Omberry Farm

Fladbury
Cross

Craycombe
Farm

EVESHAM ROAD

Wood
Norton

3   A44

CH

Radio
Mast

47

Wychavon Way

WR10

River Avon

2

Fernhill
Farm

BUTT
FURLONG

Recn
Gd

Wayside

WESTON
ORCHARD

STATION ROAD

LC

Allot
Gdns

Woodcote

Fladbury

LC

Fladbury
CE Aided
Fst Sch

1 OLD RECTORY GN
2 CHEQUERS LA

1

Allsprings

LAZY LANE

FARM STREET

PO

CHURCH STREET

PAYNES LA

BROADWAY LA

Lock

MILL BANK

Maltings

Weir

46

99   A   00   B   C   00   D   01   E   F

147
135

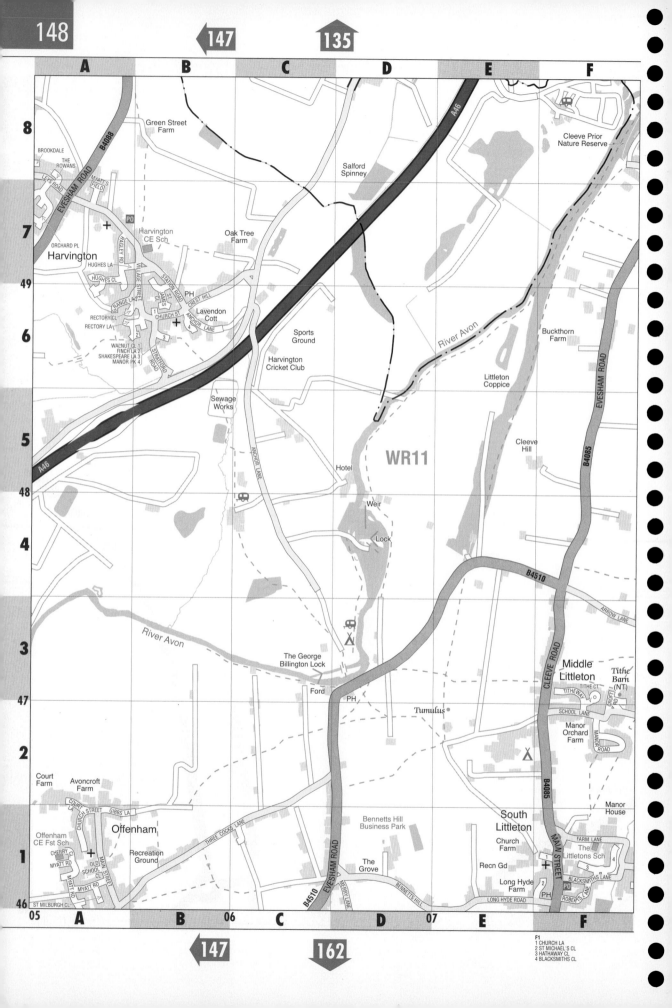

147
162

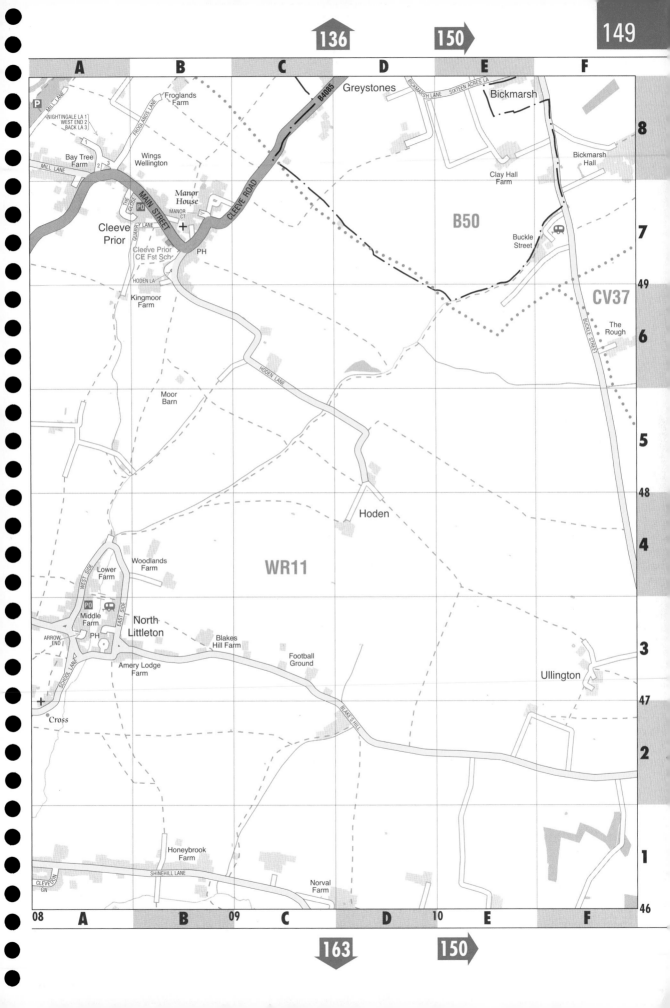

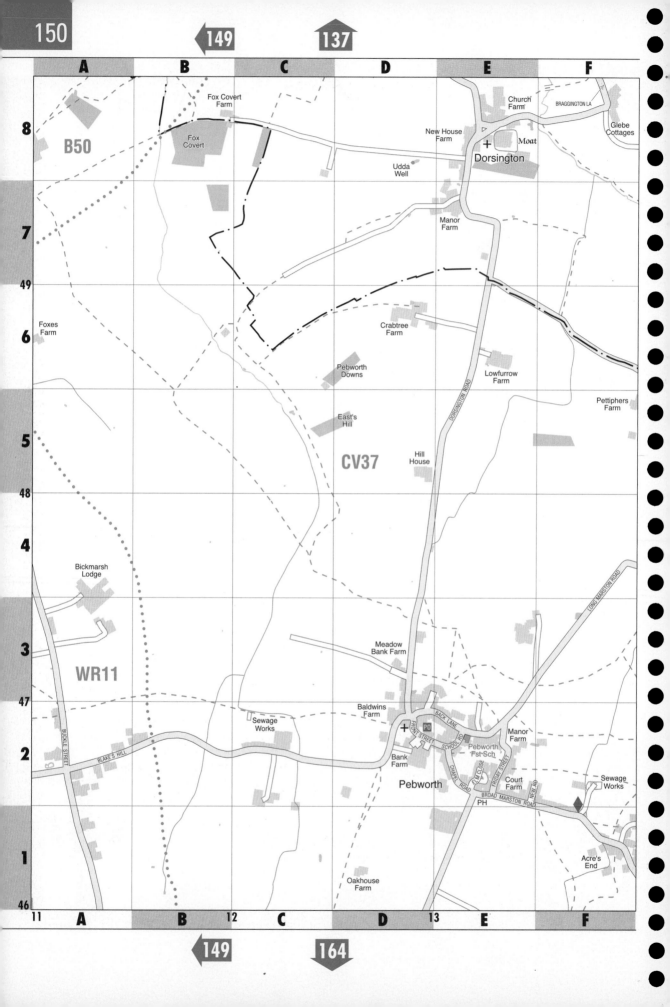

A   B   C   D   E   F

8

B50

Fox Covert
Farm

Fox
Covert

Church
Farm

BRAGGINGTON LA

New House
Farm

Glebe
Cottages

Moat

Dorsington

Udda
Well

7

49

Foxes
Farm

Manor
Farm

6

Crabtree
Farm

Pebworth
Downs

Lowfurrow
Farm

Pettiphers
Farm

East's
Hill

5

CV37

Hill
House

48

4

Bickmarsh
Lodge

DORSINGTON ROAD

LONG MARSTON ROAD

3

WR11

Meadow
Bank Farm

47

Sewage
Works

Baldwins
Farm

BACK LANE

Manor
Farm

2

BUCKLE STREET

BLAKE'S HILL

Bank
Farm

FRONT STREET

PO

SCHOOL RD

Pebworth
Fst Sch

ELM CLOSE

FRIARY STREET

Court
Farm

NEW RD

Sewage
Works

Pebworth

CHAPEL ROAD

PH

BROAD MARSTON ROAD

1

Acre's
End

Oakhouse
Farm

46

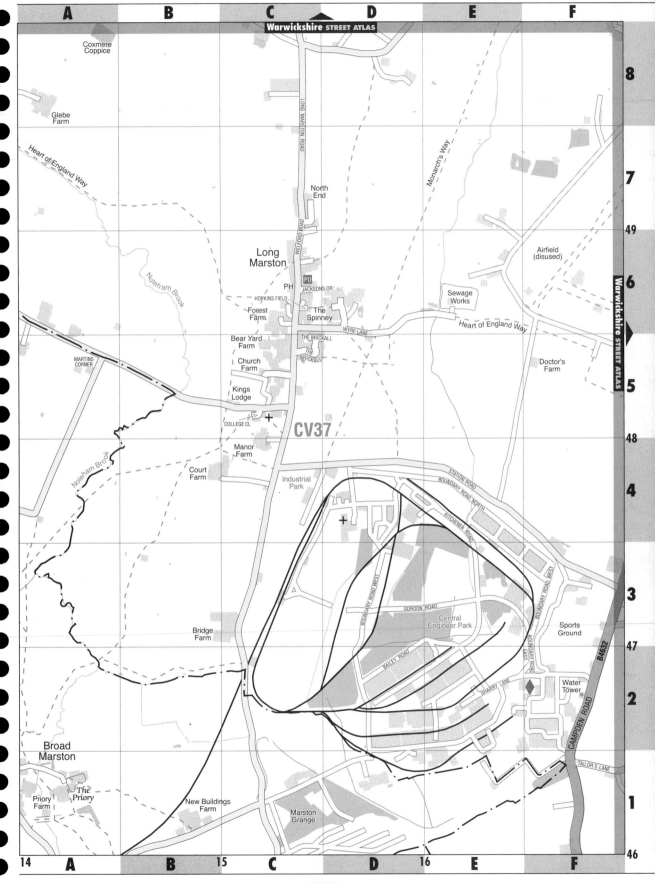

Coxmere Coppice

Glebe Farm

Heart of England Way

LONG MARSTON ROAD

North End

WELFORD ROAD

Noleham Brook

Long Marston

PH

PO

JACKSONS OR

HOPKINS FIELD

Forest Farm

The Spinney

Monarch's Way

Sewage Works

Heart of England Way

Airfield (disused)

MARTINS CORNER

Bear Yard Farm

THE BRICKALL

THE BRICKALL

WYRE LANE

Doctor's Farm

Church Farm

Kings Lodge

COLLEGE CL

CV37

Noleham Brook

Manor Farm

Court Farm

Industrial Park

STATION ROAD

BOUNDARY ROAD NORTH

KITCHENER ROAD

BOUNDARY ROAD WEST

GORDON ROAD

Central Engineer Park

BOUNDARY ROAD WEST

BOUNDARY ROAD EAST

Sports Ground

B4632

Bridge Farm

BAILEY ROAD

SHARRY LANE

Water Tower

CAMPDEN ROAD

Broad Marston

TAILOR'S LANE

Priory Farm

The Priory

New Buildings Farm

Marston Grange

8
7
49
6
48
5
4
47
3
2
1
46

14   A   B   15   C   D   16   E   F

F8
1 BACK LA
2 VICTORIA RD
3 GRANGE RD
4 ORCHARD RD

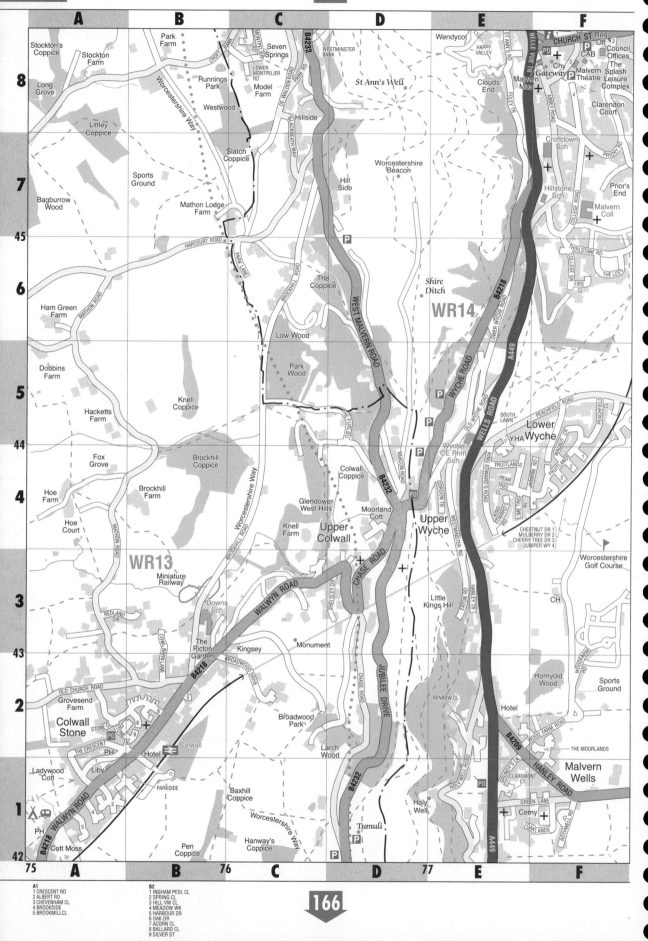

A1
1 CRESCENT RD
2 ALBERT RD
3 CHEVENHAM CL
4 BROOKSIDE
5 BROOKMILLCL

B2
1 INGHAM PEDL CL
2 SPRING CL
3 HILL VW CL
4 MEADOW WK
5 HARBOUR DR
6 OAK DR
7 ACORN CL
8 BALLARD CL
9 SILVER ST

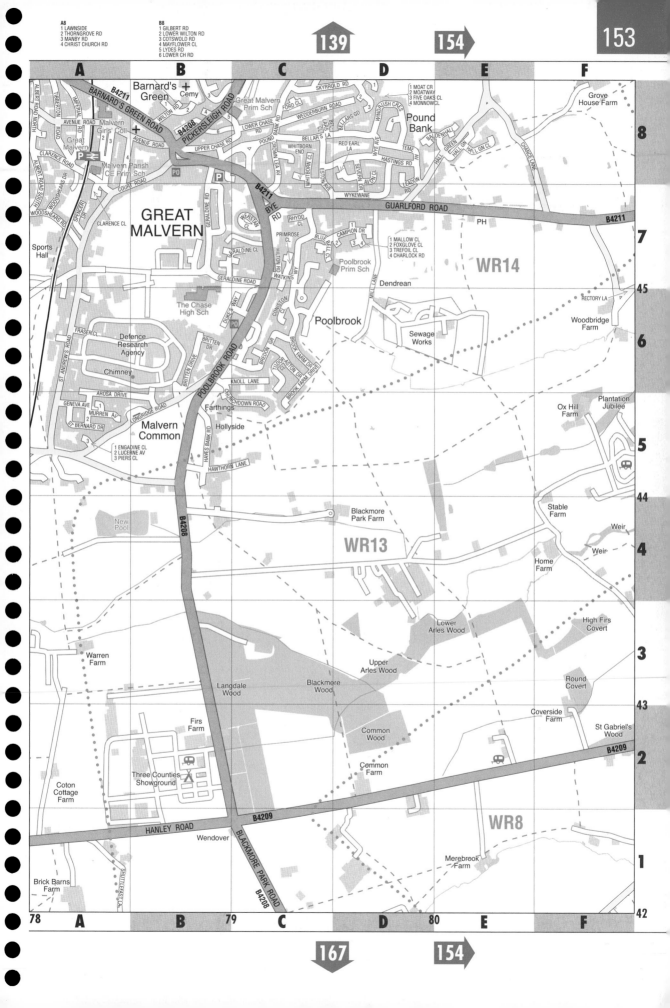

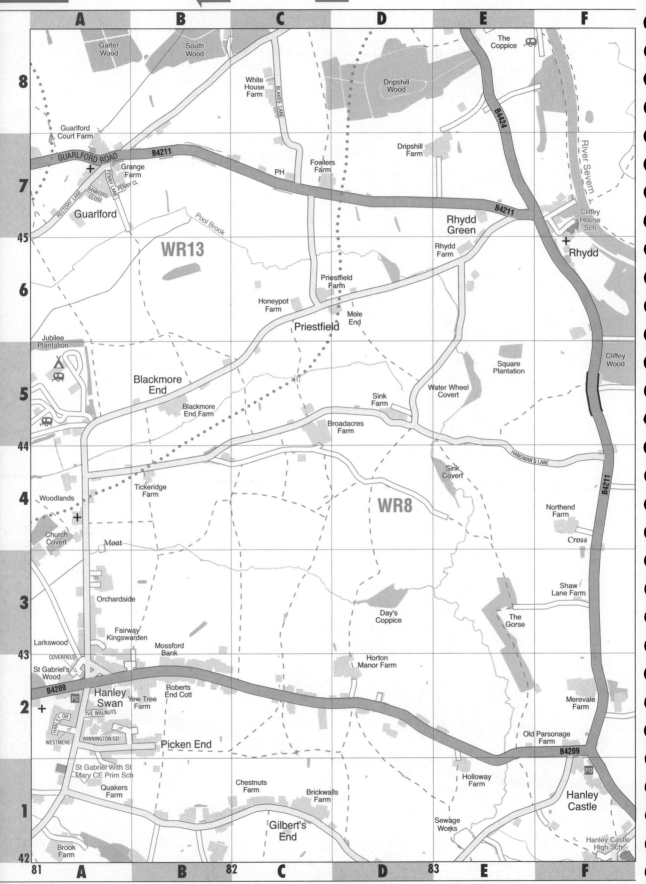

153
140

A   B   C   D   E   F

8

Garter Wood

South Wood

White House Farm

BLAKES LANE

Dripshill Wood

The Coppice

Guarlford Court Farm

7

GUARLFORD ROAD   B4211

PH

Fowlers Farm

Dripshill Farm

B4424

River Severn

+

Grange Farm

PENNY LANE   PENNY CL

RECTORY LANE   BAMFORD CLOSE

Guarlford

Pool Brook

B4211

Rhydd Green

Cliffey House Sch

45

WR13

Rhydd Farm

+ Rhydd

6

Priestfield Farm

Honeypot Farm

Mole End

Priestfield

Jubilee Plantation

Water Wheel Covert

Square Plantation

Cliffey Wood

5

Blackmore End

Blackmore End Farm

Sink Farm

Broadacres Farm

HANGMAN'S LANE

44

Tickeridge Farm

Sink Covert

B4211

4

Woodlands

+

WR8

Northend Farm

Cross

Church Covert

Moat

Shaw Lane Farm

3

Orchardside

Day's Coppice

The Gorse

Larkswood

Fairway Kingswarden

Mossford Bank

COVERFIELD

43

St Gabriel's Wood

Horton Manor Farm

Merevale Farm

B4209

Hanley Swan

Roberts End Cott

Yew Tree Farm

2

+

THE WALNUTS

HANLEY   OR

Old Parsonage Farm

WESTMERE

WINNINGTON GD

Picken End

B4209

PO

St Gabriel With St Mary CE Prim Sch

Chestnuts Farm

Brickwalls Farm

Holloway Farm

Hanley Castle

1

Quakers Farm

Sewage Works

Brook Farm

Gilbert's End

Hanley Castle High Sch

42

81   A   B   82   C   D   83   E   F

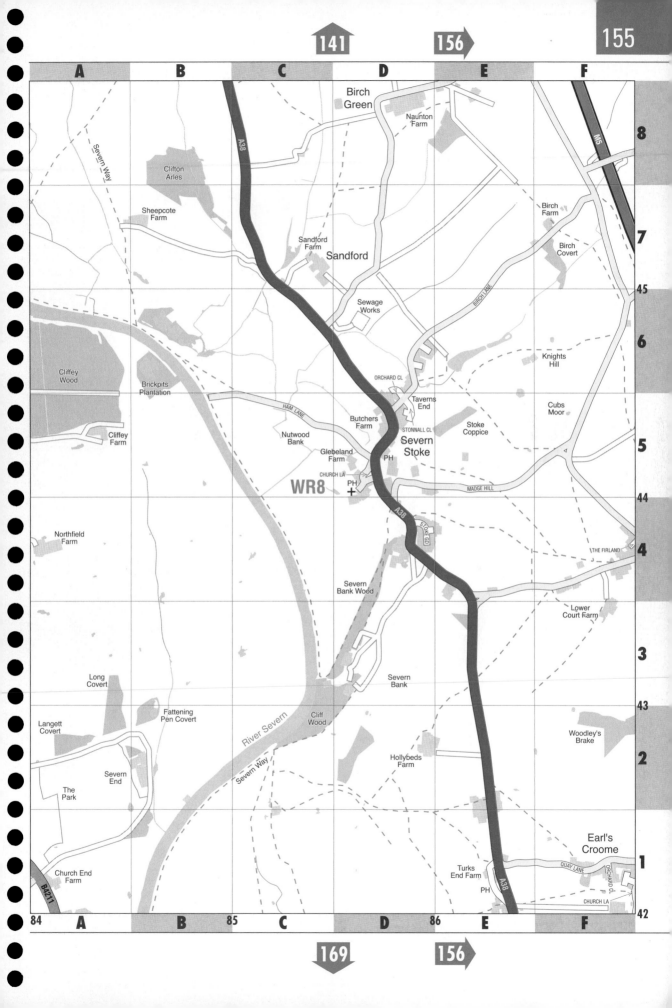

A   B   C   D   E   F

8

Birch
Green

Naunton
Farm

M5

Severn Way

Clifton
Arles

Birch
Farm

7

Sheepcote
Farm

Sandford
Farm

Birch
Covert

Sandford

45

BIRCH LANE

Sewage
Works

6

Cliffey
Wood

Knights
Hill

Brickpits
Plantation

ORCHARD CL

Taverns
End

Cubs
Moor

HAM LANE

Butchers
Farm

Cliffey
Farm

Nutwood
Bank

STONNALL CL

Stoke
Coppice

5

Glebeland
Farm

PH

Severn
Stoke

WR8

CHURCH LA

PH
✝

MADGE HILL

44

A38

Northfield
Farm

STOKE GD

THE FIRLAND

4

Severn
Bank Wood

Lower
Court Farm

Severn
Bank

3

Long
Covert

43

Fattening
Pen Covert

Cliff
Wood

Woodley's
Brake

Langett
Covert

River Severn

Severn Way

2

Severn
End

Hollybeds
Farm

The Park

Earl's
Croome

1

Turks
End Farm

QUAY LANE

ORCHARD CL

B4211

Church End
Farm

A38

PH

CHURCH LA

84   A   B   85   C   D   86   E   F   42

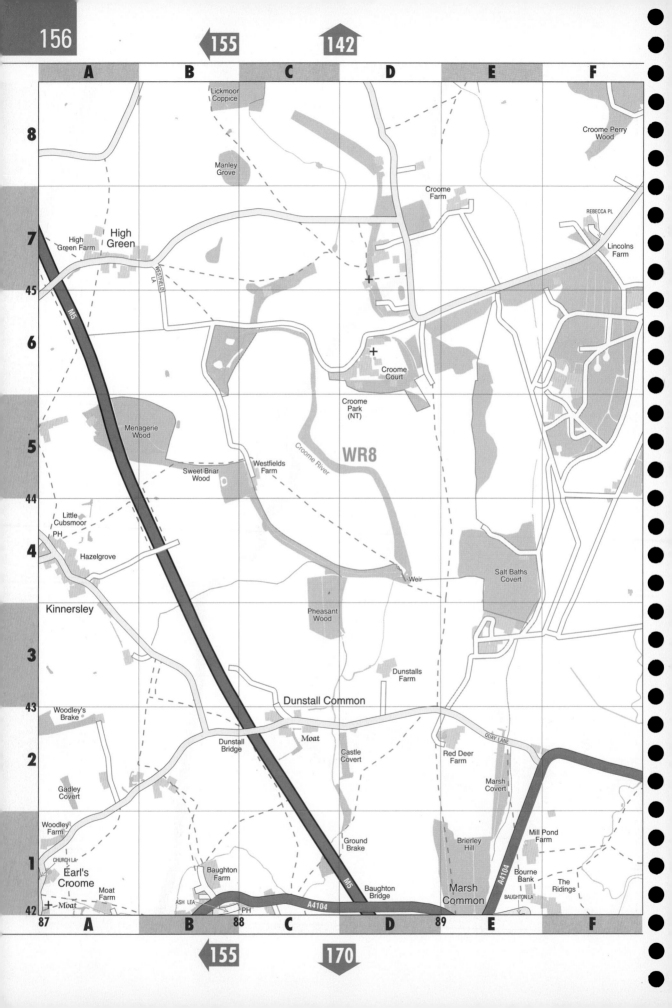

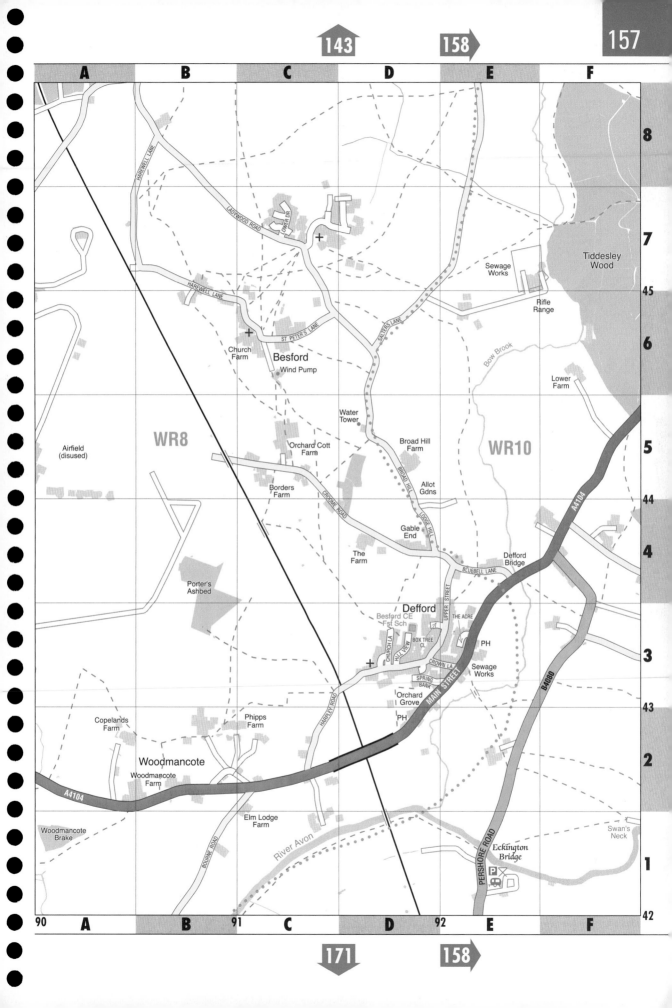

157
144

C8
1 HOLLOWAY
2 ABBOTS GRANGE
3 ORCHARD CL

D8
1 HEAD ST
2 ST AGATHAS RD
3 ST AGATHA'S CL
4 MONKS CL
5 LITTLE PRIEST LA
6 LOWER PRIEST LA

7 CHURCH ST
8 CHURCH ROW
9 BETJEMAN CL
10 CHURCH WK
11 MASONS RYDE

A B C D E F

8

Tiddesley Wood

PERSHORE

HUNTER RD
CONINGSBY DRIVE
EMC CL
OLD STILES
THREE SPRINGS ROAD
A4104
NEW ROAD
ABBEYCROFT
Abbey Park Fst & Mid Sch
ORCHARD ROAD
FARLEIGH ROAD
WOODWARD ROAD
ABBOTS ROAD
St ANDREW'S ROAD
FULBERT RD
FARLEIGH ROAD
BIRLINGHAM CLOSE
DEFFORD ROAD

LONG HEDGES

Cemetery Farm
Cemy

NEWLANDS
The Holy Redeemer RC Prim Sch
Site of Abbey (Benedictine)
Abbey Park
Pershore Liby
ABBEY ROAD
NOGAINS

Football Ground
KING GEORGE'S WY
Leisure Centre
Superstore
HIGH STREET
PO
Weir
Locks
B4536
B4084
MANOR GD
Sports Ground
Pershore Cottage
H

Wicklands Farm
YORK LANE
TIMBER DOWN
WICK HO CL
Wick Farm

7

Orchard Farm

The Spinney

DEFFORD ROAD
B4536
CORNMORE

45

6

Tiddesley Wood
A4104

River Avon

1 HANSON WY
2 PERSCORAN WY
3 GREAT CALCROFT

Allot Gdns

Pershore Bridge
BRIDGE STREET
P
Pershore & Hindlip Coll

Hazel Wood
Sports Ground

C7
1 THREE SPRINGS RD
2 WOODWARD CL
3 FULBERT RD
4 CORNMORE
5 LITTLE PENNY ROPE
6 SMITHS WY

Pensham Hill Cottages
PENSHAM HILL
Avonbank

Mary Brook Farm

5

P
Home Farm
Pensham

WR10

44

Pensham Farm

4

Upper End
The Court
The Ridings

Pensham Fields Farm

Marybrook Bridge

Lilworth Farm

3

PH
CHURCH STREET

Woodfield Farm

River Avon

43

2

Birlingham

Hall Farm

Kents Farm

QUAY LANE
Lower End Farm

1

Lower End Farm

River Avon

Berwick Brook

Ringsmere
Joes Farm

Great Comberton
Tibbetts Farm
RUSSELL STREET
CHURCH LANE
Wayside
Eastwood
MONGCROFT RD
Blackberry Farm
Westwood

42

93 A B 94 C D 95 E F

157
172

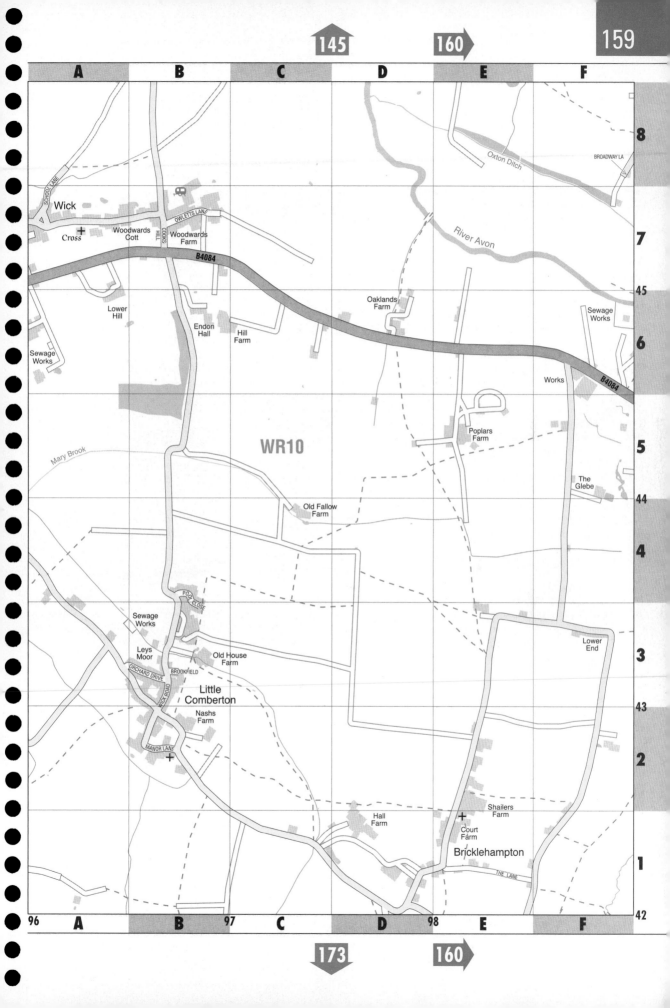

A B C D E F

8

Oxton Ditch
BROADWAY LA

River Avon

7

Wick

Cross

Woodwards
Cott

Woodwards
Farm

OWLETTS LANE

COOKS HILL

SCHOOL LANE

B4084

45

Lower
Hill

Endon
Hall

Hill
Farm

Oaklands
Farm

Sewage
Works

6

Sewage
Works

Works

B4084

WR10

Poplars
Farm

5

Mary Brook

Old Fallow
Farm

The
Glebe

44

4

POOL CLOSE

Sewage
Works

Lower
End

3

Leys
Moor

Old House
Farm

ORCHARD DRIVE

BROOKFIELD

Little
Comberton

WICK ROAD

43

Nashs
Farm

2

MANOR LANE

Shailers
Farm

Hall
Farm

Court
Farm

Bricklehampton

1

THE LANE

42

96 A B 97 C D 98 E F

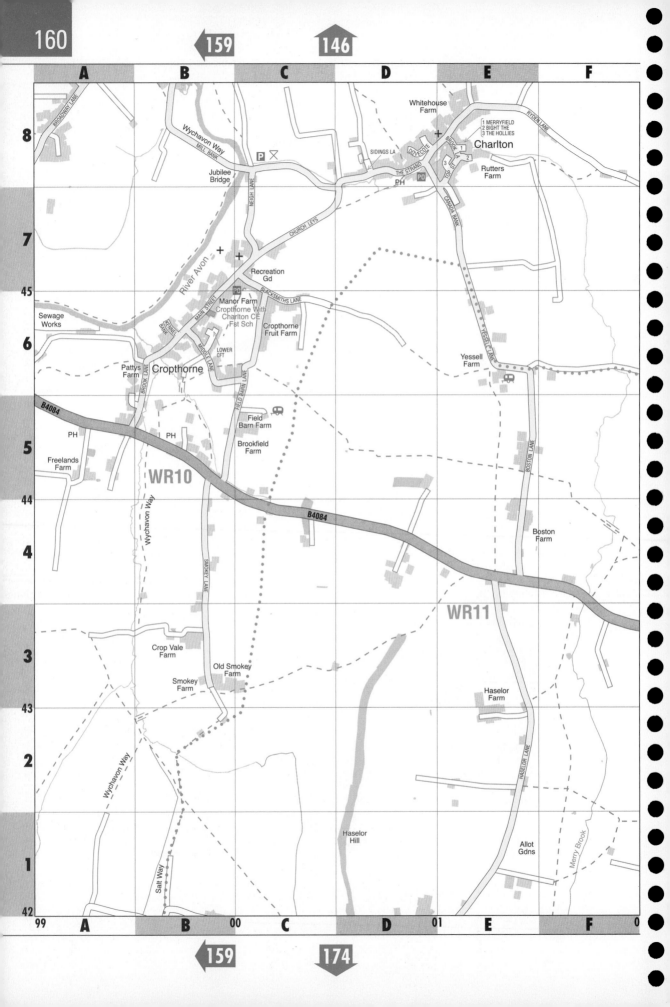

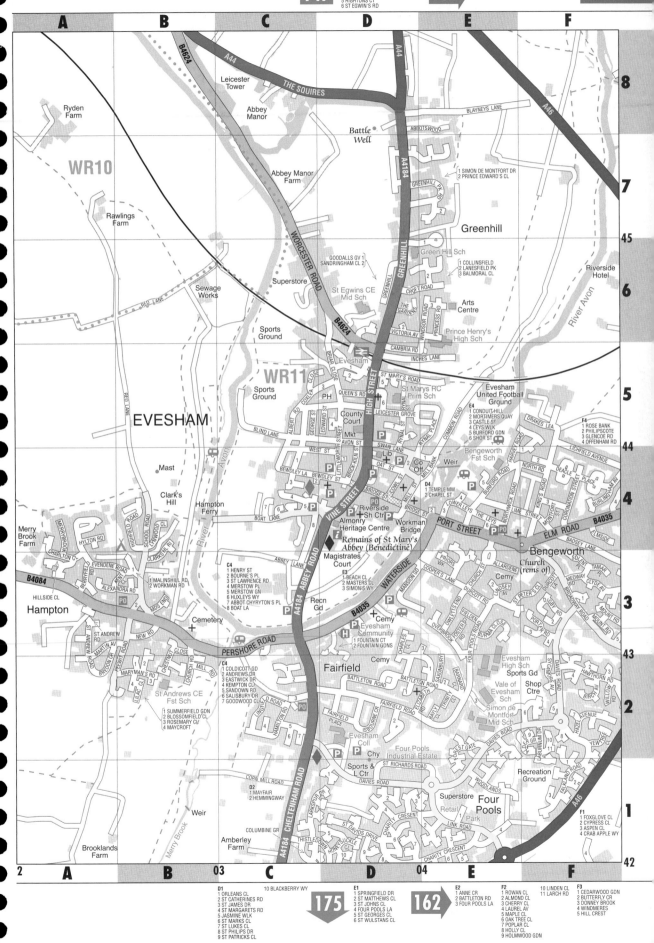

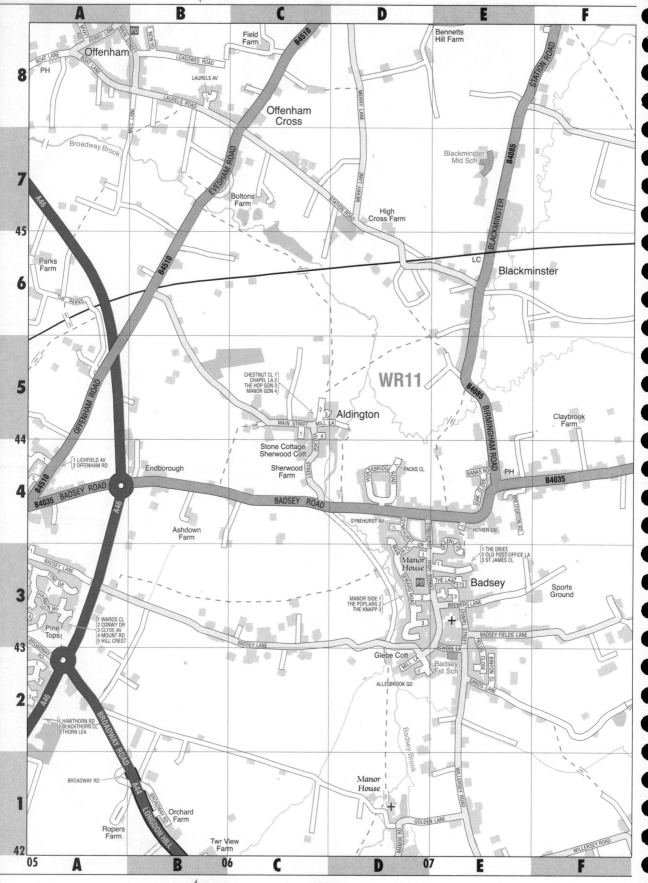

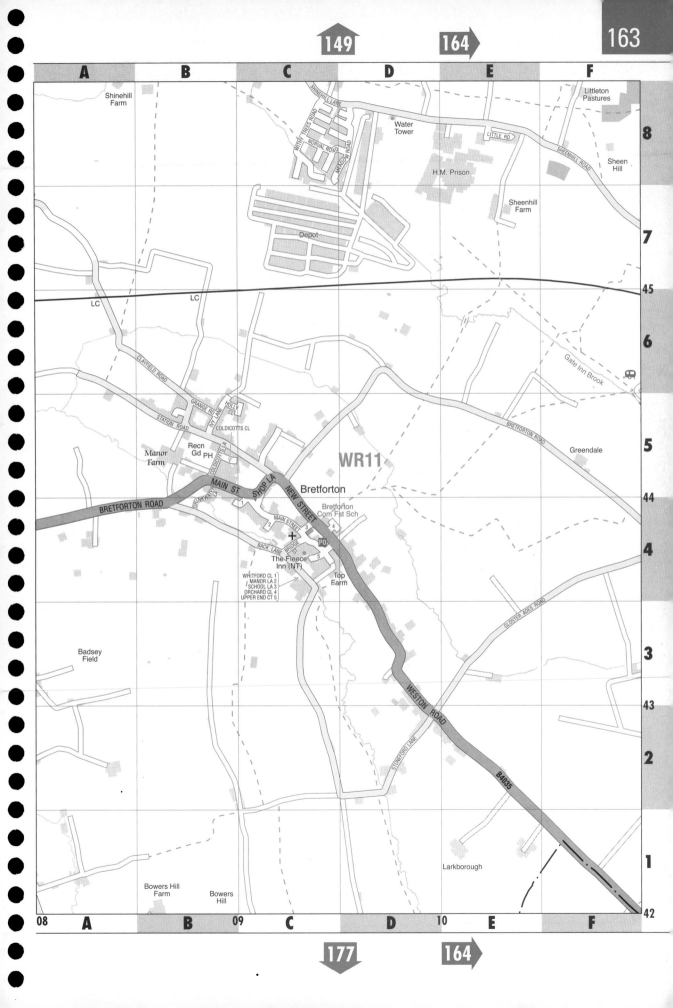

163 150

A B C D E F

163 178

8
7
45
6
5
44
4
3
43
2
1
42

11 A B 12 C D 13 E F

Tump Bew Hill

Bew Hill Farm

CV37

Pebworth Fields Farm

Baylis's Hill

Blenheim Farm

BUCKLE STREET

Works

SHEENHILL ROAD

Grove Farm

STRATFORD ROAD

Peace Egg Farm

Honeybourne

STEPHENSON WAY

Kite's Hill

Bushy Hill

Bushy Hill Buildings

STATION ROAD

DUDLEY RD
HARVARD AVE
PEBRIE DR
FERNIHOUGH AV
WESTBOURNE
GROVE AV
HUDSON
BEAUFORT END

Domestic Fowl Trust & Honeybourne Rare Breeds

Woodpeckers

Norton Hall Farm

Cemy

STRATFORD ROAD

PH Gate Inn Bridge

Woodcote Manor Farm

MICKLETON ROAD

LC

New Hill

Dairyfield Covert

Honeybourne

Corner Farm

WR11

GL55

CORNER FARM DR

BRETFORTON RD
GREEN CL
SCHOOL
STREET
TEAPES
PIECE
CHIPPE
HIGH STREET

PO

GLOSTER ABES RD
MANOR CL

Honeybourne First Sch

Mill Mound

BRICK WALK

Manor Farm

The Green Farm

PODEN LANE

Poden Farm

Recreation Ground

Weston Fields Farm

Far Poden Farm

WESTON ROAD

Moat

Long Stretch Farm

PODEN LANE

Tower Farm

Sewage Works

HONEYBOURNE ROAD

Honeybourne Airfield Industrial Estate

Works

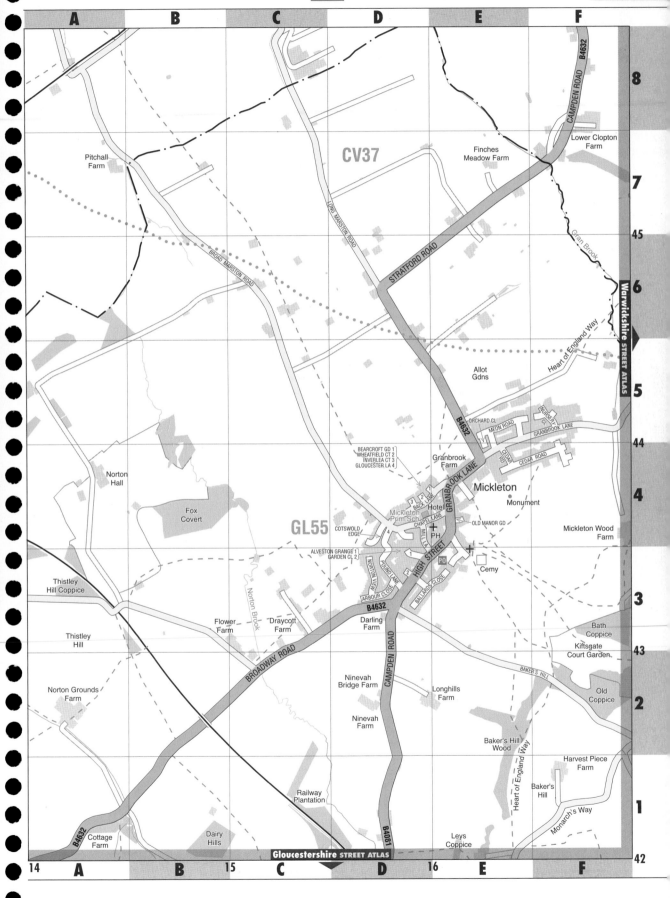

A B C D E F

8

7

45

6

Warwickshire STREET ATLAS

5

44

4

43

3

2

42

1

CV37

Pitchall Farm

BROAD MARSTON ROAD

LONG MARSTON ROAD

STRATFORD ROAD

Finches Meadow Farm

Lower Clopton Farm

CAMPDEN ROAD

B4632

Gran Brook

Heart of England Way

Allot Gdns

B4632

ORCHARD CL

MEON ROAD

NURSERY CL

GRANBROOK LANE

CEDAR ROAD

CEDAR ROAD

Mickleton

Monument

Norton Hall

Fox Covert

BEARCROFT GD 1
WHEATFIELD CT 2
INVERLEA CT 3
GLOUCESTER LA 4

Granbrook Farm

GL55

BACK LANE

Mickleton Prim Sch

CHAPEL LANE

Hotel

GRANBROOK LANE

MILL LA

Old Manor Gd

Mickleton Wood Farm

COTSWOLD EDGE

PH

Cemy

ALVESTON GRANGE 1
GARDEN CL 2

HIGH STREET

BALLARDS CLOSE

PO

NORTON VIEW

POUND LANE

ARBOUR CLOSE

Thistley Hill Coppice

Norton Brook

Flower Farm

Draycott Farm

Darling Farm

B4632

Bath Coppice

Kiftsgate Court Garden

BAKER'S HILL

Thistley Hill

BROADWAY ROAD

CAMPDEN ROAD

Ninevah Bridge Farm

Longhills Farm

Old Coppice

Norton Grounds Farm

Ninevah Farm

Baker's Hill Wood

Harvest Piece Farm

Heart of England Way

Baker's Hill

Railway Plantation

B4081

Leys Coppice

Monarch's Way

B4632

Cottage Farm

Dairy Hills

14 A B 15 C D 16 E F

E7
1 RICHMONDS PITCH
2 KINGS RD
3 WOODLANDS CL
4 WELLS CL
5 HEATHLANDS CL

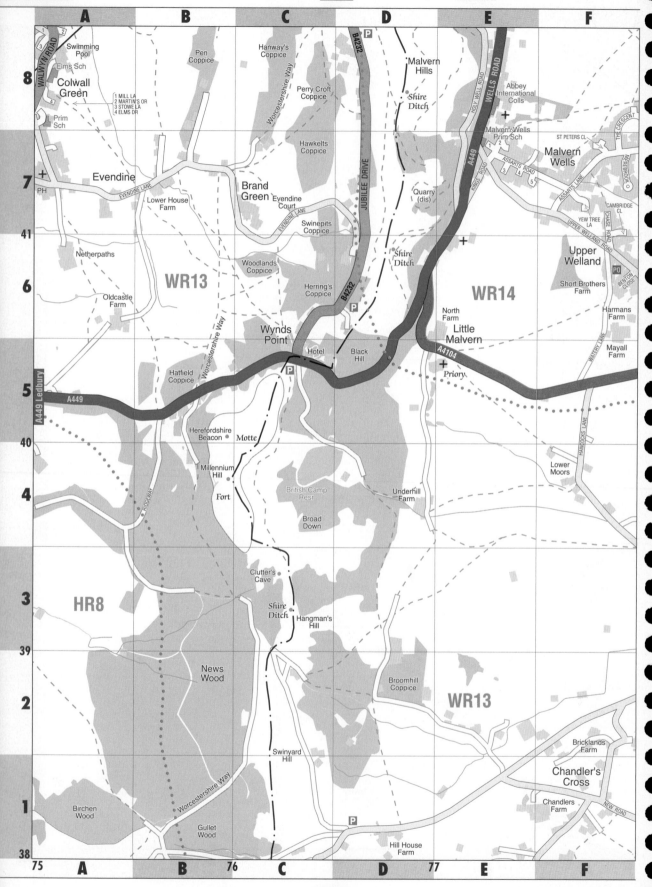

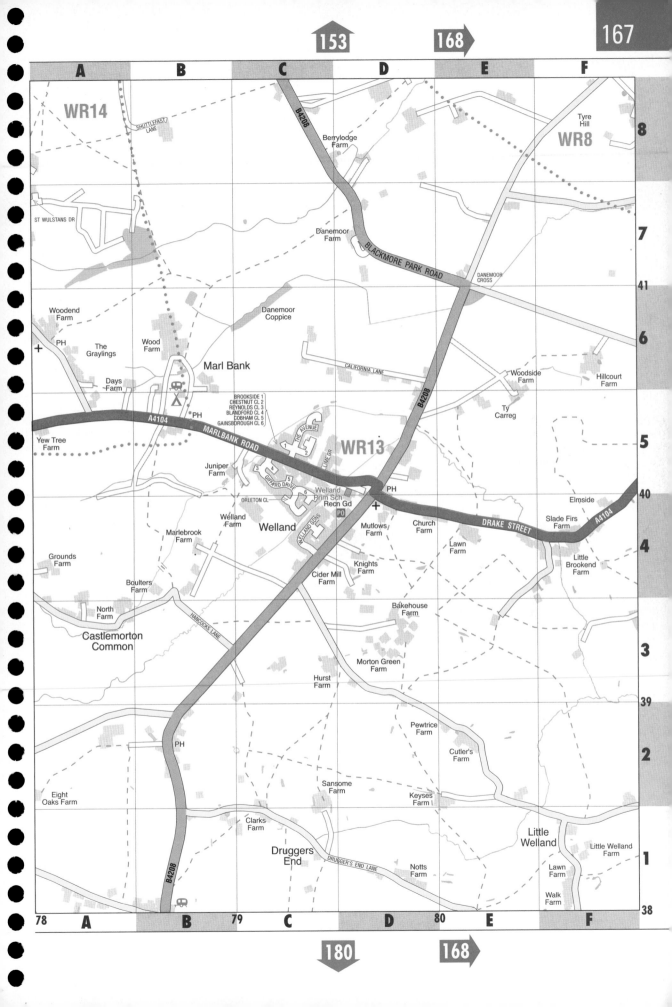

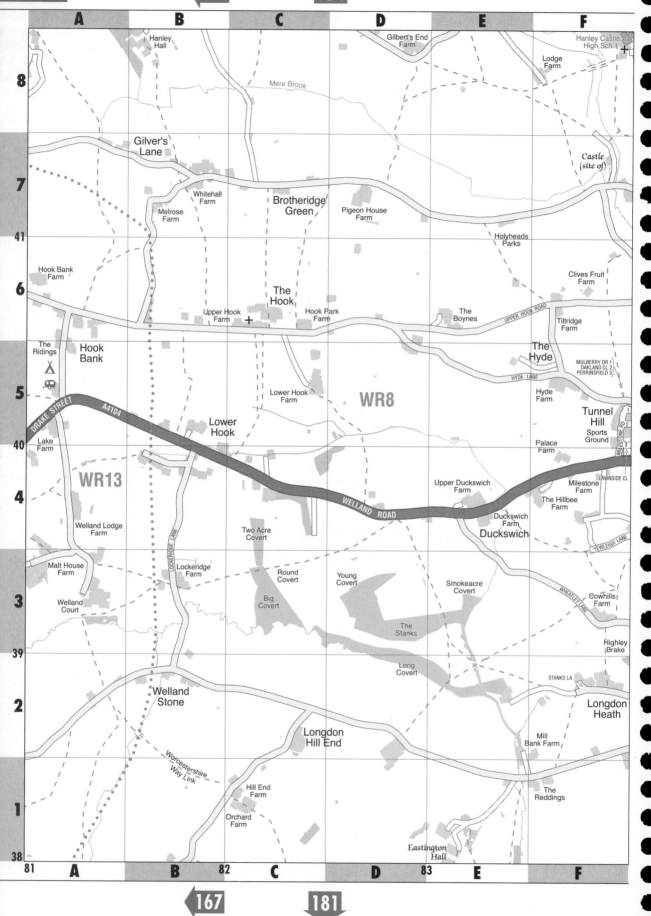

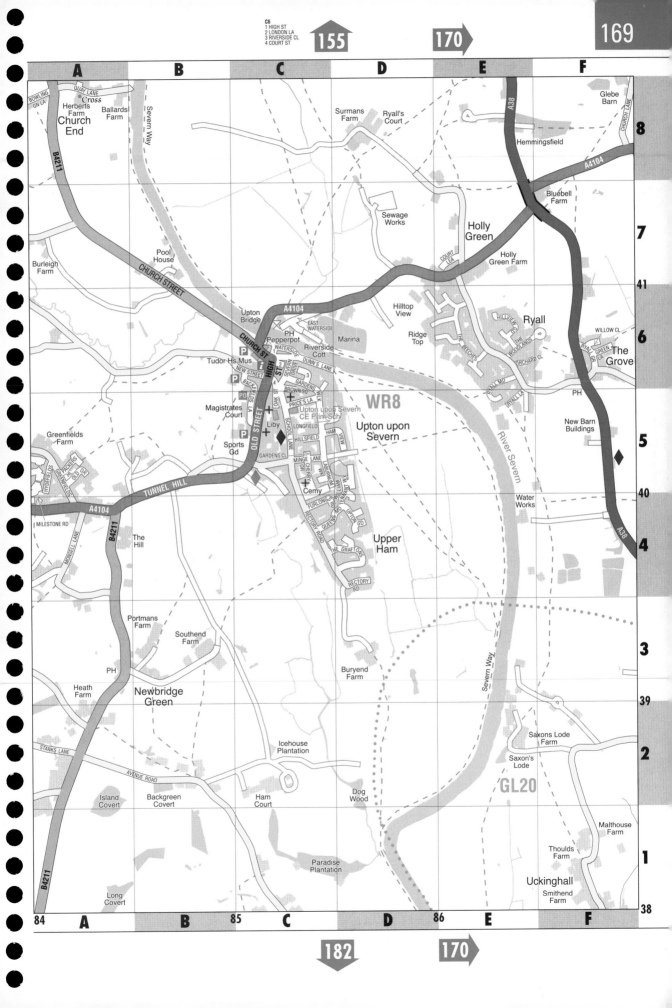

A · B · C · D · E · F

A4104

Baughton

A4104

Baughton Hill Farm

M5

Baughton Hill

BAUGHTON LANE

8

7

41

Smithmoor Common

Moat

Manor Farm

WR8

Strensham Service Area North

6

Soudley Farm

Glebe Farm

+

Hill Croome

5

Green Street

Green Street Farm

Wooshill Farm

40

Bramble Farm

Black Covert

4

Naunton

GREEN LANE

Bests Farm

Fowlers Farm

Ley Coppice

3

Ley Farm

39

Stratford

Harbour Wood

2

Phelp's Farm

Ripple Farm

Wain House Ripple Farm

GL20

1

Furlongs Farm

Whorley Grove

A38

M50

38

87 · A · B · 88 · C · D · 89 · E · F

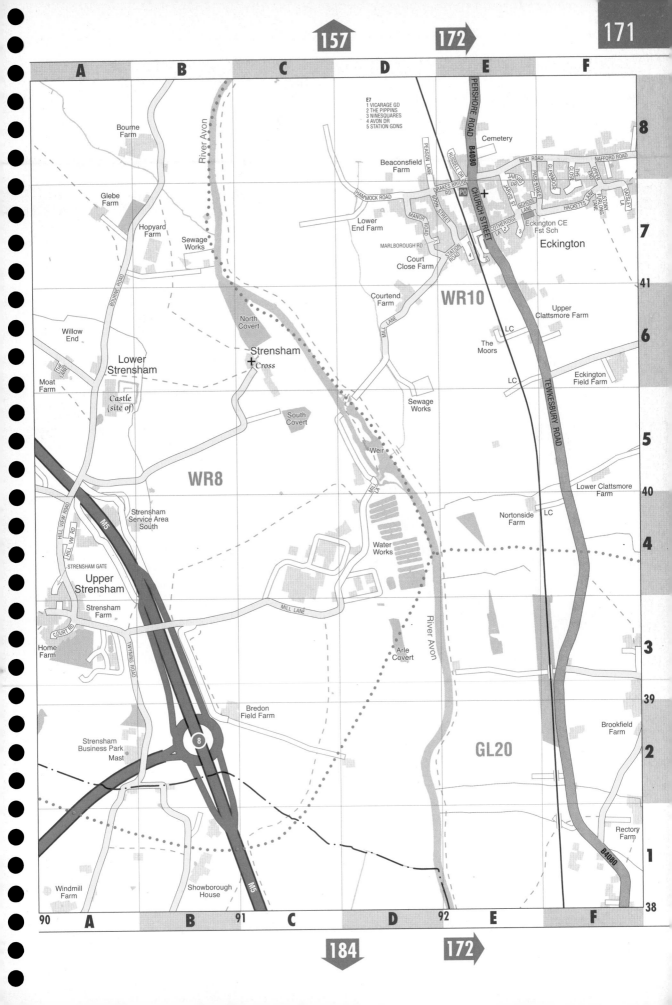

A   B   C   D   E   F

E7
1 VICARAGE GD
2 THE PIPPINS
3 NINESQUARES
4 AVON DR
5 STATION GDNS

Bourne Farm

River Avon

Glebe Farm

Hopyard Farm

Sewage Works

Willow End

Lower Strensham

THE LANE

BOURNE ROAD

Moat Farm

Castle (site of)

North Covert

Strensham Cross

South Covert

Weir

WR8

HILL VIEW ROAD

HILL VW RD

M5

STRENSHAM GATE

Upper Strensham

Strensham Service Area South

Strensham Farm

COURT RD

TWYNING ROAD

Home Farm

Strensham Business Park Mast

8

Windmill Farm

Showborough House

Bredon Field Farm

MILL LANE

MILL LA

Water Works

Arle Covert

River Avon

GL20

Beaconsfield Farm

PEASON LANE

HAMMOCK ROAD

Lower End Farm

MANOR ROAD

BOON STREET

MARLBOROUGH RD

Court Close Farm

STATION ROAD

Courtend Farm

MILL LANE

Sewage Works

DRAKES BRIDGE

RUSSELL END RD

CHURCH STREET

B4080

PERSHORE ROAD

Cemetery

NEW ROAD

JARVIS DR

JARVIS ST

GLENMOOR

UPPER END

THE CLOSE

PASS STREET

SCHOOL LANE

COTHERIDGE LA

Eckington CE Fst Sch

HACKETTS LANE

STONY FURLONG LANE

NAFFORD ROAD

OAKSLEY LA

DAISLEY LA

Eckington

WR10

The Moors

Upper Clattsmore Farm

LC

LC

Eckington Field Farm

TEWKESBURY ROAD

Lower Clattsmore Farm

Nortonside Farm

LC

Brookfield Farm

Rectory Farm

B4080

8

90   91   92

41   40   39   38

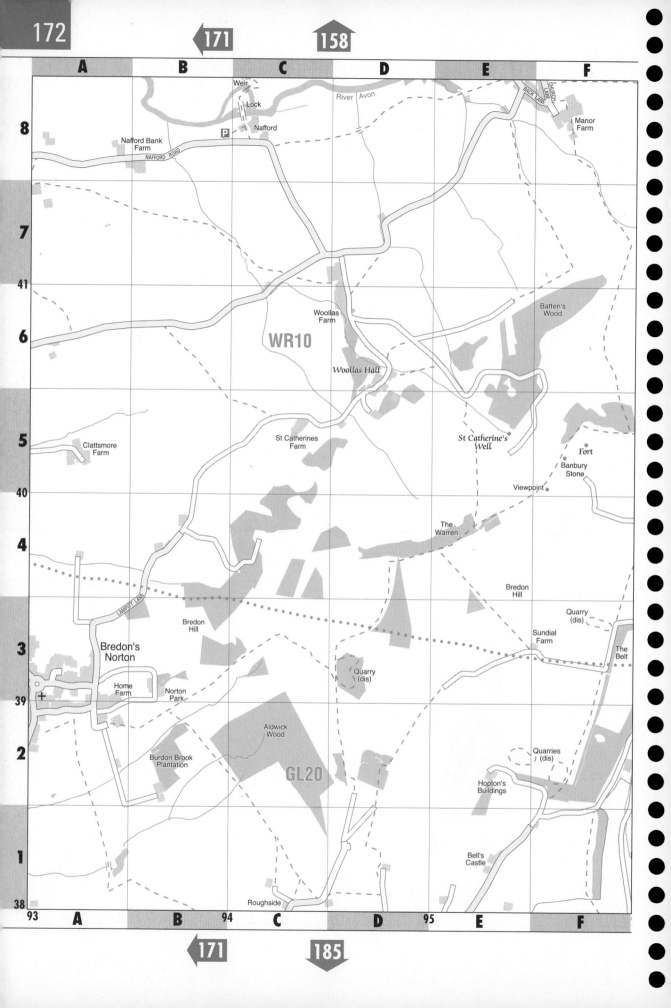

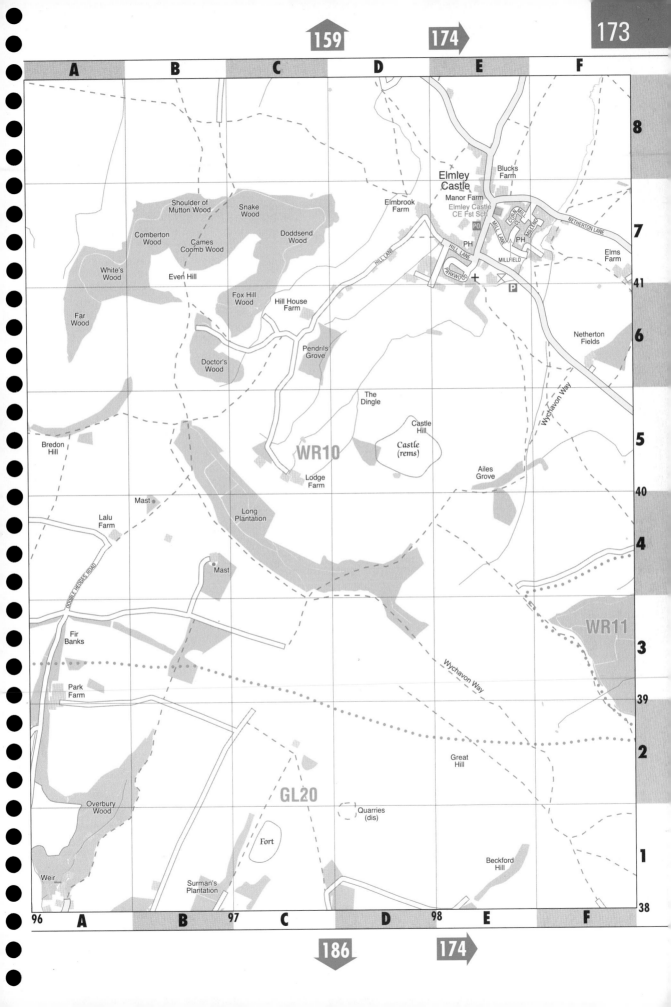

159
174

A B C D E F

8

7

41

6

Elmley Castle

Blucks Farm

Manor Farm

Elmbrook Farm

Elmley Castle CE Fst Sch

Shoulder of Mutton Wood

Snake Wood

Doddsend Wood

Comberton Wood

Cames Coomb Wood

White's Wood

Even Hill

PH

HILL LANE

PARKWOS

PO

MILL LANE

COAL MILL

MILL END

PH

MILLFIELD

NETHERTON LANE

Elms Farm

Far Wood

Fox Hill Wood

Hill House Farm

HILL LANE

Pendrils Grove

Doctor's Wood

Netherton Fields

6

The Dingle

Castle Hill

Castle (rems)

Wychavon Way

WR10

Bredon Hill

Ailes Grove

5

Lodge Farm

40

Mast

Long Plantation

Lalu Farm

DOUBLE HEDGES ROAD

4

Mast

WR11

Fir Banks

Wychavon Way

3

Park Farm

39

Great Hill

2

GL20

Overbury Wood

Quarries (dis)

Fort

Beckford Hill

1

Weir

Surman's Plantation

38

96 A B 97 C D 98 E F

173
160

A B C D E F

8

Chapel
Farm

Netherton

Chapel
(remains of)

Upper Haselor
Farm

Upper
Haselor

Coppice
Farm

7

Wychavon Way

Netherton Lane

Haselor Lane

Merry Brook

WR10

41

6

Furzehill
Brake

Furzehill
Farm

5

Manor
Farm

Middle
Farm

Kersoe

Kersoe
Farm

Furze
Hill

Ballard's
Farm

STATION ROAD

WR11

40

4

Northfield
Farm

Sandfield
Farm

3

Ashton
Wood

39

Ashwood

Holcomb
Nap

2

Nap
Coppice

GORSE
HL

CORNFIELD WAY

WOOD LA

Bredon Hill
Mid Sch

Sandfield Lane

ELMLEY ROAD

COTTON'S LANE

PO

HILLSIDE

Ashton under Hill

GL20

1

BAKER'S LANE

Little Owl
Farm

Carrant
Brook Farm

A46

CHELTENHAM ROAD

BRIDEWELL
DR

CHURCHILL
RD

BARN LA

West End
Farm

38

99 A B 00 C D 01 E F

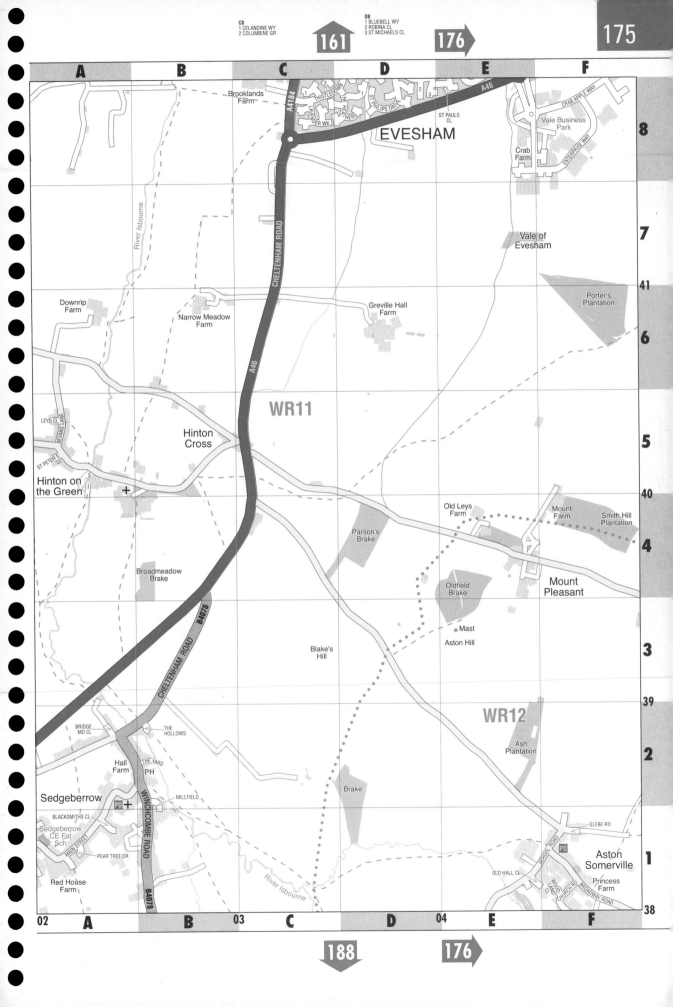

175
162

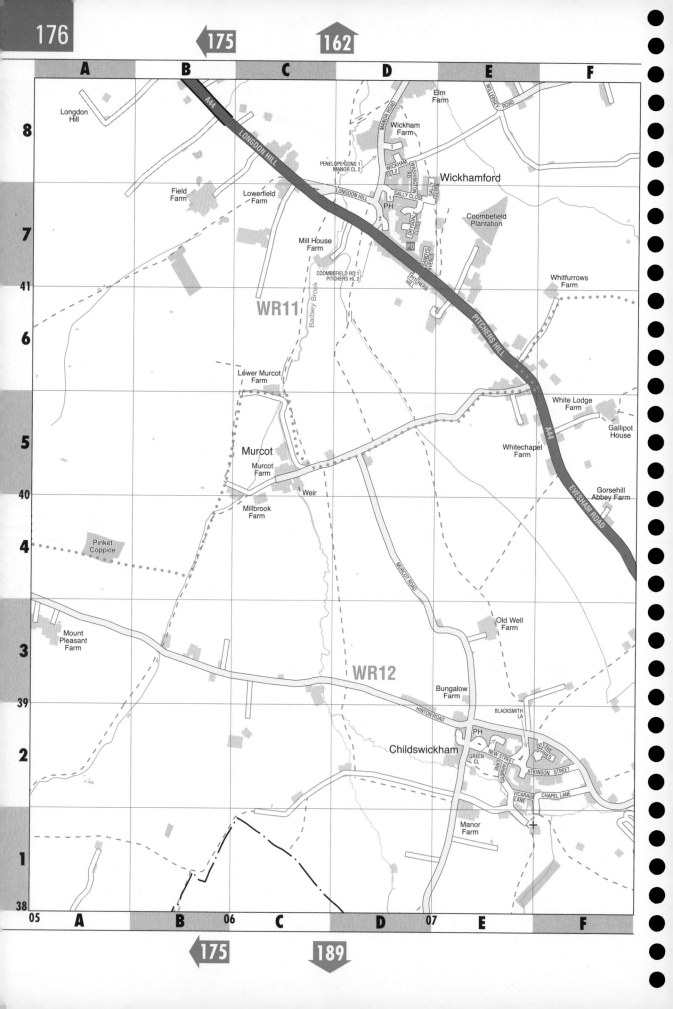

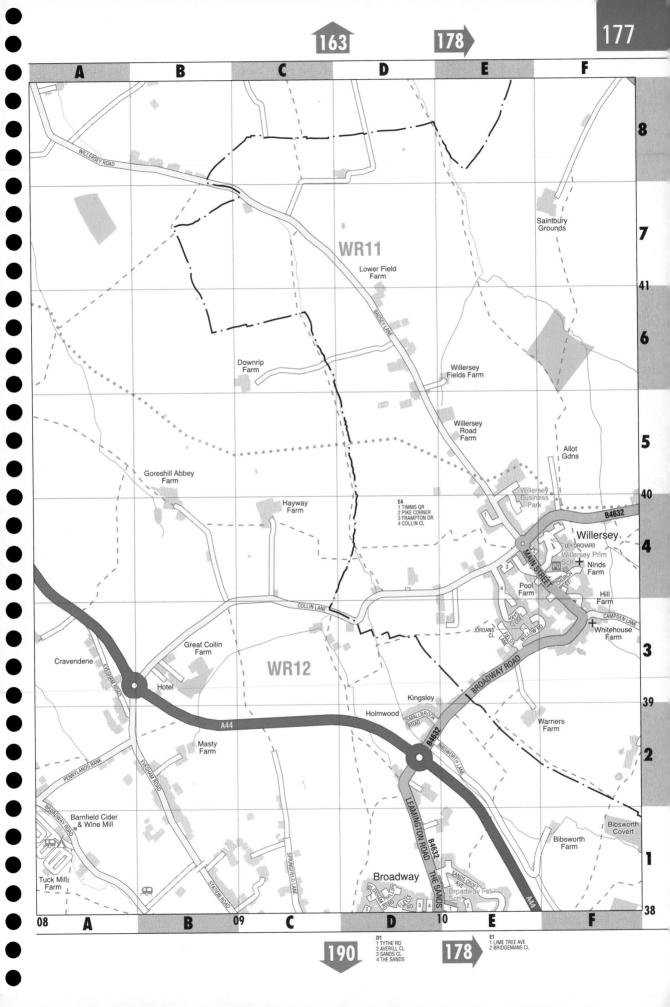

177
164

	A	B	C	D	E	F

8

B4035

Works

B4632

Manor House

Glebe Farm

Manor Farm

B4035

B4632

Gardners Farm

ASTON RD

7

HONEYBOURNE ROAD

Works

B4035

Lower Fields Farm

Brook Bend

PO

PH

CIDERMILL OR

Weston-sub-Edge

Manor Farm

Merrivale Fruit Farm

BUCKLE STREET

DOVER'S VW

Aston Subedge

41

PARSONS LANE

CHAPEL LA

Middle Farm

WR11

6

Witt's End

The Lynches Wood

Manor House (site of)

Phillips Farm

Broad Close Farm

Westwood

5

Cross

Vale Farm

Earthwork

Top Farm

GL55

The Lynches Wood

Saintbury Cross Farm

Ledge Plantation

40

Oaklands Farm

B4632

Middle Hill Farm

Dover's Hill

NT

Glebe Farm

4

Upper Wall Farm

Saintbury

Park Farm

P

Kingcombe Lane

Saintbury Coppice

Lane End

DYER'S LANE

3

Tumulus

CAMPDEN LANE

Weston Park Farm

39

Earthwork

Kiftsgate Stone

WR12

BUCKLE STREET

Campden Wood

2

Willersey Hill

Quarry (dis)

Weston Park

THE NARROWS

Broadway Golf Course

Cotswold Way — The Mile Drive

1

Long Barrow

CH

Saintbury Hill

Saintbury Hill Farm

Hotel

38

11	A	B	12	C	D	13	E	F

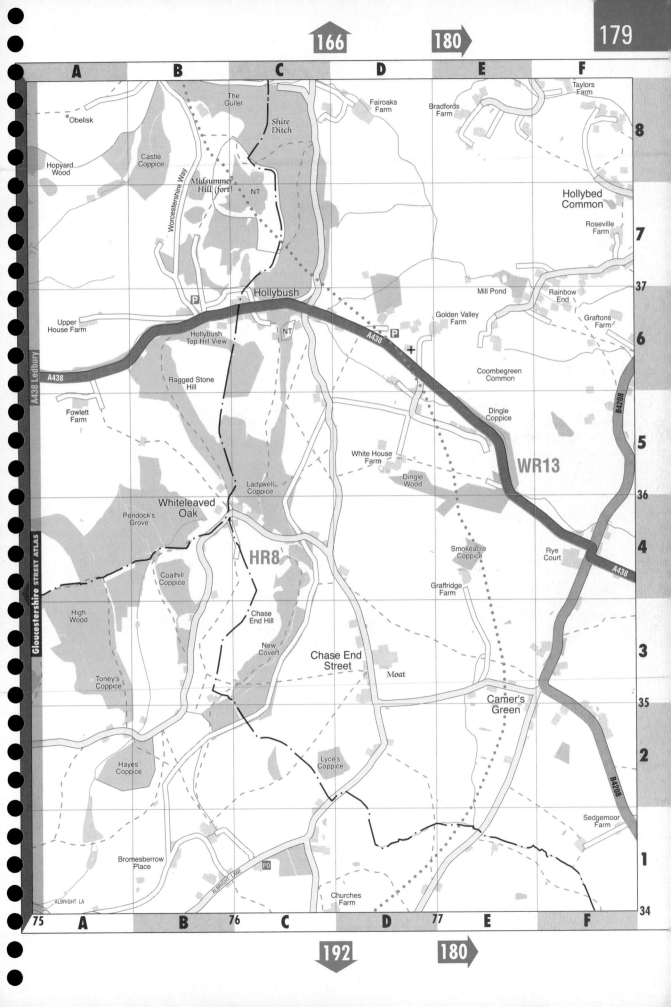

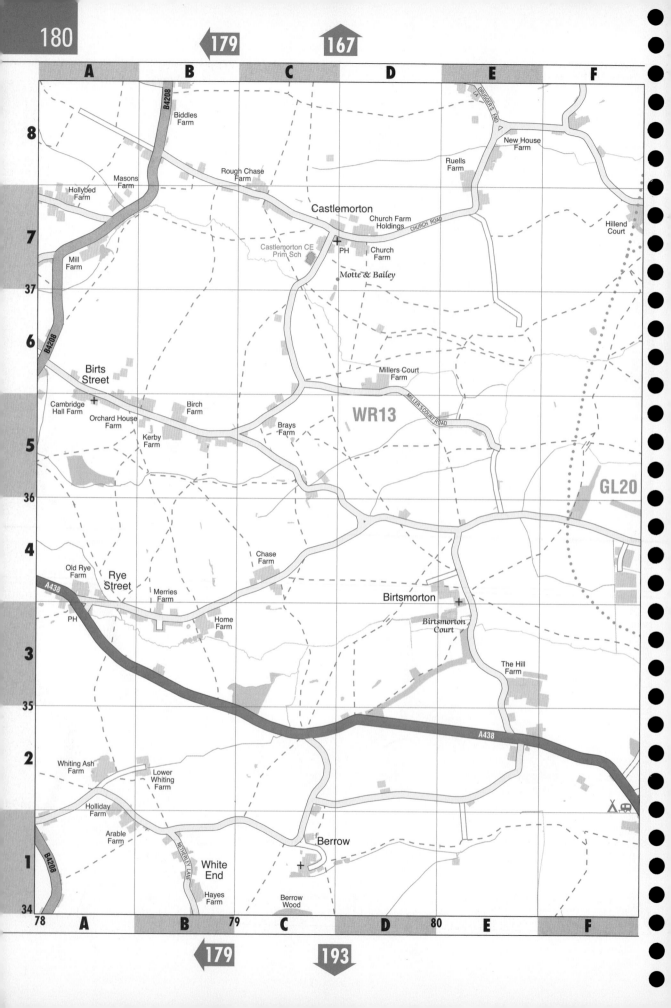

A B C D E F

8

Biddles Farm

Hollybed Farm

Masons Farm

Rough Chase Farm

Ruells Farm

New House Farm

Hillend Court

Castlemorton

Church Farm Holdings

CHURCH ROAD

7

Mill Farm

Castlemorton CE Prim Sch

PH

Church Farm

37

Motte & Bailey

B4208

6

Birts Street

Millers Court Farm

MILLER'S COURT ROAD

WR13

Cambridge Hall Farm

Birch Farm

Orchard House Farm

Kerby Farm

Brays Farm

5

GL20

36

4

Old Rye Farm

Rye Street

Chase Farm

Birtsmorton

A438

Merries Farm

Home Farm

Birtsmorton Court

PH

The Hill Farm

3

35

A438

2

Whiting Ash Farm

Lower Whiting Farm

Holliday Farm

Arable Farm

NETHERLEY LANE

White End

Berrow

1

B4208

Hayes Farm

Berrow Wood

34

78 A B 79 C D 80 E F

181
169

A **B** **C** **D** **E** **F**

B4211

Long Covert

Holdfast

Hall

8

Glover Hill Farm

FERRY LANE

Bank Farm

WR8

Green Farm

Manor Farm

7

37

Heath Hill Farm

Hen and Chicken Covert

The Barn Farm

M50

Churchend Farm

Queenhill

6

Severn Way

Bushley Brook

Woodend Bridge

River Severn

5

Bredon Sch (Pull Court)

36

Gunnice Farm

The Grove

GL20

4

B4211

Chambers Court

Gullers End Farm

Pipers End Farm

Guller's End

Weir

Hill House Farm

Mossgreen Shrubbery

3

M50

Slades Green Farm

Broadfields Farm

Windmill Tump

35

Piper's End

The Woodlands

Aggberrow Wood

Yeandley Farm

Longdon Hall

Elmwood Barn

Green Farm

Slades Green

Orchard Farm

Bushley Green

2

GREEN STREET

Tilterdown Farm

Wheypools Farm

Hill Wood

1

Buckbury Farm

The Rampings

Sarn Hill Wood

WOOD STREET

Buckbury

B4211

Buckbury End

Upper Green Farm

Wood Street Farm

34

84 **A** **B** **85** **C** **D** **86** **E** **F**

181
195

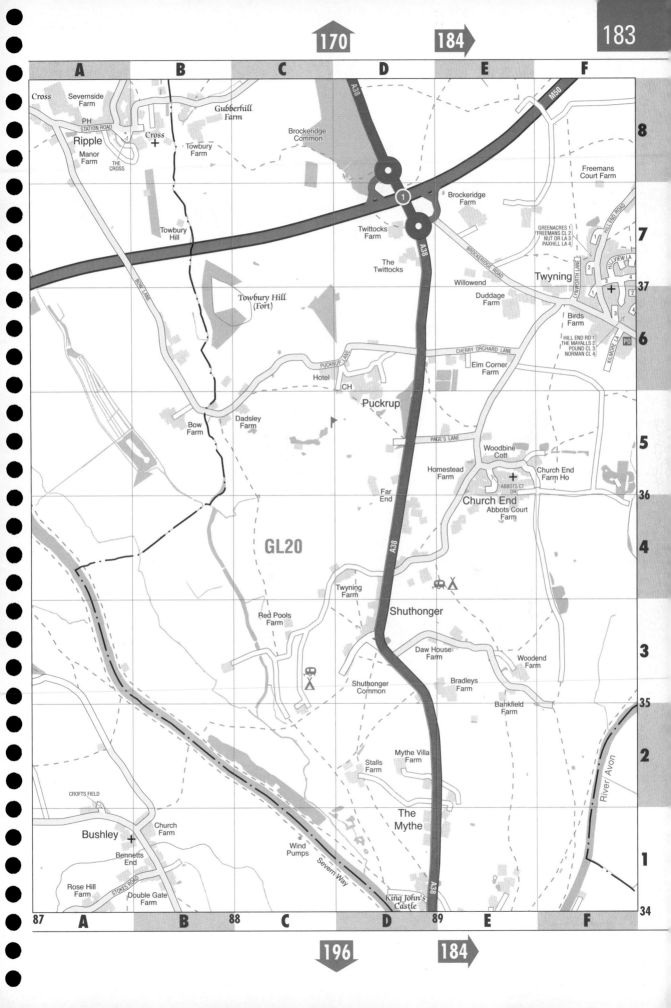

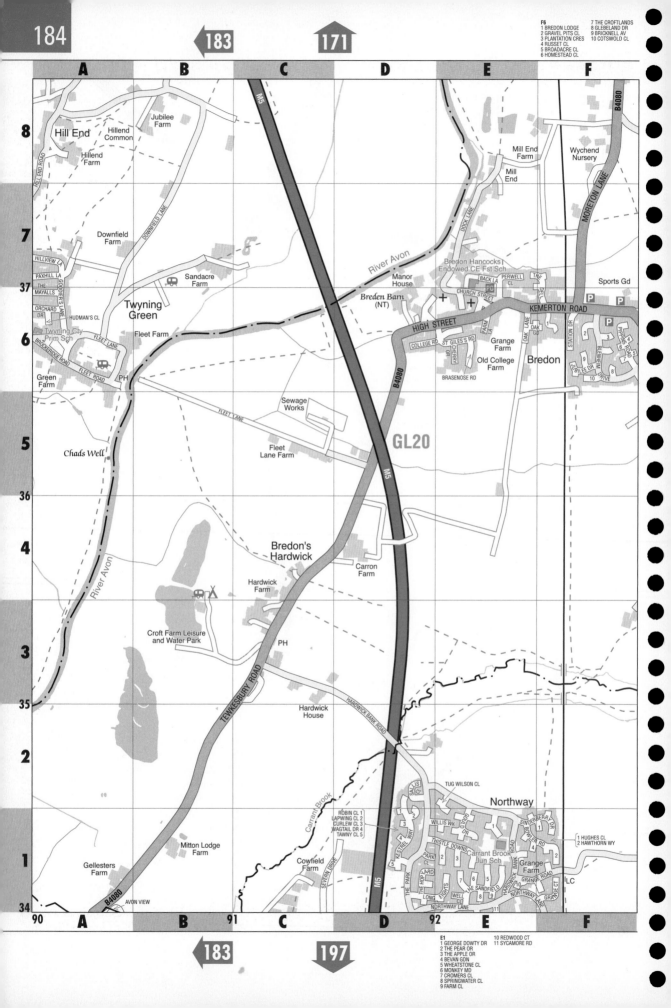

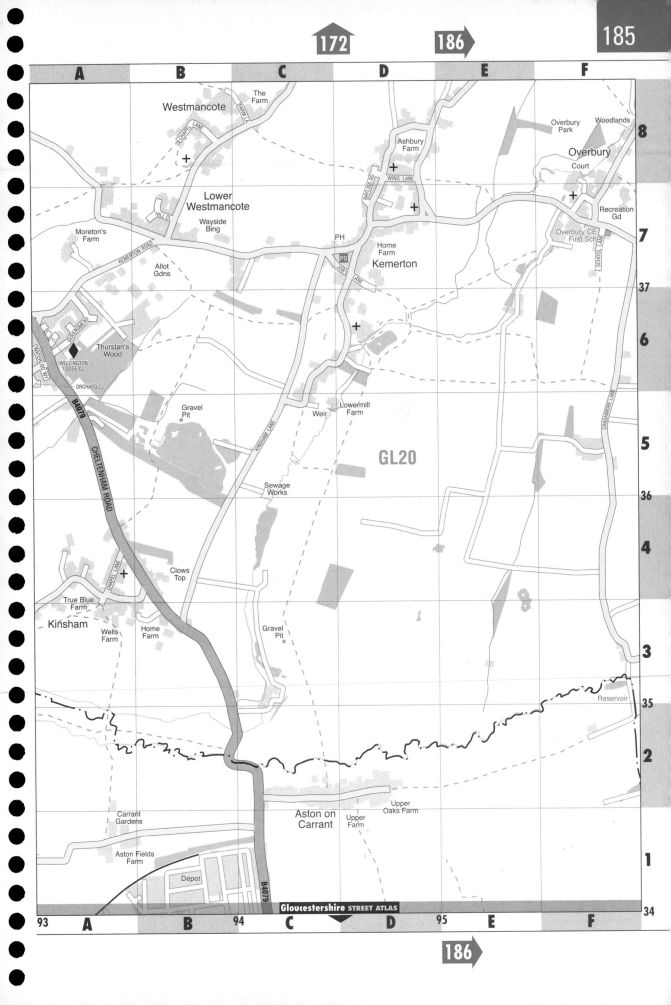

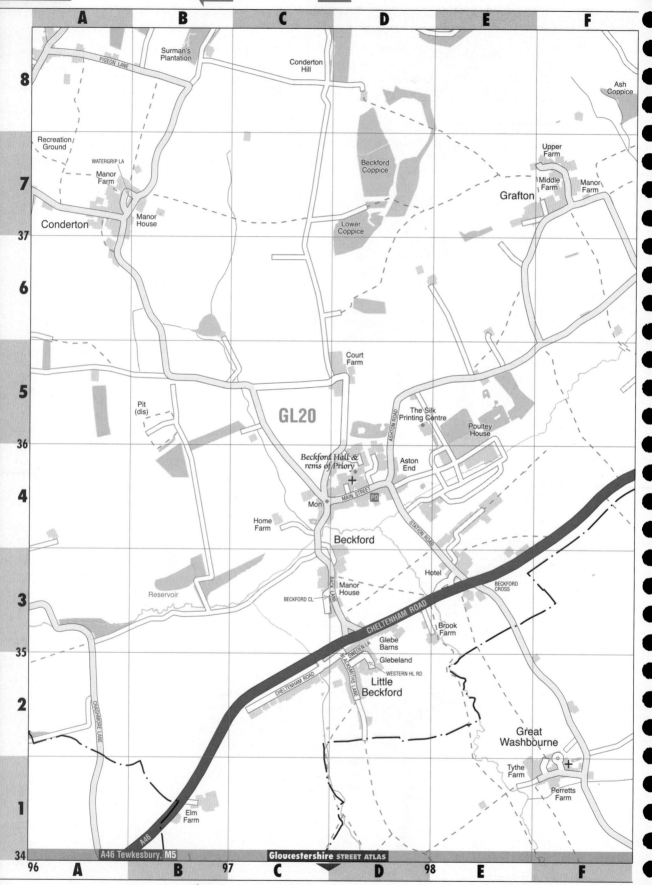

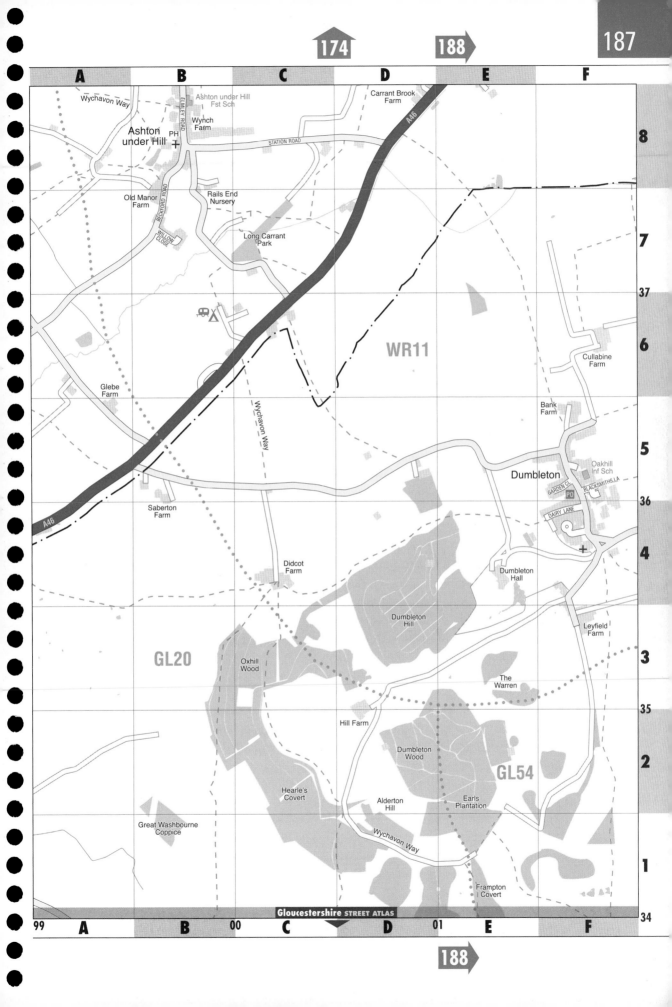

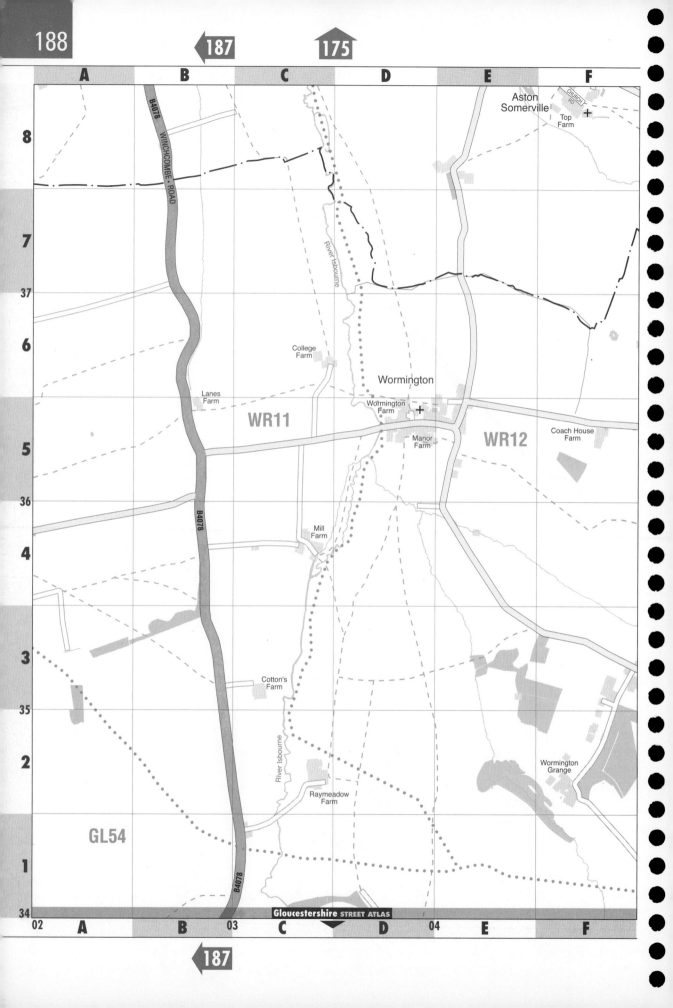

A B C D E F

8

7

37

6

5

36

4

3

35

2

1

34

B4078

WINCHCOMBE ROAD

B4078

B4078

River Isbourne

River Isbourne

College Farm

Lanes Farm

WR11

Wormington

Wormington Farm

Manor Farm

WR12

Coach House Farm

Aston Somerville

Top Farm

CHURCH RD

Mill Farm

Cotton's Farm

Raymeadow Farm

Wormington Grange

GL54

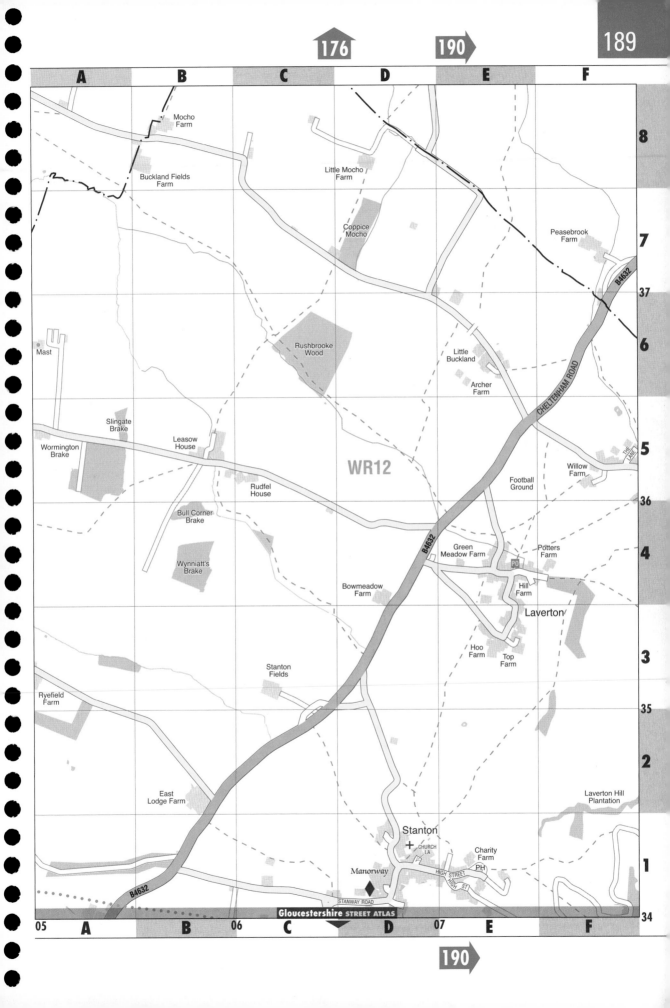

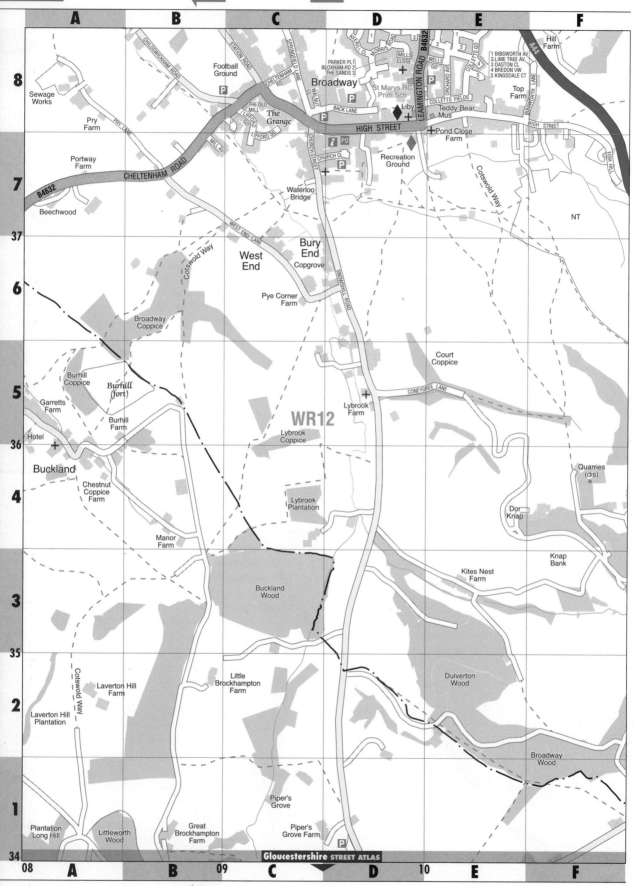

Sewage Works

Pry Farm

Portway Farm

B4632 CHELTENHAM ROAD

Beechwood

CHELDSWICKHAM ROAD

STATION ROAD

Football Ground

P

THE OLD MILL

The Grange

LIFFORD CL

LIFFORD RD

MILL AV

CHELTENHAM RD

SPRINGFIELD LANE

WALNUT

BACK LANE

CHURCH STREET

Broadway

PARKER PL 1
BLOXHAM RD 2
THE SANDS 3

ASHILL CL

MORRIS ROAD

MILLS CLOSE

St Marys RC Prim Sch

Liby

HIGH STREET

B4632

LEAMINGTON ROAD

P

WELLS GD

P

ORCHARD AVE

COLLETTS GD

COLLETTS FIELDS

Teddy Bear Mus

1 BIBSWORTH AV
2 LIME TREE AV
3 DASTON CL
4 BREDON VW
5 KINGSDALE CT

Hill Farm

A44

Top Farm

BISWORTH LANE

HIGH STREET

FISH HILL

i PO

CHURCH CL

P

Recreation Ground

Pond Close Farm

Cotswold Way

NT

Waterloo Bridge

WEST END LANE

Colswold Way

West End

Bury End

Copgrove

SNOWSHILL ROAD

Pye Corner Farm

Broadway Coppice

Court Coppice

Burhill Coppice

Burhill (fort)

Garretts Farm

Burhill Farm

CONEYGREE LANE

Lybrook Farm

WR12

Lybrook Coppice

Hotel

Buckland

Quarries (dis)

Chestnut Coppice Farm

Dor Knap

Lybrook Plantation

Manor Farm

Knap Bank

Buckland Wood

Kites Nest Farm

Cotswold Way

Laverton Hill Farm

Little Brockhampton Farm

Dulverton Wood

Laverton Hill Plantation

Broadway Wood

Piper's Grove

Plantation Long Hill

Littleworth Wood

Great Brockhampton Farm

Piper's Grove Farm

P

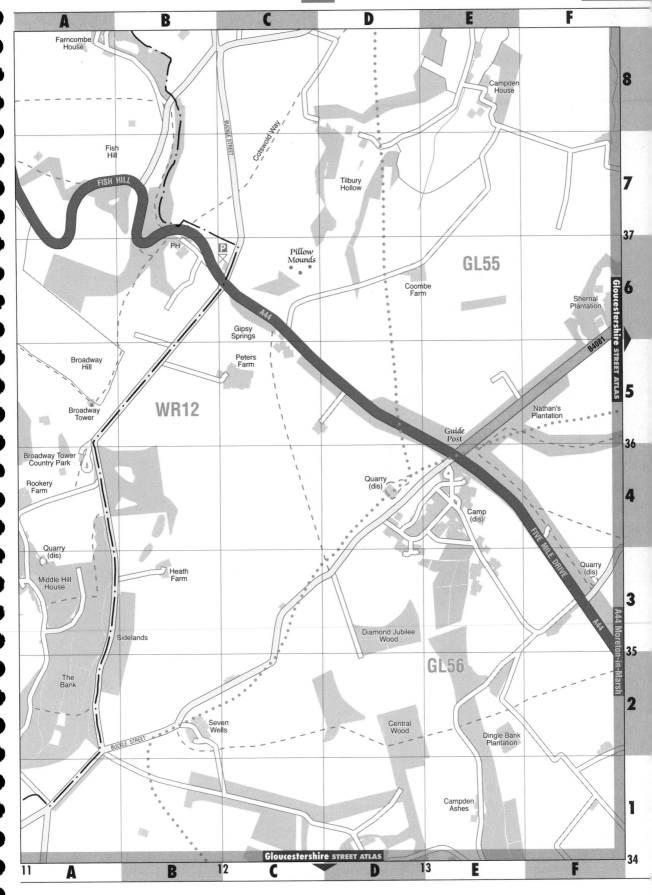

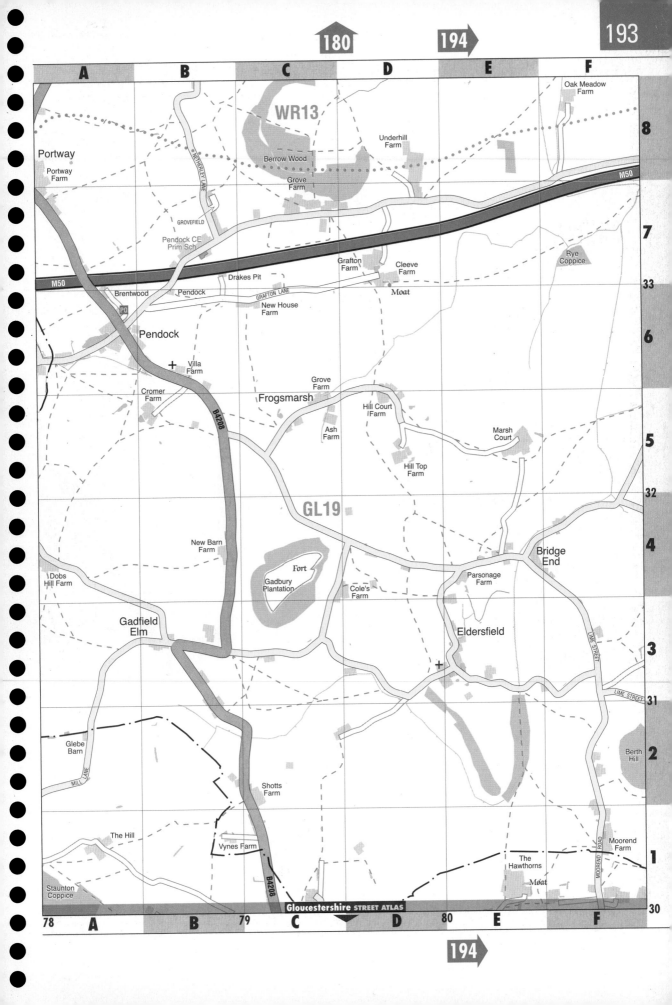

A   B   C   D   E   F

8

Priors
Court

A438

M50   A438

M50

Downend

Dean
Covert

Downend
Coppice

7

Hillenders

Beech
Coppice

33

Hooze
Farm

6

Hardwick
Green

Hardwick
Farm

Mitre
Farm

5

Newbarn

GL19

Swinley
Green

Swinley
Court

32

Dunshill
Farm

4

Oak
Grove

Nashend
Farm

Little Dunshill
Farm

3

Moat

Linkend
Farm

Sports
Gd

Pigeon House
Farm

Palmers End
Farm

Cranley
Farm

LINKEND ROAD

Moores
Farm

31

Hardwick Hay
Farm

Linkend

Eldersfield Lawn
CE Prim Sch

2

Hillfield
House

POOLHAY
CL

Corse
Lawn

LIME STREET

Hotel

Lime
Street

PH

Hallings
Farm

Elm
Farm

Stewards
Farm

1

Moat

Plough
Farm

Walnut
Tree Farm

Lucas
Farm

Slad
Farm

Walk
Farm

Wrights
Farm

Villa
Farm

B4211

30

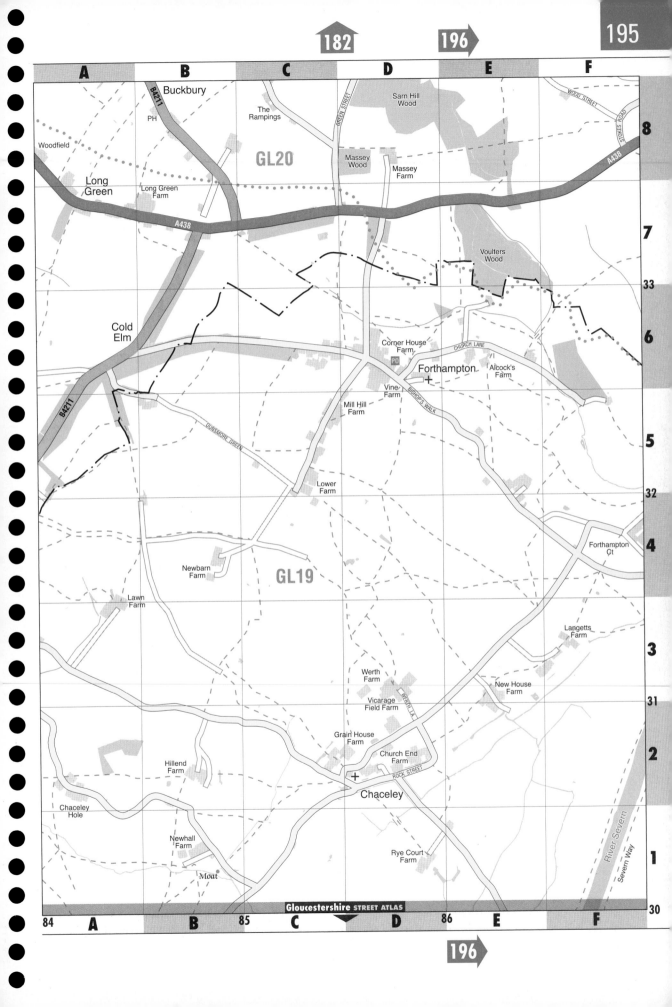

A B C D E F

8

7

33

6

5

32

4

3

31

2

1

30

Buckbury

B4211

PH

Woodfield

Long
Green

Long Green
Farm

A438

GL20

The
Rampings

GREEN STREET

Sarn Hill
Wood

Massey
Wood

Massey
Farm

WOOD STREET

STOKES ROAD

A438

Cold
Elm

B4211

DUNSMORE GREEN

Corner House
Farm

PO

Forthampton

Vine
Farm

Mill Hill
Farm

BISHOP'S WALK

CHURCH LANE

Alcock's
Farm

Voulters
Wood

Lower
Farm

Newbarn
Farm

GL19

Lawn
Farm

Forthampton
Ct

Langetts
Farm

Werth
Farm

Vicarage
Field Farm

Grain House
Farm

Hillend
Farm

WERTH LA.

New House
Farm

Church End
Farm

ROCK STREET

Chaceley

Chaceley
Hole

Newhall
Farm

Moat

Rye Court
Farm

River Severn

Severn Way

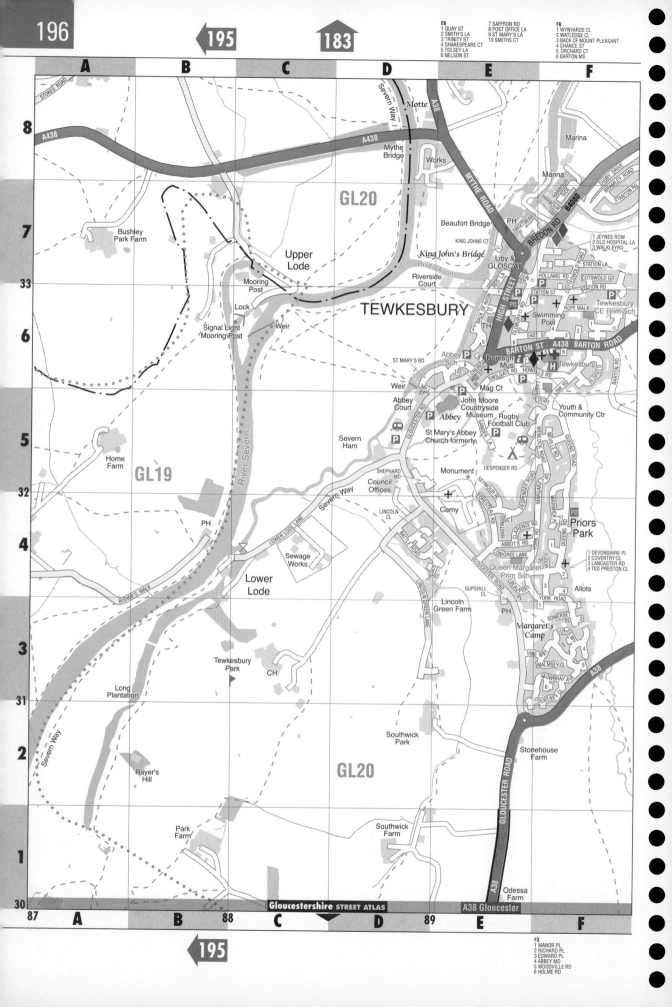

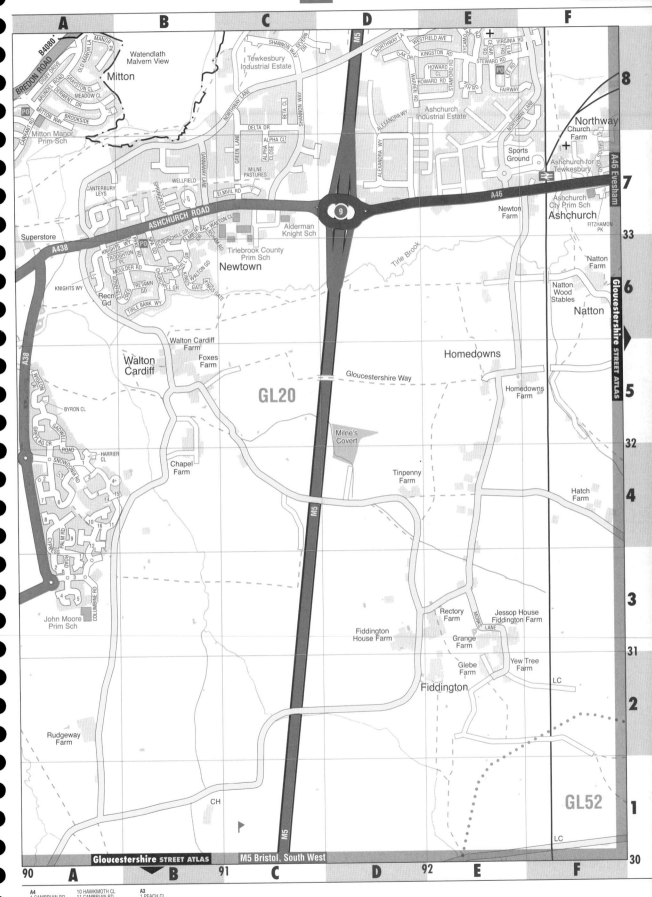

A4
1 CAMBRIAN RD
2 MILLENNIUM CL
3 BUCKINGHAM CL
4 LEXINGTON CL
5 ARLINGTON RD
6 CLIFFORD AVE
7 LONGTOWN RD
8 HOLMOAK CL
9 LAUREL AV
10 HAWKMOTH CL
11 CAMBRIAN RD
12 BELLFLOWER RD
13 HEVER CL
14 MUSKET CL
15 CHARLES CL
16 WOODRUSH RD

A3
1 PEACH CL
2 LIME RD
3 MONTEREY RD
4 THATCHAM RD
5 RICHMOND RD

Ludlow

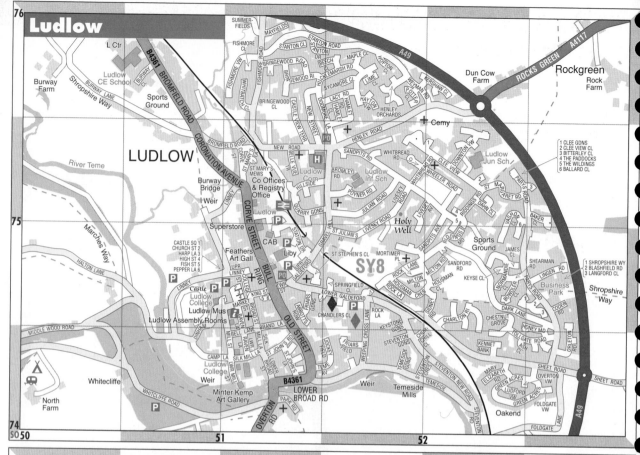

Stratford-upon-Avon

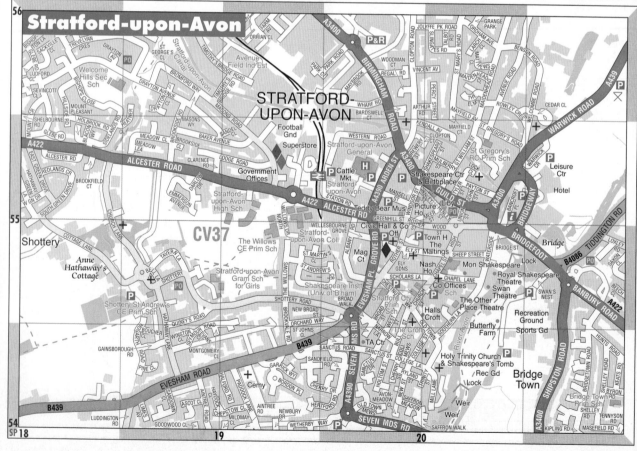

Index

Church Rd 6 Beckenham BR2.........53 C6

Place name	**Location number**	**Locality, town or village**	**Postcode district**	**Page and grid square**
May be abbreviated on the map	Present when a number indicates the place's position in a crowded area of mapping	Shown when more than one place has the same name	District for the indexed place	Page number and grid reference for the standard mapping

Public and commercial buildings are highlighted in magenta   **Places of interest** are highlighted in blue with a star★

Abbreviations used in the index

Acad	Academy	Comm	Common	Gd	Ground	L	Leisure	Prom	Prom
App	Approach	Cott	Cottage	Gdn	Garden	La	Lane	Rd	Road
Arc	Arcade	Cres	Crescent	Gn	Green	Liby	Library	Recn	Recreation
Ave	Avenue	Cswy	Causeway	Gr	Grove	Mdw	Meadow	Ret	Retail
Bglw	Bungalow	Ct	Court	H	Hall	Meml	Memorial	Sh	Shopping
Bldg	Building	Ctr	Centre	Ho	House	Mkt	Market	Sq	Square
Bsns, Bus	Business	Ctry	Country	Hospl	Hospital	Mus	Museum	St	Street
Bvd	Boulevard	Cty	County	HQ	Headquarters	Orch	Orchard	Sta	Station
Cath	Cathedral	Dr	Drive	Hts	Heights	Pal	Palace	Terr	Terrace
Cir	Circus	Dro	Drove	Ind	Industrial	Par	Parade	TH	Town Hall
Cl	Close	Ed	Education	Inst	Institute	Pas	Passage	Univ	University
Cnr	Corner	Emb	Embankment	Int	International	Pk	Park	Wk, Wlk	Walk
Coll	College	Est	Estate	Intc	Interchange	Pl	Place	Wr	Water
Com	Community	Ex	Exhibition	Junc	Junction	Prec	Precinct	Yd	Yard

Index of localities, towns and villages

A

Abberley	60 F4
Abberton	133 A8
Abbeydale	70 F5
Abbots Morton	121 B2
Abbot's Salford	135 D1
Abbotswood	142 E7
Ab Lench	133 E4
Acton	64 A3
Aggborough	27 F4
Aldington	162 D5
Alfrick	124 F7
Alfrick Pound	124 E5
Alvechurch	51 B6
Alveley	1 C5
Amblecote	5 F7
Ankerdine Hill	111 D6
Areley Kings	43 E1
Arrow	122 F6
Arrowfield Top	34 C2
Ashchurch	197 F7
Ashton under Hill	174 B1
Aspley Heath	53 D2
Astley	62 C4
Astley Cross	62 E8
Aston Bank	37 E1
Aston Fields	68 A7
Aston on Carrant	185 C1
Aston Somerville	175 F1
Aston Subedge	178 F7
Astwood Dodderhill	86 A7
Astwood Worcester	115 D7
Astwood Bank	89 F1
Atch Lench	134 C2
Avonbank	158 E6

B

Badger's Hill	146 D6
Badsey	162 E3
Bank's Green	69 B3
Bank Street	76 B2
Barbourne	115 A6
Barnard's Green	153 B8
Barnettbrook	29 D5
Barnt Green	50 A7
Bartley Green	18 E8
Barton	136 F3
Bastonford	127 A2
Batchley	70 B3
Bateman's Green	35 E6
Battenton Green	82 E8
Baughton	170 B8
Baynhall	141 C3
Bayton	40 B7
Bayton Common	40 E6
Beach Hay	23 F1
Beckford	186 D4
Beech Lanes	9 E6
Belbroughton	30 B7
Bell End	31 C7
Belle Vale	7 E5
Bell Heath	31 E8
Bengeworth	161 F3
Beoley	71 D7
Berrington	55 B3
Berrington Green	55 C2
Berrow	180 C1
Berrow Green	98 F1
Berry Hill	84 E5
Besford	157 C6
Bevere	102 A3

Bewdley	26 B2
Bickley	38 B2
Bickmarsh	149 E8
Bidford-on-Avon	136 E4
Billesley	21 C6
Billesley Common	21 A5
Birch Acre	52 D7
Birch Berrow	79 C6
Birchen Coppice	27 B1
Birch Green	155 D8
Birchwood	124 E1
Birdsgreen	1 D7
Birlingham	158 B2
Birmingham	20 C5
Birtsmorton	180 D4
Birts Street	180 A6
Bishampton	132 F3
Blackheath	7 E8
Blackminster	162 E6
Blackmore End	154 B5
Blackpole	115 F7
Blackstone	26 D1
Blackwell	50 A5
Blakebrook	27 B6
Blakedown	14 C2
Blakeshall	12 E7
Bliss Gate	41 F6
Bluntington	29 E1
Bockleton	93 E7
Boraston	37 D1
Boraston Dale	37 C1
Boreley	82 C7
Bournes Green	30 C2
Bourneville	19 E7
Bournheath	48 D8
Bouts	108 B2
Bowling Green	127 B3

Bradley Green	106 F6
Brand Green	166 C7
Brandwood End	20 D4
Bransford	126 C6
Branson's Cross	53 C2
Brayswick	140 C8
Bredicot	117 B2
Bredon	184 F6
Bredon's Hardwick	184 C4
Bredon's Norton	172 A3
Bretforton	163 C5
Brickfields	115 F6
Bricklehampton	159 E1
Bridge End	193 F4
Brierley Hill	6 F8
Bringsty Common	110 C3
Broad Alley	65 D3
Broad Common	65 B4
Broadfields	55 A5
Broad Green	50 A1
Broad Green Broadwas	112 E4
Broad Heath	77 A7
Broad Marston	151 A2
Broadmore Green	127 A8
Broadwas	112 C3
Broadwaters	13 B1
Broadway	190 D8
Brockamin	125 D8
Brockencote	46 D8
Brockmanton	92 B4
Bromsgrove	67 D7
Brook End	141 D8
Broom	136 B8
Broombank	39 C1
Broome	15 A2
Broom Hill	30 D3
Brotheridge Green	168 C7

Broughton Green	105 F7
Broughton Hackett	117 F2
Bryan's Green	65 D5
Buckbury	182 A1
Buckland	190 A4
Buckridge	24 A1
Bugle Gate	63 C4
Burcot	49 E4
Burford	55 E6
Burlish Park	43 F6
Bury End	190 C6
Bushley	183 A1
Bushley Green	182 E2
Buttonoak	10 A1

C

Cakebole	46 B5
California	9 F2
Callow End	140 F7
Callow Hill	89 A7
Callow Hill Rock	41 E8
Camer's Green	179 E3
Carpenter's Hill	52 F1
Castle Hill	99 E3
Castlemorton	180 C7
Castlemorton Common	167 A3
Catchems End	26 C5
Catshill	49 A8
Caunsall	13 B7
Chaceley	195 D2
Chadbury	147 A2
Chaddesley Corbett	46 E8
Chadwick	63 E7
Chandler's Cross	166 F1

Charford 67 F7
Charlton 160 E8
Charlton Hartlebury . . .44 E3
Chase End Street 179 D3
Chatley 102 C7
Chawson 84 C2
Cherry Orchard 128 D7
Childswickham 176 E2
Church End Hanley
 Castle 169 A8
Church End Twyning . .183 E4
Church Hil 71 C6
Churchill 14 C3
Churchill 130 E7
Church Lench 134 B3
Cladswell 108 F2
Claines 102 C2
Clanbrook 4 A7
Cleeve Prior 149 A7
Clent 15 F3
Cleobury Mortimer . . .22 C4
Clevelode 140 E2
Clifton 141 B1
Clifton Hill 98 B6
Clifton upon Teme . . .97 E8
Cobbler's Corner 112 F7
Cobley Hill 50 E4
Cock Bevington 135 B6
Cofton Hackett 33 C3
Cold Elm 195 A6
Coldheart 93 A6
Coles Green 125 D4
Collett's Green 127 C4
Collington 95 E5
Colwall Green 166 A8
Colwall Stone 152 A2
Comberton 28 B5
Comhampton 63 F2
Compton 3 B6
Conderton 186 A7
Cookhill 109 A1
Cookley 13 A6
Cooksey Corner 66 C5
Cooksey Green 66 B8
Coombeswood 8 C7
Copcut Droitwich 103 D8
Copcut Salwarpe 103 C7
Coreley 37 D8
Corse Lawn 194 E2
Cotheridge 113 B2
Cotteridge 19 E5
Coughton 109 F5
Crabbs Cross 89 A6
Cradley 7 D6
Cradley Heath 7 D8
Cranhill 137 D7
Cropthorne 160 B6
Cross Bank 42 A7
Crossway Green 63 F6
Crowcroft 125 D1
Crowle 117 E4
Crowle Green 117 E6
Crown East 114 A2
Cruise Hill 88 D4
Crumpfiled 88 E8
Crumpton Hill 138 B6
Cutnall Green 65 B6

D

Dagtail End 89 E3
Darbys Green 111 E5
Dawshill 127 C5
Dayhouse Bank 17 A1
Deabley 123 B8
Deblin's Green 140 B7
Defford 157 D3
Diglis 128 B8
Dines Green 114 C2
Ditchford Bank 87 E5
Doddenham 112 A5
Dodford 48 A5
Dordale 30 E1
Dormston 119 F8
Dorsington 150 E8
Doverdale 64 E1
Dowles 25 F6
Drakelow 12 B5
Drakes Broughton . . .144 A6
Drakes Cross 36 A6
Draycott 141 C4
Drayton 30 B4
Droitwich Spa 84 C4
Druggers End 167 C1
Duckswich 168 E4
Dumbleton 187 F5
Dunhampstead 104 C5
Dunhampton 64 A1
Dunley 62 B7

Dunnington 135 D7
Dunsley 4 C4
Dunstall Common 156 C3

E

Eachway 32 F6
Eardiston 59 B5
Earl's Common 105 F3
Earl's Croome 155 F1
Earlswood 53 F8
Eastham 57 F6
Eckington 171 F7
Edgiock 108 D5
Edvin Loach 96 B1
Edwyn Ralph 95 C1
Egdon 130 D3
Eggs Tump 192 C8
Elcock's Brook 88 E5
Eldersfield 193 E3
Elmbridge 65 F4
Elmley Castle 173 E7
Elmley Lovett 65 A8
Elms Green 60 B2
Enfield 70 D5
Evendine 166 A7
Evesham 161 B5

F

Fairfield 31 D3
Fairfield Evesham 161 D2
Fairfield Wolverley
 and Cookley 12 B3
Far Forest 24 B2
Feckenham 107 E7
Fenn Green 1 E3
Fernhill Heath 102 F3
Fiddington 197 E2
Fingerpost 24 D1
Finstall 49 D1
Fladbury 146 B1
Fladbury Cross 146 A3
Flyford Flavell 119 D2
Foley Park 27 C2
Footrid 39 E2
Forshaw Heath 53 C7
Forthampton 195 E6
Foster's Green 87 D7
Four Pools 161 E1
Foxlydiate 69 F3
Franche 12 C1
Frankley 18 B2
Frankley 18 B5
Frankley Green 18 A5
Frankley Hill 17 F3
Frith Common 59 A8
Frog Pool 81 E8
Frogsmarsh 193 C5

G

Gadfield Elm 193 B3
Gallows Green 86 B2
Gallowstree Elm 4 A6
Gilbert's End 154 C1
Gilver's Lane 168 B7
Golder Field 92 F6
Good's Green 11 A7
Goom's Hill 121 A2
Goosehill Green 105 B7
Gorst Hill 41 E7
Grafton 186 E7
Grafton Flyford 119 B5
Great Comberton 158 F1
Great Malvern 139 D2
Great Washbourne . . .186 E2
Great Witley 61 B1
Greenhill 28 A8
Greenhill Evesham . . .161 E7
Greenlands 90 A8
Green Lane 90 C6
Green Street Kempsey .141 F6
Green Street Ripple . .170 A5
Greenway 41 E2
Greystones 149 D8
Griffin's Hill 19 D8
Grimes Hill 36 B4
Grimley 101 F6
Guarlford 154 A7
Guller's End 182 C3

H

Habberley 27 A6
Haden Cross 8 A8
Hadley 83 E4
Hadzor 85 D1
Hagley 15 D6
Halesowen 8 D4
Hales Park 25 F3
Hall Flat 49 C7
Hall Green 21 E8
Hallow 101 D1
Hallow Heath 101 D3
Ham Green 88 E4
Hampton 161 A3
Hampton Lovett 84 D7
Hanbury 87 A4
Hanley Castle 154 F1
Hanley Child 76 E7
Hanley Swan 154 A2
Hanley William 77 F3
Harbours Hill 86 F8
Hardwick Green 194 A6
Harpley 96 F7
Hartle 30 F6
Hartlebury 45 A2
Hartlebury Common . . .44 C2
Hartsgreen 2 C4
Harvington 29 B2
Harvington 148 A7
Hasbury 7 E3
Hasluck's Green 21 F2
Hatfield Hatfield and
 Newhampton 93 E4
Hatfield Norton Juxta
 Kempsey 129 B1
Hawbridge 143 A4
Hawcross 192 C1
Hawford 102 B6
Hawkesley 34 F8
Hawne 8 A5
Haybridge 38 C8
Hayley Green 7 C1
Headless Cross 89 D8
Headley Heath 35 C6
Heath Green 52 F3
Heightington 42 D3
High Green 156 A7
High Lane 96 D6
Highter's Heath 21 B2
Highwood 57 F3
Hill Croome 170 D5
Hill End Droitwich Spa .85 B4
Hill End Twyning 184 A8
Hill Furze 146 B5
Hillpool 29 E5
Hill Side 99 B7
Himbleton 105 C2
Hindlip 103 B2
Hinton Cross 175 B5
Hinton on the Green . .175 A5
Hipplecote 111 E8
Hoden 149 D4
Holbeache 11 A2
Holberrow Green 108 B3
Holdfast 182 C8
Hollow Court 106 D1
Hollybed Common . . .179 F7
Hollybush 179 C6
Holly Green 169 E7
Hollywood 36 B8
Holt 82 D2
Holt End 71 F8
Holt Fleet 82 C4
Holt Heath 82 B3
Holy Cross 15 E2
Homedowns 197 E5
Homer Hill 7 B6
Honeybourne 164 A5
Hoobrook 27 C8
Hook Bank 168 A5
Hopwood 34 B3
Horsham 111 C8
Howsen 113 D1
Huddington 118 C7
Hunnington 17 B8
Hunt End 89 C5
Hurcott 28 C8
Hurst Green 8 F8

I

Illey 17 E8
Inkberrow 120 F7
Inkford 35 F1
Interfield 138 F3
Ipsley 71 C2
Iron Cross 135 C5

Iverley 14 B7

K

Kemerton 185 D7
Kempsey 141 D7
Kendal End 33 C2
Kersoe 174 A5
Kerswell Green 141 D2
Kidderminster 27 D4
King's End 127 D4
King's Green 192 D8
King's Heath 20 E7
King's Norton 19 E2
Kingswood Lower 24 C7
Kington 120 A4
Kinnersley 156 A3
Kinsham 185 A3
Kinver 3 F4
Kitwell 18 A7
Knighton 121 D6
Knighton on Teme . . .57 A8
Knightwick 111 A3
Knowle Fields 121 E8
Kyre 75 F3
Kyre Green 75 C2
Kyrewood 56 B4

L

Ladywood 103 A7
Lakeside 71 A3
Lapal 8 F3
Laughern Hill 99 E2
Laverton 189 E3
Lea End 34 F3
Leapgate 44 E5
Leigh 126 A7
Leigh Sinton 125 F2
Leigh Sinton House
 Farm 126 A2
Lem Hill 24 A2
Lenchwick 147 C3
Leysters 73 E4
Libbery 118 E3
Lickey 33 A3
Lickey End 49 C6
Lickhill 43 E5
Lifford 20 B5
Lime Street 194 A1
Lincomb 63 C6
Lindridge 58 D7
Lineholt 63 D1
Lineholt Common 63 E3
Linkend 194 D2
Linley Green 123 B7
Linthurst 50 A6
Little Beckford 186 D2
Little Comberton 159 B3
Little Eastbury 114 D7
Little Hereford 54 C6
Little Inkberrow 120 C8
Little London 38 A3
Little Malvern 166 E6
Little Welland 167 F1
Little Witley 81 A4
Littleworth Feckenham . .88 B1
Littleworth Norton Juxta
 Kempsey 129 D1
Lodge Park 70 F2
Long Bank 25 C1
Longbridge 33 C4
Longdon 181 F5
Longdon Heath 168 F2
Longdon Hill End 168 C2
Long Green 195 A8
Longley Green 124 C1
Long Marston 151 C6
Lowbands 192 E3
Lower Bach 92 A7
Lower Bentley 87 E8
Lower Broadheath . . .113 C5
Lower Clent 15 D4
Lower Hook 168 B5
Lower Howsell 139 B6
Lower Illey 17 D7
Lower Lode 196 C4
Lower Moor 145 E3
Lower Sapey 97 B5
Lower Strensham 171 A6
Lower Town 102 E4
Lower Westmancote . .185 B7
Lower Wick 127 C6
Lower Wolverton 130 F2
Lower Wyche 152 F5
Low Habberley 26 F8

Lulsley 111 E4
Lydiate Ash 32 C3
Lye 6 E6
Lye Head 42 B7
Lyppard Grange 116 B4

M

Madeley Heath 31 E7
Madresfield 139 E4
Major's Green 36 D8
Malvern Common 153 B5
Malvern Link 139 B4
Malvern Wells 152 F1
Mamble 39 F3
Mappleborough Green .72 A1
Marl Bank 167 B6
Marlbrook 32 C1
Marlcliff 136 C2
Marsh Common 156 E1
Martin Hussingtree . . .103 C5
Martley 99 A4
Matchborough 71 E1
Meadow Green 110 F6
Menithwood 59 D7
Mere Green 86 D1
Mickleton 165 E4
Middle Littleton 148 F3
Middleton 54 B8
Middleton on the Hill . .73 A6
Middletown 90 D1
Milson 38 C6
Mitton 197 B8
Monkwood Green 100 E5
Moons Moat 71 F5
Morton Spirt 121 E2
Morton Underhill 107 E3
Moseley 101 A3
Mount Pleasant 88 D5
Murcot 176 C5
Mustow Green 28 F1

N

Napleton 141 E5
Nash 37 A4
Nash End 10 E8
Natton 197 F6
Naunton 170 B4
Naunton Beauchamp . .132 B5
Neen Savage 22 D7
Neens Hill 39 B4
Neen Sollars 39 A5
Netherton 174 A8
Newbridge Green 169 B3
New End 108 F4
Newland 139 C6
Newland Common . . .104 A5
Newnham Bridge 57 D7
Newtown Ashchurch . .197 C6
Newtown Droitwich . . .84 E4
Newtown Martley 112 B8
Nineveh Bayton 39 E8
Nineveh Kyre 75 E6
Noah's Green 107 C7
Norchard 64 A6
Northfield 19 B4
North Littleton 149 B3
North Piddle 119 B1
Northway 184 E2
Northwick 115 A8
Norton 5 D2
Norton Norton and
 Lenchwick 147 D4
Norton Norton Juxta
 Kempsey 129 C2
Noutard's Green 62 E2

O

Oakall Green 101 A6
Oakenshaw 89 E6
Ockeridge 80 F1
Oddingley 104 C4
Offenham 148 A1
Offenham Cross 162 C8
Offmore Farm 28 A6
Oldbury 9 C7
Oldfield 83 B6
Old Hills 140 E6
Old Storridge Common .124 F3
Old Swinford 6 A2
Oldwood 55 E2
Ombersley 83 A4
Orleton 59 B2

Outhill	72 E1
Outwood	47 B5
Overbury	185 F8
Overend	7 E6

P

Park End	42 D7
Park Farm	90 C8
Park Gate	48 B3
Pebworth	150 D2
Pedmore	6 B1
Pendock	193 B6
Pensax	60 B6
Pensham	158 C5
Peopleton	131 B2
Perryfields	48 E4
Pershore	144 C2
Phepson	105 C4
Picken End	154 B2
Pie Corner	95 D7
Pin's Green	139 E8
Pinvin	144 E6
Piper's End	182 B3
Piper's Hill	87 A7
Pirton	142 C3
Pixham	141 A6
Playley Green	192 C4
Podmoor	45 E5
Pole Elm	140 F8
Poolbrook	153 D6
Porchbrook	41 B2
Portway	53 A5
Portway Pendock	193 A8
Potter's Cross	4 A5
Pound Bank Malvern	153 D8
Pound Bank Rock	41 B8
Pound Green	10 B2
Powick	127 E5
Powick Hams	127 E5
Priestfield	154 C6
Primsland	104 A8
Priors Park	196 F4
Puckrup	183 D5
Pudleston	92 E4
Purshull Green	47 A3

Q

Quarry Bank	7 A8
Queenhill	182 D6
Quinton	8 F5

R

Radford	120 D3
Rainbow Hill	115 D5
Ramsden	143 E2
Ravenhills Green	111 E1
Redcross	46 C8
Redditch	70 C2
Red Hill	128 F8
Redmarley D'Abitot	192 A4
Rednal	33 C6
Rhydd	154 F6
Rhydd Green	154 E7
Ribbesford	26 B1
Ridgeacre	9 D6
Ripple	183 A8

Riverside	70 F6
Rochford	57 A6
Rock	41 C3
Romsley	17 A4
Romsley	2 A2
Romsley Hill	17 A2
Ronkswood	115 F2
Rous Lench	133 E7
Rowney Green	51 E3
Rubery	33 B7
Rumbush	36 E3
Rushbrook	53 D3
Rushock	46 C3
Rushwick	127 B8
Ryall	169 E6
Rye Street	180 A4

S

Sailors Bank	113 F8
Saintbury	178 B4
St George's	70 F4
St John's	114 F1
St Michaels	74 C8
St Peter The Great	128 E6
Sale Green	105 A1
Saleway	104 F4
Salford Priors	135 F3
Salwarpe	103 B8
Sambourne	90 B1
Sandford	155 D7
Sankyns Green	81 D6
Sapey Bridge	111 A5
Sapey Common	78 C5
Sedgeberrow	175 A2
Selly Oak	19 B8
Severn Stoke	155 D5
Sharpway Gate	86 E7
Shatterford	11 C7
Shell	105 E4
Shelsley Beauchamp	79 C2
Shelsley Walsh	79 A3
Shenley Fields	18 E7
Shenstone	45 F8
Sheriff's Lench	146 F7
Shernal Green	104 D7
Sherrard's Green	139 D1
Shoulton	101 A2
Shrawley	81 E6
Shurnock	108 B6
Shuthonger	183 D3
Sidemoor	48 F4
Silver Street	35 F5
Sinton	83 B2
Sinton Green	101 B6
Slades Green	182 C2
Sledge Green	181 A1
Smallwood	70 E2
Smethwick	9 E8
Smite Hill	103 F2
Smith End Green	125 F5
Sneachill	130 B7
Snead Common	60 C7
Sneads Green	64 E4
Snuff Hill	31 D1
Solihull	21 E2
Solihull Lodge	21 E2
Southcrest	70 D1
South Littleton	148 E1
Spennells	28 A2
Spernall	91 B1
Spetchley	116 F1
Springfield	21 E5

Spurtree	56 A7
Stakenbridge	14 E3
Stambermill	6 C6
Stanbrook	140 E8
Stanford Bridge	78 F8
Stanford on Teme	78 C8
Stanklyn	28 D2
Stanley	1 A3
Stanton	189 D1
Staple Hill	49 C8
Stirchley	20 B7
Stitchin's Hill	125 B4
Stock Green	106 F2
Stockton on Teme	59 E3
Stock Wood	107 C2
Stoke Bliss	76 E2
Stoke Heath	67 D5
Stoke Pound	68 A4
Stoke Prior	67 C4
Stoke Wharf	67 D3
Stoke Works	67 C1
Stone	28 D3
Stonebow	144 A7
Stonehall	142 C6
Stonepits	120 D7
Stoney Hill	49 A2
Stony Cross	54 B3
Storridge	138 A6
Stoulton	143 B8
Stourbridge	5 D4
Stourport-on-Severn	43 C6
Stourton	4 F7
Stratford	170 C2
Strensham	171 C6
Structon's Heath	80 E8
Studley	90 F4
Suckley	124 A3
Suckley Green	123 F7
Suckley Knowl	123 E7
Summerfield	45 A8
Summerhill	27 A5
Sutton Farm	27 B4
Sweet Green	76 E2
Swinesherd	129 B8
Swinley Green	194 F5
Sytchampton	64 A1

T

Tanner's Green	36 A1
Tanwood	30 B2
Tanworth-In-Arden	53 F2
Tardebigge	69 B7
Tedstone Delamere	97 A2
Tedstone Wafer	96 D3
Ten Acres	20 B8
Tenbury Wells	55 F4
Terry's Green	53 F7
Tewkesbury	196 D6
The Bourne	119 E5
The Burf	62 F4
The Grove	169 F6
The Hook	168 C6
The Hyde	168 F5
The Lakes	25 F4
The Mythe	183 D1
The Ramplings	182 C1
The Walshes	43 F1
Thomas Town	90 B3
Thornbury	94 E4
Throckmorton	145 E8
Tibberton	117 A7
Tidbury Green	36 E4

Tilsop	37 C7
Timberhonger	47 F1
Titton	63 D8
Tolladine	115 F4
Torton	45 B5
Trimpley	11 C1
Trotshill	116 D4
Tunnel Hill	168 F5
Turleygreen	1 C7
Turves Green	19 A1
Twyford	147 E1
Twyning	183 F7
Twyning Green	184 B6

U

Uckinghall	169 F1
Ullington	149 F3
Uphampton	82 E6
Upper Arley	10 D5
Upper Bentley	69 A1
Upper Catshill	32 B2
Upper Colwall	152 D4
Upper Ham	169 D4
Upper Hamnish	92 A3
Upper Haselor	174 E8
Upper Howsell	138 F6
Upper Lode	196 C7
Upper Moor	145 C4
Upper Rochford	57 A4
Upper Sapey	77 E3
Upper Strensham	171 A4
Upper Welland	166 F6
Upper Wick	127 C7
Upper Wolverton	130 C2
Upper Wyche	152 E4
Upton Snodsbury	118 C1
Upton upon Severn	169 D5
Upton Warren	67 A3

W

Wadborough	143 A4
Walcot	144 B5
Walker's Heath	20 B1
Walkwood	89 B6
Walton Cardiff	197 B5
Walton Pool	16 A2
Wants Green	112 C7
Wapping	90 E5
Waresley	64 A8
Warley Woods	9 E8
Warndon	116 B6
Warstock	21 C3
Washford	90 E7
Weatheroak Hill	35 B1
Weavers Hill	89 C4
Webheath	70 A2
Weethley	122 A4
Weethley Bank	122 B2
Weethley Gate	122 B1
Welland	167 C4
Welland Stone	168 B2
Weoley Castle	19 A8
Westacre	84 D3
West End	190 C6
West Hagley	15 A5
West Heath	34 B7
Westlands	84 D5
West Malvern	138 C1
Westmancote	185 B8

Weston-sub-Edge	178 D7
Whatmore	37 C3
Whitbourne	111 A6
Whitbourne Ford	98 A1
White End	180 B1
White Ladies Aston	130 E6
Whiteleaved Oak	179 B4
Whitlock's End	36 E6
Whittington Kinver	4 D2
Whittington	129 B6
Whyle	92 D6
Wichenford	100 B6
Wick	159 A7
Wick Episcopi	127 E7
Wickhamford	176 E8
Wilden	44 D6
Wildmoor	31 F4
Willersey	177 F4
Willow Green	99 C1
Windmill Hill	143 D7
Winnall	63 B4
Winterfold	46 B8
Winyates	71 E2
Wirehill	90 B5
Withybed Green	50 F6
Withymoor Village	6 C8
Witnells End	11 C8
Witton	84 E1
Witton Hill	80 D1
Wofferwood Common	123 A4
Wolferlow	96 B8
Wollaston	5 E6
Wollescote	6 E4
Wolverley	12 C5
Wood Bevington	135 B8
Woodcock Hill	18 E8
Woodcote Green	47 C6
Wood End	53 F3
Woodgate	68 B2
Woodgate	9 A1
Woodgates Green	38 A1
Woodgate Valley	9 C3
Woodgreen	116 C5
Wood Green	62 E9
Woodhampton	54 E7
Woodmancote	157 B2
Wood Norton	146 F3
Woodrow	29 D3
Woodrow	90 B7
Woodsfield	139 F6
Woolmere Green	87 A3
Woonton	73 B1
Worcester	115 B1
Worlds End	101 A4
World's End	9 D5
Worles Common	60 B6
Wormington	188 D6
Worms Ash	48 C6
Wribbenhall	26 B4
Wychbold	66 E1
Wynds Point	166 C6
Wyre Piddle	145 E3
Wythall	36 B3

Y

Yardley Wood	21 E5
Yarhampton	61 F3
Yarhampton Cross	61 D3
Yearsett	123 C8
Yieldingtree	29 F8

A

Ab Lench Rd WR10 ....133 F4
Abberley Ave DY13 .....43 D1
Abberley Cl
Halesowen B63 ....7 F2
Redditch B98 ....71 C5
Abberley Dr WR9 ......84 E1
Abberley Hall WR6 ......60 F1
Abberley Parochial Prim Sch
WR6 ....60 F4
Abberley Rd B68 ....9 B8
Abberley View 4 WR3 ..115 C5
Abberton Cl B63 ....8 C3
Abberton House 4 B97 .70 A4
Abberton Rd WR10 ....133 A4
Abbey Cl
Bromsgrove B60 ....49 C2
3 Callow End WR2 ......140 F8
Abbey Cres B63 ....7 D4
Abbey Int Colleges
WR14 ....166 E8
Abbey La WR11 ....161 C3
Abbey Mdw 4 GL20 ......196 F3
Abbey Pk Fst & Mid Sch
WR10 ....158 C8
Abbey Rd
Evesham WR11 ....161 C3
Great Malvern WR14 ......152 F8
Halesowen B63 ....7 C4
Kidderminster DY11 ......27 A6
Pershore WR10 ....158 D8
Redditch B97 ....70 E4
Worcester WR2 ....114 F1
Abbey Sch GL20 ....196 E6
Abbey Trad Ind Area
B97 ....70 E5
Abbey View Rd WR10 ..144 E5
Abbeycroft WR10 .....158 C8
Abbeydale Rd B31 ......19 A2
Abbeyfields Dr B80 .....90 E6
Abbot Chyryton's Pl 7
WR11 ....161 C4
Abbot Rd B63 ....16 C8
Abbot's Rd GL20 ....196 E4
Abbots Cl WR2 ....114 E3
Abbots Ct Dr GL20 .....183 E5
Abbots Grange 2
WR10 ....158 C8
Abbots Rd
Birmingham B14 ....20 E7
Pershore WR10 ....158 C7
Abbots Wood Cl B98 ...72 A3
Abbotswood WR11 ....161 D8
Abbotts Cl DY13 ....44 D6
Abdon Ave B29 ....19 C7
Acacia Ave DY12 ....26 C3
Acacia Cl WR4 ....115 E5
Acacia Ct DY8 ....5 E6
Acacia Rd B30 ....19 E8
Acanthus Rd B98 ....71 F6
Acheson Rd B28, B90 ....21 F3
Ackleton Gr B29 ....9 F1
Aconbury Cl WR5 .....116 B3
Acorn Cl
Birmingham, Bournville
B30 ....19 E8
7 Colwall Stone WR13 ...152 B2
Acorn Ct B45 ....33 D7
Acorn Gdns B30 ....20 A7
Acorn Gr WR10 ....144 D2
Acorn Rd Catshill B61 ....49 B8
Halesowen B62 ....8 C8
Acorns The B61 ....49 A8
Acre La 3 Droitwich WR9 .84 E3
Redditch B97 ....69 E2
Acre The WR8 ....157 E3
Acreage WR6 ....110 F6
Acres Rd DY5 ....6 E8
Acton Cl B98 ....71 D5
Adam St DY11 ....27 C5
Adam's Hill DY9 ....15 E4
Adams Brook Dr B32 .....9 B1
Adams Ct DY10 ....28 A7
Adams Hill B32 ....9 B1
Adams House 3 DY11 ...27 C6
Addenbrook House B64 ..7 F8
Addenbrooke Cres
DY11 ....27 A1
Addison Rd
Birmingham, King's Heath
B14 ....20 F7
Worcester WR3 ....115 C6
Addyes Way WR9 .....103 E8
Adelaide Cl
8 Kempsey WR5 ....141 C6
11 Worcester WR3 ......115 B6
Adelaide St B97 ....70 D4
Admiral Pl WR5 ....128 F5
Adrian Cl 3 WR9 ....85 A1
Adstone Gr B31 ....19 A1
Agatha Gdns WR3 ......103 A2
Agenoria Dr DY8 ....5 F5
Aggborough Cres DY10 ..27 E3
Aggborough Stadium
(Kidderminster Harriers FC)
DY10 ....27 F4
Agmore La B60 ....50 B3
Agmore Rd B60 ....50 B4
Ainsdale Cl DY8 ....5 F2
Ainsdale Gdns B63 ....7 D2
Aintree Cl Catshill B61 ...32 A1
Kidderminster DY11 ......27 D8
Aintree Rd WR10 ......144 E4
Aire Croft B31 ....19 B1
Albany Cl DY10 ....28 B6
Albany Ct 1 B62 ....9 A7
Albany Rd WR3 ....115 D4
Albany Terr WR1 ....115 B4
Albemarle Rd DY8 ....5 F2
Albert Bradbeer Inf Sch
B31 ....33 F7
Albert Bradbeer Jun Sch
B31 ....33 F7
Albert Cl B80 ....90 E4
Albert Dr B63 ....7 F2
Albert Pk Mews WR14 ..138 F3
Albert Pk Rd WR14 ....138 F4
Albert Rd
Birmingham, King's Heath
B14 ....20 F7
Bromsgrove B61 ....67 E8
2 Colwall Stone WR13 ..152 A1
Evesham WR11 ....161 C5
Halesowen B63 ....7 F3
Kidderminster DY10 ......27 F6
Oldbury B68 ....9 C8
Worcester WR5 ....115 D1
Albert Rd N WR14 .....138 F2
Albert Rd S WR14 .....153 A8
Albert St
7 Droitwich WR9 ....84 E3
Redditch B97 ....70 E5
Stourbridge DY8 ....5 F5
Stourbridge, Lye DY9 .....6 E5
Alberta Cl WR2 ....127 E7
Albion Rd WR14 ....138 E4
Albion Terr B50 ....136 C7
Alborn Cres B38 ....34 D8
Albright & Wilson House
B68 ....9 E7
Albright La HR8 ....179 A1
Albrighton Rd B63 ....7 F3
Albury Rd B80 ....90 E4
Alcester Gdns B14 ......20 F7
Alcester Heath B49 ....109 C4
Alcester Highway B98 ..89 F8
Alcester Rd
Feckenham B96 ....107 E7
Finstall B60 ....49 F1
Hollywood B47 ....35 F5
Lickey End B60 ....49 D5
Portway B48 ....52 F7
Studley B80 ....90 E3
Tardebigge B60, B97 .....69 B7
Alcester Rd S
Birmingham, Alcester
Lane's End B14 ....20 E6
Birmingham, Highter's Heath
B14 ....20 F2
Alcester St B98 ....70 E4
Aldborough La 4 B97 ...70 B5
Aldbourne Way B38 .....34 E7
Aldbury Rd B14 ....21 A3
Aldeford Dr DY5 ....6 D8
Alder Ave DY10 ....27 E8
Alder Cl Hollywood B47 ..36 B6
Worcester WR4 ....115 D4
Alder Gr Droitwich WR9 .103 F8
Evesham WR11 ....161 F2
Halesowen B62 ....8 E6
Alder La B30 ....19 C6
Alder Way B60 ....49 B2
Alderbrook Cl B97 ......70 B5
Alderbrook Rd 1 WR9 ...84 C1
Alderhanger La B98 .....72 C8
Alderlea Cl DY8 ....6 A2
Alderley Rd B61 ....67 D8
Alderman Knight Sch
GL20 ....197 C7
Aldermans La B97 ......70 B6
Aldermere Rd DY11 .....27 C8
Alderminster Cl B97 ....89 E4
Alderney Gdns B38 .....19 D1
Alders Cl B98 ....71 A3
Alders Dr B98 ....71 F4
Alders The B62 ....16 F4
Aldersey Cl 10 WR5 ....128 D6
Aldersey Rd WR5 ......128 D6
Aldersmead Rd B31 .....19 C1
Aldgate Dr DY5 ....6 C7
Aldington Cl B98 ....70 F1
Aldridge Rd B68 ....9 B8
Alexander Ave WR9 .....84 D1
Alexander Cl B61 ....32 A1
Alexander Hill DY5 ......6 F8
Alexander Patterson Specl
Sch The DY10 ....13 C2
Alexander Rd WR2 .....115 A1
Alexandra Hospl The
B98 ....90 C6
Alexandra La WR14 ....138 F3
Alexandra Rd
Birmingham, Stirchley
B30 ....20 A7
Evesham WR11 ....161 A3
Great Malvern WR14 ....138 F3
Halesowen B63 ....7 F4
Alexandra Way GL20 ...197 D7
Alford Cl B45 ....33 C7
Alfred Ct B60 ....67 E2
Alfred St B14 ....20 F7
Alfreda Ave B47 ....36 A8
Alfreds Well B61 ....48 C6
Alhambra Rd B60 ....49 C1
Alicante Cl 1 WR14 .....139 B1
Alice Ottley Jun Sch The
WR1 ....115 B4
Alison Dr DY8 ....5 E3
Alison Rd B62 ....8 F3
All Saints Ave DY12 .....26 C4
All Saints Rd B14 ....20 E7
All Saints' CE Sch DY13 .44 D5
All Saints' Rd B61 ....49 A3
Allardene WR11 ....161 E3
Allen Cl B80 ....90 E3
Allendale Ave B80 ....90 E3
Allendale Cres B80 ......90 E3
Allendale Ct B80 ....90 E3
Allens Croft Prim Sch
B14 ....20 C5
Allens Croft Rd B14 ....20 C6
Allens Farm Rd B31 .....18 E3
Allensmore Cl B98 ......71 F2
Allesborough Dr 5
WR10 ....144 C1
Allesbrook Gdns
WR11 ....162 D2
Allwell Dr B14 ....20 F2
Allwood Gdns B32 ....9 A2
Allwood House B97 ....70 C3
Alma St Halesowen B63 ...7 C5
Worcester WR3 ....115 B6
Almond Ave DY11 ....27 B8
Almond Cl
Birmingham B29 ....19 A6
2 Evesham WR11 ......161 F2
Almond Way DY13 ......43 D5
Almonry Her Ctr★
WR11 ....161 D4
Alperton Dr DY9 ....6 E2
Alpha Cl GL20 ....197 C7
Alton Cl B97 ....70 B1
Alton Pk WR2 ....140 F7
Alton Rd WR5 ....128 E5
Alvechurch CE Fst & Mid Sch
B48 ....51 B6
Alvechurch Highway
Lydiate Ash B60 ....32 D2
Redditch B98 ....70 F3
Alvechurch House B60 ..49 B3
Alvechurch Rd
Birmingham B31 ....34 B7
Halesowen B63 ....7 F2
Alvechurch Sta B48 .....51 A4
Alveley Cl B98 ....71 D4
Alveley Prim Sch WV15 ..1 C6
Alveston Cl B98 ....71 C2
Alveston Grange GL55 .165 D3
Alveston Rd B47 ....36 A7
Alwold Ct B29 ....9 F2
Alwold Rd B29 ....9 F2
Amber Terr DY10 ....27 F5
Amber Way B62 ....8 C6
Ambergate Cl 8 B97 ....70 B5
Amberley Cl WR4 ......115 F7
Amblecote Prim Sch
DY8 ....5 F7
Amblecote Rd
Brierley Hill DY5 ....6 D8
Kidderminster DY10 ......28 B5
Ambleside B32 ....9 C1
Ambleside Dr
Brierley Hill DY5 ....6 C8
Worcester WR4 ....115 F5
Ambleside Way B60 ....49 B1
Ambrose Cl WR2 ....114 D3
Amersham Cl B32 ....9 E5
Amery Cl WR5 ....128 D8
Amos Gdns WR4 ....116 C3
Amos Rd DY9 ....6 F2
Amphlett Ct 1 B60 ......49 A2
Amphlett Way WR9 .....85 E8
Amroth Cl B45 ....33 B7
Amroth Gdns 7 WR4 ...116 B7
Amwell Gr B14 ....20 F3
Anchor La
3 Fladbury WR10 ......146 A1
Harvington WR11 ......148 B6
Anchorfields DY10 ......27 F6
Andressy Mews B61 .....49 A5
Andrew Cl WR2 ....114 E4
Andrew Rd B63 ....8 A3
Andrews Cl DY5 ....6 E8
Andrews Dr 2 WR11 ...161 C2
Angel Pas DY8 ....6 A5
Angel Pl 9 WR1 ....115 B3
Angel St
Bentley Pauncefoot B97 ...88 C8
Upper Bentley B97 ....69 B1
Worcester WR1 ....115 B3
Angelo House B13 ......21 D7
Ankadine Rd DY8 ....6 B6
Ankerage Gn WR4 ......116 B4
Ankerdine Ave 1 DY13 ..43 D1
Ankerdine Ct B63 ....8 A3
Ankerdine Rd WR2 .....113 D5
Ann Rd B47 ....36 A3
Anne Cres 1 WR11 ....161 E2
Annscroft B38 ....19 D2
Ansley Cl B98 ....71 F1
Anton Cl DY12 ....26 D5
Apley Rd DY8 ....5 E7
Apollo Rd DY9 ....7 A5
Apperley Way B63 ....7 B7
Appian Cl B14 ....20 E5
Apple Orch Cl WR14 ...139 C1
Apple Orch The 3 GL20 184 E1
Apple Tree Cl
Crowle WR7 ....117 F4
Kidderminster DY10 .....28 B7
Apple Tree Rd 3 WR10 .144 D2
Apple Tree Wlk WR9 ....83 A4
Appleby Cl B14 ....20 D5
Appleton Ave DY8 ....6 A2
Appleton Cl B30 ....19 E8
Appleton House B31 ....18 E5
Appletree Cl B31 ....18 F1
Appletree La
Inkberrow WR7 ....121 A5
Redditch B97 ....70 B5
Appletrees Cres B61 ....49 A5
Apsley Cl B68 ....9 A7
Apsley Croft B38 ....20 B2
Apsley Rd B68 ....9 A7
Aqueduct La B48 ....50 F7
Aqueduct Rd B90 ....21 E1
Arboretum Rd WR1 ...115 C3
Arbour Cl GL55 ....165 D3
Archer Cl
Great Malvern WR14 ....138 E4
Studley B80 ....90 D4
Archer Ct DY9 ....6 E2
Archer Rd
Birmingham B14 ....21 C4
Redditch B98 ....70 E4
Archer Terr B97 ....70 C1
Archer's Way WR15 .....55 E6
Archers Cl 8 WR9 ......84 E3
Ardarth Rd B38 ....20 A2
Arden Cl DY8 ....5 E7
Arden House B60 ....49 B3
Arden Leys B94 ....53 D2
Arden Rd
Birmingham, Rubery
B45 ....18 A1
Hollywood B47 ....36 A6
Worcester WR5 ....128 D5
Arden Way WV15 ....1 C5
Ardencote Rd B13 ....21 A6
Ardens Cl B98 ....72 A2
Ardingley Wlk DY5 ......6 B7
Ardley Rd B14 ....21 A5
Areley Comm DY13 .....43 E1
Areley Comm Fst Sch
DY13 ....43 E1
Areley Ct DY13 ....43 E2
Areley La DY13 ....43 E3
Arkle Cl WR9 ....104 B8
Arkle Rd WR9 ....104 B8
Arkwright Rd B32 ....9 C5
Arley Arboretum★
DY12 ....10 C6
Arley Cl
Kidderminster DY11 .....27 A2
Redditch B98 ....71 D5
Arley Dr DY8 ....5 E3
Arley La DY12 ....10 F6
Arley Sta DY12 ....10 C5
Arlington Ct DY8 ....6 B4
Arlington Gr B14 ....21 B2
Arlington Rd
Birmingham B14 ....21 B3
5 Walton Cardiff GL20 ..197 A4
Armstrong Cl DY8 ......6 B6
Arnold Gr B30 ....19 D4
Arosa Dr WR14 ....153 A5
Arran Pl WR5 ....128 F6
Arrow Croft WR9 ....84 E4
Arrow End WR11 ......149 A3
Arrow House 1 B68 .....9 B8
Arrow La WR11 ....148 F3
Arrow Rd N B98 ....71 A4
Arrow Rd S B98 ....71 A4
Arrow Vale Com High Sch
B98 ....71 E2
Arrow Valley Pk★ B98 ..71 B4
Arrow Wlk B38 ....20 B1
Arrowdale Rd B98 ....71 A3
Arrowfield Gn B38 ......34 D7
Arrowsmith Ave WR2 ..114 F3
Arthur Dr (Road 2)
DY11 ....27 E1
Arthur Dr DY11 ....44 E8
Arthur St B98 ....71 B3
Artingstall House B30 ..20 B8
Arum Cl 4 WR14 ......139 C3
Arundel Ct 13 B29 .....19 C7
Arundel Dr WR5 ....128 E8
Arundel Rd
Birmingham B14 ....21 A1
Bromsgrove B60 ....49 B1
Tewkesbury GL20 ......197 A8
Ascot Cl WR3 ....102 F3
Ascot Ct 11 B29 ....19 C7
Ascot Rd WR10 ....144 E4
Ascot Way B61 ....32 B1
Ash Ave WR4 ....115 E5
Ash Cl WR14 ....139 C3
Ash Ct DY8 ....6 A4
Ash Dr B61 ....32 B1
Ash Gr Evesham WR11 ..161 E2
Kidderminster DY11 ......27 B7
Stourbridge DY9 ....6 D3
14 Stourport-on-Severn
DY13 ....43 E4
Ash La Alvechurch B48 ...34 D2
Martin Hussingtree
WR3 ....103 C5
Ash Lea WR8 ....156 B1
Ash Rd GL20 ....197 E8
Ash Tree Rd
Birmingham B30 ....20 A6
Redditch B97 ....70 B5
Ashbourne Ridge B63 ....7 D5
Ashbrook Dr B45 ....33 B8
Ashbrook Gr B30 ....20 C8
Ashbrook Rd B30 ....20 C8
Ashburton Rd B14 ......20 D5
Ashbury Covert 3 B30 ...20 C3
Ashby WR4 ....116 C6
Ashchurch Cty Prim Sch
GL20 ....197 F7
Ashchurch for Tewkesbury
Sta GL20 ....197 F7
Ashchurch Ind Est
GL20 ....197 E8
Ashchurch Rd GL20 ....197 B7
Ashcott Cl B38 ....19 D2
Ashcroft Rd WR1 ......115 B4
Ashdale Ave WR10 ....144 D2
Ashdale Dr B14 ....21 A1
Ashdene Cl
Hartlebury DY11 ....45 A2
Kidderminster DY10 .....28 C5
Ashdown Cl
Birmingham, Frankley
B45 ....18 A2
7 Great Malvern WR14 ..139 B1
Worcester WR2 ....128 A7
Ashenden Cl 4 WR9 ...103 F8
Ashfield Cres DY9 ....7 A3
Ashfield Ct B38 ....19 E4
Ashfield Gr B63 ....7 E2
Ashfield House B28 .....21 E3
Ashgrove Cl B60 ....32 D1
Ashill Rd B45 ....33 B7
Ashley Cl DY8 ....5 D2
Ashley Ct B45 ....33 A1
Ashley Rd
Kidderminster DY10 .....13 B1
Worcester WR5 ....128 D6
Ashmead Dr B45 ......33 C4
Ashmead Rise B45 .....33 C4
Ashmore Rd B30 ....19 F5
Ashmores Cl B97 ......89 D5
Ashorne Cl B98 ....90 D8
Ashperton Cl B98 ......70 E1
Ashpool WR6 ....111 A6
Ashton Cl B97 ....70 B1
Ashton Rd GL20 ......186 D5
Ashton under Hill Fst Sch
WR11 ....187 B8
Ashville Dr B63 ....8 A5
Ashwater Dr B14 ....20 D2
Aspen Cl 3 WR11 .....161 F1
Aspen Gr B47 ....36 B5
Aspen Wlk DY13 ....43 E5
Aspens Way B61 ....49 A6
Aspley Heath B94 ......53 D2
Aspley Heath La B94 ...53 D2
Assarts La WR14 .....166 F7
Assarts Rd WR14 .....166 E7
Astbury Ct 4 B68 ....9 B7
Aster Ave DY11 ....12 D1
Astles Rock Wlk DY7 ....3 F3
Astley Ave B62 ....8 F6
Astley CE Prim Sch
DY13 ....62 C5
Astley Cl B98 ....90 A7
Astley Cres B62 ....8 F5
Astley Ct 8 DY13 ......62 E8
Astley Gdns DY13 ......62 E6
Astley Orch WR15 .....58 B5
Astley Rd B60 ....49 C1
Astley Vineyard★ DY13 ..62 F4
Aston Cl 1 WR5 ......141 C7
Aston Dr WR14 ....153 C6
Aston Fields Mid Sch
B60 ....68 C8
Aston Fields Trad Est 2
B60 ....67 F6
Aston Rd
Aston Subedge GL55 ...178 F7
Bromsgrove B60 ....67 F6
Astons Cl DY5 ....6 D7
Astons Fold DY5 ....6 D7
Astwood Bank Fst Sch
B96 ....89 E2
Astwood La
Astwood Bank B96 ......89 C2
Dodderhill WR9 ....85 F8
Feckenham B96 ....107 E8
Inkberrow B96 ....108 A8
Astwood Rd WR3 .....115 D5
Atch Lench Rd WR11 ..134 B3
Atcham Cl B98 ....71 F3
Atcheson Cl B80 ....90 E4
Athelstan Rd WR5 ....115 D1
Atherstone Cl
Redditch B98 ....71 F1
Solihull B90 ....21 E2
Athol Cl B32 ....18 D8
Atkinson St WR12 ....176 E2
Attwood Bsns Ctr 2 DY9 ..6 F5
Attwood St
Halesowen B63 ....7 F5
Stourbridge DY9 ....6 F5
Atworth Cl B98 ....90 B5
Atyed Cl WR14 ....139 C1
Aubrey Rd B32 ....9 E7
Auckland Cl WR4 .....116 D5
Auckland House B32 ....9 F4
Audley Dr DY11 ....27 A8
Audnam DY8 ....5 F8
Augustine Ave B80 .....90 D4
Austcliff Cl B97 ....89 D6
Austcliffe La DY10 .....13 C5
Austcliffe Rd DY10 .....13 A5
Austen Cl 7 WR2 .....127 C2
Austin Rd B60 ....67 E7
Austin Rise B31 ....33 F7
Austrey Gr B29 ....19 A8
Autumn Terr WR5 .....115 D2
Auxerre Ave B98 ......90 B8
Auxerre House B98 ....90 B8
Avalon Rd B60 ....49 C2
Avebury Gr B30 ....20 C7
Avebury Rd B30 ....20 C8
Avenbury Cl B98 ......71 F1
Avening Cl WR4 ......115 F7
Avenue Rd
Astwood Bank B96 ......89 E1

Avenue Rd continued
Birmingham, King's Heath
B14 . . . . .20 D8
Great Malvern WR14 . . .153 A8
Upton upon Severn WR8 . .169 A2
9 Worcester WR2 . . . .114 F1
Avenue The
Birmingham, Eachway
B45 . . . . .32 E7
Blackwell B60 . . . . . .50 A6
Blakedown DY10 . . . . .14 B2
Hartlebury DY11 . . . . .64 A8
Summerfield DY11 . . . .44 F8
Welland WR13 . . . . . .167 C5
2 Worcester WR1 . . . .115 C3
Worcester WR2 . . . . .128 A8
Averill Cl
2 Broadway WR12 . . .177 D1
Broadway WR12 . . . . .190 D8
Aversley Rd B38 . . . . .34 E8
Avery Ct 6 B68 . . . . .9 B7
Avery Dell Ind Est B30 . .20 A6
Avill Gr DY11 . . . . . .27 C7
Avocet Dr
Kidderminster DY10 . . . .28 A2
4 Stourport-on-Severn
DY13 . . . . .44 B2
Avon Cl Bromsgrove B60 . .67 F6
Great Malvern WR14 . . .153 C8
Worcester WR4 . . . . .115 F4
Avon Dr
4 Eckington WR10 . . .171 E7
Wythall B47 . . . . . . .35 E2
Avon Gn WR10 . . . . . .145 A3
Avon House 3 B68 . . . .9 B8
Avon Rd Halesowen B63 . .7 B5
Kidderminster DY11 . . . .27 B3
Pershore WR10 . . . . .144 E2
Stourbridge DY8 . . . . .5 F3
Worcester WR4 . . . . .115 F3
Avon St WR11 . . . . . .161 D5
Avon View GL20 . . . . .184 A1
Avonbank Cl B97 . . . . .89 C6
Avoncroft Mus of Historic
Bldgs ★ B60 . . . . . .67 E5
Avoncroft Rd B60 . . . . .67 D6
Avondale 6 WR9 . . . . .84 D1
Axborough La DY10 . . . .13 D4
Aycliffe Rd WR5 . . . . .128 D5
Aylesmore Cl B32 . . . . .9 C1
Aymestrey Sch WR2 . . .114 A1
Aynall La SY8 . . . . . .54 A3

B

Babylon La WR10 . . . . .132 F3
Baccabox La B47 . . . . .35 E7
Bacchurst Pl 4 WR4 . . .116 C5
Bach Camp Fort ★ HR6 . .92 B5
Bach Mill Dr B28 . . . . .21 D3
Back La Beckford GL20 . .186 C3
Bredon GL20 . . . . . . .184 E7
Bretforton WR11 . . . . .163 C4
Broadway WR12 . . . . .190 D8
Cleeve Prior WR11 . . . .149 A8
Great Comberton WR10 . .172 E8
1 Great Malvern WR14 . .152 F8
Mickleton GL55 . . . . .165 D4
Pebworth CV37 . . . . .150 E2
Stone DY10 . . . . . . .45 F8
Back La N WR1 . . . . . .115 B4
Back La S WR1 . . . . . .115 B4
Back of Avon GL20 . . . .196 E6
Back of Mount Pleasant 3
GL20 . . . . .196 F6
Back Rd B38 . . . . . . .19 F2
Back Way WR10 . . . . . .145 D3
Back Wlk WR1 . . . . . .115 B4
Backfields La WR8 . . . . .169 C6
Badbury Cl B80 . . . . . .90 D4
Badbury Gdns B80 . . . .90 D4
Badger Brook La B96 . . . .89 D1
Badger Cl Martley WR6 . . .96 A4
Redditch B98 . . . . . .71 D3
Badger Gdns WR5 . . . .128 E5
Badger St DY9 . . . . . .6 C6
Badger Way B60 . . . . .50 B5
Badgers Croft B62 . . . . .8 B7
Badgers The B45 . . . . .33 A2
Badgeworth Dr WR4 . . .116 A8
Badhams The GL20 . . . .181 F5
Badland Ave DY10 . . . .12 F1
Badon Covert B14 . . . . .20 D2
Badsey Cl B31 . . . . . .19 C4
Badsey Fields La
WR11 . . . . .162 E3
Badsey Fst Sch WR11 . .162 E3
Badsey La
Evesham WR11 . . . . .161 F4
Willersey WR11 . . . . .177 D6
Badsey Rd WR11 . . . . .162 A4
Baffin Rd 7 WR2 . . . . .127 F6
Bagehott Rd WR9 . . . .103 E8
Bagley Dr DY5 . . . . . .6 A4
Bagley St DY9 . . . . . .6 C6
Bagnell Rd B13 . . . . . .20 F7
Bailey Rd CV37 . . . . . .151 D2
Bainbrigge Ave WR9 . . . .85 A2
Baker's Hill GL55 . . . . .165 E2
Baker's La WR11 . . . . .174 B1
Bala Cl 2 DY13 . . . . . .43 F5
Bala Way WR5 . . . . . .128 E6
Balaams Wood Dr B31 . . .18 B1
Balaclava Rd B14 . . . . .20 E8
Bald's La DY9 . . . . . . .6 F5
Balden Rd B32 . . . . . .9 B3
Baldenhall WR14 . . . . .153 D8

Baldwin Rd
Bewdley DY12 . . . . . .25 F4
Kidderminster DY10 . . . .28 B7
Stourport-on-Severn
DY13 . . . . .44 B4
Baldwins La B28 . . . . .21 F4
Balholm B62 . . . . . . .8 C5
Ballarat Wlk DY8 . . . . .5 F5
Ballard Cl 8 WR13 . . . .152 B2
Ballards Cl GL55 . . . . .165 D3
Balliol Rd WR4 . . . . . .115 E3
Balmoral Cl
Evesham WR11 . . . . .161 G6
Fernhill Heath WR3 . . . .103 A4
Great Malvern WR14 . . .139 C6
Halesowen B62 . . . . . .8 D7
Balmoral Ct DY10 . . . . .28 A5
Balmoral Rd B32 . . . . .18 B7
Bamburgh Cres WR4 . . .116 C6
Bamford Cl WR13 . . . . .154 A7
Bangham Pit Rd B31 . . .18 B6
Bank Farm Cl DY9 . . . . .6 C1
Bank Rd WR6 . . . . . . .80 E3
Bank St
Great Malvern WR14 . . .138 F2
Stourbridge DY9 . . . . .6 F5
Worcester WR1 . . . . .115 B2
Bank The B50 . . . . . .136 D2
Banks Gn B97 . . . . . .69 B2
Banks Rd WR11 . . . . .162 E4
Bankside Cl WR3 . . . . .115 A7
Bannals La WR15 . . . . .76 C2
Bannercroft WR6 . . . . .110 F6
Banners La
Halesowen B63 . . . . . .7 D6
Redditch B97 . . . . . .89 E5
Banners St B63 . . . . . .7 D6
Bannut Tree La DY7 . . . .3 C5
Bant Mill Rd B60 . . . . .49 A1
Barass Ave WR4 . . . . .116 C5
Barbara Rd B28 . . . . . .21 E4
Barberry House B38 . . . .19 F1
Barbers Cl 1 WR4 . . . .115 F6
Barbers La WR6 . . . . . .99 B5
Barbourne Cres 9 WR1 115 A5
Barbourne La WR1 . . . .115 A5
Barbourne Prep Sch
WR1 . . . . .115 A6
Barbourne Rd WR1 . . . .115 B5
Barbourne Terr WR1 . . .115 A5
Barbourne Wlk 4 WR1 . .115 A5
Barbrook Dr DY5 . . . . . .6 B7
Barclay Rd B67 . . . . . .7 A8
Bardenholme Gdns DY9 . .6 D3
Barford Cl B98 . . . . . .71 F1
Barford Cres 5 B38 . . . .20 C2
Bark Piece B32 . . . . . .9 C3
Barker St WR3 . . . . . .115 D5
Barkers La
Cleobury Mortimer DY14 . .22 D4
Wythall B47 . . . . . . .36 A1
Barley Cres WR4 . . . . .116 B5
Barley Croft B60 . . . . .67 E6
Barley Mow La B61 . . . .49 B8
Barlich Way B98 . . . . .71 A2
Barlow Cl B45 . . . . . .17 E2
Barn Cl Birmingham B30 . .20 B6
Blackheath B64 . . . . . .7 E2
Halesowen B63 . . . . . .7 E2
Stoke Heath B60 . . . . .67 E6
Stourbridge DY9 . . . . .6 C4
Worcester WR2 . . . . .127 E8
Barn Croft B32 . . . . . .9 E1
Barn La
Birmingham, King's Heath
B13 . . . . .21 A7
Sedgeberrow WR11 . . . .174 F1
Barn Owl Pl DY10 . . . . .28 A2
Barn Owl Wlk DY5 . . . . .6 C6
Barn Piece B32 . . . . . .9 B4
Barnard Cl WR11 . . . . .161 E2
Barnard's Gn Rd
WR14 . . . . .153 A4
Barnes Hill B29 . . . . . .9 F2
Barnes Pl 1 WR5 . . . . .128 D6
Barnes Way WR5 . . . . .128 D6
Barneshall Ave WR5 . . .128 C6
Barnetts Cl DY10 . . . . .28 B4
Barnetts Gr DY10 . . . . .28 A4
Barnetts La 1 DY10 . . . .28 A4
Barnfield Cider & Wine Mill ★
WR12 . . . . .177 A1
Barnfield Rd
Bromsgrove B61 . . . . .48 B8
Halesowen B62 . . . . . .8 D7
2 Stourport-on-Severn
DY13 . . . . .43 F1
Barnfields WR11 . . . . .22 B3
Barnpark Covert 9 B14 . .20 C2
Barns Croft Way 6 B14 . .84 C1
Barnsdale Cres B31 . . . .18 E4
Barnsley Hall Rd B61 . . . .49 A6
Barnsley Rd B61 . . . . . .49 B4
Barnswood Cl B63 . . . . .7 C5
Barnt Gn Junc B45 . . . . .50 D8
Barnt Gn Rd B45 . . . . .33 C3
Barnwood Cl B98 . . . . .71 D5
Barnwood Rd B32 . . . . .9 F4
Baron Bsns Ctr WR9 . . . .6 C5
Barrack La B63 . . . . . .7 B6
Barracks Rd DY13 . . . . .44 C1
Barrar Cl DY8 . . . . . . .5 E4
Barratts Cl 5 DY12 . . . .26 A3
Barratts House B14 . . . .20 E2
Barratts Rd B38 . . . . . .20 A1

Barratts Stile La 4 DY12 26 A3
Barrett Cl DY10 . . . . . .28 B6
Barrett Rise WR14 . . . .139 A2
Barrie Ave DY10 . . . . . .28 C7
Barrington Rd B45 . . . . .32 E7
Barron Rd B31 . . . . . .19 B3
Barrow Cl B98 . . . . . . .71 F3
Barrow St WR1 . . . . . .115 C4
Barsham Dr DY5 . . . . . .6 C8
Barston Rd B68 . . . . . .9 B7
Bartestree B98 . . . . . .71 F1
Bartholemews La B61 . . . .48 F5
Bartleet Rd B98 . . . . . .90 E8
Bartley Dr B31 . . . . . .18 E8
Bartley Gn Tech Coll
B32 . . . . .9 C1
Bartley House B32 . . . . .18 D8
Bartley Woods B32 . . . . .9 B2
Barton Croft B28 . . . . .21 F4
Barton Lodge Rd B28 . . .21 E4
Barton Mews 6 GL20 . . .196 F6
Barton Rd
Tewkesbury GL20 . . . .196 F6
Welford-on-Avon CV37 . .137 D3
Barton St GL20 . . . . . .196 E6
Bascote Cl B97 . . . . . .70 B1
Basil Gr B31 . . . . . . .18 E4
Basil Rd B31 . . . . . . .18 E4
Basin Rd B60 . . . . . . .188 B8
Baskerville Rd DY10 . . . .12 F1
Bassett Rd B63 . . . . . .7 A6
Bassnage Rd B63 . . . . .7 E2
Batchelor Cl B31 . . . . .18 E4
Batchley Fst Sch B97 . . .70 B4
Batchley Rd B97 . . . . . .70 C4
Batemans La B47 . . . . .35 E5
Bates Hill B97 . . . . . . .70 D4
Bates La B94 . . . . . . .53 F1
Bath Ct 4 B29 . . . . . .19 B7
Bath Dr DY7 . . . . .3 A5
Bath Mdw B63 . . . . . . .7 E5
Bath Mews DY8 . . . . . .5 F5
Bath Rd Kempsey WR5 . .128 C1
Stourbridge DY8 . . . . .5 F5
7 Worcester WR5 . . . .115 C1
Batham Rd DY10 . . . . .28 A8
Batheaston Cl B38 . . . . .34 D7
Batsford Cl B98 . . . . . .90 B5
Batsford Rd WR5 . . . . .128 E5
Batson Rise DY5 . . . . . .6 A8
Battenhall Ave WR5 . . .128 D8
Battenhall Pl 7 WR5 . . .115 D1
Battenhall Rd WR5 . . . .115 D1
Battenhall Rise WR5 . . .128 E7
Battens Cl B98 . . . . . .70 F3
Battens Dr B98 . . . . . .71 D3
Battisto Wlk WR14 . . . .139 C1
Battle Rd
Tewkesbury GL20 . . . .196 D4
Worcester WR5 . . . . .128 D8
Battle Well ★ WR11 . . . .161 D8
Battleton Rd 2 WR11 . . .161 E2
Baughton La
Earl's Croome WR8 . . . .156 C1
Hill Croome WR8 . . . . .170 F7
Baveney Rd WR2 . . . . .114 E6
Baverstock Rd B14 . . . .20 E1
Baverstock Sch B14 . . . .20 E2
Bawdsey Ave WR14 . . . .139 B2
Baxter Cl DY10 . . . . . .27 F7
Baxter Gdns DY10 . . . . .27 F7
Bay Tree Cl B38 . . . . . .34 D8
Bayford Ave B31 . . . . .33 E6
Baylie Ct DY8 . . . . . . .5 F5
Baylie St DY8 . . . . . . .5 F4
Bayliss Cl B31 . . . . . .19 B5
Bayliss Rd GL20 . . . . .185 D7
Bayly Cl WR11 . . . . . .161 D2
Baynham Dr WR5 . . . . .129 A8
Bays Mdw WR9 . . . . . .85 A5
Bayston Rd B14 . . . . . .20 E3
Bayton CE Prim Sch
DY14 . . . . .40 A7
Beach Cl
Birmingham B31 . . . . .19 C1
1 Evesham WR11 . . . .161 E3
Beach Dr B63 . . . . . . .8 A5
Beach Rd DY13 . . . . . .43 A5
Beach St B63 . . . . . . .8 A5
Beacon Cl B45 . . . . . .33 A6
Beacon Hill B45 . . . . . .32 F5
Beacon La Kinver DY7 . . .2 F3
Marlbrook B60, B45 . . . .32 E4
Upper Arley WV15 . . . . .2 D3
Beacon Rd WR14 . . . . .152 D4
Beacon Rise DY9 . . . . . .6 B8
Beacon View B45 . . . . .33 A6
Beaconhill Dr WR14 . . . .114 E6
Beaconside Prim Sch
B45 . . . . .32 E6
Beaks Hill Rd B38 . . . . .19 E2
Beale St DY8 . . . . . . .5 F5
Bean Croft B32 . . . . . .9 B3
Bear Hill B48 . . . . . . .51 B5
Bear La B48 . . . . . . .51 B5
Bearcroft Ave WR4 . . . .116 B6
Bearcroft Gdn GL55 . . . .165 D4
Bearhill Dr B48 . . . . . .51 B5
Beauchamp Ave DY11 . . .27 D3
Beauchamp Ct DY11 . . . .27 D3
Beauchamp La
Callow End WR2 . . . . .127 F1
Powick WR2 . . . . . . .128 A1
Beauchamp Rd
Birmingham B13 . . . . .21 C5
1 Great Malvern WR14 . .138 F4

Beaudesert Cl B47 . . . . .36 A6
Beaudesert Rd B47 . . . .36 A6
Beaufort Ave DY11 . . . .27 A7
Beaufort End WR11 . . . .164 C5
Beaufort Pl GL20 . . . . .196 E4
Beaufort St B98 . . . . . .70 E4
Beaulieu Cl DY11 . . . . .27 D8
Beaumaris House B31 . . .18 D6
Beaumont Dr DY5 . . . . .6 B7
Beaumont Lawns B60 . . .32 D1
Beaumont Rd
Birmingham B30 . . . . .19 F6
Halesowen B62 . . . . . .8 E8
Beauty Bank B64 . . . . . .8 A8
Beauty Bank Cres DY8 . . .5 F6
Beauty Bank Prim Sch
DY8 . . . . .5 F6
Beaver Cl 2 WR2 . . . . .127 E5
Beaver Pk B50 . . . . . . .7 F6
Beckett Cl Redditch B98 . .70 F5
Worcester WR3 . . . . .115 A8
Beckett Dr WR3 . . . . . .115 B8
Beckett Rd WR3 . . . . . .115 A8
Beckfield Cl B14 . . . . . .20 E2
Beckford Cl GL20 . . . . .186 C3
Beckford Cross GL20 . . .186 C3
Beckford Hall ★ GL20 . . .186 C4
Beckford Rd WR11 . . . .187 B7
Beckman Rd DY9 . . . . . .6 C2
Becks The B48 . . . . . .51 A7
Bedcote Pl DY8 . . . . . .6 B5
Bedford Cl 2 WR10 . . . .144 C1
Bedlam Wood Rd B31 . . .18 B8
Bedwardine Rd 14 WR2 . .114 F1
Beech Ave
Birmingham, Quinton B32 . .9 D7
Drakes Broughton WR10 . .143 F6
Halesowen B62 . . . . . .8 C8
Worcester WR3 . . . . .115 C7
Beech Cl
1 Great Malvern WR14 . .139 D5
Kinver DY7 . . . . .4 B4
Beech Ct
Birmingham B45 . . . . .33 D7
Birmingham, Bournville
B30 . . . . .19 E4
Beech Farm Croft B31 . . .19 A4
Beech Gr B31 . . . . . . .21 A5
Beech Hill House B32 . . .18 C8
Beech Hurst 1 B38 . . . .34 E8
Beech Pk Dr B45 . . . . .50 C8
Beech Rd
Birmingham, Bournville
B30 . . . . .19 E4
Bromsgrove B61 . . . . .48 F4
Hollywood B47 . . . . . .36 A6
Stourbridge DY9 . . . . . .5 F3
Beech Tree Cl B97 . . . . .70 B4
Beech Wlk B38 . . . . . .34 F8
Beechcombe Cl 2
WR10 . . . . .144 C1
Beechcote Ave DY10 . . .12 C2
Beechcroft Dr B61 . . . . .49 B4
Beechcroft Est B63 . . . . .7 C6
Beechcroft Rd DY11 . . . .27 A8
Beechdale B68 . . . . . . .9 B7
Beecher Pl B63 . . . . . .7 D5
Beecher Rd B63 . . . . . .7 D5
Beecher Rd E B63 . . . . .7 D5
Beeches Cl B45 . . . . . .33 D8
Beeches Ct B45 . . . . . .33 D8
Beeches Farm Dr B31 . . .34 A7
Beeches Inf Sch The
B45 . . . . .18 B3
Beeches Mews DY9 . . . .14 F4
Beeches Rd DY11 . . . . .12 C1
Beeches The
Mamble DY14 . . . . . .40 A4
Ryall WR8 . . . . .169 E6
Upton Warren B61 . . . . .67 A5
Beeches View Ave B63 . . .7 C4
Beeches Way B31 . . . . .34 A7
Beechfield Cl B62 . . . . .8 C8
Beechfield Dr
2 Kidderminster DY11 . .12 C1
Kidderminster DY11 . . . .27 C8
Beechlawn Dr DY7 . . . . .4 E7
Beechtree La DY10 . . . .13 C6
Beechtree Pk B50 . . . . .136 C6
Beechwood Ct
1 Birmingham B30 . . . .20 C3
Blackheath B64 . . . . . .8 A7
Beechwood Rd
Birmingham, King's Heath
B14 . . . . .20 E5
Smethwick B67 . . . . . .9 F8
Beehive Cl B61 . . . . . .32 A1
Beeston Cl DY5 . . . . . .6 A8
Beeston Gdns 14 WR4 . .116 C6
Beeston Rd DY10 . . . . .13 A5
Begonia Cl 2 WR5 . . . .128 C4
Beilby Rd B30 . . . . . . .20 B5
Belbroughton CE Fst Sch
DY9 . . . . .30 D4
Belbroughton Cl B98 . . .70 F5
Belbroughton Rd
Blakedown DY10 . . . . .14 D1
Clent DY9 . . . . .15 D2
Halesowen B63 . . . . . .7 E2
Stourbridge DY9 . . . . . .6 E2
Belfont Trad Est B62 . . . .8 C4
Belfry Dr DY8 . . . . . . .5 E3
Belfry Rd WR9 . . . . . .103 F8
Belgrave Rd B62 . . . . . .8 D8
Bell Gn La B38 . . . . . .35 B5
Bell Heath Way B32 . . . .9 B2

Bell Hill B31 . . . . . . .19 A5
Bell Holloway B31 . . . . .18 F5
Bell La
Birmingham, Northfield
B31 . . . . .19 A4
Broadheath WR2 . . . . .113 F5
Hanley WR6 . . . . . . .77 A7
Studley B80 . . . . .90 A4
Bell Mdw DY9 . . . . . . .15 B8
Bell Mdw Way B14 . . . .20 E1
Bell Mead B80 . . . . . . .90 E4
Bell Row 6 DY13 . . . . .44 A3
Bell Sh Ctr The B31 . . . .19 A4
Bell St DY8 . . . . .6 A5
Bellar's La WR14 . . . . .153 C8
Bellars Cl WR14 . . . . .153 C8
Bellars Gdns WR14 . . . .153 D8
Belle Orch
Kidderminster DY11 . . . .27 B5
Tenbury Wells WR15 . . .55 F5
Belle Vale B63 . . . . . . .7 E5
Belle Vue Cl B61 . . . . .32 C5
Belle Vue Dr B62 . . . . . .8 E6
Belle Vue Terr WR14 . . .152 E8
Bellfield B97 . . . . . . .70 B1
Bellfield House B14 . . . .20 D1
Bellfield Jun & Inf Sch
B14 . . . . .18 F4
Bellflower Rd 12 GL20 . .197 A4
Bellman's Cross DY12 . . .13 F4
Bells Farm Cl B14 . . . . .20 C2
Bells Farm Inf & Jun Sch
B14 . . . . .20 C2
Bells La DY10 . . . . . . .20 D2
Bellwood Rd B31 . . . . .18 F4
Belmont Cl B97 . . . . . .70 B1
Belmont Covert B31 . . . .19 B6
Belmont Dr
Birmingham, Rubery
B45 . . . . .33 A6
Great Malvern WR14 . . .138 E4
Stourbridge DY9 . . . . . .6 F4
Belmont St WR3 . . . . .115 D5
Belstone Cl B14 . . . . . .20 D6
Belton Gr B45 . . . . . . .33 C8
Belvedere Cl DY10 . . . . .28 A5
Belvedere Cres DY12 . . .26 C5
Belvedere Dr B61 . . . . .49 A4
Belvide Gr B29 . . . . . .19 B8
Belvoir Bank WR14 . . . .138 E3
Belvoir Rd B60 . . . . . . .49 C1
Ben Nevis Way DY8 . . . . .6 A6
Benbow Cl WR14 . . . . .152 E2
Bengeworth Fst Sch
WR11 . . . . .161 E4
Bengrove Cl B98 . . . . . .90 A4
Bennett St 2 DY11 . . . .27 C6
Bennetts Farm Pk ★
WR2 . . . . .127 F6
Bennetts Hill WR11 . . . .148 D1
Bennetts Hill Bsns Pk
WR11 . . . . .148 D1
Bensfield WR6 . . . . . .126 C5
Benson Rd B14 . . . . . .21 B1
Bent Ave B32 . . . . . . .9 D6
Bentham Ave WR4 . . . .116 C3
Bentham Ct B31 . . . . . .18 F5
Bentley Cl B97 . . . . . .70 D3
Bentley Gr B29 . . . . . .18 F8
Bentley La B97 . . . . . .88 C7
Bentmead Gr B38 . . . . .20 A1
Benton Cl B98 . . . . . . .71 E8
Benton's La WR14 . . . .166 F6
Benton's Ct DY11 . . . . .27 C6
Beoley Fst Sch B98 . . . .71 E8
Beoley Gr B45 . . . . . .33 A7
Beoley La Beoley B98 . . .71 F8
Portway B98 . . . . . . .53 B1
Beoley Rd E B98 . . . . . .71 A4
Beoley Rd W B98 . . . . .71 A4
Berberry Cl B30 . . . . . .19 D6
Berkeley Bsns Pk
WR4 . . . . .116 C7
Berkeley Cl
Bromsgrove B60 . . . . .68 B8
Redditch B98 . . . . . .72 A3
Whittington WR5 . . . .129 B7
Berkeley Cres DY13 . . . .44 A1
Berkeley Prec DY11 . . . .20 F2
Berkeley Rd B90 . . . . .21 D3
Berkeley St 3 WR1 . . . .115 A5
Berkeley Way WR11 . . . .116 C3
Berkeswell Cl B98 . . . . .71 C3
Berkley Gdns WR3 . . . .102 F2
Bernie Crossland Wlk
DY10 . . . . .27 F3
Bernwall Cl DY8 . . . . . .5 F4
Berrill Cl WR9 . . . . . . .85 B1
Berrington Cl B98 . . . . .71 D2
Berrington Gdns WR15 . .55 C4
Berrington Rd WR15 . . .55 C4
Berrow Hill (fort) ★
WR6 . . . . .98 E2
Berrow Hill Rd 3 DY11 . .12 B1
Berrow View WR6 . . . . .67 D7
Berrowhill La B96 . . . . .88 B2
Berry Cl 6 WR2 . . . . . .127 C2
Berry Dr B45 . . . . . . .33 A1
Berry La B61 . . . . . . .47 C2
Berryfield Rd WR11 . . . .161 A3
Berrymound View B47 . . .36 C2
Berwick Gr WR5 . . . . .128 C2
Berwick St WR5 . . . . .128 C2
Besford CE Fst Sch
WR8 . . . . .157 D3
Besford Gr B31 . . . . . .18 D3

Bestmans La WR5 ....141 D5
Beta Cl GL20 ....197 C8
Beta Gr B14 ....21 C4
Betjeman Cl 9 WR10 .158 D8
Betjeman Ct DY10 ....28 B5
Betony Rd WR14 ......139 C4
Bettle Cl 4 WR10 .....143 F6
Betton Rd B14 ....20 E4
Bevan Gdns 4 GL20 ..184 E1
Bevans Cl WR11 ....175 A5
Bevere Cl WR3 ....102 A1
Bevere Cl S 1 WR3 ...102 A1
Bevere Dr WR3 ....102 A1
Bevere La WR3 ....102 A3
Bevere Vivas Gall ★
WR3 ....102 A3
Beverley Cl
Astwood Bank B96 .....89 C2
Kidderminster DY11 ....26 F6
Beverley Ct 1 B62 .....9 A6
Beverley Ct Rd B32 ....9 C6
Beverley Rd B45 ....33 A7
Beverley Way WR14 ..138 E6
Bewdley High Sch
DY12 ....26 C2
Bewdley Hill DY11 .....27 B5
Bewdley La WR11 .....161 C4
Bewdley Mus ★ DY12 ..26 B3
Bewdley Rd
Birmingham B30 ....20 B8
Kidderminster DY11 ....27 C6
1 Stourport-on-Severn
DY13 ....44 A4
Bewdley Rd N DY13 ...43 D7
Bewdley St WR11 .....161 C4
Bewdley Sta DY12 .....26 C3
Bewell Cl B45 ....48 F4
Bewell Head B61 ......48 F4
Bewlay Cl DY5 ....6 B7
Bibsworth Ave
Birmingham B13 ......21 D8
Broadway WR12 ......190 E8
Bibsworth La WR11 ..177 D2
Bibury Rd B28 ....21 E7
Bickington Rd B32 .....9 D1
Bickmarsh La B50 ....136 D1
Bicknell Croft B14 .....20 E2
Bicton Ave 8 WR5 ...128 E6
Bidavon Ind Est B50 ..136 E6
Biddles Hill B94 ....53 C6
Bidford Rd
Bidford-on-Avon B50 ..136 C7
Birmingham B31 ....18 E3
Bidford-on-Avon CE Prim
Sch B50 ....136 D5
Bigbury La DY13 ....44 D6
Bight The WR10 ......160 E8
Bigwood Dr B32 ....9 D1
Bilberry Cl DY13 ......43 E5
Bilberry Dr B45 ....33 A6
Bilberry Rd B14 ....20 C6
Bilbrook Gr B29 ....9 F2
Bilbury Cl B97 ....89 C6
Bilford Ave WR3 .....115 D3
Bilford Rd WR3 ......115 C7
Billesley La
Birmingham B13 ......21 A8
Portway B48 ....52 E6
Billesley Prim Sch B13 .21 C6
Bills La B90 ....36 F8
Billy La B45, B60 ......50 A7
Bilton Ind Est B38 .....34 E8
Bine La DY14 ....41 F6
Binswood Rd B62 ......9 A7
Binton Cl B98 ....71 F1
Binton Croft B13 ......20 F8
Binton Rd B90 ....21 F1
Binyon Cl WR11 ......162 E2
Birch Ave
Birmingham B31 ....18 C1
Evesham WR11 ......161 F2
Worcester WR4 ......115 E4
Birch Cl B30 ....19 E6
Birch Coppice WR9 ..103 F8
Birch Ct B30 ....19 E4
Birch Dr DY8 ....5 E6
Birch Gr Alveley WV15 ..1 C6
Oldbury B68 ....9 D7
Birch La Oldbury B68 ...9 D7
Severn Stoke WR8 ...155 E6
Birch Rd
Birmingham, Eachway
B45 ....32 E6
Oldbury B68 ....9 D7
Birch Tree Rd 3 DY12 .25 F2
Birch Wlk B68 ....9 D8
Birchen Coppice Fst Sch
DY11 ....27 B2
Birchen Coppice Mid Sch
DY11 ....27 B2
Birchensale Farm B97 .70 B5
Birchensale Mid Sch
B97 ....70 C4
Birchensale Rd B97 ...70 C5
Birches La B48 ....50 F6
Birches The DY13 .....44 B3
Birchfield
Halesowen B63 ....7 E2
Worcester WR3 ......115 C6
Birchfield Cres DY9 ...6 F3
Birchfield Ct B97 .....70 B2
Birchfield Dr B97 .....43 E5
Birchfield Rd
Kidderminster DY11 ...27 B5
Redditch B97 ....70 B2

Birchfield Rd continued
Stourbridge DY9 ....6 F3
Birchgate DY9 ....6 F4
Birchtree Gr 4 WR10 .144 D2
Birchwood Cl DY11 ....27 A7
Birchwood Rd WR14 .138 E6
Birchwoods B32 ....9 B2
Birchy Cl B90 ....36 F6
Birchy Leasowes La
B90 ....36 E5
Bird Cage Wlk B38 ....19 F2
Bird's Barn La DY7 ....3 C2
Birdie Cl B38 ....19 D1
Birdlip Cl WR4 ....116 A6
Birdlip Gr B32 ....9 C6
Birdwell Croft B13 ....20 F6
Birkdale Ave B60 ......50 A5
Birkdale Cl DY8 ....5 F2
Birkdale Gr B29 ....20 A8
Birley Gr B63 ....7 C1
Birlingham Cl WR10 .158 C7
Birmingham House B60 ..9 B3
Birmingham & Midland Mus
of Transport ★ B47 ...35 E3
Birmingham Great Pk
B45 ....33 B8
Birmingham Rd
Alvechurch B48 ....51 B7
Badsey WR11 ....162 E5
Blakedown DY10 ......14 C2
Hagley DY9 ....15 D7
Halesowen B63 ....8 B4
Hopwood B31, B48 ....34 B4
Kidderminster DY10 ...28 D7
Lickey End B60, B61 ...49 B6
Lydiate Ash B45, B61 ..32 D5
Marlbrook B61 ....32 B1
Redditch B97, B98 ....70 E8
Sambourne B49 ......109 F7
Studley B80, B98 .....90 C4
Birmingham St
Halesowen B63 ....8 B3
Stourbridge DY8 ....6 B5
Birstall Way B38 ......34 C8
Bisell Way DY5 ....6 C6
Biset Ave DY10 ....28 B5
Bishop Challoner RC Sch
B14 ....20 F8
Bishop Cl B45 ....17 E1
Bishop Hall Cres B60 .67 E7
Bishop Perone High Sch
WR3 ....115 C5
Bishop St DY13 ....44 A5
Bishop's Ct B31 ......19 B3
Bishop's Wlk GL19 ..195 D6
Bishops Ave WR3 ....115 C5
Bishops Gate B31 ....19 A2
Bishops Wlk B64 ....8 A6
Bishops Wood La DY3 .63 E4
Bishopstone Cl B98 ...71 E7
Bisley Cl WR4 ....116 A7
Bissell Cl B28 ....21 F6
Bissell St B32 ....9 A6
Bittell Cl B31 ....33 F7
Bittell Ct B31 ....33 F7
Bittell Farm Rd B48 ...34 A2
Bittell La B45 ....50 E8
Bittell Rd
Alvechurch B48 ....51 A8
Barnt Green B45 ......50 E8
Bittern Rd WR5 ......128 D5
Bittern Wlk DY5 ....6 C6
Bittern Wood Rd DY10 .28 B3
Black Haynes Rd B29 .19 A6
Black Horse La 7 DY10 .27 E6
Black Lake La B60,
B97 ....69 A2
Black Soils Rd B98 ...71 F5
Black Thorne Cl 4
WR9 ....104 A4
Blackberry La B63 .....8 A2
Blackberry Way 10
WR11 ....161 D1
Blackburne Rd B28 ...21 F6
Blackbushe Cl B17 ....9 F7
Blackdown Cl B45 ....18 A2
Blackford Cl
Halesowen B63 ....7 D2
Kidderminster DY11 ...27 A1
Blackfriars Ave WR9 ..84 C7
Blackheath Way
WR14 ....152 C8
Blackminster WR11 ..162 E6
Blackminster Cty Mid Sch
WR11 ....162 E7
Blackmore La B60 ....49 A3
Blackmore Pk Rd
Malvern Wells WR13 .153 C1
Welland WR13 ....167 D7
Blackmore Rd WR14 .138 E5
Blackpole Ind Est
WR4 ....115 F8
Blackpole Rd WR4 ...102 F1
Blacksmiths Bank B63 .63 D1
Blacksmiths Cl
Sedgeberrow WR11 ..175 A1
4 South Littleton WR11 .148 F1
Blacksmiths La
Beckford GL20 ....186 D2
Childswickham WR12 .176 E2
Cropthorne WR10 ....160 C7
Dumbleton WR11 ....187 F5
Hill & Moor WR10 ...145 E3
South Littleton WR11 .148 F1
Blackstitch La B97 ...70 A1
Blackstone Mdws Cntry Pk ★
DY12 ....43 C8

Blackthorn Cl
Birmingham B30 ......19 C6
Evesham WR11 ......162 A2
Blackthorn Ct B98 ....71 E1
Blackthorn Rd
Birmingham, Bournville
B30 ....19 D6
Worcester WR4 ......115 C6
Blackwell La 1 B97 ...70 B5
Blackwell Rd B45, B60 .50 B5
Blackwell St DY10 ....27 C6
Blackwood Rd B60 ....49 B2
Blaenwern Dr B63 .....7 B7
Blagdon Cl 12 WR5 ..128 E6
Blagdon Rd B63 ....8 A6
Blair Cl WR4 ....116 B6
Blake Ave WR9 ....84 D1
Blake Hall Cl WR5 .....6 C7
Blake Rd B61 ....49 B8
Blake St WR5 ....128 E8
Blake's Hill
North & Middle Littleton
WR11 ....149 D2
Pebworth WR11 .....150 A2
Blakebrook DY11 ......27 C6
Blakebrook Cl DY11 ...27 C6
Blakebrook Gdns DY11 .27 C6
Blakebrook Day Specl Sch
DY11 ....27 C6
Blakedown CE Prim Sch
DY10 ....14 C1
Blakedown Rd B63 .....7 F1
Blakefield Gdns WR2 .114 F1
Blakefield Rd WR2 ...114 F1
Blakefield Wlk
8 Worcester WR2 ...114 F1
2 Worcester WR2 ...114 F1
Blakemere Cl B98 .....71 F3
Blakemore Cl B32 .....9 F3
Blakeney Ave WR2 ...114 F1
Blakeney Cl 4 WR5 ..128 E6
Blakenhurst WR11 ...147 F8
Blakes Field Dr B45 ...33 A1
Blakes La WR13 .....154 C8
Blakeshall La DY11 ...12 D5
Blanchettes Ave WR3 .115 A8
Blanchettes St 3 WR3 .115 A8
Blayneys La WR11 ...161 E8
Blaze La
Astwood Bank B96, B97 .89 A3
Feckenham B96 ......88 F2
Bleachfield Rd B98 ....71 F8
Blenheim Cl 8 B50 ..136 D5
Blenheim Cres B60 ...68 A8
Blenheim Dr GL20 ...184 F6
Blenheim Rd WR2 ...114 E3
Blessed Edward Oldcorne RC
High Sch WR5 ......128 D8
Blind La
Evesham WR11 .....161 C5
Tanworth-In-A B94 ...53 D1
Blissgate Rd DY14 ....41 F7
Blithe Cl DY8 ....6 A8
Blithfield Dr DY5 ......6 A8
Blockhouse Cl 8 WR1 .115 C2
Blockley Cl B97 ....69 E2
Bloomfield Rd WR2 ..127 F5
Bloomfield St N B63 ...7 F5
Bloomfield St W B63 ...7 F4
Bloomsbury Gr B14 ..20 C7
Blossom Cl 4 WR5 ..116 B3
Blossom Dr B61 ......49 A5
Blossomfield Cl
Birmingham B38 .....34 D8
Evesham WR11 .....161 B2
Blossomfield Ct B38 ..34 D8
Blount House DY11 ...27 B8
Blount Terr WR3 ......27 D3
Bloxham Rd WR12 ...177 D1
Blue Ball La B63 ......7 C7
Blue Bell Cl WR14 ...153 C7
Blue Bird Pk B62 .....17 B7
Blue Cedars DY8 ......5 C6
Bluebell Croft B31 ....18 F4
Bluebell La B45 ......157 E4
Bluebell Way 1 WR11 .175 D8
Blythe Cl B97 ....89 D7
Blythesway B48 ......51 A6
Blythsford Rd B28 ....21 F4
BMI Droitwich Spa
WR9 ....84 F3
Boat La
8 Evesham WR11 ...161 C4
Offenham WR11 .....162 A8
Bobs Coppice Wlk DY5 ..6 F7
Bockleton Rd
Bockleton WR15 ......93 C8
Tenbury WR15 ....55 E1
Bodenham Cl B98 .....71 D3
Bodenham Rd
Birmingham B31 .....18 E1
Oldbury B68 ....9 B8
Bodiam Cl 1 WR4 ...116 C6
Bog La 2 WR15 ......55 E4
Boleyn Rd B45 ....17 E2
Bolney Rd B32 ....9 E4
Bolston Rd WR5 .....128 C8
Bolton Ave WR4 .....116 C5
Bomers Field B45 .....33 C4
Bomford Hill WR4 ...116 B4
Bond St
Birmingham, Stirchley
B30 ....20 A7
Great Malvern WR14 .139 A4
Bondfield Rd B13 .....21 B6
Bonfire Hill DY9 ......31 E6

Boon St WR10 ....171 D7
Boot Piece La B97 ....70 B5
Booton Ct DY10 ....13 A1
Boraston Bank WR15 ..56 A7
Boraston Dr WR15 ....56 A6
Boraston La
Burford WR15 ....56 A7
Tenbury Wells WR15 ..55 F6
Borderway WR15 .....55 F6
Bordesley Abbey ★ B98 .70 F6
Bordesley La B98 .....70 E6
Boreley La WR9 ....63 D1
Borough Cres DY8 .....5 E5
Borough Ct B63 ....8 B4
Borrington Gdns DY10 .28 B4
Borrington Rd DY10 ...28 B5
Borrowdale Cl DY5 ....6 B8
Borrowdale Dr WR4 .116 A5
Borrowdale Rd B31 ..18 C3
Bosbury Rd WR14 ...139 A5
Bosbury Terr B30 .....20 B7
Bosmere Cl B31 ......18 F3
Boston La WR11 .....160 E5
Bott La DY9 ....6 E6
Boughton Ave WR4 ..114 E1
Boughton Cl WR2 ...114 E1
Boughton Pk Cl WR2 .127 E8
Boughton St WR2 ...114 F1
Boulters La B97 ....89 D6
Boultons La B97 ......89 D6
Boundary Rd E CV37 .151 F2
Boundary Rd N CV37 .151 E1
Boundary Rd W CV37 .151 D3
Bourlay Cl B45 ....17 E2
Bourne Ave Catshill B61 .31 F1
Halesowen B62 ....8 F4
Bourne Cl
Birmingham B13 .....21 D6
6 Droitwich WR9 .....84 C3
Bourne Gn B32 ....9 E6
Bourne Gn
Defford WR8 ....157 B1
Strensham WR8 .....171 A6
Bourne St WR3 ......115 B6
Bourne Way Gdns B29 .20 A8
Bourne's Pl 2 WR11 .161 C4
Bournebrook Cres B62 ..9 A4
Bournes Cl B63 ....7 E4
Bournes Cres B63 .....7 E4
Bournes Hill B63 ......7 E4
Bourneheath Rd B61 .31 D2
Bournville Coll of F Ed
B30 ....19 C7
Bournville Inf Sch B30 .19 E7
Bournville Jun Sch B30 .19 E7
Bournville La B30 ....19 E6
Bournville Mews B30 .19 E5
Bournville Sch & Sixth Form
B30 ....19 C6
Bournville Sta B30 ...20 A7
Bouts La WR7 ....108 B2
Bow Hill WR2 ....140 F7
Bow La GL20 ....183 B7
Bowbrook Cl WR10 ..131 B2
Bowbrook House
(Preparatory Sch)
WR10 ....131 B1
Bowden Gn WR9 ....103 F8
Bower Bank 2 DY13 ..43 E2
Bower Hill WR9 ....84 D2
Bower Hill Dr 4 DY13 .43 E2
Bower La DY5 ....7 A8
Bowes Rd B45 ....32 E7
Bowler Rd GL20 .....184 E1
Bowling Gn La WR8 .169 A8
Bowling Gn Rd
Bowling Green WR2 .127 B3
Stourbridge DY8 ....5 E5
Bowmore Rd B60 .....49 B6
Bowness Dr 2 WR4 .116 A5
Bowood Cres B31 ....19 B2
Bowood Ct B97 ....70 D4
Bowood Dr 2 WR5 ..128 E6
Bowpatch Cl DY13 ....62 D8
Bowpatch Rd DY13 ...43 D1
Box Tree Cl WR8 ....157 D3
Boxbush Dr WR7 ....143 A8
Boxnott Cl B97 ....70 A2
Bozward St WR2 ....114 F2
Bozzards Bank WR9 ..63 C1
Brabham Cl DY11 .....12 D1
Braceby Ave B13 .....21 C6
Braces La B60 ....32 C1
Bracken Cl WR2 .....114 E4
Bracken Gr B61 ......32 A1
Bracken Way B38 ....34 D6
Brackendale Way B29 ..9 D4
Brackenfield Rd B63 ...7 E3
Brades Cl B63 ....7 B7
Bradford La DY9 .....30 D5
Bradford Pl WR5 ....116 A1
Bradley Dr WR14 ....138 E5
Bradley Rd B30 ....5 F6
Bradley Thursfield Ct
DY11 ....27 E7
Bradleys Cl B64 ....7 E7
Bradmore Gr B29 .....19 A8
Bradnock Cl B13 .....21 C7
Bradshaw Ave B38 ...19 D1
Bradstock Rd B30 ....20 C4
Bradwell House B31 ..18 B2
Braggaton La CV37 .137 E1
Braggs Farm La B90 .36 F4
Braid Cl B38 ....19 D1
Brake La DY8 ....14 E6
Brake The DY8 ....14 F6
Bramber Way DY8 .....5 F2

Bramble Cl
Birmingham, Shenley Fields
B31 ....18 F6
5 Great Malvern WR14 .139 C3
Bramble Gdns 5 WR5 .116 B3
Brambles The DY9 .....6 D3
Brambling Rise DY10 .28 B1
Brambling Wlk DY5 ...6 C6
Bramcote Rd B32 .....9 C5
Bramhope Cl WR4 ...116 A4
Bramley Ave WR4 ...114 E6
Bramley Cl
Bowling Green WR2 .127 C3
Crowle WR7 ....117 F4
Bramley Dr B47 ......36 B6
Bramley Pl WR4 .....114 E6
Bramley Rd GL20 ...196 F7
Bramley Way
1 Bewdley DY12 .....25 F3
Bidford-on-Avon B50 .136 D5
Brampton Cl DY10 ...13 B4
Bramshaw Cl B14 ....20 F2
Branch Rd B38 ....34 E8
Branches Cl 2 DY12 .25 F2
Branden Rd B48 ......51 A5
Brandheath La B96 ..109 A4
Brandon Cl B31 ......19 B1
Brandon Gr B31 ......33 F7
Brandon Rd DY5 ......6 C8
Brandon Way DY5 .....6 E8
Brandwood Gr B14 ...20 D5
Brandwood House B14 .20 D7
Brandwood Pk Rd B14 .20 C4
Brandwood Rd B14 ...20 D5
Branscombe Cl B14 ..20 D5
Bransford Rd WR2 ..114 E1
Brantwood WR4 .....116 A5
Brantwood Cl 6 WR9 .85 A1
Brantwood Rd 2 WR9 .104 A8
Brasenose Rd GL20 .184 E6
Brassie Cl B38 ....19 D1
Brayford Ave DY5 .....6 B7
Braymoor Rd WR1 ..115 B4
Breaches La B98 ......90 D6
Breakback Rd B61 ...67 D8
Bream Cl 3 WR5 ....128 C5
Brecknell Rise DY10 ..27 F8
Brecon Ave
Bromsgrove B61 .....49 A5
Warndon WR4 ....116 D6
Brecon Cl
5 Droitwich WR9 .....84 C1
Inkberrow WR7 .....120 F6
Brecon Dr DY8 ....6 B6
Breden Barn (NT) ★
GL20 ....184 D6
Bredicot La WR7 ....117 D4
Bredon Ave
Kidderminster DY11 ..27 A1
Stourbridge DY9 ......6 C5
Bredon Cl WR7 .....120 E8
Bredon Cres WR11 ..161 A2
Bredon Ct B63 ....8 A3
Bredon Gr WR14 ....153 C6
Bredon Hancocks Endowed
CE Fst Sch GL20 ....184 E7
Bredon Hill Mid Sch
WR11 ....174 C2
Bredon House B98 ....90 B7
Bredon Lodge 1 GL20 .184 F6
Bredon Rd
Bromsgrove B61 .....67 D7
Stourbridge DY8 ......6 B6
Tewkesbury GL20 ...196 E2
Bredon Sch (Pull Court)
GL20 ....182 E5
Bredon View
Broadway WR12 ....190 E4
Redditch B97 ....89 D8
Bredon Way 4 DY13 ..43 D1
Breedon Gdns B98 ...71 A3
Breedon Rd B30 ......20 A5
Brennand Cl B68 ......9 C8
Brennand Rd B68 .....9 B8
Brensham Rd GL20 .197 B7
Brent Rd B30 ....20 D8
Brent Wood Cl 6 WR5 .115 F1
Brentford Rd B14 ....21 A5
Bretforton Com Fst Sch
WR11 ....163 C4
Bretforton Rd WR11 .162 E4
Brett Dr B32 ....18 C3
Brett Young Cl DY10 .28 B5
Brettell La DY8 ....5 F8
Brewers La WR11 ...162 E3
Brewery Wlk 1 WR1 .115 B4
Briar Cl Evesham WR11 .161 D5
Lickey End B60 ......49 C6
Briar Hill
Bluntington DY10 .....29 E1
Chaddesley Corbett DY10 .46 E8
Briar Mill WR2 ....84 D3
Briar Way 16 DY13 ...43 D3
Briars Hollow WR9 ...84 D3
Briars The DY9 ......14 F4
Brick Kiln La B47 .....35 F4
Brick Kiln St DY5 ......7 A8
Brickall The CV37 ...151 C5
Brickfields Rd WR4 .115 E5
Brickhouse La B60 ...67 C4
Brick-kiln St WR11 ..161 D4
Bricknell Ave 9 GL20 .184 F6
Brickyard La
Drakes Broughton &
Wadborough WR10 .144 A3
Studley B80 ....90 C4
Bridewell Dr WR11 ..174 F1
Bridge Mdw Cl WR11 .175 A2

Bridge Piece B31 ......19 B2
Bridge Rd Alveley WV15 ...1 D6
Cookley DY11 ....13 A6
Bridge St
Bretforton WR11 ......163 C4
Evesham WR11 ....161 D4
Halesowen B63 ....7 C7
Hill & Moor WR10 ...145 D2
1 Kidderminster DY10 ...27 E5
Pershore WR10 ......158 E2
Redditch B97 ....70 B4
Stourport-on-Severn DY13 ...43 F3
Worcester WR1 ....115 B2
Bridge Trad Ctr The B64 .7 D8
Bridgeburn Rd B31 ...18 E8
Bridgemans Cl WR12 ..177 E1
Bridgnorth Rd
Kidderminster Foreign
DY11 ....11 F4
Kinver DY7 ....4 B7
Stourbridge DY7 ....5 C6
Bridgnorth Row 1
WR4 ....116 C7
Bridgwater Rd WR4 ...116 D7
Bridle Mead B38 .....34 D7
Bridle Rd DY8 ....5 D6
Bridley Moor Rd B97 ...70 C5
Bridport House B31 ...18 E7
Brier Mill Rd B63 .....8 C3
Briery Cl B64 ....7 F7
Briery Rd B63 ....7 E3
Brigfield Cres B13 ....21 B5
Brigfield Rd B13 .....21 B5
Bright Ave WR4 ......116 C4
Bright St DY8 ....5 D6
Brightstone Rd B45 ...18 B2
Brimstone Cl 7 WR5 ..128 E5
Brimstone La B61 ....48 D7
Brindle Brae DY7 ......4 A4
Brindley Ct 1 B68 .....9 B7
Brindley Heath Jun Sch
DY7 ....6 A5
Brindley Rd WR4 ....116 B7
Brindley St DY13 .....43 F5
Brine Pits La WR11 ...66 C1
Bringewood Gr B32 ...18 B8
Brinklow Cl B98 ......90 D8
Brinklow Rd B29 ......9 F2
Brinton Cl DY11 ......27 C3
Brinton Cres DY11 ...27 C3
Briseley Cl DY5 ....6 D8
Bristol Ct 15 B29 .....19 C7
Bristol Rd B29 ....19 D8
Bristol Rd S
Birmingham B31 ......18 F2
Birmingham, Longbridge
B31, B45 ....33 C7
Briston Cl DY5 ....6 C8
Britannia B98 ....70 F3
Britannia Gdns 1 DY13 ..44 B1
Britannia Rd WR1 ....115 B4
Britannia Sq WR1 ...115 B4
Britford Cl B14 ......20 F3
Britten Dr WR14 .....153 B6
Britten St B97 ....70 D4
Broach Rd DY13 .....44 B1
Broad Acres B31 ....18 E6
Broad Gd Rd B98 ....71 B2
Broad Heath Cl B97 ...70 B5
Broad Hill WR10 ....157 D5
Broad La
Birmingham B14 ......20 F4
Bishampton WR10 ...133 A3
Tanworth-In-A B98 ...53 E4
Broad Marston Rd
Mickleton GL55 .....165 B6
Pebworth CV37 .....150 E2
Broad Mdw La B30 ...20 B3
Broad St
Bromsgrove B61 ......48 F4
Kidderminster DY10 ...27 E7
Worcester WR1 .....115 B2
Broadacre Cl 5 GL20 ..184 F6
Broadclose La WR7 ...120 C7
Broadcott Ind Est B64 ...8 A8
Broadfield Cres WR3 ..102 F3
Broadfield Gdns WR4 ..116 B6
Broadfields DY9 .....15 A6
Broadheath CE Prim Sch
WR2 ....113 F7
Broadheath WR11 ...103 E8
Broadhidley Dr B32 ...9 B1
Broadlands Dr WR14 ..138 C1
Broadmeadow Dr B30 ..20 B3
Broadmeadow House
B32 ....18 D2
Broadmeadow Inf Sch
B30 ....20 B2
Broadstone Rd B63 ...7 B4
Broadwas CE Prim Sch
WR6 ....112 B3
Broadwas Cl B98 ....71 C5
Broadwaters Dr
Hagley DY9 ....15 B4
Kidderminster DY10 ...28 A8
Broadway Ave 8 B9 ...8 A2
Broadway 6 WR10 ...146 A1
Broadway Fst Sch
WR12 ....177 E1
Broadway Gr WR2 ...114 C4
Broadway La WR10 ..146 A1
Broadway Rd
Aston Somerville WR12 ..175 F1
Broadway WR12 .....177 A2
Evesham WR11 ......161 F1
Weston Subedge GL55 ..165 C2

Broadway Rd continued
Kidderminster DY11 ...12 D1
Willersey WR12 .....177 E3
Broadway Teddy Bear Mus★
WR12 ....190 F2
Broadway The DY8 ....5 D3
Broadwood Dr WR3 ..152 B2
Brockamin La WR6 ...125 F8
Brockeridge Rd GL20 ..183 E7
Brockhampton Cl 4
WR4 ....115 F7
Brockhampton Est (NT)★
WR6 ....110 A3
Brockhill La
Alvechurch B48 ......35 B2
Beoley B98 ....52 F2
Norton Juxta Kempsey
WR5 ....128 F5
Tardebigge B97 ......69 E8
Brockhill Rd WR13 ..152 C3
Brockley's Wlk DY7 ...4 C3
Brockmoor Cl DY9 ....6 C2
Brockton Pl 2 DY13 ..43 F5
Brockworth Rd B14 ...20 C2
Bromfield Rd WR7 ....70 D2
Bromford Ct B31 .....19 B1
Bromford Dell B31 ...19 C4
Bromley St WR9 ......6 F6
Brompton Dr DY5 ....6 B7
Brompton Pool Rd 2 B28 ..21 E3
Bromsgrove Highway
Bromsgrove B60 .....49 D1
Redditch B97 ....70 B2
Tardebigge B60, B97 ..69 C6
Bromsgrove Lower Sch
B60 ....48 F1
Bromsgrove Mus★ B61 ..49 A3
Bromsgrove Private Hospl
B60 ....50 B1
Bromsgrove Rd
Clent DY9 ....15 D4
Dodford B61 ....48 D6
Droitwich WR9 ......85 A4
Halesowen B63 ....8 C4
Kidderminster DY10 ...28 F2
Redditch B97 ....70 B1
Romsley B62 ....17 A5
Studley B80 ....90 D2
Bromsgrove Sch B61 ..48 F1
Bromsgrove St
Halesowen B63 ....8 C4
Kidderminster DY10 ...27 E6
Worcester WR3 .....115 B6
Bromsgrove Sta B60 ..68 B7
Bromwall Rd B13 ....21 B6
Bromwich La
Stourbridge DY9 .....15 B8
Worcester WR2 .....115 A1
Bromwich Rd WR2 ...115 A1
Bromyard Rd
Kyre WR15 ....75 E6
Stoke Bliss WR15 ....76 A3
Tenbury WR15 ....56 B2
Tenbury Wells WR15 ..55 F4
Worcester WR2 .....114 C1
Bromyard Terr WR2 ..115 A2
Bronsil Cl WR5 ......129 A8
Bronsil Dr WR14 ....138 F6
Bronte Dr DY10 .....28 C6
Brook Cl Kempsey WR5 ..141 D8
Solihull B90 ....21 F1
Brook Cres Hagley DY9 ..15 B5
Stourbridge DY9 ......6 F3
Brook Dr B32 ....9 D1
Brook Farm Dr WR4 ..153 C5
Brook Fields Cl B60 ...32 C1
Brook Holloway DY9 ...6 F4
Brook La
Birmingham, Billesley
B13 ....21 B7
Birmingham, Harborne
B32 ....9 F5
Charlton WR10 .....160 E8
Cropthorne WR10 ...160 B6
Brook Pk Trad Est 4 DY9 ..6 F5
Brook Rd
Birmingham, Eachway
B45 ....32 E2
Bromsgrove B61 .....48 E1
Fairfield B61 ....31 C2
Stourbridge DY8 ......6 B3
Brook Side WR5 ....141 C8
Brook St Brierley Hill DY5 ..7 A2
Kidderminster DY11 ...27 C6
Redditch B98 ....71 A4
Stourbridge DY8 ......5 E1
Stourbridge, Lye DY9 ...6 F5
Worcester WR1 .....115 B5
Brook Vale 4 DY12 ...26 C3
Brook Wlk B32 ....9 D2
Brookdale
Harvington WR11 ...147 F8
Kidderminster DY10 ...27 F8
Brookdale Cl B45 ....18 A1
Brookend Dr B45 ....32 F7
Brookend La WR5 ...128 F1
Brookfield
2 Great Malvern WR14 ..139 B5
Little Comberton WR10 ..159 B3
Brookfield Cl B97 ....89 D4
Brookfield House B97 ..30 C7
Brookfield Rd DY13 ...43 F5
Brookhampton Cl B97 ..89 E4
Brookhouse La B97 ...88 E4
Brookhouse Rd B45 ...49 F7
Brookland Rd DY9 ...15 A4
Brooklands Dr
Birmingham B14 .....20 E5

Brooklands Dr continued
Kidderminster DY11 ...12 D1
Brooklands La B98 ...71 B5
Brooklea Gr B38 .....20 A1
Brooklyn Ct WR7 ...120 E6
Brookmans Ave B32 ...9 D4
Brookmeadow Ct B28 ..21 D6
Brookmill Cl WR3 ...115 A7
Brookpiece House B14 ..20 E2
Brookside
Birmingham, Northfield
B31 ....18 F5
4 Colwall Stone WR13 ..152 A1
Tewkesbury GL20 ...197 A8
Welland WR13 .....167 C5
Brookside Ave B13 ...21 B7
Brookside Cl
Alvechurch B48 ......51 B6
Halesowen B63 ....7 D3
Brookside Dr B61 ....48 F8
Brookside Rd WR2 ..114 D3
Brookside Way WR10 ..14 B2
Brookthorpe Cl WR4 ..116 A7
Brookvale Cl B61 ....49 B4
Brookwillow Rd B63 ...7 E1
Brookwood Ave B28 ..21 D5
Brookwood Dr B45 ...50 C8
Broom Cl B60 ....49 B2
Broom Cres DY10 ....28 A6
Broom Dr B14 ....20 A4
Broom Mdw Rd WR3 ..102 F3
Broome Cl 5 B63 .....8 A3
Broome La
Blakedown DY9 ......14 F2
Hagley DY9 ....15 B2
Broomehill Cl DY9 ....6 C7
Broomfield Cl DY11 ...27 C7
Broomfield Gn DY11 ...27 C7
Broomfield Rd DY11 ...27 C7
Broomhall 10 WR5 ..128 F2
Broomhall Gn 10 WR5 ..128 E5
Broomhall La WR5 ..128 D2
Broomhall Way WR5 ..128 D4
Broomy Cl DY13 .....43 D5
Broseley Ave B31 ....34 B8
Brotherton Ave B97 ...69 F2
Broughton Cres B31 ..33 D8
Broughton Dr DY9 ....6 D3
Brown Sq WR9 .....169 C6
Brown St WR2 .....128 A8
Brown Westhead Pk
DY10 ....12 F3
Brownes Way WR2 ..101 C2
Brownheath Rd
Martin Hussingtree WR3 ..103 E3
Salwarpe WR9 .....104 D3
Browning Cl
Kidderminster DY10 ...28 B6
Worcester WR3 .....115 B7
Browning Twr B31 ...19 C3
Brownsea Cl B45 ....17 F1
Bruce Rd DY10 ......28 B7
Brueton Ave B60 ....68 A8
Brueton Dr B98 ......71 A3
Brunel Cl 4 DY13 ....44 A5
Brunswick Cl 4 WR4 ..127 F6
Brunswick Gate DY8 ...6 A1
Bryher Wlk B45 .....17 E1
Bryndale Ave B14 ...20 C4
Brynside Cl B14 ......20 D2
Bryony Rd B29 ......19 B7
Buck St WR2 ....114 F2
Buckbury Cl DY9 .....6 D2
Buckfast Cl B61 .....48 D1
Buckholt Dr WR4 ...116 A4
Buckingham Cl
Great Malvern WR14 ..139 C6
3 Walton Cardiff GL20 ..197 A4
Buckingham Ct B29 ..19 D8
Buckle St
Bickmarsh WR11 ...149 F6
Chipping Campden
WR12 ....191 A2
Honeybourne WR11 ..164 A7
Pebworth WR11 ....150 A7
Saintbury GL55 .....178 C7
Willersey WR12 ....178 B2
Buckle Wood WR3 ..115 D6
Buckleys Gn B48 ....51 A6
Buckleys The B48 ...51 A6
Bucknall Cres B32 ...18 A8
Bucknall House B14 ..20 E6
Buckridge Cl B38 ....34 D7
Bulford Cl B14 ......20 D2
Bull Ring 4 Halesowen B63 ..8 B3
Kidderminster DY10 ...27 E6
Bullfinch Cl 6 WR5 ..128 D5
Bullus Rd 3 DY13 ...44 A4
Bumble Hole La B61 ..48 E7
Bungay Lake La B61 ..47 F3
Bunns Rd WR5 .....128 D6
Buntsford Dr B60 ....67 F6
Buntsford Hill B60 ...67 F5
Buntsford Pk Rd B60 ..67 F6
BUPA S Bank Hospl
...................128 C8
Burcher Gn DY10 ....28 B5
Burcot Ave B60 .....49 B4
Burcot House B60 ...49 B3
Burcot La
Bromsgrove, Burcot B60 ..49 B3
Bromsgrove, Stoney Hill
B60 ....49 C4
Burdett Pl WR4 .....116 C4
Burdock House B38 ...19 F1

Burdock Rd B29 .....19 A6
Burfield Rd B63 ......7 C5
Burford CE Prim Sch
...................55 F5
Burford Cl WR4 ....116 A7
Burford Ct DY8 ....6 A4
Burford Gdns 5 WR11 ..161 E4
Burford House Gdns★
WR15 ....55 C5
Burford La B49, B80 ..91 E1
Burford Pk Rd B38 ...34 C8
Burford Rd
Evesham WR11 .....161 E4
Hollywood B47 ....36 A6
Burgesses The DY7 ...4 B3
Burghley Dr DY11 ...27 C6
Burghley Wlk DY5 ...6 B8
Burleigh 5 WR15 ....55 E4
Burleigh Rd WR2 ...114 D3
Burley Cl B90 ....21 F2
Burley Way B38 .....34 C8
Burlingham Ave WR11 ..161 F4
Burlington Cl DY10 ...28 B4
Burlish Cl DY13 .....43 F6
Burlish Crossing DY13 ..43 F6
Burlish Mid Sch DY13 ..43 F6
Burlish Top Nature Reserve★
DY13 ....43 F7
Burma Rd WR11 ....161 E3
Burman Rd B90 .....21 F2
Burnell Cl B50 .....136 C5
Burnham Cl 3 WR5 ..128 E5
Burnham Gr B29 ....19 A8
Burnhill Gr B31 .....19 C1
Burnlea Gr B31 .....19 C1
Burns Cl
Kidderminster DY10 ...28 B6
Redditch B97 ....89 C8
Stourbridge DY8 ......6 A8
Burnsall Rd WR4 ...116 A4
Burnside Way B31 ...33 F7
Burnt Mdw Rd B98 ...71 F6
Burnt Oak Dr DY8 ....6 B5
Burnthorn La DY13 ...62 B8
Burnthorne La DY13 ..43 C1
Burrington Rd B32 ...18 A8
Burrish St WR9 ......84 F3
Burrows Cl WR14 ...139 C1
Burton La B70 ....70 F3
Burtree Ave WR4 ...116 A4
Bury Mound Ct B90 ..21 C2
Bush La WR2 ....140 D7
Bush Wlk 4 WR2 ...115 A4
Bushley Cl B98 ......90 A7
Butcher's Wlk WR3 ..103 A3
Butchers La B63 .....7 C7
Bute Cl B45 ....17 E1
Butler St B96 ....89 E1
Butler's Hill La B97 ...70 B5
Butt Furlong WR10 ..146 A2
Butter Wlk B38 .....34 C8
Buttercup Cl DY10 ...27 E8
Buttercup Dr B60 ....49 C6
Butterfly Cres 2 WR11 ..161 E3
Buttermere Cl DY5 ...6 B7
Buttermere Dr
Birmingham B32 ......9 A3
Worcester WR4 ....116 A6
Buttermere Rd DY13 ..43 A6
Button Bridge La DY12 ..10 A6
Butts La DY10 ......28 B1
Butts The 11 WR1 ..115 A4
Bye Rd WR14 ....153 C7
Byefields 5 WR5 ...141 C6
Byfield Rise WR5 ...115 D2
Bylands Cl B61 ......48 E1
Byford Cl B98 ......70 B4
Byland Cl WR5 ......116 A2
Byron Cl
2 Bowling Green WR2 ..127 C2
Great Malvern WR14 ..139 A2
Kidderminster DY10 ...28 B5
Walton Cardiff GL20 ..197 A5
Byron Rd B97 ....89 D8
Byron Way B61 .....49 A8

C

Caban Cl B31 ....18 C6
Cadbury Coll B38 ....19 C4
Cadbury World★ B30 ..19 F7
Cairndhu Dr DY10 ...28 B7
Caister Ave WR4 ...116 C5
Cakebole La DY10 ...46 B5
Calder Cl
8 Droitwich WR9 .....84 D1
Droitwich WR9 .....103 D1
Calder Rd
Stourport-on-Severn
DY13 ....43 E7
Worcester WR5 .....115 D2
Caldwall Cres DY11 ...27 C5
Caldy Ave WR5 ....128 E6
Caldy Wlk
5 Birmingham B45 ...17 F1
7 Stourport-on-Severn
DY13 ....43 E6
Caledonia DY5 ....6 D7
Cales Ave WR14 ...138 E4
Calewood Rd DY5 ....6 D7
Calgary Dr WR2 ...127 C4
California House B32 ...9 E2
California La WR13 ..167 D4
California Way B32 ...9 F3
Callcott Dr DY5 ......6 D7
Callow Cl 7 DY13 ...43 D1
Callow End CE Prim Sch
WR2 ....140 E7

Callow Hill La
Feckenham B97 ......88 F6
Redditch B97 ....89 B6
Callow Hill Rd B48 ...51 A6
Callowbridge Rd B45 ..32 F7
Callowbrook La B45 ...32 F7
Callows La 2 DY10 ...27 E6
Callows Mdw WR15 ..55 E2
Calverley Rd B38 ....34 D8
Camberwell Dr 9 WR5 ..128 E5
Cambrai Dr
Birmingham B28 .....21 F8
Worcester Norton WR5 ..128 F4
Cambria Cl B90 ......36 E7
Cambria Rd WR11 ..161 D5
Cambrian Rd
11 Walton Cardiff GL20 ..197 A4
1 Walton Cardiff GL20 ..197 A4
Camelot Dr WR14 ..166 F7
Cameo Dr DY8 ....5 F8
Camford Gr B14 ....20 F3
Camino Rd B32 ......9 F3
Camp Hill WR14 ...138 C1
Camp Hill Ave
8 Worcester WR5 ...115 D8
Camp Hill Rd WR5 ..115 D1
Camp La
Birmingham, King's Norton
B38 ....19 F3
Grimley WR2 ....101 E4
Shelsley Beauchamp WR6 ..60 E1
Camp Wood Cl B30 ..19 F8
Campden Cl B97 ....89 D6
Campden La WR12 ..177 F3
Campden Rd
Mickleton GL55 .....165 D2
Quinton CV37 ......151 F2
Campion Cl 3 B38 ...34 F8
Campion Dr WR14 ..153 D7
Campion Gr B63 .....7 D3
Campion House 2 B38 ..34 F8
Campion Way WR12 ..26 D5
Can La WR11 ....135 A3
Canada Bank WR10 ..160 E7
Canada Way WR2 ...127 C4
Canal Side Hopwood B48 ..34 B2
Worcester WR3 .....115 B6
Canal St DY8 ....5 F6
Cangle La WR4 ....116 C5
Cannon St WR5 ....128 E8
Canterbury Cl B80 ...90 C4
Canterbury Leys GL20 ..197 A7
Canterbury Rd
Kidderminster DY11 ...26 F7
Worcester WR5 .....115 F2
Cantlow Rd B13 ....21 A6
Canvey Cl B45 ......17 E1
Capcroft Rd B13 ....21 B6
Capern Gr B32 ....9 F5
Captain's La WR9 ..104 C6
Captains Pool Rd DY10 ..28 A1
Carden Cl 11 WR1 ..115 C2
Carden St WR1 ....115 C2
Cardinal Cres B61 ...48 C1
Cardinal Dr DY10 ...28 B3
Cardington Cl B98 ...71 F3
Cardy Cl B97 ....70 B4
Careless Gn DY9 .....6 F4
Carisbrooke Ave 18
WR4 ....116 C6
Carisbrooke Dr B62 ..8 D3
Carlisle Rd WR5 ...116 A2
Carlton Ave DY9 .....6 C1
Carlton Cl
Kidderminster DY11 ...27 A8
Redditch B97 ....70 B1
Carlton Rd WR14 ...138 F3
Carlyle Ave DY10 ...28 B6
Carlyle Rd B60 ......68 B8
Carmel Gr B32 ....9 B1
Carnforth Rd B60 ...49 B1
Carnoustie Cl B61 ...67 D8
Carol Ave B61 ....48 D3
Carol Cres B63 ......7 F5
Carol Gdns DY8 .....5 F8
Carpenter Glade B63 ..7 D5
Carpet Trades Way
DY11 ....27 D7
Carrant Brook Jun Sch
GL20 ....184 E1
Carrant Rd GL20 ...197 A7
Carriage Ct WR4 ...114 F3
Carrock Fell 1 WR4 ..116 A5
Carroll Wlk DY10 ...28 C5
Carter Ave DY11 ....27 B4
Carter Ct DY11 .....27 C4
Carter's La
Birmingham B62 ......9 A3
Halesowen B62 ....8 F4
Carters Cl
Bromsgrove B61 .....67 D7
10 Worcester WR4 ...115 D7
Carthorse La B97 ....70 B5
Cartland Rd B14, B30 ..20 C7
Cartmel Cl WR4 ...116 B6
Cartwright Rd WR4 ..116 F1
Cartwright St B60 ...67 D2
Carver Gdns DY8 ....5 E2
Caslon Cres DY8 ....5 D4
Caslon Flats B63 .....7 C4
Caslon Prim Sch B63 ..7 C4
Caslon Rd B63 ......7 C6
Castell Pl 2 WR4 ...116 C6
Castle Cl WR15 .....56 A6

Castle Croft B68 ....9 D8
Castle Gr DY8 ....6 B3
Castle Hts B64 ....8 B8
Castle La DY12 ....26 C4
Castle Pl WR1 .....115 C1
Castle Rd
　Birmingham B29 ......19 B8
　Birmingham, King's Norton
　B30 ....19 F4
　Cookley DY10 ....13 A4
　Kidderminster DY11 ....27 E5
　Studley B80 ....90 F4
Castle Rd E B68 ....9 D8
Castle Rd W B68 ....9 C8
Castle St
　Astwood Bank B96 .....89 E2
　3 Evesham WR11 ....161 E4
　Kinver DY7 ....4 A3
　Worcester WR1 .....115 A3
Castle The DY8 ....6 B3
Castle Toot★ DY14 ......22 E5
Castleditch La B98 .....89 E7
Castlemorton CE Prim Sch
　WR13 ....180 C7
Catbrook WR3 ....115 D6
Cathcart Rd DY8 ....5 E5
Cathedral Ave DY11 ...27 A6
Catherine Cl B60 ....67 F8
Catherine Rd WR2 ...127 C4
Catherton Cl DY14 .....22 B4
Catherton Rd DY14 .....22 B5
Catshill Fst Sch B61 ...49 A8
Catshill Mid Sch B61 ...48 F8
Caunsall Rd DY11 ......13 B6
Causey Farm Rd B63 ...16 C8
Cavendish Cl
　Birmingham B38 ....20 B1
　Marlbrook B60 ....32 C1
Cavendish Dr
　Hagley DY9 ....14 F4
　Kidderminster DY10 ....28 B7
Cavendish Rd B62 ....8 F4
Cavendish St WR5 ....128 C1
Caynham Cl B98 ....71 D4
Caynham Rd B32 ....18 B6
Cecil Rd WR5 ....115 D2
Cecil St DY8 ....5 F5
Cecilia Ave WR2 ....114 E5
Cecilia Pl WR2 ......114 E6
Cedar Ave
　Great Malvern WR14 ...139 B3
　Madresfield WR13 ....139 F4
　Worcester WR4 .....115 C6
Cedar Cl Alveley WV15 ...1 C6
　Birmingham B30 ......19 E6
　Droitwich WR9 .....103 F8
　Oldbury B68 ....9 C8
　Stourbridge DY8 ......5 D2
　Stourport-on-Severn DY13 ..43 F2
Cedar Cres DY11 ....27 C6
Cedar Dr
　Birmingham, West Heath
　B31 ....34 B7
　Bromsgrove B60 ......49 A1
　Kidderminster DY11 ...27 C7
Cedar Gdns DY7 ....3 F6
Cedar Gr DY9 ....15 A6
Cedar Pk Rd B97 ....70 D4
Cedar Rd
　Birmingham B30 ......19 E6
　Mickleton GL55 .....165 E4
　Northway GL20 .....197 E8
　Redditch B97 ....70 E4
Cedar Rise **15** DY13 ....43 E4
Cedar Terr 49 A1
Cedar View B97 ....70 C4
Cedar Way B31 ....18 F1
Cedarwood Gdns **1**
　WR11 ....161 F3
Celandine Dr WR5 ....128 D4
Celandine Way WR11 ..175 C8
Celvestune Way WR9 ...84 D2
Cemetery Rd
　Redditch B97 ....70 D3
　Stourbridge DY9 ....6 E5
Centenary Cl **1** B31 ...19 A1
Central Ave
　Birmingham B31 ......33 F8
　Blackheath, Cradley Heath
　B64 ....7 D7
　Stourbridge DY9 ......6 E3
Central Rd B60 ....49 A2
Centre Ct B63 ....8 B3
Centre La B63 ....8 B3
Centreway The B14 ....21 D4
Chaceley Ct B97 ....89 D8
Chacewater Ave WR3 ..115 A7
Chacewater Cres
　WR3 ....115 A7
Chadbury Rd
　Halesowen B63 ....8 C3
　Norton & Lenchwick
　WR11 ....147 B2
Chadcote Way B61 .....31 F1
Chaddersley Cl **2** B45 ...17 F1
Chaddesley Cl B98 .....70 F1
Chaddesley Corbett Endowed
　Fst Sch DY10 ....46 E8
Chaddesley Dr **7** DY9 ....6 B1
Chaddesley Gdns **2**
　DY10 ....28 A5
Chaddesley Rd
　Birmingham B31 ......19 D2
　Halesowen B63 ....7 F2
　Kidderminster DY10 ...28 A5

Chadsgrove Sch B61 ...48 F8
Chadwich La DY9 ......31 F7
Chadwick WR4 ....116 C4
Chadwick Ave B45 .....33 B6
Chadwick Bsns Pk
　DY13 ....63 D7
Chadwick La DY11 .....44 E2
Chadwick Mews B98 ...90 A7
Chadwick Rd DY9 ....6 D3
Chale Gr B14 ....21 A3
Chalfont Cl WR3 ....115 B7
Chalfont Pl DY9 ....6 C1
Chalford Dr WR4 .....116 A7
Chalgrove Ave B38 ....19 E1
Challenger Cl **5** WR14 ..139 B1
Chalybeate Cl B45 ....17 F1
Chamberlain La B49 ..109 C4
Chamberlain Rd
　Birmingham B13 ......21 A6
　Worcester WR2 .....127 C7
Champney DY10 ....27 E2
Chance Croft B68 ....9 B8
Chance La WR14 .....153 E8
Chance St **4** GL20 ....196 F6
Chancel Way B62 ....8 C6
Chandler Ave DY7 ....3 F5
Chandlers Cl B97 .....89 D7
Channon Dr DY5 ....6 D8
Chanston Ave B14 ....20 E4
Chantry Cl B47 ....36 A7
Chantry Dr B62 ....9 A6
Chantry High Sch The
　WR6 ....99 B5
Chantry Rd DY7 ....5 C7
Chantry The **1** WR10 ..146 A1
Chapel Cl
　3 Bidford-on-Avon B50 ..136 D4
　Blackheath B64 ....8 B8
　Leigh WR13 ....126 A4
Chapel Ct
　Astwood Bank B96 .....89 E1
　Kidderminster DY10 ...13 A1
Chapel Dr B47 ....35 F3
Chapel Hill DY9 ....6 B1
Chapel House La B63 ...7 C6
Chapel La
　Aldington WR11 .....162 C5
　Belbroughton DY9 ....31 D7
　Beoley B98 ....71 F8
　Bransford WR6 .....126 D4
　Bredon GL20 ....185 A4
　Childswickham WR12 ..176 F2
　Lindridge WR6 ....59 D7
　Mickleton GL55 .....165 D4
　Ombersley WR9 ....83 A4
　Redmarley D'abitot
　GL19 ....192 A1
　Rock DY14 ....24 E1
　Romsley B62 ....16 C6
　Rowney Green B48 ....51 F4
　5 Stourport-on-Severn
　DY13 ....62 E8
　Upton Snodsbury WR7 ..131 C8
　Weston-sub-Edge GL55 ..178 D6
　Wyre Piddle WR10 ...145 B3
　Wythall B47 ....35 E2
Chapel Mews WR9 ....85 E8
Chapel Pl DY13 ....27 D6
Chapel Pl Alveley WV15 ...1 C5
　Astwood Bank B96 .....89 E1
　Kempsey WR5 ....141 C7
　Pebworth CV37 .....150 E2
Chapel St
　Astwood Bank B96 .....89 E1
　Badsey WR11 ....162 E3
　Bromsgrove B60 ......49 A2
　2 Evesham WR11 ....161 D4
　Hagley DY9 ....15 A5
　Halesowen B63 ....8 A3
　Kidderminster DY11 ...27 D6
　Redditch B97 ....70 D1
　Stourbridge, Lye DY9 ....6 E5
　Stourbridge, Wollaston
　DY8 ....6 A4
Chapel Wlk
　Birmingham B30 ......20 A2
　Bromsgrove B60 ......49 A2
Chapelfield Mews
　Birmingham B45 ....32 F6
　Stourbridge DY9 ......6 A4
Chapelfield Rd B45 ....33 A7
Chapman's Hill B62 ...17 B1
Charfield Cl B30 ....19 D7
Charford Fst Sch 67 F7
Charford Rd B60 ....67 F8
Charity Cres WR11 ...161 D1
Charlecot Rd WR9 .....85 A1
Charlecote Cl B98 .....71 D7
Charlecott Cl B13 ....21 D7
Charles Ave DY10 .....13 A1
Charles Cl
　Evesham WR11 .....161 D1
　15 Walton Cardiff GL20 ..197 A4
Charles Dickens Cl **2**
　WR9 ....103 E8
Charles Hastings Way
　WR5 ....116 B2
Charles Henry Rd WR9 ..85 A3
Charles Rd
　Halesowen B63 ....7 F4
　Stourbridge DY8 ......5 E4
Charles St
　Kidderminster DY10 ...27 F6
　Redditch B97 ....70 C1
　6 Worcester WR1 ...115 C2
Charles Way WR14 ...139 C3
Charlock Rd WR14 ...153 D7

Charlotte Bronte Dr **3**
　WR9 ....103 E8
Charlotte Cl B30 ....20 A6
Charlton Cl WR11 ....161 A3
Charlton Dr B64 ....7 D7
Charlton La DY11 .....44 F4
Charnwood Cl
　Birmingham B45 ......18 B3
　Brierley Hill DY5 ....6 B8
　3 Worcester WR2 ...127 F7
Charnwood Ct DY9 .....6 E2
Charter Cres B64 ....8 B8
Charter Pl **2** WR1 ...115 B3
Chartist La GL19 .....192 A1
Chartwell Grange B64 ...8 A7
Chase End Cl WR5 ....128 E7
Chase High Sch The
　WR14 ....153 B6
Chase Rd
　Colwall WR14 ....152 D2
　Great Malvern WR14 ..166 F7
Chaston Rd DY7 ....120 C6
Chatcombe Dr WR4 ...116 A7
Chatham Rd B31 ....19 A3
Chatsworth Rd B62 .....8 A7
Chatterton Wlk **4** DY10 ..28 B6
Chaucer Cl DY8 ....6 A8
Chaucer Cres DY11 ...28 C5
Chaucer House B63 .....7 B5
Chaucer Rd B60 ....68 B8
Chawn Hill DY9 ....6 C3
Chawn Pk Dr DY9 ......6 C3
Chawnhill Cl DY9 ....6 C3
Chawson Fst Sch WR9 ..84 E1
Chawson La WR9 ......84 C1
Chawson Rd WR9 ......84 E2
Cheapside **1** DY13 .....44 A4
Checketts Cl
　Pershore/Pinvin WR10 ..144 E7
　Worcester WR3 .....115 B7
Checketts La WR3 ...115 B8
Chedworth Cl
　Birmingham B29 ......19 B6
　Redditch B98 ....71 C5
　Worcester WR4 .....116 A7
Chedworth Dr WR4 ...116 A7
Chells Gr B13 ....21 B5
Chelmarsh Cl B98 .....71 C7
Chelmsford Dr WR5 ..115 F1
Chelsea Cl B32 ....19 F4
Chelsea Ct **6** B29 .....19 B7
Chelston Rd B31 ....18 E2
Cheltenham Ave B61 ..32 B1
Cheltenham Rd
　Beckford GL20 ....186 C2
　Bredon GL20 ....185 A5
　Broadway WR12 .....190 A7
　Buckland WR12 .....189 F5
　Evesham WR11 .....161 C1
　Hinton on the Green
　WR11 ....175 B3
　Sedgeberrow WR11 ...174 F1
Chelworth Rd B38 ....20 B2
Chepstow Ave WR4 ...116 B6
Chepstow Dr B61 ......32 B1
Chepstow Gr B45 .....33 B6
Chequers Cl
　Great Malvern WR14 ..139 C5
　3 Stourport-on-Severn
　DY13 ....62 F8
Chequers La
　1 Dodderhill WR9 .....66 E1
　Dodderhill WR9 ....85 F8
　Fladbury WR10 .....146 B1
　Worcester WR2 .....115 A2
Cherhill Covert **7** B14 ..20 C2
Cherington Cl
　Redditch B98 ....71 F1
　8 Worcester WR4 ...115 F7
Cherington Rd B29 ...20 A8
Cherrington Cl B31 ...18 F7
Cherrington Gdns DY9 ..15 C7
Cherry Cl
　16 Bewdley DY12 .....25 F3
　2 Droitwich WR9 .....85 B1
　3 Evesham WR11 ...161 F2
　Offenham WR11 .....148 A1
Cherry Cres B61 ......48 E2
Cherry Gr DY8 ....5 E4
Cherry Hill Ave B45 ...50 C8
Cherry Hill Dr B45 ...50 C8
Cherry Hill Rd B45 ...50 C8
Cherry Orch
　Bredon GL20 ....184 E6
　Holt WR6 ....82 B3
　Kidderminster DY10 ...27 F6
　Pershore WR10 .....144 D1
　Upton upon Severn WR8 ..169 C5
Cherry Orch Ave B63 ...7 F5
Cherry Orch Cres B63 ...7 F6
Cherry Orch Dr B61 ...48 E3
Cherry Orch Fst Sch
　WR10 ....144 E1
Cherry Orch La GL20 ..183 E6
Cherry Orch Prim Sch
　WR5 ....128 D7
Cherry Orch Rd WR10 ..145 D3
Cherry Pit La B98 .....53 A1
Cherry St Halesowen B63 ...7 F5
　Stourbridge DY8 ......5 E4
　Worcester WR5 .....128 C8
Cherry Tree Cres
　WR11 ....135 F3
Cherry Tree Dr WR14 ..152 F4
Cherry Tree La B63 ....7 D1
Cherry Tree Wlk
　Astley & Dunley DY13 ...62 E7
　Redditch B97 ....70 B4

Cherry Tree Wlk *continued*
　6 Worcester WR1 ....115 B3
Cherry Wlk B47 ....36 B5
Cherrytree Ct DY9 .....6 E3
Cherwell Cl WR4 .....115 F4
Cheshire Cl DY8 ....5 D7
Cheshire Gr DY11 .....27 A7
Cheslyn Gr B14 ....21 A3
Chessetts Gr B13 .....21 A6
Chesshire Ave DY13 ...62 E8
Chester Cl **1** WR5 ...115 F1
Chester Ct **5** B29 .....19 B7
Chester Pl **2** WR14 ..138 F4
Chester Rd
　Blackheath B64 ....7 C8
　Kinver DY7 ....3 F7
Chester Rd N DY10 ....28 A7
Chester Rd S DY10 ...27 F4
Chester Rise B68 ....9 B8
Chesterfield Cl B31 ...19 B2
Chesterfield Ct B38 ...19 F1
Chesterton Cl B97 .....89 D4
Chesterwood B47 .....36 A6
Chesterwood Rd B13 ..20 F6
Chestnut Cl
　Aldington WR11 .....162 C5
　Drakes Broughton
　WR10 ....144 A6
　Evesham WR11 .....161 B1
　Hill & Moor WR10 ...145 D3
　Stourbridge DY8 ......5 D3
　Welland WR13 .....167 C5
Chestnut Ct DY11 .....27 B8
Chestnut Dr
　Birmingham, Rednall
　B45 ....33 D4
　Great Malvern WR14 ..152 F4
Chestnut Gr
　Kidderminster DY11 ...27 B8
　Kinver DY7 ....3 F5
Chestnut La WR7 .....120 E7
Chestnut Pl B14 ....20 E8
Chestnut Rd
　Astwood Bank B96 .....89 E1
　Bromsgrove B61 ......48 F4
　Oldbury B68 ....9 C7
Chestnut Spinney **5**
　WR9 ....103 F8
Chestnut Wlk
　Ombersley WR9 ....83 A5
　Worcester WR1 .....115 B8
Cheswick Cl B98 ....72 A3
Chesworth Rd B60 ....49 B1
Cheveley Ave B45 ....33 B7
Chevenham Cl **3** WR13 ..152 A1
Cheverton Rd B31 ....18 E4
Chevington La WR10 ..143 E2
Cheviot Cl
　Stourport-on-Severn
　DY13 ....62 D8
　Worcester WR4 .....115 F4
Cheviot Rd DY8 ....6 A6
Cheviot Way B63 ....7 D2
Cheyne Gdns B28 .....21 E3
Cheyne Wlk DY5 ....6 C7
Chichester Ave DY11 ..12 C1
Chichester Dr B32 ....9 A5
Chilcote Cl B28 ....21 F4
Chilcote Prim Sch B28 ..21 F4
Childe Rd DY14 ....22 C4
Childswickham Rd
　WR12 ....190 B8
Chilham Pl **4** WR4 ...116 C6
Chiltern Cl
　Great Witley WR6 ....61 A1
　Halesowen B63 ....7 D1
　Stourport-on-Severn
　DY13 ....62 D8
　2 Worcester WR4 ...115 F4
Chiltern House B98 ...71 E1
Chiltern Rd DY8 ....6 B6
Chilton Rd B14 ....21 D4
China Cnr WR11 .....164 A4
Chinn Brook Rd B13 ..21 C5
Chip Cl B38 ....19 D2
Chirbury Gr B31 ....19 B1
Chirk Cl DY10 ....27 E2
Chirton Gr B14 ....20 D6
Chiseldon Croft B14 ..21 A3
Chorley Rd **2** WR9 ....84 F3
Christ & St Mary's Cath
　WR1 ....115 C1
Christ Church Rd
　4 Great Malvern WR14 ..153 A8
　Worcester WR4 .....115 C6
Christina Cl **3** WR5 ..141 C7
Christine Ave WR2 ...127 C7
Christopher Rd B62 ....8 E3
Christopher Whitehead High
　Sch WR2 ....115 A1
Church Ave Clent DY9 ...15 F3
　Stourbridge DY8 ......6 A7
　Stourport-on-Severn
　DY13 ....44 A4
Church Cl
　Broadway WR12 .....190 C7
　Inkberrow WR7 .....120 E7
　Upper Sapey WR6 ....77 E4
　Wythall B47 ....35 F3
Church Croft B63 ....8 A4
Church Ct
　Astwood Bank B96 .....89 E2
　Stourbridge DY8 ......6 A7
Church Down Cl B97 ..89 D6
Church Dr
　Birmingham B30 ......20 B7

Church Dr *continued*
　Cookhill B49 ....109 A2
　10 Stourport-on-Severn
　DY13 ....44 A4
Church End **1** WR10 ..132 F4
Church Farm
　Wick WR10 ....145 A3
　Wyre Piddle WR10 ...145 A4
　Wyre Piddle WR10 ...145 A4
Church Farm Barn & Cotts
　DY10 ....14 B3
Church Gn E B98 ....70 E4
Church Gn W B97 .....70 E4
Church Gr B13 ....21 C5
Church Hill
　Belbroughton DY9 ....30 D6
　Beoley B98 ....71 D8
　Birmingham, Frankley Green
　B32 ....18 B6
　Birmingham, Northfield
　B31 ....19 B3
　Kinver DY7 ....3 F2
　Rushock WR9 ....46 C3
Church Hill Mid Sch
　B98 ....71 D6
Church Hill Way B98 ..71 D6
Church La
　2 Bishampton WR10 ..132 F4
　Broadheath WR2 .....114 A7
　Broadwas WR6 .....112 B3
　Bromsgrove B61 ......48 F2
　Cookhill B49 ....109 A2
　Cotheridge WR6 .....113 B2
　Defford WR8 ....157 D3
　Dodderhill WR9 ....66 E1
　Earl's Croome WR8 ...156 A1
　Flyford Flavell WR7 ..119 D1
　Forthampton GL19 ...195 E6
　Great Comberton WR10 ..158 F1
　Halesowen B63 ....8 B4
　Hallow WR2 ....101 D1
　Hill & Moor WR10 ...145 D3
　Himbleton WR9 .....105 D2
　Little Witley WR6 .....81 A4
　Mamble DY14 ....39 F4
　Martin Hussingtree WR3 ..103 B4
　Norton & Lenchwick
　WR11 ....147 E4
　Norton Juxta Kempsey
　WR5 ....129 B3
　Oddingley WR9 .....104 C3
　Ombersley WR9 ....83 A3
　Pershore/Pinvin WR10 ..144 F6
　Rock DY14 ....24 B2
　Severn Stoke WR8 ...155 D5
　1 South Littleton WR11 ..148 F1
　Stanton WR12 .....189 D1
　Stoulton WR7 ....143 B8
　Suckley WR6 ....123 F4
　Tibberton WR9 .....117 A6
　Upper Sapey WR6 ....77 E4
　Upton Snodsbury WR7 ..131 C8
　Whittington WR5 .....129 C3
Church Lench CE Prim Sch
　WR11 ....134 A3
Church Leys WR10 ...160 C7
Church Rd Alveley WV15 ...1 C5
　Aston Somerville WR12 ..175 F1
　Astwood Bank B96 .....89 E2
　Belbroughton DY9 ....30 D6
　Birmingham, Northfield
　B31 ....19 A4
　Bromsgrove B61 ......48 F2
　Castlemorton WR13 ..180 D7
　Catshill B61 ....48 F8
　Crowle WR7 ....117 E4
　Dodford B61 ....47 F7
　Evesham WR11 .....161 B2
　Great Malvern WR14 ..139 A4
　Halesowen B63 ....7 C7
　Redditch, St George's
　B97 ....70 E4
　Redditch, Webheath B97 ..69 F2
　Stock & Bradley B96 ..106 F7
　Stourbridge, Lye DY9 ...6 E5
　Stourbridge, Old Swinford
　DY8 ....6 B3
　Worcester WR3 .....115 D5
Church Row **8** WR10 ..158 D8
Church St
　Bidford-on-Avon B50 ..136 E4
　Birlingham WR10 ...158 A3
　Bredon GL20 ....184 E6
　Broadway WR12 .....190 C7
　Bromsgrove B61 ......48 F2
　Cleobury Mortimer DY14 ..22 C4
　Eckington WR10 .....171 E7
　Evesham WR11 .....161 B3
　Fladbury WR10 .....146 B1
　Great Malvern WR14 ..152 F8
　Hagley DY9 ....15 A5
　Hanley Castle WR8 ...169 B7
　Harvington WR11 ...148 B6
　Kempsey WR5 ....141 B7
　Kidderminster DY10 ...27 E6
　Offenham WR11 .....148 A1
　7 Pershore WR10 ...158 D8
　Stourbridge DY8 ......6 A5
　Studley B80 ....90 E3
　2 Tenbury Wells WR15 ..55 E5
　Tewkesbury GL20 ...196 E6
　Upton upon Severn WR8 ..169 C6
　Willersey WR11 .....177 F4
　Worcester WR1 .....115 C4
　Wyre Piddle WR10 ...145 A3
Church Terr **5** WR2 ...114 F1
Church View DY12 ....26 A3
Church View Gdns **2** DY7 ..4 A4

Church Wlk
  Kidderminster DY11 .....27 C6
  Little Hereford SY8 ......54 C5
  🔟 Pershore WR10 .....158 D8
  Stourport-on-Severn
  DY13 ....43 E2
Churchdown Rd WR14 .153 B6
Churchfield Terr WR6 ...60 F4
Churchfields
  Bromsgrove B61 ....48 F3
  Kidderminster DY10 .....27 C6
Churchfields Cl B61 .....48 F3
Churchfields Gdns B61 ..48 F3
Churchfields Rd B61 .....48 F3
Churchill & Blakedown Sta
  DY10 ....14 C2
Churchill Ave
  Great Malvern WR14 ...139 B6
  Stourbridge DY8 ....6 A7
Churchill Dr
  Great Malvern WR14 ...139 B6
  Stourbridge DY8 ....6 A7
Churchill Gr GL20 .....197 B6
Churchill La DY10 ......14 B3
Churchill Rd
  Catshill B61 ....32 A1
  Halesowen B63 ....7 F2
  Sedgeberrow WR11 .....174 F1
Churchstone Cl B61 .....48 F8
Churchward Cl DY8 ....6 B6
Churchway Piece
  WR7 ....120 E7
Churchwell Ct B63 ....8 B2
Cider Ave DY5 ....6 E6
Cidermill Orch GL55 ...178 D2
Cinders La WR15 ....74 D6
Cinders Rd WR15 ....55 D1
Cirencester Cl B62 .....49 B2
Cirencester Pl 🔟 WR4 .116 B7
City East 7 D8
City Walls Rd WR1 .....115 C2
Cladswell Cl B49 ......109 A2
Cladswell La B49 ......109 A2
Cladsworth House 🔟
  B97 ....70 A4
Claerwen Ave DY13 .....43 E2
Claerwen Dr B18 ....18 E5
Claines CE Prim Sch
  WR3 ....102 C3
Claines Cres DY10 .....28 B5
Claines La WR3 ....102 C2
Claines Rd
  Birmingham B31 ....19 C4
  Halesowen B63 ....7 D5
Clanbrook Rd DY7 ....3 C4
Clandon Cl B14 ....20 C2
Clapgate La B32 ....9 C2
Claphill La
  Rushwick WR2 ....114 B1
  Worcester WR2 ....127 B8
Clarage House B62 ......8 D8
Clare Ct B90 ....21 D2
Clare Rd 🔟 WR14 ......139 B1
Clare St 🔟 WR1 ......115 C2
Clare Witnell Cl DY11 ..27 B8
Clare's Rd DY9 ....27 C6
Claremont Ct WR14 ....152 E6
Claremont Way B63 ......8 A3
Clarence Cl WR14 ......153 A7
Clarence Rd
  Great Malvern WR14 ...153 A8
  Tewkesbury GL20 ......196 E4
Clarence St DY10 ....27 F6
Clarence Way DY12 .....26 B4
Clarendon Cl B97 ....70 B5
Clarendon Pl B62 ....9 A6
Clark St DY8 ....5 E4
Clarke St 🔟 B97 ....70 E3
Clarks Hill Rise WR11 .161 B3
Clarkson Gdns 🔟 B18 ..116 C4
Clarkson Pl Ind Est DY5 .6 E6
Clatterbach La DY9 .....16 A4
Clattercut La WR9 ......46 E3
Claughton Cl DY11 .....27 C5
Claughton St DY11 .....27 C5
Clavedon Cl B31 ....18 E7
Claverdon Rd B97 ......89 D4
Claverdon House B13 ...21 B4
Claverham Cl WR2 .....128 A8
Claverton WR7 ....143 B7
Clay Dr B32 ....9 A5
Claybrook Dr B98 ......90 F7
Claybrook Fst Sch B98 ..71 F1
Claycroft Pl DY9 ....6 E5
Claydon Gr 🔟 B14 .....21 A3
Clayfield DY14 ....138 E4
Clayfield Rd DY11 .....163 B6
Clayfields B96 ....88 F3
Clayhall Rd 🔟 WR9 ....85 A1
Claypit La B61 ....31 E1
Clayton Dr B60 ....68 B7
Clayton Gdns B45 ......33 C4
Clearwell Rd B98 ......71 C3
Clee Ave DY11 ....27 C2
Clee Hill Rd
  Burford WR15 ....55 E8
  Nash SY8 ....37 A6
Clee Rd Birmingham B31 .34 A8
  Cookley DY10 ....13 B5
  Stourbridge DY8 ....6 A6
Clee View WR9 ....84 E5
Cleeve Cl Redditch B98 ..71 C6
  Stourport-on-Severn
  DY13 ....62 D8
Cleeve Dr B18 ....116 A4
Cleeve Prior CE Fst Sch
  WR11 ....149 B7
Cleeve Rd
  Bidford-on-Avon B50 ..136 D2
  Birmingham B14 ....21 C4

Cleeve Rd continued
  Cleeve Prior WR11 .....149 B7
  South Littleton WR11 ..148 F1
Clensmore St DY10 .....27 D7
Clent Ave
  Kidderminster DY11 .....27 B1
  Redditch B97 ....89 D7
Clent Dr DY9 ....15 D6
Clent Fst Sch DY9 ......15 F2
Clent House
  Bromsgrove B60 ....49 B3
  Halesowen B63 ....8 A2
Clent Rd
  Birmingham, Rubery
  B45 ....32 E8
  Oldbury B68 ....9 D8
  Stourbridge DY8 ....6 A6
Clent View Rd
  Birmingham B32 ....9 A1
  Halesowen B63 ....7 C5
  Stourbridge DY8 ....5 C2
Clent Way B32 ....18 A8
Cleobury Cl B97 ....70 B5
Cleobury La B90 ....36 F4
Cleobury Mortimer Cty Prim
  Sch DY14 ....22 B4
Cleobury Rd DY12 ......25 E3
Clerkenwell Cres
  WR14 ....139 A2
Clevedon Gn WR11 ....149 A1
Cleveland Dr B45 ....33 A2
Cleveland Dr DY8 ....5 E4
Cleves Dr B45 ....32 E8
Cleves Rd B45 ....32 E8
Clewer Croft WR13 ....125 F2
Clewley Gr B32 ....9 B5
Clews Rd B98 ....89 F7
Clewshaw La B38 ......35 C4
Cliff Rock Rd B45 ......33 B7
Cliffey House Sch
  WR8 ....154 F7
Clifford Ave 🔟 GL20 ..197 A4
Clifford Cl WR9 ....103 E7
Clifford Rd WR9 ....103 E7
Clifton Cl DY8 ....90 E8
Clifton Rd Halesowen B62 .8 E8
  Kidderminster DY11 .....27 A1
  Wolverley & Cookley
  DY10 ....13 C3
Clifton upon Teme Prim Sch
  WR6 ....97 E7
Clinic Dr DY9 ....6 E5
Clive Rd Birmingham B32 ..9 F7
  Bromsgrove B60 ....68 B8
  Redditch B97 ....70 D5
Clivedon Way B62 ....8 B7
Cloister Dr B63 ....8 D3
Cloisters The B80 ......90 D4
Clonmel Rd B30 ....20 A6
Close The
  Birmingham, Beech Lanes
  B17 ....9 F7
  Birmingham, Griffin's Hill
  B29 ....19 D8
  Cleeve Prior WR11 .....149 A4
  Eckington WR10 ......171 F8
  Halesowen B63 ....7 D6
  Hollywood B47 ....36 A5
  Hunnington B62 ....17 A7
  Wyre Piddle WR10 ....145 B4
Clover Cl B38 ....19 D2
Clover Dr B32 ....9 D2
Clover Rd B29 ....19 A7
Cloverdale B60 ....67 C3
Clowes Wood La B94 ...53 F8
Clows Top Rd
  Abberley WR6 ....60 E5
  Bayton DY14 ....40 C6
Club View B38 ....19 C7
Clun Rd B31 ....18 F6
Clunbury Rd B31 ....34 A8
Clusters The DY9 ....6 E5
Clyde Ave
  Evesham WR11 ....161 F3
  Halesowen B62 ....8 E8
Clydes Dale Rd WR14 .104 B8
Clydesdale Cl 🔟 WR9 .104 B8
Clydesdale Rd B32 .....9 B6
Coach Cotts B45 ....50 D8
Coalash La B60 ....68 C2
Coalbourn La DY8 ......5 F7
Coalbourne Gdns B63 ...7 C5
Coalbournhill Glassworks★
  DY8 ....5 F7
Coates Rd DY10 ....28 B7
Cob La B30 ....19 C6
Cobden Ave WR4 .....116 C4
Cobden St
  Kidderminster DY11 .....27 D5
  Stourbridge DY8 ....5 E5
Coberley Cl WR4 ......116 A6
Cobham Cl
  Bromsgrove B60 ....67 F7
  Welland WR13 ....167 C5
Cobham Cres DY12 ....26 A3
Cobham Ct 🔟 WR9 ....84 F3
Cobham Ct Mews DY9 ..15 D6
Cobham Rd
  Halesowen B63 ....8 B4
  Kidderminster DY10 .....27 C4
  Pershore/Pinvin WR10 .144 E4
  Stourbridge DY8 ....6 B2
Cobley Hill B48 ....50 B4
Cobnall Rd B61 ....48 E2
Cobs Field B30 ....19 C6
Cochrane Cl DY9 ....15 C8
Cock Hill La B45 ....32 F8

Cocksheds La B62 ....8 C8
Cockshot La B96 ......106 D1
Cockshot Rd WR14 ....138 F2
Cockshute Hill WR9 ....85 B2
Cockshutt La B61 ......48 D7
Cocksmead Croft B14 ..20 D5
Cocksmoor House B14 ..20 D7
Cockthorpe Cl B17 ......9 F7
Codsall Rd B64 ....7 E8
Cofton Church La B45 ..33 D3
Cofton Cl B97 ....70 B5
Cofton Ct B45 ....33 D7
Cofton Gr B31 ....33 E6
Cofton Lake Rd B45 ....33 C3
Cofton Prim Sch B31 ...34 A6
Cofton Rd B31 ....34 B7
Cokeland Pl B64 ....7 D8
Cold Comfort La B49 ..122 F8
Coldbath Rd B13 ......21 B8
Coldfield Dr B98 ....89 E7
Coldicott Gdns 🔟
  WR11 ....161 C2
Coldicotts Cl WR11 ...163 B5
Coldicotts Rd WR11 ...163 B5
Cole Bank Rd B28 .....21 E8
Cole Gn B90 ....21 F2
Cole Hill WR5 ....115 D1
Cole Valley Rd B28 ....21 D6
Colebourne Rd B13 ....21 D6
Colebrook Croft B90 ...21 F2
Colebrook Rd B90 .....21 F2
Coleford Cl B97 ....70 A2
Colemeadow Rd
  Birmingham B13 ....21 B6
  Redditch B98 ....71 F6
Coleridge Cl
  Redditch B97 ....89 C8
  Worcester WR5 ....115 C6
Colesborne Cl 🔟 WR4 .115 F7
Colesbourne Ave B14 ..20 C2
Coleshill Cl B97 ....89 C5
Coleside Ave B13 ......21 D7
Coley Pits La WR9 .....66 E3
Coleys La B31 ....19 A2
Colford Cl 🔟 WR9 .....84 C1
Colin Rd WR3 ....102 A1
Colleen Ave B30 ....20 B3
College Cl
  Cleobury Mortimer DY14 .22 C5
  Long Marston CV37 ...151 C5
College Dr 🔟 WR15 ...55 E4
College Gn B90 ....84 E1
College Gr WR14 ......152 F6
College Precincts 🔟
  WR1 ....115 C2
College Rd
  Birmingham, Quinton B32 .9 A6
  Bredon GL20 ....184 D6
  Bromsgrove B60 ....49 A2
  Great Malvern WR14 ...152 F7
  Kidderminster DY10 .....27 E4
  Stourbridge DY8 ....6 A4
  Upton Snodsbury WR7 .131 C8
College St WR1 ......115 C2
College Wlk
  Birmingham B29 ....19 D8
  Bromsgrove B60 ....49 A2
  Tenbury WR15 ....74 C8
College Yd 🔟 WR1 ...115 C2
Collett Cl DY8 ....6 A6
Collett's Gn Rd WR2 ..127 B3
Colletts Fields WR12 .190 E8
Colletts Gdns WR12 ..190 E8
Colley Gate B63 ....7 C6
Colley La B63 ....7 C6
Colley La Prim Sch B63 ..7 C6
Colley Orch B63 ....7 C6
Collier Cl 🔟 WR12 ...177 E4
Collin La WR12 ....177 C3
Collings Ave 🔟 WR4 ..116 C3
Collins Cl B32 ....9 A5
Collinsfield WR11 .....161 E6
Collinson Cl B98 ......71 A1
Collis Cl B60 ....67 E7
Collis St DY8 ....5 F8
Colman Hill B63 ....7 D5
Colman Hill Ave B63 ...7 D6
Colmers Farm Inf Sch
  B45 ....33 B8
Colmers Farm Jun Sch
  B45 ....33 B8
Colmers Fst Sch B45 ..33 B8
Colmers Wlk B31 .....18 D1
Colmore Ave B14 ......20 D7
Colmore Inf Sch B14 ..20 D7
Colmore Jun Sch B14 ..20 D7
Colmore Rd B14 ......20 D7
Coln Cl B31 ....18 F6
Colonial Ind Pk B64 ....7 D7
Colshaw Rd DY8 ....5 E4
Coltishall Cl 🔟 WR5 .128 C6
Colts La B98 ....71 D3
Columbia Dr WR2 ....127 E7
Columbine Gr WR11 ..161 C1
Columbine Rd GL20 ..197 A3
Colwall Gn CE Prim Sch
  WR13 ....166 A8
Colwall Sta WR13 ....152 B2
Colworth Rd B31 ......18 F4
Comber Croft B13 .....21 D8
Comber Rd DY7 ....4 A3
Comber Gr DY7 ....4 A3
Comber Rd DY7 ....3 F2
Comberton Ave B28 ...28 B5
Comberton Ct 🔟 DY10 ..28 A5
Comberton Fst Sch
  DY10 ....28 B4
Comberton Gdns DY10 .28 B5
Comberton Hill DY10 ..27 F5

Comberton Mans 🔟
  DY10 ....28 A5
Comberton Mid Sch
  DY10 ....28 B4
Comberton Pk Rd DY10 .28 B4
Comberton Pl DY10 ....27 F5
Comberton Rd DY10 ...28 B4
Comberton Terr DY10 ..27 F5
Comhampton La DY13 ..63 F3
Commandery Civil War Ctr
  The★ WR1 ....115 C1
Commandery Rd WR5 .115 C1
Common Barn La DY10 .13 D5
Common La
  Mappleborough Green
  B80 ....72 B3
  Neen Savage DY14 ....22 A7
Common Rd WR11 ....161 E5
Common The WR6 .....60 E3
Compa The DY7 ....4 A3
Compton Cl Kinver DY7 ..3 F5
  Redditch B98 ....70 E2
Compton Gdns DY7 .....3 F5
Compton Gr B63 ....7 C4
Compton Grange B64 ...7 C8
Compton Rd
  Halesowen B62 ....8 F5
  Kinver DY7 ....3 F5
  Stourbridge DY9 ....6 D2
  Worcester WR5 ......115 D1
Condover Rd B31 ......34 B8
Conduit Hill 🔟 WR11 .161 E4
Coney Gn DY8 ....6 B5
Coney Gn Cl 🔟 WR4 ..116 B6
Coney Gn Dr B31 ......33 F8
Coneygree La WR12 ..190 D5
Congleton Cl B97 ......70 B5
Conifer Cl DY5 ....6 C8
Conifer Dr B31 ....19 B3
Conifer Gr B61 ....48 F3
Conifer Paddock B62 ...8 E8
Conigre La GL20 .....196 F6
Coningsby Dr WR5 .....27 A8
Conisborough 🔟 WR4 .116 C5
Coniston Cl
  Birmingham B28 ....21 F7
  Bromsgrove B60 ....49 B1
  Great Malvern WR14 ...153 C6
  Worcester WR4 ......116 A5
Coniston Cres DY13 ...43 F6
Coniston House DY10 ..27 E6
Coniston Way DY12 ....25 E3
Connaught Cl 🔟 WR5 .128 C6
Connaught Cl 🔟 WR5 .128 C6
Connaught Rd B60 .....49 C1
Conningsby Dr WR10 .158 B8
Connops Way DY9 ......6 E5
Conolly Dr B45 ....18 B1
Consort Rd B30 ....20 A3
Constance Rd WR3 ....114 F8
Conway Ave B32 ....9 B6
Conway House B31 ....18 D6
Conway Rd B60 ....49 B1
Conwy Dr WR11 ......162 A3
Cook's La WR13 ......192 E7
Cookes Croft B31 ......19 B2
Cookley Cl B63 ....7 F2
Cookley La DY10 ....13 A5
Cookley Sebright Endowed
  Fst Sch DY10 ....13 A5
Cooks Cross WV15 .....1 C1
Cooks Hill WR10 .....159 B7
Cooksey Gn La
  Elmbridge WR9 ....65 D3
  Upton Warren WR9 ....66 A7
Coombe Hill B64 ....8 B7
Coombefield Rd
  WR11 ....176 D7
Coombes La B31 ....33 F7
Coombes Rd B62 ....8 B7
Coombs Rd
  Halesowen B62 ....8 B7
  Worcester WR3 ......115 B7
Coombswood Way B65 ..8 B8
Cooper Cl B60 ....67 E6
Cooper's La WR11 ....161 E3
Coopers Cl 🔟 WR4 ...115 F6
Coopers Hill B48 ......50 E6
Copcut La WR9 ....84 A1
Cope Rd WR3 ....115 B7
Copelands Dr DY7 ......4 A3
Copenhagen St 🔟 WR1 .115 C2
Copperbeech Cl B32 ....9 F5
Coppice Ave DY9 ....6 F3
Coppice Cl
  Birmingham, Eachway
  B45 ....32 F2
  Great Malvern WR14 ..138 C6
  Hallow WR2 ....101 D3
  Redditch B97 ....70 C3
Coppice Hollow B32 ...9 B1
Coppice Hts DY11 .....27 B1
Coppice Prim Sch The
  B47 ....36 A6
Coppice Rd B64 ....7 E7
Coppice The
  Birmingham, Frankley
  B31 ....18 C2
  Hagley DY8 ....14 F5
Coppice Trad Est DY11 .44 B8
Coppice Way WR9 .....84 C5
Copse Cl B31 ....19 A2
Copsewood Ave WR5 .116 B3

Copston Gr B29 ....19 B8
Copyholt La
  Stoke Prior B60 ....68 D3
  Upper Bentley B60, B97 .69 A3
Corbett Ave WR9 ......84 F2
Corbett Cl B60 ....68 B8
Corbett Cres DY8 ......6 A7
Corbett Dr B60 ....67 C1
Corbett Hospl 🔟 DY8 ...5 F7
Corbett House 🔟 DY8 ..5 F8
Corbett Rd
  Hollywood B47 ....36 A7
  Kidderminster DY11 .....27 A8
Corbett St WR9 ....84 F2
Corbizum Ave B80 .....90 D4
Cordle Marsh Rd DY12 .26 C5
Corfe Ave WR4 ......116 C6
Corfe Cl B32 ....9 F5
Coriander Cl
  Birmingham B45 ......18 B2
  Stoke Prior B60 ......67 C1
Corinne Cl B45 ....33 A6
Corley Ave B31 ....19 B3
Corley B90 ....21 E1
Cormorant Gr DY10 ...28 B3
Cormorant Rise WR2 .128 A6
Corn Mill Cl B32 ....9 E1
Corn Mill Rd WR11 ...161 C1
Corn Mkt 🔟 WR1 ....115 C2
Cornbow Ctr B63 ....8 B3
Cornbrook Rd B29 ....18 F7
Corndon Cl DY11 ......27 B2
Corner Farm Dr WR11 .164 A1
Corner La B97 ....69 E2
Corner Stone Ctry Club
  B31 ....19 B5
Cornerway B38 ....34 F7
Cornfield Ave B60 .....67 D6
Cornfield Rd B31 ......19 B4
Cornfield Way WR11 ..174 B2
Corngreaves Rd B64 ...7 E7
Corngreaves Trad Est
  B64 ....7 D7
Corngreaves Wlk B64 ...7 E7
Cornhampton Cl 🔟 B97 .70 B5
Cornhill Gr B30 ....20 C7
Cornmeadow Gn WR3 .102 B1
Cornmeadow La WR3 .102 B1
Cornmill Cl WR10 ....173 E7
Cornmore WR10 .....158 B7
Cornwall Ave
  Kidderminster DY11 .....12 C1
  Oldbury B68 ....9 B8
Cornwall Gdns 🔟 WR15 .55 E5
Cornwall Rd
  Birmingham, Rubery
  B45 ....17 E1
  Stourbridge DY8 ....5 D8
Cornwell Cl B98 ......90 B5
Coronation Ave WR2 .127 B8
Coronation Rd 🔟 WR4 .139 B5
Coronation St WR11 ..161 F4
Coronation Terr B60 ...68 B7
Coronation Way DY10 .28 B5
Corporation St DY10 ..27 E5
Corrie Croft B33 ......18 B7
Corron Hill B63 ....8 B4
Corser St DY8 ....6 A3
Corvedale Rd B29 ....19 A6
Corville Rd B62 ....8 F6
Corwen Croft B31 ....18 E6
Cosford Cl B98 ....71 F1
Cosgrove Cl WR4 ....115 F8
Costers La B98 ....71 F2
Cote La Enville DY7 ....3 F8
  Kinver DY7 ....4 A7
Cotford Rd B14 ....21 A2
Cotheridge Cl B98 ....90 B5
Cotheridge Ct★ WR6 .113 A2
Cotheridge La WR10 ..171 E7
Cotland WR3 ....115 D5
Coton Gr B90 ....21 E2
Cotsgrove Cl WR14 ...43 D1
Cotswold Ave 🔟 DY13 .43 D1
Cotswold Cl
  Birmingham B45 ......18 B2
  🔟 Bredon GL20 .....184 F6
  Kidderminster DY11 .....27 C2
Cotswold Croft B63 ....7 C1
Cotswold Edge GL55 .165 D4
Cotswold Gdns GL20 .196 F7
Cotswold House 🔟 B14 .21 A3
Cotswold Rd
  🔟 Great Malvern WR14 .153 B8
  Stourbridge DY8 ....6 B6
Cotswold Way
  Bromsgrove B61 ....49 A5
  Worcester WR4 ......115 F8
Cottage Dr B60 ....32 D1
Cottage Farm La B60 ..32 D1
Cottage Gdns B45 .....32 F6
Cottage La B60 ....32 C1
Cottages The B63 ......7 E6
Cotteridge Inf & Jun Sch
  B30 ....20 A5
Cotteridge Rd B30 ....20 A4
Cotteswold Rd GL20 ..196 F6
Cotton Pool Rd B61 ...48 E2
Cotton's La WR11 ....174 A1
Cottrells Cl B14 ......21 C4
Coughton CE Prim Sch
  B49 ....109 F5
Coughton La B49 ....109 E4
Countinghouse Way 🔟
  B60 ....67 E6

County Cl
Birmingham, Stirchley
B30 ....20 C6
Birmingham, Woodgate
B32 ....9 D3
County La DY7 ......14 D8
County Pk Ave B62 ......8 D3
Coupass Cotts B96 ..107 D7
Court Cl DY11 ....12 B1
Court Dr [3] DY13 .....43 F4
Court La WR11 ......148 A2
Court Lea WR8 ......169 E7
Court Oak Gr B32 ......9 F6
Court Oak Rd B32 ......9 F6
Court Rd
Great Malvern WR14 ...153 A7
Strensham WR8 ....171 A3
Court St [7] Stourbridge DY8 6 A4
[4] Upton upon Severn
WR8 ....169 C6
Court Way B50 ......136 D4
Courtland Cl [4] WR3 ..102 A1
Courtney DY10 ....27 E2
Courtney Cl GL20 ....196 F3
Courtway Ave B14 ......21 B1
Courtyard The B60 ......67 D2
Coventry Ave WR2 ....128 A7
Coventry Cl GL20 ....196 F4
Coventry Highway B98 .71 C4
Coventry St
Kidderminster DY10 ......27 F6
Stourbridge DY8 ....6 A5
Covercroft [3] WR9 ......84 F3
Coverfield WR8 ......154 A2
Covers The B80 ....90 E6
Covert La DY8 ....5 D2
Cow La WR9 ....64 B1
Cowl Barn La WR13 ...152 B3
Cowl St WR11 ......161 D4
Cowleigh Bank WR14 ..138 D4
Cowleigh Rd WR14 ....138 D3
Cowper Wlk DY10 ......28 C6
Cowslip Cl
[1] Birmingham, Hawkesley
B38 ....34 F8
Birmingham, Selly Oak
B29 ....19 A7
Cowslip Wlk DY5 ....6 C6
Cox Cl B50 ....136 E5
Coxcroft Ave DY5 ....6 F8
Coxlea Cl WR11 ......161 C5
Coxwell Dr WR14 ....139 B3
Crab Apple Way
[4] Evesham WR11 ......161 F1
Evesham WR11 ....175 F3
Crab Mill Cl B38 ....34 E7
Crabbe La WR8 ......143 C2
Crabbe St DY9 ....6 F5
Crabbs Cross La B97 ...89 E5
Crabmill La B38 ....35 D8
Crabtree Cl
Birmingham B31 ....19 C2
Hagley DY8 ....15 B6
Redditch B98 ....71 A2
Crabtree Dr B61 ....48 F3
Crabtree La B61 ....48 E3
Cradley CE Prim Sch
B63 ....7 C7
Cradley Cl B98 ....71 F2
Cradley Fields B63 ......7 D5
Cradley Forge DY5 ......7 A8
Cradley Heath Factory Ctr
B64 ....7 B8
Cradley Heath Sta B64 ..7 B8
Cradley High Sch B63 ...7 B6
Cradley Rd B64 ....7 C8
Cralves Mead WR15 ....55 E5
Cranberry Dr [3] DY13 ..43 E4
Cranbourne Cl B45 ......18 B2
Cranbourne Rd DY8 ......6 B4
Crane Dr WR2 ....128 A6
Crane St DY11 ....27 C6
Cranesbill Dr WR5 ....128 D5
Cranesbill Rd B29 ......19 A6
Cranham Cl B97 ....70 B1
Cranham Dr WR4 ......116 A7
Cranham Prim Sch
WR4 ....115 F7
Cranmoor Cres B63 ......8 A5
Crashmore La
Beckford GL20 ....186 A2
Overbury GL20 ....185 F5
Craufurd Ct DY8 ....6 A3
Craufurd St DY8 ....6 A3
Crawford Cl B50 ......136 C4
Crendon Cl B80 ....90 E5
Crescent Grange Rd The
DY9 ....6 C4
Crescent Pl WR15 ......55 F3
Crescent Rd
[1] Colwall Stone WR13 ..152 A1
Kidderminster DY11 ......27 C5
Crescent The
Blackheath, Cradley Heath
B64 ....8 A7
Bromsgrove B60 ....48 F1
Colwall Stone WR13 ....152 A2
Great Malvern WR14 ...166 F7
Hagley DY8 ....14 F5
Hindlip WR3 ....103 B1
Tenbury Wells WR15 ....55 F3
Wolverley & Cookley
DY10 ....13 B4
Cressage Ave B31 ......19 A1
Cresswell Ave WR3 ....102 E2

Crest Hill WR11 ......148 B6
Crest The
Birmingham B31 ....34 C7
Edwyn Ralph HR7 ....95 C1
Crest View B14 ....21 B4
Crestwood Ave DY11 ....27 A5
Creswick Gr B45 ....33 C7
Cricketers Mdw B64 ......7 F7
Cricklewood Dr B62 ......8 D3
Crickley Dr WR4 ......116 A7
Crimmond Rise B63 ......7 E5
Croft Bank
Great Malvern WR14 ...138 C1
Mathon WR14 ....152 B8
Croft Cl WR8 ....71 D3
Croft Farm Dr WR14 ...138 B1
Croft Farm Leisure & Water
Pk★ GL20 ....184 B3
Croft Rd
Evesham WR11 ....161 D6
South Littleton WR11 ...148 F2
Upton Snodsbury WR7 ..131 C8
Worcester WR1 ....115 B3
Croft The
Birmingham B31 ....19 B2
Blakedown DY10 ....14 C2
Church Lench WR11 ....134 A3
Kidderminster DY11 ......27 A4
Croft Wlk WR1 ......115 B3
Croftdown Rd B32 ......9 F6
Croftdown Sch WR14 ...152 F2
Crofters Cl DY8 ....6 B4
Crofters End WR9 ......84 D6
Croftlands The [7] GL20 .184 F6
Crofts Field GL20 ....183 E4
Crofts Cl
Astwood Bank B96 ......89 B2
Feckenham B96 ....88 F2
Croftwood Rd DY9 ......6 D4
Cromdale Dr B63 ....7 D3
Cromers Cl [7] GL20 ...184 E1
Crompton Ave B50 ....136 E5
Crompton Rd B45 ......17 D1
Cromwell Cres WR5 ...128 E8
Cromwell Cres La
WR5 ....128 E8
Cromwell Cl B31 ......18 E8
Cromwell Rd
[4] Bowling Green WR2 ..127 C2
Great Malvern WR14 ...139 A4
Cromwell St WR1 ......115 D3
Crookbarrow Rd WR5 ..128 F4
Crookbarrow Way
WR5 ....129 A5
Crookham Cl B17 ....9 F7
Crooks La B80 ....90 D3
Croome Cl
Drakes Broughton
WR10 ....144 A6
Redditch B98 ....71 F1
Croome Rd
Defford WR8 ....157 C5
Worcester WR2 ....127 F7
Cropredy Rd B31 ......34 B8
Cropthorne Cl B98 ......90 B7
Cropthorne Dr B47 ......36 B7
Cropthorne House B98 .49 B3
Cropthorne With Charlton CE
Fst Sch WR10 ......160 C6
Cross Farms La B45 ....17 E7
Cross St Halesowen B63 ..8 A3
Stourbridge DY8 ....5 E5
Tenbury Wells WR15 ....55 E4
Cross The Ripple GL20 .183 A4
Stourbridge DY8 ....6 E6
[10] Worcester WR1 ....115 B3
Cross Wlks DY9 ....6 E5
Crossgate Rd B98 ......90 C7
Crossley Ret Pk DY11 ..27 D6
Crossley Wlk B60 ......67 E7
Crossroads The WR1 ..130 B8
Crowhurst Rd B31 ......33 E7
Crowle CE Fst Sch
WR7 ....117 E5
Crowle Dr DY9 ....6 C5
Crown Cl
Broadheath WR2 ......114 A7
Bromsgrove B61 ....48 F2
Crown Ctr The★ [2] DY8 ..6 A5
Crown E Heritage
Woodland★ WR2 ....113 F7
Crown E La
Broadheath WR2 ......113 E4
Rushwick WR2 ....114 A2
Crown La Defford WR8 .157 D3
Dodderhill WR9 ....66 C2
Hartlebury DY13 ....63 E8
Iverley DY10 ....14 C7
Kidderminster DY10 ......27 E6
Stourbridge DY9 ....5 F5
Crown Lea Ave WR14 ..153 C8
Crown Mdw
Alvechurch B48 ....51 A7
Broadheath WR2 ......114 A7
Crown Rd B30 ....20 A4
Crown St WR3 ....115 B6
Crowngate Sh Ctr
WR1 ....115 B3
Crowther Gdns B63 ......7 C7
Crowther St DY11 ......27 C6
Cruiseill La B97 ....88 D5
Crumpfields La
Feckenham B97 ....88 E8
Redditch B97 ....69 F1
Crumpton Hill Rd
WR13 ....138 B6
Crundalls La DY12 ......26 B5

Crundelend La WR6 .....60 B2
Crutch La
Dodderhill WR9 ....85 A7
Droitwich WR9 ....85 A4
Upton Warren WR9 ......66 B4
Crychan Cl B45 ....18 B2
Culford Dr B32 ....18 C8
Culmington Rd B31 ....33 F8
Cumberland Rd B68 ......9 B7
Cumberland St WR1 ...115 B5
Cumbrian Croft B63 ......7 D2
Cur La B97 ....69 D3
Curdale Cl DY14 ....22 B4
Curdale Rd B32 ....18 B8
Curlew Cl
Kidderminster DY10 ......28 B2
Northway WR20 ......184 D1
Curslow La
Chaddesley Corbett DY10 ..45 F5
Kidderminster DY10 ......28 F1
Stone DY10 ....45 F8
Curtis Cl B60 ....68 F8
Cutlers Rough Cl B31 ..18 F5
Cutnall Gn CE Fst Sch
WR9 ....65 B5
Cutsdean Cl B31 ....18 F6
Cutts Pool WR7 ......131 C8
Cutty Sark Dr [2] DY13 ..44 B2
Cygnet Cl B48 ....51 A7
Cypress Cl [2] WR11 ...161 F1
Cypress Ct DY10 ......28 A4
Cypress Gr B31 ....18 E1
Cypress Rd GL20 ......197 A4
Cypress St WR3 ......115 B6
Cypress Way B31 ......33 F8
Cyprus Ave B96 ....89 D2
Cyprus Cl B29 ....19 A7
Cyril Rd WR3 ....115 D4

Dace Rd [7] WR5 ......128 C5
Dacer Cl B30 ....20 B5
Dad's La B13 ....20 D8
Daddlebrook Rd WV15 ...1 C6
Daffodil Way B31 ......33 E8
Dagnell End Rd B98 ....71 B7
Dagtail La B97 ....89 D3
Daimler Rd B14 ....21 D3
Dainton Gr B32 ....9 C1
Dairy Ct B68 ....9 D7
Dairy La
Dumbleton WR11 ......187 F4
Redditch B97 ....70 A5
Daisy Farm Rd B14 ......21 B3
Dalbury Cl [5] WR14 ...138 F4
Dalbury Rd B28 ....21 E5
Dale Cl B61 ....48 F7
Dale Hill B60 ....49 F6
Dale Rd Halesowen B62 ...8 F8
Redditch B98 ....70 F5
Stourbridge DY9 ....5 F2
Daleview Rd B14 ....21 C4
Damar Croft B14 ....20 D4
Damascus Way DY12 ...26 C4
Dame Elizabeth Cadbury Sch
& Sixth Form B30 ......19 D7
Dame Ellen Pinsent Specl
Sch B13 ....21 A7
Damson Cl B97 ....89 C6
Damson Way DY12 ......26 C4
Danbigh Cl [3] B29 .....19 C7
Dane Gr B13 ....20 D8
Danebury Pk WR14 ....138 D3
Danemoor Cross
WR13 ....167 E7
Danes Cl WR3 ....102 E3
Danescroft [4] DY13 ....43 F4
Danford Cl DY8 ....6 A4
Danford Rd B47 ....35 F6
Danube Cl WR9 ......103 D8
Danzey Cl B98 ....90 B5
Danzey Gr B14 ....20 C3
Dark La
Astley & Dunley DY13 ...62 C6
Astwood Bank B96 ......89 D1
Belbroughton DY9 ......30 F8
Grimley WR2 ....101 C5
Hollywood B38, B47 .....35 E7
Kinver DY7 ....4 B3
Ombersley WR9 ....63 F1
Rock DY14 ....41 E7
Romsley B62 ....16 F4
Stock & Bradley B96 ...107 A3
Stoke Heath B60 ....67 D6
Dark Orch WR15 ....55 E3
Darris Rd B29 ....20 A8
Dart Rd WR5 ....115 F3
Dartmoor Cl B45 ....18 A2
Darwin Cl [6] WR5 ....141 C6
Daston Cl WR12 ......190 E8
Dauntsey Covert B14 ...20 D2
Davena Dr B29 ....9 E2
Davenham Cl WR14 ....139 A1
Davenham Rd B60 ......49 C1
Davenport Dr B60 ......49 B1
Daventry Gr B32 ......19 D6
Davids The B31 ....19 C5
Davies Rd WR11 ......161 D1
Dawberry Cl B14 ......20 C6
Dawberry Fields Rd
B14 ....20 D5
Dawberry Rd B14 ....20 C6
Dawn Rd B31 ....18 E6
Dawson Cl [3] WR2 ....127 F6
Dawson Rd B61 ....48 E2
Daybrook Cl B97 ....70 B5

Dayhouse Bank B62 ....17 B1
De La Bere Cl [8] WR11 ..161 D5
De Salis Dr WR9 ....84 D7
De Salis Ct WR9 ....84 D7
De Walden Rd WR14 ...138 C1
De Wyche Cl WR9 ......85 E8
De Wyche Rd WR9 ......85 E8
Deacle Pl WR11 ......161 F4
Deal Cres WR4 ....116 C7
Deal Gr B31 ....19 A3
Dean Cl Stourbridge DY8 ..6 B6
[1] Tenbury Wells WR15 ..55 F6
Deane Cl [5] WR2 ....127 C2
Deans Cl B98 ....71 D5
Deanscroft Dr B60 ......49 C6
Deansford La DY10 .....29 B6
Deansway
Bromsgrove B61 ....48 E2
Worcester WR1 ....115 B2
Deansway House WR1 ..28 A7
Deansway The DY10 ....28 A7
Dearmont Rd B31 ......33 E7
Debdale Ave WR4 ......116 B5
Dee Way WR4 ....115 F3
Deelands Rd B45 ....32 F8
Deeley Cl B64 ....7 E7
Deepwood Gr B32 ......18 B8
Deer Ave WR5 ....128 F6
Deer Barn Hill B98 .....71 A1
Deerhurst Cl B98 ....71 C7
Defford Cl B97 ....69 E1
Defford Rd WR10 ......158 A7
Delamere Rd
Bewdley DY12 ....26 C4
Birmingham B28 ....21 F7
Great Malvern WR14 ...139 B1
Tedstone Delamere HR7 .96 E2
Dell The
Birmingham, Shenley Fields
B31 ....18 D6
Bredon DY13 ....184 E7
Stourbridge DY8 ....5 E6
Della Dr B32 ....18 D8
Dellow Gr B48 ....51 A5
Dellows Cl B38 ....34 D7
Dellway Ct DY8 ....5 E5
Delph Dr DY5 ....6 E7
Delph La DY5 ....6 E7
Delphinium Cl [3] DY11 ..12 C1
Delrene Rd B28, B90 ...21 F3
Delta Dr GL20 ....197 C8
Denaby Gr B14 ....21 D4
Dencer Cl B45 ....33 A8
Dencil Cl B63 ....7 D5
Dene Hollow B13 ....21 C7
Dene Rd DY8 ....5 F3
Denehurst Cl B45 ....33 A1
Denford Cl B14 ....20 D5
Denholme Gr B14 ....21 A3
Denison Cl WR14 ......139 B2
Dennis Hall Rd DY8 ......6 A8
Dennis St DY8 ....6 F8
Denshaw Rd B14 ....20 D6
Dent Cl WR5 ....115 D2
Denton Rd WR5 ....7 A4
Denver Rd B14 ....21 A2
Derby Rd [1] WR5 ....115 C1
Derick Burcher's Mall [5]
DY10 ....27 E6
Derries The WR3 ......103 A3
Derwent Ave DY13 ....43 F5
Derwent Cl [2] WR4 ...115 F5
Derwent Dr
[6] Bewdley DY12 ......25 F4
Tewkesbury GL20 ......197 A8
Derwent Gr [8] WR9 ....84 C1
Derwent House DY10 ...27 F7
Derwent Rd B30 ....20 C8
Derwent Way B60 ......49 B1
Desborough House [8]
B14 ....21 A3
Despenser Rd GL20 ...196 E4
Dettonford Rd B32 ......18 B8
Devil's Spittleful Nature
Reserve★ DY12 ......26 C3
Devon Cl
Inkberrow WR7 ....120 F6
Kidderminster DY11 .....12 C1
Devon Ct [3] B29 ....19 B7
Devon Rd
Birmingham B45 ....17 F1
Smethwick B67 ....9 E7
Stourbridge DY8 ....5 E7
Worcester WR5 ....115 F1
Devonport Cl [3] B97 ...70 B5
Devonshire Pl GL20 ...196 F4
Dewberry Cl [9] DY13 ..43 E4
Dewsbury Cl B96 ....89 C1
Dial Cl B14 ....20 C5
Dial La DY8 ....5 E8
Dice Pleck B31 ....19 C2
Dickens Cl [9] B14 .....21 A3
Dickens Heath Rd B90 ..36 F5
Didcot Cl B97 ....89 C5
Digby Dr GL20 ....196 F7
Digby Rd WR11 ......161 F3
Diglis Dock Rd WR5 ...128 B7
Diglis La WR5 ....128 C8
Diglis Rd WR5 ....115 C1
Dilmore Ave WR3 .....102 E3
Dilmore La WR3 ......102 E4
Dilwyn Cl B98 ....71 D3
Dimmingsdale Bank B32 .9 C4
Dimsdale Gr B31 ....18 D3
Dimsdale Rd B31 ....18 D3
Dinchall Rd WR5 ......129 A8

Dinedor Cl B98 ....71 D3
Dineley Cl [3] WR10 ...131 B2
Dineley Rd WR10 .....131 B2
Dines Gn Prim Sch
WR2 ....114 D2
Dingle Ave B64 ....7 E8
Dingle Cl B30 ....19 D7
Dingle End WR7 ......120 F6
Dingle Mead B14 ....20 C4
Dingle Rd Leigh WR6 ..125 D8
Stourbridge DY9 ....6 C2
Dingleside B98 ....70 E2
Dingleside Mid Sch
B98 ....90 B8
Dinmore Ave B31 ....19 B4
Dinmore Cl
Redditch B98 ....71 D3
[4] Worcester WR5 ....128 E5
Ditchford Cl B97 ....89 D4
Ditton Gr B31 ....33 F6
Dixon Ct DY10 ....28 C8
Dixon St DY10 ....27 E5
Dobbins Oak Rd DY9 ....6 E1
Dobes La DY10 ....46 C7
Dock La GL20 ....184 E2
Dock The Catshill B61 ..49 A8
Stourbridge DY9 ....6 F5
Dockar Rd B31 ....18 E2
Dockery Ave WR4 ....116 A5
Doctors Hill
Bournheath B61 ....48 B8
Stourbridge DY9 ....6 C3
Dodderhill Rd WR9 ......85 A5
Doddington Gr B32 ......18 B8
Dodford Cl B45 ....32 F7
Dodford Ct B61 ....48 C6
Dodford Fst Sch B61 ...48 A5
Dodford House B60 ......49 B3
Dodford Rd B61 ....31 D1
Dog La Bewdley DY12 ..26 B3
Ombersley DY13 ....63 E3
Upton Warren B61 ......66 C6
Dogkennel La B63 ......8 B3
Dogwood Cl WR14 ....139 C3
Dolben La B98 ....71 D3
Dolday WR1 ....115 B2
Dolphin Cl WR2 ......114 E4
Dolphin Rd B98 ....71 A5
Domar Rd DY11 ....27 B7
Domestic Fowl Trust &
Honeybourne Rare Breeds★
WR11 ....164 A5
Dominic Dr B30 ....19 D4
Don Rd WR4 ....115 F3
Donney Brook [3] WR11 .161 F3
Donnington Cl B98 ......71 C5
Doran Cl B63 ....7 D1
Dorchester Rd DY9 ......6 D2
Dordale Cl B31 ....18 C1
Dordale Rd DY9 ....30 C8
Dordon Cl B90 ....21 E1
Dormie Cl B38 ....19 D1
Dormouse Croft WR5 ..128 F6
Dormston Cl B98 ....70 F1
Dormston Dr B29 ....9 F2
Dormy Dr B31 ....34 A7
Dornie Dr B38 ....19 F1
Dornton Rd B30 ....20 C8
Dorothy Cres [5] WR3 ..102 A1
Dorrels Orch [3] WR10 .132 F4
Dorridge Cl B97 ....70 B1
Dorset Cl B45 ....17 F2
Dorset Cotts B30 ....20 A6
Dorset Ct [3] B29 ......19 B7
Dorset Rd DY8 ....5 D8
Dorsett Rd [3] DY13 ...43 F5
Dorsington Rd CV37 ...150 E5
Dorstone Covert B14 ...20 C2
Dorville B38 ....34 D8
Dotterel Pl B31 ....28 A1
Double Hedges Rd
WR10 ....173 A3
Douglas Rd B47 ....36 A7
Doulton Cl B32 ....9 F3
Dove Cl
Kidderminster DY10 ......28 B2
Worcester WR4 ....115 F3
Dove Dr DY8 ....6 A8
Dove Gdns B38 ....20 B2
Dove Ridge DY8 ....6 A7
Dovecote WR10 ......160 D8
Dovecote Rd
Bromsgrove B61 ....48 E1
Droitwich WR9 ....85 A1
Dovedale Ct [19] B29 ...19 C7
Dovedale Dr B28 ....21 F5
Dover Ave WR4 ......116 C6
Dover Ct B32 ....18 A7
Dover's View GL55 ....178 D7
Doverdale Ave DY10 ....28 B5
Doverdale Cl
Droitwich WR9 ....84 E2
Halesowen B63 ....7 E5
Redditch B98 ....90 B7
Doverdale La
Hampton Lovett WR9 ....83 F8
Ombersley WR9 ....64 D1
Doveridge Rd B28 ......21 E5
Doversley Rd B14 ......20 C5
Doveton House DY8 .....6 A3
Dowar Rd B45 ....33 C7
Dowland Gdns [3] DY13 .114 D3
Dowler's Hill Cres B98 ..90 A8
Dowles Cl B29 ....19 B6
Dowles Croft [2] WR9 ..84 E3
Dowles Manor★ DY12 ..25 F5

Dowles Rd
Bewdley DY12 . . . . .26 A4
Kidderminster DY11 . . . . . . .27 B2
Upper Arley DY12 . . . . .25 F5
Downcroft Ave B38 . . . . . .19 E2
Downfield La GL20 . . . . .184 B7
Downing Ct 5 B68 . . . . .9 B7
Downing St B63 . . . . .8 A5
Downland Cl B38 . . . . .19 F1
Downs Sch WR13 . . . . . . .152 B3
Downsell House B97 . . . . .70 A2
Downsell Rd B97 . . . . .70 A2
Dragons La WR13 . . . . . .125 E1
Dragoon Fields B60 . . . . .68 B8
Drake Ave WR2 . . . . .114 D3
Drake Cres
Kidderminster DY11 . . . . . . .27 A7
Kidderminster Foreign
DY11 . . . . .26 F7
Drake St WR13 . . . . .167 E4
Drakelow La DY11 . . . . . . .12 C5
Drakes Bridge Rd
WR10 . . . . .171 D7
Drakes Cl B97 . . . . .89 C6
Drakes Cross Par B47 . . . .36 A5
Drakes Hill Cl DY8 . . . . . . .5 C4
Drakes Lea WR11 . . . . . .161 F5
Drapers WR4 . . . . .115 F6
Drawbridge Rd B90 . . . . .36 E8
Draycote Cl 2 B97 . . . . . .70 B5
Draycott Cl 9 B97 . . . . . . .70 B5
Draycott Dr B31 . . . . .18 E7
Drayton Rd
Belbroughton DY9 . . . . .30 B5
Birmingham B14 . . . . .20 F8
Drew Cres DY9 . . . . .6 D2
Drew Rd DY9 . . . . .6 D3
Drews Holloway B63 . . . . . .7 D5
Drews Holloway S B63 . . . .7 D5
Drews House B63 . . . . . . .20 D1
Drews Mdw Cl 1 B14 . . . .20 C2
Driffield DY8 . . . . .5 D4
Drift The WR11 . . . . .162 E3
Driftwood Cl B38 . . . . .34 D7
Drinkwater La WR11 . . . .163 B4
Drive The
Bowling Green WR2 . . . . . .127 B3
Halesowen B63 . . . . .8 A3
Halesowen, Cradley B63 . . . . .7 D5
Hindlip WR3 . . . . .103 B2
Hopwood B48 . . . . .34 B3
Redditch B97 . . . . .69 C7
Worcester WR3 . . . . .115 B8
Droitwich High Sch
WR9 . . . . .84 D3
Droitwich Rd
Feckenham B96 . . . . .107 A4
Fernhill Heath WR3 . . . . . .103 A3
Hartlebury DY10 . . . . .45 A6
Worcester WR3 . . . . .115 C8
Droitwich Spa Brine Baths★
WR9 . . . . .84 F3
Droitwich Spa Lido Pk★
WR9 . . . . .85 A3
Droitwich Spa Sta WR9 . .84 E3
Droitwich Sports & Leisure
Ctr WR9 . . . . .84 D3
Drovers Pl 3 WR9 . . . . . .84 D5
Drovers Way
Bromsgrove B60 . . . . .67 E6
2 Droitwich WR9 . . . . .84 D5
Worcester WR3 . . . . .115 C7
Drugger's End La
WR13 . . . . .167 C1
Druids La B14 . . . . .20 D1
Drumbles La 2 WR4 . . . .116 C4
Drummond Rd
Bromsgrove B60 . . . . .68 B8
Stourbridge DY9 . . . . .6 F4
Drury La
Martin Hussingtree
WR3 . . . . .103 C5
Redmarley D'abitot GL19 . .192 B4
Stourbridge DY8 . . . . .6 A5
Dry Mill La DY12 . . . . .25 C1
Drybrook Cl B38 . . . . .34 E8
Dryden Cl WR3 . . . . .115 C6
Drysdale Cl WR11 . . . . . .176 D7
Duck Mdw WR4 . . . . .116 B4
Dudley Cl WR2 . . . . .114 D3
Dudley Rd Halesowen B63 . .8 B5
Honeybourne WR11 . . . . . .164 B5
Stourbridge DY9 . . . . .6 E6
Dudley St DY10 . . . . .27 E6
Dudnill Gr B32 . . . . .18 A8
Dufton Rd B32 . . . . .9 E4
Dugard Way WR9 . . . . . .103 E7
Dugdale Ave B50 . . . . . . .136 C5
Dugdale Dr WR4 . . . . .116 C3
Duke of Edinburgh Way
WR14 . . . . .139 B5
Duke St DY8 . . . . .6 A6
Duke's Way WR14 . . . . . .153 B6
Dukes Rd B30 . . . . .20 A3
Dukes Way GL20 . . . . . . .196 F3
Dulais Cl B98 . . . . .70 E1
Dulvern Gr B14 . . . . .20 D5
Dumble Pit La B48 . . . . . . .52 F7
Dumbleton La WR11 . . . . .159 B6
Dumphouse La B48 . . . . . .52 C3
Dunard Rd B90 . . . . .21 D4
Dunbar Cl
Birmingham B32 . . . . .9 D1
Kidderminster DY10 . . . . . . .28 C6

Dunchurch Cl B98 . . . . . . .71 F1
Dunchurch Dr B31 . . . . . . .18 E7
Dunclent Cres DY10 . . . . .28 B5
Dunclent La DY10 . . . . . . .28 E3
Duncombe St DY8 . . . . . . .5 D5
Dunedin Dr B45 . . . . .33 B1
Dunedin House B32 . . . . . . .9 F4
Dunhampton Dr DY10 . . . .13 B1
Dunkirk Dr WR5 . . . . . . .129 A4
Dunley Rd
Astley & Dunley DY13 . . . . . .61 F8
Rock DY12 . . . . .42 F2
Dunlin Dr DY10 . . . . .27 F2
Dunlop Rd DY9 . . . . .89 D5
Dunmore Rd DY12 . . . . . . .26 D5
Dunmow Ave WR4 . . . . . .116 C3
Dunnigan Rd B32 . . . . .9 F3
Dunnington Ave DY10 . . . .13 A1
Dunnington CE Prim Sch
B49 . . . . .135 D8
Dunns Bank DY5 . . . . .6 F7
Dunsford Cl DY5 . . . . .6 F7
Dunslade Cres DY5 . . . . . . .6 F8
Dunsley Dr DY7 . . . . .4 C4
Dunsley Rd Kinver DY7 . . . .4 B4
Stourbridge DY8 . . . . .5 C4
Dunsmore Dr DY5 . . . . .6 F8
Dunsmore Gn GL19 . . . . .195 B5
Dunstall Cl B97 . . . . .70 B2
Dunstall Gr B29 . . . . .18 F8
Dunstall Rd B63 . . . . .7 D3
Dunster Cl
Birmingham B30 . . . . .20 C4
6 Worcester WR4 . . . . . . .116 B7
Durant Cl B45 . . . . .17 D1
Durcott La WR11 . . . . . . .161 F3
Durcott Rd WR11 . . . . . . .161 F3
Durham Cl B61 . . . . .48 E4
Durham Rd
Stourbridge DY8 . . . . .5 D8
Worcester WR5 . . . . .116 A3
Durnford Croft B14 . . . . . .20 E1
Dursley La B98 . . . . .72 A3
Dusthouse La B60 . . . . . . .68 D7
Dutton St 2 WR3 . . . . . .115 D4
Duxford DY7 . . . . .89 B8
Dwellings La B32 . . . . .9 F5
Dyas Rd B47 . . . . .36 A7
Dyer's La GL55 . . . . .178 F3
Dyson Dr WR14 . . . . .139 D1
Dyson Perrins CE High Sch
The WR14 . . . . .138 F5

E

Eachway B45 . . . . .32 F6
Eachway Farm Cl B45 . . . .33 A6
Eachway La B45 . . . . .33 A6
Eadie Mews B97 . . . . .70 D1
Eagle Cl 4 WR5 . . . . .128 C5
Eagle Croft B14 . . . . .20 E2
Eagle La DY14 . . . . .22 C4
Eagle Rd B98 . . . . .71 E5
Eagle Trad Est B63 . . . . . . .8 A4
Eardisley Cl B98 . . . . .71 F1
Earls Cl B97 . . . . .69 F2
Earls Comm Rd WR9 . . . .106 C1
Earls Ferry Gdns B32 . . . .18 B7
Earls High Sch The B63 . . .8 B4
Earls Way B63 . . . . .8 B4
Earlsdon Rd WR2 . . . . . . .127 F8
Earlswood Sta B94 . . . . . . .36 D1
Earlswood Trad Est
B94 . . . . .53 C6
Early River Pl 5 DY12 . . .25 F3
Easemore Rd B98 . . . . . . .70 F5
Easenhall La B98 . . . . .71 E1
Easinghope La WR6 . . . . .111 F6
Easmore Cl B14 . . . . .20 D2
East Cl WR9 . . . . .85 E8
East Comer WR2 . . . . . . .114 E4
East Pk Dr WR9 . . . . .84 D4
East Rd Bromsgrove B60 . . .49 A1
Stourport-on-Severn
DY13 . . . . .44 B5
East Side WR11 . . . . .149 A3
East St Brierley Hill DY5 . . . .7 A8
Kidderminster DY10 . . . . . . .27 F6
Tewkesbury GL20 . . . . .196 B6
Worcester WR1 . . . . .115 C4
East Waterside WR8 . . . . .169 C6
Eastbank Dr WR3 . . . . . . .115 A7
Eastern Hill B96 . . . . .89 F2
Easterton Croft B14 . . . . .20 E1
Eastfield Cl WR11 . . . . . .162 E3
Eastgrove Gottage Gdn★
WR6 . . . . .81 D5
Eastham Rd B13 . . . . .21 C6
Eastleigh Dr B62 . . . . .17 A4
Eastnor Cl
Kidderminster DY10 . . . . . . .27 E2
Redditch B97 . . . . .70 E1
Worcester WR5 . . . . .128 E1
Easton Gr B47 . . . . .36 B7
Eastville B31 . . . . .19 B3
Eastward Rd WR14 . . . . . .138 F6
Eastwick Dr 3 WR11 . . . .161 C2
Eastwood Cl B96 . . . . .89 E1
Eastwood Dr DY10 . . . . . . .28 B5
Easy Row WR1 . . . . .115 B3
Eathorpe Cl B34 . . . . .71 E1
Eaton Cl WR14 . . . . .152 E3
Ebmore Dr B14 . . . . .20 D2
Ebrington Cl B14 . . . . .20 D4
Ebrington Dr WR4 . . . . . .116 B7
Ebrington Rd WR14 . . . . .138 C2

Ebsdorf Cl 4 B50 . . . . . .136 D5
Ebury Rd B30 . . . . .20 B4
Echells Cl B61 . . . . .48 D2
Eckersall Rd B38 . . . . .19 E3
Eckington CE Fst Sch
WR10 . . . . .171 F7
Eckington Cl B98 . . . . .90 B8
Eckington Wlk B38 . . . . . .34 E7
Eddy Rd DY10 . . . . .27 E7
Eden Cl Birmingham B31 . . .33 E8
Studley B80 . . . . .90 D3
Edenfield Cl B97 . . . . .70 A3
Edenhall Rd B32 . . . . .9 B6
Edenhurst Rd B31 . . . . . . .33 F7
Edgar St 2 WR1 . . . . . . .115 C1
Edge Hill DY7 . . . . .3 F5
Edge View Cl DY7 . . . . .3 F5
Edge View Wlk DY7 . . . . . .3 F5
Edgecliff High Sch DY7 . . . .4 B5
Edgehill Rd B31 . . . . .19 B1
Edgewood Cl B64 . . . . .7 F8
Edgewood Dr B45 . . . . . . .33 B1
Edgewood Rd
Birmingham, King's Norton
B38 . . . . .34 C1
Birmingham, Rednall
B45 . . . . .33 B6
Edgeworth Cl
Redditch B98 . . . . .71 C5
1 Worcester WR4 . . . . . . .116 A7
Edgioake La B96 . . . . .108 E6
Edgmond Cl B98 . . . . .71 D4
Edinburgh Cl DY10 . . . . . .27 E8
Edinburgh Rd B68 . . . . . . .9 B8
Edison Gr B32 . . . . .9 D5
Edith Berry Ct 2 WR14 . . .139 F1
Edith Wlk WR14 . . . . .138 F1
Edmonton Cl 6 WR2 . . . .127 F6
Ednall La B60 . . . . .48 F1
Edward Cl 3 WR5 . . . . . .115 D1
Edward Pl 3 GL20 . . . . . .196 F3
Edward Rd
Birmingham, Highter's Heath
B14 . . . . .21 A1
Halesowen B63 . . . . .7 F4
Oldbury B68 . . . . .9 C8
Edward St
Evesham WR11 . . . . .161 D5
Redditch B97 . . . . .70 D4
Edward's La WR7 . . . . . . .130 C6
Edwin Ave (Road 4)
DY10 . . . . .27 F1
Edwin Cres B60 . . . . .67 F7
Edwin Ct B60 . . . . .67 F7
Edwin Rd B30 . . . . .20 B7
Effingham Rd B13 . . . . . . .21 C7
Egdon La WR7 . . . . .130 C2
Egg La
Belbroughton DY9, DY10 . . .30 A5
North Claines WR3 . . . . . .102 C6
Egghill La B31, B45 . . . . . .18 B3
Eggington Rd DY8 . . . . .5 D6
Egginton Rd B28 . . . . .21 E5
Egremond Gdns 2
WR4 . . . . .116 C5
Egret Ct DY10 . . . . .28 A1
Eider Cl DY10 . . . . .28 B1
Elan Ave DY13 . . . . .43 E7
Elan Cl Bewdley DY12 . . . . .25 F4
Cookley DY10 . . . . .13 B4
Elan Rd B31 . . . . .18 C2
Elbury Mount Prim Sch
WR4 . . . . .115 F6
Elbury Mount Schools
WR4 . . . . .116 A6
Elbury Pk Rd WR4 . . . . . .116 A6
Elderberry Cl
Stourbridge DY8 . . . . .5 D5
6 Stourport-on-Severn
DY13 . . . . .43 E4
Elderfield Rd B30 . . . . .20 B3
Eldersfield Cl B98 . . . . . . .71 E7
Eldersfield Lawn CE Prim Sch
GL19 . . . . .194 D3
Eldon Rd
Birmingham, Woodgate
B32 . . . . .9 A3
Halesowen B62 . . . . .8 F3
Eldorado Cl B80 . . . . .90 D4
Eleanor Harrison Dr
DY11 . . . . .13 B5
Elford Cl B14 . . . . .20 E5
Elgar Ave WR14 . . . . .139 C1
Elgar Birthplace (Museum)
The★ WR2 . . . . .113 F4
Elgar Cres WR9 . . . . .103 F8
Elgar Ct 3 WR3 . . . . .115 D4
Elgar Dr WR5 . . . . .141 C6
Elgar Mews 2 B60 . . . . . . .48 F2
Elgar Ret Pk WR4 . . . . . .115 E7
Elgar Tech Coll WR3 . . . .115 D7
Elgin Cl DY8 . . . . .6 A7
Eliot Rd WR3 . . . . .115 C6
Eliot Wlk DY10 . . . . .28 C6
Elizabeth Ave
Droitwich WR9 . . . . .85 A3
Worcester WR3 . . . . .102 B1
Elizabeth House DY9 . . . . . .6 E5
Elizabeth Rd
Evesham WR11 . . . . .161 D2
Halesowen B63 . . . . .8 A6
Elizabeth Way B97 . . . . . .70 D5
Elkstone Cl 3 WR4 . . . . . .116 A7
Elkstone Covert B14 . . . . .20 C2
Ellbrook Cl 6 B97 . . . . . . .70 B5
Ellenbrook Cl B98 . . . . . . .89 D8
Ellerdene Cl B98 . . . . .89 D8
Ellerside Gr B31 . . . . .18 F2
Ellerslie Cl DY5 . . . . .6 D8

Ellerslie Rd B13 . . . . .21 C7
Elliot Gdns B45 . . . . .33 B5
Elliott Cl 1 B50 . . . . .136 D5
Ellis Rd WR2 . . . . .115 A1
Ellison Ave WR2 . . . . .114 E5
Ellsdon Rise WR5 . . . . . . .141 C7
Elm Cl Cookley DY10 . . . . . .13 B4
Pebworth CV37 . . . . .150 E2
Stourbridge DY8 . . . . .5 D2
Elm Croft B68 . . . . .9 C7
Elm Ct WR5 . . . . .70 D4
Elm Dr Blakedown DY10 . . .14 B3
Hartlebury DY10 . . . . .64 D8
Elm Gn Cl WR5 . . . . .128 C5
Elm Gr Bromsgrove B61 . . .49 A4
Kinver DY7 . . . . .4 C3
Stourport-on-Severn
DY13 . . . . .62 D8
Elm Link Cl 1 WR2 . . . . . .127 C1
Elm Pl Cookley DY10 . . . . . .13 B4
Harvington DY10 . . . . .29 B3
Elm Rd
Birmingham, Bournville
B30 . . . . .19 F8
Drakes Broughton
WR10 . . . . .144 A6
Evesham WR11 . . . . .161 F4
Kidderminster DY10 . . . . . . .28 A5
Northway WR20 . . . . .197 E8
Redditch B97 . . . . .70 D4
Worcester WR2 . . . . .115 A3
Elm Tree Gr B63 . . . . .7 D6
Elm Tree Rd B30 . . . . .20 A6
Elmbridge Cl B43 . . . . .7 D5
Elmbridge La
Elmbridge WR9 . . . . .66 A4
Rushock WR9 . . . . .46 D1
Elmbury Dr GL20 . . . . . . .197 B6
Elmcroft Ave B32 . . . . .9 A1
Elmdale B62 . . . . .9 A7
Elmdale Cres B31 . . . . . . .18 E4
Elmdale Dr DY10 . . . . .28 C5
Elmdale Gr B31 . . . . .18 E4
Elmdale Rd WR3 . . . . .115 B8
Elmfield Gdns WR5 . . . . . .115 D1
Elmfield Rd 1 WR11 . . . . . .45 A1
Elmfield Rudolf Steiner Sch
DY8 . . . . .6 A3
Elmfield Wlk 1 DY13 . . . . .43 E4
Elmhurst Cl WR7 . . . . .89 D4
Elmley Castle CE Fst Sch
WR10 . . . . .173 E7
Elmley Cl
Elmley Lovett WR9 . . . . . . .65 B6
Great Malvern WR14 . . . . .139 B1
Kidderminster DY11 . . . . . . .27 B3
Elmley Gr B30 . . . . .20 B2
Elmley House 9 B97 . . . . . .70 A4
Elmley La WR9 . . . . .65 B6
Elmley Rd WR11 . . . . .174 B1
Elms Cl B38 . . . . .34 C8
Elms Dr WR13 . . . . .166 A8
Elms Sch WR13 . . . . .166 A8
Elmside WR11 . . . . .161 F4
Elmstone Cl B97 . . . . .89 C5
Elmvil Rd GL20 . . . . .197 C7
Elmwood Gr B47 . . . . .36 A6
Elmwoods B32 . . . . .9 B2
Elsma Rd B68 . . . . .9 C8
Elton Rd 6 DY12 . . . . .25 C4
Eltric Rd WR3 . . . . .115 B8
Ely Cl
Kidderminster DY11 . . . . . . .27 A6
Worcester WR5 . . . . .116 A1
Ely Gr B32 . . . . .9 C4
Embassy Ind Est 1 DY9 . . .6 F5
Emerald Rd WR2 . . . . . . .114 E3
Emery Ct DY10 . . . . .27 E7
Emes Cl WR10 . . . . .158 C3
Emperor Dr WR5 . . . . . . .128 F5
Emsmore Gr B14 . . . . .20 D6
Emsworth Gr B14 . . . . .20 D6
Endeavour Pl DY13 . . . . . .44 B7
Enfield Ind Est B97 . . . . . .70 D5
Enfield Rd B97 . . . . .89 D5
Engadine Cl WR14 . . . . . .153 A5
Engadine Rd B60 . . . . .49 C1
Engine La
Stourbridge DY9 . . . . .6 D6
7 Stourport-on-Severn
DY13 . . . . .44 A3
Enigma Bsns Pk
WR14 . . . . .139 C4
Ennerdale Cl WR4 . . . . . .116 A5
Ennerdale Dr B63 . . . . .7 D2
Ennerdale Rd DY13 . . . . . .43 F6
Enterprise Dr DY9 . . . . .6 F6
Enterprise Way WR11 . . .175 E8
Enville Pl DY7 . . . . .5 F5
Enville Rd DY7 . . . . .3 F6
Enville St DY7 . . . . .5 F5
Epping Cl B45 . . . . .18 B2
Epsom Cl
Fernhill Heath WR3 . . . . . .102 F3
Redditch B97 . . . . .89 C6
Epsom Ct 16 B29 . . . . .19 C7
Epsom Rd B61 . . . . .37 F8
Erica Cl Birmingham B29 . . .19 A8
Kidderminster DY11 . . . . . . .12 D1
Erneley Cl 1 DY13 . . . . . . .43 F1
Ernest Ct B38 . . . . .20 A1
Erwood Cl B97 . . . . .70 B2
Eskdale Cl 7 WR4 . . . . . .115 F6
Eskdale Wlk DY5 . . . . .6 B8
Esmond Cl B30 . . . . .19 C5
Essex Cl
3 Bowling Green WR2 . . . .127 C2
Worcester WR2 . . . . .114 C2
Essex Ct 5 B29 . . . . .19 C7

Essex Gdns DY8 . . . . .5 D7
Eston Ave WR14 . . . . .153 C8
Eton Dr DY8 . . . . .6 A3
Eton Wlk DY9 . . . . .15 A6
Ettingley Cl B98 . . . . .90 B5
Etwall Rd B28 . . . . .21 E6
Eunal Ct B97 . . . . .89 E5
Evans Cl DY11 . . . . .12 C3
Evelench La WR9 . . . . . . .117 B8
Evendene Rd WR11 . . . . . .161 A3
Evendine Cl WR5 . . . . . . .128 D8
Evendine La WR13 . . . . . .166 A7
Evenlode Cl B98 . . . . .70 F1
Everard Cl 4 WR2 . . . . . .114 E5
Everard Pl 5 WR2 . . . . . .114 E5
Evers St DY5 . . . . .7 A8
Eversley Cl WR14 . . . . . . .139 B2
Eversley Gr WR14 . . . . . . .139 B2
Evertons Cl WR9 . . . . .84 E1
Eves Croft B32 . . . . .9 C1
Evesham Arts Ctr★
WR11 . . . . .161 E6
Evesham Coll WR11 . . . . .161 D2
Evesham Com Hospl
WR11 . . . . .161 D3
Evesham Ctry Pk★
WR11 . . . . .147 E1
Evesham High Sch
WR11 . . . . .161 E2
Evesham House B60 . . . . . .49 B3
Evesham Mews 9 B97 . . . .70 E3
Evesham Rd
Astwood Bank B96 . . . . . . .108 E8
Broadway WR12 . . . . .177 B2
Childswickham WR12 . . . . .176 F5
Church Lench WR11 . . . . . .134 A2
Cleeve Prior WR11 . . . . . . .148 F5
Cookhill B49 . . . . .122 B7
Fladbury WR10 . . . . .146 C3
Harvington WR11 . . . . . . .148 A7
Hill & Moor WR10 . . . . . . .145 D3
Norton & Lenchwick
WR11 . . . . .147 F5
Redditch B96, B97 . . . . . . .89 E3
Salford Priors WR11 . . . . .135 E2
Stoulton WR7 . . . . .130 C6
Temple Grafton B50 . . . . .137 D7
Weethley B49 . . . . .122 B4
Evesham Sports & Leisure
Ctr WR11 . . . . .161 D1
Evesham Sq 3 B97 . . . . . .70 E3
Evesham Sta WR11 . . . . .161 D5
Evesham Wlk 2 B97 . . . . .70 E4
Eveson Rd DY8 . . . . .5 E2
Ewloe Cl DY10 . . . . .27 E1
Exchange St DY10 . . . . . . .27 E6
Exe Croft B31 . . . . .34 B8
Exeter Cl DY11 . . . . .27 A6
Exeter Rd WR5 . . . . .116 A2
Exford Cl DY5 . . . . .6 B7
Exhall Cl B98 . . . . .71 D5
Exmoor Ct B61 . . . . .49 A5
Exmoor Dr B61 . . . . .49 A4
Eymore Cl B29 . . . . .19 B6
Eyton Cl B98 . . . . .71 D3

F

Fabian Cl B45 . . . . .18 A2
Fabricius Ave WR9 . . . . . .84 F2
Facet Rd B38 . . . . .20 A2
Factory La B61 . . . . .48 F1
Fairbairn Ave WR3 . . . . . .115 B8
Fairbourne Gdns B97 . . . . .89 C7
Fairfax Rd B31 . . . . .34 A8
Fairfield Cl WR4 . . . . .115 F5
Fairfield Dr DY7 . . . . .4 B3
Fairfield Fst Sch B61 . . . . .31 D3
Fairfield House B60 . . . . . .49 B3
Fairfield La DY11 . . . . .12 B3
Fairfield Pl WR11 . . . . . . .161 D2
Fairfield Rd
Birmingham B14 . . . . .20 E8
Bournheath B61 . . . . .31 D1
Evesham WR11 . . . . .161 D2
Halesowen B63 . . . . .8 A2
Fairfield Rise DY8 . . . . .5 D5
Fairford Cl B98 . . . . .71 E7
Fairlie Cres B38 . . . . .19 D1
Fairlight Dr B45 . . . . .33 A1
Fairmead Rise B38 . . . . . . .19 E1
Fairmile Rd B63 . . . . .8 A6
Fairmont Rd B60 . . . . .68 B8
Fairoak Dr B60 . . . . .67 E6
Fairway Birmingham B31 . . .18 E3
Northway GL20 . . . . .197 D6
Fairway Dr B45 . . . . .32 F6
Fairway Prim Sch B38 . . . .19 D1
Fairway The
Birmingham B38 . . . . .19 D2
Worcester WR4 . . . . .116 A4
Fairways WR10 . . . . .144 D1
Fairways Ave DY8 . . . . .5 E2
Fairways Cl DY8 . . . . .5 E2
Fairways Wlk 3 WR10 . . .144 D1
Fakenham Croft B17 . . . . . .9 F7
Falcon Cl
Droitwich Spa WR9 . . . . . .104 B8
Kidderminster DY10 . . . . . . .27 E2
5 Worcester WR5 . . . . . . .128 C5
Falcon Cres B50 . . . . .136 E5

Falcon Rise DY8 . . . . .5 C6
Falcon View B30 . . . . .20 A4
Falconry Ctr★ DY9 . . . . . .14 F3
Falfield Gr B31 . . . . .33 E7
Falkland Croft B30 . . . . . .20 B6
Falkland Rd WR11 . . . . . .161 F1
Fallow Wlk B32 . . . . .9 A2
Fallowfield Ave B28 . . . . .21 F5
Fallowfield Rd B63 . . . . . . .7 D3
Fallowfields CI B61 . . . . . .48 E3
Falmouth WR4 . . . . .116 D6
Falstaff Ave B47 . . . . .36 A6
Falstaff Dr WR9 . . . . .103 E8
Falstaff House B13 . . . . . .21 D7
Fancott Rd B31 . . . . .19 A5
Far Moor La B98 . . . . .72 A3
Far Wood Rd B31 . . . . . . .18 E8
Faraday Ave B32 . . . . .9 D5
Faraday Ct B32 . . . . .9 D5
Farfield
  Kidderminster DY10 . . . .27 F5
  Stoke Prior B60 . . . . . . .67 F4
Farfield CI B31 . . . . .19 B2
Farfield Studios DY10 . . .27 F5
Farlands Dr DY8 . . . . .6 A3
Farlands Rd DY8 . . . . .6 A3
Farleigh Rd WR10 . . . . . .158 C8
Farley La WR14 . . . . .139 B4
Farley St WR2 . . . . .114 E4
Farlie CI **2** WR5 . . . . . .141 C6
Farlow CI B98 . . . . .71 D3
Farlow Rd B31 . . . . .19 C3
Farm Bank Rd WR9 . . . . .84 B7
Farm CI
  Kidderminster DY11 . . . .27 B2
  9 Northway GL20 . . . . .184 E1
  Worcester WR3 . . . . . . .115 C7
Farm La Bredon GL20 . . . .184 D4
  South Littleton WR11 . . .148 F1
Farm Rd Redditch B98 . . .71 A3
  Stourport-on-Severn
  DY13 . . . . .44 B4
Farm St WR10 . . . . .146 A1
Farmbrook CI **6** WR2 . .114 D1
Farmcote CI B97 . . . . .89 D4
Farmcroft Rd DY9 . . . . .6 E2
Farmdale Gr B45 . . . . .33 A6
Farmers Ct
  6 Droitwich WR9 . . . . .84 D5
  Halesowen B63 . . . . .7 F4
Farmers La WR12 . . . . . .176 E2
Farmers Rd B60 . . . . .67 F2
Farmers Way WR9 . . . . . .84 D5
Farmside CI DY9 . . . . .7 A3
Farnborough CI B98 . . . . .71 F1
Farnbury Croft B38 . . . . . .20 B2
Farndale CI DY5 . . . . .6 B6
Farne Ave WR5 . . . . .128 E6
Farnham Gn **10** WR4 . . .116 C6
Farren Rd B31 . . . . .18 D1
Farrier CI B60 . . . . .67 E6
Farrier St **7** WR1 . . . . .115 B3
Farriers Way WR9 . . . . . .84 D4
Farthing B97 . . . . .70 B5
Fastlea Rd B32 . . . . .9 D1
Fatherless Barn Cres
  B63 . . . . .7 D5
Faulkner CI DY8 . . . . .5 E4
Fawley Gr B14 . . . . .20 B5
Fearnings Cotts B97 . . . . .89 D5
Featherbed La B97 . . . . . .89 C5
Featherstone Rd B14 . . . . .20 E6
Feckenham CE Sch
  B96 . . . . .88 E1
Feckenham House B60 . . .49 B3
Feckenham Rd
  Astwood Bank B96 . . . . . .89 E2
  Redditch, Headless Cross
  B97 . . . . .89 C8
  Redditch, Hunt End B97 . .89 C4
Feckenham Wyldemoor
  Nature Reserve★
  B96 . . . . .107 E5
Felbrigg CI DY5 . . . . .6 D8
Feldon La B62 . . . . .8 E7
Fels Ave WR4 . . . . .116 C3
Felton CI B98 . . . . .71 E1
Fen CI DY13 . . . . .27 E8
Fennel Rd DY5 . . . . .6 C7
Fenton Rd B47 . . . . .36 A4
Fenwick CI B97 . . . . .70 B1
Ferguson Dr DY11 . . . . . . .27 A1
Fern Rd WR2 . . . . .114 E4
Fernbank CI B63 . . . . .7 E2
Ferndale Catshill B61 . . . . .32 A1
  Hagley DY9 . . . . .15 A5
  Hartlebury DY13 . . . . . . .44 C3
  3 Worcester WR3 . . . .102 C3
Ferndale Cres DY11 . . . . . .27 B8
Ferndale Pk DY9 . . . . .15 C8
Ferndale Rd B28 . . . . .21 F8
Ferney Hill Ave B97 . . . . .70 C3
Fernhill Gr WR14 . . . . . . .139 A1
Fernihough Ave WR11 . .164 B5
Fernleigh B60 . . . . .49 A1
Fernwood CI B98 . . . . .90 B5
Fernwood Croft B14 . . . . . .20 E6
Fernwoods B32 . . . . .9 B2
Ferry CI WR2 . . . . .114 F4
Ferry La
  Offenham WR11 . . . . . . .162 A8
  Ripple GL20 . . . . .182 E4
Field Ave B31 . . . . .18 F5
Field Barn La WR10 . . . .160 C5

Field CI Bromsgrove B60 . .67 E6
  Worcester WR4 . . . . . . .115 E6
Field Cottage Dr DY8 . . . . .6 B3
Field End **7** DY13 . . . . . .43 E4
Field Farm La B98 . . . . . . .71 D2
Field La Birmingham B32 . .18 B8
  Clent DY9 . . . . .15 D4
  Stourbridge DY8 . . . . .6 A3
  Tenbury SY8 . . . . .54 D2
Field Rd WR4 . . . . .115 E6
Field Wlk WR5 . . . . .128 D7
Fielden CI WR11 . . . . . . .161 E3
Fielden Row WR4 . . . . . .116 C3
Fieldfare WR14 . . . . .138 D6
Fieldfare Ct DY10 . . . . . . .28 A1
Fieldfare Rd DY9 . . . . .6 D4
Fieldhead CI **3** WR2 . . .114 D1
Fieldhouse La B62 . . . . . . .16 E4
Fields CI WR11 . . . . .162 E2
Fields La WR12 . . . . .177 E3
Fieldways CI B47 . . . . .36 A7
Fiery Hill Dr B45 . . . . .50 C8
Fiery Hill Rd B45 . . . . .50 C8
Fimbrell CI DY5 . . . . .6 A8
Finch La WR11 . . . . .148 B6
Finchfield CI DY8 . . . . .5 C4
Findon CI B97 . . . . .70 A5
Findon St DY10 . . . . .27 F6
Finmere Rd B28 . . . . .21 F8
Finsbury Dr DY5 . . . . .6 C7
Finstall Fst Sch B60 . . . . .49 B1
Finstall Rd
  Bromsgrove B60 . . . . . . .68 C8
  Finstall B60 . . . . .49 D1
Fir Croft DY5 . . . . .6 C8
Fir Gr Birmingham B14 . . .20 F5
  Stourbridge DY8 . . . . .5 D6
Fir Tree CI B97 . . . . .70 D4
Fir Tree Rd WR3 . . . . . . .102 F3
Fir Way WR4 . . . . .115 E6
Firbank CI B30 . . . . .19 E7
Fircroft B31 . . . . .18 F8
Fircroft CI B60 . . . . .67 D6
Fircroft Coll B29 . . . . .19 D8
Firecrest Way DY10 . . . . .28 B1
Firhill Croft B14 . . . . .20 D2
Firland The WR8 . . . . . . .155 F4
Firlands CI WR3 . . . . . . .102 F3
Firmstone Ct DY8 . . . . .5 E7
Firmstone St DY8 . . . . .5 E7
Firs CI
  Great Malvern WR14 . . . .152 F6
  Marlbrook B60 . . . . .32 D1
Firs CI The DY10 . . . . .28 A5
Firs Ind Est DY13 . . . . . . .44 B7
Firs The DY10 . . . . .28 A5
Firsby Rd B32 . . . . .9 E5
First Ave WR2 . . . . .128 A7
First Mdw Piece B32 . . . . .9 E4
Firtree Dr Birmingham B14 .21 B5
  Halesowen B62 . . . . .8 E8
Firth Pk Cres B62 . . . . .8 E8
Fish Hill
  Broadway WR12 . . . . . . .190 F7
  Redditch B97 . . . . .70 F4
Fish House La B60 . . . . . . .67 E4
Fish St WR1 . . . . .115 B2
Fisher CI B45 . . . . .17 C2
Fishers Dr B90 . . . . .36 F5
Fishing Line Rd B97 . . . . .70 E5
Fiskin La WR4 . . . . .116 C3
Fitcher CI WR2 . . . . .114 E6
Fitz Roy Ave B17 . . . . .9 F7
Fitzgerald PI DY5 . . . . .6 B6
Fitzhamon Pk GL20 . . . . .197 F7
Fitzroy Rd B31 . . . . .18 D3
Fitzwilliam CI **2** WR2 . .114 D3
Five Mile Dr GL56 . . . . . .191 F4
Five Oaks CI WR14 . . . . .153 D8
Five Ways Blackheath B64 . .7 C8
  Churchill DY10 . . . . .28 B6
Fladbury CE Aided Fst Sch
  WR10 . . . . .146 B1
Fladbury CI B98 . . . . .90 B8
Flag Mdw Wlk WR1 . . . . .115 B5
Flanders CI B98 . . . . .71 D5
Flatlea B31 . . . . .18 F4
Flats The B61 . . . . .48 F3
Flavel Rd B60 . . . . .67 E7
Flavell CI B32 . . . . .9 B1
Flax CI B47 . . . . .36 A5
Flax Gdns B38 . . . . .34 F8
Flax Piece WR7 . . . . .131 C8
Flaxley CI B98 . . . . .72 A4
Fleece Inn (NT) The★
  WR11 . . . . .163 C4
Fleece Rd WR12 . . . . . . .177 D1
Fleet La GL20 . . . . .184 B4
Fleet Rd GL20 . . . . .184 A6
Fleetwood Ave WR2 . . . .127 B2
Fleming Rd B32 . . . . .9 D5
Fletcher St DY9 . . . . .6 F5
Fletton Gr B14 . . . . .21 A3
Flint CI DY10 . . . . .27 E2
Florence Ave WR9 . . . . . .84 E1
Florence CI **4** WR5 . . .141 C6
Florence Rd B14 . . . . .20 F8
Flyford CI B98 . . . . .70 F1
Flyford Croft B29 . . . . . . .19 F2
Flyford Flavell Fst Sch
  WR7 . . . . .119 E1
Fockbury Mill La B61 . . . .48 E5
Fockbury Rd B61 . . . . . . .48 B5
Fold The B38 . . . . .20 A1
Foley Ave WR5 . . . . .128 F5
Foley Bsns Pk DY11 . . . . .44 C8
Foley Dr DY11 . . . . .44 B8
Foley Gdns B60 . . . . .67 E6

Foley Gr DY11 . . . . .44 B8
Foley Ind Est DY11 . . . . . .27 D3
Foley Inf Sch DY7 . . . . . . .4 A3
Foley Pk Fst Sch DY11 . . .27 D3
Foley Rd Stourbridge DY9 . .6 C2
  Worcester WR2 . . . . . . .115 A1
Foley St DY7 . . . . .4 A4
Foley Terr WR14 . . . . . . .152 E8
Foley Wlk **3** WR2 . . . .128 A8
Folkes Rd DY9 . . . . .7 A6
Folly Rd WR6 . . . . .124 F7
Folly The B97 . . . . .89 D8
Ford Abbey HR6 . . . . .92 E1
Ford CI WR4 . . . . .153 C8
Ford La WR9 . . . . .85 B6
Ford Rd B61 . . . . .48 E1
Fordbridge CI B97 . . . . . . .70 C1
Forde Hall La B94 . . . . . . .72 F8
Forde Way Gdns B38 . . . .34 D7
Forder Gr B14 . . . . .21 A2
Fordhouse La B30 . . . . . . .20 B6
Fordhouse Rd B60 . . . . . . .49 B1
Fordraught La B62 . . . . . . .17 B1
Fordrough The
  Birmingham B31 . . . . . . .19 C1
  Hollywood B90 . . . . .36 C7
Fords Rd B90 . . . . .36 E7
Foredraft CI B32 . . . . .9 C2
Foredraft St B63 . . . . .7 D5
Foredraught B80 . . . . .90 E4
Foredraught La WR9 . . . .104 A1
Foredrift CI B98 . . . . .70 E2
Foregate St
  Astwood Bank B96 . . . . . .89 E1
  Worcester WR1 . . . . . . .115 B3
Foregate St Sta WR1 . . .115 B3
Forelands CI B61 . . . . .67 D8
Forest CI **10** Bewdley DY12 25 F3
  3 Bewdley DY12 . . . . . .26 A3
  Lickey End B60 . . . . .49 B6
  Worcester WR4 . . . . . . .114 E4
Forest Dale B45 . . . . .33 B6
Forest Dr DY7 . . . . .3 F3
Forest Gate WR11 . . . . . .161 E2
Forest La B60 . . . . .87 D5
Forest Rd B68 . . . . .9 C7
Forest The WR9 . . . . .84 D8
Forest View WR9 . . . . .89 E6
Forest Way B47 . . . . .36 A6
Forester Way DY10 . . . . . .27 E3
Foresters Rd GL20 . . . . .196 E5
Forfar Wlk B38 . . . . .19 D2
Forge Dr B61 . . . . .48 F3
Forge La
  Belbroughton DY9 . . . . . .30 D7
  Blackheath B64 . . . . .7 B8
  Blakedown DY10 . . . . . . .14 B1
  Halesowen B62 . . . . .8 C5
Forge Mdws WR6 . . . . . . .97 E7
Forge Mill Needle Mus★
  B98 . . . . .70 F6
Forge Mill Rd B98 . . . . . . .70 F6
Forge Rd DY8 . . . . .5 F6
Forge The B60 . . . . .7 B8
Forge Trad Est B62 . . . . . . .8 C5
Forhill House B38 . . . . . . .34 F3
Forrell Gr B31 . . . . .34 B7
Forresters Rd WR15 . . . . .55 F6
Forshaw Heath La B94 . . .53 A7
Forshaw Heath Rd B94 . . .36 C1
Forsythia CI B31 . . . . .18 F8
Fort Royal★ WR5 . . . . . .115 C1
Fort Royal Hill WR5 . . . .115 C1
Fort Royal La **2** WR5 . .115 D1
Forth Gr B38 . . . . .34 E8
Forth Way B62 . . . . .8 E8
Fort-Mahon PI **8** DY12 . .25 F3
Forward Cotts B48 . . . . . .50 F6
Fossil Dr B45 . . . . .33 A7
Foster Ave B80 . . . . .90 E3
Foster Cres **3** DY7 . . . . .4 A4
Foster Dr WR9 . . . . .65 B5
Foster PI DY8 . . . . .5 E6
Foster Rd WR11 . . . . . . .161 B3
Foster St Kinver DY7 . . . . . .4 A4
  6 Stourbridge DY8 . . . . .6 A5
Foster St E DY8 . . . . .6 A5
Fosters Gn B60 . . . . .87 D7
Fotheringhay WR4 . . . . . .116 D6
Foundry St
  9 Stourport-on-Severn
  DY13 . . . . .44 A4
  Worcester WR1 . . . . . . .115 C2
Fountain CI B31 . . . . .33 E6
Fountain Ct **1** WR11 . . .161 D3
Fountain Gdns **2** WR11 161 D3
Fountain PI **12** WR1 . . .115 A5
Four Acres B32 . . . . .9 C4
Four Dwellings High Sch
  B32 . . . . .9 B5
Four Dwellings Inf Sch
  B32 . . . . .9 C5
Four Dwellings Jun Sch
  B32 . . . . .9 C5
Four Oaks CI B98 . . . . . . .89 C8
Four Pools Ind Est
  WR11 . . . . .161 D2
Four Pools La **3** WR11 . .161 E2
Four Pools Rd WR11 . . . .161 E2
Fourlands Rd B31 . . . . . . .18 E6
Fowler Ave **5** WR4 . . . .116 C3
Fowler PI **2** DY13 . . . . . .44 A5
Fownhope CI B98 . . . . .71 E3
Fox Covert DY8 . . . . .5 B5
Fox Dr WR5 . . . . .128 F5
Fox Hill B29 . . . . .19 C8
Fox Hill CI B29 . . . . .19 C8
Fox Hollies Rd B28 . . . . . .21 F7

Fox Hollow CI B45 . . . . . . .33 C7
Fox La Bromsgrove B61 . . .67 E8
  Chaddesley Corbett DY10 .46 D6
  Kempsey WR5 . . . . .142 A8
  Lindridge WR6 . . . . .59 D7
  Norton Juxta Kempsey
  WR5 . . . . .129 A1
Foxcote CI B98 . . . . .71 F4
Foxcote La B63, DY9 . . . . .7 B4
Foxes CI B60 . . . . .50 B5
Foxes Hill WR5 . . . . .141 D6
Foxes Mdw B30 . . . . .19 F4
Foxes Ridge B64 . . . . .7 E8
Foxfield B31 . . . . .18 F4
Foxfield Dr DY8 . . . . .6 A3
Foxglove CI
  1 Evesham WR11 . . . . .161 F1
  Great Malvern WR14 . . . .153 D7
Foxglove Rd WR5 . . . . . .128 C4
Foxglove Way B60 . . . . . . .49 C6
Foxhill Barns B48 . . . . . . .50 E5
Foxhill La B48 . . . . .50 E5
Foxholes La
  Feckenham B97 . . . . .88 F6
  Redditch B97 . . . . .89 A6
Foxholes The DY10 . . . . . .27 F8
Foxhollies Dr B63 . . . . .7 E4
Foxhollow B61 . . . . .67 D8
Foxhope CI B38 . . . . .20 B2
Foxhunt Rd B63 . . . . .7 D5
Foxhunter CI WR9 . . . . . .104 B3
Foxland Ave B45 . . . . .33 C7
Foxlea Rd B63 . . . . .7 D1
Foxlydiate Cres B97 . . . . .70 A4
Foxlydiate La B97 . . . . . . .69 F3
Foxlydiate Mews **3** B97 .70 A4
Foxwalks Ave B61 . . . . . . .67 D8
Foxwell St WR5 . . . . .128 E8
Foyle CI B38 . . . . .19 F1
Fradley CI B30 . . . . .19 D4
Framlingham CI **7**
  WR5 . . . . .128 D6
Frampton CI B30 . . . . .19 D7
Frampton Dr **3** WR12 . .177 E4
Frances Rd B30 . . . . .20 A5
Franche Fst Sch DY11 . . . .27 B8
Franche Mid Sch DY11 . . .27 B8
Franche Rd **6** DY11 . . . .12 B1
Franchecourt Dr DY11 . . .12 B1
Franchise St DY11 . . . . . . .27 C5
Francis Rd
  Bromsgrove B60 . . . . . . .67 F7
  Stourbridge DY9 . . . . .5 C5
  3 Stourport-on-Severn
  DY13 . . . . .43 E6
Francis Wlk B31 . . . . .34 A7
Frankley Ave B62 . . . . .8 F5
Frankley Beeches Rd
  B31 . . . . .18 D3
Frankley Com High Sch
  B45 . . . . .17 F1
Frankley Gn B32 . . . . .17 D5
Frankley Gn La B32 . . . . .17 E5
Frankley Hill La B32 . . . . .18 A4
Frankley Ind Pk B45 . . . . .18 B1
Frankley La B31, B32 . . . .18 D6
Frankley Lodge Rd B31 . .18 D4
Frankley Rd B68 . . . . .9 B8
Franklin CI **1** WR2 . . . .127 F6
Franklin Rd B30 . . . . .19 F5
Franklin Way B30 . . . . . . .19 F6
Franklin's La WR11 . . . . .134 C5
Frankton CI B98 . . . . .90 E8
Fraser CI WR14 . . . . .153 A6
Freda Eddy Ct **3** DY10 . .27 C6
Frederick Eary House
  B98 . . . . .90 B7
Frederick Rd (Road 1)
  DY10 . . . . .27 F1
Frederick Rd
  Great Malvern WR14 . . . .138 F4
  Oldbury B68 . . . . .9 D7
Fredericks CI DY8 . . . . .5 A8
Freeman Ct DY11 . . . . . . .27 B3
Freemans CI B20 . . . . . . .183 F7
Freemantle Dr WR5 . . . .141 C6
French CI WR10 . . . . .144 C1
Frenchlands La WR2 . . . .113 C7
Freshwater Dr DY5 . . . . . . .6 B8
Friar St Droitwich WR9 . . .84 F3
  9 Worcester WR1 . . . .115 C2
Friars Gorse DY7 . . . . .5 C8
Friday Ct **7** DY10 . . . . .136 D5
Friday Furlong B50 . . . . . .136 D5
Friday St CV37 . . . . .150 E2
Friesland Dr WR3 . . . . . .115 D7
Fringe Gn B60 . . . . .68 A7
Fringe Gn CI B60 . . . . .68 A7
Fringe Mdw Rd B98 . . . . . .71 F6
Froggery La WR7 . . . . . . .143 A8
Froglands La WR11 . . . . .149 B8
Frogmill Com Jun Sch
  B45 . . . . .18 B2
Frogmill Rd B45 . . . . .18 B2
Frome Way B14 . . . . .20 D6
Front Cotts B48 . . . . .50 F6
Front St CV37 . . . . .150 D2
Froxmere CI WR7 . . . . . . .117 F5
Froxmere Rd WR7 . . . . . .117 F5
Fruitlands WR14 . . . . . . .152 E4
Fry CI WR5 . . . . .116 C4
Fryer Rd B31 . . . . .34 B7
Fryers CI DY14 . . . . .22 B4
Fugelmere CI B17 . . . . .9 F7
Fulbert Rd WR10 . . . . . . .158 C7
Fulbrook CI B98 . . . . .71 C6
Fulbrook Gr B29 . . . . .18 F8

Fulford Hall Rd B90,
  B94 . . . . .36 D3
Fulmar Cres DY10 . . . . . . .28 B2
Fulton CI B60 . . . . .49 B1
Fulwood Ave B62 . . . . .8 F8
Furlong Ct B63 . . . . .7 C6
Furlong La B63 . . . . .7 D6
Furlong Mdw B31 . . . . . . .19 C2
Furlongs CI **1** DY14 . . . .22 D5
Furlongs Rd
  Cleobury Mortimer DY14 . .22 C5
  Pershore WR10 . . . . . . .144 E2
  Upton upon Severn WR8 . .169 C4
Furlongs The DY8 . . . . .6 B3
Furnace Hill B63 . . . . .8 B5
Furnace La B63 . . . . .8 B5
Furness CI **3** WR4 . . . .115 F5
Furrows The B60 . . . . .67 D6
Furze La B98 . . . . .72 A4

G

Gaddesby Rd B14 . . . . . . .20 F8
Gadwell Rd GL20 . . . . . . .197 A5
Gainsborough CI
  WR13 . . . . .167 C5
Gainsborough Hill DY8 . . . .6 A3
Gainsborough Mews
  DY11 . . . . .27 B5
Gainsborough Trad Est
  DY9 . . . . .6 C4
Gainsford Dr B62 . . . . .8 B6
Galahad Way DY13 . . . . . .43 F4
Gallipoli Dr WR5 . . . . . . .128 F4
Galton Rd B67 . . . . .9 F8
Galtons La DY9 . . . . .31 A7
Gamekeepers Dr **13**
  WR4 . . . . .115 F6
Gamson CI DY10 . . . . .27 E4
Ganborough CI B98 . . . . . .71 E1
Gander La GL20 . . . . .196 E5
Gannaway La GL20 . . . . .197 B7
Gannow Gn La B45 . . . . . .17 D1
Gannow Manor Cres
  B45 . . . . .17 E2
Gannow Manor Gdns
  B45 . . . . .17 F1
Gannow Rd B45 . . . . .32 E7
Gannow Wlk B45 . . . . . . .32 E7
Garden CI
  Birmingham, Frankley
  B45 . . . . .18 A2
  Dumbleton WR11 . . . . . .187 F5
  Mickleton GL55 . . . . . . .165 D3
Garden Stiles WR10 . . . .158 C8
Gardeners CI DY11 . . . . . .27 C8
Gardens CI WR8 . . . . . . .169 C5
Gardens The WR11 . . . . .161 D6
Gardens Wlk WR8 . . . . . .169 C6
Gardners CI **8** WR4 . . .115 F6
Gardners Mdw DY12 . . . . .26 B3
Garganey Ct DY10 . . . . . . .27 F1
Garibaldi Terr B60 . . . . . . .49 A1
Garland Cres B62 . . . . .8 E8
Garland Dr DY13 . . . . .43 D6
Garland Way B31 . . . . .19 C4
Garrard CI WR11 . . . . . . .135 F3
Garratts Wlk B14 . . . . .20 E1
Garth Ct WR5 . . . . .141 B7
Garth The B14 . . . . .21 D4
Garway CI B98 . . . . .71 E1
Gas Sq B61 . . . . .48 F1
Gateley CI B98 . . . . .72 A4
Gateley Rd B68 . . . . .9 D7
Gauden Rd DY9 . . . . .6 D2
Gaunts The B48 . . . . .51 B6
Gawtree Way **6** WR4 . .116 C5
Gay Hill La B38 . . . . .35 B8
Gaydon CI B98 . . . . .70 F1
Gayfield Ave DY5 . . . . .6 D8
Gaymore Rd DY10 . . . . . .13 B5
Gazala Dr WR5 . . . . .129 A4
Gedney CI B90 . . . . .21 C3
Geneva Ave WR14 . . . . . .153 A5
Geneva Ct WR3 . . . . .115 A8
Geneva Cres WR7 . . . . . .117 F4
Genners App B31 . . . . . . .18 D8
Genners La B31 . . . . .18 D7
Gentian CI B31 . . . . .18 D7
Geoffrey Chaucer Wlk **4**
  WR9 . . . . .103 E8
Geoffrey Rd B90 . . . . .21 F3
George Baylis Rd WR9 . . .84 E5
George Dance CI **2**
  DY10 . . . . .28 B6
George Dowty Dr **1**
  GL20 . . . . .184 E1
George La WR10 . . . . . . .145 B4
George Law Ct DY10 . . . . .27 F5
George Rd
  Alvechurch B48 . . . . .51 A5
  Halesowen B63 . . . . .7 F4
George St
  1 Bromsgrove B61 . . . .48 F2
  Evesham WR11 . . . . . . .161 C5
  Kidderminster DY10 . . . . .27 F6
  Worcester WR1 . . . . . . .115 C2
George Wlk **5** B97 . . . . .70 E3
George's Elm La B50 . . . .136 E8
Georgina Ave WR2 . . . . .128 A8
Gerald Rd DY8 . . . . .5 E7
Geraldine CI WR14 . . . . .153 B7
Geraldine Rd WR14 . . . . .153 B7
Gheluvelt Ave DY10 . . . . .27 F7
Gheluvelt St CI **6** DY13 . .43 F4
Gibb La B61 . . . . .49 A8
Gibbet La Kinver DY7 . . . . .4 E5

Gibbet La continued
  Stourbridge DY7 ....5 B4
Gibbons Cres
  1 Stourport-on-Severn
  DY13 ....43 F4
  7 Stourport-on-Severn
  DY13 ....44 A4
Gibbs Cl WR10 ....145 E3
Gibbs Hill B31 ....34 C7
Gibbs La WR11 ....148 A1
Gibbs Rd Redditch B98 ..71 A5
  Stourbridge DY9 ....7 A5
Gibraltar DY7 ....4 B4
Gibson Gr WR14 ......138 E3
Giffard Dr WR13 ......167 C5
Gig Bridge La WR10 ..144 C2
Gigmill Way DY8 ......5 E4
Gigmill Prim Sch DY8 ..5 E3
Gilbanks Rd DY8 ......5 D7
Gilbert Rd
  Bromsgrove B60 ......67 E7
  1 Great Malvern WR14 ..153 B8
Gilbert Scott Way DY10 .27 F7
Gilbertstone Cl B98 ...70 E1
Gildas Ave B38 ......20 A1
Gilgal DY13 ....44 A4
Gillam St WR3 ....115 C5
Gilmour Cres WR3 ....102 C1
Gilt Edge Club Leisure Ctr
  DY13 ....44 A8
Gimble Wlk B17 ......9 F7
Gipsy La Kinver DY7 ...4 A1
  Wolverley & Cookley DY11 .3 F1
Gisburn Cl **5** B97 ....70 B5
GK Davies Trad Est DY9 .7 A6
Glade The
  Great Malvern WR14 ..139 C1
  Stourbridge DY9 ......6 E5
Gladstone Dr DY8 .....5 D6
Gladstone Rd DY8 ....5 D6
Glasbury Croft B38 ...34 E7
Glasshouse Hill DY8 ..6 B3
Glastonbury Cl WR14 ..27 A6
Glastonbury Rd B14 ..21 C1
Gleads Croft B62 .....9 A3
Glebe Cl
  Bidford-on-Avon B50 ..136 D4
  Redditch B98 ....71 D2
  Worcester WR2 ......114 F2
Glebe La DY8 ....5 E4
Glebe Rd Alvechurch B48 .51 A7
  Aston Somerville WR12 ..175 F1
Glebe The
  Belbroughton DY9 .....30 E6
  Beoley B98 ....71 F7
  Great Witley WR6 .....61 B1
Glebeland Dr **8** GL20 .184 F6
Glen Devon Cl B45 ...18 A2
Glen Rd DY8 ....5 F3
Glen Rise B13 ....21 C6
Glen Side B32 ....9 D2
Glen The B60 ....50 A5
Glenavon Rd B14 ....21 A3
Glencoe Rd **3** WR11 ..161 F4
Glendale **3** WR9 ....84 D1
Glendale Cl B63 .....8 B4
Glendene Cres B38 ...34 C7
Glenelg Dr B60 ......50 A5
Glenelg Dr DY8 ......6 B2
Glenfield Cl B97 .....89 D1
Glengarry Cl B32 ....18 B7
Glenhill Dr B38 ......35 A8
Glenmoor WR10 .....171 F8
Glenmore Dr B38 ....19 D2
Glenridding Cl **3** WR4 .116 A5
Glenroyde B38 ....34 E7
Glenthorne Ave WR4 ..115 F5
Glenwood Cl DY5 ....6 D8
Glenwood Rd B38 ....34 D8
Gloster Ades Rd
  WR11 ....163 E3
Gloucester Cl WR14 ..139 C5
Gloucester Dr WR13 ..139 F3
Gloucester La GL55 ..165 D4
Gloucester Rd B60 ...196 D5
Gloucester Way DY12 ..26 B4
Glover Cl B28 ....21 F6
Glover St B98 ....70 E3
Glyn Farm Rd B32 ....9 C4
Glyn Rd B32 ....9 D6
Glynn Cres B63 ......7 B7
Glynside Ave B32 ....9 D6
Goblins Cl WR5 .....128 F4
Goddard Rd WR1 ....115 B5
Godson Cres DY11 ...27 C3
Godson Pl DY11 .....27 C3
Godson's Cl WR15 ...55 F5
Goffs Cl B32 ....9 F3
Goldcrest Dr DY10 ...28 B2
Golden Acres WV15 ..1 C6
Golden Cross La B61 ..32 B1
Golden Hind Dr DY13 ..44 A2
Golden La WR11 .....162 D1
Goldfinch Cl B38 ....19 D8
Goldfinch Rd DY9 ....6 C3
Goldsmith Rd
  Birmingham B14 .....20 D8
  Worcester WR4 .....115 F6
Goldsmith Wlk DY10 ..28 C5
Goldthorn Pl DY11 ...27 C2
Goldthorn Rd DY11 ...27 C2
Goldthorne Cl B97 ...70 C1
Goldthorne Wlk B14 ..20 F3
Gomeldon Ave B14 ...20 D3
Gooch Cl DY8 ....6 B6
Goodalls Gr WR11 ...161 D6
Goodier's La GL20 ...184 A7
Goodleigh Ave B45 ...33 E6

Goodman Cl B28 .....21 F6
Goodrest Ave B62 ....9 A5
Goodrest Croft B14 ..21 C4
Goodrest La B38 .....34 F6
Goodrest Wlk WR3 ..115 C5
Goodrich Covert **10** B14 ..20 C2
Goodson Rd WR14 ...139 C5
Goodwin Cl DY11 ....27 C7
Goodwood Ave WR5 ..128 E8
Goodwood Cl
  7 Evesham WR11 ....161 C2
  Fernhill Heath WR3 ...102 F2
  5 Worcester WR5 ...128 E8
Goodwood Rd
  Catshill B61 ....32 B1
  Great Malvern WR14 ..139 A4
  Pershore/Pinvin WR10 ..144 E4
Goodwyn Ave B68 ....9 C7
Goosehill Cl B98 .....71 E1
Goosehill La WR9 ....86 A2
Gorcott Hill B98 .....72 C5
Gordon Dr CV37 .....151 D3
Gordon Terr WR12 ...152 E4
Gorleston Gr B14 ....21 B2
Gorleston Rd B14 ....21 B2
Gorse Cl
  Birmingham, Selly Oak
  B29 ....19 A8
  5 Droitwich WR9 ....104 A8
Gorse Gn La DY9 ....31 C8
Gorse Hill WR11 ....174 B2
Gorse Hill Prim Sch
  WR4 ....115 F4
Gorse Hill Rd WR4 ..115 F5
Gorse Mdw Dr B45 ..50 B8
Gorsey Cl B96 ......108 E8
Gorsey La B47 ....36 A3
Gorsly Piece B32 ....9 C4
Gorsty Hill Rd B65 ...8 B8
Gorsy Rd B32 ....9 D5
Gorsymead Gr B31 ..18 C2
Goscote Cl B97 ......70 A5
Gould Ave E DY11 ...27 A2
Gould Ave W DY11 ..27 A1
Gould Dr GL20 ......184 E1
Gower House B62 ...8 F6
Gower Rd B62 ......8 F6
Gracemere Cres B28 ..21 E3
Gracewell Homes B13 ..21 D8
Grafson Pl WR9 .....84 D1
Grafton Cl
  Great Malvern WR14 ..138 F3
  Redditch B98 ....90 B7
Grafton Cres B60 ....67 E8
Grafton House B60 ..49 B3
Grafton La
  Bidford-on-Avon B50 ..136 F6
  Bromsgrove B61 ......67 C7
  Pendock GL19 ....193 C6
Grafton Rd B90 .....21 C2
Graftons The WR8 ...169 C4
Graham Rd
  Great Malvern WR14 ..138 F1
  Halesowen B62 ......8 C8
  6 Worcester WR2 ...114 F1
Grainger's La B64 ...7 D8
Graith Cl B28 ....21 E3
Grammar Sch La B63 ..8 A4
Grampian Rd DY8 ....6 A6
Granary Rd B60 .....67 E6
Granbrook La GL55 ..165 E4
Granby Cl B98 ......71 F6
Grand Stand Rd WR1 ..115 A3
Grange Ave WR3 ....102 A1
Grange Cres
  Birmingham B45 .....32 F8
  Halesowen B63 ......8 B3
Grange Ct
  Northway GL20 .....184 F1
  1 Redditch B98 .....70 F4
  Stourbridge DY9 .....6 C4
Grange Farm Dr B38 ..34 D8
Grange Hill Rd B38 ..19 E1
Grange La
  Alvechurch B48 ......51 B3
  Broadheath WR2 ....113 E5
  Fernhill Heath WR3 ..102 D2
  Harvington WR11 ....148 A6
  Stourbridge DY9 .....6 D4
  Worcester WR2 .....127 B8
Grange Rd
  Bidford-on-Avon B50 ..136 E4
  Birmingham, King's Heath
  B14 ....20 E8
  Blackheath B64 ......8 B8
  Bretforton WR11 ....163 B5
  Broadheath WR2 ....114 A7
  3 Great Malvern WR14 ..152 F8
  Halesowen B63 ......8 C3
  Kidderminster DY11 ..27 B7
  Northway GL20 .....184 E1
  2 Redditch B98 .....70 F4
  Stourbridge DY9 .....6 C4
Grange Rise B38 ....34 F7
Grange Sch The
  North Claines WR3 ...102 D3
  Stourbridge DY9 .....6 D4
Grange The B62 .....8 F6
Grange Way WR4 ...116 D3
Grangers La B98 ....90 B5
Granhill Cl B98 ......90 A8
Granshaw Cl B38 ....19 F1
Grant Ct B30 ....20 A5
Granton Cl B14 .....20 D5
Granton Rd B14 ....20 D5

Granville Cl B60 .....49 B1
Granville Crest DY10 ..28 B6
Granville Rd B64 .....8 B8
Grasmere Cl DY10 ...27 E7
Grasmere Dr WR4 ...116 A5
Grasmere Gr DY13 ..43 F6
Grasshopper Ave
  WR5 ....128 C5
Grassington Dr WR4 ..116 A4
Grassmere Dr DY8 ...5 F3
Grassmoor Rd B38 ..19 E2
Gratham Cl DY5 .....6 B7
Gravel Bank B32 ....9 D2
Gravel Pit La B48 ....51 B3
Gravel Pits Cl **2** GL20 ..184 F6
Gray Cl DY10 ....28 B6
Grayling Cl WR5 ....128 C5
Grayling Rd DY9 ....6 C6
Grayshott Cl B61 ...48 E3
Grayston Cl GL20 ...197 A8
Grayswood Pk Rd B32 ..9 C6
Grayswood Rd B31 ..33 F7
Grazebrook Croft B32 ..18 D8
Grazing La B97 ......69 F2
Grazings The DY7 ...4 C3
Great Barn La B97 ..70 B1
Great Calcroft WR10 ..158 D7
Great Cornbow **5** B63 ..8 B3
Great Farley Dr B31 ..18 C1
Great Hockings La B97 ..69 E2
Great House Rd WR2 ..114 F1
Great Malvern Prim Sch
  WR14 ....153 C8
Great Malvern Sta
  WR14 ....153 A8
Great Oaty Mdw WR4 ..116 B5
Great Stone Rd B31 ..19 A3
Great Western Way
  DY13 ....44 A5
Great Witley CE Prim Sch
  WR6 ....80 B8
Greatfield Rd DY11 ..27 B4
Greaves Gdns DY11 ..12 B1
Greaves Sq B38 .....20 B1
Green Acres Rd B38 ..34 D8
Green Bower Dr B97 ..49 A5
Green Cl
  Childswickham WR12 ..176 E2
  Honeybourne WR11 ..164 A4
  Studley B80 ....90 E3
  Wythall B47 ....36 A3
Green Cover WR4 ...116 A4
Green Ct B28 ....21 F6
Green Dr B32 ....9 C1
Green Dragonfly WR5 ..128 F6
Green Gables B47 ...36 A7
Green Hill Bath Rd **8**
  WR5 ....115 C1
Green Hill Cl B60 ...49 D6
Green Hill London Rd **10**
  WR5 ....115 C1
Green Hill Pl **11** WR5 ..115 C1
Green Hill Sch WR11 ..161 E6
Green La
  Birmingham, Hawkesley
  B38 ....34 E8
  Birmingham, Quinton B32 ..9 C6
  Broadheath WR2 ....114 A6
  Catshill B61 ....32 A1
  Feckenham B97 .....88 F6
  Great Malvern WR14 ..152 E1
  Hadzor WR9 ....85 C1
  Inkberrow B96 ......108 A3
  Redditch B97 ....89 A7
  Ripple WR8 ....170 B4
  Ryall WR8 ....169 F6
  Solihull B90 ....21 E1
  Stourbridge DY9 .....6 E5
  Studley B80 ....90 B5
  Tewkesbury GL20 ...197 C7
  Tibberton WR9 .....104 B3
  Worcester WR10 ....102 A2
Green Leys WR10 ...133 A4
Green Leys Cres WV15 ..1 C6
Green Mdw WR9 ....15 B7
Green Mdw Prim Sch
  B29 ....18 F7
Green Mdw Rd B29 ..19 A7
Green Pk Rd
  Birmingham B31 .....18 E2
  Bromsgrove B60 ....49 B2
Green Slade Cres B60 ..32 E1
Green St Bushley GL20 ..182 D1
  Kidderminster DY10 ..27 E5
  Stourbridge DY8 .....5 F5
Green St Ind Est DY10 ..27 E5
Green Sward La B98 ..71 D1
Green The
  Birmingham B31 .....18 C2
  Birmingham, King's Norton
  B38 ....19 F2
  4 Birmingham, Quinton
  B32 ....9 A6
  Bluntington DY10 ....29 E1
  Hagley DY9 ....14 F4
  Pershore/Pinvin WR10 ..144 F7
Green Wickets B13 ..20 E6
Green Wlk B17 ......9 F7
Greenacres
  Birmingham B32 .....9 E2
  Twyning GL20 ......183 F7
Greenacres La DY12 ..26 A4
Greenacres Rd
  Bromsgrove B61 .....48 D2
  Worcester WR2 .....114 D2
Greenaleigh Rd B14 ..21 D3
Greenbank
  Barnt Green B45 ....50 D8

Greenbank continued
  2 Droitwich WR9 ....85 B2
Greenbank Rd DY12 ..25 E2
Greenbush Dr B63 ...8 A5
Greendale Cl B61 ...49 B8
Greenfield Ave
  Marlbrook B60 ......32 D1
  Stourbridge DY8 .....5 F5
Greenfield Cl **2** WR4 ..116 B4
Greenfield Cotts B48 ..51 A5
Greenfield Prim Sch
  DY8 ....5 F5
Greenfields
  Redditch B98 ....70 E2
  Upton upon Severn WR8 ..169 A5
Greenfields Cl **1** WR10 ..143 F6
Greenfields Rd **3** WR14 ..138 F5
Greenfinch Cl DY10 ..28 B3
Greenfinch Rd DY9 ..6 D3
Greenford Cl B97 ...70 B5
Greenford Gdns WR2 ..114 C5
Greenford Rd B14 ...21 C3
Greenhill Blackwell B60 ..49 F4
  Evesham WR11 ......161 D6
Greenhill Ave DY10 ..27 F7
Greenhill Cl WR15 ..55 F5
Greenhill Ct B62 ....8 E7
Greenhill Dr WR14 ..139 A1
Greenhill Gdns B62 ..8 D6
Greenhill Ind Est DY10 ..28 A7
Greenhill La WR2 ...101 D2
Greenhill Oak DY10 ..27 F7
Greenhill Pk Rd WR11 ..161 D7
Greenhill Rd B62 ...8 D7
Greenhurst B45 .....33 A1
Greenlands WR8 ....71 A1
Greenlands Bsns Ctr
  B98 ....71 B2
Greenlands Dr B98 ..89 F8
Greenleas Gdns B63 ..8 C3
Greenleys WR11 ....162 E3
Greenoak Cres B30 ..20 C8
Greenroyde DY9 ....6 B1
Greens Croft Way
  WR7 ....120 C7
Greensforge La DY7 ..4 C7
Greenside B60 ......67 C2
Greenslade Croft B31 ..19 A2
Greenslade Rd B90 ..21 C2
Greenvale B31 ......18 F5
Greenvale Ave B38 ..34 E7
Greenway Gdns B38 ..34 E7
Greenway The
  Bowling Green WR2 ..127 C3
  Hagley DY9 ....14 F5
  Rock DY14 ....41 D2
Greenways
  Birmingham B31 .....18 F8
  Halesowen B63 .....7 C6
Greenwood Cl B14 ..20 E5
Greenwoods The DY8 ..5 E5
Gregory Ave B29 ....19 A8
Gregory Rd DY8 ....5 D5
Gregory's Bank WR3 ..115 C5
Gregory's Mill St WR3 ..115 B6
Grendon Cl B98 .....71 D1
Grendon Rd B14 ....21 A3
Grendon Sch B14 ...21 A3
Grenville Rd WR2 ...114 D2
Gresham Rd
  Birmingham B28 .....21 F6
  Worcester WR2 .....114 D1
Grey Gn La DY12 ...26 B5
Grey's Rd B80 ......90 E3
Greyfriars Dr B61 ...48 D2
Greyhound La DY8 ..5 D2
Greylag Cres GL20 ..197 A5
Greystone Cl B98 ...71 C5
Griffin Cl B31 ....19 B6
Griffin Rd DY10 .....27 E4
Griffins Brook Cl B30 ..19 D7
Griffins Brook La B30 ..19 D6
Grigg Gr B31 ....18 E1
Grimley & Holt CE Prim Sch
  WR2 ....101 F6
Grimley Cl B98 .....70 F1
Grimley La B60 .....68 E6
Grimley Rd **2** B31 ..19 D2
Grimpits La B38 ....35 A7
Grisedale Dr B45 ...116 A6
Gristhorpe Rd B29 ..20 A8
Grit La WR14 ....138 E6
Grizedale Cl B45 ...18 B2
Grosmont Ave WR14 ..116 D6
Grosvenor Ave DY10 ..28 A6
Grosvenor Cl **6** WR9 ..85 B1
Grosvenor Cres **5** WR9 ..85 A1
Grosvenor Ct DY9 ..6 B1
Grosvenor Gdns B61 ..49 B5
Grosvenor House B97 ..70 E4
Grosvenor Sh Ctr B31 ..19 A4
Grosvenor Sq B28 ..21 F5
Grosvenor Way
  Brierley Hill DY5 ....6 E7
  Droitwich WR9 .....85 A1
Grosvenor Wood **12** DY12 ..25 F2
Grove Ave Halesowen B63 ..7 F3
  Honeybourne WR11 ..164 B5
Grove Cres WR2 ....114 D1
Grove Field WR4 ...116 B7
Grove Gdns B61 ....49 A6
Grove Jun Sch WR14 ..139 B2
Grove Mdw **4** DY14 ..22 D5
Grove Mews B31 ....34 B8
Grove Rd
  Birmingham, King's Heath
  B14 ....20 D6
  Stourbridge DY9 .....6 F3

Gib - Hal 211

Grove St B98 ....70 E4
Grove The
  Birmingham, Rednall
  B45 ....33 D4
  Birmingham, West Heath
  B31 ....34 B8
  Stourport-on-Severn
  DY13 ....44 B2
  Studley B80 ....90 D3
  Worcester WR3 .....115 B8
Grove Villas B64 ....7 D7
Grove Way WR12 ...114 B1
Grovefield GL19 ....193 B7
Grovelley La B31, B45 ..33 E5
Grovewood Dr **2** B38 ..19 E1
Grovewood Rd WR14 ..139 C4
Grundy's La WR14 ..152 E1
Guardian Ct
  Birmingham, Frankley
  B31 ....18 D3
  3 Bromsgrove B60 ..49 A2
Guardian House B68 ..9 C7
Guardians Way B31 ..18 E8
Guarlford Rd
  Great Malvern WR14 ..153 D7
  Guarlford WR13 ....154 A7
Guild Ct **4** B60 ....48 F2
Guild Rd B60 ....48 F1
Guildford Ct
  Kidderminster DY11 ..27 A6
  Worcester WR5 .....115 F2
Guildford Cl **12** B29 ..19 C7
Guinness Cl B98 ....89 D8
Guiting Cl B97 .....70 B1
Guiting Rd B29 .....19 A7
Gullane Cl B38 .....19 D1
Gullswood Cl B14 ..20 D2
Gunbarrel Ind Ctr B63 ..7 F6
Gunner La B45 .....32 D7
Gunners La B80 ....90 E4
Gunnings La WR10 ..132 E4
Gupshill Cl GL20 ...196 E4
Gurneys La **5** WR9 ..85 A3
Gutter The DY9 ....31 E7
Guy's Wlk B61 .....49 A5
Gypsy La B97 ......69 C5

H

Habberley La
  Kidderminster DY11 ..27 A8
  Kidderminster Foreign
  DY11 ....26 F8
Habberley Rd
  Bewdley DY12 ......26 E5
  Kidderminster DY11 ..27 B7
Habberley St **1** DY11 ..27 C6
Habberley Valley Nature
  Reserve★ DY11 .....26 E8
Hacketts La WR10 ..171 F7
Hackmans Gate La DY9 ..30 B7
Hadcroft Grange DY9 ..6 C4
Hadcroft Rd DY9 ...6 C4
Haddon Croft B63 ..7 C1
Haden Cl B64 ......8 A7
Haden Cross Dr B64 ..8 A7
Haden Hill Rd B63 ..8 B6
Haden Pk Rd B64 ..7 F7
Hadendale B64 .....8 A7
Hadley Cl B47 ......36 A5
Hadzor House **5** B97 ..70 A4
Hadzor La WR9 ....85 C2
Hadzor Rd B68 .....9 D8
Hafren Cl B45 ......18 B2
Hafren Way DY13 ..43 E4
Haggs Mdw WR4 ...116 C5
Haig Pl B13 ....21 A7
Hailsham Cl **8** WR5 ..128 E8
Haines Ave
  Worcester WR4 .....116 C3
  Wyre Piddle WR10 ..145 A4
Halas Ind Est B62 ..8 C5
Haldon Gr B31 .....33 E7
Hales Pk **14** DY12 ..25 F3
Hales Rd B63 ......8 A4
Halesbury Ct B63 ..7 F2
Halesbury Sch B62 ..8 E7
Halescroft Sq B31 ..18 E6
Halesmere Way B63 ..8 C3
Halesowen CE Prim Sch
  B63 ....8 B4
Halesowen Coll
  (e-commerce Ctr) B62 ..8 C8
Halesowen Coll (Walton
  Campus) B63 ......8 A3
Halesowen Coll
  (Whittingham main campus)
  B63 ....8 B5

Halesowen Ind Pk B62 ...8 B6
Halesowen Rd
 Halesowen B62 ....8 F6
 Lydiate Ash B61 ....32 C3
Halfcot Ave DY9 ....6 C3
Halfkey Rd WR13 ......138 D6
Halfshire La DY10 ......14 B1
Halifax Ct DY11 ....27 B8
Halifax Dr WR2 ....127 F7
Hall Cl WR4 ....116 A5
Hall Dale Cl B28 ....21 F5
Hall Dr DY9 ....15 D6
Hall Gn WR14 ....153 E8
Hall Gn Cl WR14 ....153 E8
Hall Gn Inf Sch B28 ....21 F7
Hall Gn Jun Sch B28 ...21 F7
Hall Gn Sch B28 ....21 E8
Hall La DY9 ....15 D6
Hall Mdw DY9 ....15 D7
Hall St DY8 ....6 A3
Halladale B38 ....19 F1
Hallow CE Prim Sch
 WR2 ....101 D2
Hallow Rd
 Broadheath WR2 ....114 A7
 Worcester WR2 ....114 E6
Hallowfields Cl B98 ......70 E1
Halls Farm La DY12 .....11 C1
Hallstead Rd B13 ....21 B5
Ham Dingle Prim Sch
 DY9 ....6 C2
Ham La Powick WR2 ....127 C4
 Severn Stoke WR8 ....155 C5
 Stourbridge DY9 ....6 C2
Ham View WR8 ....169 C5
Hamble Cl WR5 ....115 E2
Hambleton Rd B63 ....7 D2
Hambury Dr B14 ....20 D7
Hamgreen La B97 ....88 E5
Hamilton Ave
 Halesowen B62 ....8 C3
 Stourbridge DY8 ....5 D6
Hamilton Cl
 [1] Bowling Green WR2 ...127 C2
 Lickey End B60 ....49 C6
Hamilton Dr
 Birmingham B29 ....19 D8
 Studley B80 ....90 D3
Hamilton Rd
 Evesham WR11 ....161 C2
 Kidderminster DY11 ......27 B3
 Redditch B97 ....89 C8
 [18] Worcester WR5 .....115 C2
Hamlet Gdns B28 ....21 F8
Hamlet Rd B28 ....21 F8
Hammer Bank DY5 ....7 A8
Hammersley Cl B63 ......7 C7
Hammock Rd WR10 .....171 D7
Hammond Cl [9] WR9 ....85 A1
Hammond Way B60 ......6 A7
Hampden Cl DY5 ....7 A8
Hampden Rd WR14 ......139 A4
Hampshire Ct [1] B29 ....19 B7
Hampstall La DY13 ......63 A4
Hampstead Glade B63 ...8 C2
Hampton Ave B60 ....68 A8
Hampton Cl
 Redditch B98 ....90 B7
 Worcester WR2 ....114 E3
Hampton Dr DY7 ....4 B4
Hampton Gdns DY9 ......6 D3
Hampton Lovett Ind Est
 WR9 ....84 C7
Hampton Rd WR9 ....84 F4
Hams Way WR2 ....127 E2
Hanbury Ave WR2 ......127 F8
Hanbury CE Fst Sch
 B60 ....86 F5
Hanbury Cl
 Bromsgrove B60 ....68 A8
 Halesowen B63 ....7 F1
Hanbury Ct DY8 ....6 A4
Hanbury Hall (NT) ★
 B60 ....86 C4
Hanbury Hill DY8 ....6 A4
Hanbury House B97 ......70 B4
Hanbury Pk ★ B60 ......86 C4
Hanbury Pk Rd WR2 ....127 F7
Hanbury Rd Hadzor WR9 .85 C3
 Hanbury B60 ....87 A6
 Stoke Heath B60 ....67 D4
Hanbury St WR9 ....85 A3
Hancocks La
 Castlemorton WR13 ......167 B3
 Welland WR13 ....166 F4
Handbury Rd WR14 .....139 A5
Handley Gr B31 ....18 C2
Hanging La B31 ....18 E2
Hangman's La WR8 ......154 E4
Hanley Castle High Sch
 WR8 ....154 F1
Hanley Cl B63 ....7 E4
Hanley Orch WR8 ....154 A2
Hanley Rd
 Great Malvern WR14 .....152 F1
 Malvern Wells WR13 .....153 B1
Hanley Terr WR14 ......152 E3
Hannon Rd B14 ....20 E5
Hanover Ct B97 ....89 D8
Hanover Pl B60 ....48 F1
Hanover St B60 ....48 F1
Hansom Rd B32 ....9 C5
Hanson Way WR10 ......158 D2
Hanstone Rd DY13 ......43 F1
Happy Land N WR2 .....114 F1

Happy Land W WR2 ....114 E1
Happy Valley
 Great Malvern WR14 .....138 E1
 Malvern WR14 ....152 E8
Harberrow Cl DY9 ....15 A6
Harbinger Ave WR14 ....139 B1
Harbinger Rd B38 ....20 B2
Harborne Rd B68 ....9 E8
Harborough Wlk DY9 ....6 A2
Harbour Cl B50 ....136 C4
Harbour Dr [5] WR13 ...152 B2
Harbour View GL20 .....196 F7
Harbours Cl B61 ....67 D7
Harbours Hill DY9 ....31 E6
Harbourside GL20 ......196 F7
Harbury Cl B98 ....71 D1
Harcourt Rd
 Blackheath B64 ....7 F8
 Mathon WR13 ....152 B6
Harden Ct B31 ....18 E1
Harden Manor Ct B63 ...8 C3
Harden Vale B63 ....7 E5
Hardnott Row WR4 .....116 D6
Hardwick Bank Rd
 GL20 ....184 D3
Hardwick Dr B62 ....8 A7
Hardwick La B80 ....91 B6
Hardwicke Cl WR2 ......115 A3
Hardwicke Way DY9 .....6 D5
Hardwike Wlk B14 ....20 D2
Hardy Ave DY10 ....28 A6
Hardy Ct WR3 ....115 C6
Harebell Gdns B38 ......34 F8
Haresfield Cl
 Redditch B97 ....70 D3
 [15] Worcester WR4 ....115 F6
Harewell La WR8 ....157 B8
Harewood Cl B28 ....21 E5
Hargrave Rd B90 ....21 D1
Hargreaves Ct DY11 ....27 C3
Harland Cl B61 ....48 D3
Harlech Cl
 Birmingham B32 ....18 A7
 [15] Worcester WR4 ....116 C6
Harlech Way DY10 ......27 E2
Harlestones House DY8 ..5 F7
Harlstones Cl DY8 ....6 A8
Harman's Hill WR9 ......105 E5
Harmon Rd DY8 ....5 C5
Harold Davies Dr [1]
 DY13 ....43 F2
Harold Evers Way DY10 .27 F7
Harpers Rd
 Birmingham, Highter's Heath
 B14 ....21 A1
 Birmingham, Northfield
 B31 ....19 A2
Harpley Rd WR8 ....157 C2
Harport Rd B98 ....71 A1
Harrier Cl GL20 ....197 A4
Harriers Gn DY10 ....28 B8
Harriers Ind Est DY10 ...27 F5
Harringay Dr DY8 ....5 E3
Harrington Rd WR2 .....114 D1
Harris Cl [6] WR9 ....84 E3
Harris Ind Pk B60 ....67 E2
Harrison House B14 .....20 F3
Harrison Rd B97 ....89 C8
Harrop Way DY8 ....5 E8
Harrow Cl Hagley DY9 ...15 A6
 Stoke Heath B60 ....67 E6
Harrow Croft WR2 ......114 C1
Harry Cheshire Com High
 Sch DY11 ....27 B6
Harry Taylor Fst Sch The
 B97 ....89 C6
Harry Taylor House
 B98 ....71 A4
Hartford Rd B60 ....49 B1
Hartland Rd B31 ....33 E6
Hartle La DY9 ....30 F6
Hartlebury Castle ★
 DY11 ....44 F3
Hartlebury Cl B98 ....71 E2
Hartlebury Comm Nature
 Reserve ★ DY13 ......44 C2
Hartlebury Ind Est
 DY10 ....45 D1
Hartlebury Ind Sch
 DY11 ....45 A2
Hartlebury Rd
 Halesowen B63 ....7 C1
 Stourport-on-Severn
 DY13 ....44 C3
Hartlebury Sch DY11 ....44 F3
Hartlebury Sta DY11 ....45 B2
Hartlebury Trad Est
 DY10 ....64 D8
Hartmann Cl [7] DY14 ...22 C4
Harton Way B14 ....20 C5
Hartsbourne Dr B62 .....8 D4
Hartside Cl B63 ....7 D2
Hartswell Dr B13 ....20 F6
Harvard Ave WR11 .....164 B6
Harvest Cl
 Birmingham B30 ....20 B6
 Stoke Heath B60 ....67 E6
Harvey Mews B30 ......19 D7
Harvey Rd WR11 ....161 E4
Harvey Wlk WR3 ....115 D5
Harvey Works Ind Est
 B63 ....7 F6
Harvine Wlk DY8 ....5 E3
Harvington CE Sch
 WR11 ....148 B7
Harvington Cl
 Kidderminster DY11 .....12 A1

Harvington Cl continued
 Redditch B97 ....70 B5
Harvington Hall ★ DY10 .29 B1
Harvington Hall La
 Chaddesley Corbett DY10 .46 C8
 Harvington DY10 ....29 B1
Harvington Rd
 Birmingham B29 ....19 A8
 Bromsgrove B60 ....68 A8
 Halesowen B63 ....7 F1
 Oldbury B68 ....9 A8
Hasbury CE Prim Sch
 B63 ....7 F2
Hasbury Cl B63 ....7 E2
Hasbury Rd B32 ....18 B8
Haseley Cl B98 ....71 E1
Haselor La WR11 ....160 E2
Haslucks Gn Rd B90 ....36 E7
Hastings Cl WR6 ....99 A3
Hastings Dr WR14 ......116 C6
Hastings Pl GL20 ....196 E4
Hastings Rd
 Bromsgrove B60 ....67 E7
 Great Malvern WR14 .....153 D8
Haswell Rd B63 ....7 D4
Hatfield Bank WR5 ......129 A1
Hatfield Cl B98 ....71 E1
Hatfield La WR5 ....129 B2
Hatfield Rd DY9 ....6 C4
Hathaway Cl
 [3] South Littleton WR11 .148 F1
 [5] Worcester WR2 .....114 D3
Hatherton Gr B29 ....9 F1
Haunch La B13 ....21 A5
Haven The B14 ....21 D4
Haverford Dr B45 ....33 B6
Havergal Wlk B63 ....7 B4
Hawfinch Rise DY10 ....28 A3
Hawford Dovecote (NT) ★
 WR3 ....102 B6
Hawford Lock La WR3 ..102 A4
Hawford Pl WR9 ....84 D1
Hawkes Cl B30 ....20 A7
Hawkesbury Rd B90 ....21 F1
Hawkesley CE & Methodist
 Prim Sch B38 ....34 E7
Hawkesley Cres B31 ....19 A1
Hawkesley Dr B31 ......33 F8
Hawkesley End B38 .....34 E7
Hawkesley Mill La B31 ..18 F2
Hawkesley Sq B38 ......34 E7
Hawkestone Rd B29 ....19 A7
Hawkhurst Rd B14 ......20 F2
Hawkins Cl WR2 ....114 D3
Hawkley Row WR4 .....116 C5
Hawkmoor Gdns B38 ....35 A8
Hawkmoth Cl [10] GL20 ..197 A4
Hawksbury Cl B98 ......71 D5
Hawkstone Cl DY11 .....27 D8
Hawkswood Gr B14 .....21 B3
Hawkwood Cl WR14 ....138 E3
Hawkwood Cres WR2 ...114 E4
Hawne Cl B63 ....7 E6
Hawne La B63 ....7 F6
Hawnelands The B63 ....7 F5
Hawthorn Coppice DY9 .15 A6
Hawthorn Cres DY12 ...25 E2
Hawthorn Croft B68 .....9 D7
Hawthorn Gr DY11 ......27 A6
Hawthorn La
 Great Malvern WR13 .....153 B5
 Newland WR2 ....139 F8
 Powick WR2 ....126 F1
Hawthorn Rd
 Brierley Hill DY5 ....7 A8
 Bromsgrove B61 ....49 B4
 Evesham WR11 ....161 F2
 Redditch B97 ....70 A4
 Worcester WR4 ....115 E4
Hawthorn Way GL20 ....184 F1
Hawthorne Cl WR10 ....143 F7
Hawthorne Dr B47 ......36 B6
Hawthorne Rd
 Birmingham, King's Norton
 B30 ....19 D5
 Halesowen B63 ....7 E2
Hawthorne Way DY7 ....4 C3
Hawthorne Wlk [6] WR9 .103 F8
Hawthorns The
 Hagley DY9 ....14 F4
 [1] Kidderminster DY10 ..28 A5
 Oldbury B68 ....9 D7
Hay Cl
 Kidderminster DY11 .....27 C7
 Worcester WR4 ....116 A4
Hay Gn DY9 ....6 D5
Hay Gn Cl B30 ....19 D6
Hay Gn La B30 ....19 D6
Hay La WR9 ....104 E7
Haybridge Ave DY8 .....14 F5
Haybridge High Sch
 DY8 ....14 F6
Haydock Rd B61 ....32 B1
Haydon Way
 Sambourne B49 ....109 F8
 Studley B49 ....90 F4
Haye La
 Mappleborough Green
 B80 ....72 B1
 Ombersley WR9 ....83 C5
Hayes Bank Rd WR13 ..153 B5
Hayes Croft B38 ....34 F7
Hayes La Stourbridge DY9 .7 A6
 Tenbury WR15 ....54 F3
Hayes Rd DY11 ....12 C3
Hayes The
 Birmingham B31 ....34 C7

Hayes The continued
 Stourbridge DY9 ....7 A5
Hayes Trad Est DY9 .....7 A6
Hayfield Cl [7] WR2 .....114 D1
Hayford Cl WR9 ....71 A5
Hayle Cl B38 ....20 B2
Hayley Gn Rd B32 ......18 B8
Hayley Pk Rd B63 ......16 C8
Hayling Cl
 Birmingham B45 ....17 F1
 [4] St. Peter the Great County
 WR5 ....128 E6
Hayloft Cl B60 ....67 E6
Haylofts The B63 ....7 C1
Haynes Cl B61 ....49 B8
Haynes House B97 ......70 D2
Hays Cl WR12 ....177 E3
Hayseech B64 ....8 A7
Hayseech Rd B63 ....7 F6
Haysfield The WR14 ....139 C4
Hayslan Ave WR14 .....139 B2
Hayslan Gn WR14 ......139 B2
Hayslan Rd WR14 ......139 B2
Haytor Ave B14 ....20 D5
Haywood Dr B62 ....8 C8
Haze Croft WR4 ....116 B4
Hazel Ave WR11 ....161 C4
Hazel Cl
 Droitwich Spa WR9 ......103 F8
 [4] Worcester WR4 ......115 F5
Hazel Croft B31 ....19 A3
Hazel Dr B47 ....36 B5
Hazel Gr DY8 ....5 C3
Hazel Rd
 Birmingham B45 ....32 F6
 Redditch B97 ....70 C5
Hazelbank B38 ....19 E2
Hazeldene DY13 ....44 C3
Hazeldene Rd B63 ......7 D2
Hazelgrove WV15 ....1 D6
Hazelhurst Rd B14 ......20 E7
Hazelmere Rd B28 ......21 F8
Hazels The DY9 ....14 F5
Hazelton Cl B61 ....49 C8
Hazelton Rd B61 ....32 C1
Hazelwell Cres B30 .....20 B6
Hazelwell Fordrough
 B30 ....20 B6
Hazelwell La B30 ....20 B7
Hazelwell Rd B30 ......20 A6
Hazelwell St B30 ....20 A7
Hazelwood Cl DY11 .....27 B4
Hazewood Cl [7] WR5 ...115 F1
Hazlitt Gr B30 ....19 D4
Head St [1] WR10 ......158 D8
Headless Cross Dr B97 ..70 D5
Headley Croft B38 ......34 D8
Headley Heath La B38 ..35 B6
Heale Cl B63 ....7 A7
Heath Cl
 Birmingham B30 ....19 D5
 Bromsgrove B60 ....67 E6
 Cleobury Mortimer DY14 .22 B4
 Hallow WR2 ....101 D3
Heath Croft B31 ....34 A7
Heath Dr
 Kidderminster DY10 .....13 B1
 Worcester WR5 ....128 E5
Heath End Rd DY9 ......31 D7
Heath Farm Rd DY8 .....5 E3
Heath House B14 ....20 F2
Heath La
 Kidderminster DY10 .....28 C1
 Stone DY10 ....45 D8
 Stourbridge DY8 ....6 A4
Heath Rd
 Birmingham B30 ....19 D5
 Hollywood B47 ....36 A7
 Worcester WR4 ....115 E4
Heath Rd S B31 ....19 B4
Heath Rise B14 ....21 A1
Heath St DY8 ....5 F4
Heath The WR6 ....82 B3
Heathcote Rd B30 ......20 A5
Heather Cl WR5 ....128 C1
Heather Dr
 Birmingham B45 ....32 F6
 Kinver DY7 ....3 F4
Heather House B38 ......19 F1
Heathers The WR11 ....175 D8
Heathfield Cres DY11 ...27 B4
Heathfield Gdns DY8 ....5 F4
Heathfield Rd
 Bewdley DY12 ....26 C4
 Birmingham, King's Heath
 B14 ....20 F8
 Halesowen B63 ....7 E3
 Hartlebury DY13 ....44 C1
 Norton & Lenchwick
 WR11 ....147 D3
 Redditch B97 ....70 A1
Heathfield Sch DY10 ....12 F2
Heathlands Cl [5] WR14 .166 E7
Heathlands Dr B31 ......19 A1
Heathlands The
 Stourbridge DY8 ....6 B4
 Stourport-on-Severn
 DY13 ....44 B3
Heathleigh Rd B38 .....34 C8
Heathside Dr B38 ....20 B2
Heathy Farm Cl B32 ....9 A2
Heathy Rise B32 ....9 A2
Hebb St WR1 ....115 B4
Hebden Gr B28 ....21 E3
Hedera B98 ....71 F6
Hedgefield Gr B63 ......7 C4
Hedgerows The B62 ....16 F4
Hedges Way B60 ....49 B1

Heightington Pl DY13 ...43 E1
Heightington Rd
 Ribbesford DY12 ....25 F1
 Rock DY14 ....41 F6
Heights The WR5 ......116 B3
Helford Cl B63 ....115 C2
Helmsley Cl DY5 ....6 C8
Heming Rd B98 ....90 E8
Hemming St DY11 ......27 C4
Hemming Way DY10 ....46 E8
Hemmings Cl DY9 ....5 F5
Hemmingway [2] WR11 .161 D2
Hemplands Rd DY8 .....5 F5
Hemsby Cl [9] WR5 .....128 D6
Hemyock Rd B29 ....19 B8
Henderson Ct [7] B68 ...9 B8
Henley Dr
 [7] Droitwich WR9 ......85 A1
 Droitwich WR9 ....104 A8
Henley Pl WR14 ....138 F3
Henlow Rd B14 ....21 A2
Hennals Ave B97 ....69 F2
Henry Fowler Cl [2]
 WR11 ....161 D5
Henry St
 [1] Evesham WR11 .....161 C4
 Worcester WR1 ....115 B5
Henry Wlk B60 ....67 E7
Hentland Cl B98 ....71 D4
Henwick Ave WR2 .....114 F3
Henwick Rd WR2 ......114 F3
Herbert Austin Dr B60 ..32 E1
Herbert St B98 ....70 E4
Hereford & Worcester Cty
 Mus ★ DY11 ....44 F3
Hereford Cl
 Birmingham B45 ....18 A2
 Kidderminster DY11 .....27 A5
Hereford Rd B68 ....9 B7
Hereward Rise B62 .....8 C5
Heriotts Ct [7] WR9 .....85 A3
Heritage Way [7] WR9 ..84 F3
Hermitage Way [2] DY13 .62 F8
Hern Rd DY5 ....6 C6
Herne Field [5] WR4 ....116 C5
Herne's Nest DY12 ......26 A2
Hernehurst B32 ....9 C6
Heron Cl Alvechurch B48 .51 A7
 Worcester WR2 ....128 A3
Heron Pl WR2 ....85 B3
Heron Way B45 ....32 F7
Herondale Cres DY8 ....5 C4
Herondale Rd DY8 ......5 C4
Heronfield Cl B98 ....71 C5
Heronfield Dr B31 ......33 F6
Herons Gate Rd DY7 ...2 F5
Heronswood Rd
 Birmingham B45 ....33 B6
 Kidderminster DY10 .....28 A2
Hestia Dr B29 ....19 E8
Hetherington Cl [2]
 WR5 ....141 C7
Hetherington Rise
 WR4 ....116 C3
Hever Ave WR4 ....116 C6
Hever Cl [13] GL20 .....197 A4
Hewell Ave B60 ....67 F7
Hewell Cl
 Birmingham B31 ....33 F7
 Redditch B97 ....69 C6
Hewell La
 Barnt Green B45 ....50 D8
 Redditch B60, B97 ......69 D8
Hewell Rd
 Barnt Green B45 ....50 D8
 Redditch B97 ....70 D4
Hexton Cl B90 ....21 D2
Heycott Gr B38 ....20 C2
Heydon Rd B60 ....49 D1
Heythrop Gr B13 ....21 D8
Hickman St DY9 ....6 C6
Hickmans Cl [2] B62 ....9 A6
Hidage The WR5 ....142 D8
Hidcote Cl [5] WR5 .....128 D5
Higgins La B32 ....9 C5
High Ave B64 ....7 F8
High Clere B64 ....8 A7
High Elms La
 Bentley Pauncefoot B60 ..87 E8
 Upper Bentley B60 ....68 E1
High Farm Rd
 Halesowen, Hasbury B63 ..7 F3
 Halesowen, Hurst Green
 B62 ....8 F8
High Haden Cres B64 ...8 A8
High Haden Rd B64 .....8 A8
High Heath Cl B30 ......19 D5
High House Dr
 Barnt Green B45 ....32 F3
 Inkberrow WR7 ....120 E7
High House La B60 ......69 A6
High La HR7 ....96 D5
High Leasowes B63 .....8 A4
High Mdw Rd B38 ......20 A2
High Mdws B60 ....67 D4
High Pk Rd B63 ....7 C5
High St
 Astwood Bank B96 ....89 E1
 Badsey WR11 ....162 D3
 Belbroughton DY9 ....30 D2
 Bewdley DY12 ....26 B3
 Bidford-on-Avon B50 ....136 C4
 Birmingham, King's Heath
 B14 ....20 E8
 Birmingham, Quinton B32 .9 A6
 Blackheath B64 ....7 F8
 Bredon GL20 ....184 D6

High St *continued*
Brierley Hill, Quarry Bank DY5 7 A8
Broadway WR12 190 D8
Bromsgrove B61 49 A2
Cleobury Mortimer DY14 22 B4
Droitwich WR9 85 A3
Evesham WR11 161 D5
Feckenham B96 107 D7
1 Halesowen B63 8 B3
Honeybourne WR11 164 B4
Inkberrow WR7 120 E7
Kidderminster DY10 27 E6
Kinver DY7 4 B3
Mickleton GL55 165 D3
Pershore WR10 144 D1
Solihull B90 21 D2
Stanton WR12 189 D1
Stourbridge DY8 5 E7
Stourbridge, Amblecote DY8 5 F7
Stourport-on-Severn DY13 44 A3
Studley B80 90 E4
Tewkesbury GL20 196 E6
1 Upton upon Severn WR8 169 C6
Worcester WR1 115 C2
High Timbers B45 17 F1
High Trees Cl B98 89 E7
Highbury Ct B13 20 F7
Highbury Rd B14 20 D8
Highclere DY12 26 A2
Highclere Dr DY12 26 A2
Highcrest Cl B31 34 A7
Highfield WR2 140 F8
Highfield Ave B97 89 D8
Highfield Cl
Birmingham B28 21 D5
Droitwich WR9 84 F2
Great Malvern WR14 139 A4
Highfield Cres B63 7 D6
Highfield La
Birmingham B32 9 B4
Clent DY9 16 A3
1 Halesowen B63 8 A3
Highfield Mews B63 7 D6
Highfield Pl B14 21 D5
Highfield Rd
Birmingham, Yardley Wood B14, B28 21 D5
Bromsgrove B61 67 E8
Cookley DY10 13 A5
Evesham WR11 161 B4
Great Malvern WR14 138 F4
Halesowen B63 7 D5
Kidderminster DY10 28 A8
Redditch B97 89 D8
Studley B80 90 D4
Highfields B61 48 E1
Highfields Prim Sch B65 8 C8
Highgate Cl DY11 27 A4
Highgrove Ct DY10 13 A1
Highland House B62 8 C8
Highland Rd WR4 115 E4
Highland Ridge B62 8 E5
Highland Way B98 90 A7
Highlands Cl DY11 27 A5
Highley Cl
Kidderminster DY11 27 B2
Redditch B98 71 E4
Highlow Ave DY11 12 C1
Highmore Dr B32 18 C8
Highpark Ave DY8 5 D5
Highter's Heath Inf & Jun Sch B14 21 B3
Highter's Heath La B14 21 A2
Highters Cl B14 21 B2
Highters Rd B14 21 A3
Hightown B63 7 C6
Hightree Cl B32 9 B1
Highwood Croft B38 19 D1
Hilary Gr B31 18 F4
Hill Ave The WR5 128 C8
Hill Bank DY9 6 F5
Hill Bank Rd
Birmingham B38 20 A2
Halesowen B63 7 D6
Hill Cl Birmingham B31 19 C1
Bredon GL20 185 B7
Pershore WR10 144 C1
Hill Crest 5 WR11 161 F3
Hill Croft Rd B14 20 C6
Hill End Rd GL20 183 F6
Hill Farm WR7 120 E7
Hill Furze Rd WR10 133 C1
Hill Gr Cres DY10 28 A4
Hill La
Alvechurch B47, B48 35 D1
Bentley Pauncefoot B60 87 E6
Bromsgrove B60 48 F1
Clent DY9 15 E4
Elmley Castle WR10 173 D7
Hill Rd Lulsley WR6 111 E3
Pirton WR8 142 D3
Hill Rise View B60 49 C6
Hill Side WR5 141 C8
Hill St
Brierley Hill, Quarry Bank DY5 7 A8
Halesowen B63 8 A3
Kidderminster DY11 27 D6
Stourbridge DY8 5 F4
Stourbridge, Lye DY9 6 F5
Stourbridge, Amblecote DY8 5 F8
Worcester WR5 115 D3
Hill The B32 9 E2
Hill Top B97 69 F1
Hill Top Ave B62 8 E7
Hill Top La WR9 83 B4
Hill Top Rd B31 18 F3
Hill View WR8 157 D3
Hill View Cl
3 Colwall Stone WR13 152 B2
Great Malvern WR14 139 B5
Hill View Rd
Bidford-on-Avon B50 136 E5
Strensham WR8 171 A4
Worcester WR2 127 F7
Hillaire Cl B38 20 C2
Hillary Rd DY13 44 D7
Hillboro Rise DY7 4 A5
Hillborough La B50 137 C5
Hillbrow Cres B62 8 F8
Hillcrest Ave B63 7 B7
Hillcrest Ind Est B64 7 D8
Hillcrest Pk B47 52 F8
Hillcrest Rd B62 17 A4
Hillcrest Rise WR3 102 A1
Hillcrest Sch & Sixth Form Ctr B32 9 E3
Hillcroft House B14 20 F2
Hillditch La DY11 44 E2
Hillery Rd WR5 128 F8
Hillfields Rd DY5 6 B7
Hillgrove Gdns DY10 28 A4
Hillmeads Rd B38 20 A1
Hillmorton Cl B98 71 E6
Hillsfield WR8 169 C5
Hillside
Ashton under Hill WR11 174 B1
Redditch B98 70 D2
Hillside Ave
Blackheath B65 8 B8
Brierley Hill DY5 7 A8
Halesowen B63 7 D6
Hillside Cl
Birmingham B32 18 A8
Evesham WR11 161 A3
Kidderminster DY11 27 A7
6 Stourport-on-Severn DY13 62 E8
Upton Snodsbury WR7 131 C8
Worcester WR5 115 F3
Hillside Dr
Kidderminster DY11 27 A7
Lickey End B61 49 B6
Hillside Gr DY10 13 C3
Hillstone Sch WR14 152 F7
Hilltop DY9 6 F3
Hilltop Ave DY12 26 D4
Hillview Cl
Halesowen B63 7 E6
Lickey End B60 49 C6
Hillview Dr WR14 138 E4
Hillview Gdns WR8 169 E6
Hillview La GL20 183 F7
Hillview Rd
Birmingham B45 32 E8
Lickey End B60 49 C6
Hillville Gdns DY8 6 B3
Hillwood Rd
Birmingham B31 18 E7
Halesowen B62 8 C7
Hilston Ave B63 7 F4
Hilton Ave B28 21 F4
Hilton Cl DY8 6 A7
Hilton Rd WR14 153 C7
Himbleton CE Fst Sch WR9 105 D1
Himbleton Cl B98 70 F1
Himbleton Rd WR2 114 E4
Himley Gr B45 33 B6
Hinckley Ct 3 B68 9 B7
Hindhead Rd B14 21 C4
Hindlip CE Fst Sch WR3 103 A3
Hindlip Cl Halesowen B63 7 F2
Redditch B98 72 A3
Hindlip La WR3 103 C1
Hindon Wlk B32 9 C2
Hingley Ave WR4 116 B3
Hingley Rd DY9 7 A6
Hinton Ave B48 51 A6
Hinton Fields B61 48 E7
Hinton Rd WR12 176 D2
Hiplands Rd B62 8 F4
Hipton Hill WR11 147 C5
Hirdemonsway B90 36 F5
Hither Gn WR11 162 E4
Hither Gn La B98 70 F7
Hoarstone DY8 14 F5
Hoarstone Cl DY12 26 C5
Hoarstone La DY12 26 C6
Hob Gn Prim Sch DY9 6 E2
Hob Gn Rd DY9 6 E2
Hobacre Cl B45 33 A8
Hobbis House B38 34 C7
Hobhouse Gdns 6 WR4 116 C3
Hock Coppice 4 WR4 116 B4
Hockham's La WR6 80 D2
Hockley Brook La DY9 30 F3
Hoden La WR11 149 B7
Hodge Hill Ave DY9 6 F3
Hodge Hill Cotts DY10 28 C7
Hodges The 7 WR11 161 D5
Hodgetts Dr B63 16 C8
Hoggs La B31 18 E4
Holcroft Rd
Halesowen B63 7 C5
Stourbridge DY9 6 C4
Holdens The B28 21 E6
Holder Cl 10 B50 136 D5
Holdgate Rd B29 19 C7
Holdings La WR5 128 D1
Hole Farm Rd B31 19 C5
Hole Farm Way B38 34 F7
Hole La B31 19 C5
Hollams Rd GL20 196 F7
Holland Cl 4 B50 136 D4
Holland Gn WR4 116 C3
Hollaway Ct B63 7 D5
Hollie Lucas Rd B13 20 F7
Hollies Dr B62 8 E6
Hollies La Enville DY7 2 F7
Kidderminster Foreign DY11 11 F3
Hollies Mews The 4 WR14 139 B5
Hollies Rise B64 7 F8
Hollies The
Birmingham B45 33 A1
Charlton WR10 160 E8
2 Stourport-on-Severn DY13 43 E6
Hollins La WR6 99 A3
Hollister Dr B32 9 F3
Hollow Croft B31 19 B3
Holloway
Birmingham B31 18 E5
1 Pershore WR10 158 C8
Holloway Dr
Pershore WR10 144 B1
Redditch B98 71 B3
Holloway La B98 70 F3
Holloway Pk B98 71 A3
Holloway The
Alvechurch B48 51 D3
Bluntington DY10 29 E2
Chaddesley Corbett DY10 46 E8
Droitwich WR9 85 A2
Stourbridge DY8 5 F7
Hollowfields Rd B96 106 C6
Hollows The WR11 175 B2
Hollowtree La B60 50 A3
Holly Bush Gr B32 9 D7
Holly Bush La WR6 97 A7
Holly Cl
Bretforton WR11 163 B5
Droitwich WR9 104 A8
8 Evesham WR11 161 F2
Kinver DY7 3 F5
Holly Ct DY10 27 D8
Holly Dell B38 20 B2
Holly Dr B47 36 B7
Holly Gr
Birmingham, Bournville B30 19 F8
Bromsgrove B61 48 F3
Stourbridge DY8 5 F5
Holly Hill 4 B45 17 F1
Holly Hill Meth & CE Inf Sch B45 17 F2
Holly Hill Rd B45 18 A2
Holly La B48 52 F5
Holly Mount WR4 115 E4
Holly Mount Rd WR4 115 E4
Holly Rd
Birmingham, King's Norton B30 20 A4
Bromsgrove B61 48 F4
Oldbury B68 9 C8
Stourport-on-Severn DY13 44 B4
Tenbury Wells WR15 55 F6
Holly Tree La WR2 127 B8
Holly Well La DY14 40 E6
Hollybank Gr B63 7 D1
Hollybank Rd B13 21 A6
Hollyberry Cl B98 72 A4
Hollybrow B29 19 B7
Hollybush La DY8 5 F7
Hollyfield Dr B45 33 A1
Hollyhedge Cl B31 18 D6
Hollymoor Way
Birmingham B31 18 D1
Birmingham B31 18 B1
Hollymount B62 9 A7
Hollyoak Croft B31 34 B8
Hollywood By-Pass
Birmingham B47 20 F1
Hollywood B38, B47 35 E6
Hollywood Gdns B47 36 A8
Hollywood La B47 36 B7
Hollywood Prim Sch B14 21 A1
Holman St DY11 27 C5
Holmcroft Rd DY10 28 A5
Holme Rd 6 GL20 196 F3
Holmes Dr B45 32 F6
Holmes La Hanbury B60 87 A7
Stoke Prior B60 68 B1
Holmoak Cl 8 GL20 197 A4
Holmwood Ave DY11 27 A6
Holmwood Dr B97 70 C3
Holmwood Gdns 9 WR11 161 F2
Holmwood House B97 70 C3
Holt Fleet Rd WR9 82 E4
Holt Gdns B80 90 E2
Holt Hill B98 71 F8
Holt House B61 49 A3
Holt La B62 16 D4
Holt Rd B80 90 E2
Holy Cross Gn DY9 15 E2
Holy Cross La DY9 30 E8
Holy Oaks Cl B98 71 E2
Holy Redeemer RC Prim Sch The WR10 158 D8
Holy Well Rd
Great Malvern WR14 166 E8
Malvern Wells WR14 152 E1
Holyoakes Field Fst Sch B97 70 D4
Holyoakes La B97 69 C5
Holywell La B45 32 D6
Holywell Prim Sch B45 32 D7
Home Cl B28 21 F6
Home Mdw Ct B13 21 A5
Home Mdw La B98 71 E6
Home Piece WR9 84 D2
Homedene Rd B31 18 E7
Homefield Rd WR2 115 A1
Homemead Gr B45 32 F7
Homer Hill Rd B63 7 C7
Homestead Ave WR4 116 B7
Homestead Cl 6 GL20 184 F6
Homfray Rd DY10 12 F1
Honeybourne Airfield Ind Est WR11 164 B1
Honeybourne Cl 3 B63 8 A3
Honeybourne Fst Sch WR11 164 A4
Honeybourne Rd
Alveley WV15 1 C6
Bidford-on-Avon B50 136 E2
Halesowen B63 8 C3
Weston-sub-Edge WR11 164 B1
Honeybourne Sch B28 21 F8
Honeybourne Sta WR11 164 A6
Honeybrook Cl DY11 12 D2
Honeybrook La DY11 12 B1
Honeychurch Cl B98 70 F3
Honeycomb Way B31 18 E3
Honeysuckle Cl
Birmingham B32 9 B5
Evesham WR11 161 D1
Honeywood Rd WR2 114 E4
Honister Dr WR4 116 A6
Honiton Cl B31 18 E4
Honiton Cres B31 18 E4
Honnington Ct 2 B29 9 F1
Hoo Farm Ind Est DY10 27 F1
Hoo Rd DY10 27 E4
Hoobrook Ent Ctr DY10 27 E2
Hoobrook Ind Est DY10 27 E2
Hood Gr B30 19 D4
Hood St 6 WR1 115 B2
Hoopers Cl WR13 126 A2
Hoopers La B96 89 E1
Hoosen Cl B62 9 A6
Hop Gdns The WR11 162 C5
Hop Pole Gn WR13 125 F2
Hop Pole La DY12 25 E4
Hope La WR6 97 C6
Hope St B62 8 D8
Hopedale Rd B32 9 C5
Hopehouse La WR6 99 B3
Hopgardens Ave B60 49 B2
Hopkins Field CV37 151 C6
Hopton Dr DY10 27 E1
Hopton Gr B13 21 C5
Hopton La WR6 125 B6
Hopton St WR2 114 E2
Hopwood Cl B63 8 A2
Hopwood Gr B31 33 E6
Hopyard La B98 71 D4
Hopyard The GL20 184 D1
Hordern Cres DY5 6 D8
Horn La WR6 99 B7
Hornbeam Cl
15 Bewdley DY12 25 F3
Birmingham B29 19 B7
Hornby Gr B14 21 C4
Hornsby Ave WR4 116 C3
Hornyold Ave WR14 138 E3
Hornyold Rd WR14 138 E3
Horrell Rd B90 21 F2
Horse Bridge La DY7 4 C2
Horse Fair DY10 27 E7
Horsebridge Ave WR11 162 D4
Horsford Rd WR2 114 F5
Horton La WR9 65 A2
Horton Rd DY7 3 F5
Hoskyns Ave WR4 116 C3
Hospital Bank WR14 138 E3
Hospital La WR2 127 C2
Hospital Lea Castle DY10 13 C3
Hospital Rd WR14 138 D6
Hospital Tewkesbury GL20 196 F6
Hossil La
Belbroughton DY9 30 C8
Clent DY9 15 D1
Hough Rd B14 20 D6
Houghton Ct B28 21 D4
Houldey Rd B31 19 B1
Houndsfield Cl B47 36 C6
Houndsfield Farm B47 36 B5
Houndsfield Gr B47 36 A5
Houndsfield La B47 36 C6
Housman Cl B60 67 E8
Housman Ct B60 49 A3
Housman Pk B60 49 A2
Housman Wlk DY10 28 C6
Houx The DY8 5 E8
Hoveton Cl B98 71 B2
Howard Ave B61 48 E3
Howard Cl
Bidford-on-Avon B50 136 C4
Northway GL20 197 E8
Howard Rd
Birmingham, King's Heath B14 20 E7
Northway GL20 197 D8
Redditch B98 90 C8
Worcester WR2 114 C3
Howard Rd E B13 20 F7
Howcroft Gn 3 WR4 116 B6
Howells Rd GL20 196 E6
Howlett Pl WR4 116 C3
Howley Grange Prim Sch B62 8 F5
Howley Grange Rd B62 9 A4
Howsell Rd WR14 139 A4
Howsells The WR14 139 B6
Hoyland Way B30 19 E8
Huband Cl B98 71 A5
Huddington Ct* WR7 118 C6
Hudman's Cl GL20 184 A6
Hudson Cl
Honeybourne WR11 164 B5
Pershore WR10 144 C1
Worcester WR2 127 F7
Hudson's Dr B30 20 A4
Hudswell Dr DY5 6 D8
Hughes Cl
Harvington WR11 148 A7
Northway GL20 184 F1
Hughes La WR11 148 A7
Huins Cl B98 71 A4
Hullbrook Rd B13 21 C6
Hulls La WR9 104 A3
Humber Gdns B63 7 C5
Humber Rd WR5 115 E3
Hume St DY11 27 C5
Humphrey Ave B60 67 F7
Humphries Dr DY10 27 F2
Hungary Cl DY9 6 C5
Hungary Hill DY9 6 C5
Hungerford Rd DY8 5 E2
Hungerpit Wlk WR3 115 B6
Hunnington Cl B32 9 A4
Hunnington Cres B63 8 B2
Hunscote Cl B90 21 F1
Hunscote House B90 21 F1
Hunslet Cl B32 9 F4
Hunslet Rd B32 9 F4
Hunstanton Ave B17 9 F8
Hunstanton Cl
Brierley Hill DY5 6 C7
5 Worcester WR5 128 D6
Hunt Ave WR4 116 C4
Hunt End La B97 89 C5
Hunter Rise WR10 158 C8
Hunters Hill Sch B60 49 F6
Hunters Rise B63 7 D1
Hunters Way WR9 84 D4
Huntingdon Cl B98 71 F2
Huntingdon Gdns B63 7 C7
Huntingtree Prim Sch B63 7 E3
Huntingtree Rd B63 7 E3
Huntlands Rd B63 7 F2
Hunts Rd B30 20 B7
Hunts Rise DY12 26 C3
Huntsmans Cl 3 WR10 143 F6
Huntsmans Dr DY7 3 F5
Hurcott Ct DY10 28 A8
Hurcott La DY10 28 C8
Hurcott Rd DY10 28 B8
Hurst Ct DY9 6 F5
Hurst Gn Prim Sch B62 8 E8
Hurst Gn Rd B62 8 F8
Hurst La WR3 102 F2
Hurst Rd WR10 144 D2
Hurst The
Birmingham B13 21 D7
2 Cleobury Mortimer DY14 22 C4
Hollywood B47 36 A6
Husum Way DY10 28 C7
Huxleys Way 6 WR11 161 C4
Huxtable Rise WR4 116 B4
Hyacinth Cl 1 WR5 128 C4
Hyatt Sq DY5 6 C7
Hyde Cl Bromsgrove B60 49 B2
Kinver DY7 4 A5
Hyde La Kinver DY7 4 A6
Upton upon Severn WR8 168 E5
Hyde Pk Cnr GL19 192 A3
Hyde The DY9 6 D2
Hydefields WR8 169 A5
Hydrangea Cl WR5 128 D4
Hylton Rd
Evesham WR11 161 A4
Worcester WR2 114 F4
Hyperion Rd DY7 5 C7
Hytall Rd B90 21 C2

I

Ibberton Rd B14 21 B3
Ibis Cl DY10 28 B3
Ibstock Cl B98 71 E4
Ibstock Dr DY8 6 A4
Ibstock House B98 71 E4
Icknield Cl B50 136 E4
Icknield Fst Sch B98 71 D1
Icknield St
Alvechurch B38 35 B2
Beoley B98 52 C2
Bidford-on-Avon B50 136 E4
Redditch, Church Hill B98 71 C7
Redditch, Ipsley B98 71 D2
Rowney Green B48 52 B6
Icknield St Dr B98 90 D7
Ideal Bldgs 7 DY11 27 D6
Ideal Wks DY9 7 A6
Idleton 7 WR4 116 C3
Idmiston Croft B14 20 F2

Ikon Ind Est DY10 ....45 D6
Ilkley Cl WR4 ....116 A4
Illey Cl B31 ....18 C1
Illey La Birmingham B32 ..18 A7
  Halesowen B62 ....17 E8
Illeybrook Sq B32 ......9 D2
Illshaw Cl B98 ....72 A4
Ilmington Cl B98 .....71 D1
Ilmington Rd B29 ......9 F1
Ilsham Gr B31 ....33 E6
Imber Rd DY10 ....28 A1
Imperial Ave DY10 .....27 F8
Imperial Gr DY10 ......27 F8
Imperial Rd WR14 ....153 A8
Impney Cl WR9 ....71 E6
Inches La WR11 ......161 D5
Inett Way WR9 ....84 C3
Infirmary Wlk [5] WR1 ..115 B3
Ingestre Rd B28 ....21 F7
Ingeva Dr B45 ....33 A1
Ingham Pedl Cl [1]
  WR13 ....152 B2
Inglemere Gr B29 ......18 F7
Ingoldsby Rd B31 .....19 C3
Inkberrow Fst Sch
  WR7 ....120 F8
Inkberrow Rd B63 ......7 F2
Inn La DY11 ....45 A2
Innage Rd B31 ....19 B4
Innage The B47 ....36 A5
Innerstone La GL19 ...192 C1
Insetton Cl B98 ......71 D4
Institute Rd B14 .....20 F8
Instone Rd B63 ....8 A3
Insull Ave B14 ......21 B1
Intended St B63 ....7 C7
Inverlea Ct GL55 ....165 D4
Inverness Rd B31 .....18 F3
Io Ctr The B98 ....90 C8
Ipsley Alders Marsh Nature
  Reserve* B98 ....71 F4
Ipsley CE Mid Sch B98 .71 E3
Ipsley Church La B98 ..71 D2
Ipsley La B98 ....71 D2
Ipsley St B98 ....70 E3
Iris Cl B29 ....19 B8
Iris Dr B14 ....20 E3
Iron Bridge Wlk DY9 ..15 B8
Ironside Cl [17] DY12 ..25 F3
Irwin Ave B45 ....33 C7
Isaac Wlk WR2 ....114 E1
Isaacs Way WR9 ......103 F7
Isbourne Cres WR11 ..161 D2
Island Dr DY10 ....27 E4
Islington B63 ....8 A4
Ismere Way DY10 .....12 F1
Ithon Gr B38 ....34 E8
Iverley Ct [6] WR15 ...55 F6
Iverley La DY10 ......14 C5
Iverley Rd B63 ....8 C4
Iverley Wlk DY9 ......6 C2
Ivor Rd B97 ....70 D2
Ivy La Bretforton WR11 .163 B5
  Fernhill Heath WR3 ...103 A2
  Romsley B62 ....16 D5
Ivy Rd B30 ....20 A6
Ivy St WR3 ....115 A6
Ivyhouse Rd B38 .....34 C8
Izod St B97 ....70 D4

J

Jack Thomson Croft
  WR11 ....135 F3
Jackdaw La WR9 ......104 B7
Jackson Cres DY13 ....43 E1
Jackson St DY9 ....6 E6
Jackson Way B32 ......9 A5
Jacksons Mdw B50 ...136 C6
Jacksons Orch CV37 ..151 C6
Jacob Cl [4] WR3 ....115 E7
Jacob Ladder WR3 ...102 D4
Jacomb Cl WR2 ......114 A7
Jacomb Dr WR2 ......114 A7
Jacomb Rd WR2 .....114 A7
Jakeman Cl B98 ......71 E4
Jamaica Cres WR14 ..139 A5
Jamaica Rd WR14 ....139 A5
James Cl WR1 ....115 C2
James Ct B38 ....19 F2
James Lloyd Trust Flats
  B30 ....19 C5
James Rd DY10 ....28 A8
James Scott Rd B63 ...7 A6
James St DY7 ....4 A4
Janice Gr B14 ....21 B4
Jarvis Dr WR10 ......171 E8
Jarvis St WR10 ......171 E7
Jasmin Croft B14 .....20 E3
Jasmine Cl [7] WR5 ..128 D5
Jasmine Gr B61 ....48 F4
Jasmine Rd WR14 ....152 F4
Jasmine Wlk [5] WR11 .161 D1
Jason Rd DY9 ....6 F4
Jasper Cl [5] WR4 ....127 F7
Jay Pk Cres DY10 .....28 B2
Jays Cl B98 ....72 A3
Jays Cres B48 ....34 B1
Jeal Cl B47 ....35 E2
Jelleyman Cl DY11 ...27 C6
Jennett Tree La WR2 .127 E1
Jennings Wood La
  DY13 ....43 A2
Jersey Cl B98 ....71 D7

Jerusalem Wlk DY10 ...27 E7
Jervoise Dr B31 ......19 B5
Jeynes Row GL20 ....196 F7
Jiggins La B32 ....9 D1
Jill La B96 ....90 B2
Jinnah Rd B98 ....70 E2
Jinney Ring Craft Ctr*
  B60 ....87 A5
Job's La GL20 ....185 D7
John Comyn Dr WR3 .115 C3
John Moore Countryside
  Mus* GL20 ....196 E5
John Moore Prim Sch
  GL20 ....197 A3
John Rd B62 ....8 F3
Johns Cl B80 ....90 C4
Johnson Cl B98 ....71 A5
Johnsons Gr B68 ......9 D8
Joiners Cl [3] WR4 ..115 F6
Jordans Cl Redditch B98 .89 D6
  Willersey WR12 ......177 E3
Jorden's Wlk DY12 ....26 D4
Josiah Rd B31 ....18 D2
Joyberry Dr DY8 ......6 A3
Jubilee Ave B97 ......89 D7
Jubilee Cl B50 ......136 E5
Jubilee Dr
  Bredon GL20 ....184 B4
  Colwall WR14 ......152 D2
Jubilee Dr N DY11 ....27 B2
Jubilee Dr S DY11 ....27 B2
Jubilee Rd
  Birmingham B45 .....17 E2
  Worcester WR2 .....128 A8
Jubilee Terr B60 ......67 C1
Judge Dr DY5 ....6 F7
Juggins La B94 ....53 B7
Julian Cl B61 ....49 A8
Juliet Rd B62 ....8 F3
Junction Rd
  Bromsgrove B61 .....48 E3
  Stourbridge DY8 .....5 E8
Juniper Ct DY10 ......28 A4
Juniper Rise B63 ......7 C5
Juniper Way WR14 ...152 F4
Jury La WR6 ....99 A4
Jury Rd DY5 ....6 F7
Jutland Rd B13 ....21 B8

K

Karen Way DY5 ....6 D8
Katmandu Rd B60 .....49 C1
Katrine Rd DY13 ......43 E6
Keats Ave WR3 ......115 C6
Keats Cl B98 ....6 A8
Keats House B97 ......89 C8
Keats Pl DY10 ....28 B6
Keble Cl WR4 ....115 E3
Kedleston Ct B28 .....21 F4
Kedleston Rd B28 .....21 F5
Keele Cl B98 ....71 E6
Keepers Cl WR10 ....143 F6
Keir Pl DY8 ....5 E8
Keith Winter Cl B61 ..48 F6
Kelby Cl B31 ....18 E4
Kelby Rd B31 ....18 F4
Kelling Cl DY5 ....6 C8
Kelverdale Gr B14 ...20 C4
Kelvin Cl DY11 ......27 A8
Kelvin Rd B31 ....19 B1
Kelwood Dr B63 ....8 A5
Kemelstowe Cres B63 .16 C8
Kemerton House B97 ..70 B4
Kemerton Rd GL20 ..184 E6
Kempsey Cl
  Halesowen B63 ....7 E4
  Redditch B98 ....90 B7
Kempsey Covert B38 ..34 E7
Kempsey House B32 ..18 A8
Kempsey Prim Sch
  WR5 ....141 C7
Kempsford Cl B98 ....89 F6
Kempton Cl [4] WR11 .161 C2
Kempton Ct B61 ......32 A1
Kempton Rd WR10 ...144 E4
Kempton Way DY8 .....5 E3
Kemshead Ave B31 ...33 E8
Kemsley Rd B14 ......20 F2
Kenchester Cl B98 ....71 F2
Kendal Ave B45 ......33 B7
Kendal Cl
  Bromsgrove B60 .....49 B1
  Redditch B98 ....72 A3
Kendal Ct [14] B29 ...19 C7
Kendal Dr B45 ....33 D1
Kendal End Rd B45 ..33 D1
Kendal Gn WR4 .....116 B6
Kendal Rise Rd B45 ..33 B7
Kendall St WR3 .....115 D4
Kendlewood Rd DY10 .13 B1
Kenelm Cl WR6 ......97 E8
Kenelm Rd WR6 ......97 E8
Kenelm's Ct B62 .....17 A4
Kenilworth Cl B97 ...89 D6
Kenilworth Dr DY10 ..27 E2
Kenilworth House B13 .21 A6
Kenilworth Rd B68 ....9 D7
Kenley Gr B30 ....20 B3
Kennedy Cl DY10 .....27 F3
Kennedy Ct DY8 ......5 F5
Kennedy Gr B30 .....20 B6
Kennel Bank WR6 ...160 B6
Kennels La WR3 .....102 F4
Kennet Gn WR5 .....115 D2
Kenswick Dr B63 ......8 A2

Kent Cl Evesham WR11 ..161 A3
  Great Malvern WR14 ..139 C6
  Kidderminster DY10 ...27 E3
Kent Rd Birmingham B45 ..17 F1
  Halesowen B62 ....8 F5
  Stourbridge DY8 ......5 D7
Kentmere Cl WR4 ...116 A5
Kentmere Rd B60 .....49 C1
Kenward Croft B17 ...115 B8
Kenway B47 ....36 A7
Kenwood Ave WR4 ...115 F4
Kenwood Cl WR4 ....115 F4
Kenyon Cl
  Bromsgrove B60 .....49 A1
  Stourbridge DY8 .....6 A7
Kepax Gdns WR3 ....115 A6
Keren Dr WR5 ....128 F3
Keresley Gr B29 ......9 F2
Kernthorpe Rd B14 ...20 D4
Kerry Cl B31 ....18 F4
Kerry Croft Cl B97 ...89 E5
Kerry Hill
  [3] Bromsgrove B60 ..67 E6
  Worcester WR3 .....115 E8
Kerswell Cl [2] B97 ...70 B5
Kestrel Cl DY10 ......27 F5
Kestrel Ct [6] WR5 ..128 C5
Kestrel Gr B30 ....19 D8
Kestrel Rd B63 ....7 B7
Kestrel View WR5 ....49 C7
Kestrel Way GL20 ...184 D1
Keswick Dr WR4 ....116 A6
Kettles Wood Dr B32 ..9 C2
Kewstoke Croft B31 ..18 E6
Key Ave WR4 ....116 A5
Keynell Covert B30 ...20 C2
Kidderminster Coll
  DY10 ....27 E4
Kidderminster General Hospl
  DY11 ....27 C6
Kidderminster Rd
  Bewdley DY12 ....26 C4
  Bromsgrove B61 .....48 C3
  Chaddesley Corbett DY10 .47 A6
  Droitwich WR9 ......84 C4
  Hagley DY9 ....15 B5
  Iverley DY7, DY10 ...14 C7
Kidderminster Rd S
  DY9 ....14 F3
Kidderminster Sta
  DY10 ....27 F5
Kidderminster Town Sta*
  DY10 ....27 F5
Kielder Gdns DY9 ......6 B1
Kielder Rise WR2 ...127 F6
Kiftsgate Stone*
  GL55 ....178 E2
Kilbury Dr WR5 .....129 A8
Kilcote Rd B90 ....21 C2
Kilmore La GL20 ....183 F6
Kiln Cl B80 ....90 C4
Kiln La WR13 ....126 A2
Kilpeck Cl B98 ....71 F2
Kimberley Ave DY10 ..13 B4
Kimberley Cl B98 ....71 B7
Kimbolton Dr B60 ....50 A5
Kimpton Cl B14 ......20 E2
Kineton Cl B98 ....71 D1
Kineton Croft B32 ....18 D8
Kineton House B13 ...21 A6
Kineton Rd B45 ......32 E7
King Arthur's Cl WR2 .114 E1
King Charles Ave
  WR2 ....127 C2
King Charles Cl DY11 .27 C6
King Charles I High Sch
  DY10 ....28 A5
King Charles Rd B62 ..8 F5
King Charles Sq [4] DY10 .27 E6
King Edmund Sq [1]
  WR1 ....115 B3
King Edward Ave B61 .48 F5
King Edward Rd B61 ..48 F5
King Edward VI Camp Hill
  Schs B14 ....20 D7
King Edward VI Coll DY8 .6 A6
King Edward VI Five Ways
  Sch B32 ....18 C8
King Edward's Rd
  WR14 ....152 E4
King George Ave
  Bromsgrove B61 .....48 F4
  Droitwich WR9 ......84 F1
King George Cl B61 ..48 F4
King George's Way
  [5] Pershore WR10 ..144 D1
  Pershore WR10 .....158 E8
King Johns Ct GL20 .196 E7
King St Brierley Hill DY5 ..7 A8
  Halesowen B63 ......8 A4
  Stourbridge DY8 .....5 E6
  Stourbridge, Lye DY9 ..6 F5
  Worcester WR5 .....115 C1
King St Pas DY8 ......7 A8
King Stephen's Mount
  WR2 ....114 F5
King William St DY8 ..5 F8
King's End Rd WR2 ..127 D4
King's Heath Boys Sch
  B13 ....21 A6
King's Hill WR5 .....141 C8
King's La
  Bidford-on-Avon B50 .136 B6
  Norton & Lenchwick
  WR11 ....147 D3
King's Norton Boys Sch
  B30 ....19 E4

King's Norton Girls Sch
  B30 ....19 F5
King's Norton Prim Sch
  B30 ....19 E4
King's Norton Sta B30 .19 F4
King's Rd
  Evesham WR11 .....161 F4
  Kidderminster DY11 ..27 C6
King's Sch Playing Field
  WR2 ....115 B1
Kingcomb La GL55 ..178 F3
Kingfield Rd B90 .....21 C2
Kingfisher Cl WR5 ..128 D6
Kingfisher Ct B48 ....51 A4
Kingfisher Dr DY8 .....5 C4
Kingfisher Ent Pk B98 .71 A3
Kingfisher Gr DY10 ...28 B3
Kingfisher Sh Ctr [2] B97 .70 C3
Kingfisher Way B30 ..19 D8
Kingfisher Wlk B97 ...70 D4
Kingham Cl B98 ......72 A4
Kingham Covert B14 ..20 D2
Kings Arms La DY13 ..62 E8
Kings Cl B14 ....20 C6
Kings Ct DY8 ....5 E5
Kings Gate GL20 ....197 B6
Kings Gdn B30 ....19 E4
Kings Gn Ave B30 ....19 F2
Kings Hawford Sch
  WR3 ....102 A5
Kings Norton Bsns Ctr
  B30 ....20 A4
Kings Norton High Sch
  B38 ....34 F8
Kings Rd
  Birmingham, Stirchley
  B14 ....20 C6
  [2] Great Malvern WR14 .166 E7
Kings Sch WR5 ......115 C1
Kings Terr B14 ....20 D6
Kingsbridge Rd B32 ...9 D1
Kingsbury Ave WR2 .127 F8
Kingscote Cl B98 ....71 D7
Kingsdale Ct WR12 ..190 E8
Kingsdown Rd B31 ....9 F1
Kingsfield Rd B14 ....20 D6
Kingsford La Kinver DY11 .3 C1
  Wolverley & Cookley
  DY11 ....12 C7
Kingshill Cl WR14 ..139 A1
Kingshill Dr B38 .....19 F2
Kingshurst Rd
  Birmingham B31 .....19 A3
  Solihull B90 ....21 F1
Kingsley Ave B98 ....71 A3
Kingsley Coll B98 ....90 C6
Kingsley Rd B30 .....19 D4
Kingsthorpe Rd B14 ..21 A3
Kingston Ave WR3 ..115 D6
Kingston Cl [1] WR4 .104 A8
Kingston Cl [17] B29 ..19 C7
Kingston Rd GL20 ..197 E8
Kingsway Oldbury B68 ..9 B7
  Stourbridge DY8 .....5 E8
Kingsway Dr B38 .....19 F2
Kingswood Dr B30 ...20 E2
Kingswood House B14 .20 E2
Kingswood Rd
  Birmingham, Coft Common
  B31 ....33 F7
  Hampton Lovett WR9 .84 C7
Kinlet Cl B98 ....71 E3
Kinlet Gr B31 ....19 C2
Kinlet Rd DY12 ......24 A5
Kinloss Sch WR6 .....99 D4
Kinnersley Cl B98 ...71 E3
Kinnersley Rd WR14 .138 E6
Kinnerton Cres B29 ...9 F2
Kinsey Gr B14 ....20 F4
Kinsham La GL20 ...185 C5
Kinthall La WR6 .....77 B6
Kintore Croft B32 ...18 B7
Kintyre Cl B45 ....17 E1
Kinver Ave DY11 .....27 A1
Kinver Dr DY9 ....15 C7
Kinver La DY11 ......13 B7
Kinver Rd
  Birmingham B31 .....19 D2
  Enville DY7 ....3 E8
Kinverdale DY11 .....12 B6
Kipling Cl
  Great Malvern WR14 .139 A2
  Worcester WR3 .....115 C6
Kipling Rd B30 ......19 C4
Kipling Wlk [3] DY10 ..28 B6
Kirkstone Cl DY5 ......6 B8
Kirkstone Dr WR4 ...115 F4
Kirkstone Way DY5 ...6 B8
Kirkwall Rd B32 ......9 D1
Kitchener Rd CV37 ..151 E4
Kite La B97 ....70 A5
Kitebrook Cl B98 .....71 E4
Kitswell Gdns B32 ...18 A4
Kittiwake Dr
  Brierley Hill DY5 .....6 D7
  Kidderminster DY10 ..28 B3
Kitwell Jun & Inf Sch
  B32 ....18 A7
Kitwell La B32 ....18 A4
Knapp Pl WR5 ......128 E6
Knapp The WR11 ....162 D3
Knapp Way WR14 ...138 E6
Knaresdale Cl DY5 ....6 C8
Knight House B13 ....21 A6
Knight Rd DY11 ......12 C3

Knight St WR2 ......114 F2
Knighton Rd B31 .....19 C4
Knights Way GL20 ..197 A6
Knightsford Cl B97 ...69 F2
Knoll La WR14 ......153 B6
Knoll Cl The DY11 ....27 A7
Knoll The B32 ....9 C1
Knottesford Cl B80 ...90 C3
Knotts Ave WR4 ....116 C4
Knowesley Cl B60 ...49 B2
Knowle Cl
  Birmingham B45 .....33 D7
  Redditch B98 ....71 C6
Knutswood Cl B13 ...21 D7
Kohima Dr
  Stourbridge DY8 .....5 E5
  Worcester Norton WR5 .128 F4
Kylemilne Way DY13 ..44 C3
Kyles Way B32 ....18 B7
Kyre Pk Gdns* WR15 .75 F3
Kyreside WR15 ....55 F4

L

Labrador Rd [5] WR2 .127 F6
Laburnum Cl
  Hollywood B47 ......36 A5
  Kinver DY7 ....3 F5
  Redditch B98 ....70 E2
  Stourbridge DY8 .....5 E7
Laburnum Dr WR11 ..161 F1
Laburnum Gr
  Bromsgrove B61 .....48 F4
  Kidderminster DY11 ..27 B8
Laburnum Rd
  Birmingham B30 .....19 F8
  Worcester WR4 .....115 E4
Laburnum St DY8 .....5 E7
Laburnum Trees B47 ..35 F7
Laburnum Way B31 ..19 A1
Laburnum Wlk WR8 .169 C5
Lacon Childe Sch DY14 .22 C5
Lacon Cl DY14 ....22 B4
Ladbrook Cl B98 .....89 E7
Lady Bank B32 ......18 A5
Lady Bracknell Mews
  B31 ....19 C4
Lady Grey's Wlk DY8 ..5 D5
Lady Harriet's La B98 .70 F4
Ladygo La WR2 .....101 C2
Ladygrove Cl B98 ....90 A8
Ladypool Cl B62 ......8 C4
Ladysmith Rd B63 ....7 C6
Ladywood Rd
  Besford WR8 ....157 B7
  Martin Hussingtree
  WR3 ....103 A5
Lahn Dr WR9 ....103 D8
Lakedown Cl B14 ....20 E1
Lakefield B31 ....18 F4
Lakehouse Gr B38 ...19 D3
Laker Cl DY8 ....6 A7
Lakes Cl DY11 ....27 C7
Lakes Ct DY12 ....25 F3
Lakes Halt The B94 ..53 F8
Lakes Rd The DY12 ..25 F3
Lakeside B97 ....69 D7
Lakeside Ct DY5 ......6 B8
Lakeside Ind Est B98 .71 B3
Lakewood Dr B45 ....18 B1
Lamb Bank WR14 ...138 D3
Lambert Rd WR2 ....114 E1
Lambourne Ave WR14 .139 A5
Lambourne Cl [2] B50 .136 D5
Lambourne Cres B14 .114 E6
Lambourne Dr [2] DY12 .25 F4
Lambourne Orch WR6 .82 B3
Lambourne Way DY5 ..6 B8
Lambscote Cl B90 ...21 C2
Lamont Ave B32 ......9 F3
Lampitt La GL20 ....172 A3
Lamport House [5] B14 .21 A3
Lancaster Ave B45 ...33 A6
Lancaster Cl B30 ....20 A6
Lancaster Rd [3] DY12 .25 F4
Lancelot House DY10 .28 C8
Lanchester Rd B38 ..20 A1
Lancing Cl [3] WR5 ..128 E8
Land Oak Dr DY10 ...28 B7
Lander Cl B45 ....33 A4
Landor Rd B98 ....71 A1
Landsdowne St WR1 .115 B4
Landsgate DY8 ....6 A1
Lane The
  Buckland WR12 ....189 F5
  Elmley Castle WR10 .159 E1
  Strensham WR8 ....171 A6
Lane's End WR5 ....141 B7
Lanescourt GL20 ...196 F6
Lanesfield Pk WR11 .161 E6
Langdale Cl WR4 ...116 A6
Langdale Dr WR4 ...115 F5
Langdale Rd
  [3] Stourport-on-Severn
  DY13 ....43 D1
  [10] Worcester WR1 .115 A4
Langdale Way DY9 ....6 D4
Langland Ave WR13 .139 C2
Langland Rd DY14 ...22 C5
Langland Stadium (Malvern
  Town Football Club)
  WR14 ....139 C2
Langley Cl Redditch B98 .71 D1
  [6] Worcester WR2 ..114 E5
Langley Rd [4] WR9 ..85 A1
Langstone Br B14 ....21 B3
Lankets The WR11 ...162 E3

Lannacombe Rd B31 ....33 E6
Lansbury Gn B64 ....8 B8
Lansbury Rd B64 ....8 B8
Lansdown Gn DY11 ....27 C5
Lansdowne Cl 8 WR14 .139 B1
Lansdowne Cres
　Great Malvern WR14 ...139 A1
　Studley B80 ....90 D3
　Worcester WR3 ......115 C4
Lansdowne Ct DY9 ......6 C1
Lansdowne Rd
　4 Great Malvern WR14 .138 F4
　Halesowen, Hasbury B63 ..7 D2
　Studley B80 ....90 D3
　9 Worcester WR3 ....115 B4
Lansdowne Rise 1
　WR3 ....115 C4
Lansdowne Terr
　WR14 ....139 A1
Lansdowne Wlk 1
　WR3 ....115 D4
Lapal Cl WR2 ....114 F2
Lapal La B62 ....9 A2
Lapal La N B62 ....8 E3
Lapal La S B32, B62 ....8 E3
Lapal Prim Sch B62 .....8 F4
Lappath House B32 ....18 D8
Lapwing Cl
　Kidderminster DY10 ...28 B1
　Northway GL20 ....184 D1
Lapworth Cl B98 ....89 F7
Larch Cl DY7 ....4 C3
Larch House DY8 ....5 C6
Larch Rd
　11 Evesham WR11 ....161 F2
　Worcester WR4 ....115 D4
Larches Cottage Gdns
　DY11 ....27 C3
Larches Rd DY11 ....27 C4
Larchfield Cl WR14 ....138 E4
Larchmere Dr
　Birmingham B28 ......21 F8
　Bromsgrove B61 ......48 E3
Larford Wlk DY13 ......43 F1
Lark Cl B14 ....21 A2
Lark Hill WR5 ....115 E1
Lark Hill Rd WR5 ......115 E1
Larkfield Rd B98 ......71 A1
Larkhill DY10 ....27 E7
Larkhill Rd DY8 ....5 C4
Larkhill Wlk B14 ......20 D1
Larks Rise DY14 ....22 B4
Larksfield Mews DY5 ...6 C7
Larkspur Ct B62 ....8 F7
Larkspur Dr WR11 .....161 C1
Larkspur Rd 8 WR5 ...128 D5
Lashbrooke House B45 .32 F7
Laslett St WR3 ....115 D4
Lassington Cl B98 .....71 E4
Latchford Cl B98 ......71 E6
Latimer Rd B48 ....51 A5
Laugherne Rd WR2 ....114 F3
Laughton Cl B31 ......34 B7
Launceston Pl 11 WR4 .116 C6
Launde The B28 ....21 E3
Laurel Cl
　4 Evesham WR11 ....161 F2
　9 Walton Cardiff GL20 .197 A4
Laurel Bank Mews B60 .49 F4
Laurel Cl
　Drakes Broughton WR10 .143 F6
　Redditch B98 ....70 E2
Laurel Gr
　Birmingham B30 ......19 E6
　Bromsgrove B61 ......48 F4
Laurel La B8 ....8 E3
Laurel Rd
　Birmingham, King's Norton
　B30 ....20 A4
　Worcester WR4 ....115 E5
Laurel Wood Cl 6 WR9 .104 A8
Laurel Wood Rd WR9 ..104 A8
Laurels Ave WR11 .....162 B8
Laurels The B68 ....9 B6
Laurels Rd WR11 ......162 B8
Laurence Ct B31 ......19 B5
Lavender House B38 ...34 F8
Lavender La DY8 ......5 D3
Lavender Rd WR3 .....115 A6
Lavender Wlk WR1 ....175 C8
Lavinia Rd B62 ....8 E3
Lawford Rd B90 ....21 D2
Lawley The B63 ....7 D1
Lawn Ave DY8 ....5 E4
Lawn St DY8 ....5 E4
Lawnsdown Rd DY5 ....6 F6
Lawnside 1 WR14 .....153 A8
Lawrence Ct 6 B68 ....9 B8
Lawrence St DY9 ......6 C6
Lax La DY12 ....26 B3
Laxton Ave WR11 .....114 E5
Laxton Cl WR7 ....117 C4
Laxton Dr 3 DY12 ....25 F4
Layamon Wlk WR1 ....43 F2
Laylocks La WR2 .....113 C1
Layton Ave WR14 .....139 B3
Lazy Hill B38 ....20 B2
Lazy La WR10 ....146 A1
Lea Bank Ave DY11 ...27 B5
Lea Castle Cl DY10 ...12 F1
Lea Castle Dr DY10 ...13 C2
Lea Cl WR3 ....102 B1
Lea Croft B97 ....89 D5
Lea Cswy The WR1 ....27 A4
Lea End La B48 ....34 D3
Lea Gn La B47 ....36 C5
Lea Hill Cl WR14 .....138 F2
Lea House Rd B30 ....20 A7

Lea La DY10 ....12 F4
Lea Meml CE Fst Sch
　DY14 ....24 C2
Lea Pk Rise B61 ......48 F5
Lea St DY10 ....27 F6
Lea St Fst Sch DY10 ...27 F6
Lea The Alveley WV15 ..1 C6
　Kidderminster DY11 ...27 A5
　Throckmorton WR10 ..145 E8
Lea Vale Rd DY8 ......5 F3
Lea View DY14 ....22 B4
Lea Wlk B45 ....32 F8
Lea Wood Gr DY11 ....27 A5
Lea Yield Cl B30 ......20 A7
Leabank Dr WR3 .....102 A1
Leach Gn La B45 .....33 B6
Leach Heath La B45 ...33 A7
Leadbetter Dr B61 ....48 D2
Leadon Rd WR14 .....153 D7
Leafield Gdns B8 .....8 B8
Leaholme Gdns DY9 ...6 B2
Leamington Rd WR2 ..177 D2
Leander Gdns B14 ....20 F5
Leander Rd DY9 ......6 C1
Leapgate Ctry Pk★
　DY13 ....44 C2
Leapgate La DY13 ....44 E5
Lear Cl WR2 ....114 D3
Leasow Cl 5 WR2 ....114 D1
Leasow Rd B45 ....32 F8
Leasowe DY14 ....40 B7
Leasowes Com Coll B62 .8 E6
Leasowes La B8 ......8 D4
Leasowes Rd WR11 ...162 B8
Lechlade St B63 ......7 F3
Lechlade Cl WR9 .....71 B7
Lechmere Cres
　6 Great Malvern WR14 .138 F5
　Worcester WR4 ....114 E5
Leckhampton Cl WR4 ..116 A7
Ledbury Cl B98 ....71 F2
Ledbury House B97 ...70 B4
Ledsam Gr B32 ....9 F6
Ledwych Cl WR9 .....84 D3
Ledwych Gdns WR9 ...84 E3
Ledwych Rd 1 WR9 ...84 E3
Lee Rd Blackheath B64 .7 F8
　Hollywood B47 ......36 A7
　Northway GL20 ......197 A4
Leebank Rd B63 ......7 E2
Leeds Ave WR4 ......116 C6
Lees The WR14 ......152 F6
Legion Rd B45 ....32 E7
Leicester Gr WR11 ...161 D5
Leicester St 5 WR1 ..115 B4
Leigh & Bransford Prim Sch
　WR13 ....126 B2
Leigh Gr WR9 ....84 E4
Leigh Sinton Rd
　Leigh WR13 ....126 A1
　Malvern WR13 ....125 F1
Leith Gr B38 ....34 E8
Lench Cl B97 ....70 A5
Lenchs Trust B32 .....9 E6
Lenwade Rd B68 .....9 D8
Leominster Ct B45 ...32 F8
Leominster Wlk B45 ..32 F8
Leonard Ave DY10 ...13 A1
Leonard Rd DY8 .....5 C5
Leopard Rise WR5 ...116 B3
Leslie Ave WR3 .....102 A1
Leswell Gr DY10 .....27 F6
Leswell La DY10 .....27 F6
Leswell St DY10 .....27 F6
Leven Dr WR5 ....128 E6
Lewes Gdns WR4 ....116 C6
Lewis Cl WR10 ....143 F6
Lewis Rd
　Birmingham B30 .....20 C7
　Oldbury B68 ....9 B7
　Stourbridge DY9 ....6 D5
Lewkner Almshouses The
　B48 ....51 A5
Lexington Cl 4 GL20 .197 A4
Lexington Gn DY5 ....6 C7
Ley Hill Farm Rd B31 .18 E5
Ley Hill Prim Sch B31 .18 E5
Ley Orch WR12 ......177 A4
Lindsey Ave
　Birmingham B31 .....19 C4
　Evesham WR11 .....161 E3
Leybrook Rd B45 ....33 B8
Leycester Cl B31 .....34 A7
Leycroft 4 WR9 .....85 B1
Leydon Croft B38 ....20 B2
Leylan Croft B13 .....21 D7
Leyman Cl B14 ......21 C4
Leys Cl
　Hinton on the Green
　WR11 ....175 A5
　Stourbridge DY9 ....6 C2
Leys Rd WR11 ....134 D1
Leys The
　Bidford-on-Avon B50 .136 E5
　Birmingham B31 .....19 B5
　Evesham WR11 .....161 E4
Leys Wlk 4 WR11 ....161 E4
Leysfield WR11 ......147 F7
Leysters Cl B98 ......71 E3
Leyton Cl DY5 ....6 D8
Library Way B45 .....32 F7
Lichen Gdns B38 ....34 D7
Lichfield Ave
　Evesham WR11 .....161 D4
　Kidderminster DY11 ..26 F6
　Worcester WR5 .....116 A2
Lichfield Ct B90 .....21 D2
Lichfield St DY13 ....44 A3
Lickey Coppice B45 ..33 C6
Lickey End Fst Sch B60 .49 C6
Lickey Gr DY11 ......27 B2

Lickey Grange Dr B60 .32 E1
Lickey Hills Ctry Pk★
　B45 ....33 B3
Lickey Hills Prim Sch
　B45 ....32 F3
Lickey Rd
　Birmingham B45 ....33 C6
　Stourbridge DY8 ....6 B6
Lickey Rock B60 .....32 D1
Lickey Sq B45 ....33 A2
Lickhill Lodge Fst Sch
　DY13 ....43 D5
Lickhill Mid Sch DY13 .43 F4
Lickhill Rd N DY13 ...43 D6
Liddiard Ct DY8 .....5 E6
Lifford Cl B14 ....20 C4
Lifford Gdns WR12 ..190 C1
Lifford La B30 ....20 B4
Lightning Way B31 ...34 B7
Lightoak Cl B97 .....89 C6
Lightwood La WR2 ..113 D3
Lightwoods Hill B67 ..9 E8
Lightwoods Jun & Inf Sch
　B68 ....9 D8
Lightwoods Rd DY9 ...6 C1
Lilac Ave Droitwich WR9 .104 A8
　Evesham WR11 .....161 B2
　Redditch B98 ....70 E2
Lilac Gr DY13 ....43 E4
Lilac Way B62 ....8 F8
Lilleshall Cl B98 ....71 E3
Lilley Gn Rd B48 ....52 D5
Lilley La B31 ....34 B8
Lily Gn La B97 ......70 A4
Lilycroft La B38 .....35 A7
Limbrick Cl B90 .....21 F2
Lime Ave WR5 ......115 C4
Lime Cl Alveley WV15 ..1 D6
　Hollywood B47 .....36 A5
Lime Ct DY10 ....28 A4
Lime Gr Bromsgrove B61 .48 F4
　Kinver DY7 ....4 C3
　Welland WR13 ......167 C5
Lime Kiln Cl B38 ....34 D7
Lime Rd 2 GL20 ....197 A3
Lime St
　Eldersfield GL19 ....193 F3
　Evesham WR11 .....161 E4
Lime Tree Ave
　Broadway WR12 ....177 E1
　Great Malvern WR14 .152 E4
Lime Tree Cres B97 ..70 B4
Lime Tree Gr B31 ....19 C2
Lime Tree Wlk DY13 ..43 E5
Limekiln La B14 .....21 A4
Limes The WR5 .....141 D8
Lincoln Cl WR11 ....161 D5
Lincoln Cres DY11 ...26 F6
Lincoln Ct 9 B29 ....19 C7
Lincoln Gn 2 WR1 ..115 F1
Lincoln Gn La GL20 ..196 D4
Lincoln Rd B61 .....48 E4
Lincomb La DY13 ....63 D7
Lindale Cres DY5 ...6 B6
Linden Ave
　Halesowen B62 .....8 E7
　Kidderminster DY11 ..28 A7
　5 Stourport-on-Severn
　DY13 ....43 E1
Linden Cl 10 WR11 ..161 F2
Linden Dr DY8 ......6 A3
Linden Gdns DY10 ...28 A6
Linden Glade B63 ...8 A4
Linden Rd
　Birmingham B30 ....19 E2
　6 Worcester WR4 ..115 F5
Lindens The B32 ....9 E7
Lindenwood Way B32 .20 B2
Lindridge CE Prim Sch
　WR15 ....58 D6
Lindridge Cl B98 ....72 A3
Lindridge Rd B90 ...21 F1
Lindsworth App B30 .20 C3
Lindsworth Ct 2 B30 .20 C3
Lindsworth Rd B30 ..20 C3
Lindsworth Specl Sch
　B30 ....20 C3
Lineholt Cl B98 .....90 A6
Linehouse La WR9 ..63 E1
Linehouse La
　Catshill B60 ....49 D8
　Marlbrook B60 .....32 D1
Lingen Cl B98 ......71 E3
Lingfield Rd
　Bewdley DY12 .....26 D5
　Birmingham B90 ...21 F1
Lingfield Wlk B61 ...32 B1
Link Rd Evesham WR11 .161 E1
Link Terr WR14 .....138 F2
Link Way WR14 .....139 A4
Linkend Rd GL19 ...194 E3
Links Cres B68 .....9 B8
Links Dr Birmingham B45 .33 A5
　Stourbridge DY8 ...5 E2
Links Rd
　Birmingham B14 ...21 A1
　Oldbury B68 ....9 B8
Links The DY10 .....28 A4
Links View B62 .....8 D4

Linksview Cres WR5 ..116 A2
Linkwood Ind Est DY8 .5 F6
Linley Cl WR3 ......102 A1
Linley Gr B14 ....20 C6
Linnet Cl
　Birmingham B30 ....19 E8
　Halesowen B62 .....8 B6
Linnet Rise DY10 ....27 F1
Linpole Wlk B14 ....20 D2
Linthurst Fst Sch B60 .50 A6
Linthurst Newtown
　B60 ....50 B5
Linthurst Rd B45, B60 .50 A7
Linton Cl Halesowen B63 .7 D5
　Redditch B98 ....71 F2
Linton Mews B98 ....71 F2
Lion Cl WR1 ....115 C3
Lion Hill DY13 ......44 A3
Lion La DY14 ....22 D4
Lion Pas DY8 ....5 F5
Lion Sq DY10 ....27 E6
Lion St
　Kidderminster DY10 .27 E6
　Stourbridge DY8 ...5 F5
Lionfields Cl DY10 ...13 A5
Lionfields Rd DY10 ..13 A4
Lisko Cl DY5 ....6 A8
Lisle Ave DY11 .....27 D3
Lismore Cl B45 .....17 E1
Lismore Gn 11 WR5 ..128 E6
Lister Ave WR4 .....116 C3
Lister Rd DY11 .....27 B4
Listowel Rd B14 ....20 D6
Little Acre B97 .....89 D6
Little Battenton WR9 .63 D1
Little Boughton St 4
　WR2 ....114 E1
Little Chestnut St
　WR1 ....115 C4
Little Cornbow B63 ..8 B3
Little Forge Rd B98 ..90 C8
Little Gn GL19 .....192 A4
Little Grebe Rd DY10 .28 B3
Little Hayes DY11 ...12 C3
Little Heath La B60 ..49 D6
Little Hill WR9 .....84 C2
Little Hill Gr B38 ...20 A1
Little Hill Way B38 ..20 A1
Little London 8 WR1 .115 B4
Little Mdw Croft B31 .18 E4
Little Penny Rope
　WR2 ....158 C2
Little Piece 7 WR4 ..116 B5
Little Pk B32 ....9 B4
Little Pk St 15 WR5 .115 C2
Little Priest La 5
　WR1 ....115 B4
Little Rd WR11 .....163 E8
Little Southfield St 1
　WR1 ....115 C3
Little Woods B97 ....89 E6
Littlecote Croft 1 B14 .21 C1
Littlemead Ave B90 ..36 E8
Littlemead Rd B90 ...36 E8
Littleover Ave B28 ..21 F6
Littleshaw Croft B47 .36 C4
Littleshaw La B47 ...36 C4
Littletons Sch The
　WR11 ....148 F1
Littlewood Gn B80 ..90 D3
Littleworth La B96 ..88 B1
Littleworth St WR11 .161 D4
Liverpool Rd WR5 ...115 F1
Livingstone Rd B14 ..20 E6
Livingstone St 7 WR5 .128 E8
Llangorse Cl DY13 ...43 E7
Lloyd Cl WR11 ......147 E3
Lloyds Bk B62 ......8 C8
Load St DY12 ....26 B3
Lobelia Cl
　Kidderminster DY11 .12 C1
　Worcester WR5 .....128 D5
Lock Cl B97 ....70 A4
Lock Keepers Reach
　B48 ....50 F6
Lock St WR5 ....115 C2
Lockeridge La WR8 ..168 B3
Lockington Croft B62 .8 F6
Lockside Dr DY7 ....4 B4
Lockton Rd B30 .....20 C8
Lockwood Rd B31 ...18 F4
Lodge Bank WR9 ....63 C3
Lodge Cl
　Halesowen B62 .....8 E3
　Worcester WR2 ....114 E4
Lodge Cres DY9 ....15 B5
Lodge Croft B31 ....18 E6
Lodge Dr WR14 .....138 E2
Lodge Forge Trad Est
　B64 ....7 C7
Lodge Hill WR10 ...157 D4
Lodge Pool Dr B98 ..70 F1
Lodge Rd Redditch B98 .70 E2
　5 Stourport-on-Severn
　DY13 ....44 A3
Lodgefield Rd B62 ...8 B7
Lofthouse Cres B31 ..18 F3
Lofthouse Gr B31 ...18 F3
Loftus Cl B29 ......18 F8
Lomas Dr B31 ......18 E4
Lomas La B31 ......18 E4
Lombard St DY13 ...44 A3
Lombardy Croft 3 B62 .9 A6
London La
　Bromsgrove B60 ...69 A6
　Tardebigge B60 ....69 A6
　2 Upton upon Severn
　WR8 ....169 C6

London Rd WR5 .....115 D1
Long Acre DY10 ....27 F7
Long Bank DY12 ....25 C1
Long Cl DY9 ....15 A4
Long Compton Dr DY9 .15 A6
Long Eights GL20 ...184 D1
Long Hedges WR10 .158 B7
Long Hyde Rd WR11 .148 E1
Long Innage B63 ....7 B6
Long La Halesowen B62 .8 E8
　Peopleton WR10 ...131 F1
　Pinvin WR10 ....132 A1
　Throckmorton WR10 .145 B8
Long Leasow B29 ...19 B7
Long Marston Rd
　Mickleton CV37 ....165 C7
　Pebworth CV37 ....150 F3
　Welford-on-Avon CV37 .151 C8
Long Mdw Rd B60 ..49 C6
Long Mynd B63 ....7 D1
Long Mynd Rd B31 ..18 F6
Long Nuke Rd B31 ..18 E7
Long Saw Dr B31 ...18 D1
Long Sling WR9 ....84 D1
Long Wood B30 ....19 E5
Longboat La DY13 ..44 A4
Longborough Cl B97 .89 B6
Longbow Rd B29 ...18 F7
Longbridge La B31 ..33 E8
Longbridge Sta B31 .33 D8
Longcroft The B63 ..7 E4
Longdales Rd B38 ...34 B8
Longdon Cl B98 ....90 B7
Longdon Hill
　Evesham WR11 ....162 B1
　Wickhamford WR11 .176 C8
Longfellow Cl B97 ..89 C7
Longfellow Gn DY10 .28 C6
Longfellow Rd
　Birmingham B30 ...19 D4
　Worcester WR3 ....115 C6
Longfield WR8 .....169 C5
Longfield Cl B28 ...21 F6
Longfield Rd
　Birmingham B31 ...18 E8
　Stourbridge DY9 ...6 B8
Longford Cl
　Bidford-on-Avon B50 .136 D5
　Birmingham B32 ...18 A7
Longham Croft B32 ..9 F4
Longheadland WR9 ..83 A5
Longhope Cl B98 ....72 B4
Longhurst Croft B31 .34 B7
Longlands Cl B38 ...34 C8
Longlands Rd B62 ..8 E3
Longlands The B45 ..50 D7
Longmeadow Dr 8
　WR15 ....55 F6
Longmeadow Gr B31 .34 A6
Longmoor Cl B97 ...70 B5
Longmoor Rd B63 ..7 E3
Longmore Hill DY13 .62 F6
Longmynd Way DY13 .43 D1
Longridge Rd WR14 .153 B5
Longtown Rd 7 GL20 .197 A4
Longwill Prim Sch For Deaf
　Children B31 ......19 A5
Longwood Rd B45 ..33 A7
Lord Austin Dr B60 .32 E1
Lord's Heath 4 WR4 .116 B5
Lords La B80 ....90 E2
Lordswood Cl B97 ..69 F2
Lorne Gr DY10 .....28 A6
Lorne St
　Kidderminster DY10 .28 A5
　Stourport-on-Severn
　DY13 ....44 A3
Lorrainer Ave DY5 ..6 A8
Loughmill Rd WR10 .144 C1
Loughton Gr B63 ...7 F4
Louise Croft B14 ...20 C2
Lovage Rd B98 .....71 F6
Love La
　Cleobury Mortimer DY14 .22 C4
　Hollywood B47 ....35 F7
　Stourbridge, Lye DY9 .6 F5
　Stourbridge, Old Swinford
　DY8 ....6 A3
Love Lyne
　Feckenham B97 ....88 D2
　Redditch B97 ......89 B5
Love's Gr WR1 .....115 B4
Lovell Cl B29 ......19 B6
Lovett Pl WR4 .....116 C4
Lovett Rd WR9 ....84 D7
Lovington La WR2 ..114 B7
Low Fold Cl WR2 ...114 C1
Low Rd WR11 ......134 B4
Low Thatch B38 ....34 C4
Lowans Hill View B97 .70 C4
Lowbrook La B90 ...36 D4
Lowe La Alveley WV15 .1 D2
　Wolverley & Cookley
　DY11 ....12 B2
Lowell St WR1 .....115 C4
Lower Barbourne Terr 8
　WR1 ....115 A5
Lower Beeches Rd B31 .18 C2
Lower Bentley La B60 .68 F1
Lower Bull Entry 5
　WR1 ....115 B4
Lower Chase Rd 6
　WR14 ....153 B8
Lower Chestnut St
　WR1 ....115 C4

Lower Cladswell La
B49 108 F2
Lower Comm La B97 70 B2
Lower Croft WR10 160 B6
Lower Dr WR8 157 C7
Lower Ferry La WR2 140 F7
Lower Field Terr WR5 128 C8
Lower Gambolds La
B60 68 B6
Lower Grinsty La B97 89 A8
Lower High St
Blackheath B64 7 C8
Stourbridge DY8 5 F6
Lower Higley Cl B32 9 E4
Lower Howsell Rd
Leigh WR13 126 A1
Malvern WR13 139 A8
Lower Inhedge 5 DY14 22 D5
Lower Leys WR11 161 E4
Lower Lickhill Rd DY13 43 E5
Lower Lode La GL20 196 C4
Lower Mill St DY11 27 D6
Lower Montpelier Rd
WR14 138 C1
Lower Moor B30 19 E8
Lower Parklands DY11 27 C5
Lower Pk DY12 26 B3
Lower Priest La 6
WR10 158 D8
Lower Quest Hills Rd 3
WR14 138 F4
Lower Rd WR14 138 C2
Lower Shepley La B60 49 E6
Lower St DY14 22 D4
Lower White Rd B32 9 D5
Lower Wilton Rd 2
WR14 153 B8
Lower Wyche Rd
WR14 152 E6
Lowesmoor WR1 115 C3
Lowesmoor Terr WR1 115 C3
Lowesmoor Trad Est
WR1 115 C3
Loweswater House B38 20 B1
Loweswater Rd DY13 43 E7
Lowfield Cl B62 9 A3
Lowfield La B97 70 B5
Lowhill La B45 33 D6
Lowlands La B98 71 D3
Lowndes Rd DY8 5 E6
Loxley Ave
Birmingham B14 21 C3
Solihull B90 21 F1
Loxley Cl
Birmingham B31 18 E8
Redditch B98 71 D6
Loynells Rd B45 33 B7
Lucerne Ave WR14 153 A5
Lucerne Cl 1 WR3 115 A8
Lucy Baldwin Unit Hospl
DY13 43 F5
Lucy Edwards Ct DY11 27 C5
Ludford Rd B32 9 A1
Ludgate Ave DY11 27 A4
Ludlow Ave WR4 116 B6
Ludlow House B13 21 A6
Ludlow Rd
Cleobury Mortimer DY14 22 A4
Kidderminster DY10 27 E3
Redditch B97 70 E3
Ludstone Rd B29 9 F1
Lugano Rd WR3 115 A8
Lulworth Cl B63 7 C6
Lundy Row WR5 128 E6
Lunnon La WR9 46 C2
Lunt Gr B32 9 D5
Lupton Ct B60 49 A1
Lusbridge Cl B63 7 B4
Lutley Ave B63 7 E4
Lutley Dr DY9 6 C3
Lutley Gr B32 9 B1
Lutley La B63 7 C2
Lutley Mill Rd B63 7 E4
Lutley Prim Sch B63 7 D1
Lutterworth Cl 3 WR4 115 F4
Lyall Gdns B45 17 E1
Lychgate Ave DY9 6 C1
Lydate Rd B62 8 F4
Lydbrook Covert 5 B38 34 E8
Lyddington Dr B62 8 B7
Lyde Gn B63 7 B7
Lydes Rd 5 WR14 153 B8
Lydford Terr Ave 13
WR4 116 C6
Lydham Cl B98 70 E5
Lydiate Ash Rd B60 32 C3
Lydiate Ave B31 18 D1
Lydney Cl B98 71 D7
Lydney Gr B31 18 F3
Lye Ave B32 9 A2
Lye Bsns Ctr DY9 6 F6
Lye By-Pass DY9 6 E6
Lye Cl La B32 9 A2
Lye Sta DY9 6 E6
Lye Valley Ind Est DY9 6 F6
Lyf's La WR5 141 B7
Lygon Bank WR14 138 F2
Lygon Cl B98 71 A5
Lygon Gr B32 9 E4
Lynbrook Cl B47 36 A7
Lynch La SY8 54 B4
Lyncourt Gr B32 9 B6
Lynden Cl B61 48 E3
Lyndenwood B97 70 A2
Lyndholm Rd DY10 28 A6
Lyndhurst Dr DY10 27 E8
Lyndon Cl B63 7 F4
Lyndon House B31 19 B3
Lyndon Rd B45 32 E7
Lyndworth Rd B30 20 C8
Lyneham Cl 5 WR4 115 F7
Lynfield Cl B38 34 F7
Lynn Cl WR13 125 F2
Lynval Rd DY5 6 F7
Lynwood Cl WR11 161 B4
Lynwood Dr DY10 14 C2
Lynworth La GL20 183 F6
Lyppard Grange Prim Sch
WR4 116 C4
Lysander Rd B45 18 A2
Lyth La WR9 63 B2
Lytham Cl DY8 5 F2
Lythwood Dr DY5 6 C8
Lyttelton Pl DY9 15 C6
Lyttelton Rd
Bewdley DY12 26 A4
Droitwich WR9 84 F1
Stourbridge DY8 5 D5
Lyttelton St 4 WR1 115 A5
Lyttleton Ave
Bromsgrove B60 67 E7
Halesowen B62 8 F7
Lyttleton House B63 8 A2
Lyttleton Rd WR10 144 E4
Lytton La B32 9 F3

M

Maas Rd B31 19 A4
Mabey Ave B98 70 F5
Macarthur Rd B64 7 C8
Macaulay Rise WR14 139 A2
Madeley Rd
Belbroughton DY9 31 D6
Redditch B98 71 F5
Madge Hill WR8 155 E5
Madinatul Uloom Al-Islamiya
Sch DY10 28 D1
Madley Cl B45 32 E8
Madresfield CE Prim Sch
WR13 139 E3
Madresfield Dr B63 8 B2
Madresfield Rd WR14 139 A1
Mafeking Villas B62 8 B7
Magnolia Cl
Birmingham B29 19 A7
Drakes Broughton WR10 143 F6
9 Worcester WR5 128 D5
Magpie Cl WR5 128 D5
Magpie Way DY10 28 B2
Main Rd Kempsey WR5 141 C5
Wyre Piddle WR10 145 B3
Main St
Aldington WR11 162 C5
Beckford GL20 186 D4
Bishampton WR10 132 F3
Bretforton WR11 163 B5
Church Lench WR11 134 A3
Cleeve Prior WR11 149 B7
Cropthorne WR10 160 B6
Defford WR8 157 D3
Offenham WR11 148 A1
Pershore/Pinvin WR10 144 E6
Sedgeberrow WR11 175 A1
South Littleton WR11 148 F1
Willersey WR12 177 E4
Mainstone Cl B98 71 E3
Maisemore Cl B98 71 D6
Malcolm Ave B61 48 E3
Malcolm Gr B45 33 A7
Malfield Ave B97 69 F3
Malham Pl 1 WR5 128 E6
Malham Rd DY13 43 E7
Malinshill Rd WR11 161 B3
Mallaby Cl B90 36 F8
Mallard Ave DY10 28 B3
Mallard Cl
Brierley Hill DY5 6 C7
Redditch B98 70 F5
Worcester WR2 128 A6
Mallard Pl WR9 85 B3
Mallard Rd B80 90 F4
Mallards Cl WV15 1 D5
Mallory Dr DY11 12 D1
Mallow Cl WR14 153 D7
Mallow Dr B61 48 F6
Malmsey Cl GL20 196 F3
Malpas Dr B32 18 C8
Malpass Rd DY5 6 F7
Malt House La WR11 134 B3
Malt Mill La B62 8 D8
Malt Mill La Trad Est
B62 8 D8
Malthouse Cres WR7 120 E7
Malthouse La B94 53 E7
Malthouse Pl 2 WR1 115 B2
Maltings The B80 90 D4
Malton Cl WR14 138 E6
Malton Gr B13 21 B7
Malus Cl WR14 139 C3
Malvern Ave DY9 6 C5
Malvern Cl
Broadheath WR2 114 A7
Stourport-on-Severn
DY13 62 D8
Malvern Coll WR14 152 F7
Malvern Com Hospl
WR14 139 A1
Malvern Dr DY10 27 E3
Malvern Girls' Coll
WR14 153 A8
Malvern House
7 Halesowen B63 8 A3
Redditch B97 70 C1
Malvern Link CE Prim Sch
WR14 139 A4
Malvern Link Sta
WR14 139 A4
Malvern Mus★ WR14 152 E8
Malvern Parish CE Prim Sch
WR14 153 A8
Malvern Rd
Barnt Green B45 33 A2
Bromsgrove B61 67 D7
Newland WR2 126 F1
Oldbury B68 9 B8
Powick WR2 127 D3
Redditch B97 89 D8
Worcester WR2 114 F1
Malvern Theatre★
WR14 152 F8
Malvern View
Bluntington DY10 29 E1
Kidderminster DY11 27 B1
Mamble DY14 40 E4
Malvern Wells Prim Sch
WR14 166 E7
Mamble Craft Ctr★
DY14 39 F4
Mamble Rd DY8 5 E5
Manby Rd 3 WR14 153 A8
Mandalay Dr WR5 128 F4
Mandarin Ave DY10 28 B3
Mandeville Way B61 48 F5
Manitoba Cl 3 WR2 127 E6
Manitoba Croft 2 B38 34 F8
Manning Rd WR9 84 E2
Manningford Ct B14 20 F3
Manningford Rd B14 20 E3
Manor Abbey Rd B62 8 E4
Manor Ave DY11 27 A7
Manor Ave S DY11 27 A6
Manor Cl Badsey WR11 162 D3
Droitwich WR9 85 A2
Honeybourne WR11 164 A4
Kidderminster DY11 27 A6
Stourport-on-Severn
DY13 44 B5
Wickhamford WR11 176 D8
Manor Ct
Broughton Hackett WR7 117 E1
Cleeve Prior WR11 149 B7
5 Halesowen B62 9 A7
Manor Ct Rd B60 67 F8
Manor Dr B80 91 F7
Manor Farm WR7 143 A8
Manor Farm Craft Ctr★
B94 36 F2
Manor Gdns
Aldington WR11 162 C5
Pershore WR10 158 E7
Manor House Cl B29 9 F1
Manor House La B96 89 E3
Manor La
Bretforton WR11 163 C4
Halesowen B62 8 E4
Hartlebury DY11 64 B8
Little Comberton WR10 159 B2
Lydiate Ash B61 32 C4
Stourbridge DY8 5 D3
Manor Mews B80 90 E4
Manor Pk
Harvington WR11 148 B6
Tewkesbury GL20 197 A8
Manor Pk Gr B31 18 C1
Manor Pk Specl Sch
WR2 114 F4
Manor Pl 1 GL20 196 F3
Manor Rd
Clifton upon Teme WR6 97 E8
Eckington WR10 171 D7
Hill & Moor WR10 145 D3
South Littleton WR11 148 F2
Stourport-on-Severn
DY13 44 A5
Studley B80 90 E4
Upper Bentley B97 69 B1
Wickhamford WR11 162 D1
Worcester WR2 127 F8
Wythall B47 36 A3
Manor Side WR11 162 D3
Manor Side Ind Est
B98 71 E6
Manor Way B62, B63 8 D3
Manor Way Prim Sch
B63 8 C3
Manorfield WR2 114 A7
Manse Gdns B80 90 E3
Mansell Cl B63 7 B7
Mansell Rd B97 89 D7
Mansfield Rd 1 WR14 139 C3
Mansion Ct B62 8 E7
Mansion Gdns WR11 161 D3
Mapit Pl WR4 116 C4
Maple Ave
5 Pershore WR10 144 D2
Worcester WR4 115 E4
Maple Cl
5 Evesham WR11 161 F2
Kidderminster DY11 27 B8
Kinver DY7 4 A5
Stourbridge DY8 5 D2
11 Stourport-on-Severn
DY13 43 E4
Maple Cres WV15 1 C6
Maple Croft B13 20 F5
Maple Gr WR9 103 F8
Maple House B97 70 B2
Maple Rd
Birmingham, Eachway
B45 32 F6
Birmingham, Selly Oak
B30 19 E8
Halesowen B62 8 D8
Maple Tree La B63 7 C6
Maple Way B31 18 F1
Mappleborough Gn CE Prim
Sch B98 72 B2
Mappleborough Rd
B90 21 E1
Marans Croft B38 34 D7
Marble Alley B80 90 E4
Marbury Cl B38 19 D2
March Gr DY12 26 B4
March Hare Leisure Ctr
WR7 117 F1
Marchwood Cl B97 70 A5
Marcliff Cres B90 21 C2
Marden Gr B31 34 A7
Margaret Ave B63 7 F4
Margaret Cl DY5 6 E8
Margaret Dr DY8 6 B4
Margaret Rd
Tewkesbury GL20 196 F4
Worcester WR2 128 A8
Margesson Dr B45 33 D1
Marhon Cl 5 WR9 85 B1
Marigold Cl 8 WR5 128 C5
Marion Cl WR3 115 B8
Marion Way B28 21 E7
Marjoram Cl B38 34 F8
Marjorie Ave B30 20 B3
Mark Cl
Great Malvern WR14 138 E6
Redditch B98 70 E2
Market Pl
Bromsgrove B61 48 F2
Redditch B98 70 E4
Market Sq B64 7 C8
Market St
Bromsgrove B61 48 F2
Kidderminster DY10 27 E5
Stourbridge DY8 6 A5
Tenbury Wells WR15 55 F5
Market Way DY9 15 C6
Market Wlk 4 B97 70 E4
Marl Bank WR3 115 D4
Marl Top B38 19 F2
Marlbank Rd WR13 167 B5
Marlborough Ave B60 68 A8
Marlborough Ct B60 68 B8
Marlborough Dr
Astley & Dunley DY13 62 F8
Stourbridge DY8 6 A3
Marlborough Gdns
WR14 139 B6
Marlborough Rd
WR10 171 D7
Marlborough St
2 Kidderminster DY10 27 E5
4 Worcester WR5 128 E8
Marlbrook Gdns B61 32 B1
Marlbrook La
Crowle WR9 105 A1
Marlbrook B60 32 D2
Marlcliff Gr B13 21 A6
Marldon Rd B14 20 E6
Marleigh Rd B50 136 E5
Marlfield Farm Fst Sch
B98 71 C6
Marlfield La B98 71 B4
Marlow Rd WR2 114 D2
Marlowe Cl DY10 28 B6
Marlpit La B97 70 C1
Marlpool Cl 4 DY11 12 B1
Marlpool Ct DY11 27 C8
Marlpool Dr B97 70 C3
Marlpool Fst Sch DY11 27 C8
Marlpool La DY11 12 B1
Marlpool Pl DY11 27 C8
Marquis Dr B62 8 A7
Marsden Rd B98 70 E3
Marsh Ave WR4 116 A5
Marsh Cl WR14 139 B2
Marsh End B38 35 A8
Marsh Gr DY10 27 E8
Marsh Way B61 31 F1
Marsham Rd B14 20 F3
Marshfield Cl B98 71 B7
Marshwood Croft B62 9 A3
Marston Cl DY8 5 D4
Marston Rd B29 18 F8
Mart La DY13 44 A3
Marten Croft WR5 128 F5
Martin Ave WR11 161 A2
Martin Cl
Bromsgrove B61 48 E1
Great Malvern WR14 139 C1
Martin's Orch WR13 166 A8
Martindale Cl WR4 116 B6
Martindale Wlk DY5 6 B6
Martingale Cl 4 B60 67 E6
Martins Cnr CV37 151 A5
Martins Way DY13 43 F3
Martley CE Prim Sch
WR6 99 B4
Martley Cl B98 90 B7
Martley Croft B32 9 E4
Martley Ct DY9 6 C4
Martley Dr DY9 6 C4
Martley Rd
Broadheath WR2 114 E5
Great Witley WR6 80 B7
Stourport-on-Severn
DY13 62 D8
Mary Vale Rd B30 19 F6
Maryland Dr B31 19 B5
Maryland Rd DY5 6 F7
Marylebone Cl DY8 6 A7
Maryman's Rd WR11 161 B2
Maryvale WR15 55 D4
Marywell Cl B32 18 B7
Masefield Cl WR3 115 C6
Masefield Gdns 1 DY10 28 B6
Masefield Rise B62 8 D3
Masefield Sq B31 19 C4
Mashie Gdns B38 19 D1
Maslen Pl B63 8 B3
Mason Cl
Bidford-on-Avon B50 136 E5
Great Malvern WR14 139 B3
Redditch B97 89 D7
Mason La B94 36 F1
Mason Rd
Kidderminster DY11 27 C6
Redditch B97 89 D8
Masonleys Rd B31 18 D3
Masons Cl B63 7 C6
Masons Dr WR4 115 F6
Masons Ryde 11 WR10 158 D8
Masshouse La B38 19 F1
Masters Cl 2 WR11 161 E3
Masters La B62 8 E8
Matchborough Ctr B98 71 E1
Matchborough Way
B98 71 E1
Math Mdw B32 9 F5
Mathon Rd
Great Malvern WR14 138 C1
Mathon WR13 152 A6
Matravers Rd WR14 139 B2
Matthew La (Road 3)
DY10 27 F1
Matthias Cl WR14 139 A5
Maughan St DY5 7 A8
Maund Cl B60 67 E7
Maund St WR2 114 E4
Maurice Rd B14 20 E5
Mavis Gdns B68 9 B8
Mavis Rd B31 18 E1
Mawley Hall★ DY14 22 F3
Max Rd B32 9 D5
Maxstoke Cl
Birmingham B32 18 A7
Redditch B98 71 D1
May Ave WR4 115 E4
May Farm Cl B47 36 A6
May La Birmingham B14 20 F5
Hollywood B47 36 A7
May Tree Hill WR9 104 A8
May Trees B47 35 F6
Mayalls The GL20 183 F6
Maybank WR14 139 C3
Mayberry Cl
Birmingham B14 21 B2
5 Stourport-on-Severn
DY13 43 E4
Maycroft WR11 161 B2
Mayfair
1 Evesham WR11 161 D2
Stourbridge DY9 6 D2
Mayfield Ave WR3 115 C5
Mayfield Cl Catshill B61 31 F1
Kidderminster DY11 27 A8
Mayfield Ct DY11 27 C7
Mayfield Rd
Birmingham, Stirchley
B30 20 A6
Great Malvern WR14 139 C2
Halesowen, Hasbury B63 7 E2
Pershore WR10 144 D2
Worcester WR3 115 D5
Mayfields The B98 70 E2
Mayflower Cl
4 Great Malvern WR14 153 B8
2 Stourport-on-Severn
DY13 44 A2
Mayflower Rd WR9 85 B2
Mayford Gr B13 21 B6
Mayhurst Cl B47 36 C6
Mayhurst Rd B47 36 B6
Maynard Ave DY8 5 D3
Maypole Cl
Bewdley DY12 26 C3
Blackheath B64 7 B8
Maypole Dr DY8 5 E5
Maypole Fields B63 7 A7
Maypole Gr B14 21 B2
Maypole Hill B63 7 A7
Maypole La B14 21 A2
Mayswood Gr B32 9 D4
Maytree Rd WR10 145 D3
McConnell Cl B60 68 B7
McCormick Ave 2 WR4 116 C3
McIntyre Rd WR2 114 F2
McNaught Pl 12 WR1 115 B4
Meaburn Cl B29 19 A7
Mead The WR2 114 E4
Meadfoot Ave B14 20 F3
Meadow Brook Rd B31 18 F5
Meadow Cl
Kempsey WR5 141 C6
Kington WR7 119 E4
Tewkesbury GL20 197 A8
Meadow Croft
Hagley DY9 14 F4
Wythall B47 36 A3
Meadow Ct WR5 141 B7
Meadow Gn WR5 110 F6
Meadow Gn Prim Sch
B47 36 A3
Meadow Hill Cl DY11 27 A5
Meadow Hill Rd B38 19 E2
Meadow La B48 51 B6

Meadow Mill WR15 .....55 F3
Meadow Mills Ind Est DY10 ....27 E5
Meadow Rd
Birmingham, Quinton B32 ...9 A6
Catshill B61 ....48 F8
Droitwich WR9 ....84 E4
Great Malvern WR14 ...139 A2
Halesowen B62 ....8 C8
Honeybourne WR11 .....163 D8
Worcester WR3 ....102 B1
Wythall B47 ....36 A3
Meadow Rise
Bewdley DY12 ....26 D5
Birmingham B30 ....19 E7
2 Tenbury Wells WR15 ...55 F6
Meadow St B64 ....7 F8
Meadow View
Birmingham B13 ....21 C8
9 Stourport-on-Severn DY13 ....62 E8
Meadow Way WR9 ......84 D5
Meadow Wlk
Birmingham B14 ....20 E1
Blackheath B64 ....7 D8
4 Colwall Stone WR13 ..152 B2
Meadowbank Dr WR2 ..114 D1
Meadowbrook Cl WV15 ..1 C5
Meadowbrook Rd B63 ....7 E3
Meadowfield Rd B45 ....33 A6
Meadowhill Cres B98 ...70 F5
Meadowhill Rd B98 .....70 F5
Meadowpark Rd DY8 ....5 D8
Meadows End WR11 ...161 B3
Meadows Fst Sch B61 ...49 A3
Meadows Prim Sch The B31 ....18 E1
Meadows The
Bidford-on-Avon B50 ..136 C4
Stourbridge DY9 ....15 B7
Meadowsweet Ave B38 ..34 E6
Meadowsweet Pl DY10 ..28 D7
Meadowvale Rd B60 ....49 C6
Meadvale Rd B45 ....33 B6
Meadway The B97 ......70 C1
Mears Coppice DY5 .....6 E6
Mearse La
Barnt Green B45 ....33 A1
Belbroughton DY9 ......31 B6
Cookhill WR7 ....108 E2
Meaton Gr B32 ....18 B8
Meaton La DY14 ....23 E8
Meddins Cl 1 DY7 ......4 A4
Meddins La DY7 ....3 F4
Meddins Rise DY7 ....3 F4
Medici Rd B60 ....49 C2
Medway Gr B38 ....34 E8
Medway Rd
Evesham WR11 ....161 F3
Worcester WR5 ....115 E2
Meer End B38 ....34 D7
Meeting House La B31 ..19 A4
Meir Rd B98 ....90 C8
Melbourne Ave B61 ....48 E4
Melbourne Cl B61 .....48 E3
Melbourne Rd
Bromsgrove B61 ....48 E3
Halesowen B63 ....8 B5
Melbourne 7 WR3 ....115 B6
Melbury Gr B14 ....20 E5
Melchett Rd B30 ....20 A4
Melen St B97 ....70 D4
Melfort Gr B14 ....21 A3
Melrose Ave DY8 ....6 A2
Melrose Cl
Birmingham B38 ....19 F1
Worcester WR2 ......114 F3
Melstock Rd B14 ....20 D7
Melton Rd B14 ....20 F8
Melzer House DY7 .....27 E7
Mendip Cl
Bromsgrove B61 ....49 A5
Great Malvern WR14 ..139 B1
Mendip Cl Kenwood Ave WR4 ....115 F4
Mendip House B98 .....71 D6
Mendip Rd
Halesowen B63 ....7 D1
Stourbridge DY8 ....6 B6
Menin Cres B13 ....21 B7
Menin Rd B13 ....21 B8
Menston Cl WR4 ......116 A4
Menteith Cl DY13 .....43 E7
Meon Rd GL55 ....165 E5
Meon Rise DY9 ....6 C3
Mercia Cl B60 ....67 F7
Mercot Cl B98 ....90 A6
Mere Hall* WR9 .....105 E8
Mere Rd DY8 ....5 E3
Merebrook WR14 .....166 F3
Meredith Gn DY11 ....27 A1
Meres Rd B63 ....7 C5
Merevale Cl B98 ....90 D8
Merganser Way DY10 ..28 B3
Merick Rd WR14 .....139 C4
Meriden Ave DY8 ....5 D6
Meriden Cl Redditch B98 ..72 A3
Stourbridge DY8 ....5 D6
Meridian Pl B60 ....49 A1
Merino Ave B31 ....34 A8
Merlin Dr DY10 ....28 B3
Merrick Cl B63 ....7 D2
Merricks Cl 1 DY12 ...25 F3
Merricks La 7 DY12 ..25 F3
Merriemont Dr B45 ....33 A1
Merrill Gdns B60 .....32 D2
Merriman's Ct 1 WR3 .115 C5

Merriman's Hill Rd WR3 ....115 C5
Merriman's Wlk 5 WR3 115 C5
Merrishaw Rd B31 .....34 A8
Merritt's Brook La B31 ..18 C5
Merritts Brook Cl B29 ..19 A5
Merritts Hill B31 ......18 E6
Merry La WR11 ....148 D1
Merrybrook WR11 ....161 A4
Merryfield WR10 .....160 E8
Merse Rd B98 ....71 E6
Mersey Gr B38 ....34 E8
Mersey Rd WR5 ......115 E2
Merstow Gn 5 WR11 .161 C4
Merstow Pl 4 WR11 ..161 C4
Merton Cl
4 Bewdley DY12 .....25 F4
Kidderminster DY10 ..28 B7
Worcester WR4 ......115 E3
Merton Rd B32 ....139 A4
Michael Cres WR14 ..138 F5
Michaelwood Cl B97 ..69 F2
Michelle Cl B13 ....21 A5
Mickleton Cl B98 .....89 E7
Mickleton Prim Sch GL55 ....165 D4
Mickleton Rd GL55 ..164 D5
Middle Acre Rd B32 ...9 E2
Middle Dr B45 ....33 D4
Middle Field Rd B31 ..19 D2
Middle Hollow Dr WR4 ....116 A3
Middle House Dr B60 ..32 D1
Middle La
Cropthorne WR10 ....160 B6
Hadzor WR9 ....104 C7
Wythall B38 ....35 D5
Middle Leasowe B32 ...9 A4
Middle Mdw Ave B32 ..9 C5
Middle Piece Dr WR4 ..70 B1
Middle Pk Cl B29 .....19 B8
Middle Pk Rd B29 ....19 C8
Middle Rd
Stock & Bradley B96 .106 E3
Upper Bentley B60 ...69 A2
Wildmoor B61 ....31 F4
Worcester WR4 ......114 F1
Middle St WR1 ......115 C3
Middlefield Gdns B62 ..8 F8
Middlefield House B14 ..20 F2
Middlefield La DY9 ...15 B6
Middlefield Rd B60 ...68 B7
Middlehill Rise B32 ....9 D3
Middlehouse La WR7 ..70 E6
Middlemore Cl B80 ...90 D4
Middlemore Rd B31 ..19 B3
Middles Ave WR4 ....116 B4
Middleton Cl B98 .....71 F2
Middleton Gdns
Birmingham B30 ......19 D4
1 Worcester WR4 ...116 B5
Middleton Grange B30 ....19 E4
Middleton Hall B30 ..19 E4
Middleton Hall Rd B30 ..19 E4
Middleton Rd
Birmingham B14 ......20 F7
Bromsgrove B61 ......48 F4
Kidderminster DY11 ..12 C1
Middletown B80 ......90 D1
Middletown La B96, B80 ....90 D1
Middletree Rd B63 ....7 C7
Midhurst Cl 1 WR5 ..128 E8
Midhurst Rd B30 .....20 B3
Midland Rd
Birmingham B30 .....19 F5
Worcester WR5 ......115 D1
Midsummer Hill (fort)* HR8 ....179 C8
Midsummer Mdw WR7 ....120 F6
Midvale Dr B14 ....20 D2
Mikado Rd B60 ....49 D1
Milcote Cl B98 ....90 A7
Milcote Rd B29 ....19 A8
Mile Post La B96 .....108 B5
Milebrook Gr B32 ....18 B8
Milestone Dr DY9 ....14 F4
Milestone Rd WR14 ..168 F4
Milford Ave 4 DY13 ..43 E6
Milford Cl B97 ....89 C6
Milford Rd B14 ....20 E8
Milhill Rd B98 ....71 E1
Mill Ave W12 ....190 D1
Mill Bank
Evesham WR11 ......161 F4
Fladbury WR10 ......146 B1
Mill Cl
Bidford-on-Avon B50 .136 B7
Blakedown DY10 .....14 B2
Bromsgrove B60 .....67 F6
Hollywood B47 ......36 A1
4 Stourport-on-Severn DY13 ....44 B4
Mill Fields DY7 ....4 B3
Mill Gdns B14 ....21 D5
Mill La Aldington WR11 162 C5
Badsey WR11 ....162 D2
Bidford-on-Avon B50 .136 B7
Birmingham, Northfield B31 ....19 A2
Birmingham, Woodgate Valley B32 ....9 E2
Blakedown DY10 .....14 B2
Bromsgrove B61 .....48 F2
Cleeve Prior WR11 ..149 A8
Colwall Stone WR13 .166 A8

Mill La continued
Dodderhill WR9 ......66 E1
Drakes Broughton & Wadborough WR8 ..143 C5
Earlswood B94 ....53 D8
Eckington WR10 .....171 D6
Elmley Castle WR10 ..173 C4
Feckenham B96 .....107 D8
Halesowen B63 ....8 C4
Kidderminster, Blakebrook DY11 ....27 D6
Kidderminster, Hoobrook DY10 ....27 F2
Kinver DY7 ....4 B3
Knighton on Teme WR15 .57 C7
Lindridge WR15 ......59 A4
Malvern WR14 ......153 D6
Mickleton GL55 .....165 D4
Offenham WR11 .....162 B7
Pershore WR10 .....144 D2
Redmarley D'abitot GL19 192 F4
Rous Lench WR7 ....120 D3
Staunton GL19 .....193 A2
Stourport-on-Severn DY13 ....44 B4
Strensham WR8 .....171 C3
Wildmoor B61 ....31 F3
Wolverley & Cookley DY11 ....12 D2
Wythall B47, B94 ....36 B1
Mill La WR10 ....144 C3
Mill Lodge Prim Sch B90 ....21 E2
Mill Mound* WR11 ..164 A4
Mill Pleck B80 ....90 E3
Mill Pool Cl DY9 ......15 A4
Mill Pool Pl DY14 .....22 D5
Mill Race La DY8 ......6 A4
Mill Rd Blackheath B64 ..7 E7
Evesham WR11 .....161 B2
Stourport-on-Severn DY13 ....44 B4
Mill St Evesham WR11 161 B4
Halesowen B63 ....7 C7
Kidderminster DY11 ..27 D6
Redditch B97 ....70 D4
Tewkesbury GL20 ...196 B6
Worcester WR5 .....115 C1
Mill Wlk The B31 .....18 F1
Mill Wood Dr WR4 ..116 B4
Millbank Cotts WR11 ..27 D6
Millbrook Cl WR3 ...115 A7
Millbrook Ct B62 ......8 A7
Millbrook Dr B31 .....33 E8
Millbrook Rd B14 ....20 C6
Millbrook Way DY5 ...6 B8
Millcroft Cl B32 ......9 E2
Milldale Cl DY10 .....27 E8
Millend WR10 ....173 D6
Millennium Cl 2 GL20 197 A4
Miller Cl B60 ....67 E6
Miller St WR9 ....84 F3
Miller's Ct Rd WR13 .180 D5
Millers Bank B50 ....136 B7
Millers Cl 12 WR4 ...115 F6
Millers Ct
1 Kidderminster DY11 .27 D6
Solihull B90 ....21 F2
Millers Gn WR4 ......60 F4
Millfield Birmingham B31 ..19 A4
Elmley Castle WR10 .173 E7
Hinton on the Green WR11 ....175 B2
Millfield Gdns 2 DY11 ..27 D6
Millfield Rd B61 ......48 E1
Millfield View B61 .....7 E4
Millhams Rd WR4 ...116 B5
Millhaven Ave B30 ...20 B6
Millmead Rd B32 .....9 E1
Millpool Gdns B14 ...20 F3
Millpool Hill B14 .....20 F4
Millrace Rd B98 ......70 E5
Millridge Way DY11 ..64 E8
Mills Cl WR12 ....190 D8
Millsborough Rd B98 ..70 F8
Millside B28 ....21 F5
Milne Pastures GL20 .197 C7
Milner Way B13 ......21 D8
Milret Cl 2 WR5 ....115 C5
Milston Cl B14 ....20 E1
Milton
Kidderminster DY11 ..27 A6
Redditch B97 ....89 C8
Worcester WR5 .....115 C6
Milton Dr DY9 ....15 D7
Milton House B63 .....7 B5
Milton Rd B61 ....49 A8
Milverton Cl B63 ......8 A6
Milverton Ct 3 B62 ...9 A7
Milward Sq 8 B97 ....70 E3
Mimosa Cl B29 ....19 B7
Minett Ave WR2 ....127 B8
Minge La WR8 ......169 C5
Minley Ave B17 ....9 F7
Minster Rd 5 DY13 ..44 A4
Minster Wlk B61 .....48 E8
Minter Ave WR9 .....84 F2
Minton Mews B60 ...68 B8
Minton Rd B32 ....9 F4
Minworth Cl B97 .....70 B2
Miranda Cl B45 ......18 A2
Mitcheldean Cl B98 ..89 E7
Mitcheldean Covert B14 ....20 D2
Mitre Cl B61 ....49 A3
Mitre Rd DY9 ....6 C5
Mitten Ave B45 ......18 A1

Mitton Cl DY13 ....44 A4
Mitton Gdns DY13 ....44 A3
Mitton Manor Prim Sch GL20 ....197 A8
Mitton St DY13 ....44 A4
Mitton Way GL20 ...197 A8
Moat Bank GL20 .....181 F5
Moat Coppice B62 .....9 A1
Moat Cres WR14 ....139 D1
Moat Farm Dr B32 ....9 A1
Moat Farm La WR14 132 F3
Moat House Ct B80 ...90 F8
Moat Mdws B32 ....9 A1
Moatfield Mid Sch B98 71 E1
Moatway WR14 .....139 C1
Moatway The B38 .....34 E7
Modbury Ave B32 .....9 D1
Moffit Way 13 DY13 ..43 E4
Mogul La B63 ....7 A7
Moira Cres B14 ....21 C4
Monarch Dr WR2 ...114 E6
Monarch Pl 7 WR2 ..114 E6
Monckton Rd B68 .....9 A7
Money La B61 ....32 A7
Mongcroft Rd WR10 158 F1
Monk Way B30 ....90 D4
Monks Cl 4 WR10 ..158 D8
Monks Dr B80 ....90 D4
Monks La GL20 .....197 E3
Monks Path B97 .....69 F4
Monks Way WR10 ..131 B2
Monksfield La WR2 ..126 E1
Monkshood Retreat B38 ....34 F8
Monksway B38 ....20 B1
Monkswood Rd B31 ..19 C2
Monkwood Nature Reserve* WR6 ....100 E6
Monmouth Rd
Birmingham B32 .....18 D8
Smethwick B67 ....9 A8
Monnow Cl
Droitwich WR9 ......103 A8
Great Malvern WR14 .153 D8
Monsell La WR8 ....169 A4
Monsieurs Hall La B61 .48 A3
Monterey Rd 3 GL20 197 A8
Montfort St WR11 ...161 E4
Montfort Wlk B32 .....9 A2
Montgomerie WR2 ..127 B2
Montgomery Cl B61 ..32 A1
Montgomery Cres DY5 ..6 F7
Montpelier Rd WR14 138 C1
Montreal Cl WR2 ...127 E6
Monument Ave DY9 ...6 E4
Monument La
Barnt Green B45 .....32 F4
Hagley DY9 ....15 D7
Monyhull Hall Rd B30 .20 C3
Monyhull Hospl B14 ..20 D3
Moons Moat Dr B98 ..71 E5
Moons Moat Fst Sch B98 ....71 D5
Moons Pk B98 ....71 E6
Moor Hall Dr DY9 ...16 A1
Moor Hill Dr 5 DY13 ..43 F4
Moor House B14 .....20 C2
Moor Leasow B31 ....19 C2
Moor St WR1 ....115 B3
Moorcroft Cl B97 ....89 B6
Moorcroft Gdns B97 ..89 B6
Moorend Rd GL19 ..193 F1
Moorfield Dr
Bromsgrove B61 .....48 F3
Halesowen B63 ....8 A5
Moorfoot Ave B63 .....7 F2
Moorgate Cl B98 .....71 E6
Moorgate Rd B60 ....68 A2
Moorhall La DY13 ....43 E3
Moorlands Rd WR14 138 F2
Moorlands The WR14 152 F2
Moorpark Rd B31 ....19 A1
Moors Ave DY11 .....45 B2
Moors Croft B32 ......9 B1
Moors La
Birmingham B31 .....18 E7
Feckenham B96 .....107 E7
Moors The WR11 ...115 A4
Moorside Rd B14 .....21 D3
Moorsom Way B60 ...68 B7
Moray Cl B62 ....8 E8
Mordiford Cl B98 .....89 E7
Moreland Rd WR9 ...84 E2
Morelands The B31 ..19 B1
Morella Cl 13 DY12 ..25 F3
Moreton B32 ....9 F5
Moreton La GL20 ...184 F7
Moreton Pl 1 WR1 ..115 B2
Morgan Cl B80 ....90 F2
Morillon Ct DY10 ....28 A1
Morlich Rise DY5 ......6 B8
Morning Pines DY9 ...5 E4
Morningside WR15 ...55 F6
Morrin Cl WR3 ......102 B1
Morris Ave WR3 ....115 B4
Morris Field Croft B28 .21 E4
Morris Rd WR12 ....190 D6
Morris Wlk B60 ......67 E8
Morsefield La B98 ....71 D1
Mortimer Gdns 5 DY14 .22 C4
Mortimer Gr DY12 ..26 C4
Mortimers Cl B14 ...21 B1
Mortimers Quay 2 WR11 ....161 E4
Mortlake Ave WR5 ..128 F8
Mortlake Dr WR6 .....99 A4
Morton Ave WR3 ....102 B2
Morton Hall La B96 .107 F3

Morton House B97 ....70 A3
Morton La B97 ....89 B7
Morton Rd
Brierley Hill DY5 ......6 D7
Fernhill Heath WR3 ..102 E2
Harvington DY10 ....29 B2
Morvale Ct DY9 ....6 E5
Morvale Gdns DY9 ....6 E5
Morvale St DY9 ....6 E5
Mosel Dr WR9 ......103 D8
Moseley Rd WR2 ...101 B3
Moss Gr B14 ....20 D6
Moss La Beoley B98 ..71 F8
Mappleborough Green B98 ....72 A7
Moss La Cl B98 ......71 F8
Mossfield Rd B14 ....20 F7
Mostyn Rd DY13 ....43 E6
Moulder Rd GL20 ...197 A6
Moule Cl DY11 ....27 C6
Mounds The B38 .....34 E8
Moundsley Gr B14 ...21 A3
Moundsley House B14 .20 F2
Mount Carmel RC Fst Sch B97 ....70 A2
Mount La B14 ....15 E4
Mount Orch 4 WR15 .55 E4
Mount Pleasant
Pershore WR10 .....144 D2
Redditch B97 ....70 D2
3 Tenbury Wells WR15 55 F4
Mount Pleasant Barns 1 WR10 ....144 D2
Mount Pleasant La DY13 ....63 F4
Mount Rd
Evesham WR11 .....161 F3
Fairfield B61 ....31 C2
Stourbridge, Stambermill DY8 ....6 B5
Mount St Halesowen B63 .8 A3
Redditch B98 ....70 E3
Stourbridge DY8 ......6 B5
Mount Vernon Dr B61 .49 A5
Mountain Ash Dr DY9 ..6 C4
Mountbatten Rd WR14 ....139 C2
Mountfield Cl B14 ...21 A2
Mountford Rd B90 ...21 D1
Mountserrat Rd B60 .49 B1
Mouse La DY11 ......27 B8
Mousehall Farm Rd DY5 .6 D7
Mousesweet Wlk B64 ..7 B8
Mowbray Ave GL20 .196 F3
Mowbray Cl B45 .....18 A2
Moyle Dr B63 ....7 B7
Mucklow Hill B62 .....8 D5
Mucklow Hill Trad Est B62 ....8 C5
Muirfield Gdns B38 ..19 D1
Mulberry Dr
Great Malvern WR14 .152 F4
Upton upon Severn WR8 168 F5
Mulberry Rd B30 .....19 C5
Mulberry Terr WR4 .115 C4
Mulberry Tree Hill WR9 ....104 A8
Mull Cl B45 ....17 E1
Mullion Croft B38 ...19 E1
Munro Cl DY10 ......28 C6
Munsley Cl B98 ......71 F2
Munslow Gr B31 .....33 F8
Murcot Rd WR12 ...176 D4
Murcroft Rd DY9 .....6 E1
Murren Ave WR14 ..153 A4
Mus of Worcester Porcelain The* WR1 ....115 B1
Museum of Local Life* WR1 ....115 C2
Musket Cl 14 GL20 .197 A4
Musketts Ct B97 .....70 B2
Muskoka DY12 ....25 F3
Myatt Gr WR11 .....148 A1
Myatt's Field WR11 .148 A7
Mynors Cres B47 ....36 A6
Myrtle Ave
Birmingham, Highter's Heath B14 ....20 F2
Redditch B98 ....70 E2
Mythe Rd GL20 .....196 E8
Myton Dr B90 ....21 D1
Mytton Rd B30 ......19 C5

N

Nafford Gr B14 ......20 F2
Nafford Rd WR10 ...171 F8
Nailers Cl Birmingham B32 18 D7
Stoke Heath B60 ....67 E6
Nailers Ct 3 B60 .....48 F2
Nailsworth Cl 9 WR4 115 F7
Nailsworth Rd B98 ...70 F2
Nairn Cl Birmingham B28 .21 F5
Redditch B98 ....71 E4
Nantmel Gr B32 .....18 C8
Napleton La WR5 ...141 D6
Napton Cl B98 ....71 D1
Napton Gr B29 ....9 F2
Narrow La B62 ....8 E8
Narrow Wlk 11 WR2 .114 F1
Narrows The GL55 ..178 E2
Naseby Cl B98 ....71 D6
Naseby Dr B63 ....7 D2
Naseby House 4 B14 .21 A3

Nash Cl Martley WR6 . . . .99 A4
Worcester WR3 . . . . .102 A1
Nash Ct (School) SY8 . .37 A4
Nash Gn WR13 . . . . .126 A2
Nash La DY9 . . . . .30 D7
Nash Rd B98 . . . . .71 B1
Nashe Cl DY10 . . . . .28 C5
Naunton Cl B29 . . . . . . .19 A7
Navenby Cl B90 . . . . . . .21 C3
Navigation Rd WR5 . . . .128 B7
Naylor Cl DY11 . . . . .27 B3
Near Lands Cl B32 . . . . . .9 B4
Near Oak House B32 . .18 D8
Nearhill Rd B38 . . . . . . .34 C8
Neason Cl **8** WR4 . . . .116 B4
Needle Cl B80 . . . . .90 E4
Needle Mill La B98 . . . .70 E6
Neigh La WR10 . . . . .160 C7
Nelson Rd
Stourport-on-Severn
  DY13 . . . . .44 B1
Worcester WR2 . . . . . . .114 F2
Nelson St **6** GL20 . . . .196 E6
Nene Cl DY8 . . . . .6 A5
Nesfield Cl B38 . . . . . . .19 C1
Nestor House B13 . . . .21 D7
Netheravon Cl B14 . . . .20 D1
Nethercote Gdns B90 . .21 A1
Netherdale Rd B14 . . . .21 A1
Netherend Cl B63 . . . . . .7 A7
Netherend La B63 . . . . . .7 B7
Netherfield Sq B63 . . . . .7 A7
Netherfield B98 . . . . . . .90 A8
Netherley La
Berrow WR13 . . . . .180 B1
Pendock GL19 . . . . .193 B8
Netherton La
Bewdley DY12 . . . . .26 C2
Netherton WR10 . . . . . .173 F7
  8 Worcester WR1 . . .115 B3
Netherton Rd
Astley & Dunley DY13 . .62 A8
Rock DY13 . . . . .61 E7
Netherwood La
Crowle WR9 . . . . .117 D8
Oddingley WR9 . . . . . . .104 D1
Netley House B32 . . . . . .9 F5
Neville Ave DY11 . . . . . .27 D3
Neville Cl B98 . . . . .71 A5
Neville Ct
Birmingham B13 . . . . . .20 F6
Kidderminster DY11 . . . .27 D3
Neville Rd Solihull B90 . .36 F8
Tewkesbury GL20 . . . . .196 F5
New Bank St WR3 . . . . .115 B6
New Bldgs B63 . . . . .7 A7
New Chawson La WR9 . .84 C1
New England B62 . . . . . . .8 E7
New Farm Cl DY9 . . . . . . .6 C4
New Forest Cl DY14 . . .24 C2
New Inn La
Salford Priors WR11 . . .135 C2
Shrawley WR6 . . . . .62 D1
New Inns La B45 . . . . . .17 E1
New John St B62 . . . . . . .8 C8
New Mdw Cl B31 . . . . . .19 B2
New Mdw Rd B98 . . . . .71 B3
New Pool Rd B64 . . . . . . .7 B8
New Rd
Astwood Bank B96 . . . . .89 E1
Bewdley DY12 . . . . .26 D5
Birmingham B45 . . . . . . .32 F7
Bromsgrove B60 . . . . . . .49 A1
Bromsgrove, Sidemoor
  B61 . . . . .48 E3
Castlemorton WR13 . . .166 F1
Cleobury Mortimer DY14 . .22 D5
Doverdale WR9 . . . . .64 F3
Eckington WR10 . . . . . .171 E8
Evesham WR11 . . . . . . .161 B3
Fairfield B61 . . . . .31 E2
Halesowen B63 . . . . .8 B4
Hanley WR6 . . . . .58 C1
Hollywood B47 . . . . .36 A8
Kidderminster DY10 . . . .27 E5
Offenham WR11 . . . . . .162 B8
Pebworth CV37 . . . . . . .150 E2
Pershore WR10 . . . . . . .158 C8
Rock DY14 . . . . .24 B2
Stourbridge DY8 . . . . . . .6 A5
Studley B80 . . . . .90 E3
Wolverley & Cookley
  DY11 . . . . .13 B7
Worcester WR2 . . . . . . .115 A2
New Rd Est WR6 . . . . .124 A3
New St
Birmingham, Frankley
  B45 . . . . .18 A1
Bretforton WR11 . . . . . .163 C5
Brierley Hill DY5 . . . . . . .7 A8
Childswickham WR12 . .176 A1
Stourbridge DY8 . . . . . . .5 F5
Stourport-on-Severn DY13 . .43 F3
Upton upon Severn WR8 .169 C6
Worcester WR1 . . . . . . .115 C2
New Wharf Cotts B60 . .69 B7
New Wlk **3** B97 . . . . .70 E4
New Wood Cl DY7 . . . . . .5 C8
New Wood Dr B31 . . . . .18 D1
New Wood La DY10 . . . .29 B8
Newall House B97 . . . . .70 D2
Newark Gn WR4 . . . . . .116 D6
Newbold Ct B63 . . . . . . .8 B3

Newborough Gr B28,
  B90 . . . . .21 F3
Newborough Rd B28 . . .21 F4
Newbourne Hill B48 . . .51 E4
Newburn Croft B32 . . . . .9 B5
Newbury Cl Catshill B61 . .32 B1
Halesowen B62 . . . . .8 D3
Newbury Rd WR2 . . . . .114 F2
Newcastle Cl **3** WR5 . .115 F1
Newent Cl B98 . . . . .72 A3
Newent Rd B31 . . . . . . .19 C4
Newey Cl B45 . . . . .33 A6
Newey Rd B28 . . . . .21 F6
Neweys Hill WR3 . . . . .115 A7
Newfield Cres B63 . . . . . .8 A5
Newfield Gdns DY9 . . . .15 A4
Newfield La B63 . . . . .8 B5
Newfield Pk Prim Sch
  B63 . . . . .8 A5
Newfield Pl DY9 . . . . . . .15 A4
Newfield Rd DY9 . . . . . .15 A4
Newhouse La B61 . . . . .66 D8
Newick Gr B14 . . . . .20 C4
Newland B98 . . . . .90 B7
Newland Comm Rd
  WR9 . . . . .104 A5
Newland Cres WR2 . . . .127 D8
Newland Dr WR9 . . . . . .84 F1
Newland Gdns B64 . . . . . .7 E7
Newland Rd WR9 . . . . . .84 F1
Newlands WR10 . . . . . .158 C8
Newlands Cl DY11 . . . . .27 C7
Newlands Dr B62 . . . . . . .8 E7
Newlands Rd B30 . . . . . .20 C7
Newlands The B80 . . . . .90 D3
Newlyn Rd
Birmingham B31 . . . . . .18 F3
Blackheath B64 . . . . .7 D8
Newman Coll Cl B32 . . .18 C8
Newman Coll of Higher Ed
  B32 . . . . .18 C8
Newman Way B45 . . . . .33 A6
Newport Cl B97 . . . . . . .89 B6
Newport St **3** WR1 . . .115 B2
Newton Cl
  5 Bewdley DY12 . . . .25 F4
Crowle WR7 . . . . .117 F4
Redditch B98 . . . . .90 A6
Newton Rd WR9 . . . . . .68 A7
Newton Works B60 . . . .68 A6
Newtown Hospl WR5 . .116 B2
Newtown La
Romsley B62 . . . . .17 D2
Wildmoor B62 . . . . .31 D8
Newtown Rd
Great Malvern WR14 . . .138 E3
Worcester WR4 . . . . . . .115 D3
Nibletts Hill B61 . . . . . .48 B7
Nibley Cl **11** WR4 . . . .115 F7
Nigel Ave B31 . . . . .19 A5
Nightingale Ave WR4 . .116 C3
Nightingale Cl WR9 . . .104 B7
Nightingale Cres DY5 . . .6 D7
Nightingale Dr DY10 . . .28 B2
Nightingale La WR11 . . .144 B8
Nightingale Rd WR14 . .139 C2
Nimmings Cl B31 . . . . . .33 F6
Nimmings Rd B62 . . . . . .8 D8
Nina Cl DY13 . . . . .44 B3
Nine Acres Gn **6** WR4 .116 B4
Nine Days La B98 . . . . . .90 B6
Ninesquares **3** WR10 . .171 E7
Nixon Ct WR2 . . . . .140 F8
No Man's Gn La DY7 . . . .2 F6
Noble View WR14 . . . . .138 D3
Nodbury Hill WR7 . . . . .120 F6
Node Hill B80 . . . . .90 D3
Node Hill Cl B80 . . . . . .90 D3
Noel Ct B97 . . . . .89 C8
Nogains WR10 . . . . .158 D7
Nonsuch Prim Sch B32 . .9 D2
Noonan Cl B97 . . . . .70 B2
Norbury Cl B98 . . . . .71 B7
Norchard La WR10 . . . .131 B1
Norfolk Cl
Birmingham B30 . . . . . .20 B6
Worcester WR2 . . . . . . .114 C3
Norfolk Cl **6** B29 . . . . .19 C7
Norfolk House B30 . . . .20 A3
Norfolk Rd
Birmingham B45 . . . . . .17 F2
Oldbury B68 . . . . .9 B7
Stourbridge DY8 . . . . . . .5 D8
Norgrove La B97 . . . . . .88 D6
Norham Pl WR4 . . . . . .116 C6
Norlan Dr B14 . . . . .20 F3
Norley Gr B13 . . . . .21 C7
Norman Ave B32 . . . . . . .9 E7
Norman Cl
Twyning GL20 . . . . .183 F6
  5 Worcester WR4 . . .116 B6
Norman Rd B31 . . . . . . .19 B3
Norrington Gr B31 . . . . .18 C3
Norrington Rd B31 . . . .18 D3
North Bromsgrove High Sch
  B60 . . . . .49 B3
North Croft WR4 . . . . . .127 E8
North E Worcestershire Coll
  (Bromsgrove Campus)
  B60 . . . . .49 B3
North E Worcestershire Coll
  (Redditch Campus)
  B98 . . . . .70 E4
North End La WR9 . . . . .19 B3
North Hill Gdns WR14 . .138 E3
North Malvern Rd
  WR14 . . . . .138 E2

North Rd
Bromsgrove B60 . . . . . . .49 A2
Evesham WR11 . . . . . . .161 F4
Stourport-on-Severn
  DY13 . . . . .44 A5
North St WR9 . . . . .84 F3
North Wlk
Birmingham B31 . . . . . .19 C1
Malvern WR14 . . . . . . .138 E2
Northampton La WR9 . .82 F7
Northbrook Cl WR3 . . . .115 B6
Northcliffe Hts DY11 . . .27 C7
Northcote St **12** WR3 . .115 B6
Northfield Children's Farm★
  B31 . . . . .18 C4
Northfield Cl
Fernhill Heath WR3 . . . .102 F3
Redditch B98 . . . . .71 D6
Northfield Manor Jun & Inf
  Sch B29 . . . . .19 B7
Northfield Rd B30 . . . . .19 E4
Northfield Sta WR1 . . . .115 C4
Northfield Sta B31 . . . . .19 B2
Northgate B64 . . . . .7 D8
Northgate Cl DY11 . . . . .27 A4
Northleach Ave B14 . . . .20 D2
Northleach Cl
Redditch B98 . . . . .71 B5
  1 Worcester WR4 . . .115 F7
Northleigh CE Prim Sch
  WR14 . . . . .138 D4
Northside B98 . . . . .89 E7
Northumberland Ave
  DY11 . . . . .27 D3
Northway La GL20 . . . . .184 D1
Northwick Ave WR3 . . .115 A6
Northwick Cl WR3 . . . . .115 A7
Northwick Manor Jun & Inf
  Sch WR3 . . . . .115 A7
Northwick Rd
Evesham WR11 . . . . . . .161 E4
Worcester WR3 . . . . . . .102 A1
Northwick Wlk WR3 . . .115 A7
Northwood Halt Sta
  DY12 . . . . .25 F7
Northwood La DY11 . . . .10 F1
Northwood Way DY5 . . . .6 B8
Norton Cl
Birmingham B31 . . . . . .19 A3
Redditch B98 . . . . .71 F2
Worcester WR5 . . . . . . .128 C6
Norton Gate B38 . . . . . .19 C1
Norton Juxta Kempsey CE Fst
  Sch WR5 . . . . .129 C1
Norton La B47, B90,
  B94 . . . . .36 E3
Norton Mews B61 . . . . .49 A4
Norton Rd
Kempsey WR5 . . . . .128 E4
Kidderminster DY10 . . . .28 B6
Stourbridge DY8 . . . . . . .5 E2
Norton Terr B30 . . . . . . .20 B6
Norton View
Birmingham B14 . . . . . .20 D7
Mickleton GL55 . . . . . . .165 D3
Nortune Cl B38 . . . . . . .19 D2
Norval Rd WR14 . . . . . .163 C8
Norwich Ave B64 . . . . . . .7 E7
Norwich Dr B17 . . . . .9 F8
Norwich Rd WR5 . . . . .115 F2
Norwood Ave B64 . . . . . .7 E7
Nuffield Cl B31 . . . . . . .18 E2
Nuffield Dr WR9 . . . . . .84 C3
Nunnery Ave WR9 . . . . .84 E2
Nunnery La
  5 Worcester WR5 . . .115 F1
Worcester WR5 . . . . . . .129 A8
Nunnery Way WR5 . . . .116 C1
Nunnery Wood High Sch
  WR5 . . . . .116 A1
Nunnery Wood Nature
  Reserve★ WR5 . . . . . .116 B2
Nunnery Wood Prim Sch
  WR5 . . . . .115 F1
Nursery Cl
Birmingham B30 . . . . . .19 F5
Hagley DY9 . . . . .15 A4
Kidderminster DY11 . . . .27 B8
Mickleton GL55 . . . . . . .165 F5
  2 Pershore WR10 . . .144 D1
Nursery Dr B30 . . . . . . .19 F5
Nursery Gdns B90 . . . . .36 E8
Nursery Gr
  5 Kidderminster DY11 . .12 B1
Kidderminster DY11 . . . .27 B8
Nursery Rd
Bewdley DY12 . . . . .26 B4
Birmingham B30 . . . . . .19 E5
Great Malvern WR14 . . .138 D4
Worcester WR2 . . . . . . .127 E8
Nursery Wlk **15** WR2 . .114 F1
Nut Orch La GL20 . . . . .183 F7
Nutbush Dr B31 . . . . . . .18 D6
Nutfield Wlk B32 . . . . . . .9 F5
Nutgrove Cl B14 . . . . . . .20 F7
Nuthatch Dr DY5 . . . . . . .6 C7
Nuthurst Gr B14 . . . . . . .20 F2
Nuthurst Rd B31 . . . . . .33 F6

O

Oak Apple Cl DY13 . . . .62 E7
Oak Apple Rd B61 . . . . .49 B8
Oak Ave
Madresfield WR13 . . . . .139 F4
Worcester WR4 . . . . . . .115 E5
Oak Barn Rd B62 . . . . . . .8 E8

Oak Bridge Ct WR15 . . . .55 F3
Oak Cl Badsey WR11 . . .162 E4
Kinver DY7 . . . . .4 C3
Oak Cotts B14 . . . . .21 C2
Oak Cres WR14 . . . . . . .139 C1
Oak Ct Halesowen B63 . . .7 C1
Stourbridge DY8 . . . . . . .6 A4
Oak Dr
  6 Colwall Stone WR13 . .152 B2
Hartlebury WR9 . . . . . . .64 E8
Northway GL20 . . . . . . .197 D8
Oak Farm Rd B30 . . . . .19 E5
Oak Gdns GL20 . . . . . . .184 F6
Oak Gr Birmingham B31 . .18 E1
Kidderminster DY10 . . . .28 A5
Oak Hill Fst Sch B98 . . .71 A2
Oak La GL20 . . . . .184 E6
Oak Leasow B32 . . . . . . .9 B4
Oak Pk Ind Est DY10 . . .45 C2
Oak Rd Catshill B61 . . . .49 B8
Oldbury B68 . . . . .9 C7
Oak St WR8 . . . . .169 C5
Oak Tree Ave B97 . . . . . .70 B4
Oak Tree Cl
  6 Evesham WR11 . . . .161 F2
  4 Tenbury Wells WR15 . .55 F5
Oak Tree Cres B62 . . . . . .8 F6
Oak Tree Dr WR9 . . . . . .65 B5
Oak Tree House B30 . . . .19 E7
Oak Tree La
Birmingham B29 . . . . . .19 E8
Cookhill B49 . . . . .109 A2
Hollywood B47 . . . . .36 B6
Sambourne B96 . . . . . . .90 B2
Oak Tree Pk B30 . . . . . .71 F6
Oak Tree Rd WR11 . . . .147 F1
Oak Trees B47 . . . . .36 A7
Oak Wlk The B31 . . . . . .19 A1
Oakalls Ave B60 . . . . . . .49 B2
Oakcroft B13 . . . . .21 C7
Oakden Pl DY11 . . . . . . .27 C7
Oakdene DY13 . . . . .44 B3
Oakdene Dr B45 . . . . . . .50 C8
Oakenshaw Rd B98 . . . .71 A1
Oakfield Cl WR5 . . . . . .141 D6
Oakfield Dr
Birmingham B45 . . . . . .33 D4
Kempsey WR5 . . . . .141 C6
Oakfield Rd
Great Malvern WR14 . . .139 A4
Kidderminster DY11 . . . .27 B5
Ombersley WR9 . . . . . . .83 A5
Stourbridge, Wollescote
  DY9 . . . . .6 F2
Oakham Cl B98 . . . . . . .90 A5
Oakham Dr WR9 . . . . . .84 C2
Oakham House **7** B14 . .21 A3
Oakham Pl WR9 . . . . . . .84 C2
Oakhampton Rd DY13 . .62 E8
Oakhill Ave DY10 . . . . . .27 E4
Oakhill Dr DY5 . . . . .6 B7
Oakhill Infants Sch
  WR11 . . . . .187 F5
Oakhurst Dr B60 . . . . . .49 A3
Oakland Ave WR9 . . . . .84 E1
Oakland Cl WR8 . . . . . .168 F5
Oakland Gr B61 . . . . . . .49 B4
Oaklands
Birmingham, Northfield
  B31 . . . . .18 F4
Great Malvern WR14 . . .152 E1
Halesowen B62 . . . . .9 A4
Worcester WR5 . . . . . . .116 B3
Oaklands The
  1 Droitwich WR9 . . . .103 F8
Halesowen B62 . . . . .8 F6
Kidderminster DY11 . . . .28 A7
Oaklands Way B31 . . . . .18 C1
Oakleaf Cl B32 . . . . .9 C2
Oakleaf Rise DY14 . . . . .24 C2
Oakleigh B31 . . . . .19 C2
Oakleigh Ave WR2 . . . .101 C2
Oakleigh Heath WR2 . .101 C2
Oakleigh Rd
  2 Droitwich WR9 . . . .84 C1
Stourbridge DY8 . . . . . . .6 B2
Oakley House B60 . . . . .49 A1
Oakley Rd B30 . . . . .20 B5
Oakly Rd B97 . . . . .70 D3
Oakridge Cl
Redditch B98 . . . . .71 C7
  2 Worcester WR4 . . .116 A7
Oaks The
Birmingham, Hawkesley
  B38 . . . . .34 F7
  1 Kempsey WR5 . . . .141 C6
Stoke Bliss WR15 . . . . . .75 F3
Oaktree Cl B48 . . . . .51 A7
Oaktree Farm Mobile Homes
  Pk B94 . . . . .53 B7
Oakwood Ct B63 . . . . . . .8 A4
Oakwood Dr B14 . . . . . .20 D4
Oakwood Rd
  9 Bewdley DY12 . . . .25 F3
  2 Bewdley DY12 . . . .25 F3
Hollywood B47 . . . . .36 A6
Oasis The DY9 . . . . .15 F5
Oasthouse Cl B60 . . . . .67 D6
Oat St WR11 . . . . .161 D4
Oatlands Wlk **3** B14 . . .20 C2
Oatsley La WR10 . . . . . .171 F7
Oberon Cl B45 . . . . .18 A2
Ockam Croft B31 . . . . . .19 C2
Oddingley Rd B31 . . . . .19 C2
Odnall La DY9 . . . . .15 F3
Offenham CE Fst Sch
  WR11 . . . . .148 A1
Offenham Cl B98 . . . . . .71 B6

Offenham Covert B38 . .34 E8
Offenham Rd **4** WR11 . .161 F1
Offerton La WR3 . . . . . .103 F1
Offley St WR3 . . . . .115 B6
Offmoor Rd B32 . . . . . . .18 B8
Offmore Cr DY10 . . . . . .28 C6
Offmore Farm Cl DY10 . .28 C6
Offmore Fst Sch DY10 . .28 B6
Offmore La DY10 . . . . . .28 A6
Offmore Rd DY10 . . . . . .27 F6
Offwell Rd B98 . . . . .71 D1
Ogbury Cl B14 . . . . .20 C2
Ogilvy Sq WR3 . . . . . . .115 A8
O'key's La WR3 . . . . . . .103 A2
Old Bakery Ct DY9 . . . . .15 A5
Old Bank Top B31 . . . . .19 B2
Old Barn Rd B30 . . . . . .19 D6
Old Birmingham Rd
Alvechurch B48 . . . . . . .51 B8
Catshill B60 . . . . .49 C8
Marlbrook B60, B45 . . . .32 E1
Old Bowling Gn Cl
  WR15 . . . . .55 E6
Old Chawson La **4** WR9 .84 C1
Old Chester Rd S DY10 . .27 E2
Old Church Rd WR13 . . .152 A2
Old Coach Rd WR9 . . . . .84 E2
Old Cres Ct **9** B68 . . . . .9 B8
Old Crest Ave B98 . . . . .70 E2
Old Crown Cl B32 . . . . . .9 B1
Old Dr The WR3 . . . . . . .103 C2
Old Farm Gr B14 . . . . . .21 D5
Old Forge Rd WR6 . . . . .110 F6
Old Forge Bsns Ctr
  B98 . . . . .90 C8
Old Forge Dr B98 . . . . . .90 C8
Old Forge Gdns **4** DY11 . .45 B2
Old Forge Trad Est DY9 . .6 E6
Old Glebe Pastures
  WR10 . . . . .131 B1
Old Gr Gdns DY9 . . . . . . .6 D1
Old Hall Cl
Aston Somerville WR12 . .175 E1
Stourbridge DY8 . . . . . . .6 A8
Old Ham La DY9 . . . . . . .6 D2
Old Hawne La B63 . . . . . .8 A5
Old Hill WR7 . . . . .119 D2
Old Hill Sta B64 . . . . . . .8 A8
Old Hollow WR14 . . . . .138 C3
Old Hospl La GL20 . . . .196 F6
Old House La B62 . . . . . .17 B1
Old La B48 . . . . .52 C4
Old Lime Gdns B38 . . . .34 E8
Old Malvern Rd WR2 . . .127 C3
Old Manor Cl WR10 . . . .145 C3
Old Manor Gdns GL55 . .165 E4
Old Manor La GL20 . . . .197 A8
Old Mdw Rd B31 . . . . . .34 F8
Old Mill Cl B90 . . . . .21 D2
Old Moat Dr B31 . . . . . .19 B3
Old Northwick La
  WR3 . . . . .114 F8
Old Oak Rd B38 . . . . . . .20 A2
Old Orch WR8 . . . . .169 A5
Old Pk B29 . . . . .19 A5
Old Portway B38 . . . . . .34 E7
Old Post Office La
  WR11 . . . . .162 E3
Old Quarry Cl B45 . . . . .32 F8
Old Rd
Clifton upon Teme WR6 . .97 F7
Powick WR2 . . . . .127 F5
Old Rd N WR5 . . . . .141 C7
Old Rd S WR5 . . . . .141 B5
Old Rectory Cl WR2 . . .127 E3
Old Rectory Gn WR10 . .146 B1
Old Rectory La B48 . . . .51 B7
Old Sch Cl WR11 . . . . . .148 A1
Old Sch La WR15 . . . . . .55 F6
Old St WR8 . . . . .169 C5
Old Sta Rd B60 . . . . . . .49 A1
Old Stone Cl B45 . . . . . .17 F1
Old Stratford Rd B60 . . .49 C2
Old Swinford CE Prim Sch
  DY8 . . . . .6 A3
Old Town Cl B38 . . . . . .19 F2
Old Turnpike Rd WR7 . .117 F6
Old Vicarage Cl **3** WR5 . .141 C6
Old Vicarage Gdns B80 . .90 E4
Old Wharf Rd DY8 . . . . . .5 F6
Old Woodyard The DY9 . .15 D3
Old Wyche Rd WR14 . . .152 E5
Oldacre Rd B68 . . . . .9 A7
Oldbury Cl B98 . . . . .71 B6
Oldbury Pk Prim Sch
  WR2 . . . . .114 F3
Oldbury Rd
Broadheath WR2 . . . . . .114 B4
Tewkesbury GL20 . . . . .196 E6
Worcester WR2 . . . . . . .114 C3
Oldfield GL20 . . . . .196 F6
Oldfield Dr DY8 . . . . .6 A3
Oldfield La WR9 . . . . . . .83 C7
Oldfields Blackheath B64 . .7 D8
Hagley DY9 . . . . .15 A4
Oldhouse Farm Cl B28 . .21 F6
Oldington La DY11 . . . . .44 B8
Oldington Trad Est
  DY11 . . . . .27 B1
Oldnall Cl DY9 . . . . .6 F1
Oldnall Rd
Kidderminster DY10 . . . .28 A4
Stourbridge B63, DY9 . . .7 A4
Oldswinford Hospl Sch
  DY8 . . . . .6 A4
Oldwood Rd WR15 . . . . .55 D1
Olive Dr B62 . . . . .8 C8
Olive Gr DY13 . . . . .43 F4

Olive Hill Prim Sch B62 ....8 D7
Olive Hill Rd B62 ......8 D8
Olive La B62 ....8 D8
Olive Pl B14 ....20 E7
Olliver Cl B62 ....9 A3
Olympus Gdns DY13 ....44 C3
Ombersley Cl B98 ......90 C7
Ombersley Endowed Fst Sch
WR9 ....83 B4
Ombersley Pk★ WR9 .83 A3
Ombersley Rd
Droitwich WR9 .....84 C3
Halesowen B63 ......7 F2
Worcester WR3 ....102 A1
Ombersley St E 4 WR9 .84 E3
Ombersley St W WR9 .84 E3
Ombersley Way WR9 ..84 D2
Ongrils Cl WR10 ....144 C1
Ontario Cl
Birmingham B38 .....35 A8
Worcester WR2 ....127 E6
Open Field Cl B31 ...19 C2
Orangery The DY9 ...15 D7
Orchard Ave WR12 ..190 E8
Orchard Cl
Bidford-on-Avon B50 .136 D5
Bredon GL20 ......185 A6
Bretforton WR11 ...163 C4
Earl's Croome WR8 ..155 F1
Hagley DY9 ....15 B4
Halesowen B63 ......7 C6
Hallow WR2 ......101 D1
Mickleton GL55 ....165 E5
3 Pershore WR10 ..158 C8
Rock DY14 ....41 F6
Ryall WR8 ....169 E6
Severn Stoke WR8 ..155 D6
3 Stourport-on-Severn
DY13 ....44 B4
Worcester WR2 ....127 B8
Orchard Cres B60 ....67 C3
Orchard Croft B45 ...50 D8
Orchard Ct 5 GL20 ..196 F6
Orchard Dr
Birmingham B31 .....33 F7
Little Comberton WR10 .159 A3
Twyning GL20 .....184 A6
Orchard End DY14 ....22 C5
Orchard Gdns WR6 ..77 E3
Orchard Gr
Cookhill B96 ....108 E7
Cookley DY11 ......13 A6
Kinver DY7 ....4 B4
Norton Juxta Kempsey
WR5 ....129 D1
Orchard Holmes WV15 .1 C6
Orchard Lea The 7 WR9 .85 A1
Orchard Mead WR7 ..120 E7
Orchard Pl
Harvington WR11 ...147 F7
Redditch B80 ......90 F8
Orchard Rd
Bromsgrove B61 .....48 F4
4 Great Malvern WR14 .152 F8
Pershore WR10 ....158 C8
Wolverley & Cookley
DY10 ....13 C4
Orchard Ridge GL20 .181 F5
Orchard Rise
Bewdley DY12 ......26 A3
Droitwich WR9 .....103 E8
Orchard St
Kidderminster DY10 ..27 E6
Redditch B98 ......70 E3
Worcester WR5 ....128 C3
Orchard The
Bewdley DY12 ......25 E3
Bowling Green WR2 .127 C3
Bromsgrove B61 .....48 E4
Orchard Villas
Fairfield B61 ......31 D2
Wythall B47 ......35 F1
Orchard Way
Bransford WR6 .....126 C5
Callow End WR2 ....140 F7
Hollywood B47 .....36 A8
Studley B80 ....90 E2
Orchardlea WR10 ...132 A5
Orchards The
Astwood Bank B96 ...89 D1
Hollywood B47 .....36 A7
2 Kidderminster DY11 .12 B1
Orcheston Wlk B14 ..20 D2
Orchid Cl WR5 .....128 C4
Orford Way WR14 ..139 C1
Oriel Cl WR4 ......115 E3
Oriole Gr DY10 .....28 B2
Orleans Cl 1 WR11 ..161 D1
Orleton Cl B63 ......7 C4
Orleton La WR15 .....58 F4
Ormande Cl B63 .....7 E3
Orme Cl DY5 ....6 B8
Ormond Rd B45 .....17 F1
Ormscliffe Rd B45 ...33 B6
Orwell Cl DY5 ......6 F8
Orwell Dr B38 ......34 C8
Orwin Gn 1 WR4 ...116 B3
Osborne Cl
Brierley Hill DY5 .....6 F8
Kidderminster DY10 ..28 B6
Osborne Rd WR14 ..139 A3
Osier Cl WR5 ......128 C2
Osmaston Rd DY8 ....5 F2
Osmington Gr B63 ...7 D6
Osnor Ct B60 ....68 B7
Osprey Cl WR2 ....128 A6
Osprey House B80 ...90 D4
Osprey Pk Dr DY10 ..28 B3

Ostler Dr WR2 ......114 E3
Oswald St B98 ......70 E3
Oswestry Cl B97 .....89 C7
Other Rd B98 ......70 E4
Otherton La WR11 ...113 E1
Otley Cl WR4 ......116 A3
Ottawa Cl WR2 ....127 E7
Otter Cl B98 ....72 A3
Otter La WR5 ......128 E1
Ottilie Hild Sch B60 .67 E5
Oulton Cl DY11 .....12 D1
Ounty John La DY8 ...6 A1
Our Lady & Kenelm RC Sch
B63 ....8 A4
**Our Lady of Fatima RC Prim
Sch** B17 ....9 C7
**Our Lady of Lourdes RC Prim
Sch** B13 ....21 D5
**Our Lady Queen of Peace RC
Prim Sch** WR4 ....114 F1
Out Wood Dr B31 ...18 D1
Outfields B13 ......20 E6
Outwood Cl B98 ....89 E6
Over Brunton Cl B31 .19 B2
Overbrook WR11 ...161 E3
Overbury CE Fst Sch
GL20 ....185 D2
Overbury Cl
Birmingham B31 ....19 C3
Halesowen B63 ......8 B2
Overbury Rd B31 ...19 C3
Overdale B96 ......89 E1
Overdale Rd B32 ....9 E5
Overend Rd B63, B64 ..7 C5
Overfield Rd B32 .....9 F1
Owens Croft B38 ....20 A1
Owlets End B50 ....136 F3
Owletts End 4 B61 .161 E3
Owletts La
Pershore/Pinvin WR10 .144 F7
Wick WR10 ......159 B7
Owlhill La WR9 .....63 E2
Ox Leasow B32 ......9 C2
Oxbow Way DY10 ...27 E8
Oxenton Croft B63 ...7 D2
Oxford Cl WR5 ....115 D1
Oxford Ct 8 B29 ....19 C7
Oxford Dr DY8 ......5 F4
Oxford St
Birmingham, Stirchley
B30 ....20 A7
Kidderminster DY10 ..27 E5
Oxhill Cl B98 ......71 E4
Oxhill Rd B90 ......21 C2
Oxleasow Rd B98 ...71 E4
Oxley Gr B29 ......19 A8
Oxwood La B32 ....17 D4

P

Packers Hill WR8 ...169 A5
Packhorse Cl WR2 ..114 E3
Packhorse La B38, B47 .35 E6
Packington Rd
Droitwich WR9 .....84 E2
3 Worcester WR2 ..114 E1
Packs Cl WR11 .....162 D4
Packwood Cl B97 ...69 F1
Packwood Rd 1 B29 ..9 F1
Padbury House B18 .18 D5
Paddock Cl
Bidford-on-Avon B50 .136 C5
Pershore WR10 ....144 C4
Paddock La B98 ....89 E7
Paddock The
Birmingham B31 ...19 C4
Stoke Heath B60 ...67 D6
Stourbridge DY9 ...15 C8
Paddock Way DY9 ..84 D5
Paddocks Rd B47 ...35 F6
Paddocks The
Cleobury Mortimer DY14 .22 C5
Norton & Lenchwick
WR11 ....147 C3
Padgets La B98 .....71 D4
Padgewell Hill 1 WR9 .84 D1
Padmore Cl WR1 ...115 C3
Padua Rd B13 ......21 C5
Page's La GL20 ....183 D5
Paget Cl B61 ......48 E2
Pagnall Gr B13 .....21 C6
Painswick Cl
Redditch B98 ......89 E6
Worcester WR4 ....116 A7
Painswick Rd B28 ...21 F7
Pakefield Rd B30 ...20 C3
Palfrey Rd DY8 ......5 D5
Palm Croft DY5 .....6 C8
Palm Rd GL20 .....197 A4
Palmcourt Ave B28 .21 E7
Palmers Gn
13 Worcester WR2 ..114 F1
2 Worcester WR2 ..114 E1
Palmers Rd B98 ....71 F5
Palmyra Rd B60 ...49 C2
Pamela Rd B31 ....19 A3
Paper Mill Cotts B97 .69 E5
Paper Mill Dr B98 ...71 B5
Paper Mill La WR9 ..66 E2
Papworth Dr B61 ...48 F5
Par Gn B38 ....19 D1
Parade The B64 ....7 E8
Paradise Ct B28 ...21 E6
Paradise La B28 ...21 E6
Paradise Row B60 ..48 F2
Pargeter St DY8 .....5 F4
Parish Gdns DY9 ....6 C1

Parish Hill B61 .....31 D1
Park Ave
Birmingham, King's Norton
B30 ....20 A5
Stourport-on-Severn DY13 .43 F4
Studley B80 ....90 E3
Worcester WR3 ....115 A6
Park Butts Ringway
DY11 ....27 D6
Park Cl Bewdley DY12 .26 B8
Great Malvern WR14 .139 B4
Northway GL20 ....184 D1
Park Cres DY13 .....43 F4
Park Croft B47 .....36 A5
Park Ct
Kidderminster DY11 ..27 D5
Redditch B98 ......71 A3
Park Dingle DY12 ...25 E2
Park Farm Ind Est B98 .90 C7
Park Gate Rd DY10 ..13 B2
Park Hall Mews WR1 .135 D4
Park La Bewdley DY12 .25 E2
Halesowen B63 ......7 B6
Hallow WR2 ......114 D8
Harvington WR10 ...29 A2
Kidderminster DY11 ..27 D6
Rushock WR9 ......46 D2
Upper Sapey WR6 ...78 C5
West Malvern WR14 .152 C6
Worcester WR3 ....115 A5
Park Rd Brierley Hill DY5 ..6 F8
Great Malvern WR14 .152 E4
Hagley DY9 ....15 B6
Halesowen B63 ......7 B5
Park Rd W DY8 .....5 D5
Park Ridge Dr B63 ..7 B6
Park Rise DY11 .....27 D5
Park Row
Kidderminster DY11 ..27 D5
Stourbridge, Lye DY9 ..6 F5
Stourbridge, Stambermill
DY8 ....6 A5
Stourbridge, Amblecote
DY8 ....5 F8
Park St Gdns DY11 .27 D6
Park The
Northway GL20 ....184 D1
Redditch B97 ......69 C7
Park View B49 ...122 F6
Park View Rd
Birmingham B31 ...18 F3
Stourbridge DY9 ....6 F4
Park View Terr WR3 .115 A6
Park Way
Birmingham B45 ...33 B8
Droitwich WR9 .....84 D4
Redditch B98 ......71 A5
Park Wlk Brierley Hill DY5 .6 F8
4 Redditch B97 ...70 E2
Parkbrook Ind Est 5 DY9 .6 F5
Parkdale Cl B31 ....34 A7
Parker House B14 ..20 F3
Parker Pl
Broadway WR12 ...190 D8
Kidderminster DY13 ..44 C7
Parkes Pas 2 DY13 ..44 A3
Parkes Quay 1 DY13 .44 A3
Parkfield B32 ......9 A2
Parkfield Cl
Halesowen B62 .....9 A5
Hartlebury DY11 ...45 A2
Redditch B98 ......71 B6
Parkfield La WR2 ..114 D7
Parkfield Rd DY8 ....6 B5
Parkland Ave DY11 ..27 B5
Parkland Rd 2 WR3 .102 A1
Parklands Cl B97 ...70 A5
Parklands The
3 Droitwich WR9 ..103 F8
Stourbridge DY9 ....6 D3
Parks The WR11 ...162 A6
Parkside Birmingham B32 .9 C2
Colwall WR13 .....152 B1
Parkside Mid Sch B61 .49 A3
Parkside Way B31 ...18 C1
Parkstone Ave B61 ..67 D8
Parkview Fst Est B38 .19 F3
Parkwood WR10 ...173 E2
Parkwood Rd B61 ..48 E3
Parlows End B38 ...34 D7
Parmington Cl B97 ..89 B6
Parry Rd WR1 .....27 B3
Parsonage Dr
Birmingham B45 ...33 D4
Halesowen B63 ......7 A7
Parsonage La WR9 ..82 F4
Parsonage Way WR4 .116 D5
Parson's Hill B30 ...20 B2
Parsons La
Hartlebury DY11 ...44 F1
Redmarley D'abitot GL19 .192 E3
Weston-sub-Edge GL55 .178 D6
Parsons Rd B98 ....70 E2
Partons Rd B14 ....20 D6
Partridge Cl 3 WR5 .128 D5
Partridge Gr DY10 ..28 A2
Partridge House B97 .70 D2
Partridge La
Broadheath WR2 ...114 A6
Redditch B97 ......89 A7
Partridge Rd DY8 ....5 C4
Pass St WR10 .....171 E8
Pastures Wlk B38 ...34 D7
Pat Davis Ct DY10 ..27 E7

Patch La B98 ......89 F6
Paternoster Row 4
DY11 ....27 D6
Pathway The B14 ...20 C5
Patios The DY11 ....27 C7
Patricia Ave B14 ....21 C4
Patterdale Dr WR4 .116 A5
Patterdale Way DY5 ..6 B8
Pavilion Gdns B61 ..48 F5
Paxford Cl B98 .....71 B6
Paxford Way B31 ...18 C6
Paxhill La GL20 ....183 F7
Paxton Cl B60 .....49 B1
Paxton Rd DY9 .....7 A4
Paynes La WR4 ....146 A1
Peabody Ave WR4 ..116 C4
Peach Cl 1 GL20 ...197 A3
Peach Ley Rd B29 ..18 F7
Peachfield Cl WR14 .152 F5
Peachfield Rd WR14 .152 E5
Peachley Cl 8 B63 ..8 B3
Peachley Gdns WR2 .113 F7
Peachley La WR2 ..113 F8
Peacock Cl 8 WR5 .128 E5
Peacock Mews WR3 .27 E8
Peacock Rd B13 ....20 F6
Peak Rd DY8 ......6 B6
Peakman Cl B45 ....33 A6
Peakman St B98 ....70 E4
Pear Orch The 2 GL20 .184 E1
Pear Tree Cl
Great Malvern WR14 .152 E4
Kidderminster DY10 ..28 B7
Solihull B90 ......21 D2
Pear Tree Cres B90 .21 C2
Pear Tree Dr
Leigh WR13 ......126 A2
Sedgeberrow WR11 .175 A1
Pear Tree Gr B90 ...21 D2
Pear Tree Way
Crowle WR7 ......117 E4
2 Dodderhill WR9 ..66 E1
Pearl La DY13 .....43 D1
Pearmain Cl WR2 ..114 E6
Pearman Rd B45 ...17 D1
Pearmans Croft B47 .36 A6
Pearson St DY9 ......6 F4
Peart Dr B80 ......90 C4
Peartree Dr DY8 .....6 A2
Peason La WR10 ...171 D8
Pebble Cl DY8 ......6 B5
Pebworth Cl B98 ...90 B7
Pebworth Ct DY11 ..71 C7
Pebworth Fst Sch
CV37 ....150 E2
Peckingham St 2 B63 .8 B3
Pedmore CE Prim Sch
DY9 ....6 C1
Pedmore Cl B98 ....90 B7
Pedmore Ct Rd DY9 .15 B7
Pedmore Hall La DY9 .15 C8
Pedmore La Hagley DY9 .15 F8
Stourbridge DY9 ....6 E1
Pedmore Rd DY9 ....6 D5
Peel St DY11 ......27 D5
Peel Wlk B17 ......9 F7
Peewit Rd WR11 ...161 B2
Pegasus Ct B62 .....8 F5
Pegleg Wlk 2 B14 ..20 C2
Pelham Lodge DY10 .28 A5
Pelham Rd WR9 ...103 E8
Pemberton Cres DY10 .13 C3
Pembridge Cl
Birmingham B32 ...18 A7
Redditch B98 ......71 C7
Pembroke Ave WR15 .55 F5
Pembroke Pl WR4 ..116 D5
Pembroke Way DY13 .43 E6
Penbury St WR3 ...115 B7
Pendeen Rd B14 ...21 C4
Pendennis Cl B30 ..19 D5
Pendock CE Prim Sch
GL19 ....193 B7
Pendragon Cl WR14 .139 C3
Penelope Gdns WR11 .176 D8
Penfields Rd DY9 ....6 B6
Penhill Cres WR2 ..114 D3
Peninsula Rd WR5 .129 A4
Penlu Rd 7 WR15 ..55 F6
Penmanor B60 .....68 D8
Penmanor Cl WR2 .114 E2
Penn Hall La WR6 ..59 E7
Penn La B94 ......53 C4
Pennard Gr B32 .....9 F4
Pennine Rd B61 ...49 A5
Pennine Way DY8 ...6 A1
Penny Cl WR13 ....154 A7
Penny La WR13 ....154 A7
Pennyacre Rd B14 ..20 D2
Pennyfold Cl B97 ...70 A5
Pennylands Bank
WR12 ....177 A2
Penrice Rd WR9 ....84 E1
Penrith Cl
Brierley Hill DY5 .....6 B8
Worcester WR4 ....116 A6
Penrith Croft B32 ...18 D8
Pensax CE Prim Sch
WR6 ....60 A6
Pensax Rd Pensax WR6 .60 A5
Stockton on Teme WR6 .59 F3
Pensby Cl B13 .....21 D8
Pensford Rd B31 ...19 C3
Pensham Hill WR10 .158 E6
Penshurst Rd B60 ..49 C1
Penstock Ct DY10 ..28 C8
Penzer Dr B45 .....50 D8
Peplins Way DY8 ....6 A3
Pepper Hill DY8 ....6 A4

Oli - Pig **219**

Pepper St WR7 ....120 F6
Pepper Wood Dr B31 .18 C1
Pepperpot★ WR8 ..169 C6
Pepperwood Cl B61 .31 C2
Perch Rd WR5 .....128 C5
Percheron Way
7 Droitwich WR9 ...85 B1
Droitwich WR9 ....104 B8
Perdiswell Leisure Ctr
WR3 ....115 D7
Perdiswell Prim Sch
WR3 ....115 D7
Perdiswell St WR3 .115 B7
Peregrine Gr DY10 ..28 A2
Perivale Way DY8 ...6 A8
Perkins Cl WR11 ...135 D4
Perrett Wlk 5 DY11 .27 D6
Perrie Dr WR11 ...164 B5
Perrin Ave WR11 ...27 B4
Perrins Cl WR14 ..138 E4
Perrins Field WR8 .168 F5
Perrins La DY9 ......6 F4
Perrins Rise DY9 ....6 F4
Perry Ct B68 ....9 B7
Perry Hill Cres B68 ..9 B7
Perry Hill House B68 .9 C8
Perry Hill La B68 ...9 B7
Perry Hill Rd B68 ...9 B7
Perry La Bromsgrove B61 .48 F2
Hartlebury DY10 ...45 B5
Perry Mill Rd 2 WR10 .131 C2
Perry Wood Cl WR5 .115 E1
Perry Wood Wlk WR5 .115 E1
Perrycroft Cl WR3 .102 F3
Perryfields Cl B98 ..89 F6
Perryfields Cres B61 .48 F5
Perryfields High Sch
B68 ....9 A8
Perryfields Prim Sch
B68 ....9 A7
Perryfields Rd B61 ..48 D4
Perrymill La B96 ...90 B1
Perscoran Way WR10 .158 F6
Pershore & Hindlip Coll
WR10 ....158 F6
Pershore Cottage Hospl
WR10 ....158 C8
Pershore Ct DY11 ..27 D5
Pershore High Sch
WR10 ....144 E3
Pershore La WR3 ..103 D2
Pershore Rd
Birmingham, Breedon Cross
B30 ....20 A5
Birmingham, Ten Acres
B30 ....20 B8
Eckington WR10 ...157 E1
Evesham WR11 ....161 C3
Halesowen B63 ......8 A2
Kidderminster DY11 ..27 A6
Upton Snodsbury WR7 .131 C3
Pershore Rd S B30 ..19 F3
Pershore Sta WR10 .144 E5
Pershore Trad Est
WR10 ....144 E4
Perton Gr B29 .....19 A8
Perwell Cl GL20 ...184 E7
Pestilence La B48 ..51 C8
Peter's Finger B60 ..48 F1
Peter's Hill Prim Sch
DY5 ....6 C7
Peter's Hill Rd DY5 ..6 C6
Peterborough Cl WR5 .115 A6
Peterbrook Cl B98 ..89 F7
Peterbrook Prim Sch
B90 ....21 D2
Peterbrook Rd B90 ..21 D1
Peterbrook Rise B90 .21 D1
Peters Ave B31 ....18 F2
Petersbourne Ct B28 .21 F8
Petersfield Ct B28 ..21 F8
Petersfield Rd B28 ..21 F8
Petland Trad Ctr B98 .71 D4
Pettitt Cl B14 .....20 E2
Petton Cl B98 .....71 E7
Petunia Cl WR5 ...128 C5
Pevensey Cl 9 WR5 .128 E8
Pevensey Rd B60 ...49 C1
Peverell Dr B28 ....21 F7
Pheasant Cl DY10 ..28 A2
Pheasant La B98 ...89 F7
Pheasant St WR1 ..115 C3
Philip Rd Halesowen B63 .7 F3
Worcester WR3 ...102 B1
Philipscote 2 WR11 .161 E4
Phillips Gr GL19 ...192 B3
Phillips Rd WR12 ..177 D1
Phillips Terr B98 ...70 E4
Pickenham Rd B14 .21 A1
Pickering Croft B32 ..9 D1
Pickering Gn 7 WR4 .116 C6
Pickersleigh Ave
WR14 ....139 B4
Pickersleigh Cl
Great Malvern WR14 .139 A4
6 Halesowen B63 ..8 A3
Pickersleigh Gr WR14 .139 B2
Pickersleigh Rd WR14 .139 B1
Picton Gdn The★
WR13 ....152 B3
Picton Cl WR14 ...21 B6
Pierpoint St 4 WR1 .115 B3
Piers Cl WR14 ....153 A5
Pig Pen The★ WR6 .123 A7
Pigeon La GL20 ...186 A8

Pike Cnr 2 WR12 ......177 E4
Pike Hill B60 ....50 A7
Pikes Pool La B60 .....49 E2
Pikes The B45 ....32 F8
Pilgrim Rd WR9 ....85 B2
Pillow Mounds★
 WR12 ....191 C6
Pinchers Cl DY9 ......30 E7
Pine Cl
 Fernhill Heath WR3 .....103 A3
 Kinver DY7 ....4 C3
Pine Ct DY9 ....6 B1
Pine Gr Barnt Green B45 .32 F2
 Birmingham B14 ....21 A5
Pine Tree Cl B97 ....69 F3
Pine Way WR4 ....115 E6
Pine Wlk
 Birmingham B31 ....19 B3
 Stourbridge DY9 ....6 D3
 2 Stourport-on-Severn
 DY13 ....43 E4
Pine Woods B32 ....9 A2
Pineapple Gr B30 ......20 C8
Pineapple Rd B30 ......20 C7
Pinedene DY13 ....44 C3
Pinehurst Dr B38 ......19 F3
Pineridge Dr DY11 .....27 B5
Pines The B45 ....18 A1
Pinetree Rd 1 DY12 ...25 F2
Pineview B31 ....18 F2
Pinewall Ave B38 ......20 A1
Pinewood Cl
 Birmingham, Eachway
 B45 ....32 D8
 1 Kidderminster DY11 ...12 C1
Pinewood Dr B32 ....9 A1
Pinewoods
 Birmingham B31 ....18 F8
 Halesowen B62 ....14 F4
Pinewoods Ave DY9 ....14 F4
Pinewoods Cl DY9 .....14 F4
Pinewoods Ct DY9 .....14 F4
Pinfield Dr B45 ....33 B1
Pink Gn La B98 ....72 B8
Pinkett St WR3 ....115 A7
Pinkham DY14 ....22 D4
Pinkham La DY14 ......22 D5
Pinkus Cl 3 WR4 .....116 C3
Pinner Gr B32 ....9 E4
Pinta Dr DY13 ....44 B3
Pintail Gr DY10 ....28 B3
Pinvin CE Fst Sch
 WR10 ....144 C4
Pinvin House B97 ......70 A3
Pioneer B97 ....70 D4
Piper Pl DY8 ....5 F8
Pipers Cl B61 ....67 D7
Pipers Gn B28 ....21 F5
Pipers Rd B98 ....90 D7
Pipit Cl DY10 ....28 A2
Pippen Field WR4 .....116 C5
Pippin Ave B63 ....7 B7
Pippin Cl 6 B50 ......136 D5
Pippins The 2 WR10 ..171 E7
Pirie Ave WR4 ....116 C3
Pit Leasow Cl B30 .....20 B8
Pitcairn Cl B30 ....20 B6
Pitcairn Dr B62 ....8 B5
Pitchard Cl HR7 ....96 D7
Pitchcroft La WR1 ....115 A5
Pitcheroak Cotts B97 ...70 A4
Pitcheroak Specl Sch
 B97 ....70 B4
Pitchers Hill WR11 ....176 D7
Pitclose Rd B31 ....19 B1
Pitfields Cl B68 ....9 A8
Pitfields Rd B68 ....9 A8
Pitman Rd B32 ....9 C5
Pitmaston Prim Sch
 WR2 ....127 E4
Pitmeadow House B14 ..20 E2
Pitt Ave WR4 ....116 B3
Pitt St DY10 ....13 A1
Pitts La DY10 ....27 E5
Pixham Ferry La WR5 ..141 B5
Plane Tree Cl DY10 .....27 F7
Planetree La B60 ......49 B2
Plantation Cres 5 GL20 184 F6
Plantation Dr WR4 ....116 C5
Plantation Sch WR6 .....82 B3
Platts Cres DY8 ....5 E8
Platts Dr DY8 ....5 F8
Platts Rd DY8 ....5 F8
Playdon Gr B14 ....21 A3
Players Ave WR14 .....159 A5
Pleasant Harbour DY12 .26 B4
Pleasant St DY10 ....27 E7
Pleck House B14 ......20 C1
Pleck The
 Bidford-on-Avon B50 ...136 D4
 Inkberrow WR7 ....120 E8
Pleck Wlk B38 ....20 A1
Plimsoll Gr B32 ....9 C5
Plimsoll St DY11 ....27 D5
Plough Ave B32 ....9 A6
Plough Croft 12 WR4 ..116 B5
Plough La
 Oddingley WR9 ....104 B2
 Rock DY14 ....24 C1
Plough Rd WR9 ....117 A7
Ploughmans Cl 11 WR4 115 F6
Ploughmans Way 1
 WR9 ....84 D5

Ploughmans Wlk B60 ...67 D6
Plover Gr DY10 ....28 B1
Plovers Rise 7 WR5 ...141 C6
Plymouth Cl
 Birmingham B31 ....34 A7
 Redditch B97 ....70 C1
Plymouth Cl B97 ......70 C1
Plymouth Dr B45 ......50 A8
Plymouth Rd
 Barnt Green B45 ....50 A8
 Birmingham B30 ....20 B7
 Redditch B97 ....70 D2
Pochard Cl DY10 ....27 F1
Poden La
 Aston Subedge GL55 ...178 E8
 Honeybourne GL55 .....164 D4
Pointon Way WR9 ......84 C6
Polden Cl B63 ....7 C1
Pole Elm Cl 2 WR2 ...140 F8
Polesworth Cl B98 ......71 D1
Polly Brooks Yd DY9 ....6 E5
Polo Fields DY9 ....6 B1
Pomeroy Rd B32 ....9 C1
Pool Bank B98 ....70 E2
Pool Cl WR10 ....159 B4
Pool Field Ave B31 .....18 E7
Pool Furlong DY9 ......15 E1
Pool Rd Halesowen B63 ..8 B3
 Studley B80 ....90 E4
Poolbrook Prim Sch
 WR14 ....153 D7
Poolbrook Rd WR14 ...153 B5
Poole St DY8 ....5 E4
Pooles Ct DY10 ....27 E7
Poolhead La
 Earlswood B94 ....53 C7
 Tanworth-In-A B94 ......53 E5
Pooltail Wlk B31 ....18 D1
Pope Iron Rd WR1 ....115 A5
Popes La
 Astwood Bank B96 ......89 E2
 Birmingham B30, B31,
 B38 ....19 D3
Poplar Ave
 Birmingham, King's Heath
 B14 ....20 F4
 Worcester WR4 ....115 C6
Poplar Cl Catshill B61 ..48 F8
 7 Evesham WR11 ......161 F2
Poplar Cres DY8 ....5 D3
Poplar Dr B45 ....50 D8
Poplar La B62 ....14 A4
Poplar Piece WR7 .....120 F6
Poplar Rd
 Kidderminster DY11 .....27 C4
 Redditch B97 ....70 A3
 Stourbridge DY8 ....5 E3
 Wichenford WR6 ....99 E5
Poplar Row DY11 ....27 C4
Poplar Trees B47 ......36 C4
Poplars La
 Astwood Bank B96 ......89 A1
 Feckenham B96 ....107 F8
Poplars The
 Badsey WR11 ....162 D3
 Bidford-on-Avon B50 ...136 D5
Poplars Trad Est B80 ...90 D6
Poplarwoods B32 ....9 B2
Popular Ave WR10 ....145 A4
Porlock Cres B31 ....18 D3
Porlock Rd DY8 ....6 A4
Port St WR11 ....161 E4
Portefields Rd WR4 ....115 F4
Porter Rd WR11 ......161 E1
Porters Mill La WR9 ..102 E6
Portersfield Ind Est B64 .7 D8
Portersfield Rd B64 .....7 C8
Portland Cres DY9 ......6 B1
Portland Dr DY9 ....6 B1
Portland Rd
 1 Droitwich WR9 ....85 B2
 Great Malvern WR14 ...138 F1
Portland St WR5 ......115 B1
Portland Wlk WR2 ....115 B1
Portman Rd B13 ....20 F7
Portrush Ave B38 ......19 D1
Portsdown Rd B63 ......7 D2
Portway Pl DY10 ....13 A5
Post Office La
 Bransford WR6 ....126 D6
 Fernhill Heath WR3 ....103 A3
 Kempsey WR5 ....141 D7
 8 Tewkesbury GL20 ...196 E6
Post Office Wlk B96 ...89 E1
Poston Croft B14 ......20 D3
Potters Cl WR4 ....115 F6
Pouk La WR6 ....77 F6
Pound Bank Rd WR14 .139 C1
Pound Cl GL20 ....183 F6
Pound La
 Birmingham B32 ....17 F3
 Mickleton GL55 ....165 D3
 Rock DY14 ....41 C7
Pound Rd B14 ....20 E2
Poverty B96 ....89 E2
Powderham Ave WR4 ..116 C6
Powell Ave B32 ....9 A6
Powell St 7 B63 ....8 B3
Powell's Row WR1 ....115 A1
Power Sta Rd DY13 ....44 B2
Powick Bridge★ WR2 ..127 E5
Powick CE Prim Sch
 WR2 ....127 D3
Powlers Cl DY9 ....6 E2
Powyke Ct Cl WR2 ....127 D3

Pratts La
 Mappleborough Green
 B80 ....91 A8
 Redditch B80 ....90 F7
Preece Cl WR14 ....138 F6
Premier Bsns Ctr 3 DY9 .6 F5
Premier Ct B30 ....20 C3
Prescot Rd DY9 ....6 C3
Prescott Dr WR4 ......116 A8
Prestbury Cl
 Redditch B98 ....72 A3
 6 Redditch WR4 ......115 F7
Presthope Rd B29 ......19 B7
Preston Cl B98 ....71 B6
Prestwich Ave WR5 ...115 F1
Prestwood Dr Kinver DY7 .4 A4
 Stourbridge DY7 ....5 B7
Prestwood Rd
 Birmingham B29 ....19 B8
 Stourton DY7 ....4 E6
Price Rd WR9 ....7 A6
Price St WR3 ....115 B6
Price's La WR8 ....169 C5
Pridzor Rd WR9 ....85 A4
Priest La 6 WR10 ....144 C1
Priest Mdw Cl B96 .....89 D1
Priestfield Rd B97 ......89 E5
Priestley Cl B63 ....7 B6
Primrose Cl
 Blackheath B64 ....7 B8
 Great Malvern WR14 ...153 C7
 Lickey End B60 ....49 C6
Primrose Cres WR5 ...128 C5
Primrose Croft B28 .....21 F5
Primrose Dr 10 WR5 ..128 C5
Primrose Gdns B38 .....34 F8
Primrose Hill B38 ....35 A8
Primrose Hill Prim Sch
 B38 ....34 F8
Primrose La B28 ....21 F5
Primrose Twr B38 ......34 E8
Primrose Woods B32 ....9 B2
Primsland Dr 3 WR9 ...85 B1
Primsland Pl 3 WR9 ..104 A8
Primsland Way WR9 ..103 E8
Prince Andrew Cres
 B45 ....17 E2
Prince Charles Cl B45 ..17 E2
Prince Edward Dr B45 ..17 E2
Prince Edward's Cl
 WR11 ....161 E7
Prince Henry's High Sch
 WR11 ....161 E6
Prince of Wales La B14 .21 C3
Prince Philip Cl B45 ....17 E2
Prince Rd B30 ....20 A3
Prince Rupert Ave
 WR2 ....127 B2
Prince Rupert Rd
 3 Stourport-on-Severn
 DY13 ....43 E2
 16 Worcester WR5 ....115 C2
Prince St B64 ....7 D8
Princes Ave 2 WR9 ...103 F8
Princes Rd DY8 ....5 D3
Princess Anne Dr B45 ..17 E2
Princess Cres B63 ......7 E6
Princess Margaret Ave 6
 WR14 ....139 B5
Princess of Wales Com Hospl
 The B61 ....49 A4
Princess Rd WR11 ....161 E6
Princess Way DY13 ....43 E1
Prior Ave B60 ....67 C3
Prior Cl DY10 ....28 C5
Priors Grange WR11 ..135 E4
Priors Oak B97 ....70 B4
Priors Wlk WR11 .....161 E1
Priory Cl DY8 ....6 B3
Priory Ct Stourbridge DY8 .6 B3
 Studley B80 ....90 E5
Priory Farms 11 WR9 ..84 F3
Priory House B63 ....7 F5
Priory La WR9 ....84 F3
Priory Rd
 Birmingham, Stirchley
 B14 ....20 C7
 Birmingham, Warstock
 B28 ....21 D3
 Dodford B61 ....48 A6
 Great Malvern WR14 ...152 F4
 Halesowen B62 ....8 F4
 Kempsey WR5 ....141 D7
 Worcester WR2 ....127 F8
Priory Sq B80 ....90 E5
Priory The 1 DY13 ....44 A5
Pritchard Cl DY12 .....26 C3
Pritchett Rd B31 ....34 B7
Private Way B45 ....33 C4
Proctors Barn La B98 ..71 B4
Prophets Cl B97 ....70 D3
Prospect Gdns DY8 ......6 A4
Prospect Hill
 Kidderminster DY10 .....27 E6
 Redditch B97 ....70 E4
 Stourbridge DY8 ....6 A4
Prospect La DY10 ......27 E6
Prospect Pl 9 WR5 ...115 C1
Prospect Rd
 Halesowen B62 ....8 C5
 Stourport-on-Severn
 DY13 ....44 B4
Prospect Rd N B98 .....71 A4
Prospect Rd S B98 .....71 A4
Prospect Row DY8 ......6 A3
Prospero Cl B45 ....18 A2
Proud Cross Ringway
 DY11 ....27 C6

Providence Ct B64 ....7 C8
Providence Dr DY9 ......6 E6
Providence Ind Est DY9 ..6 E6
Providence Rd B61 .....48 F3
Providence St
 Stourbridge DY9 ....6 F6
 5 Worcester WR1 ....115 C2
Pry Cl The WR15 ....59 A8
Pry La WR12 ....190 A8
Puckrup La GL20 .....183 C6
Pudford La Martley WR6 ..98 F7
 Shelsley Beauchamp WR6 .79 E1
Pulley La WR9 ....103 E7
Pulley La 4 DY13 .....44 A4
Pump St
 Great Malvern WR14 ...138 E3
 Kidderminster DY10 .....27 C4
 Worcester WR1 ....115 C2
Pumphouse La
 Bentley Pauncefoot B97 ..88 B8
 Blackwell B45, B60 .....49 F7
 Hanbury B60 ....86 E3
 Redditch B97 ....69 D1
Purbeck Cl B63 ....7 D1
Purbeck Croft B32 ......9 F4
Purefoy Rd B13 ....21 C5
Purleigh Ave WR4 ....116 C5
Purliou The WR14 ....152 D5
Purshall Cl B97 ....70 C3
Purshull Gn La
 Elmbridge WR9 ....47 A2
 Upton Warren B61 ......66 B8
Purslow Gr B31 ....19 A1
Putney La B62 ....17 B1
Puxton Dr DY11 ....12 D1
Puxton La DY11 ....27 C7
Pyke Rd GL20 ....197 B7

Q

Quail Pk Dr DY10 ......28 A2
Quantock Cl
 Birmingham B45 ....18 B2
 Halesowen B63 ....7 D2
Quantock Dr DY10 .....28 A6
Quantock Rd DY8 ....6 B6
Quantry La DY9 ....31 F8
Quarrington Gr B14 ....21 A3
Quarry Bank DY11 .....45 A2
Quarry Hill B63 ....7 F2
Quarry House Cl B45 ...17 F1
Quarry La
 Birmingham B31 ....19 A2
 Bromsgrove B61 ....67 D8
 Cleeve Prior WR11 ....149 B7
 Halesowen B63 ....8 A2
Quarry Pk Rd DY8 ......15 A8
Quarry Rd B29 ....19 A8
Quarry The DY10 ......27 F8
Quarry Wlk B45 ....33 F4
Quay La
 Earl's Croome WR8 ....155 F1
 Great Comberton WR10 158 F2
 Hanley Castle WR8 ....169 A8
Quay St
 1 Tewkesbury GL20 ...196 E6
 Worcester WR1 ....115 B2
Quebec Cl WR2 ....127 E6
Queen Elizabeth Dr
 WR10 ....144 D1
Queen Elizabeth Rd
 Birmingham B45 ....17 E2
 Kidderminster DY10 .....28 B5
Queen Margaret Prim Sch
 GL20 ....196 E4
Queen St
 Astwood Bank B96 ......89 E1
 Brierley Hill, Quarry Bank
 DY5 ....7 A8
 Droitwich WR9 ....85 A3
 Halesowen B63 ....8 A4
 Kidderminster DY10 .....27 E7
 Redditch B98 ....27 E7
 Stourbridge, Wollaston DY8 ..5 F6
 Worcester WR1 ....115 C3
Queen St Pas DY5 ......7 A8
Queen's Cl WR14 .....138 E4
Queen's Cotts B97 .....70 B4
Queen's Cres DY8 ......6 A7
Queen's Dr WR14 .....138 E1
Queen's Pk Rd B32 .....9 F6
Queen's Rd
 Evesham WR11 ....161 D5
 Great Malvern WR14 ...138 E3
 Stourbridge DY8 ....6 A7
 Stourport-on-Severn DY13 .43 F1
Queen's Way DY12 .....26 C4
Queens Ave B14 ....20 E8
Queens Dr B30 ....20 A4
Queens Dr The B62 .....8 C5
Queens Hill DY9 ....30 D7
Queens Mead WR8 ....169 C4
Queens Rd GL20 ......196 E6
Queensmead GL20 ....185 A6
Queensway
 2 Bidford-on-Avon B50 136 C5
 Halesowen B63 ....8 B3
 Oldbury B68 ....9 B8
 Stourbridge DY9 ....6 E2
 Wichenford WR6 ....100 B6
Queenswood Dr 4
 WR5 ....128 C6
Quest Hills Rd WR14 ..138 F4
Quibery Cl B98 ....71 F3
Quincy Rise DY5 ....6 C7
Quinneys Ct B50 .....136 E4

Quinneys La
 Bidford-on-Avon B50 ...136 E4
 Redditch B98 ....90 B6
Quinton Church Prim Sch
 B32 ....9 A6
Quinton Cl B98 ....71 D1
Quinton Expressway B32 .9 B4
Quinton La B32 ....9 C6
Quinton Rd W B32 ......9 D4
Quisters 13 WR4 ......116 B5

R

Race Field 3 WR4 ....116 B5
Racecourse La DY8 ......5 F1
Racecourse Rd WR10 ..144 E4
Racks La WR9 ....83 B5
Radbourne Dr B63 ......7 A7
Radcliffe Dr B62 ....8 E6
Raddens Rd B62 ....8 F3
Raddlebarn Farm Dr
 B29 ....19 F8
Raddlebarn Rd B29 .....19 F8
Radford Ave DY10 .....27 E7
Radford Ct DY10 ......27 E7
Radford House 2 B97 ..70 A4
Radford Rd
 Alvechurch B48 ....51 D7
 Birmingham B29 ....19 A6
 Flyford Flavell WR7 ....119 D2
 Rous Lench WR11 ......120 D1
Radley Rd DY9 ....6 F4
Radnor Cl B45 ....18 B2
Radnor Croft 3 WR3 ..115 E7
Radnor House B31 ......18 D6
Radnor Rd B68 ....9 B7
Radway Cl 8 WR8 .....71 B6
Raglan Ct B60 ....49 A1
Raglan St WR3 ....115 B6
Ragley Cres B60 ....68 A8
Ragley Hall★ B49 ......122 E4
Ragley House 8 B97 ...70 A4
Ragley Rd WR11 ......148 A7
Raglis Cl B97 ....70 A1
Rail Gd 6 WR10 ......144 C1
Railway Cl B60 ....90 D4
Rainbow Hill WR3 .....115 D4
Rainford Way B38 ......34 C8
Rainthorpe Ave 3 WR5 128 E6
Raleigh Cl WR2 ....114 D2
Ralphs Mdw B32 ....9 D2
Ramble Cl WR7 ....120 F6
Ramillies Dr WR5 .....128 E4
Ramsden Cl B29 ....19 B7
Ramsey Cl B45 ....17 F1
Ramsons Cl WR14 ....139 C3
Randall Ave B48 ....51 A6
Randle Rd DY9 ....6 C4
Randwick Cl 14 WR4 ..115 F6
Randwick Dr WR4 ....115 F7
Ranelagh Rd WR14 ...139 C5
Rangeways Rd DY11 ...27 A8
Rangeworthy Cl B97 ...89 C7
Rannoch Ave 10 WR5 .128 E6
Rannoch Cl
 Brierley Hill DY5 ....6 B8
 Stourport-on-Severn
 DY13 ....43 E7
Ransom Rd WR5 ......128 C7
Ran-Tan The B97 ......89 E5
Rathmore Cl DY8 ....5 E2
Rathvilly Sch B31 ......19 B3
Raven Dr WR5 ....128 D5
Raven Hays Rd B31 ....18 C2
Raven Scroft Dr 1 WR9 .85 B2
Raven St DY13 ....43 F3
Ravenhayes La B32 .....18 A6
Ravens Bank Dr B98 ...71 D6
Ravens Bank Fst Sch
 B98 ....71 D6
Ravenscroft DY9 ....5 C6
Ravenshill Cl 2 WR5 ..128 E5
Ravenshill Rd B14 .....21 D4
Ravenshill Wood Nature
 Reserve★ WR6 ......124 D8
Ravensmere Rd B98 ....71 B1
Raybon Croft B45 ......33 A6
Rea Ave B45 ....32 E8
Rea Cl B31 ....34 A7
Rea Fordway B45 ......17 F1
Rea Valley Dr B31 .....19 B2
Rea Way WR2 ....114 D2
Reabrook Rd B31 ......33 F8
Reades Piece WR11 ...164 A4
Rear Cotts B48 ....50 F6
Reaside Cres B14 ......20 B5
Reaside Dr B45 ....18 B1
Reaside Mid Sch B45 ...17 E1
Rebecca Pl WR8 ......156 F7
Rebekah Gdns WR9 ...103 F7
Recreation Rd B61 .....48 F3
Rectory Cl
 Broadheath WR2 ....114 A7
 Harvington WR11 ......148 A6
 Stourbridge DY8 ....6 B3
Rectory Ct B97 ....70 D1
Rectory Gdns
 Hartlebury DY11 ....45 A3
 Stourbridge DY8 ....6 B3
 Worcester WR2 ....115 A2
Rectory La
 Guarlford WR13 ....154 A7
 Hartlebury DY11 ....45 A3
 Harvington WR11 ......148 A6
 Madresfield WR14 .....139 D3
 Malvern WR13 ....153 F6
 Rock DY14 ....41 B5

Rectory La continued
Shrawley WR6 . . . . .81 D7
1 Stourport-on-Severn
DY13 . . . . .43 E2
Upton Warren B61 . . . . .66 F3
Rectory Rd
Birmingham B31 . . . . . . .19 B3
Redditch B97 . . . . .70 D1
Stourbridge DY8 . . . . . . .6 B3
Upton upon Severn WR8 .169 C4
Red Brick Cl B64 . . . . . .7 D7
Red Ditch La GL19 . . . . .192 A2
Red Earl La WR14 . . . . .153 D8
Red Hill Bewdley DY12 . .26 B2
Redditch B98 . . . . .70 F2
Stourbridge DY8 . . . . . . .6 B4
Red Hill CE Prim Sch
WR5 . . . . .128 E8
Red Hill Cl B80 . . . . . . .90 E6
Red Hill Gr B38 . . . . . . .34 F7
Red Hill La WR5 . . . . . .128 F7
Red Hill Pl B62 . . . . . . .17 A7
Red House Rd DY13 . . . .62 D8
Red La Evesham WR11 . .161 B5
Tewkesbury GL20 . . . . .196 E6
Red Leasowes Rd B63 . . . .8 A3
Red Lion St
Alvechurch B48 . . . . . . .51 B6
Redditch B98 . . . . .70 E4
Red Sands Rd DY10 . . . .27 E8
Redbrook Covert 7 B38 . .34 E8
Redcar B61 . . . . .32 B1
Redcliffe St WR3 . . . . .115 A7
Reddings The B47 . . . . .36 A5
Redditch Rd
Alvechurch, Arrowfield Top
B48 . . . . .51 B8
Alvechurch, Rowney Green
B48 . . . . .51 C3
Birmingham B31, B38 . . .34 C8
Hopwood B48 . . . . .34 B1
Stoke Heath B60 . . . . . .67 D5
Studley B80 . . . . .90 D5
Redditch Ringway B97 . .70 D4
Redditch Sta B97 . . . . . . .70 D4
Redfern WR5 . . . . .115 F1
Redgate Ave WR15 . . . . .55 E4
Redgate Cl B38 . . . . . . .19 D2
Redhall Rd B32 . . . . .9 E7
Redhill Cl DY8 . . . . .6 B4
Redhill Ct DY8 . . . . .6 B4
Redhill La B45, B61 . . . .32 C5
Redhill Rd B38 . . . . .34 D7
Redhill Sch DY8 . . . . .6 B4
Redlake Dr DY9 . . . . . . .15 B8
Redlake Rd DY9 . . . . .6 B1
Redland Cl B60 . . . . . . .32 C1
Redland Dr WR3 . . . . . .152 A3
Redland Rd WR14 . . . . .139 A4
Redlands 4 WR9 . . . . . .144 D1
Redmarley CE Prim Sch
GL19 . . . . .192 A3
Redmead Cl B30 . . . . . . .19 C4
Rednal Hill Jun & Inf Schs
B45 . . . . .33 C7
Rednal Hill La B45 . . . . .33 A6
Rednal Mill Dr B45 . . . . .33 C7
Rednal Rd B38 . . . . .19 E1
Redstart Ave DY10 . . . . .28 B2
Redstone Cl B98 . . . . . . .71 C6
Redstone La 4 DY13 . . . .62 F8
Redwing Cl WR4 . . . . . .138 D6
Redwing Ct DY10 . . . . . .28 A1
Redwood Cl
Birmingham B30 . . . . . . .19 E4
Worcester WR4 . . . . . . .115 E6
Redwood Croft B14 . . . . .20 E7
Redwood Ct 10 GL20 . . .184 E1
Redwood Rd
Birmingham B30 . . . . . . .19 E4
Kinver DY7 . . . . .4 C3
Reedham Cl WR3 . . . . . .115 A7
Reedmace Cl B38 . . . . . .34 F8
Reeve Ct DY10 . . . . .28 A1
Reeves Rd B14 . . . . .20 C6
Regan House B13 . . . . . .21 D7
Regency Dr B38 . . . . . . .19 F2
Regency Gdns B14 . . . . .21 C3
Regency Rd 3 WR14 . . .139 B5
Regent Cl 8 A4
Regent Ct 4 B62 . . . . . . .9 A7
Regent Mews B60 . . . . . .67 E8
Regent St B30 . . . . .20 A7
Regents Pk Rd B60 . . . . .49 C2
Regiment Cl WR5 . . . . . .128 E4
Regina Cl
Birmingham B45 . . . . . . .17 E2
Worcester WR2 . . . . . . .127 F6
Renfrew Gdns DY11 . . . . .27 C5
Rennie Gr B32 . . . . .9 E7
Renshaw Ind Est B80 . . . .90 B4
Reservoir La 5 WR3 . . . .115 D4
Reservoir Rd
Birmingham, Rednall
B45 . . . . .33 C3
Kidderminster DY11 . . . . .27 C3
Resolution Way 3 DY13 . .44 B2
Retreat St B96 . . . . .89 E1
Retreat The B64 . . . . .7 E7
Reyde Cl B97 . . . . .70 A2
Reynard Cl B97 . . . . .69 F3
Reynolds Cl WR13 . . . . .167 C5
Reynolds Ct 8 B68 . . . . . .9 B8
Rhayader Rd B31 . . . . . .18 E5
Rhuddlan Way DY10 . . . .27 E1
Rhydd Cl WR14 . . . . . . .153 C7
Ribbesford Cl B63 . . . . . . .7 D6

Ribbesford Dr DY13 . . . .43 E4
Ribbesford Rd DY13 . . . .43 C2
Ribble Cl WR5 . . . . .115 E2
Ribblesdale Rd B30 . . . . .20 A8
Ribston Cl 2 WR2 . . . . .114 E5
Richard Pl 2 GL20 . . . . .196 F3
Richard's Cl WR14 . . . . .138 E5
Richards Cl B31 . . . . .33 F6
Richardson Cl WR9 . . . . .85 E6
Richardson Dr DY8 . . . . . .5 E8
Richmond Ct
4 Birmingham B29 . . . .19 C7
Halesowen B63 . . . . .7 A5
Stourbridge DY9 . . . . . . .6 B1
Richmond Gdns DY8 . . . . .5 F7
Richmond Gr DY8 . . . . . . .5 E8
Richmond Pl B14 . . . . . . .20 F8
Richmond Rd
Bewdley DY12 . . . . .25 F4
Birmingham, Eachway
B45 . . . . .32 C7
Great Malvern WR14 . . .139 A4
Hollywood B47 . . . . .36 C7
5 Walton Cardiff GL20 . .197 A3
Worcester WR5 . . . . . . .115 D2
Richmond St B63 . . . . . . .8 A4
Richmonds Pitch **1**
WR14 . . . . .166 E7
Rickets Cl DY13 . . . . . . .44 B7
Rickett's La 12 WR9 . . . .84 F3
Ricketts Pl DY12 . . . . . . .26 B3
Rickyard Cl B29 . . . . . . .19 A6
Rickyard La B98 . . . . . . .71 D5
Rickyard Piece B32 . . . . . .9 C6
Riddings Cl DY12 . . . . . .26 C5
Riddings The DY9 . . . . . . .6 D2
Ridgacre La B32 . . . . .9 C6
Ridgacre Rd B32 . . . . .9 C6
Ridgacre Rd W B32 . . . . . .9 A6
Ridge Cl B13 . . . . .21 C6
Ridge Gr DY9 . . . . .6 C5
Ridge Prim Sch The DY8 . . .5 C5
Ridgefield Rd B62 . . . . . . .8 C7
Ridgemount Dr B38 . . . . .34 D8
Ridgewater Cl B45 . . . . . .33 B6
Ridgeway WR13 . . . . . . .166 B4
Ridgeway Ave B62 . . . . . .9 A6
Ridgeway Cl B80 . . . . . . .90 E2
Ridgeway Mid Sch The
B96 . . . . .108 E8
Ridgeway The
Cookhill B96 . . . . .109 A6
Droitwich WR9 . . . . .84 C7
Stourport-on-Severn DY13 .43 F5
Worcester WR5 . . . . . . .115 A7
Ridgeway Trad Est B96 . . .89 E1
Ridgewood Ave DY8 . . . . .5 C7
Ridgewood High Sch
DY8 . . . . .5 C5
Ridgmont Croft B32 . . . . . .9 E5
Ridings La B98 . . . . .71 B6
Ridleys Cross DY13 . . . . .62 E6
Ridsdale Cl WR11 . . . . . .135 E4
Rifle Range Rd DY11 . . . .27 B3
Rigby Hall B60 . . . . .68 C8
Rigby Hall Sch B60 . . . . . .68 C8
Rigby La B60 . . . . .68 C8
Rightons Ct 5 WR11 . . . .161 D5
Riley Rd B14 . . . . .21 D3
Rilstone Rd B32 . . . . .9 F5
Ringway The DY10 . . . . . .27 D6
Ringwood Dr B45 . . . . . . .18 A1
Ripley Gdns WR4 . . . . . .116 D6
Ripon Rd
Birmingham B14 . . . . . . .21 C4
Worcester WR5 . . . . . . .116 A3
Ripple Rd
Birmingham B30 . . . . . . .20 B7
Droitwich WR9 . . . . .84 C2
Rise Ave B45 . . . . .33 A7
Rise La WR15 . . . . .56 B6
Rise The B48 . . . . .34 B4
Rissington Ave B29 . . . . .20 A8
River Brook Dr B30 . . . . .20 B8
River Sch The WR3 . . . . .102 D2
Riverside Studley B80 . . .90 F5
1 Tenbury Wells WR15 . .55 E5
Riverside Cl
Lickey End B60 . . . . .49 C6
3 Upton upon Severn
WR8 . . . . .169 C6
Riverside Cres B28 . . . . .21 D4
Riverside Ct B38 . . . . . . .19 D3
Riverside N DY12 . . . . . . .26 B4
Riverside Rd 3 WR9 . . . . .85 A3
Riverside Way WR9 . . . . .85 B3
Riversleigh Dr DY8 . . . . . .5 E8
Riverview Cl WR2 . . . . . .114 F6
Riverway DY12 . . . . .26 B4
Rivington Cl DY8 . . . . .5 E8
Roach Cl 1 WR5 . . . . . .128 E5
Road No 1 DY10 . . . . . . .27 E2
Road No 2 DY10 . . . . . . .27 E2
Road No 3 DY10 . . . . . . .27 E2
Roberts La
South Littleton WR11 . . .148 F1
Stourbridge DY9 . . . . . . .15 B8
Robeson Cl WR9 . . . . . . .85 B3
Robin Cl
Northway GL20 . . . . . . .184 D1
Worcester WR5 . . . . . . .128 D5
Robin Ct DY10 . . . . .28 A2
Robin Hood Cres B28 . . . .21 E7
Robin Hood Croft B28 . . .21 F6

Robin Hood La
Birmingham B28 . . . . . . .21 F6
Birmingham B28 . . . . . . .21 E7
Robin's Cl DY8 . . . . .6 A3
Robina Cl 1 WR11 . . . . .175 D8
Robins Hill Dr B48 . . . . . .51 A5
Robinsfield Dr B31 . . . . . .34 A7
Rochester Cl B97 . . . . . . .89 C8
Rochester Rd B31 . . . . . .19 A4
Rochester Wlk DY10 . . . . .28 C5
Rochford Cl
Birmingham B45 . . . . . . .32 E7
Halesowen B63 . . . . .7 F2
Rock Ave B45 . . . . .33 C7
Rock Cotts 6 DY11 . . . . . .27 D6
Rock Hill
Bromsgrove B61 . . . . . . .67 D7
Inkberrow WR7 . . . . . . .120 F6
Rock La WR6 . . . . .78 C4
Rock St GL19 . . . . .195 D2
Rockford Rd B98 . . . . . . .89 F5
Rockhill La B96 . . . . .107 F8
Rockingham Hall Gdns
DY9 . . . . .15 D7
Rockingham La WR4 . . . .116 D6
Rockley Bank 3 DY14 . . . .22 C5
Rockley Gr B45 . . . . .33 B7
Rockwell La B48 . . . . . . .51 E4
Rocky La B61 . . . . .48 E7
Rocky Wall DY7 . . . . .3 E4
Rodborough Cl WR4 . . . .116 A7
Rodborough Dr WR4 . . . .116 A7
Roden Ave DY10 . . . . . . .28 A7
Rodway Cl DY5 . . . . .6 D7
Rogers Hill WR3 . . . . . . .115 C4
Rolan Dr B90 . . . . .36 E8
Roman Ct B38 . . . . .35 B8
Roman Rd (Sandy La)
DY8 . . . . .5 C3
Roman Way
Bromsgrove B61 . . . . . . .49 B4
Droitwich Spa WR9 . . . . .84 F4
Great Malvern WR14 . . .139 C5
Salwarpe WR9 . . . . .84 C1
Roman Way Bsns Pk
WR9 . . . . .84 E5
Roman Way Fst Sch
B98 . . . . .71 E3
Romany Rd B45 . . . . .17 D1
Romany Way DY8 . . . . . . .5 C3
Romilly Cl DY8 . . . . .5 E6
Romney Cl B28 . . . . .21 F7
Romsley Cl
Birmingham B45 . . . . . . .32 E8
Halesowen B63 . . . . .8 B2
Redditch B98 . . . . .71 F3
Romsley Hill Grange
B62 . . . . .16 F1
Romsley La
Romsley WV15 . . . . .2 A2
Upper Arley DY12 . . . . . .11 B8
Romsley Rd
Birmingham B32 . . . . . . .18 B8
Stourbridge DY9 . . . . . . .6 C5
Romsley View WV15 . . . . .1 C6
Rona Gdns WR5 . . . . . . .128 E6
Ronhill Cres DY14 . . . . . .22 C5
Ronhill La DY14 . . . . .22 C5
Ronkswood Cres WR5 . . .115 E3
Ronkswood Hill WR4 . . . .115 E3
Ronkswood Jun Sch
WR5 . . . . .115 F3
Rookery Cl B97 . . . . .70 E6
Rookery Rd WR5 . . . . . . .141 C7
Rookery The B62 . . . . . . .9 A2
Rooks Mdw DY9 . . . . .15 B6
Rope Wlk GL20 . . . . .196 F6
Rosafield Ave B62 . . . . . . .8 F6
Rose Ave Alvechurch B48 . .51 A5
Droitwich WR9 . . . . .85 A3
Oldbury B68 . . . . .9 C7
Worcester WR5 . . . . . . .115 D1
Rose Bank
1 Evesham WR11 . . . . .161 F4
Worcester WR5 . . . . . . .115 D1
Rose Cotts B30 . . . . .20 A6
Rose Dene 12 DY13 . . . . .43 E4
Rose Hill
Barnt Green B45 . . . . . . .33 B4
Worcester WR5 . . . . . . .115 D1
Rose Hill Sch WR4 . . . . . .115 F6
Rose La B61 . . . . .48 A6
Rose Terr
Barnt Green B45 . . . . . . .50 D8
Worcester WR5 . . . . . . .115 D1
Rosebay Ave B38 . . . . . . .34 F8
Roseberry Gdns DY10 . . . .13 C3
Rosebriars B90 . . . . .36 E7
Rosedale WR6 . . . . .60 E4
Rosedale Cl B97 . . . . .70 A4
Rosefield Cres GL20 . . . .197 A6
Rosehall Cl B98 . . . . .89 E6
Roseleigh Rd B45 . . . . . . .33 B6
Rosemary Ave WR2 . . . . .114 E3
Rosemary Cl 1 WR11 . . . .161 B2
Rosemary Dr B60 . . . . . . .67 C1
Rosemary La DY8 . . . . . . .5 D3
Rosemary Rd
Halesowen B63 . . . . .7 E2
Kidderminster DY10 . . . . .28 B7
Stourbridge DY8 . . . . . . .5 D3
Rosemoor Dr DY5 . . . . . . .6 B7
Rosemoor Gdns 5 WR5 128 E6
Rosemount B32 . . . . .9 E5
Rosenhurst Dr 6 DY12 . . .26 A3
Rosetti Cl DY10 . . . . .28 C6
Rosewood Cl WR3 . . . . . .102 C1
Rosewood Dr B45 . . . . . . .50 C7
Roslin Cl B60 . . . . .49 B1

Rossees La WR6 . . . . . . .99 D7
Rossendale Cl
Fernhill Heath WR3 . . . . .102 F3
Halesowen B63 . . . . .7 D6
Rothesay Croft B32 . . . . .18 B7
Rothley Wlk B38 . . . . . . .34 C8
Rothwell Rd WR14 . . . . .152 F1
Rough Hill Dr B98 . . . . . .89 F6
Rough Mdw 9 WR4 . . . . .116 A6
Rough The B97 . . . . .89 D8
Round Hill Ave DY9 . . . . . .6 C1
Round Hill Wharf DY11 . . .27 D5
Round Saw Croft B45 . . . .32 F8
Roundabout The B31 . . . .18 D1
Roundhills Rd B62 . . . . . . .8 F8
Roundlea Rd B31 . . . . . . .18 E7
Rousay Cl B45 . . . . .17 F1
Rowan Ave WR4 . . . . . . .115 E4
Rowan Cl
Bromsgrove B61 . . . . . . .48 E2
Droitwich WR9 . . . . .103 F8
1 Evesham WR11 . . . . .161 F2
Hollywood B47 . . . . .36 B5
Rowan Cres B97 . . . . .70 A4
Rowan Ct B30 . . . . .20 A2
Rowan Rd B97 . . . . .70 A4
Rowan Way B31 . . . . .33 F8
Rowanberry Cl 4 DY13 . . .43 A5
Rowans The WR11 . . . . .148 A8
Rowantrees B45 . . . . .33 B5
Rowborough Cl B96 . . . . .89 E2
Rowbrook Cl B90 . . . . . . .36 B5
Rowcroft Covert B14 . . . .20 E2
Rowheath Rd B30 . . . . . .19 E5
Rowheath House B30 . . . .19 F4
Rowland Ave B80 . . . . . . .90 E3
Rowland Hill Ave WR11 . .27 B5
Rowland Hill Ctr 9 DY10 .27 E6
Rowland Way (Road 1a)
DY11 . . . . .27 E1
Rowley Hill St WR2 . . . .114 F2
Rowley Hill View B64 . . . .7 F8
Rowney Croft B28 . . . . . .21 E4
Rowney Gn La B48 . . . . . .51 F5
Rowntree Gdns WR4 . . . .116 C2
Roxall Cl DY10 . . . . .14 C2
Roxboro House B97 . . . . .71 E4
Royal Albert Cl 6 WR5 . .115 C1
Royal Cl DY5 . . . . .6 C8
Royal Gram Sch WR1 . . . .115 B4
Royal Oak Rd B62 . . . . . . .8 B7
Royal Orthopaedic Hospl The
B31 . . . . .19 B5
Royal Sq 4 B97 . . . . .70 E3
Royal Worcester Cres
B60 . . . . .49 C1
Rozel Ave DY10 . . . . .13 B1
Rubery Farm Gr B45 . . . .32 F7
Rubery Field Cl B45 . . . . .18 B1
Rubery La B45 . . . . .18 A1
Rubery La S B45 . . . . . . .32 F8
Ruckley Rd B29 . . . . .19 B8
Rudge Rd 3 WR11 . . . . .161 D5
Rufford Prim Sch DY9 . . . . .6 C5
Rufford Rd DY9 . . . . .6 D5
Rufford St DY9 . . . . .6 D5
Rugby Rd DY8 . . . . .5 D7
Rumbow B63 . . . . .8 A4
Rumbow La B90, B94 . . . .36 A1
Rumbush La B94 . . . . . . .53 D3
Runcorn Cl B98 . . . . .89 F8
Rush Gn B32 . . . . .9 E2
Rush La B98 . . . . .71 B6
Rushall Cl DY8 . . . . .5 E8
Rushbrook Cl B64 . . . . . .20 C4
Rushbrook La B94 . . . . . .53 D3
Rusher's Cl WR10 . . . . . .144 C1
Rushleigh Rd B90 . . . . . . .36 A6
Rushmead Gr B45 . . . . . .33 A7
Rushock Cl B98 . . . . .90 C7
Rushock Trad Est WR9 . . . .46 A2
Rushwick Prim Sch
WR2 . . . . .127 C8
Rushy Piece B32 . . . . .9 D3
Ruskin Ave DY10 . . . . . . .28 C6
Ruskin Cl B68 . . . . .9 B8
Russel Croft B60 . . . . . . .68 A7
Russell Cl
Bowling Green WR2 . . . .127 C6
Great Malvern WR14 . . .139 B3
Russell Dr
Eckington WR10 . . . . . .171 E8
Great Malvern WR14 . . .139 B3
Russell Rd DY10 . . . . .27 F4
Russell St WR10 . . . . . . .158 F1
Russet Cl
4 Bredon GL20 . . . . . .184 F6
1 Worcester WR4 . . . . .114 C5
Russet Way B31 . . . . .18 E6
Russett Way 1 DY12 . . . .25 F4
Ruth Chamberlain Ct **3**
DY11 . . . . .27 D6
Ruthall Cl B29 . . . . .19 C7
Rutherford Rd B60 . . . . . .68 B7
Rutland Cl 3 B29 . . . . . . .19 C7
Rutland Dr B60 . . . . .68 A8
Rutland Pl
9 St. Peter the Great County
WR5 . . . . .128 E6
Rutley Gr B32 . . . . .9 F4
Rutters Mdw B32 . . . . . . .9 E4
Ryall Gr WR8 . . . . .169 F6
Ryall Mdw WR8 . . . . . . .169 E5
Rydal Cl
Stourport-on-Severn DY13 .43 F6
5 Worcester WR4 . . . . .115 F5

Rydal Way B28 . . . . .21 F7
Ryde Pk Rd B45 . . . . . . .33 C7
Ryden La WR10 . . . . . . .160 E8
Rye Cl WR3 . . . . .85 A2
Rye Croft Hollywood B47 . .36 A5
Stourbridge DY9 . . . . . . .6 E2
Rye Hill La WR7 . . . . . . .117 E2
Ryebank Rd B30 . . . . . . .19 C5
Ryefield Cl DY9 . . . . .15 A4
Ryefields Rd B60 . . . . . . .67 C3
Ryegrass La B97 . . . . . . .89 C6
Ryeland 5 WR3 . . . . . . .115 E5
Ryeland La
Elmley Lovett WR9 . . . . .45 F8
Hartlebury WR9 . . . . . . .64 F8
Ryelands WR10 . . . . .145 A4
Ryemarket DY8 . . . . .6 A5
Ryland Cl B63 . . . . .7 E2
Rynal Pl WR11 . . . . .161 E5
Rynal St WR11 . . . . .161 D5
Ryton Cl B98 . . . . .71 D1
Ryvere Cl 2 DY13 . . . . . .43 F2

S

Sabrina Ave WR3 . . . . . .115 A6
Sabrina Dr DY12 . . . . . . .26 A4
Sabrina Terr 18 WR1 . . .115 A5
Sabrina Wlk WR3 . . . . . .115 A7
Saddlers B63 . . . . .7 B5
Saffron House 3 B38 . . . .34 E8
Saffron Rd 7 GL20 . . . . .196 E6
Sage Croft B31 . . . . .18 F5
Sagebury Dr B60 . . . . . . .67 C1
St Agatha's Cl
7 Pershore WR10 . . . . .144 D1
3 Pershore WR10 . . . . .158 D8
St Agathas Rd
8 Pershore WR10 . . . . .144 D1
2 Pershore WR10 . . . . .158 D8
St Agnes Cl B80 . . . . . . .90 C4
St Alban's Ave DY11 . . . .27 A7
St Alban's RC Prim Sch
B14 . . . . .20 F4
St Albans Cl WR5 . . . . . .115 F3
St Albans House B32 . . . . .9 F5
St Ambrose B62, B65 . . . . .8 C3
St Ambrose RC Prim Sch
DY10 . . . . .27 F6
St Andrew Rd 6 WR11 . . .161 A3
St Andrew's Cl 8 WR9 . . .84 F3
St Andrew's Dr WR9 . . . . .84 F2
St Andrew's Fst Sch
B45 . . . . .50 D8
St Andrew's Rd
Great Malvern WR14 . . .153 A6
Pershore WR10 . . . . . . .158 C7
St Andrew's St WR9 . . . . .84 F3
St Andrews CE Fst Sch
WR11 . . . . .161 B2
St Andrews Cl DY8 . . . . . .5 F2
St Andrews Gn DY10 . . . .27 E4
St Andrews Rd 9 WR9 . . .84 F3
St Andrews Way B61 . . . .67 D8
St Ann's Rd WR14 . . . . .138 E1
St Anne's CE Mid Sch
DY12 . . . . .25 F2
St Anne's Cl WR3 . . . . . .102 B1
St Anne's Rd
Blackheath B64 . . . . .7 C8
Worcester WR3 . . . . . . .102 B1
St Anns Sch WR5 . . . . . . .129 E6
St Asaphs Ave B80 . . . . . .90 D4
St Audrie's Ct WR5 . . . . .128 E5
St Augustine Dr WR9 . . . .85 A4
St Augustine's Cl WR9 . . .85 A4
St Augustine's RC High Sch
B97 . . . . .89 D7
St Barnabas CE Fst & Mid
Sch WR10 . . . . .143 F6
St Barnabas CE Fst Sch
DY11 . . . . .12 B1
St Barnabas CE Prim Sch
WR3 . . . . .115 D5
St Bartholomew's Rd 5
DY13 . . . . .43 E2
St Bede's RC Mid Sch
B98 . . . . .70 F4
St Bernard Dr WR14 . . . .153 A4
St Brigid's RC Prim Sch
B31 . . . . .18 F3
St Catherine's Hill
WR5 . . . . .115 D1
St Catherine's Rd B60 . . .50 A5
St Catherine's Vale 2
WR5 . . . . .115 C1
St Catherines Cl B60 . . . .50 A5
St Catherines Rd 2
WR11 . . . . .161 D1
St Cecilia Cl DY10 . . . . . .27 E2
St Chad's Rd B45 . . . . . . .32 F7
St Chads Rd B80 . . . . . . .90 C4
St Clement's CE Prim Sch
WR2 . . . . .114 F2
St Clement's Cl 3 WR2 115 A2
St Clement's Ct 1 WR2 115 A2
St Clement's Gdns
WR2 . . . . .115 A2
St Columba's RC Prim Sch
B45 . . . . .33 D7
St Columbas Dr B45 . . . . .33 D7
St David's Cl 1 DY13 . . . .43 E6
St Davids Dr
Birmingham B32 . . . . . . .9 B5

St Davids Dr continued
Evesham WR11 . . . . .161 D1
St Davids Rd GL20 . . . . .197 F7
St Denis Rd B29 . . . . . . .19 B7
St Dunstan's Cl WR5 .128 C8
St Dunstan's Cres
18 Worcester WR5 . . . .115 C1
Worcester WR5 . . . . . .128 C8
St Dunstan's La WR5 . .57 A4
St Dunstan's RC Prim Sch
B14 . . . . .20 F8
St Egwin's Cl WR11 . .147 D3
St Egwin's Rd 6 WR11 .161 D5
St Egwine Cl WR3 . . . .115 C5
St Egwins CE Mid Sch
WR11 . . . . .161 D6
St Francis CE Prim Sch
B30 . . . . .154 A1
St Gabriel With St Mary CE
Prim Sch WR8 . . . . . .154 A1
St George's CE Fst Sch
Kidderminster DY10 . . . . .27 F7
Redditch B98 . . . . .70 F3
St George's CE Prim Sch
WR1 . . . . .115 B5
St George's Cres 4 WR9 85 A3
St George's Ct B30 . . . .19 E7
St George's Gdns 3 B98 .70 F4
St George's La N WR1 .115 B5
St George's La S WR1 .115 B5
St George's Pl DY10 . . . .27 E7
St George's Rd DY8 . . . .5 D2
St George's Sq WR1 . . .115 B5
St George's Terr DY10 . .27 E7
St George's Wlk WR1 . .115 B5
St Georges Cath Sch
WR1 . . . . .115 A5
St Georges Cl 5 WR11 .161 E1
St Georges Ct 10 DY10 . .27 E6
St Georges Rd B98 . . . .70 F4
St Giles Row DY8 . . . . . .6 A6
St Giles's Rd GL20 . . . .184 E6
St Godwald's Cres B60 .68 B8
St Godwald's Rd B60 . .68 C7
St Heliers Rd B31 . . . . .18 F4
St Hubert's RC Prim Sch
B68 . . . . .9 C8
St James CE Prim Sch
DY8 . . . . .5 D7
St James Cl
Badsey WR11 . . . . .162 E3
Harvington WR11 . . . . .148 B6
Norton Juxta Kempsey
WR5 . . . . .129 C1
St James Ct B60 . . . . . .49 A3
St James Dr 3 WR11 . .161 D1
St James Prim Sch
WR14 . . . . .138 C1
St James' RC Jun & Inf Sch
B45 . . . . .33 A7
St James's & the Abbey
WR14 . . . . .138 C1
St James's Dr WR14 . .138 F2
St John Fisher RC Fst Sch
B98 . . . . .71 D6
St John Fisher RC Prim Sch
B31 . . . . .34 B7
St John St B61 . . . . . . .48 F2
St John's WR2 . . . . . . .115 A1
St John's Ave DY11 . . . .27 B6
St John's CE Foundation Mid
Sch B61 . . . . .48 F1
St John's CE Fst Sch
Kidderminster DY10 . . . . .27 B6
Stourport-on-Severn
DY13 . . . . .44 A6
St John's CE Mid Sch
DY11 . . . . .27 B6
St John's Cl
6 Kidderminster DY11 . .27 C6
Worcester WR3 . . . . . .102 B1
St John's La DY12 . . . . .25 A2
St John's Rd
Halesowen B63 . . . . .7 E4
Stourbridge DY8 . . . . . . .6 A5
Stourport-on-Severn
DY13 . . . . .44 A5
St John's St 5 DY11 . . .27 C6
St Johns Cl 3 WR11 . . .161 E1
St Johns Ct B31 . . . . . .19 B1
St Johns Wood B45 . . .33 B5
St Joseph's Cl WR9 . . .84 D2
St Joseph's RC Prim Sch
WR9 . . . . .84 D2
St Josephs Ave B80 . . .90 D4
St Josephs Prim Sch
WR14 . . . . .138 C1
St Josephs RC Prim Sch
Birmingham B30 . . . . . .19 F5
Worcester WR4 . . . . . .116 B7
St Judes Ave B80 . . . . .90 D4
St Judes Cl B14 . . . . . .20 F2
St Judes Ct B14 . . . . . .20 F7
St Judes RC Jun & Inf Sch
B14 . . . . .20 F2
St Kenelm's CE Sch
B62 . . . . .17 A4
St Kenelm's Rd B62 . . .16 E5
St Kenelms Ave B63 . . . .7 A4
St Kitts Cl 5 WR14 . . .138 F5
St Laurence CE Inf Sch
B31 . . . . .19 B4
St Laurence CE Jun Sch
B31 . . . . .19 B4
St Laurence Cl B48 . . . .51 B6

St Laurence Rd B31 . . . .19 B5
St Laurence Way 3
B50 . . . . .136 D5
St Lawrence Cl 4 WR2 .127 F7
St Lawrence Rd 3
WR11 . . . . .161 C4
St Loye's Cl B62 . . . . . . .8 D8
St Luke's CE Fst Sch
B97 . . . . .70 D1
St Luke's Cotts B97 . . .70 D1
St Lukes Bsns Ctr B64 . . .7 E8
St Lukes Cl 7 WR11 . . .161 D1
St Margarets Dr B63 . . . .7 F2
St Margarets Rd 4
WR11 . . . . .161 D1
St Mark's Cl WR5 . . . .128 C7
St Mark's Rd DY9 . . . . . .6 D5
St Marks Cl 6 WR11 . . .161 D1
St Martins Ave B80 . . . .90 D4
St Mary's CE Prim Sch
DY10 . . . . .27 E8
St Mary's Cl
Kempsey WR5 . . . . . . .141 B7
4 Tenbury Wells WR15 . .55 E5
St Mary's Convent Sch Mount
Battenhall WR5 . . . . . .128 C8
St Mary's La
Stourbridge DY8 . . . . . . .6 B3
9 Tewkesbury GL20 . . .196 E6
St Mary's Pl 1 DY14 . . .22 C4
St Mary's Prep Sch
WR15 . . . . .56 D1
St Mary's RC Prim Sch
B80 . . . . .90 E4
St Mary's Rd
Droitwich WR9 . . . . .84 F2
Evesham WR11 . . . . . . .161 D5
Tewkesbury GL20 . . . . .196 D6
St Marys CE Prim Sch
GL20 . . . . .181 D5
St Marys RC Prim Sch
Broadway WR12 . . . . . .190 D8
Evesham WR11 . . . . . . .161 D6
St Marys Ringway DY10 .27 E6
St Matthews Cl
2 Evesham WR11 . . . . .161 E1
Salford Priors WR11 . . .135 E3
St Michael's CE Jun & Inf Sch
B32 . . . . .18 C8
St Michael's Cl
2 South Littleton WR11 .148 F1
3 Stourport-on-Severn
DY13 . . . . .44 A4
St Michael's Coll WR15 .74 C8
St Michaels Cl WR3 . . .115 B8
St Michaels Ct 3 WR11 175 D8
St Milburgh Cl WR11 . .148 A1
St Moritz Cl WR3 . . . . .114 F8
St Nicholas CE Mid Sch
WR10 . . . . .144 E6
St Nicholas La WR4 . . .116 D6
St Nicholas Rd WR10 . .131 B2
St Nicholas St
Droitwich WR9 . . . . .84 A2
Worcester WR1 . . . . . .115 B3
St Nicolas Gdns B38 . . .19 F2
St Oswald's Rd WR1 . .115 B4
St Oswalds CE Fst Sch
DY10 . . . . .13 A1
St Oswalds Cl DY11 . . . .27 F8
St Patrick's Ct DY11 . . .27 B1
St Patricks Ct
Birmingham B14 . . . . . .20 E5
9 Evesham WR11 . . . . .161 D1
St Paul's Rd DY11 . . . . .27 A6
St Paul's RC Prim Sch
B38 . . . . .20 A1
St Paul's St WR1 . . . . .115 C2
St Pauls Cl WR11 . . . . .175 E8
St Peter's Church La
WR9 . . . . .85 A2
St Peter's Cl
Evesham WR11 . . . . . . .161 E3
Hinton on the Green
WR11 . . . . .175 A5
Redditch B97 . . . . .89 C5
St Peter's Cres WR9 . . .85 A3
St Peter's Dr
Martley WR6 . . . . .99 A4
St. Peter the Great County
WR5 . . . . .128 C5
St Peter's La WR8 . . . .157 C6
St Peter's RC Fst Sch
B61 . . . . .67 E8
St Peter's Rd
Droitwich WR9 . . . . .84 F2
Great Malvern WR14 . . .138 D6
Stourbridge DY9 . . . . . . .6 C1
St Peter's Wlk WR9 . . .85 A3
St Peters CE Fst Sch
WR9 . . . . .85 A2
St Peters Cl
Birmingham B28 . . . . . .21 D6
Bromsgrove B61 . . . . . .48 E1
Malvern Wells WR14 . . .166 F7
St Peters RC Prim Sch
B32 . . . . .9 C1
St Peters St 5 WR5 . . .115 C1
St Philips Dr
8 Evesham WR11 . . . . .161 D1
Evesham WR11 . . . . . . .175 D8
St Richard's Gdns 9
WR11 . . . . .84 E3
St Richards Cl WR11 . . .85 E8
St Richards Rd
Dodderhill WR9 . . . . . . .85 D1
Evesham WR11 . . . . . . .161 D1
St Saviour's Ct DY9 . . .15 A6

St Stephan's House
B97 . . . . .70 E4
St Stephen's CE Fst Sch
B98 . . . . .70 F5
St Stephen's St 5 WR3 115 B6
St Stephen's Terr 1
WR3 . . . . .115 B6
St Stephens Gdns B98 . .70 F5
St Stephens Rd B29 . . .20 B8
St Swithin's St 1 WR1 .115 C2
St Swithuns Cl WR5 . . .128 D8
St Thomas Aquinas RC Sch
B38 . . . . .19 D3
St Thomas More RC Fst Sch
B98 . . . . .90 B7
St Wulstan's Cres 1
WR5 . . . . .115 D1
St Wulstans Cl 6 WR11 161 E1
St Wulstans Dr WR14 . .167 A7
St Wulstans RC Prim Sch
DY13 . . . . .43 D4
Salamanca Dr WR5 . . .128 F4
Salcombe Dr DY5 . . . . . .6 C7
Salford Cl B98 . . . . .90 B6
Salford Priors CE Sch
WR11 . . . . .135 E4
Salisbury Cl WR5 . . . . .115 C1
Salisbury Dr
6 Evesham WR11 . . . . .161 C2
Kidderminster DY11 . . . . .26 F6
Sallis Cl WR11 . . . . . . .176 D2
Salop Rd B97 . . . . .70 D3
Salt Way Cookhill B96 . .108 D5
Feckenham B96 . . . . . .107 A8
Hadzor WR9 . . . . .85 F2
Saltbox La WR15 . . . . . .55 F2
Saltbrook Rd B63 . . . . . .7 A7
Saltbrook Trad Est B63 . .7 A7
Salter's La B97 . . . . . . .70 B5
Salters Cl WR4 . . . . . . .115 F6
Salters La Besford WR8 .143 E1
Defford WR8 . . . . .157 D6
Fladbury WR10 . . . . . . .145 E2
Saltway WR4 . . . . .84 F3
Saltwood WR4 . . . . . . .116 C6
Salwarpe Ct* WR9 . . . .84 B1
Salwarpe Gr B29 . . . . . .9 F2
Salwarpe Rd
Bromsgrove B60 . . . . . .67 F8
Droitwich WR9 . . . . .84 E3
Sam Spencer Ct DY10 . .29 A2
Sambourne La
Astwood Bank B96 . . . . .89 F1
Coughton B96 . . . . . . .109 E6
Sambourne B96 . . . . . . .90 A1
Sambourne Pk B96 . . .109 A8
Sambourne Pk La B96 . .90 A1
Samuels Rd B32 . . . . . . .9 A5
Sanctuary Cl WR2 . . . .114 E2
Sandalls Cl B31 . . . . . .18 D1
Sandals Rise B62 . . . . . .8 D3
Sandbourne Dr DY12 . . .26 C3
Sanderling Ct DY10 . . . .28 A1
Sanders Cl B97 . . . . . . .70 B4
Sanders Ind Est B61 . . .48 E1
Sanders Rd
Bromsgrove B61 . . . . . .48 E1
Salford Priors WR11 . . .135 F3
Sanderson Cl DY11 . . . .27 C5
Sandfield La WR11 . . . .174 E2
Sandfield The GL20 . . .184 E1
Sandgate Rd B28 . . . . . .21 F4
Sandhills Gn B48 . . . . . .50 E7
Sandhills La B45 . . . . . .50 D7
Sandhills Rd B45 . . . . . .50 D8
Sandhurst Ave DY9 . . . . .6 D2
Sandhurst Cl B98 . . . . . .71 C6
Sandhurst House B38 . . .20 B1
Sandiacre Way DY10 . . .28 A2
Sandles Cl WR9 . . . . . .103 F7
Sandles Rd WR9 . . . . . .103 F7
Sandmartin Way DY10 . .28 A2
Sandmere Gr B14 . . . . .21 D3
Sandmere Rd B14 . . . . .21 D3
Sandon Cl WR8 . . . . . . .71 A3
Sandon Rd DY9 . . . . .6 F4
Sandown Ct 18 B29 . . . .19 C7
Sandown Dr B61 . . . . . .32 B1
Sandown Rd 5 WR11 . .161 C2
Sandown Twr 3 B31 . . .19 A1
Sandpiper Cl
Kidderminster DY10 . . . . .28 B2
Stourbridge DY9 . . . . . . .9 F5
6 Worcester WR5 . . . .128 E6
Sandpiper Cres WR14 .138 D6
Sandpiper Gdns B38 . . .34 F7
Sandpits Cl WR6 . . . . . .99 A3
Sandpits The B30 . . . . .19 E8
Sandringham Cl
Evesham WR11 . . . . . . .161 D6
Great Malvern WR14 . . .139 C6
Sandringham Rd B62 . . .8 F8
Sandringham Way DY5 . .6 C8
Sands Cl 3 WR12 . . . . .177 D1
Sands Croft Ave
WR12 . . . . .177 E1
Sands La WR11 . . . . . . .162 E2
Sands Rd B96 . . . . .107 F1
Sands The
4 Broadway WR12 . . . .177 D1
Broadway WR12 . . . . . .190 D8
Sandstone Ave B45 . . . .33 A8
Sandstone Rd 5 DY12 . .26 A4
Sandway Gr B13 . . . . . .21 C7
Sandy Bank DY12 . . . . .26 A3
Sandy Croft B13 . . . . . .21 C7

Sandy La
Blakedown DY10 . . . . . .29 C7
Kidderminster Foreign
DY11 . . . . .12 A1
Kinver DY7 . . . . .3 F1
Stourport-on-Severn
DY13 . . . . .44 B1
Wildmoor B61, B62 . . . . .31 E5
Sandy La Ind Est DY13 . .44 B1
Sandy Rd DY8 . . . . .5 D1
Sandyacre Way DY8 . . . .6 B5
Sandy's Rd WR14 . . . . .139 C3
Sandys Ave WR9 . . . . .176 D7
Sandys Cl 2 WR10 . . . .146 A1
Sandys Rd WR9 . . . . . . .83 A5
Sandys' Rd WR1 . . . . . .115 A5
Sansome Pl WR1 . . . . .115 C3
Sansome Rd 7 WR11 . . .21 F2
Sansome Rise B90 . . . . .21 F2
Sansome Wlk WR1 . . . .115 B3
Sant Rd B31 . . . . .34 B7
Santa Maria Way DY13 . .44 B3
Santridge Ct B61 . . . . . .49 A4
Santridge La B61 . . . . . .49 A4
Sapphire Cres WR2 . . .114 E3
Sarah Seager Cl 5 DY13 .43 E6
Sarehole Mill Mus★
B13 . . . . .21 D8
Sarehole Rd B28 . . . . . .21 E8
Sargent Turner Trad Est
DY9 . . . . .6 F6
Saunders St WR3 . . . . .115 A7
Saunderton House B31 .18 E5
Savernake Cl B45 . . . . .18 A2
Saville Cl B45 . . . . .33 B7
Saxelby Cl B14 . . . . . . .20 E2
Saxelby House B14 . . . .20 E2
Saxilby Pl 1 DY13 . . . . .44 B4
Saxon Bsns Pk B60 . . . .67 E2
Saxon Cl
Clifton upon Teme WR6 . .97 E7
Studley B80 . . . . .90 E5
Saxon Wood Cl 2 B31 . .19 A4
Saxonbury WR11 . . . . . .161 E2
Saxonfields 2 B50 . . . .136 D4
Saxons Way B14 . . . . . .21 A2
Sayers Ave B14 . . . . . .138 E4
Scafell Cl WR4 . . . . . . .116 A5
Scafell Rd DY8 . . . . .6 B6
Scaife Rd B60 . . . . .68 B7
Scarfield Hill B48 . . . . .50 E5
School Ave WR11 . . . . .135 E4
School Bank WR9 . . . . .83 B4
School Dr
Bromsgrove B60 . . . . . .49 A3
Stourbridge DY8 . . . . . . .5 F8
Wythall B47 . . . . .36 A3
School La
Alvechurch B48 . . . . . . .51 B5
Badsey WR11 . . . . .162 E3
Bretforton WR11 . . . . . .163 C4
Crowle WR7 . . . . .117 E5
Eckington WR10 . . . . . .171 E7
Hagley DY9 . . . . .15 D6
Halesowen B63 . . . . .7 F2
Lickey End B60 . . . . . . .49 B6
North & Middle Littleton
WR11 . . . . .149 A3
Overbury GL20 . . . . . . .185 F7
South Littleton WR11 . . .148 F2
Upton Snodsbury WR7 . .131 C8
Upton upon Severn WR8 .169 C5
Upton Warren B61 . . . . .66 F3
Wick WR10 . . . . .159 A7
School Rd
Aston Somerville WR12 .175 E1
Birmingham B28 . . . . . .21 D6
Birmingham, Eachway
B45 . . . . .32 E6
Birmingham, Yardley Wood
B14 . . . . .21 C4
Dodderhill WR9 . . . . . . .85 E8
Elmley Lovett WR9 . . . . .65 B6
Evesham WR11 . . . . . . .161 B6
Hanbury B60 . . . . .87 A5
Pebworth CV37 . . . . . .150 E2
Salford Priors WR11 . . .135 E3
Worcester WR2 . . . . . .114 F1
School St
Honeybourne WR11 . . . .164 A4
Stourbridge DY8 . . . . . . .5 F6
Schoolhouse Cl B38 . . .20 B2
Scobell Cl 3 B98 . . . . . .90 C1
Scotland La B32 . . . . . .18 C7
Scotland Pl 3 WR15 . . .55 E5
Scots Cnr B14 . . . . .20 E8
Scots La WR13 . . . . . . .62 F5
Scott Rd B97 . . . . .89 C8
Scott's Rd DY8 . . . . .5 F6
Scribers La B28 . . . . . . .21 E4
Sculthorpe Rd DY10 . . .14 B2
Seabright Way WV15 . . . .1 C5
Seafield La Beoley B98 . .53 A2
Portway B48 . . . . .52 E4
Seaford La
Naunton Beauchamp
WR10 . . . . .132 A4
Peopleton WR10 . . . . . .131 F3
Seals Gn B38 . . . . .34 D7
Sebright Ave
3 Worcester WR5 . . . .115 C1
Worcester WR5 . . . . . .128 D8
Sebright Cl WR10 . . . . .144 C1
Sebright Gn DY11 . . . . .12 C3
Sebright Rd DY11 . . . . .12 C3
Securehold Bsns Ctr
B98 . . . . .71 B2

Sedge Ave B38 . . . . . . .19 F3
Sedge Cl WR2 . . . . . . .114 D2
Sedge Dr B61 . . . . .49 A6
Sedgeberrow CE Fst Sch
WR11 . . . . .175 A1
Sedgeberrow Covert 4
B38 . . . . .34 E8
Sedgeberrow Rd B63 . . . .8 A2
Sedgebourne Way B31 . .18 C1
Sedgefield Wlk B61 . . . .32 B1
Sedgeford DY5 . . . . .6 D8
Sedgley Cl B98 . . . . . . .70 F4
Seedgreen Cl 3 DY13 . .62 E8
Seedgreen La DY13 . . . .63 A5
Seedhouse Ct B64 . . . . . .8 B8
Segbourne Rd B45 . . . .32 F8
Selba Dr DY11 . . . . .26 F6
Selborne Gr B13 . . . . . .21 C5
Selborne Rd 7 WR1 . . .115 A5
Selborne Rd W WR1 . . .115 A5
Selby Gr B13 . . . . .21 C6
Selcombe Way B38 . . . .34 F7
Selcroft Ave B32 . . . . . . .9 F5
Selly Hall Croft B30 . . . .20 A6
Selly Oak Colls B29 . . . .19 D8
Selly Oak Rd B30 . . . . . .19 E5
Selly Oak Specl Sch
B29 . . . . .19 E8
Sellywood Rd B29,
B30 . . . . .19 E8
Selma Gr B14 . . . . .21 D5
Selsdon Rd
Kidderminster DY11 . . . . .27 B5
Wythall B47 . . . . .36 C5
Selsey Cl WR4 . . . . . . .116 A7
Senneleys Pk Rd B31 . . . .9 E1
Sensall Rd DY9 . . . . .6 F3
Serin Cl DY10 . . . . .28 A1
Serpentine The DY11 . . .27 C4
Servite Ct B14 . . . . .21 A2
Seven Acres WR4 . . . . .116 A4
Seven Acres La B98 . . . .71 C5
Seven Acres Rd
Birmingham B31 . . . . . .19 C1
Halesowen B62 . . . . .9 A5
Sevenhills Dr DY13 . . . .62 D8
Severn Cl B61 . . . . .49 A8
Severn Ct 10 WR9 . . . . .84 D1
Severn Dr
Ashchurch GL20 . . . . . .184 C1
Great Malvern WR14 . . .153 D8
Upton upon Severn WR8 .169 C6
Severn Gr DY11 . . . . . . .27 B3
Severn House 4 B68 . . . .9 B8
Severn Hts WR6 . . . . . .82 B3
Severn Rd Halesowen B63 .7 B5
Stourbridge DY8 . . . . . . .5 F3
Severn Side DY13 . . . . .44 A2
Severn Side N DY12 . . .26 B4
Severn Side S DY12 . . .26 B3
Severn Terr WR1 . . . . .115 B3
Severn Way
Bewdley DY12 . . . . .25 F3
Wythall B47 . . . . .35 E2
Severndale WR9 . . . . . .84 D1
Severnside Bsns Pk
DY13 . . . . .44 A2
Seward Rd WR11 . . . . .162 D3
Seymour Ave WR3 . . . .115 A8
Seymour Dr B98 . . . . . .71 A5
Seymour Pl GL20 . . . . .196 E5
Seymour Rd
Kidderminster DY11 . . . . .27 B8
Stourbridge DY9 . . . . . . .7 A4
Shadymoor Dr DY5 . . . . .6 C8
Shaftesbury Ave DY9 . . .6 C2
Shaftesbury Cl B60 . . . .49 B2
Shaftesbury Gn 8 WR4 116 C3
Shaftland Cross WR9 . .118 B7
Shaftsbury Ave B63 . . . .7 B7
Shakells Cl B97 . . . . . . .89 E4
Shakespeare Ave B98 . .71 A2
Shakespeare Ct 4
GL20 . . . . .196 E6
Shakespeare Dr DY10 . .28 B6
Shakespeare House
B31 . . . . .34 A8
Shakespeare La WR11 .148 B6
Shakespeare Rd
1 Worcester WR2 . . . .114 D2
Worcester WR2 . . . . . .114 D2
Shalnecote Gr B14 . . . .20 C5
Sham La WV15 . . . . .1 F3
Shambles The WR1 . . .115 C2
Shandon Cl B32 . . . . . . .9 F3
Shannon Rd B38 . . . . . .34 E7
Shannon Way
Ashchurch GL20 . . . . . .197 C8
Evesham WR11 . . . . . . .162 A3
Tewkesbury GL20 . . . . .197 C8
Shap Dr WR4 . . . . .116 B6
Shapinsay Dr B45 . . . . .17 F1
Sharman Rd WR1 . . . . .115 A5
Sharpe Rd WR2 . . . . . .128 C3
Sharps Cl B45 . . . . .33 A7
Sharpway Gate B60 . . . .86 E8
Sharry La CV37 . . . . . . .151 E2
Shatterford Wildlife
Sanctuary★ DY12 . . . .11 D6
Shaw Ave DY10 . . . . . . .28 B6
Shaw Hedge Rd DY12 . .26 C4
Shaw La Dodderhill B60 . .86 B8
Stoke Prior B60 . . . . . . .67 C3
Shaw La Ind Est B60 . . .67 C2
Shaw St WR1 . . . . .115 B3
Shawbank Rd B98 . . . . .71 B3

Shawbrook Gr 10 B14 ....21 A3
Shawbury Cl B98 .....71 E3
Shawfield B47 .....36 A5
Shawhurst Croft B47 ..36 A7
Shawhurst Gdns B47 ..36 B7
Shawhurst La B47 .....36 A6
Shaws Cl B97 .....69 F2
Shearwater Cl
  Birmingham B45 .....32 F6
  Kidderminster DY10 ....28 B1
Sheenhill Rd
  Honeybourne WR11 ....164 A7
  South Littleton WR11 ...163 F8
Sheepcote Grange B61 .48 F5
Sheepcroft Cl B97 .....69 F2
Sheepmoor Cl B17 ....9 F8
Sheepscombe Dr
  WR4 .....116 A6
Sheepwalks La DY7 ....3 A6
Sheepwash La
  Kinver DY7 .....3 C3
  Wolverley & Cookley
  DY11 .....12 C8
Sheerwater Dr DY5 ....6 B6
Sheffield Cl 4 WR5 ...115 F1
Shelah Rd B63 .....8 A6
Sheldon Cl 1 WR10 ..144 C1
Sheldon Dr B31 .....18 D2
Sheldon Pk Rd WR3 ...102 A2
Sheldon Rd B98 .....90 A8
Shelduck Cl DY10 .....28 B3
Shelfield Rd B14 .....20 C3
Shell Cnr Trad Est B62 .8 D8
Shelley Ave B97 .....27 E7
Shelley Cl Catshill B61 ..49 A8
  Redditch B97 .....89 C8
  Stourbridge DY8 .....6 A8
  Worcester WR3 .....115 C7
Shelley House B63 ....7 B5
Shelly Twr B31 .....19 C3
Shelsley Dr WR13 ....152 D3
Shelton La B63 .....7 E5
Sheltwood Cl B97 .....70 A2
Sheltwood La B60,
  B97 .....69 A3
Shenley Ct Sch B29 ..18 F7
Shenley Fields Dr B31 .18 F8
Shenley Fields Rd B29 .19 B8
Shenley Gdns B29 ....19 A7
Shenley Gn B29 .....18 F6
Shenley Hill B31 .....18 F6
Shenley La B29 .....18 F7
Shenstone Ave
  Halesowen B62 .....8 E5
  Stourbridge DY8 .....5 D3
Shenstone Cl B60 .....49 B3
Shenstone Ct
  Bromsgrove B60 .....49 B3
  Solihull B90 .....21 D2
Shenstone Flats B62 ..8 F5
Shenstone Rd B14 ....21 A1
Shenstone Trad Est B63 .8 C4
Shenstone Valley Rd
  B62 .....8 F6
Shephard Mead GL20 .196 D5
Shepherds Brook Rd
  DY9 .....6 D5
Shepherds Cl 5 WR9 ..84 D5
Shepherds Hill 4 WR9 ..84 D5
Shepherds Pool 1
  WR11 .....161 D5
Shepherds Way WR9 ..84 D5
Shepherds Wlk B60 ...67 E7
Shepley Mdw B45 ....50 B8
Shepley Rd
  Barnt Green B45 .....50 A7
  Birmingham B45 .....33 B6
Sheraton Dr DY10 ....28 B6
Sheraton Grange DY8 ..5 F2
Sheraton Rd B60 .....49 C1
Sherbourne Cl B98 ....71 D2
Sherbourne Rd
  Blackheath B64 .....8 B8
  Stourbridge DY8 .....6 B4
Sheridan Row 1 WR4 .116 C1
Sheringham Rd
  Birmingham B30 .....20 B3
  Worcester WR5 .....128 D6
Sherrard's Gn Rd
  WR14 .....139 C1
Sherratts The WR9 ....65 B6
Sherridge Rd WR6 ...125 E5
Sherriff St WR4 .....115 D3
Sherston Covert 1 B30 .20 C2
Sherwood Cl B28 .....21 F5
Sherwood House B64 ..7 F8
Sherwood La WR2 ....127 F7
Sherwood Mews B28 ..21 E6
Sherwood Rd
  Birmingham B28 .....21 E7
  Bromsgrove B60 .....68 A6
  Stourbridge DY8 .....5 E7
Sherwood Wlk B45 ....18 B2
Shetland Cl 2 WR3 ...115 E7
Shifnal Wlk B31 .....33 F8
Shilton Gr B29 .....18 F8
Shinehill La WR11 ....149 B1
Ship Wrights Cl 9 WR4 .116 B5
Shipbourne Cl B32 ....9 F5
Shipley Gr B29 .....19 A8
Shipston Cl WR4 .....115 F1
Shipston Rd B31 .....19 B1
Shire Bsns Pk WR9 ....85 B1
Shire Way WR9 .....85 B1
Shirehampton Cl B97 ..89 C6
Shireland Cl B97 .....70 A4
Shirley Cl 4 WR14 ...139 B1
Shirley Jones Cl WR9 ..84 C3

Shirley Rd
  Birmingham, King's Norton
  B30 .....20 A5
  Droitwich WR9 .....84 E1
Shirley Sta B90 .....21 F1
Shop La WR11 .....163 C5
Shor St 6 WR11 .....161 E4
Short St Halesowen B63 ..7 F5
  Stourbridge DY8 .....5 F1
Shorters Ave B14 .....21 B4
Shortlands Cl B30 ....20 A2
Shortyard The DY11 ...12 E4
Shoulton La WR2 .....101 C2
Showell Cl WR9 .....103 E7
Showell Gn WR9 .....103 E7
Showell Gr WR9 .....103 E7
Showell Rd WR9 .....103 E7
Shrawley Ave DY11 ...27 B3
Shrawley Cl
  Birmingham B45 .....32 F7
  Halesowen B63 .....8 A2
Shrawley Rd
  Birmingham B31 .....19 C2
  Fernhill Heath WR3 ...102 E3
Shrewsbury Rd DY11 ..27 A6
Shrewton Ave B14 ....20 D2
Shrub Hill WR1 .....115 D3
Shrub Hill Rd WR1 ...115 D3
Shrubbery DY10 .....13 B5
Shrubbery Ave WR1 ..115 B5
Shrubbery Cl DY10 ...27 F7
Shrubbery Rd
  Bromsgrove B61 .....48 E1
  Drakes Broughton WR10 .143 F6
  Worcester WR1 .....115 B5
Shrubbery St DY10 ...27 F7
Shrublands Ave B68 ..9 B7
Shut Mill La B62 .....16 D2
Shuttlefast La WR13 ..153 A1
Sibdon Gr B31 .....34 A8
Sidbury WR5 .....115 C1
Sidemoor Fst Sch B61 .48 E3
Sidings La WR10 .....160 D8
Sidings Rd WR8 .....142 E2
Sidings The DY9 .....15 A6
Sidlaw Cl B63 .....7 D2
Silk Printing Ctr The★
  GL20 .....186 D5
Sillins Ave B98 .....71 A3
Sillins La B97 .....88 E6
Silver Birch Dr
  Hollywood B47 .....36 B6
  Kidderminster DY10 ...28 C5
  Kinver DY7 .....3 F5
Silver Birches Bsns Pk 3
  B60 .....67 F4
Silver Innage B63 ....7 F7
Silver St Birmingham B14 .20 E8
  9 Colwall Stone WR13 ..152 B2
  Hollywood B47 .....35 E5
  Kidderminster DY10 ...27 E7
  Redditch B97, B98 ....70 E4
  Worcester WR1 .....115 C3
Silverdale B61 .....48 F4
Silverdale Ave WR5 ..115 F1
Silverfield Cl B14 ....20 E8
Silvermead Ct B47 ...35 F5
Silverstone Ave DY11 .12 D1
Silverthorne La B64 ..7 D8
Silvester Way DY5 ....6 B8
Silvington Cl B29 .....19 C7
Simcox Gdns B32 ....9 D2
Simeon's Wlk DY5 ....6 F7
Simmons Dr B32 .....9 D4
Simmons Leasow B32 .9 E2
Simms La B47 .....36 A5
Simon De Montfort Dr 1
  WR11 .....161 E7
Simon de Montfort Mid Sch
  WR11 .....161 E2
Simon Evans Cl DY14 .22 D4
Simon Rd B47 .....36 A7
Simon's Way 3 WR11 .161 E4
Sinderberry Dr GL20 .184 E1
Sinton La WR9 .....83 B3
Sinton Terr WR2 .....114 F1
Sion Ave WR10 .....13 A1
Sion Gdns 1 DY13 ...44 A3
Sion Hill WR10 .....12 F1
Sion Hill Mid Sch DY10 .13 A2
Sir George's Mall 6
  DY10 .....27 E6
Sir Hilton's Rd B31 ..34 C7
Sir Richards Dr B17 ..9 F7
Sir Theodore Pritchett Inf &
  Jun Sch B14 .....20 D2
Sir Walter's Mall 8 DY10 27 E6
Sisefield Rd B38 .....20 A1
Siskin Dr WR5 .....6 C3
Siskin Way DY10 .....28 B1
Site 7 Trading Est WR9 .65 B8
Siviter St B63 .....8 B8
Six Acres B32 .....9 C4
Six Acres Croft 3 WR4 .116 A4
Six Ashes DY14 .....22 E7
Sixteen Acres La B50 .149 E8
Skenfrith Pl 9 WR4 ..116 C6
Skiddaw Cl WR4 .....116 B5
Skilts Ave B98 .....70 F1
Skilts Sch B98 .....72 C4
Skinner Rd WR2 .....114 F1
Skinner St WR2 .....114 F1
Skipton Cres 2 WR4 .116 C7
Skomer Cl B45 .....17 C1
Skylark Way DY11 ...28 A2
Skyrrold Rd WR14 ...153 C8
Slad The DY13 .....44 D6
Sladd La DY11 .....12 A5

Slade Ave WR4 .....116 B5
Slade La Birmingham B28 .21 E3
  Shrawley WR6 .....62 D2
Slade Rd B63 .....7 C6
Sladen CE Mid Sch The
  DY10 .....27 F7
Sladepool Farm Rd
  B14 .....21 A2
Slideslow Ave B60 ....49 B2
Slideslow Dr B60 .....49 B3
Slimbridge Cl
  Redditch B97 .....89 E5
  6 Worcester WR5 ...128 C5
Slims Gate B63 .....8 A4
Sling La
  Great Malvern WR14 ..139 A1
  Hindlip WR3 .....103 B2
Sling The DY10 .....27 E6
Slingfield Mills DY10 ..27 D6
Slingfield Rd B31 ....19 C1
Slingpool Wlk WR2 ..115 A1
Slough The B97, B80 ..90 B4
Small La B94 .....53 E6
Smallbrook Rd WR12 .177 D2
Smallshire Way DY8 ..5 E8
Smallwood Almshouses
  B98 .....70 E3
Smallwood Arch 5 B98 .70 E4
Smallwood St B98 ....70 E3
Smedley Crooke Pl
  B48 .....34 C2
Smirrells Rd B28 .....21 E5
Smite La WR3 .....103 E2
Smith's La 2 GL20 ...196 E6
Smithfields 3 DY8 ....6 A5
Smiths Ave WR2 .....114 E1
Smiths Cl B32 .....9 B1
Smiths Ct 10 GL20 ...196 E6
Smiths Way WR11 ....158 C7
Smokey La WR10 .....160 B4
Snake La B48 .....51 A6
Snake Terr B48 .....51 A6
Snakes Lake La B61 ..48 D6
Sneechill WR7 .....130 B7
Snowberry Ave WR4 ..116 A4
Snowberry Cl 8 DY13 .43 E4
Snowdon Cl DY11 ....12 C1
Snowdon Gr B63 .....7 D1
Snowdon Rd DY8 .....6 B6
Snowdonia Rd GL20 ..197 A4
Snowford Cl B90 .....21 F1
Snowshill Cl
  Redditch B98 .....71 B6
  2 Worcester WR4 ...116 B7
Snowshill Dr WR12 ..190 D6
Snuff Mill Wlk DY12 ..26 A2
Solcum La DY11 .....12 D6
Solent Pl WR11 .....161 E3
Solent Rd WR11 .....161 E3
Solitaire Ave WR2 ...114 D3
Somerdale Rd B31 ....19 C4
Somerford Rd B29 ...18 F8
Somerleyton Ave DY10 .28 A5
Somerleyton Ct 3 DY10 .28 A5
Somers Cl WR13 .....125 F2
Somers Pk Ave WR14 .138 F4
Somers Pk Prim Sch
  WR14 .....138 F4
Somers Rd
  Great Malvern WR14 ..138 F3
  Halesowen B62 .....8 C5
Somers' Rd WR1 .....115 A5
Somerset Dr
  Birmingham B31 .....33 F7
  Kidderminster DY11 ...12 C1
  Stourbridge DY8 .....5 D7
Somerset Pl
  Tewkesbury GL20 ....196 F3
  Worcester WR1 .....115 B5
Somerville Rd WR4 ..115 E3
Sommerfield Rd B32 ..9 B5
Sonata Rd B60 .....49 C1
Sorrell Wlk DY5 .....6 B6
Soudan B97 .....70 C2
Souters House WR3 ..18 D8
South Ave DY8 .....5 F4
South Bank Rd B64 ..7 F8
South Birmingham Coll (Hall
  Gn Campus) B28 ....21 E8
South Bromsgrove Com High
  Sch (Tech Coll) B60 ..67 F8
South Cres B60 .....49 A1
South Croft WR2 .....127 E8
South E Quadrant 8 B98 70 E4
South Gdns DY9 .....15 A4
South Lawn WR14 ...152 E5
South Moons Moat Ind Est
  B98 .....71 D4
South Par WR11 .....115 B2
South Pk Dr WR9 ....84 D4
South Quay WR11 ....115 B2
South Rd
  Birmingham, King's Heath
  B14 .....20 D6
  Birmingham, Northfield
  B31 .....18 F2
  Bromsgrove B60 .....68 B7
  Hagley DY9 .....15 A4
  Stourbridge DY8 .....5 E4
South St
  3 Kidderminster DY10 ..27 E6
  Redditch B98 .....70 E3
  13 Redditch B98 ....115 C2
South Wlk B31 .....19 C1
Southall Ave WR3 ...115 A8
Southall Dr DY11 .....45 A1
Southam Cl B28 .....21 E8
Southam Rd B28 .....21 E8

Southbank Rd B64 ....7 F8
Southcote Gr B38 ....19 D1
Southcott Ave DY5 ...6 A7
Southcrest Gdns B97 ..70 D1
Southcrest Rd B98 ...71 A2
Southdown Rd 6 WR3 .115 C2
Southern House B13 ..21 A7
Southfield St WR1 ...115 C5
Southgate B64 .....7 D8
Southgate Cl DY11 ...27 A4
Southmead Cres WR8 .70 F3
Southmead Dr B60 ...49 B6
Southmead Gdns B80 .90 E3
Southminster Dr B14 .20 E6
Southview Ridge DY5 ..6 D7
Southville Bglws For Old
  People B14 .....21 B4
Southwick Rd B62 ....8 D8
Southwold Ave B30 ..20 C3
Southwood Cl 6 WR5 .128 C6
Southwood Covert B14 .20 C2
Sovereign Hts WR5 ...18 C1
Sovereign Rd B30 ....20 A4
Spa Gdns GL20 .....197 B7
Spa Gr B30 .....20 C8
Spa Rd WR9 .....84 F2
Spadesbourne Rd B60 .49 C6
Sparrey Dr B30 .....20 C8
Sparrowhall La WR2 .127 B3
Sparrowhawk Cl
  WR14 .....139 C4
Speedwell Gdns DY5 ..6 B6
Speedwell House B38 .20 A1
Spencer Ave DY12 ...26 C4
Spencer Dr WR14 ....153 A7
Spencer St WR2 .....27 C4
Spennells Fst Sch
  DY10 .....28 A2
Spennells Valley Rd
  DY10 .....28 A3
Spenser Rd WR2 .....114 D3
Spenser Wlk B61 .....49 D3
Spernal Ash B80 .....90 F1
Spernal La B80 .....91 B1
Spetchley Dr WR7 ....89 C6
Spetchley Pk & Gdns★
  WR5 .....129 F8
Spetchley Rd WR5 ...116 B1
Spiceland Rd B31 ....18 F6
Spies Cl B62 .....8 F6
Spies La B62 .....8 F5
Spindle Cl DY11 .....12 C1
Spindle Rd 2 WR14 .139 C3
Spinney Cl
  Birmingham B31 .....19 B3
  Kidderminster DY11 ...27 A7
Spinney Mews B97 ...70 C1
Spinney The
  Worcester WR2 .....114 E5
  Wythall B47 .....36 B4
Spion Kop WR10 .....144 C5
Spiral Cl B62 .....8 E8
Spiral Ct DY8 .....6 A4
Spire View B61 .....48 F3
Spirehouse La B60 ...49 E5
Splash Leisure Complex The
  WR14 .....152 E4
Spoon Dr B38 .....19 D2
Spreadbury Cl B17 ...9 F8
Spring Bank
  Defford WR8 .....157 D3
  Worcester WR3 .....102 E1
Spring Cl
  2 Colwall Stone WR13 ..152 B2
  Hagley DY9 .....14 F4
  Kinver DY7 .....3 F5
  3 Tenbury Wells WR15 ..55 F6
Spring Cres B64 .....7 F7
Spring Gdns
  Great Malvern WR14 ..139 B5
  Tenbury Wells WR15 ..55 F5
  Worcester WR1 .....115 C2
Spring Gr Cres DY11 ..27 B3
Spring Gr La WR15 ...55 E2
Spring Gr Rd DY11 ...27 B3
Spring Hill WR5 .....115 D2
Spring La
  Great Malvern WR14 ..139 B4
  Romsley B62 .....16 D4
  Worcester WR5 .....115 D4
Spring La N WR14 ...139 C4
Spring La S WR14 ...139 C3
Spring Mdw
  Halesowen B63 .....7 F2
  1 Worcester WR4 ...116 B4
Spring St Halesowen B63 .7 D1
  Stourbridge DY9 .....6 E4
Springbrook La B94 ..53 F7
Springfield GL20 .....197 B7
Springfield Ave
  Bromsgrove B60 .....68 A8
  Stourbridge DY9 .....6 E4
Springfield Cl 2 WR5 .128 D6
Springfield Ct B28 ...21 F8
Springfield Dr
  1 Evesham WR11 ...161 E1
  Halesowen B62 .....8 D7
Springfield Glade 1
  WR14 .....138 F5
Springfield House
  DY10 .....27 F8
Springfield La
  Broadway WR12 .....177 C1
  Kidderminster DY10 ...27 F8
Springfield Rd
  Birmingham, King's Heath
  B14 .....20 F8

Springfield Rd continued
  Halesowen B62 .....8 D7
  Worcester WR5 .....128 D6
Springhill Gdns B97 ..69 E2
Springhill Rise DY12 ..26 C4
Springs Ave B61 .....32 A1
Springside B98 .....90 C8
Springslade B32 .....9 F5
Springvale Rd B97 ...69 F2
Springwater Cl 8 GL20 .184 E1
Spruces The 14 F4
Square Cl B32 .....9 C3
Square The B48 .....51 B6
Squire's Cl WR5 .....141 C7
Squire's Wlk WR5 ...141 B6
Squires Ct DY5 .....6 C8
Squires The
  Childswickham WR12 ..176 F2
  Evesham WR11 .....161 C6
  Norton & Lenchwick
  WR11 .....147 B1
Squirrel Dr WR5 .....128 F6
Squirrels Hollow B68 .9 D7
Stable Way B60 .....67 E6
Stableford Cl
  Birmingham B32 .....9 F4
  Redditch B97 .....89 D7
Stacey Dr B13 .....21 A5
Stacey Grange Gdns
  B45 .....33 A6
Stadium Cl WR10 ....27 F4
Stafford Ave WR4 ...116 D6
Stagborough Way DY13 .43 E4
Stainburn Ave WR2 .114 D1
Stainburn Cl WR2 ...114 D2
Staite Dr DY10 .....13 A5
Stakenbridge La DY10 .14 D4
Stallard Rd WR2 .....114 E1
Stalls Farm Rd WR9 ..84 E3
Stambermill Dr DY9 ..6 D5
Stambermill House DY9 .6 D5
Stamford Rd DY5 ....6 C6
Stamford St DY8 .....5 F7
Stanage Cl 10 WR4 ..116 B5
Stanbrook Abbey
  WR2 .....140 E8
Stanbrook House Rd 4
  WR2 .....140 E8
Stanbrook Rd WR15 ..55 F6
Stanbury Rd B14 .....21 B4
Standlake House B31 ..18 E5
Stanfield Rd B32 .....9 E6
Stanford Cl B97 .....89 B6
Stanford Gr B63 .....7 C1
Stanford Rd
  Great Witley WR6 ....60 F1
  Northway GL20 .....197 E8
Stanhoe Cl DY5 .....6 D8
Stanier Rd WR4 .....116 B7
Stanklyn La Stone DY10 .28 C1
  Summerfield DY10 ...45 A8
Stanks La WR8 .....168 F2
Stanley Ave B32 .....9 E7
Stanley Cl B98 .....71 A5
Stanley Rd
  Birmingham, King's Heath
  B14 .....20 D7
  Great Malvern WR14 ..139 B1
  Oldbury B68 .....9 C1
  Stourbridge DY8 .....5 F3
  Worcester WR5 .....115 D2
Stanley Rd Prim Sch
  WR5 .....115 D2
Stanley St WR5 .....128 C7
Stanmore Cl B62 .....9 A3
Stanmore Rd WR2 ...127 C1
Stanton Fields WR10 .132 F3
Stanton Rd GL20 ....196 F7
Stanway Cl WR4 .....115 F7
Stanway Rd WR12 ...189 C1
Staple Flat B60 .....49 C8
Staple Hall Rd B31 ...19 B2
Staple Lodge Rd B31 .19 C2
Stapleford Croft B14 ..20 C2
Staplehurst Rd B28 ..21 F8
Stapleton Cl
  Redditch B98 .....71 D3
  Studley B80 .....90 D3
Stapleton Rd B80 ....90 D4
Staplow Rd WR5 .....129 A8
Star La 7 WR2 .....114 F1
Star St DY9 .....6 F5
Starling Cl 2 WR5 ...128 C5
Station App
  Barnt Green B45 .....50 D8
  Kidderminster DY10 ...27 F5
Station Cl WR7 .....143 D8
Station Cotts B60 ....50 A4
Station Dr
  Blakedown DY10 .....14 C2
  Bredon GL20 .....184 F6
  Earlswood B94 .....36 D1
  Hagley DY9 .....15 A6
Station Gdns 5 WR10 .171 E7
Station Hill 3 DY11 ..45 B2
Station La GL20 .....196 F2
Station Rd
  Alvechurch B48 .....51 A5
  Ashton under Hill WR11 .187 C8
  Beckford GL20 .....186 D4
  3 Bewdley DY12 ....26 C3
  Birmingham B13 .....20 D8
  Birmingham, King's Norton
  B30 .....19 E4

Station Rd *continued*
Birmingham, Northfield
  B31 ....19 A2
Blackheath, Haden Cross
  B64 ....8 A8
Blackwell B60 ....50 A5
Bretforton WR11 ....163 B5
Broadway WR12 ....177 B1
Central Engineer Park
  CV37 ....151 E4
Cleobury Mortimer DY14 ...22 D5
Drakes Broughton &
  Wadborough WR8 ....142 E4
Eckington WR10 ....171 E7
Fernhill Heath WR3 ....103 A4
Fladbury WR10 ....146 A2
Hagley DY9 ....15 A6
Hartlebury DY11 ....45 B2
Harvington WR11 ....148 B7
Hinton on the Green
  WR11 ....174 F5
Honeybourne WR11 ....164 B5
Offenham WR11 ....162 C7
Pershore WR10 ....144 D2
Ripple GL20 ....183 A8
Rock DY12 ....24 A5
Salford Priors WR11 ....135 F3
South Littleton WR11 ....162 F8
Stourbridge DY9 ....6 E6
Studley B80 ....90 D4
Tewkesbury GL20 ....196 F6
Wythall B47 ....36 B3
Station St Blackheath B64 ..7 C8
Bromsgrove B60 ....48 F1
4 Droitwich WR9 ....84 E3
Tewkesbury GL20 ....196 F6
Station Way B97 ......70 D3
Staveley Rd WR4 ......116 C4
Steamer Point WR14 ..139 B2
Steatite Way DY13 ....43 E5
Steel Rd B31 ....18 F2
Steelpark Rd B62 ......8 C7
Steene Gr B31 ....18 D3
Steeple Cl **3** DY14 ......22 C4
Steeples The DY8 ......6 B3
Steepwood Croft B30 ..19 D4
Stennels Ave B62 ......8 E4
Stennels Cres B62 ......8 E4
Stephenson Pl **2** DY12 ..26 C3
Stephenson Rd WR1 ..115 A4
Stephenson Terr WR1 ..115 A4
Stephenson Way
  WR11 ....164 A6
Steppes Piece B50 ..136 C5
Stepping Stones
Bidford-on-Avon B50 ..136 C5
Stourbridge DY9 ......6 B5
Sterrymere Gdns DY7 ..4 B4
Stevens Ave B32 ......9 D2
Stevens Rd DY9 ......6 D2
Stevenson Ave B98 ....70 F3
Steward Rd GL20 ....197 E8
Stewart Ct DY10 ....27 F5
Stewarts Rd B62 ......8 D7
Stewkins DY8 ......5 E8
Steynors Ave WR9 ....84 E2
Steynors Cl WR9 ....84 E2
Stilthouse Gr B45 ....33 A7
Stirchley Com Sch B30 ..20 A6
Stirchley Trad Est B30 ..20 B6
Stirling Ave WR4 ....116 C6
Stock Coppice Cl **1**
  WR4 ....116 B6
Stockhill Dr B45 ......32 F6
Stocking St DY9 ......6 F5
Stockmans Cl B38 ....34 E8
Stocks La Leigh WR13 ..126 B2
Newland WR13 ....139 C8
Stocks Rd WR6 ....124 E4
Stocks Wood B30 ....19 F8
Stockton Rd
Abberley WR6 ....60 B3
Stockton on Teme WR6 ..59 F3
Stockwell Ave DY6 ....6 D8
Stockwood La WR7 ..107 C1
Stoke Cross B60 ....68 E7
Stoke Gdns WR8 ....155 D4
Stoke La Dodderhill WR9 ..85 E7
Redditch B98 ....71 B7
Stoke Pound La
Stoke Pound B60 ....68 A4
Stoke Prior B60 ....67 F3
Stoke Prior Fst Sch
  B60 ....67 C3
Stoke Rd
Bromsgrove, Aston Fields
  B60 ....68 A7
Bromsgrove, Charford
  B60 ....67 F7
Stokes Rd GL20 ....183 A1
Stokesay Cl DY10 ....27 C4
Stokesay Gr B31 ....33 F8
Stokesay La **5** WR4 ..116 C6
Stone CE Fst Sch DY10 ..28 C2
Stone Cl Birmingham B38 ..19 F2
Colwall WR13 ....152 A1
Stone Cotts B31 ....19 A3
Stone Dr WR13 ....152 A1
Stone Hill DY10 ....28 E2
Stone La DY7 ....4 A4
Stone Yd B64 ....7 C8
Stonebow Rd
Drakes Broughton WR10 ..143 F6
Drakes Broughton &
  Wadborough WR10 ....144 A7

Stonebridge Cross Bsns Pk
  WR9 ....84 C6
Stonebrook Way B29 ..9 F2
Stonechat Cl DY10 ....28 B2
Stonecroft Ave B45 ..33 A7
Stonecrop Cl B38 ....34 F8
Stoneford La WR11 ..163 D2
Stonehenge Croft B14 ..20 D1
Stonehouse Cl B97 ....70 D1
Stonehouse Gr B32 ....9 D2
Stonehouse La
Birmingham B32 ......9 E2
Hopwood B48 ....34 E2
Stonehouse Rd B60 ..49 A1
Stoneleigh Cl
Redditch B98 ....89 F6
6 Worcester WR5 ....128 C5
Stoneleigh House B32 ..9 F5
Stonepit La WR7 ....120 E7
Stonepits La B97 ....89 D4
Stonerwood Ave B28 ..21 E8
Stoneton Gr B29 ....19 A8
Stoney Hill Cl B60 ....49 A1
Stoney La
Birmingham, Quinton B32 ..9 B6
Blackwell B60 ....50 C2
Churchill DY10 ....14 E3
Hartlebury DY13 ....64 A6
Himbleton WR9 ....105 E3
Kidderminster DY10 ....27 E8
Stoney La Ind Est DY10 ..27 E8
Stoneycroft WR3 ....102 F2
Stoneyford Gr B14 ....21 B4
Stonnall Cl WR8 ....155 D5
Stony Furlong La
  WR10 ....171 F7
Storrage La B48 ....51 E3
Storrs Way The B32 ..18 B7
Stotfold Ave WR4 ....116 C4
Stotfold Rd B14 ....20 F2
Stour DY13 ....7 E6
Stour Hill DY5 ......7 A8
Stour House **2** B68 ....9 B8
Stour La **4** DY13 ....44 A3
Stour Vale Rd DY9 ....6 F6
Stour Valley Cl DY5 ....6 D7
Stourbridge Coll (Church St
** Ctr)** DY8 ....6 A5
Stourbridge Coll (Westhill
** Ctr)** DY8 ....6 B4
Stourbridge Coll
Stourbridge DY8 ....5 E5
Stourbridge, Old Swinford
  DY8 ....6 A4
Stourbridge Juntion Sta
  DY8 ....6 B3
Stourbridge Rd
Belbroughton DY9 ....31 B7
Blakedown DY9 ....14 F1
Catshill B61 ....48 F7
Churchill DY10 ....14 A6
Churchill & Blakedown
  DY10 ....13 D2
Fairfield B61 ....31 D2
Hagley DY9 ....15 C7
Halesowen B63 ....7 F5
Kidderminster DY10 ....27 E8
Lower Clent DY9 ....15 E3
Stourbridge DY9 ......6 D5
Stourbridge Town Sta
  DY8 ....6 A5
Stourbridge Trad Est
  DY8 ....6 A6
Stourdale Rd B64 ....7 C8
Stourdell Rd B63 ....7 E6
Stourminster Sch DY10 ..28 B4
Stourport Rd
Bewdley DY12 ....26 C3
Great Witley WR6 ....61 B1
Hartlebury DY13 ....63 D8
Kidderminster DY11 ....27 C2
Stourport-on-Severn Fst Sch
  DY13 ....44 A4
Stourport-on-Severn High
** Sch** DY13 ....44 A5
Stourton Cres DY7 ......4 F7
Stourton Rd B32 ......9 B5
Stourvale Ind Est DY9 ..6 F6
Stourvale Trad Est B63 ..7 D6
Stouton Croft WR4 ....84 E4
Stow Dr DY5 ....6 B6
Stowe La WR13 ....166 A8
Strand La WR3 ....103 B4
Strand The
Bromsgrove B61 ....49 A3
Charlton WR10 ....160 D8
Stratford Rd
Bidford-on-Avon B50 ..137 A5
Birmingham B28 ....21 F7
Bromsgrove B60 ....49 A2
Harvington WR11 ....148 B6
Honeybourne WR11 ....164 B5
Mickleton CV37 ....165 D6
Strensham Bsns Pk
  WR8 ....171 A2
Strensham Gate WR8 ..171 A4
Stretton Dr B45 ....33 A2
Stretton House **7** B97 ..70 A4
Stretton Rd DY11 ....27 B4
Stroma Ave **13** WR5 ..128 E6
Stronsay Cl B45 ....17 F1
Stroud Rd B90 ....21 F2
Stuart Rd B62 ......8 F5
Stuart Rise WR5 ....128 F8
Stuarts Ct DY9 ....15 B8
Stuarts Gn DY9 ....15 B8
Stuarts Way B32 ....18 B7
Stud La WR6 ....60 C4

Studley Dr DY5 ......6 C8
Studley Gate DY8 ....5 D5
Studley High Sch B80 ....90 E3
Studley Inf Sch B80 ....90 E4
Studley Rd B98 ....71 A2
Studley St Mary's CE Jun Sch
  B80 ....90 E3
Suckley Prim Sch
  WR6 ....124 A4
Suckley Rd
Bransford WR6 ....126 B6
Leigh WR6 ....125 F5
Sudeley Ave **8** WR4 ..116 C6
Sudeley Cl WR14 ....138 F6
Sudgrove Cl **2** WR4 ..115 F7
Suffield Cl WR13 ....126 B4
Suffolk Dr
Brierley Hill DY5 ......6 C7
Worcester WR3 ....115 E7
Suffolk La WR6 ....60 F5
Suffolk Way **1** WR6 ..104 B8
Sugar Loaf La DY10 ....14 B7
Sugarbrook Ct **1** B60 ..67 F6
Sugarbrook La B60 ....68 A5
Sugarbrook Rd B60 ....68 A7
Summer Hill **6** B63 ....8 B3
Summer Hollow WR2 ..127 A8
Summer Pl DY11 ....27 C5
Summer St Redditch B98 ..70 E3
Stourbridge, Lye DY9 ......6 E5
Stourbridge, Wollaston DY8 ..5 F5
2 Worcester WR3 ....115 B6
Summercroft **7** DY13 ..62 E8
Summerfield Dr **2** B29 ..19 A7
Summerfield Gdns
  WR11 ....161 B2
Summerfield La DY11 ..44 F7
Summerfield Rd
Clent DY9 ....15 E2
Great Malvern WR14 ....139 B5
2 Stourport-on-Severn
  DY13 ....44 B4
Summerfields Ave B62 ..8 F7
Summerhill Ave DY11 ..27 C4
Summerhouse Cl B97 ..89 A6
Summervale Cl DY9 ....15 A5
Summervale Rd DY9 ....15 A5
Summerway La DY11 ..44 F6
Summit Gdns B63 ......7 F3
Summit The DY14 ....40 E4
Summit The DY9 ......6 D4
Sun St GL20 ....196 E7
Sunbury Cotts B31 ....19 A4
Sunbury Rd
Birmingham B31 ....33 E7
Halesowen B63 ....7 F4
Suncroft B32 ......9 C5
Sundbury Rise B31 ....19 B5
Sunderland Dr DY8 ....6 A8
Sunderton Rd B14 ....20 E4
Sunningdale
Bromsgrove B60 ....49 A1
Halesowen B63 ....8 E4
Sunningdale Cl
Redditch B98 ....70 F4
Stourbridge DY8 ....5 F2
Sunningdale Holiday Est
  WR6 ....111 D6
Sunningdale Rd B61 ....67 D8
Sunny Bank Rd B68 ....9 F7
Sunnymead B60 ....49 A1
Sunnyside Gdns **1** DY11 ..12 B1
Sunnyside Rd WR1 ..115 B5
Sunnyside Sch WR1 ..115 A5
Sunrise **6** WR14 ....139 B1
Surfeit Hill Rd B64 ......7 D8
Surman St WR1 ....115 B4
Sussex Rd **7** B29 ....19 C7
Sutherland Rd B64 ......7 E8
Suthill Bridge WR6 ....59 B5
Sutton Cl **8** WR8 ....71 D2
Sutton Pk Fst Sch DY11 ..27 B4
Sutton Pk Gr DY11 ....27 C3
Sutton Pk Rd DY11 ....27 B3
Sutton Pk Rise DY11 ..27 B3
Sutton Rd DY11 ....27 C4
Swale Gr B38 ....19 F1
Swaledale Cl B60 ....67 E6
Swallow Cl **1** WR5 ..128 D5
Swallow Dr DY10 ....28 A2
Swallow Pl WR9 ....104 B7
Swallowfall Ave DY8 ....5 C4
Swallowfields WR1 ....115 A6
Swan Cl Blakedown DY10 ..14 B1
9 Tenbury Wells WR15 ..55 F6
Swan Ct **8** WR15 ....55 F6
Swan Ctr **7** DY10 ....27 E6
Swan Dr WR9 ....85 B3
Swan La
Evesham WR11 ....161 D5
Fairfield B61 ....31 E3
Tenbury Wells WR15 ....55 F6
Upton Warren B61 ....66 E5
Swan Orch WR6 ....125 A7
Swan St Alvechurch B48 ..51 B5
Stourbridge DY8* 5 E5
Swan Theatre* WR1 ..115 A3
Swanley Cl B62 ......9 A3
Swanpool Wlk WR2 ..115 A1
Swans Length B48 ....51 A7
Swansbrook Gdns **4**
  B38 ....20 C2
Swansbrook La B96 ....88 E1
Swanshurst Sch B13 ....21 B7
Swarthmore Rd B29 ....19 B7
Sweden La GL20 ....186 D2

Sweetpool La DY8 ......14 F5
Swift Cl B61 ....67 E8
Swift Pk Gr DY10 ....28 B2
Swilgate Rd GL20 ....196 E6
Swinburne Rd B97 ....89 C7
Swincross Rd DY8 ......6 C1
Swindell Rd DY9 ......6 C1
Swinesherd Way WR5 ..116 C1
Swinford Old Hall DY8 ..6 B3
Swinford Rd DY8 ......6 A3
Swinton Cl
3 Worcester WR2 ....114 E1
Worcester WR2 ....127 E8
Swinton La
5 Worcester WR2 ....114 E1
Worcester WR2 ....127 E8
Swiss Hts **3** DY13 ....43 E1
Sycamore Ave
Evesham WR11 ....161 F2
Redditch B98 ....70 E2
Sycamore Cl
Great Malvern WR14 ....139 A5
Kidderminster DY10 ....27 F3
Stourbridge DY9 ......5 D2
Sycamore Ct B30 ....19 E4
Sycamore Dr B47 ....36 B6
Sycamore Rd
Birmingham, Bournville
  B30 ....19 F7
11 Northway GL20 ....184 E1
Northway GL20 ....197 E8
Worcester WR4 ....115 E5
Sycamore Terr B14 ....20 C7
Sycamores The DY9 ....14 F5
Sydnall Cl B97 ....69 F2
Sydney Rd Blackheath B64 ..7 C8
Bromsgrove B61 ....48 E3
Sydney St WR3 ....115 B6
Sylvan Ave B31 ....18 F3
Sylvan Gn B62 ......8 D5
Sylvia Ave B31 ....34 B8
Synehurst WR11 ....162 D4
Synehurst Ave WR11 ..162 D4
Synehurst Cres WR11 ..162 D4
Sytchampton Endowed Fst
** Sch** WR9 ....64 B1

T

Tabberness Cl WR6 ..112 C3
Tabbs Gdns DY10 ....28 A6
Tagwell Cl WR9 ....104 B8
Tagwell Rd **2** WR9 ....85 A1
Tailor's La CV37 ....151 F1
Talavera Rd WR5 ....128 F3
Talbot Cl **1** DY11 ....45 A1
Talbot Pass **5** DY8 ....6 A5
Talbot Rd B60 ......49 A1
Talbot St Halesowen B63 ..7 C6
Kidderminster DY11 ....27 C4
Stourbridge, Lye DY9 ....6 A5
Talbotshill La DY10 ....13 C4
Talgarth Covert B38 ....34 E7
Tall Trees Cl B61 ....48 F8
Tall Trees Dr DY9 ......6 D2
Talladale B32 ....18 B7
Tallow Hill WR5 ....115 D3
Tamar Cl WR5 ....115 E3
Tamar Pl WR11 ....161 F3
Tamar Rise DY8 ......6 A8
Tamarisk Cl
Birmingham B29 ....19 B8
North Claines WR3 ....102 E3
Tame Rd B68 ......9 B8
Tame Rise B68 ......9 B8
Tamerton Rd B32 ......9 D1
Tamworth Ave **12** WR4 ..116 C6
Tan House La WR2 ....127 C7
Tan La **2** DY13 ....43 F4
Tandy Dr B14 ....20 F3
Tandy's La DY10 ....29 E4
Tanglewood Cl
Birmingham, Quinton B32 ..9 B4
Blackwell B60 ....50 A5
Tanhouse La
Great Malvern WR14 ....138 F6
Halesowen B63 ....7 C5
Redditch B98 ....71 C6
Tanners Cl **7** WR4 ....115 F6
Tanners Gn La B47,
  B94 ....36 B2
Tanners Hill DY12 ....25 E3
Tansy WR5 ....128 D4
Tantallon Dr B32 ......9 D1
Tanwood Cl B97 ....89 A6
Tanwood Cross DY10 ..30 B2
Tanwood La DY10 ....30 A2
Tanworth La B98 ....72 C7
Tanyard Cl B48 ....51 B6
Tanyard La B48 ....51 B6
Tapenhall Rd WR3 ....102 E2
Tardebigge CE Fst Sch
  B60 ....69 B7
Tardebigge Ct B97 ....69 C6
Tardebigge House B60 ..49 B3
Tarragon Gdns B31 ....18 C2
Tarrant Gr B32 ......9 F5
Tarrington Covert **6**
  B38 ....34 E8
Tattersall **2** WR4 ....116 B3
Taunton Cl B31 ....18 C2
Tavern La WR5 ....57 C7
Tavern Orch WR4 ....116 B5
Tawny Cl DY10 ....184 D1
Tay Ave WR5 ....128 E6
Tay Gr Birmingham B38 ..34 F8
Halesowen B62 ......8 E8

Tay Rd B45 ....18 B1
Taylor Rd B13 ....20 F5
Taylor's La **3** WR1 ..115 B3
Taylors La WR5 ....128 D4
Taynton Covert **4** B30 ..20 C3
Taysfield Rd B31 ....18 E6
Tayson Way **2** WR14 ..138 F5
Teal Cres DY10 ....28 B3
Teal Rd B80 ....90 F4
Tearne St WR2 ....114 E4
Teasdale Way DY9 ......6 D4
Teasel Cl WR5 ....128 D4
Teasel Way WR3 ....102 D2
Teazel Ave B30 ....19 D6
Ted Preston Cl GL20 ..196 F4
Tedstone Rd B32 ......9 E5
Tees Gr B38 ....34 F8
Teesdale Cl **4** WR9 ....84 D1
Teeswater Cl
Bromsgrove B60 ....67 E6
1 Worcester WR3 ....115 E7
Telford Dr DY12 ....26 A3
Teme Ave
Great Malvern WR14 ....153 D8
Kidderminster DY11 ....27 B3
Teme Cres **7** WR9 ....84 D1
Teme La WR6 ....112 C1
Teme Rd Halesowen B63 ..7 B5
Stourbridge DY8 ......5 F3
Worcester WR4 ....115 F3
Teme St WR15 ....55 F5
Temeside Cl **10** WR15 ..55 F6
Temeside Way WR2 ..127 F5
Temperance St **1** WR1 ..115 C2
Temple Ave WR13 ....139 F4
Temple Cl B98 ....89 A6
Temple Mews **1** WR11 ..161 D4
Ten Acres End B30 ....20 B8
Ten Ashes La B45 ....33 C4
Tenacres Fst Sch B98 ..71 F3
Tenacres La B98 ....71 F3
Tenbury & District Hospl
  WR15 ....55 F6
Tenbury CE Prim Sch
  WR15 ....55 F4
Tenbury Cl B98 ....71 C6
Tenbury High Sch
  WR15 ....55 E3
Tenbury House **2** B63 ..8 A3
Tenbury Mead **6** WR4 ..22 C4
Tenbury Mus* WR15 ....55 F5
Tenbury Rd
Birmingham B14 ....20 E6
Cleobury Mortimer DY14 ..22 B3
Tenbury Swimming Pool
  WR15 ....55 F5
Tenbury Wells Bsns Pk
  WR15 ....56 A3
Tenbury Wells Pump Rms*
  WR15 ....55 F5
Tenby Twr **2** B31 ....19 A1
Tenby Way DY13 ....43 E5
Tenlands Rd B63 ......7 F3
Tennal Dr B32 ......9 F6
Tennal Gr B32 ......9 F6
Tennal La B32 ......9 F6
Tennal Rd B32 ......9 F6
Tennis Ct B30 ....19 D4
Tennis Wlk WR1 ....115 B4
Tennyson Cl WR3 ....115 C7
Tennyson Dr WR14 ..139 A2
Tennyson House B31 ..34 A8
Tennyson Rd B97 ....89 C6
Tennyson Way B30 ....28 C6
Tenter Ct B63 ......8 B4
Tenter Dr B63 ......8 C4
Tenterfields B63 ......8 B4
Tenterfields Prim Sch
  B63 ....8 C4
Tern Gr B38 ....19 E1
Terrace Rd WR10 ....144 F4
Terrace The B64 ......7 E8
Terrill Ct **4** WR11 ..161 D5
Terrills La WR15 ....55 F1
Terrys Cl B98 ....70 F5
Tessall La B31 ....18 D2
Tetbury Dr WR4 ....116 A6
Tetbury Gr B31 ....18 D3
Teviot Gr B38 ....34 F8
Tewkesbury Borough Mus*
  GL20 ....196 E6
Tewkesbury CE Prim Sch
  GL20 ....196 F6
Tewkesbury Ind Est
  GL20 ....197 C8
Tewkesbury Rd
Bredon GL20 ....184 B2
Eckington WR10 ....171 F6
Thackeray Rd B30 ....19 D5
Thackholme **7** WR4 ..116 C5
Thame Ct B47 ....35 E2
Thames Cl WR5 ....115 E3
Thames Dr WR9 ....84 D1
Thane Cl B80 ....90 F4
Thatcham Rd **4** GL20 ..197 A3
Thatchers Ct WR9 ....84 D5
Thatchers The B62 ......8 E8
Thatchers Way WR9 ....84 D5
Thatchway Gdns B38 ..34 F7
Thelbridge Rd B31 ....33 E6
Theocs Cl GL20 ....196 E4
Thicknall Dr DY9 ......6 C2
Thicknall La DY9 ....15 B3
Thicknall Rise DY9 ....15 A4
Third Rd B61 ....31 F4
Thirlmere Cl **4** WR4 ..116 C6
Thirlmere Dr B13 ....21 D8
Thirlmere Rd DY13 ....43 F6

Thirlmere Wlk DY5 6 B7
Thirlstane Rd WR14 152 F6
Thirsk Way B61 32 B1
Thistle Cl 11 WR5 128 D5
Thistle Downs GL20 184 D1
Thistle Gn B38 34 E7
Thistle La B32 18 B7
Thistledown WR11 161 C1
Thomas Cl WR3 102 E2
Thomson Ave B38 19 D1
Thorn Ave WR4 115 E6
Thorn Lea WR11 162 A2
Thorn Rd B30 19 E7
Thornbury La B98 71 C7
Thorncliffe Cl B97 89 A6
Thorneloe Rd WR1 115 A5
Thorneloe Wlk WR1 115 A4
Thorngrove Rd 2
WR14 153 A8
Thornham Way B14 20 D1
Thornhill Rd
Brierley Hill DY5 6 E8
Halesowen B63 7 E3
Redditch B98 71 E6
Thornhurst Ave B32 9 E7
Thorns Com Coll DY5 6 E8
Thorns Prim Sch DY5 6 E7
Thorns Rd DY5 6 E7
Thornthwaite Cl B45 18 B2
Thornton House Sch
WR5 115 D1
Three Acres La B90 36 F6
Three Cnr Cl B90 36 E8
Three Cocks La WR11 148 B1
Three Counties Showground* WR13 153 B2
Three Oaks Rd B47 36 B4
Three Springs Rd 7
WR10 144 C1
Three Springs Trading Est
WR5 115 D2
Threlfall Dr DY12 26 D4
Threshfield Dr WR4 116 A4
Throckmorton Rd
Hill & Moor WR10 145 E4
Redditch B98 90 A8
Thruxton Cl
Birmingham B14 20 F3
Redditch B98 71 E3
Thurleigh Cl DY9 6 C2
Thurlestone Rd B31 33 E7
Thurloe Cres B45 17 E1
Tibbats Cl B32 9 C3
Tibberton CE Fst Sch
WR9 117 A8
Tibberton Cl B63 8 C4
Tibberton Cl B60 67 E7
Tibberton Rd WR14 153 A8
Ticknall Cl B97 70 A4
Tidbury Cl B97 89 C6
Tidbury Gn Sch B90 36 E4
Tidworth Croft 2 B14 21 A3
Tigley Ave B32 9 D1
Tilehouse B97 70 D2
Tilehouse La B90 36 E6
Till St WR3 115 C5
Tillington Cl B98 71 E3
Tilshead Cl B14 20 E3
Timber Down WR10 158 F7
Timber La WR10 158 F7
Timberdine Ave WR5 128 C7
Timberdine Cl
Halesowen B63 7 D6
Worcester WR5 128 D7
Timberdyne Cl DY14 41 C3
Timberhonger La
Bromsgrove B61 48 B2
Dodford with Grafton B61 47 F1
Timbertree Cres B64 7 E7
Timbertree Prim Sch
B64 7 E7
Timbertree Rd B64 7 F7
Timmis Rd DY9 6 C6
Timms Gn 1 WR12 177 E4
Tinker's Cross WR3 102 D3
Tinkers' Cross WR6 113 B5
Tinkers Farm Gr B31 18 E3
Tinkers Farm Rd B31 18 E3
Tinmeadow Cres B45 33 C7
Tintern Ave WR3 115 D5
Tintern Cl
Bromsgrove B61 48 E1
Kidderminster DY11 26 F6
Tintern House B32 9 F5
Tipper Trad Est DY9 7 A5
Tipping's Hill B97 89 C5
Tiree Ave WR5 128 E6
Tirle Bank Way GL20 197 B6
Tirlebrook Cty Prim Sch
GL20 197 C6
Titania Cl B45 18 A3
Tithe Ct WR11 148 F3
Titheway WR11 148 F3
Titterstone Rd B31 34 A8
Tiverton Cl 5 WR4 116 B7
Tixall Rd B28 21 E5
Toftdale Gn WR4 116 B4
Toll House Cl WR2 127 B8
Toll House Rd B45 33 C7
Tolladine Rd WR4 115 E3
Tolley Rd DY11 27 B1
Tollgate Cl B31 33 F8
Tollhouse Dr WR2 114 F3
Tollhouse Rd B60 67 E6
Tolsey La 5 GL20 196 E6
Tomkinson Dr DY11 27 B4
Tomlan Rd B31 34 C7
Toms Town La B80 90 E3
Top Field Wlk B14 20 D2
Top Rd B61 32 A4
Top St WR10 160 E8
Topfield House B14 20 E1
Topham Ave WR4 116 B3
Topland Gr B31 18 C2
Topsham Croft B14 20 D5
Toronto Pl 5 WR2 127 E6
Toronto Gdns B32 9 E6
Torre Ave B31 18 E2
Torridon Cl DY13 43 E7
Torrs Cl B97 70 D2
Torton La DY10 45 B5
Toulouse Dr WR5 128 F4
Towbury Cl B98 89 F5
Towbury Hill (Fort)*
GL20 183 C6
Tower Croft 4 B50 136 E5
Tower Dr B61 49 A6
Tower Hill
Bidford-on-Avon B50 136 E4
6 Droitwich WR9 85 A3
Tower House Dr GL19 192 E3
Tower Rd WR1 115 A6
Towers Cl DY10 28 B5
Town Acres 11 WR4 116 A5
Towneley WR4 116 C3
Townsend Ave B61 49 B4
Townsend St 5 WR1 115 A5
Townsend Way WR14 139 D4
Toy City* WR15 75 F4
Toys La B63 7 C5
Traceys Mdw B45 33 A7
Trafalgar Ct 1 B50 136 D4
Trafford Pk The B98 70 F3
Tram St DY10 27 E5
Tranter Ave B48 51 A5
Treacle Nook 2 WR4 116 B5
Tredington Cl
1 Birmingham B29 19 A7
Redditch B98 90 B7
Tree Acre Gr B63 7 C4
Trefoil Cl
Birmingham B29 19 A7
Great Malvern WR14 153 D7
12 Worcester WR5 128 D5
Tregarron Rd B63 7 C5
Trehearn Rd WR9 85 B3
Treherne Dr DY9 6 B1
Trejon Rd B64 7 E8
Trelawney Cl 10 WR2 114 F1
Trench La
Huddington WR9 118 B8
Oddingley WR9 104 D5
Trench Wood Nature Reserve* WR9 104 F2
Trent Cl DY8 6 A4
Trent Cres B47 35 E2
Trent Rd WR5 115 F3
Tresco Cl B45 17 E1
Trescott Jun & Inf Sch
B31 18 D3
Trescott Rd
Birmingham B31 18 D4
Redditch B98 70 F3
Tretawn Gdns GL20 197 B6
Trevanie Ave B32 9 C6
Treville Cl B98 71 E3
Trevithick Cl
5 Stourport-on-Severn
DY13 44 A5
4 Worcester WR4 116 C4
Trianon Rd B60 49 C1
Trickses La B97 88 D4
Trimpley Dr DY11 27 A7
Trimpley La
Bewdley DY12 26 D5
Kidderminster Foreign
DY12 11 C5
Trimpley Rd B32 9 B1
Trinity Cl WR11 161 E2
Trinity Ct
Bromsgrove B60 68 B7
1 Kidderminster DY10 27 F6
Trinity Fields DY10 27 F6
Trinity Grange DY10 27 F7
Trinity High Sch & Sixth Form Ctr B98 70 F4
Trinity Pas 4 WR1 115 C2
Trinity Rd
Great Malvern WR14 138 E2
Stourbridge DY8 6 A8
Trinity St
3 Tewkesbury GL20 196 E6
2 Worcester WR1 115 C2
Trinity The 3 WR1 115 C3
Trippleton Ave B32 18 B8
Tristram Ave B31 19 B1
Trittiford Rd B13 21 C6
Trotshill La E WR4 116 C5
Trotshill La W WR4 116 B5
Trotshill Way WR4 116 D4
Troughton Pl GL20 197 B6
Trout Beck Dr WR4 115 F5
Troutbeck Dr DY5 6 B8
Trow Way WR5 128 B7
Troy Gr B14 20 D4
Troy Ind Est B96 90 A3
Truemans Heath La
B47, B90 36 C7
Truro Dr DY11 27 A5
Tryst The B61 49 B5
Tudbury Rd B31 18 E4
Tudor Bsns Ctr B98 70 E3
Tudor Cl
Birmingham, Highter's Heath
B14 21 A1
Tudor Cl *continued*
Birmingham, King's Heath
B13 20 F6
Great Malvern WR14 153 C6
Tudor Gdns DY8 5 E5
Tudor House Mus*
WR8 169 B6
Tudor Pl GL20 196 F4
Tudor Rd DY12 25 F3
Tudor Way WR2 114 C3
Tuer The WR11 134 A3
Tuer Way WR7 120 E7
Tuffery Cl WR3 115 B6
Tug Wilson Cl GL20 184 E2
Tugford Rd B29 19 C7
Tugwood La DY13 64 B6
Tunnel Dr B98 70 E2
Tunnel Hill
Upton upon Severn WR8 169 B4
Worcester WR4 115 F5
Tunnel La B14 20 C4
Turbary Ave WR4 116 C5
Turgo Gdns WR5 116 A1
Turner Dr DY5 6 D7
Turners Cl WR4 115 F6
Turney Rd DY8 5 F6
Turnpike Cl WR2 114 F3
Turnpike La B97 70 A4
Turnstone Rd DY10 28 A1
Turrall St WR1 115 B6
Turton St DY10 28 A8
Turves Gn
Birmingham, Turves Green
B31 19 A1
Birmingham, West Heath
B31 33 F8
Turves Gn Boys' Sch
B31 34 A8
Turves Gn Girls Sch & Tech Coll B31 19 A1
Turves Gn Prim Sch
B31 19 A1
Tutbury Row WR4 116 D6
Tutnall Cl B60 49 F1
Tutnall La Blackwell B60 50 A1
Finstall B60 49 F1
Twarnley Rise 3 WR4 116 B3
Twatling Rd B45 33 A2
Tweed Cl WR5 115 E2
Tweeds Well B32 18 B7
Twickenham Ct DY8 5 C7
Twiners Rd B98 70 F1
Twixtbears GL20 196 E7
Two Gates B63 7 C5
Two Gates La B63 7 C5
Twyning Cty Prim Sch
GL20 184 A6
Twyning Rd
Birmingham, Stirchley
B30 20 B7
Strensham WR8 171 A3
Tybridge St WR2 115 A2
Tye Gdns DY9 6 B1
Tylers Gn B38 20 B1
Tyndale WR4 116 C4
Tyndall Wlk B32 9 A2
Tyne Cl WR5 115 E2
Tyne Dr WR11 162 A3
Tynes The B60 67 E7
Tynings Cl DY11 12 B1
Tynsall Ave B97 69 F2
Tyrol Cl DY8 5 D6
Tysoe Cl B98 71 D2
Tythe Barn Cl B60 67 D6
Tythe Rd 1 WR12 177 D1
Tythebarn La B90 36 F6
Tything The WR1 115 B4

U

Uffculme Rd B30 20 D8
Uffmoor Est B63 7 E2
Uffmoor La B62 16 D7
Ullapool Cl B97 89 D5
Ullenhall La B95 72 E6
Ullswater Ave DY13 43 F6
Ullswater Cl
Birmingham B32 9 F2
Worcester WR4 116 A5
Ulverston Gn 1 WR4 115 F5
Ulwine Dr B31 19 A4
Umberslade Rd B29 20 A8
Underhill Cl B98 89 F6
Underwood Cl B97 89 A7
Unicorn Hill B97 70 D4
Union La WR9 84 E3
Union Pl WR3 115 A7
Union St
Kidderminster DY10 27 E7
Redditch B98 70 F3
Stourbridge, Lye DY9 6 E5
Stourbridge, Stambermill
DY8 6 A4
Worcester WR1 115 C2
Unwin Cres DY8 5 E5
Upland Gr B61 49 A4
Upland Rd B61 49 B4
Uplands B63 7 E2
Upleadon Cl B97 89 A6
Upper Arley CE Fst Sch
DY12 10 D5
Upper Chase Rd
WR14 153 B8
Upper Cl B32 9 D3
Upper Crossgate Rd
B98 90 C8
Upper End WR10 171 F8
Upper End Ct WR11 163 C4
Upper Ferry La WR2 140 E7
Upper Field Cl B98 71 C6
Upper Gambolds La
B60 68 C5
Upper Gd WR4 116 B5
Upper Hall Cl B98 71 D2
Upper Hook Rd WR8 168 E6
Upper House WR6 124 F6
Upper Howsell Cl 4
WR14 138 F5
Upper Howsell Rd
WR14 138 F5
Upper Mdw Rd B32 9 C5
Upper Norgrove House
B97 69 F1
Upper Pk St WR5 115 D1
Upper St WR8 157 E3
Upper Tything WR1 115 B4
Upper Welland Rd
WR14 166 F7
Upper Wick La WR2 127 C8
Upton Cl B98 71 F3
Upton Gdns WR8 169 D4
Upton Rd
Callow End WR2 140 E8
Kidderminster DY10 12 F1
Powick WR2 127 E2
Upton Snodsbury CE Fst Sch
WR7 131 C8
Upton Snodsbury Rd
WR10 144 E7
Upton upon Severn CE Prim Sch WR8 169 C5
Usmere Rd
Kidderminster DY10 12 F1
Kidderminster DY10 27 F8
Uxbridge Ct DY11 27 D5

V

Valbourne Rd B14 20 C4
Vale Bsns Pk WR11 175 F8
Vale Cl B32 9 F3
Vale Ct B64 7 D7
Vale Ind Est DY11 27 C1
Vale of Evesham Sch
WR11 161 E2
Vale Rd DY13 44 A3
Vale St DY8 6 A8
Vale Wildlife Visitor Ctr*
WR11 147 E1
Valencia Rd B60 49 D1
Valentines Cl 3 WR9 104 B8
Valerian DY10 27 E2
Valley Cl
Kidderminster Foreign
DY11 26 E8
Redditch B97 89 A6
Valley Farm Rd B45 33 A6
Valley Rd Blackheath B64 7 E7
Bournheath B61 48 E7
Halesowen B62 8 F8
Stourbridge DY9 6 F6
Valley Stad (Redditch FC)
B97 70 C4
Valley View DY12 25 E2
Valley Way WR9 84 D2
Vancouver Cl 1 WR2 127 E6
Vandra Cl WR14 139 B5
Vardon Way B38 19 D1
Varlins Way B38 34 D6
Vaughan Rd DY14 22 B4
Vauxhall Rd DY8 6 A5
Vauxhall St WR3 115 D5
Vawdrey Cl
4 Stourport-on-Severn
DY13 43 E1
1 Stourport-on-Severn
DY13 62 E8
Vaynor Dr B97 89 D8
Vaynor Fst Sch The
B97 89 C7
Ventnor Cl B68 9 C7
Venus Bank 1 DY12 26 A3
Vera Roberts Way
DY11 27 B3
Verbena Cl B60 67 C1
Verbena Rd B31 18 F6
Vernon Cl Halesowen B62 8 D8
Martley WR6 99 A4
Redditch B98 71 A5
Vernon Ct 2 B68 9 B7
Vernon Gr WR9 84 D3
Vernon Pk Rd 16 WR2 114 F1
Vernon Rd
Halesowen B62 8 C8
Stourport-on-Severn
DY13 44 A4
Vernon Trad Est B62 8 C8
Veronica Cl B29 19 A6
Verstone Croft B31 19 A3
Vestry Ct DY8 5 E6
Vetch Field Ave WR4 116 B4
Vicar St
Kidderminster DY10 27 E6
Worcester WR3 115 D4
Vicarage Bank WV15 1 B5
Vicarage Cl
Birmingham, Stirchley
B30 20 C7
Brierley Hill DY5 6 C8
Bromsgrove B60 68 B8
Hallow WR2 101 D1
Vicarage Cres
Kidderminster DY10 27 F5
Redditch B97 70 C3
Vicarage Ct DY7 4 A3
Vicarage Dr DY7 4 A3
Vicarage Gdns 1 WR10 171 E7
Vicarage Hill B94 53 F3
Vicarage La
Childswickham WR12 176 E2
North Claines WR3 102 C3
Vicarage Rd
Birmingham, King's Heath
B14 20 D7
Brierley Hill DY5 6 C7
Stone DY10 28 E2
Stourbridge DY8 5 D7
Stourbridge, Lye DY9 6 F5
Vicarage Rd S DY9 6 E5
Vicarage View B97 70 D3
Vicars Wlk DY9 6 E2
Victor Bsns Ctr B98 71 B3
Victoria Ave
Droitwich WR9 84 F1
Evesham WR11 161 D6
Halesowen B62 8 F6
Worcester WR5 115 D1
Victoria Ct
6 Halesowen B62 9 A7
2 Kidderminster DY10 27 F6
Victoria La WR3 115 A6
Victoria Mews B45 50 D8
Victoria Pass 4 DY8 6 A5
Victoria Pk Rd WR14 139 B4
Victoria Pl
Kidderminster DY11 27 B2
5 Worcester WR5 115 D1
Victoria Rd
Bidford-on-Avon B50 136 C5
Birmingham, Stirchley
B30 20 A7
Bromsgrove B61 49 A3
Dodford B61 47 F6
2 Great Malvern WR14 152 F8
Halesowen B62 8 D8
Victoria Specl Sch B31 19 A5
Victoria Sq 5 WR9 84 F3
Victoria St
Halesowen B63 8 A4
7 Redditch B98 70 E4
Stourbridge DY8 6 A5
Worcester WR3 115 A6
Victory Cl 1 DY13 44 B2
Viewfields 6 WR5 116 B3
Vigornia Ave WR3 115 D5
Villa St DY8 6 A8
Village St
Aldington WR11 162 C5
Harvington WR11 148 B7
Village The WR6 97 E8
Villette Gr B14 21 C4
Villiers Rd B60 67 E7
Villiers St DY10 28 A5
Vimiera Cl WR5 128 F4
Vimy Rd B13 21 B8
Vincent Rd WR5 115 D2
Vine Ct B64 7 D8
Vine La Clent DY9 15 F3
Halesowen B63 8 B3
Kyre WR15 75 C5
Vine St Evesham WR11 161 D4
Kidderminster DY10 28 A8
Redditch B97 70 D4
Worcester WR3 115 A7
Vine Way GL20 196 E3
Vines La WR9 84 F4
Vineyard Rd B31 18 F5
Vinnall Gr B32 18 B8
Vintners Cl 5 WR4 115 F6
Violet La DY9 15 E4
Viols Wlk 4 DY14 22 C4
Virginia Rd GL20 197 E8
Vista Gn B38 20 B1
Vivian Ave WR2 127 C8
Vyrnwy Gr B38 34 E8

W

Wadborough Rd
Norton Juxta Kempsey
WR5 129 C1
Stoulton WR7 143 A7
Waggon La
Churchill DY10 14 A3
Churchill & Blakedown
DY10 13 F3
Waggon Pl 6 WR4 116 B5
Waggon Wlk B38 34 C8
Waggoners Cl 1 B60 67 E6
Wagtail Dr GL20 184 D1
Wain Gn WR4 116 B5
Wainwright Rd WR4 116 B8
Wake Gn Rd B13 21 D8
Wakefield Cl WR5 115 F2
Wakeford Rd B31 19 C1
Wakeman St 10 WR3 115 B6
Walcot La WR10 143 F5
Waldrons Moor B14 20 C5
Walford Gn B32 18 B7
Walford Wlk 7 B97 70 E3
Walker Ave
Brierley Hill DY5 6 D7
Stourbridge DY9 6 E3
Walker Dr DY10 13 A1
Walkers Heath Rd B38 20 B1
Walkers La WR5 129 A7
Walkers Rd B98 71 E6
Walkley Rd GL20 196 F7

Walkmill Dr WR9 ....85 D8
Walkwood CE Mid Sch
 B97 ....89 C8
Walkwood Cres B97 ...89 C6
Walkwood Rd B97 ....89 D6
Walkworth Ave 6 WR4 .116 C6
Wall Well B63 ....7 F3
Wall Well La B63 .....7 F3
Wallace Rise B64 .....7 F3
Wall's Rd B60 ......67 C3
Wallcroft Cl WR2 ...114 E4
Wallhouse La
 Feckenham B97 ......88 B5
 Hanbury B97 ....87 F5
Walmead Croft B17 ...9 F7
Walmers Cres WR4 ..116 C7
Walmers Wlk The B31 .18 D1
Walmesley Way B31 ...18 E3
Walmley Cl B63 ......7 B7
Walnut Ave WR4 ....115 F5
Walnut Cl
 Broadway WR12 ....190 C8
 Harvington WR11 ...148 B6
 Stourbridge DY9 .....6 B1
Walnut Cres WR14 ...152 F4
Walnut La B60 ......68 D8
Walnut Way B31 .....33 F8
Walnuts The B45 ....154 A2
Walter Nash Rd E DY11 .27 B2
Walter Nash Rd W
 DY11 ....27 A1
Walters Cl B31 ......33 F6
Walters Rd B68 ......9 B6
Waltham Cl B61 .....48 E1
Waltham House B38 ...20 B1
Walton Ave B65 .....8 B8
Walton Cl Halesowen B63 .7 F2
 Kidderminster DY11 ..27 B2
 Redditch B98 ....71 E3
 2 Stourport-on-Severn
 DY13 ....43 D1
 Tewkesbury GL20 ...197 B7
Walton Ct B63 ....7 F3
Walton Dr DY9 ......6 C5
Walton Gdns GL20 ..197 B6
Walton Gr B30 ......20 B2
Walton La
 Elmley Lovett DY10 ..45 D2
 Grimley WR2 ....101 C5
Walton Pool La DY9 ..15 F2
Walton Rd
 Bromsgrove B61 .....49 B4
 Elmley Lovett DY10 ..45 D2
 Stourbridge DY8 .....6 A6
Walton Rise DY9 ....16 A3
Walwyn Cl
 Colwall Stone WR13 .152 A1
 Great Malvern WR13 .152 C3
Wannerton Rd DY10 ..14 B1
Wansbeck Gr B38 ....34 E8
Wapping La B98 .....72 B7
Warbage La
 Belbroughton DY9 ....30 F1
 Dodford B61 ....48 A7
Warbank Cl B48 .....51 A6
Warbler Pl DY10 .....28 A2
Ward Rd 2 DY13 ....44 B1
Wardle Way DY11 ....12 B3
Wardoor Place' 1 WR4 .116 C5
Wards Cl WR1 ......162 A3
Wareham House B28 ..21 E3
Wareham Rd B45 ....18 B2
Waresley Ct Rd DY11 .45 A1
Waresley Pk DY11 ...64 A8
Waresley Rd DY11 ...45 A1
Warley Croft B69 .....8 E8
Warmington Rd B47 ..36 A6
Warmstry Ct 4 WR1 .115 B2
Warndon Bsns Pk
 WR4 ....116 A8
Warndon Gn WR4 ...116 A6
Warndon Infants Sch
 WR4 ....116 B6
Warndon Jun Sch
 WR4 ....116 B6
Warndon La WR4 ...116 C6
Warndon Way WR4 ..116 D7
Warple Rd B32 ......9 C5
Warren La B45 ......33 B3
Warren Rd
 Birmingham, Stirchley
 B30 ....20 A6
 Northway GL20 .....197 D8
Warrens End 1 B38 ..19 F1
Warstock La B14 ....21 A4
Warstock Rd B14 ....21 A3
Warston Ave B32 ....9 D3
Warstone Cl DY10 ...26 D4
Warwards La B29 ....20 A8
Warwick Ave B60 ...68 A8
Warwick Dr DY9 ....90 D3
Warwick Ct 1 B80 ...19 C7
Warwick Hall Gdns
 B60 ....68 A8
Warwick Highway B98 .71 C2
Warwick Pl GL20 ...196 F5
Warwick Rd B68 .....9 D7
Warwick St DY13 ....44 A1
Wasdale Rd B31 .....18 F4
Waseley Cl 3 WR5 ..128 E5
Waseley Hills Ctry Pk*
 B45 ....32 C8
Waseley Hills High Sch
 B45 ....32 D7
Waseley Rd B45 .....32 E8

Washbrook Cl 3 WR4 .116 B7
Washford Dr B98 ....90 D7
Washford Ind Est B98 .90 D8
Washford La B98 ....90 D8
Washington Rd WR11 .176 D8
Washington St
 Kidderminster DY11 ..27 C5
 3 Worcester WR1 ...115 C4
Washpole La WR9 ...104 B4
Wassage Way WR4 ...84 D7
Wassage Way N WR9 .84 C7
Wassage Way S WR9 .84 C7
Wassell Ct B63 ......7 E2
Wassell Gr Rd
 Hagley DY9 ....15 F8
 Halesowen B63 ......7 A2
Wassell Rd
 Halesowen B63 ......7 E2
 Stourbridge DY9 .....6 E2
Wassell Wood Nature
 Reserve* DY12 ......26 D7
Wast Hill Gr B38 ....34 F7
Wasthill La B38, B48 ..34 D5
Watchetts Gn 1 WR4 .116 C4
Watchman Ave DY5 ...6 B6
Watchtower Rd DY13 ..44 D6
Water Croft 5 WR4 ..116 C5
Waterfall Rd DY5 .....6 D7
Waterford Cl WR3 ..115 A7
Watergrip La GL20 ..186 A7
Waterhaynes Cl B45 ..33 A6
Waterlade Cl 2 DY11 .45 B2
Waterlaide Rd DY11 ..45 A2
Waterloo Cres B50 ..136 E5
Waterloo Ind Est B50 .136 E6
Waterloo Pk B50 ...136 E6
Waterloo Rd
 Bewdley DY12 ......25 F2
 Bidford-on-Avon B50 .136 E6
 Birmingham, King's Heath
 B14 ....20 E8
Waterloo St DY10 ....27 E6
Waterloo Way GL20 ..185 A6
Waterside
 Droitwich WR9 ......85 A3
 Evesham WR11 .....161 D3
 Upton upon Severn WR8 .169 C6
Waterside Cl 2 WR9 ..85 A3
Waterside Grange
 DY10 ....27 E8
Waterside Orch B48 ..34 B2
Waterside View DY5 ..6 B8
Waterworks Dr B31 ..18 D4
Waterworks Rd WR1 .115 A5
Watery La
 Alvechurch B48 .....35 C1
 Belbroughton DY9 ...29 F7
 Birmingham B62 .....9 A3
 Hopwood B48 ....34 F2
 Portway B48 ....52 D7
 Redditch B98 ....71 B2
 Welland WR14 .....166 F5
 Worcester WR2 ....114 E1
Watford Rd B30 .....19 F5
Watkins Gdns B31 ...19 C4
Watkins' Way WR14 .153 C7
Watledge Cl 2 GL20 .196 F6
Watleys Cl 5 B50 ...136 D5
Watt Cl 3 DY13 .....44 A4
Watts Rd B80 ....90 E2
Watwood Rd B28, B90 .21 F3
Waugh Dr B63 ......16 D8
Wavell Rd DY5 ......6 F7
Waveney Rd 5 WR9 ..84 D1
Waverley Cl DY10 ....28 A8
Waverley Cres B62 ...16 F4
Waverley Pk WR5 ...128 C7
Waxland Rd B63 .....8 B2
Way Croft B63 ......8 B2
Waystone La DY9 ....30 D4
Weather La DY13 ....62 F4
Weatheroak Cl WR9 ..85 A3
Weatheroak Hill B48 .35 B1
Weatheroaks B62 ....9 A7
Weaver Cl WR9 .....85 A3
Weavers Cl B97 .....89 D4
Weavers Hill B97 ....89 D4
Webb La B28 ....21 E6
Webheath Fst Sch B97 .70 A4
Wedderburn Rd WR14 .153 C8
Wedgberrow Cl WR9 ..84 F2
Wedgewood Rd B32 ..9 D5
Wedley Pl WR4 .....116 C3
Weethley House 6 B97 .70 A4
Weights Farm B97 ...70 C7
Weights Cl B97 .....70 C7
Weir La WR2 ......128 A7
Weirbrook Cl B29 ....19 C7
Welbeck Cl B62 .....8 E6
Welbeck Dr DY11 ....27 B5
Welbeck Gr B32 .....9 A1
Welches Cl B31 .....19 B5
Welcome Dr B61 ....32 A1
Welford Cl B98 .....89 F5
Welford Rd
 Bidford-on-Avon B50 .137 A3
 Long Marston CV37 .151 C6
Well Cl Northway GL20 .184 E1
 Redditch B98 ....89 E5
Well La Little Witley WR6 .81 B4
 Rushock WR9 ....46 B2
Well Mdw B45 ......33 A6
Welland Cl WR9 .....84 D1
Welland Dr DY8 .....6 D4
Welland Gdns WR13 .167 C4
Welland Prim Sch
 WR13 ....167 C5

Welland Rd
 Halesowen B63 ......8 A2
 Upton upon Severn WR8 .168 D4
Wellesbourne Cl WR8 .70 E4
Wellfield GL20 ......197 B7
Wellington Cl 4 WR1 .115 C2
Wellington Ct
 Birmingham, Beech Lanes
 B32 ....9 F5
 Kidderminster DY11 ..27 C5
Wellington House B32 .9 F4
Wellington Lodge Cl
 GL20 ....185 A6
Wellington Rd
 Bromsgrove B60 .....68 A8
 Ombersley WR9 .....83 A5
Wellington St 5 B98 ..70 E4
Wellington Twr 4 B31 .19 A1
Wellmead Wlk B45 ...32 F8
Wells Cl
 4 Great Malvern WR14 .166 E7
 Kidderminster DY11 ..27 A6
Wells Gdns WR12 ...190 E8
Wells Rd
 Great Malvern WR14 .166 E8
 Malvern Wells WR14 .152 E5
 Worcester WR5 ....116 A4
Welsh House Farm Com Sch
 B32 ....9 F4
Welsh House Farm Rd
 B32 ....9 F4
Wendron Cl B60 .....49 B2
Wendron Rd B14 ....20 D4
Wenlock Cl B63 .....7 B2
Wenlock Dr B61 .....49 A5
Wenlock Rd
 Stourbridge DY8 .....6 B4
 Tewkesbury GL20 ..196 F5
Wenlock Way 1 DY13 .43 E1
Wensleydale B14 ....84 D1
Wensleydale Dr WR3 .115 E7
Wentworth Dr B60 ...50 A5
Wentworth Rd DY8 ...5 E7
Wentworth Rise B62 ..8 D3
Wentworth Way 3 WR3 .115 F7
Weoley Castle Rd B29 .9 F1
Weoley Hill B29 .....19 C8
Werstan Cl WR14 ...153 C7
Werth La GL19 .....195 D2
Wesley Cl
 Halesowen B63 ......7 B8
 Stourport-on-Severn
 DY13 ....43 E1
Wesley Ct B64 ......7 F8
Wesley Wlk B60 .....67 E7
Wesson Gdns B63 ....8 A3
Wessons Rd B50 ...136 E5
West Ave B98 ......70 E4
West Bvd B32 ......9 F4
West Cl B60 ....67 F6
West End WR11 ....149 A8
West End La WR12 ..190 F2
West End Villas B38 ..19 F2
West Heath Hospl B38 .34 C8
West Heath Jun & Inf Sch
 B38 ....34 C8
West Heath Rd B31 ..19 B1
West Hill Ct B14 ....20 C4
West Malvern Rd
 Great Malvern WR14 .138 C1
 West Malvern WR14 .152 D6
West Mead Dr B14 ...20 E6
West Midland Safari Pk*
 DY12 ....26 E3
West Midlands (Private)
 Hospl B13 ....7 D5
West Mill Croft B38 ..34 E7
West Pk Ave B31 ....18 E2
West Rd Bromsgrove B60 .49 A2
 Halesowen B63 ......7 B6
West Rd S B63 ......7 B6
West Side WR11 ....149 A4
West St Brierley Hill DY5 .6 F8
 Droitwich WR9 ......84 E3
 Evesham WR11 .....161 C4
 Redditch B98 ....70 E3
 Stourbridge DY8 .....5 F5
West Way B31 ......34 B7
Westacre Dr DY5 ....6 F8
Westacre Mid Sch
 WR9 ....84 D3
Westbourne WR11 ..164 B5
Westbourne Cl B61 ..48 E1
Westbourne Rd B62 ..8 E7
Westbourne St 1 DY12 .26 C3
Westbourne Terr B61 ..48 E1
Westbury Ave WR9 ..84 C5
Westbury House B97 ..70 B2
Westbury St B13 ....115 C3
Westcliff Pl B31 ....18 F4
Westcombe Gr B32 ...9 A1
Westcote Ave B31 ...18 C4
Westcroft Gr B38 ....19 D3
Westcroft St 5 WR9 ..84 E3
Westcroft Way B14 ..21 B1
Westdean Cl B62 ....8 C4
Western Ave B62 ....8 E4
Western Bsns Pk B62 .8 B7
Western Hill Cl B96 ..89 C1
Western Hill Rd GL20 .186 D2
Western Rd
 Blackheath B64 .....7 C8
 Hagley DY9 ....15 B4
 Stourbridge DY8 .....5 F4
Westfield Ave
 Birmingham B14 ....21 B1
 Northway GL20 .....197 D8

Westfield Cl WR3 ...102 F3
Westfield La WR8 ...156 B7
Westfield Rd
 Birmingham B13 ....20 D8
 Brierley Hill DY5 .....6 F8
 Fernhill Heath WR3 .102 E3
Westfields B61 ......48 F8
Westgate B61 ......21 E3
Westhaven Dr B31 ...18 E7
Westhaven Pl 8 WR2 .114 E5
Westhead Rd DY10 ..13 A4
Westhead Rd N DY10 .13 A4
Westhill Coll (Univ
 Birmingham) B29 ...19 D8
Westhill Rd B38 ....19 D4
Westholme Croft B30 .19 E8
Westholme Rd B50 ..136 D5
Westhouse Gr B14 ...20 D4
Westland Gdns DY8 ..5 F7
Westlands Fst Sch
 WR9 ....84 D5
Westlea Cl WR2 ....114 C1
Westlyn Cl WR14 ...139 B3
Westmead Ave B80 ..90 E4
Westmere WR8 ....154 A2
Westminster Bank
 Great Malvern WR14 .138 C1
 West Malvern WR14 .152 C8
Westminster Cl B61 ..48 D1
Westminster Ct 2 B60 .49 A2
Westminster Dr B14 ..20 E6
Westminster Rd
 Birmingham, Stirchley
 B29 ....20 A8
 Great Malvern WR14 .152 E4
 Kidderminster DY11 ..27 A6
 Worcester WR5 ....115 F2
Westmount Cl 2 WR2 .127 F6
Weston Hill WR6 ...112 D4
Weston Rd WR10 ...146 A1
Weston Pk* GL55 ..178 E3
Weston Rd
 Bretforton WR11 ...163 D3
 Honeybourne WR11 .164 B3
Westonbirt Cl 1 WR5 .128 E5
Westonhall Rd B60 ..67 D4
Westray Cl B45 .....17 F1
Westridge Rd B13 ...21 C6
Westside Dr B32 ....9 D1
Westview Cl WR2 ..114 C2
Westville Ave DY11 ..27 A5
Westward Rd WR14 .138 C3
Westwood Ave
 Droitwich WR9 ......84 C1
 Stourbridge DY8 .....5 D3
Westwood Cl WR9 ...84 C2
Westwood Dr B45 ...18 B1
Westwood La HR6 ...94 A3
Westwood Pk* WR9 ..84 B4
Westwood Rd WR9 ..84 D4
Westwood Way WR9 ..84 C3
Wey Cl WR9 ....84 D2
Weyburn Cl WR2 ...127 E6
Wharf La B60 ......50 B1
Wharf Rd B30 ......20 A2
Wharfedale Ave 7 WR9 .84 C1
Wharfedale Dr WR14 .116 A5
Wharrington Cl B98 ..90 A8
Wharrington Hill B98 .90 A8
Wheatcroft Ave DY12 .26 C4
Wheatcroft Cl B62 ...8 F8
Wheatfield Ave WR5 .128 C5
Wheatfield Cl GL55 .165 D4
Wheatfield View B31 .18 D6
Wheatley Cl B68 .....9 C8
Wheatley La WR8 ...168 B3
Wheatley Rd B68 ....9 D8
Wheatmill Cl DY10 ..14 B2
Wheatridge Rd B60 ..67 E6
Wheatstone Cl 5 GL20 .184 E1
Wheeler Cl WR14 ...27 F6
Wheeler Orch WR15 .55 E3
Wheeler S DY8 .....5 F5
Wheeler's La B13 ....21 A7
Wheelers La B13 ....20 F7
Wheelers La Inf Sch
 B13 ....20 F7
Wheelers La Jun Sch
 (Annexe) B13 ......21 A4
Wheelers La Jun Sch
 B13 ....20 F7
Wheeley Rd B48 ....50 D5
Wheelwright Cl
 Bromsgrove B60 .....67 E6
 Worcester WR4 ....115 E6
Whetty La B45 .....32 F7
Whettybridge Rd B45 .32 E6
Whimbrel Gr DY10 ..28 A1
Whinchat Gr DY10 ..28 A2
Whinfield Rd
 Dodford B61 ....48 B6
 Worcester WR3 ....102 B1
Whiston Gr B29 .....19 B8
Whitborn Cl WR14 ..153 C7
Whitborn End WR14 .153 C8
Whitbourne VC Prim Sch
 WR6 ....110 F6
Whitburn Cl DY11 ...27 B5
Whitchurch Cl B98 ..89 F6
Whitcomb's Orch WR14 .22 C3
Whitcot Gr B31 .....33 F8
Whitcroft Rd WR10 .144 D1
White Castle WR4 ..116 D6
White Cl WR9 ......6 C2
White Cottage Gdn*
 WR9 ....106 C1
White Heart Cl 18 DY12 .25 F3

White Hill
 Birmingham B31 ....19 B6
 Kinver DY7 ....3 E5
 Worcester WR4 ....116 A4
White House Ct WR6 .124 A6
White House Dr B45 ..33 A2
White Ladies Cl WR1 .115 B4
White Ladies Wlk 6
 WR1 ....115 B4
White Rd B32 ......9 D6
Whitebeam Croft 3 B38 .19 E1
Whitefriars Dr B63 ...8 A4
Whitegate Dr WR4 ...27 A3
Whitehall Cl WR2 ...127 C8
Whitehall Cl B63 .....8 B4
Whitehall Rd
 Blackheath B64 .....7 C8
 Halesowen B63 .....8 B4
 Stourbridge DY8 .....6 B2
Whitehill La B29, B31 .19 A5
Whitehill Rd DY11 ...27 A4
Whitehorse Cl 4 WR2 .127 E6
Whitehouse La B98 ..71 E4
Whitehouse Pl B45 ..32 F6
Whitehouse Rd DY10 .27 D4
Whitemoor La B96 ..109 B7
Whitepits La B48 ....52 F4
Whitesmith Croft B14 .20 E8
Whitestone Rd B63 ...8 A6
Whitethorn Gr 3 WR14 .139 C3
Whitewood Cl WR5 .129 A8
Whitewood Way WR5 .129 A8
Whitford Bridge Rd
 B60 ....68 A2
Whitford Cl
 Bretforton WR11 ...163 C4
 Bromsgrove B61 ....67 D8
Whitford Gdns B61 ..48 D2
Whitford Hall Dodderhill Sch
 WR9 ....85 A4
Whitford Rd B61 ....48 D2
Whitland Cl B45 ....33 B6
Whitland Dr B14 ....20 F3
Whitlenge La DY10 ..45 C3
Whitley Ct Rd B32 ...9 C6
Whitlock Gr B14 ....21 A3
Whitlocks End Halt
 B90 ....36 E7
Whitmore Rd
 Stourbridge DY8 .....5 D5
 Worcester WR4 ....114 D1
Whitney Ave DY8 ....5 D6
Whittakers Cl 1 WR10 .144 D1
Whittal Cl WV15 ....1 C5
Whittall Dr E DY11 ..27 B1
Whittall Dr W DY11 ..27 A1
Whittingham Rd B63 .8 A5
Whittington CE Prim Sch
 WR5 ....129 B6
Whittington Cl B14 ..20 E5
Whittington Hall La
 Kinver DY7 ....4 F2
 Stourbridge DY7 .....5 B3
Whittington Rd
 Stourbridge DY8 .....5 E3
 Worcester WR5 ....129 A8
Whitville Cl DY11 ...27 C7
Whyle La HR6 ......92 D5
Whynot Cl B60 .....67 C2
Whynot St B63 .....8 A5
Wichenford Dovecote (NT)*
 WR6 ....100 B4
Wick House Cl WR10 .158 F7
Wick Rd WR10 ....159 B2
Wickham Cl WR11 ..176 D8
Wickham Rd B80 ...90 F4
Wicklow Cl B63 .....7 D1
Wide Acres B45 ....17 F1
Widney House B97 ..70 C4
Wigeon La GL20 ...197 A6
Wigland Way B38 ...20 A1
Wigley Bank Rd DY7 .3 D6
Wigorn House B67 ...9 F8
Wigorn La DY9 .....15 B8
Wike La B96 ....109 C8
Wilberforce Pl 9 WR4 .116 C3
Wild Goose La B98 ..90 D8
Wildacres DY8 .....5 C6
Wilde Cl B14 ......20 D4
Wilden Cl B31 .....18 C3
Wilden Ind Est DY13 .44 C6
Wilden La
 Kidderminster DY10 ..27 E1
 Stourport-on-Severn
 DY13 ....44 C6
Wilden Top Rd DY13 .44 D5
Wildmoor La B61 ....32 A3
Wilfred Cl 3 WR3 ...115 D5
Wilkes Way 9 B50 ..136 D5
Willersey Bsns Pk
 WR12 ....177 E5
Willersey Prim Sch
 WR12 ....177 F4
Willersey Rd
 Badsey WR11 ......162 F1
 Birmingham B13 ....21 D8
Willes Ct 2 B62 ....9 A7
Willett Rd WR9 ....103 F8
Willetts Dr B63 .....7 B4
Willetts Rd B31 .....19 A1
William Bullock Cl
 DY13 ....43 F3
William Coley Pl 3 DY13 .43 F1
William Shakespeare Pl 7
 WR9 ....103 F8
William St B97 .....70 E4

William Tennant Way
WR8 . . . . .169 D4
Willis St DY11 . . . . .27 C5
Willis Wlk GL20 . . . . . . .184 D1
Willmore Gr 4 B38 . . . . . .34 F8
Willow Bank Cl WR10 . . .145 A8
Willow Brook Rd B48 . . . .51 A7
Willow Cl
  Ashton under Hill WR11 . .187 B7
  Bromsgrove B61 . . . . .48 E2
  Fernhill Heath WR3 . . . . .103 A3
  Hagley DY9 . . . . .14 F5
  4 Pershore WR10 . . . . .144 C1
  Ripple WR8 . . . . .169 F6
Willow Coppice B32 . . . . .9 C1
Willow Ct B61 . . . . .48 E3
Willow Dr WR3 . . . . .103 F8
Willow End DY9 . . . . .6 D3
Willow Gdns B61 . . . . . . .48 E3
Willow Gr WR14 . . . . . . .139 A3
Willow Hts B64 . . . . .8 A8
Willow Pk Dr DY8 . . . . . . .6 B2
Willow Rd
  Birmingham, Bournville
    B29, B30 . . . . .19 F8
  Bromsgrove B61 . . . . .48 E3
  Evesham WR11 . . . . .161 F2
  Kinver DY7 . . . . .4 C3
  Martley WR6 . . . . .112 C8
  Wichenford WR6 . . . . . . .99 D1
  Willersey WR12 . . . . . . .177 E3
Willow St WR5 . . . . .115 C1
Willow Tree Dr B45 . . . . . .50 D8
Willow Way
  Redditch B97 . . . . .70 B4
  Studley B80 . . . . .90 E2
Willowdene DY13 . . . . . . .44 C3
Willowfield Dr DY11 . . . . .12 C1
Willows The
  Hollywood B47 . . . . .36 A6
  Stourport-on-Severn
    DY13 . . . . .44 C3
Willowsbrook Rd B62 . . . . .8 F8
Willowslea Rd WR3 . . . . .102 A1
Willsbridge Covert 8
  B14 . . . . .20 C2
Willson Croft B28 . . . . . . .21 D3
Wilmcote Cl B61 . . . . .67 D8
Wilmcote House B97 . . . . .70 B4
Wilmington Rd B32 . . . . . . .9 B8
Wilmore La B47 . . . . .35 F4
Wilmot Rd WR14 . . . . . . .138 F5
Wilsford Cl B14 . . . . .20 D1
Wilson Rd DY11 . . . . .45 A1
Wilson St 4 WR3 . . . . . . .115 D4
Wilton Ave DY11 . . . . .27 B8
Wilton Rd WR14 . . . . . . .153 B8
Wiltshire Ct 10 B29 . . . . . .19 C7
Wiltshire Dr B63 . . . . .7 B7
Wimbledon Dr DY8 . . . . . . .6 B2
Winbrook DY12 . . . . .26 A3
Winchcombe Dr WR4 . . . .115 F7
Winchcombe Rd
  WR11 . . . . .175 B2
Winchester Ave
  Kidderminster DY11 . . . . . .27 A6
  Worcester WR2 . . . . .127 F8
Winchester Cl DY9 . . . . . . .15 A6
Winchester Dr DY8 . . . . . . .6 A3
Winchester Gdns B31 . . . . .19 A3
Winchfield Dr B17 . . . . .9 F7
Windermere Dr WR4 . . . . .115 F7
Windermere House
  DY10 . . . . .27 E7
Windermere Way 1
  DY13 . . . . .43 F5
Winding Mill N DY5 . . . . . . .6 E7
Winding Mill S DY5 . . . . . . .6 E7
Windles Row 8 WR4 . . . . .116 B5
Windmeres 4 WR11 . . . . .161 F1
Windmill Ave B45 . . . . .32 E8
Windmill CE Mid Sch
  DY13 . . . . .43 E1
Windmill Cl
  Birmingham B31 . . . . .19 C5
  4 Stourport-on-Severn
    DY13 . . . . .43 F1
  1 Stourport-on-Severn
    DY13 . . . . .62 F8
  3 Worcester WR1 . . . . .115 B4
Windmill Dr B97 . . . . .89 C6
Windmill Gdns B97 . . . . . .89 B6
Windmill Hill
  Birmingham B31 . . . . .19 B5
  Halesowen B63 . . . . .7 D5
  Temple Grafton B49 . . . . .137 C8
Windmill La
  Inkberrow WR7 . . . . .120 E7
  Kempsey WR5 . . . . .141 C8
  Stoulton WR7 . . . . .143 D8
Windmill Rd B90 . . . . .21 E2
Windrush Cl
  Redditch B97 . . . . .89 D6
  Worcester WR5 . . . . .115 C1
Windrush Cres WR14 . . . .153 D6
Windrush Gr B29 . . . . .20 A8
Windrush House B31 . . . . .18 E5
Windrush Rd B97 . . . . .36 B7
Winds Point DY9 . . . . .15 A6
Windsor Ave WR2 . . . . . . .114 E2
Windsor Cl
  Birmingham, Coft Common
    B31 . . . . .34 A6
  Birmingham, Frankley
    B45 . . . . .18 A2
  Halesowen B63 . . . . .7 F3
  Newland WR14 . . . . .139 C6
Windsor Cres DY7 . . . . .3 F4

Windsor Ct B38 . . . . .19 F1
Windsor Dr
  Astley & Dunley DY13 . . . . .62 F8
  Kidderminster DY10 . . . . . .27 E7
Windsor Gdns B60 . . . . . . .49 A2
Windsor High Sch B63 . . . . .7 F4
Windsor Holloway DY7 . . . . .4 C1
Windsor Rd
  Birmingham, Stirchley
    B30 . . . . .20 B5
  Droitwich WR9 . . . . .103 F8
  Evesham WR11 . . . . .161 E6
  Halesowen B63 . . . . .7 F4
  Redditch B97 . . . . .70 D5
  Stourbridge DY8 . . . . .5 E3
Windsor St B60 . . . . .49 A2
Windsor View B32 . . . . . . .18 B7
Winforton Cl B98 . . . . .71 E3
Wing La GL20 . . . . .185 D8
Wingate B30 . . . . .19 F4
Wingfield Ave WR4 . . . . . .116 C7
Winnall La DY13 . . . . .63 B4
Winnington Cl WR6 . . . . . .97 E8
Winnington Gdns
  WR8 . . . . .154 A2
Winnipeg Cl WR2 . . . . . . .127 C6
Winnipeg Rd B38 . . . . .35 A8
Winsford Cl B63 . . . . .8 A6
Winslow Ave WR9 . . . . . . .85 B3
Winslow Cl B98 . . . . .71 F3
Winsmore WR2 . . . . .127 E3
Winston Dr B62 . . . . .17 A4
Winston Rd DY11 . . . . .13 A6
Winstone Cl B98 . . . . .71 A4
Winterbourne Croft
  B14 . . . . .20 C1
Winterburn Rd WR2 . . . .114 E6
Winterfold Cl DY10 . . . . . .28 B6
Winterfold House Sch
  DY10 . . . . .46 A8
Wintour Wlk B60 . . . . .67 E7
Winward Rd B98 . . . . .71 F1
Winwood Ct DY8 . . . . .5 F4
Winwood Heath Rd
  B62 . . . . .16 E2
Winwoods Gr B32 . . . . . . .18 A8
Winyate Hill B98 . . . . .71 A2
Winyates Crafts Ctr ★
  B98 . . . . .71 E3
Winyates Ctr B98 . . . . . . .71 E3
Winyates Way B98 . . . . . . .71 E4
Wirehill Dr B98 . . . . .70 F1
Wirlpiece Ave WR4 . . . . . .116 C5
Wirral Rd B31 . . . . .18 F6
Wiseacre Croft B90 . . . . . .21 E2
Wiselack Pl 7 WR4 . . . . . .116 B4
Wishaw Cl Redditch B98 . . .90 A8
  Solihull B90 . . . . .21 E2
Wisley Way B32 . . . . .9 F5
Wistaria Cl B31 . . . . .19 A6
Witherford Cl B29 . . . . . . .19 C8
Witherford Way B29 . . . . .19 C8
Withers Rd WR2 . . . . .115 A1
Withincroft 5 WR4 . . . . . .116 B4
Withington Covert B14 . . . .20 D2
Withy Trees Rd WR11 . . . .163 C8
Withybed Cl B48 . . . . .51 A6
Withybed La
  Alvechurch B48 . . . . .51 A6
  Inkberrow WR7 . . . . .120 D8
Withymoor Rd DY8 . . . . . . .6 A7
Witley Ave B63 . . . . .7 E4
Witley Cl DY11 . . . . .27 B2
Witley Ct ★ WR6 . . . . . . .80 D6
Witley Rd
  1 Birmingham B31 . . . . .19 D2
  Holt WR6 . . . . .81 E3
Witley Way DY13 . . . . .62 D8
Witton Ave WR2 . . . . .84 D1
Witton Bank B62 . . . . .8 F7
Witton Mid Sch WR2 . . . . .84 E1
Witton St DY8 . . . . .5 F4
Wivelden Ave DY13 . . . . . .44 D6
Wixford Rd B50 . . . . .137 A8
Woburn Cl B61 . . . . .48 D1
Woburn Dr
  Brierley Hill DY5 . . . . .6 B8
  Halesowen B62 . . . . .8 B7
Wold Wlk B13 . . . . .21 C6
Wolferlow Medieval Village
  of ★ HR7 . . . . .96 B8
Wollaston Ct DY8 . . . . .5 C6
Wollaston Rd
  Stourport-on-Severn DY7 . . .5 C7
  Stourbridge, Amblecote
    DY8 . . . . .5 F8
Wollescote Bsns Pk 6
  DY9 . . . . .6 F5
Wollescote Prim Sch
  DY9 . . . . .6 F4
Wollescote Rd DY9 . . . . . . .6 D3
Wolsey Cl WR4 . . . . .115 C3
Wolverhampton Rd
  Kidderminster DY10 . . . . . .13 A1
  Oldbury B68 . . . . .9 D8
  Stourton DY7 . . . . .4 E7
Wolverhampton Rd S
  B32 . . . . .9 E7
Wolverley Ave DY8 . . . . . . .5 C6
Wolverley High Sch
  DY11 . . . . .12 D4
Wolverley Rd
  Birmingham B32 . . . . .18 B8
  Halesowen B63 . . . . .7 F3
  Kidderminster DY11 . . . . . .12 B1
Wolverley Sebright Prim Sch
  DY11 . . . . .12 D3
Wolverly Rd DY10 . . . . . . .13 A2

Wolverton Cl B98 . . . . .71 E2
Wolverton Rd B45 . . . . . . .33 C6
Wood Croft B47 . . . . .36 B6
Wood Ct B97 . . . . .70 C1
Wood End Dr B45 . . . . .50 A8
Wood End La B94 . . . . .53 F5
Wood End Sta B94 . . . . . . .53 F4
Wood Farm Rd WR14 . . . .152 E2
Wood Hill Cl WR4 . . . . . . .116 B4
Wood La
  Ashton under Hill WR11 . . .174 B2
  Birmingham, Woodgate
    B32 . . . . .9 A1
  Cookhill B96 . . . . .108 F3
  Earlswood B94 . . . . .36 E1
  Edwyn Ralph HR7 . . . . . . .95 B2
  Fairfield B61 . . . . .31 C3
Wood Leason Ave
  WR4 . . . . .116 B5
Wood Leasow B32 . . . . .9 A1
Wood Leigh B63 . . . . .8 A6
Wood Piece Cl 4 WR4 . . . .116 B7
Wood Piece La B98 . . . . . . .71 D7
Wood St Bushley GL20 . . . .182 E1
  Kidderminster DY11 . . . . . .27 C5
  Stourbridge DY8 . . . . .5 D6
  Stourbridge, Lye DY9 . . . . . .6 F5
Wood Terr
  Sambourne B96 . . . . .90 B1
  Worcester WR1 . . . . .115 B4
Woodbank Dr B61 . . . . . . .48 F8
Woodberrow La B97 . . . . . .89 D6
Woodbine Rd 6 B45 . . . . .115 A5
Woodbridge Cl WR5 . . . . .128 C6
Woodbrooke Rd B30 . . . . . .19 E7
Woodbury Cl
  Great Witley WR6 . . . . . . .61 B1
  Halesowen B62 . . . . .8 F8
  Hartlebury DY11 . . . . .45 A1
  Redditch B97 . . . . .89 A6
Woodbury La WR5 . . . . . . .129 C3
Woodbury Pk Holt WR6 . . . .82 B3
  Norton Juxta Kempsey
    WR5 . . . . .129 D3
Woodbury Rd
  Halesowen B62 . . . . .9 A8
  Kidderminster DY11 . . . . . .27 B2
  Stourport-on-Severn DY13 . .43 F5
Woodbury Rd N DY13 . . . . .43 F5
Woodbury Rise WR14 . . . .138 E3
Woodchester DY9 . . . . . . .15 B4
Woodcock Cl
  Birmingham B31 . . . . .18 C1
  Tanworth-In-A B94 . . . . . .53 E3
Woodcock Hill Jun & Inf Sch
  B31 . . . . .18 E7
Woodcock La B31 . . . . .18 E8
Woodcombe Cl DY5 . . . . . . .6 B7
Woodcote Cl B98 . . . . .71 E3
Woodcote La
  Belbroughton DY9 . . . . . . .30 E1
  Dodford with Grafton B61 . . .47 D5
Woodcroft Cl
  Blackheath B64 . . . . .7 F8
  Blackwell B60 . . . . .49 F5
Woodend Cl B97 . . . . .70 B2
Woodfall Ave B30 . . . . .19 F5
Woodfarm Rd WR14 . . . . .152 F2
Woodfield DY9 . . . . .30 E7
Woodfield Ave
  Blackheath B64 . . . . .7 D8
  Stourbridge DY9 . . . . .6 F2
Woodfield Cl B98 . . . . .71 A5
Woodfield Cres DY11 . . . . .27 D5
Woodfield La
  Ombersley WR9 . . . . .83 A6
  Romsley B62 . . . . .31 D8
Woodfield Mid Sch
  B98 . . . . .71 A2
Woodfield Rd
  Birmingham, King's Heath
    B13 . . . . .20 F8
  1 Droitwich WR9 . . . . . .85 A3
Woodfield St 4 DY11 . . . . .27 C6
Woodfields WR9 . . . . .85 A4
Woodgate Bsns Pk B32 . . . .9 B2
Woodgate Dr B32 . . . . .9 A1
Woodgate Gdns B32 . . . . . .9 A1
Woodgate House B32 . . . . .70 B4
Woodgate Jun & Inf Sch
  B32 . . . . .9 B1
Woodgate La B32 . . . . .9 A2
Woodgate Rd
  Bentley Pauncefoot B60 . . .87 D8
  Stoke Prior B60 . . . . .68 B1
Woodgate Valley Ctry Pk ★
  B32 . . . . .9 C3
Woodgate Way DY9 . . . . . .30 E7
Woodglade Croft B38 . . . . .19 E2
Woodgreen Cl B97 . . . . . . .89 B7
Woodgreen Croft B68 . . . . . .9 C7
Woodgreen Dr WR4 . . . . . .116 C2
Woodgreen Rd B68 . . . . . . .9 C7
Woodhall Cl WR9 . . . . .83 A5
Woodhall La WR9 . . . . .83 A5
Woodham Cl B45 . . . . .17 C1
Woodhampton Cl 6
  DY13 . . . . .62 F8
Woodhouse Orch DY9 . . . .30 E7
Woodhouse Prim Sch
  B32 . . . . .9 E6
Woodhouse Rd B32 . . . . . . .9 E5
Woodland Ave
  Hagley DY8 . . . . .14 F5
  Kidderminster DY11 . . . . . .27 C7
Woodland Cl
  Aston Somerville WR12 . . .175 F1

Woodland Cl continued
  2 Drakes Broughton
    WR10 . . . . .143 F6
  Stourbridge DY9 . . . . .6 D2
  Worcester WR3 . . . . .115 C6
Woodland Dr B45 . . . . .33 A2
Woodland Gr DY10 . . . . . . .13 C3
Woodland Rd
  Birmingham, Northfield
    B31 . . . . .19 B3
  Dodford B61 . . . . .47 F6
  Halesowen B62 . . . . .8 D8
  Redditch B97 . . . . .70 B5
  Suckley WR6 . . . . .124 A3
  Worcester WR3 . . . . .115 C6
Woodland Rise
  Blackheath B64 . . . . .7 F8
  2 Cleobury Mortimer DY14 22 D5
Woodlands WR11 . . . . . . .161 E1
Woodlands Cl
  3 Great Malvern WR14 . .166 E7
  1 Hartlebury DY11 . . . . .45 B2
Woodlands Pk Rd B30 . . . . .19 C5
Woodlands Rd
  Birmingham, Rubery
    B45 . . . . .32 D7
  Cookley DY10 . . . . .13 A4
Woodlands The
  Blackheath B64 . . . . .8 A7
  Ryall WR8 . . . . .169 E6
  Stourbridge DY9 . . . . .6 A2
Woodleaves B47 . . . . .35 F8
Woodleigh WR10 . . . . . . .143 F6
Woodleigh Ct B38 . . . . . . .19 F1
Woodleys The B14 . . . . . . .21 B4
Woodman Cl B63 . . . . .8 C3
Woodman La DY9 . . . . .15 E4
Woodman Rd
  Birmingham B14 . . . . .21 A1
  Halesowen B63 . . . . .8 C3
Woodmancote 10 WR4 . . .115 F7
Woodmans Way WR4 . . . . .84 D5
Woodmeadow Rd B30 . . . . .20 B3
Woodpecker Gr DY10 . . . . .28 B2
Woodridge Ave B32 . . . . . .18 C8
Woodridge Rd B63 . . . . .8 A5
Woodrow Cl B61 . . . . .31 F1
Woodrow Ctr B98 . . . . .90 B8
Woodrow Dr B98 . . . . .90 B7
Woodrow Fst Sch B98 . . . . .90 B7
Woodrow La
  Bluntington DY10 . . . . . . .29 E3
  Catshill B61 . . . . .32 B2
Woodrow N B98 . . . . .90 A7
Woodrow S B98 . . . . .90 B7
Woodrow Wlk B98 . . . . . . .90 A7
Woodrush Dr B47 . . . . .36 A5
Woodrush High Sch The
  B47 . . . . .36 A6
Woodrush Rd 16 GL20 . . . .197 A4
Woods La Blackheath B64 . . .7 C8
  Brierley Hill DY5 . . . . .6 D7
Woodshears Dr WR14 . . . .153 A7
Woodshears Rd WR14 . . . .153 A7
Woodshill Ave B45 . . . . . . .33 A2
Woodside Ave B97 . . . . . . .70 B2
Woodside Dr B45 . . . . .50 B8
Woodside House B13 . . . . .21 A7
Woodside Way B32 . . . . . . .18 A8
Woodstock House B13 . . . . .21 A7
Woodstock Rd WR2 . . . . . .114 E3
Woodthorpe Dr
  Bewdley DY12 . . . . .26 A4
  Stourbridge DY9 . . . . .6 D3
Woodthorpe Gdns B14 . . . .20 E5
Woodthorpe Prim Sch
  B14 . . . . .20 E5
Woodthorpe Rd B14 . . . . . .20 E5
Woodvale Dr B28 . . . . .21 E4
Woodvale Rd
  Birmingham, Woodgate
    B32 . . . . .9 A1
  Birmingham, Yardley Wood
    B28 . . . . .21 A4
Woodville Rd
  Birmingham, King's Heath
    B14 . . . . .20 F8
  5 Tewkesbury GL20 . . .196 F3
Woodward Cl WR10 . . . . . .158 C7
Woodward Parks 5
  WR10 . . . . .146 A1
Woodward Pl DY9 . . . . .6 C4
Woodward Rd
  Kidderminster DY11 . . . . . .27 C4
  Pershore WR10 . . . . .158 C7
Woolaston Rd B98 . . . . . . .90 C8
Woolhope Cl B98 . . . . .71 F3
Woolhope Rd WR5 . . . . . . .129 A8
Woollas Hall ★ WR10 . . . .172 D6
Woolmead Row WR4 . . . . .116 D5
Wooton Cl B97 . . . . .70 A4
Wootton Rd B31 . . . . .34 A6
Worboys Rd WR2 . . . . .127 F8
Worcester 6th Form Coll
  WR5 . . . . .129 A8
Worcester City Art Gall &
  Mus ★ WR1 . . . . .115 B3
Worcester Cl DY9 . . . . .15 C4
Worcester Coll of Tech
  WR1 . . . . .115 B2
Worcester Cross 3 DY10 27 E5
Worcester House 4 B63 . . .8 A3
Worcester La WR5 . . . . .15 B7
Worcester Porcelain Works ★
  WR5 . . . . .115 C1
Worcester Racecourse ★
  WR1 . . . . .115 A3

Worcester Rd
  Bromsgrove B61 . . . . .48 F1
  Dodderhill WR9 . . . . .66 E1
  Evesham WR11 . . . . .161 C7
  Great Witley WR6 . . . . . . .61 A1
  Hagley DY9 . . . . .14 F3
  Harvington DY9, DY10 . . . .29 C4
  Kidderminster DY10 . . . . . .27 C2
  Mustow Green DY10 . . . . .28 F1
  Newland WR2 . . . . .126 F1
  Oldbury B68 . . . . .9 A8
  Ombersley WR3 . . . . .102 A7
  Pershore WR10 . . . . .144 C1
  Pirton WR8 . . . . .142 B4
  St. Peter the Great County
    WR5 . . . . .128 C4
  Stoke Heath B61 . . . . .67 B4
  Stone DY10 . . . . .45 D7
  Stourport-on-Severn
    DY13 . . . . .44 B3
  Wyre Piddle WR10 . . . . . .145 A4
Worcester Shrub Hill Sta
  WR4 . . . . .115 D3
Worcester Sixth Form Coll
  WR5 . . . . .116 A1
Worcester Sq 1 B97 . . . . .70 E4
Worcester St
  Kidderminster DY11 . . . . . .27 E5
  Stourbridge DY8 . . . . .6 A4
  Stourport-on-Severn
    DY13 . . . . .44 B4
Worcester Swimming Pool &
  Fitness Ctr WR1 . . . . . . .115 B4
Worcester Univ Coll
  WR2 . . . . .114 F4
Worcester Woods Ctry Pk ★
  WR5 . . . . .116 B1
Worcestershire Royal Hospl
  WR5 . . . . .116 B2
Worcestershire Sch of Ag
  WR6 . . . . .99 A3
Word Hill B17 . . . . .9 F7
Wordsley Cl B98 . . . . .71 B7
Wordsworth Ave
  Redditch B97 . . . . .89 C8
  Worcester WR3 . . . . .115 C6
Wordsworth Cres DY10 . . . .28 B6
Wordsworth Gn WR14 . . . .139 C4
Wordsworth House
  Birmingham B31 . . . . .34 A8
  Halesowen B63 . . . . .7 B5
Workman Rd WR11 . . . . . .161 B3
World's End Ave B32 . . . . . .9 D5
World's End Jun Sch
  B32 . . . . .9 D5
World's End La B32 . . . . . . .9 D5
Worth Cres DY13 . . . . .43 D5
Worthen Gr B31 . . . . .34 A8
Worthings The B30 . . . . . . .20 B6
Worton Rd DY9 . . . . .6 E2
Wrekin Cl Halesowen B63 . . .7 C1
  Kidderminster DY11 . . . . . .27 B6
Wrekin Dr
  Bromsgrove B61 . . . . .49 A5
  Stourbridge DY9 . . . . .6 D4
Wrekin Wlk 5 DY13 . . . . . .43 D1
Wren Ave WR14 . . . . .139 C2
Wren Cl WR3 . . . . .102 E3
Wribbenhall Fst Sch
  DY12 . . . . .26 C5
Wribbenhall Mid Sch
  DY12 . . . . .26 C3
Wright St B63 . . . . .8 B4
Wroxall Cl DY5 . . . . .6 C8
Wroxall Gr B13 . . . . .21 A6
Wryflatt 3 WR4 . . . . .116 C5
Wych Rd WR9 . . . . .84 E2
Wychall La B38 . . . . .19 E2
Wychall Pk Gr B38 . . . . . . .19 D2
Wychall Prim Sch B31 . . . .19 C2
Wychall Rd B31 . . . . .19 C3
Wychbold Cl B97 . . . . .89 A6
Wychbold Cl DY9 . . . . .15 C8
Wychbold Fst Sch WR9 . . . .85 E8
Wychbury Ct B63 . . . . .8 A3
Wychbury Dr WR9 . . . . . . .15 C7
Wychbury Grange DY9 . . . . .6 C1
Wychbury Rd
  Birmingham B32 . . . . .18 B7
  Brierley Hill DY5 . . . . .6 E8
  Stourbridge DY9 . . . . .6 E2
Wyche Ave B14 . . . . .20 D4
Wyche CE Prim Sch
  WR14 . . . . .152 E4
Wyche Cotts B60 . . . . .67 C1
Wyche Rd WR14 . . . . .152 E5
Wychelm Cl 2 WR5 . . . . . .128 C8
Wychelm Farm Rd B14 . . . .21 A1
Wychwood Dr B97 . . . . . . .89 D6
Wye Ave WR14 . . . . .153 D8
Wye Cl Droitwich WR9 . . . .103 E8
  Worcester WR5 . . . . .115 C2
Wykewane WR14 . . . . .153 D7
Wyld's Gn WR5 . . . . .115 C2
Wynall La S DY9 . . . . .6 F3
Wyndbrook La GL19 . . . . .192 F7
Wyndham Gdns B30 . . . . . .19 D4
Wynds Covert B14 . . . . . . .20 D2
Wynds Point B31 . . . . .19 B5
Wynfield Gdns B14 . . . . . . .20 F5
Wynn Cl DY12 . . . . .26 D5
Wynniattes Way WR6 . . . . .60 F3
Wynstead Covert 6 B14 . . .20 C2
Wynyards Cl 1 GL20 . . . . .196 F6
Wyre Cl B45 . . . . .18 B1

Wyre Forest Nature
  Reserve★ DY12 ....25 B5
Wyre Hill Bewdley DY12 ..25 F2
  Pinvin WR10 ....144 F4
Wyre La CV37 ....151 D6
Wyre Rd
  Pershore WR10 ....144 E3
  Stourbridge DY8 ....5 E7
Wyrebrook Gdns WR15 .57 A7
Wythall Gn Way B47 ...35 E3
Wythall Rd B63 ....8 A2
Wythall Sta B47 ......36 C4
Wythwood Cl DY9 ......6 D1
Wythwood Gr B47 .....36 C6
Wythwood Rd B47 .....36 C6

Y

Yard The WR11 ....175 B2
Yardley Cl B98 ....71 E3
Yardley St DY9 ....6 C6
Yardley Wood Com Prim Sch
  B14 ....21 D4

Yardley Wood Rd B13,
  B14 ....21 B5
Yardley Wood Sta B28 ..21 D5
Yardley Works DY9 ......6 C5
Yarn Cl B47 ....36 A5
Yarnborough Hill DY8 ...6 A2
Yarnbury Cl B14 ....20 E1
Yarningale Cl B98 ......89 F6
Yarningale Rd B14 ....20 D5
Yarnold La
  Bournheath B61 ....48 C8
  Fairfield B61 ....31 C1
Yarranton Cl 2 DY13 ..62 E8
Yarrow Cl WR5 ....128 D4
Yarrow Dr B38 ....34 F8
Yates Hay Rd WR14 ...138 F5
Yeadon Cl B97 ....70 A1
Yellowhammer Ct
  DY10 ....28 A1
Yeoman Cl DY10 ....27 E3
Yeomans Wlk B60 .....67 E8
Yessell La WR11 ......160 E6
Yew Tree Ave DY9 .....30 E8
Yew Tree Cl
  4 Bewdley DY12 ......25 F3
  Redditch B97 ....70 A4
  Worcester WR5 ....128 F8

Yew Tree La
  Bewdley DY12 ....25 F3
Birmingham, Frankley
  B32 ....17 E3
  Fairfield B61 ....31 D2
  Fernhill Heath WR3 ...103 A3
  Malvern Wells WR14 ...166 F7
Yew Tree Pl B62 ......17 A5
Yew Tree Rd
  Halesowen B63 ....7 F3
  Kidderminster DY10 ...27 F5
Yew Tree Wlk 10 DY13 ..43 E4
Yewleigh La WR8 .....168 F4
Yewtree Cl WR11 ....161 F2
Yewtree Dr B60 ......49 B2
Yewtree Hill WR9 ...103 F8
York Ave
  Bromsgrove B61 ....48 E4
  Droitwich WR9 ....84 F1
York Cl Birmingham B30 .20 A6
  Bromsgrove B61 ....48 E4
  Malvern WR14 ....139 B5
  Studley B80 ....90 C4
York Cres DY8 ....5 D7
York Ct DY10 ....27 E7
York La WR10 ....144 F1
York Pl WR1 ....115 A4

York Pl La WR1 ......115 A4
York Rd Bewdley DY12 ..25 F4
Birmingham, King's Heath
  B14 ....20 E8
  Bromsgrove B61 ....48 E4
  Tewkesbury GL20 .....196 F4
York St
  Kidderminster DY10 ...27 E7
Stourport-on-Severn
  DY13 ....44 A3
Yvonne Rd B97 ....89 D7

Z

Zermatt Cl 2 WR3 .....115 A8
Zetland Rd WR14 .....138 F2
Zortech Ave DY13 .....44 A8
Zouche Cl DY8 ....5 E8

NG NH NJ NK

NM NN NO NP

NR NS NT NU

NX NY NZ

SC SD SE TA

SH SJ SK TF TG

SM SN SO SP TL TM

SR SS ST SU TQ TR

SW SX SY SZ TV

Any feature in this atlas can be given a unique reference to help you find the same feature on other Ordnance Survey maps of the area, or to help someone else locate you if they do not have a Street Atlas.

The grid squares in this atlas match the Ordnance Survey National Grid and are at 500 metre intervals. The small figures at the bottom and sides of every other grid line are the National Grid kilometre values (**00** to **99** km) and are repeated across the country every 100 km (see left).

To give a unique National Grid reference you need to locate where in the country you are. The country is divided into 100 km squares with each square given a unique two-letter reference. Use the administrative map to determine in which 100 km square a particular page of this atlas falls.

The bold letters and numbers between each grid line (**A** to **F**, **1** to **8**) are for use within a specific Street Atlas only, and when used with the page number, are a convenient way of referencing these grid squares.

Example   The railway bridge over DARLEY GREEN RD in grid square B1

Step 1: Identify the two-letter reference, in this example the page is in **SP**

Step 2: Identify the 1 km square in which the railway bridge falls. Use the figures in the southwest corner of this square: Eastings **17**, Northings **74**. This gives a unique reference: **SP 17 74**, accurate to 1 km.

Step 3: To give a more precise reference accurate to 100 m you need to estimate how many tenths along and how many tenths up this 1 km square the feature is (to help with this the 1 km square is divided into four 500 m squares). This makes the bridge about **8** tenths along and about **1** tenth up from the southwest corner.

This gives a unique reference: **SP 178 741**, accurate to 100 m.

Eastings (read from left to right along the bottom) come before Northings (read from bottom to top). If you have trouble remembering say to yourself "Along the hall, THEN up the stairs"!

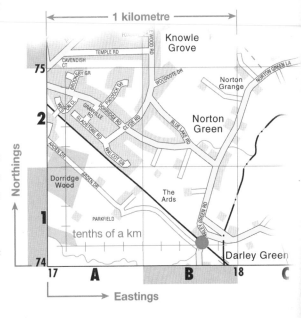

Name and Address	Telephone	Page	Grid reference

Street Atlases from Philip's

Philip's publish an extensive range of regional and local street atlases which are ideal for motoring, business and leisure use. They are widely used by the emergency services and local authorities throughout Britain.

Key features include:

◆ Superb county-wide mapping at an extra-large scale of 3½ inches to 1 mile, or 2½ inches to 1 mile in pocket editions

◆ Complete urban and rural coverage, detailing every named street in town and country

◆ Each atlas available in two handy sizes – standard spiral and pocket paperback

'The mapping is very clear... great in scope and value'

★★★★ BEST BUY   AUTO EXPRESS

1 Bedfordshire
2 Berkshire
3 Birmingham and West Midlands
4 Bristol and Bath
5 Buckinghamshire
6 Cambridgeshire
7 Cardiff, Swansea and The Valleys
8 Cheshire
9 Cornwall
10 Cumbria
11 Derbyshire
12 Devon
13 Dorset
14 County Durham and Teesside
15 Edinburgh and East Central Scotland
16 Essex
17 North Essex
18 South Essex
19 Fife and Tayside
20 Glasgow and West Central Scotland
21 Gloucestershire
22 North Hampshire
23 South Hampshire
24 Herefordshire and Monmouthshire
25 Hertfordshire
26 East Kent
27 West Kent
28 Lancashire
29 Leicestershire and Rutland
30 Lincolnshire
31 London
32 Greater Manchester
33 Merseyside
34 Norfolk
35 Northamptonshire
36 Nottinghamshire
37 Oxfordshire
38 Shropshire
39 Somerset
40 Staffordshire
41 Suffolk
42 Surrey
43 East Sussex
44 West Sussex
45 Tyne and Wear and Northumberland
46 Warwickshire
47 Worcestershire
48 Wiltshire and Swindon
49 East Yorkshire and Northern Lincolnshire
50 North Yorkshire
51 South Yorkshire
52 West Yorkshire

How to order

The Philip's range of street atlases is available from good retailers or directly from the publisher by phoning 01903 828503